Professional Microsoft® SharePoint® Designer 2007

Professional

Microsoft® SharePoint® Designer 2007

Professional
Microsoft® SharePoint® Designer 2007

Woody Windischman

Bryan Phillips

Asif Rehmani

WILEY

Wiley Publishing, Inc.

Professional Microsoft® SharePoint® Designer 2007

Published by
Wiley Publishing, Inc.
10475 Crosspoint Boulevard
Indianapolis, IN 46256
www.wiley.com

Copyright © 2009 by Wiley Publishing, Inc., Indianapolis, Indiana

Published simultaneously in Canada

ISBN: 978-0-470-28761-3

Manufactured in the United States of America

10 9 8 7 6 5 4 3 2 1

Library of Congress Cataloging-in-Publication Data is available from the publisher.

For general information on our other products and services please contact our Customer Care Department within the United States at (800) 762-2974, outside the United States at (317) 572-3993 or fax (317) 572-4002.

About the Authors

Woodrow (Woody) Windischman is a technology trainer and consultant with more than 20 years' experience in a variety of roles, allowing him to see problems holistically and come up with appropriate solutions. His SharePoint experience started even before SharePoint became a product, with predecessors such as Site Server, the Digital Dashboard Resource Kit, and the earliest versions of Microsoft FrontPage. Since then Woody's been deeply involved in the SharePoint community—first having been awarded Microsoft SharePoint MVP from October 2005 through September 2007, and then working directly for the SharePoint product team. He's active in several online SharePoint communities, including the TechNet forums.

Bryan Phillips is a software architect and senior partner with Composable Systems, LLC, specializing in service-oriented business solutions using the latest Microsoft technology. Bryan has worked professionally with Microsoft development technology since 1997 and holds the Microsoft Certified Trainer (MCT), Microsoft Certified Solution Developer (MCSD), Microsoft Certified Database Administrator (MCDBA), and Microsoft Certified Systems Engineer (MCSE) certifications. Bryan contributes regularly to the Microsoft development community by speaking on topics such as Smart Client, ASP.NET, SharePoint, SQL Server, and Mobile development; presenting DevCares courses; and blogging on topics of interest to developers. Bryan is a Microsoft Most Valuable Professional (MVP) in Client Application Development.

Asif Rehmani has been a Trainer and a Consultant working out of the Chicago office of SharePoint Solutions (`http://sharepointsolutions.com/chicago`) since early 2005. He is a SharePoint Server MVP and MCT.

Asif runs a SharePoint eLearning website (`http://sharepoint-elearning.com`), which provides numerous SharePoint Video Tutorials on various topics within SharePoint.

He has been a speaker on SharePoint topics at several conferences over the years, including Microsoft SharePoint Conference, SharePoint Connections, Advisor Live, and the Information Workers Conference. Also, he is one of the founders and active current leaders of the Chicago SharePoint User Group (`http://cspug.org`). For a more detailed bio, please visit `http://sharepoint-elearning.com/Pages/Bio.aspx`.

About the Technical Editors

Jacob J. Sanford began his career in, of all things, accounting and auditing. He graduated from Florida State University in 1997 with B.S. degrees in accounting and finance, which made him eligible to sit for the CPA exam. Although he realized in college that he was more interested in computers and technology, he decided to give accounting a chance. It didn't last. He had been dabbling in HTML and VBA when he took a job at a private software company and met David Drinkwine, who introduced him to the wonders of classic ASP. From there, he began learning as much as he could about all kinds of web application development, including ColdFusion, PhP, PhotoShop, CSS, XML, and finally ASP.NET (starting in the 1.0 and 1.1 release). He has been using ASP.NET (VB and C#—but mostly C#) for the last four or five years. He has worked at several State of Florida agencies and, in that capacity, found a fondness for pure CSS design and accessibility considerations. Most recently, he has started focusing on new technologies and tools such as Microsoft Silverlight and Visual Studio 2008.

Jacob is currently a Senior Consultant with Captaré Consulting, LLC, and is the founding leader of the Tallahassee SharePoint Experts Exchange for Developers (SPEED). He is a regular presenter at regional .NET Code Camps and at local .NET User Group meetings and is the author of *Professional ASP.NET 2.0 Design* (Wrox) and one of the authors of *Professional SharePoint 2007 Design* (Wrox).

Jacob lives in Tallahassee, Florida, with his beautiful wife, Shannan. He has two amazing sons, Matthew and Hayden, and an eternal puppy, Petey.

Coskun Cavusoglu is the Director of Consulting Services and the Chief Solution Architect of Captaré Consulting, LLC (www.captare.com). He has been architecting and implementing technology solutions for more than 10 years in both large, enterprise organizations and fast-growth midmarket firms. Coskun consults on a variety of business process practices. He has a broad range of expertise in areas such as knowledge management, business process analysis, collaboration, project management, office productivity, and application programming. As a software engineer specializing in the .NET Framework and the Office Server System, specifically Windows SharePoint Services and Microsoft Office SharePoint Server, he has extensive experience designing, implementing, and supporting Internet solutions using Microsoft technologies such as SharePoint, CRM, Project Server, Windows Server, Active Directory, Exchange, IIS, and ASP .NET 2.0/3.5.

Coskun is a technology writer, a blogger, and a published author on Microsoft server products. His latest book, which he coauthored with fellow SharePoint experts, is called *Professional Microsoft SharePoint 2007 Design* (Wrox), and his blog is located at http://sharepointblogs.com/gnarus. He also is a speaker who attends various community events, both local and international, where he talks about various SharePoint topics, and his past and future engagements can be found at his blog.

Coskun is a Microsoft Certified Professional and is also a Microsoft Certified Technology Specialist for SharePoint Portal Server 2003 and Microsoft Office SharePoint Server 2007.

Arif Ilhan Kolko earned a B.S. degree in Industrial Engineering from Purdue University, and then moved to Chicago, Illinois, to start his professional career at Chicago Metallic Corporation, an international manufacturing company, as a quality/manufacturing engineer. The companies he has worked for as an engineer and manager include the Coca-Cola Company, Pirelli Tire Company, and Networked Concepts.

Looking to merge his development skills and experience with his career interest in conducting client-based, time-sensitive projects, Ilhan joined Captaré Consulting, LLC, in October 2007. He currently serves as a Senior Consultant and the Vendor Management Office (VMO) Representative. In his professional career, Ilhan has successfully managed and delivered several process optimization, quality systems development, lean manufacturing, capital investment justification, process simulation, business development, product-system innovation, and web application design and development projects. Ilhan has been a certified Six Sigma Green Belt since 2004 and a Microsoft Certified Professional Developer (MCPD) since Spring 2008.

Ilhan received his first master's degree, summa cum laude, from DePaul University, in Marketing Analysis. He is planning to start working toward his MBA degree in Operations Management by January 2009 at a school to be decided.

Credits

Acknowledgments

Every writer needs a first book, and this is mine. While I never thought it would be easy, I have learned that a lot more goes into the planning, writing, and publishing of a work like this than you might guess. It was definitely not a solo effort, and I would like to express my deepest appreciation to the many people who helped make it possible. In particular, I would like to thank: Jerome Thiebaud, Product Manager for Microsoft Office SharePoint Designer, for encouraging me to pursue this; Katie Mohr and Maryann Steinhart of Wiley, for giving me the opportunity, helping to guide me through the process, and putting up with innumerable delays; and especially Bryan Philips (chapters 15–17) and Asif Rehmani (chapters 6–8) for joining me as coauthors to overcome some of those delays.

—*Woody*

I would like to thank Woody Windischman for giving me the opportunity to contribute to this book. I have always wanted to share my knowledge and experience with others, and this book is an excellent vehicle to do so.

I would also like to thank Todd Bleeker for his information on converting SharePoint Designer workflows for use in Visual Studio. His time and effort in developing those techniques have reduced my time on this book.

Finally, I would like to thank Jacob Sanford and Coskun Cavusoglu for their meticulous technical editing and review of my work. As this is my first published work, their patience and guidance are greatly appreciated.

—*Bryan*

First and foremost, I thank God for all the opportunities that have been sent my way throughout my life to get me to this point. In terms of mortals, I would like to first thank my beautiful wife, Anisa, for her support and understanding throughout the writing process. I know it wasn't easy putting up with my schedule at times, but I appreciate that you did. Also, thanks to my wonderful boys, Armaan and Ayaan, who always put a smile on my face when I need it the most. Thanks to my parents for the hardworking genes that they have passed on to me, which always keep me going.

On a professional note, I would like to thank Katie Mohr with Wiley Publishing for giving me the chance to contribute to this book project. Also, thanks to AC for referring me to Katie. I owe you one! A special thanks to my mentors and friends at SharePoint Solutions, Jeff Cate and Kevin Pine. The support and encouragement you have provided me through the years, to help me sharpen my instructional skills and business acumen, have not gone unnoticed. Thank you.

—*Asif*

Contents

Contents

Contents

Contents

Contents

Contents

Contents

Contents

Contents

Contents

Introduction

"Can you make it look less like SharePoint?"

Such a simple question, and yet, like someone opening the lid to Pandora's Box, the customer asking it can release a whole range of troubles into the life of a web designer. The latest release of Microsoft SharePoint products has taken the world by storm. Faster than anyone could have foreseen, businesses large and small have discovered that SharePoint addresses a range of needs, and have rushed to jump on the bandwagon.

SharePoint is not merely a web server. It is a large and complex application, with many moving parts. Some of them are easy to customize; others require a bit more finesse. Tools and guidance for that customization are few and far between. Fortunately for you, SharePoint Designer is such a tool, and this book provides the guidance. Together, they enable you to look your customer in the eye and answer with a resounding: "Yes!"

Yet SharePoint Designer can do far more than customize SharePoint sites. It is a fully-featured web design tool in its own right, with excellent support for many industry standards, as well as backward compatibility with a few nonstandard capabilities.

Who This Book Is For

This book is for anyone who has been asked the opening question. You may be an experienced web designer or a web application developer who has never used SharePoint. You may be a system administrator who needs to tweak a few things to match an existing standard. Perhaps you are a business analyst looking for ways to integrate some CRM information into the company's home page. All of you will find something useful here.

If your familiarity with SharePoint is limited, chapters 2, 3, and 4 will be indispensable for you. They cover the key features of SharePoint, and how they are viewed from the user's, administrator's, and web designer's perspectives, respectively.

This book is also for people upgrading from Microsoft FrontPage. SharePoint Designer is one of two direct successors to FrontPage. As a result, FrontPage users will find much that is familiar, as well as many things that have changed. In general, you will find that while you can edit existing sites that use legacy features, SharePoint Designer's function layout encourages a much more standards-compliant way to design new sites and content.

This book assumes you have a more than passing familiarity with designing applications for the web. A basic knowledge of JavaScript is assumed, as is an understanding of HTML tags. Some allowance is made for the rise of certain technologies in recent years. A few chapters deal with CSS, XML, and XSL, and a short introduction to each is provided where appropriate.

The book also assumes a certain willingness to explore. Although all of the core functions, menus, and toolbars of SharePoint Designer are described, this is not a *Bible* that explains each and every menu item and dialog tick in excruciating detail. If a program feature offers several options, a representative few are described, and one may be used in an example.

The book assumes you are familiar with basic Windows operations and applications. Where functions are common in many applications, they probably are not discussed at all. (You are shown where to find the Formatting toolbar, for instance, but your familiarity with the icons and meanings of Bold, Center, and the various bulleting options is assumed.) It's also assumed that you know how to point, click, cut, copy, and paste.

The later chapters move out of SharePoint Designer and into Visual Studio. They cover creating extensions to SharePoint, SharePoint Designer, or both. Examples are provided in both C# and Visual Basic .NET. Although the source is discussed and/or documented in the text, no attempt is made to teach the languages themselves, so proficiency in one of these languages is desirable. Many readers may consider these chapters optional, although system administrators should at least pay attention to chapter 18.

What This Book Covers

This book covers Microsoft Office SharePoint Designer 2007, with an emphasis on using it to customize web sites based on Microsoft SharePoint products and technologies. You will learn about Master Pages, Themes, and various Web Parts that enable you to create powerful applications with little or no code.

A short overview of SharePoint is provided to ensure that you are not flying blind when you customize SharePoint sites. At the other end of the scale, you are taken outside the box with chapters that teach you how to use Visual Studio and other tools to extend the capabilities available in both SharePoint and SharePoint Designer.

Aspects of SharePoint Designer beyond SharePoint customization are not ignored, however. You will find sections that cover the basic web-editing features, generic application of the CSS editor, and site administration functions provided by SharePoint Designer. Many elements, such as Data Views, while described in the SharePoint context, are also relevant without a SharePoint environment.

How This Book Is Structured

This book is made up of 18 chapters, in five parts. Each part brings together related tasks and content. Part I is fundamental to everything else, but the other parts do not necessarily need to be read in a particular order. They are, however, largely progressive in their complexity.

Part I, "The Basics," provides an overview of SharePoint Designer, SharePoint technology, and their relationship to one another.

Part II, "Customizing the SharePoint Look and Feel," shows how to use SharePoint Designer to customize various aspects of your sites.

Part III, "Applications without Programming," shows how SharePoint Designer can create many powerful applications that in the past would have required considerable programming effort.

Part IV, "Programming on the Client Side," demonstrates some tools provided by SharePoint and SharePoint Designer to enable even more custom interactivity.

Part V, "Beyond SharePoint Designer," takes you far past the built-in capabilities of SharePoint Designer with extensions, add-ins, migration, and conversion tools.

Web design is an intrinsically visual process, web designers tend to be visual learners, and SharePoint Designer is a visual tool. This book takes that into account by including a relatively high proportion of screenshots. There are also step-by-step exercises where appropriate. Finally, it wouldn't be a Wrox Professional book without sample code, and that is here in abundance. In this case, "code" is interpreted liberally to include markup, CSS, and scripting, in addition to compiled source.

What You Need to Use This Book

While you can learn much from this book simply by reading, to follow along with the exercises and step-by-step instructions, it will be helpful to have a few things. Most important, of course, is a copy of SharePoint Designer 2007. You should also have access to a SharePoint environment that you can use without adversely impacting production sites.

Certain examples make use of Web Parts that are only included with editions of Microsoft Office SharePoint Server 2007 or Microsoft Search Server 2008. The Express Edition of Search Server (MSSX) is available as a free download from Microsoft, and is a sufficient version of SharePoint to perform all of the exercises and examples in this book.

Chapter 8 describes Publishing layouts and content management. These are features exclusive to Microsoft Office SharePoint Server 2007. You will need access to this if you wish to follow the examples in that chapter, except for those in chapter 8.

To compile the example programs in Part V, you need Visual Studio 2005 or Visual Studio 2008, Standard Edition or higher. You also need to download the following add-ons from the Microsoft MSDN site:

The Windows SharePoint Services 3.0 Software Development Kit (WSS SDK).

The Microsoft Office SharePoint Server 2007 Software Development Kit (MOSS SDK).

Visual Studio Tools for Office (VSTO).

Visual Studio Extensions for Windows SharePoint Services (VSeWSS).

The SharePoint Designer add-in example in chapter 17 requires the SharePoint Designer 2007 Add-In project template from the Microsoft CodePlex site.

Most SharePoint designers and developers find it convenient to create a sandbox development environment containing all of the tools listed here (and other favorite development utilities) on a virtual machine (VM). All versions of SharePoint require Windows Server 2003 or Windows Server 2008, with at least 1GB of RAM to install successfully (2GB or more of RAM is recommended).

Related Products

SharePoint Designer is not the only Microsoft product created for manipulating web pages. It is closely related to Microsoft Expression Web, which sprang from the same FrontPage roots. In addition, Visual Studio is a useful tool for web designers of all stripes.

SharePoint Designer Compared to Expression Web

As with the mythical Hydra, who grows more than one head if the first is cut off, the end of FrontPage was the beginning of several children. Like SharePoint Designer, Microsoft Expression Web is a direct descendent of Microsoft FrontPage. In fact, from a basic page-editing standpoint, SharePoint Designer and Expression Web appear virtually identical.

Scratch the surface, however, and the differences become clear. Nothing says it better than the dialog shown in Figure 1, which you get when you try to open a SharePoint-based site in Expression Web. Expression Web has no capability to work on a SharePoint site.

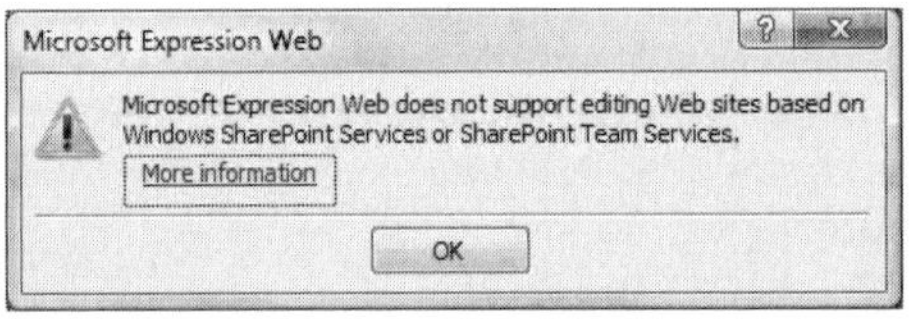

Figure I-1

SharePoint Designer, on the other hand, happily opens web sites created with most versions of SharePoint. In addition, SharePoint Designer offers more complete support for sites created using the FrontPage Server Extensions.

So, why use Expression Web? If you don't need to work with SharePoint, Expression Web provides an excellent set of tools for creating standards-based web sites. It integrates with Visual Studio, supports PHP (which SharePoint Designer does not), and includes several web site templates that are not available with SharePoint Designer.

SharePoint Designer Compared to Visual Studio

The other tool you might consider for working with SharePoint is Visual Studio. In fact, there are certain things that cannot be done with SharePoint Designer. Some of these tasks are described in Part V, "Beyond SharePoint Designer." The key is to remember that SharePoint Designer is generally used to customize SharePoint sites and manipulate existing features, whereas Visual Studio is used to develop new SharePoint functionality.

Conventions

To help you get the most from the text and keep track of what's happening, there are a number of conventions used throughout the book.

> Boxes like this one hold important, not-to-be-forgotten information that is directly relevant to the surrounding text.

Notes, tips, hints, tricks, and asides to the current discussion are offset and placed in italics like this:

As for styles in the text:

❑ New terms are *highlighted* when they're introduced.

❑ Keyboard combination strokes look like this: Ctrl+A.

❑ Filenames, URLs, and code within the text look like so: `persistence.properties`.

❑ Code is presented in two different ways:

```
Most code examples are in a monofont type with no highlighting.
Gray highlighting emphasizes code that's particularly important
in the present context.
```

❑ Code lines are sometimes longer than a book page is wide. When that happens, the ↵ character indicates that the code line continues on the next line.

Source Code

As you work through the examples in this book, you may choose either to type in all the code manually or to use the source code files that accompany the book. All of the source code used in this book is available for download at `http://www.wrox.com`. Once at the site, simply locate the book's title (either by using the Search box or by using one of the title lists) and click the Download Code link on the book's detail page to obtain all the source code for the book.

Because many books have similar titles, you may find it easiest to search by ISBN; this book's ISBN is 978-0-470-28761-3.

Once you download the code, just decompress it with your favorite compression tool. Alternately, you can go to the main Wrox code download page at `http://www.wrox.com/dynamic/books/download.aspx` to see the code available for this book and all other Wrox books.

Errata

Every effort is made to ensure that there are no errors in the text or in the code. However, no one is perfect, and mistakes do occur. If you find an error, like a spelling mistake or faulty piece of code, in one of our books, we would be very grateful for your feedback. By sending in errata you may save another reader hours of frustration, and at the same time you will be helping us provide even higher-quality information.

To find the errata page for this book, go to `http://www.wrox.com` and locate the title using the Search box or one of the title lists. Then, on the book details page, click the Book Errata link. On this page, you can view all errata that have been submitted for this book and posted by Wrox editors. A complete book list including links to each book's errata is also available at www.wrox.com/misc-pages/booklist.shtml.

If you don't spot your error on the Book Errata page, go to www.wrox.com/contact/techsupport.shtml and complete the form there to send us the error you have found. We'll check the information and, if appropriate, post a message to the book's errata page and fix the problem in subsequent editions of the book.

p2p.wrox.com

For author and peer discussion, join the P2P forums at p2p.wrox.com. The forums are a Web-based system for you to post messages relating to Wrox books and related technologies, and to interact with other readers and technology users. The forums offer a subscription feature to e-mail you topics of interest of your choosing when new posts are made to the forums. Wrox authors and editors, other industry experts, and your fellow readers are present on these forums.

At http://p2p.wrox.com you will find a number of different forums that will help you, not only as you read this book, but also as you develop your own applications. To join the forums, just follow these steps:

1. Go to p2p.wrox.com and click the Register link.
2. Read the terms of use and click Agree.
3. Complete the required information to join, as well as any optional information you wish to provide, and click Submit.
4. You will receive an e-mail with information describing how to verify your account and complete the joining process.

    You can read messages in the forums without joining P2P, but in order to post your own messages, you must join.

Once you join, you can post new messages and respond to messages other users post. You can read messages at any time on the Web. If you would like to have new messages from a particular forum e-mailed to you, click the Subscribe to this Forum icon by the forum name in the forum listing.

For more information about how to use the Wrox P2P, be sure to read the P2P FAQs for answers to questions about how the forum software works, as well as many common questions specific to P2P and Wrox books. To read the FAQs, click the FAQ link on any P2P page.

Part I
The Basics

Exploring SharePoint Designer

Microsoft Windows SharePoint Services 3.0 and Microsoft Office SharePoint Server 2007 are large and sophisticated web applications. It should come as no surprise, therefore, that the tool meant to customize them — Microsoft Office SharePoint Designer 2007 — is a large, sophisticated desktop application. This chapter explores:

❑ How SharePoint Designer fits in Microsoft's toolset.

❑ SharePoint Designer's basic editing features.

❑ SharePoint navigation.

It also provides an overview of site administration tools.

SharePoint Designer as a Web Editor

SharePoint Designer is a descendant of Microsoft FrontPage, and a close relative of Expression Web, Microsoft's dedicated Web design tool. In fact, SharePoint Designer provides a true superset of Expression Web functionality, and therefore makes an excellent all-around tool for Web design.

In addition to the SharePoint-related features, SharePoint Designer includes more features for backward compatibility with existing FrontPage-based sites than are a part of Expression Web 1.0.

For the 2007 Microsoft Office System, Microsoft has replaced many of the traditional user interface elements in several client applications, such as Microsoft Word, with what it calls the fluent user interface, the most noticeable feature of which is a tabbed mega-toolbar called the Ribbon. Microsoft has not done this in SharePoint Designer 2007, which sports menus, toolbars, and so on in all of their historical profusion. See Figure 1-1.

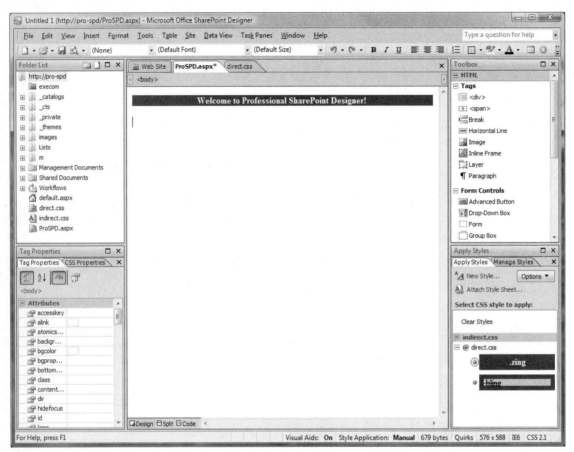

Figure 1-1

The overall interface in SharePoint Designer is very much in the mold of an Integrated Development Environment (IDE) such as Visual Studio, or web design and development tools like Adobe Dreamweaver (formerly of Macromedia). As you learn about the various tools at your disposal, you will quickly feel at home in SharePoint Designer.

If you are new to the IDE experience, you want to be aware of the need for development and design tools to manage projects consisting of many interrelated files. Some commands operate on individual files, and others work on a project as a whole. This need will surface in a number of different ways. For example, examine the File menu shown in Figure 1-2. Notice that there are two options each for Open, Close, and Recent items.

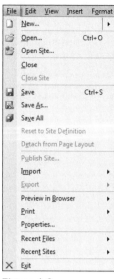

Figure 1-2

The collection of files that is treated as a project unit in SharePoint Designer is called a *site* or *web*. (This nomenclature is independent of what the corresponding structures may be called on the target server. SharePoint sites have a similar naming structure, which is detailed in chapter 3.) The Open Site, Close Site, and Recent Sites menu items are for working with an entire site. The plain Open and Close items, as well as Recent Files, Save, and Save As, are for working with individual component files within a site.

When you open an existing file-type item, the containing site (if any) also opens.

With SharePoint Designer, you are usually working against a live (though not necessarily production) environment. When combined with the duality described above, this has the result that certain changes have immediate effect, while others aren't visible unless or until you save the component you are working on. In general, changes to overall site structure (such as renaming, deleting, or moving a file) are immediate, while you need to save changes within a page or graphic file to see them on the site.

In a source-controlled or content-managed environment, your file(s) may need to go through a check-in and approval process before certain changes become visible.

The major elements of the SharePoint Designer workspace include the menu, various toolbars, the design surface (usually containing the Page Editor), the status bar, and a wide array of task panes. The workspace is quite customizable. Other than the design surface, which will resize itself based upon the remaining available space, virtually every workspace component can be resized, shown, hidden, set to float, or docked. Menu and toolbar items can be added or removed.

The menu bar cannot be hidden, but it can float and be dragged offstage, like toolbars and task panes.

The rest of this chapter describes these workspace elements in detail.

Page Editor

The Page Editor in SharePoint Designer is the design surface where you compose the elements of your page. It offers three primary modes, or views, of the page that is currently open — *Design*, *Code*, and *Split*. These modes are selected with the Page Mode toolbar, at the left along the lower window margin. When no page is open for editing, the central area of the workspace shows the Web Site structural views (covered later in this chapter).

> *All three views are available for web page file types (.htm, .aspx, and .master, for example). Files such as .css, .js, and .txt that do not have a direct visual component only have Code view and do not display the Page Mode toolbar.*

Figure 1-3 shows the Page Editor in Design view, with the menu and all of the toolbars and task panes removed. This can be accomplished either by closing or floating each item, and dragging the floated items someplace unobtrusive. (This is sometimes referred to as dragging the element offstage.) What remain are the design surface itself and the status bar.

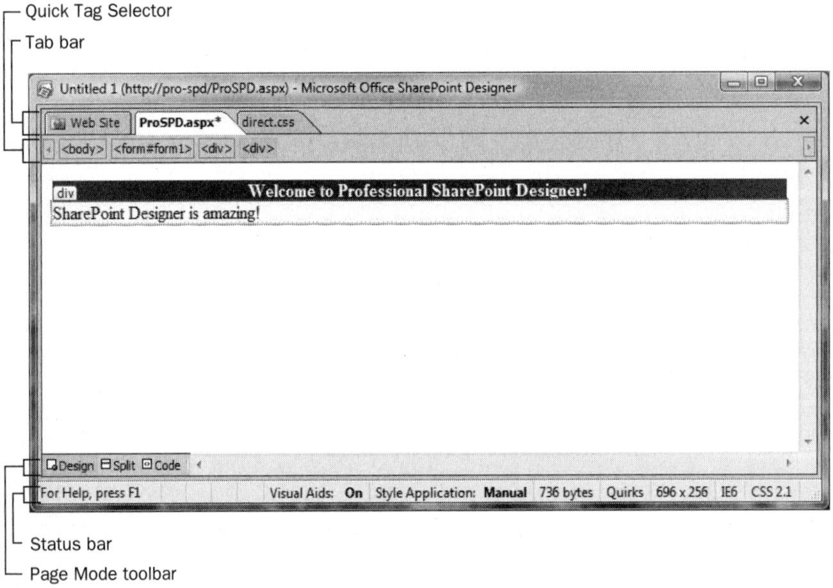

Figure 1-3

The Page Editor has the following elements (see Figure 1-3):

❑ **Tab bar:** Across the top of the Page Editor is a tab bar, which gives access to each file that is currently open in SharePoint Designer. Files that have been modified since being opened or last saved are indicated with an asterisk (*). The leftmost tab, Web Site, gives access to the site structural views (described later in this chapter).

❑ **Quick Tag Selector:** Below the tab bar is the Quick Tag Selector, which superficially appears to be a simple HTML breadcrumb, displaying the hierarchy of tags nesting down to the currently selected element; it is much more than that. Clicking a tag in the Selector immediately selects that element in the current view (hence the name). In addition, each tag in the Selector provides a context menu (as shown in Figure 1-4), allowing you to quickly adjust the parameters of the tag, create a containing tag, or even remove the tag without removing any child controls.

❑ **Status bar:** The status bar tells you all about your page design experience, but like the Quick Tag Selector, the status bar is also your active partner in the editing process. In addition to being context sensitive (the set of elements displayed on the status bar is dependent upon the current selection), many status segments also provide the option to edit the setting they are reporting.

❑ **Page Mode toolbar:** Selects which of the three editing modes to display.

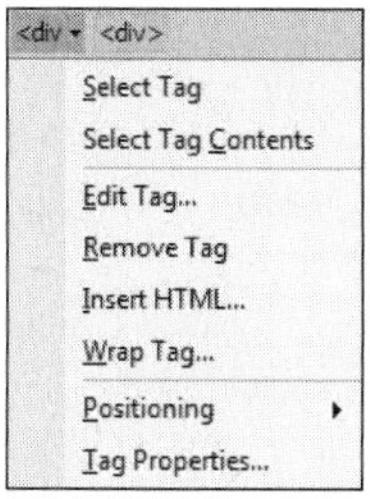

Figure 1-4

Design View

The Design view offers a what-you-see-is-what-you-get (WYSIWYG) editing experience. It supports many traditional GUI document-editing functions:

❑ Fonts, styles, and item placements in the Design view map very closely to the final page rendering.

❑ It allows you to drag and drop.

❑ You can copy, cut, and paste.

Design view also supports the use of the Ruler and Grid (with and without snap-to) options typically found in graphics and page layout programs. In addition, there is a wide array of specialty tools provided to improve your design experience. Some of them, such as Visual Aids and Table Tools, are described in this chapter, while others are covered later in the book (for instance, the CSS editing features are discussed in chapter 6).

The following sections discuss some of the features of the Design view.

Visual Aids

To assist you with your page designs, SharePoint Designer provides a number of Visual Aids. Visual Aids provide a way for you to see and access page elements that may not normally be visible, such as ActiveX controls, content placeholders, or items with a hidden attribute. Figure 1-5 shows a page with all Visual Aids enabled.

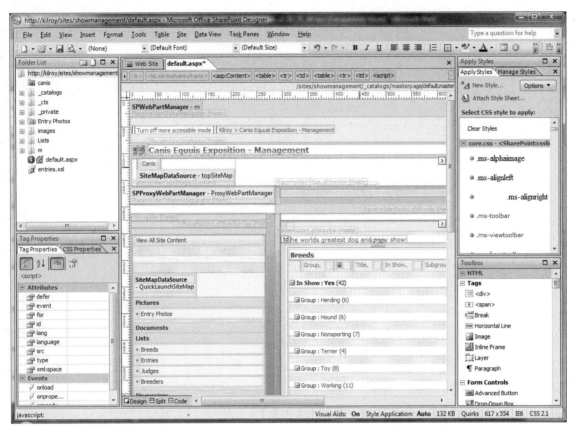

Figure 1-5

To keep your workspace uncluttered, you can enable or disable specific types of Visual Aids, either by selecting View ➪ Visual Aids (see Figure 1-6) or by right-clicking the Visual Aids segment in the status bar. You can also turn the current set of aids on and off by double-clicking the Visual Aids segment.

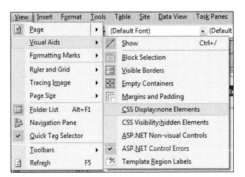

Figure 1-6

The Visual Aids view submenu is designed to remain visible as you select multiple options. This is also true of the Ruler and Grid view submenu. Visual Aids only appear in the Design and Split views, although the setting is displayed in the status bar and configurable in Code view.

Although Visual Aids can make the design of a page much easier, they also can significantly affect the layout as seen in Design view. Turn off Visual Aids occasionally to verify precise positioning. Figure 1-7 shows the same page as Figure 1-5, with the Visual Aids turned off.

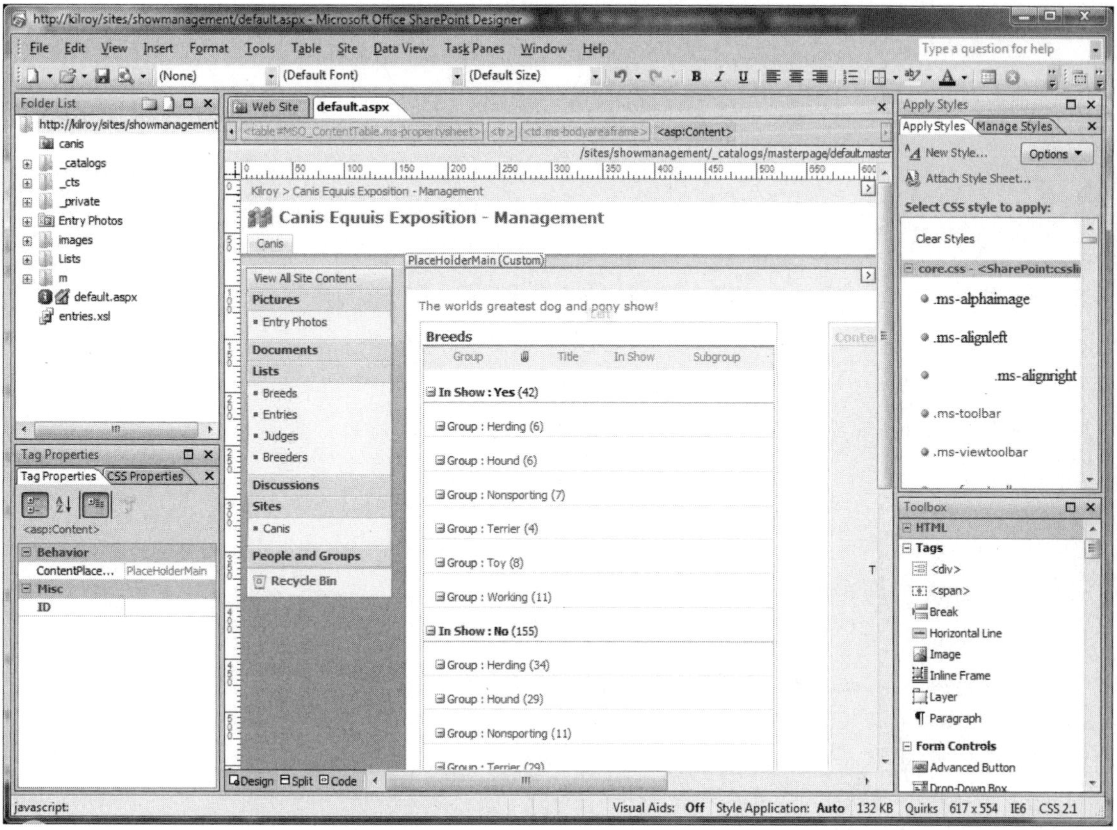

Figure 1-7

Table-Editing Tools

SharePoint Designer Design view supports traditional HTML tables in two different ways, each with a slightly different toolset:

❑　Standard tables are traditional grids of rows and columns, along with tools for merging and splitting cells, inserting rows, and so on, for the presentation of tabular information.

❑　Layout tables are of interest to web designers because tables have historically been used as a layout tool for HTML pages. SharePoint Designer's layout tables make table-based page layout much easier.

SharePoint Designer also fully supports the use of CSS for page layout, as you'll see in chapter 6.

Standard tables can be inserted two ways:

❑ Select Table ⇨ Insert Table. This summons the Insert Table dialog, shown in Figure 1-8, which allows you to set all of the core properties of the table prior to its insertion.

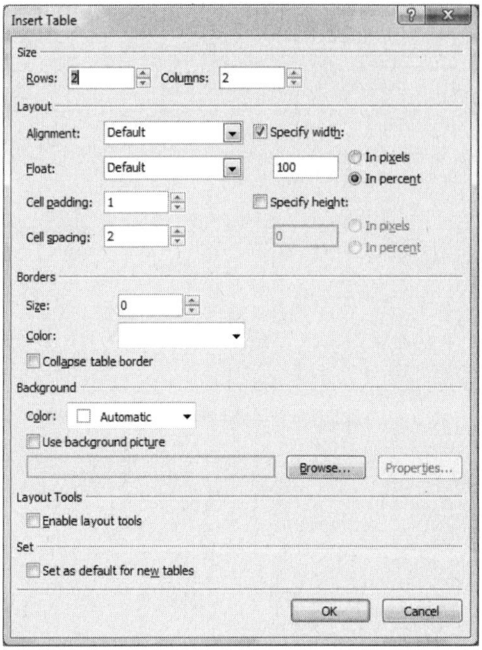

Figure 1-8

❑ Click the Table tool on the standard toolbar and drag to visually select the initial number of rows and columns, as shown in Figure 1-9.

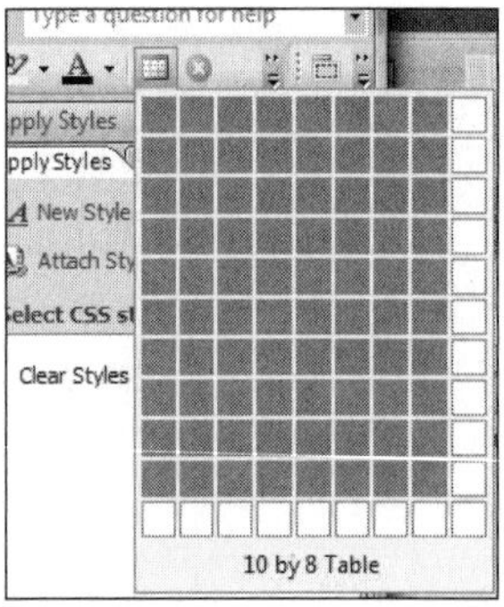

Figure 1-9

Layout tables are inserted by using the Insert Layout Table link in the Layout Tables task pane. The code generated for a layout table uses standard table, row, and cell tags, but also includes dimension styles by default. In addition, SharePoint Designer inserts HTML comments in each element, allowing it to have content automatically rearranged to follow changes to the layout. Figure 1-10 shows how both a regular table and a layout table look in Design view.

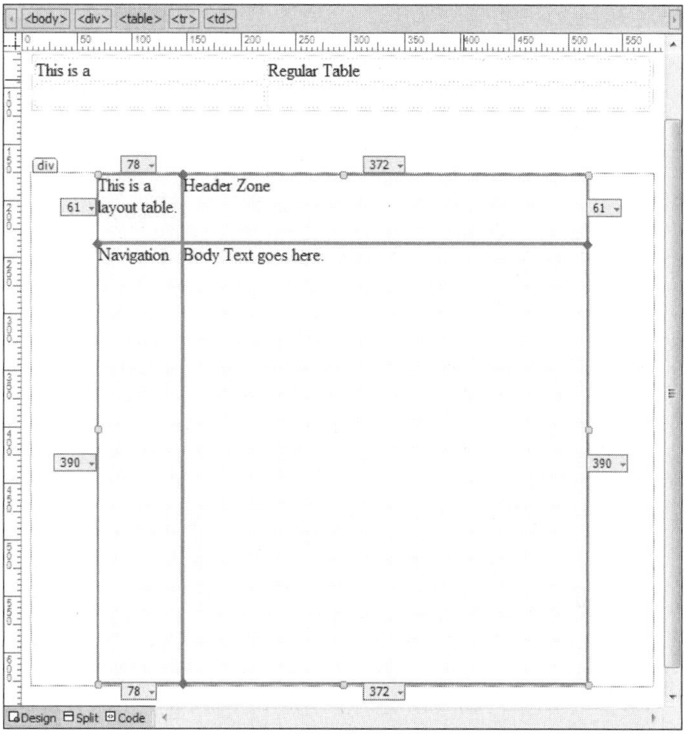

Figure 1-10

The Layout Tables task pane shows many of the options available with a layout table, including several predefined common page layouts. If you have content in a table based on one of these layouts, and later decide to change to a different layout, the content is moved to the corresponding cell in the new layout.

Page Sizes and Browser Preview

One of the most frustrating things about designing for the Web is the wide array of browsers and screen formats in which your site may be displayed. SharePoint Designer helps mitigate this problem by giving you several preview options.

First, you can fix the Design view to a set of dimensions. In the status bar, you can see the current dimensions of the window the Design view represents. Click the dimensions entry to see the menu shown in Figure 1-11, which allows you to choose from several page sizes.

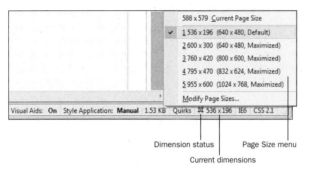

Figure 1-11

If the selected dimensions are smaller than the current design window, the width of the working area is reduced to the horizontal dimension selected. The chosen vertical dimension is shown by a dotted line across the visible area of the page.

If the selected dimensions are larger than the current design window, the workspace is expanded horizontally, and the scroll bar at the bottom of the window is activated.

> *The default page sizes represent Microsoft Internet Explorer in its default configuration. You can create your own set of dimensions to choose from.*

When a fixed page size is selected, the dimension status shows the hash symbol seen in Figure 1-11. The Page Size menu is also available under the View menu.

Design view provides a close approximation of the rendering of your page, especially with the Visual Aids turned off. However, even with the fixed page size option, SharePoint Designer cannot perfectly reproduce the environment of a web browser. To resolve this, SharePoint Designer provides the option to preview your page directly in web browsers.

Not only can a page be rendered differently in a browser than within SharePoint Designer, but different browsers and even different versions of the same browser have their own ways of rendering pages. It is best practice, therefore, to test your pages in each of the browsers you expect to view your site. SharePoint Designer's Preview in Browser function enables you to select an exact environment in which to test your pages. Figure 1-12 shows the Preview in Browser menu as selected from the icon in the Common toolbar.

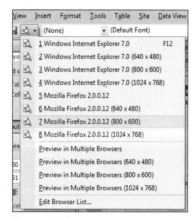

Figure 1-12

Internet Explorer and Mozilla Firefox are automatically detected by SharePoint Designer if they are installed on your workstation. In addition, you can select any other installed browser for live preview. Follow these steps to add another browser to the preview list:

1. Select Preview in Browser ⇨ Edit Browser List. The Edit Browser List dialog box appears, as shown in Figure 1-13.

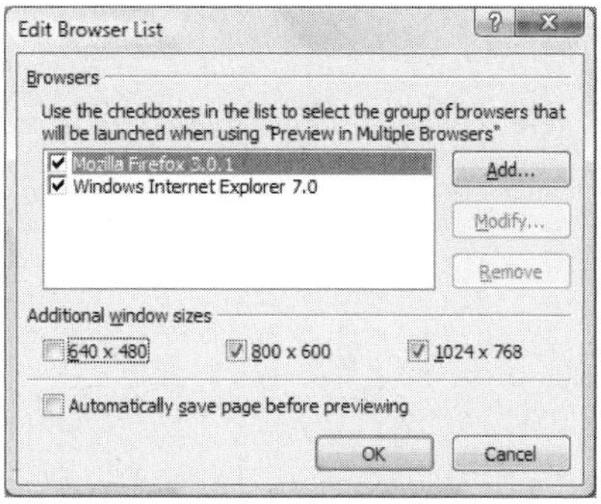

Figure 1-13

2. Click the Add button. The Add Browser dialog box appears (see Figure 1-14).

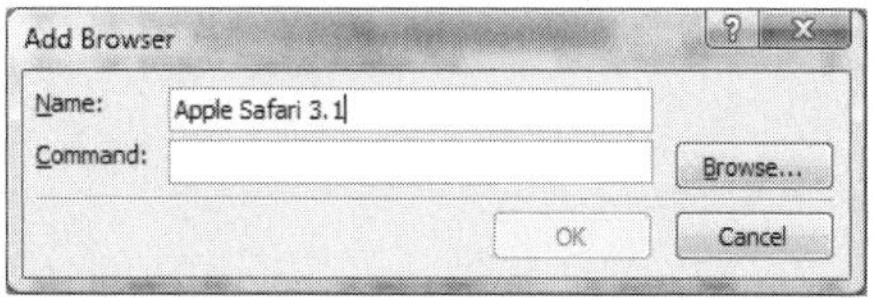

Figure 1-14

3. Type a name to represent the browser.

4. Click the Browse button to open the Add Browser window (see Figure 1-15), and navigate to the .exe file that starts the application. (You may need to look at the properties of the application's launch icon to find the file location.)

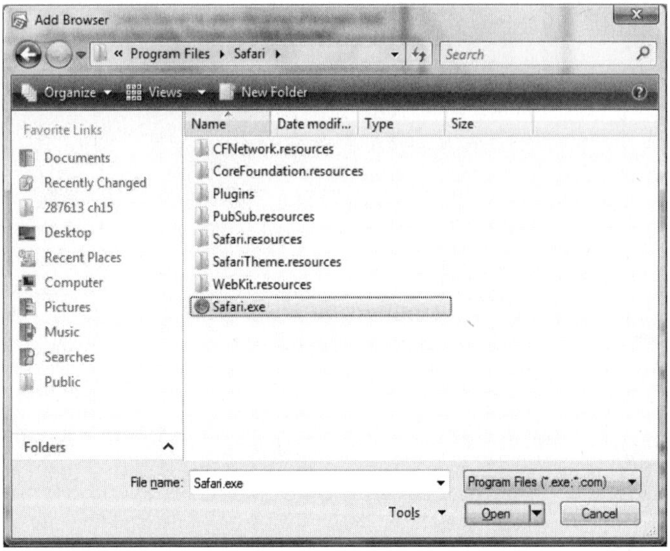

Figure 1-15

5. Click Open, and then click OK on the other two dialogs.

A page must be saved before it can be previewed in a web browser.

Code View

Although the SharePoint Designer Design view provides an easy and powerful way to create, lay out, and edit the pages of your site, at the end of the day these pages remain what they have always been — plaintext HTML and script. Fortunately, SharePoint Designer is just as adept at helping you work with code as it is with page design. Figure 1-16 shows the same page you have seen in the prior shots in SharePoint Designer's Code view.

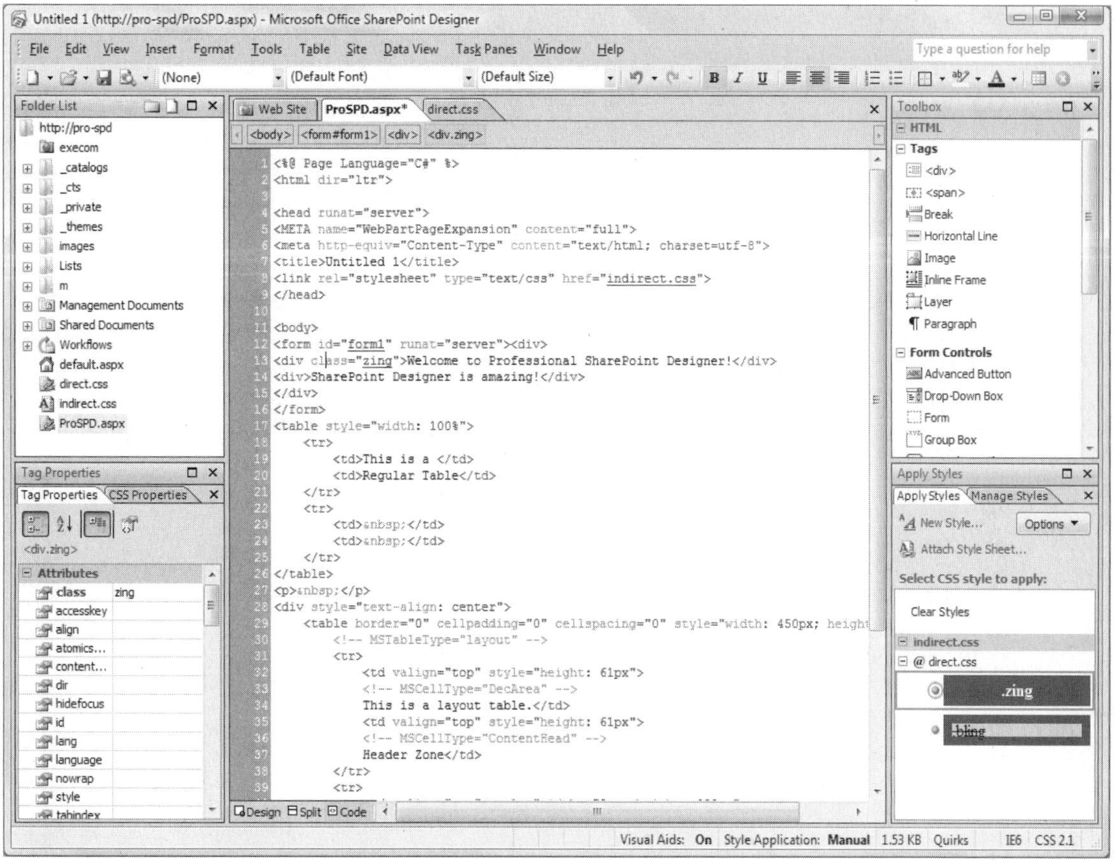

Figure 1-16

Although it may be difficult to see on a book page, Code view uses color coding to help you recognize tags delimiters, parameters, inline text, comments, and many other code elements. In fact, Code view offers all of the assistance typical of any modern development environment, and then some, as discussed in the following sections.

IntelliSense and More

IntelliSense has been a part of Microsoft development tools for more than a decade. Usually manifesting as a pop-up, it detects what you are typing and offers suggestions for completing your task. Though originally limited to program code, in SharePoint Designer Code view, IntelliSense has been expanded far beyond that. It now includes such features as:

❑   Automatic tag and brace closure.

❑   Parameter selection (as shown in Figure 1-17).

❑   CSS statement completion.

❑   Automatic code hyperlinks.

❑   Programming code completion.

Figure 1-17

Not everyone wants or needs this level of automatic assistance. You can therefore enable or disable IntelliSense for each of the available elements. The IntelliSense tab (see Figure 1-18) of the Page Editor provides a complete list of IntelliSense settings available.

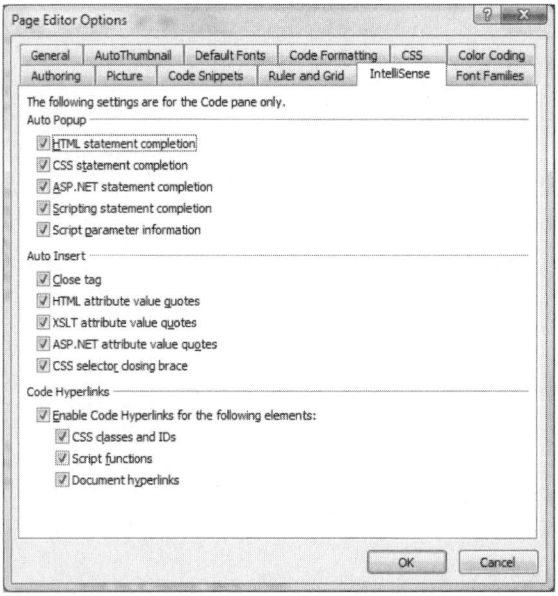

Figure 1-18

IntelliSense in Code view further helps you by being sensitive to your settings for browsers, HTML, and CSS version. For example, the primary IntelliSense options shown in Figure 1-18 are the Authoring options that are available in a tab on the Page Editor Options dialog. You can access this dialog either by clicking one of the authoring mode indicators (such as Quirks, IE6, or CSS 2.1) on the right side of the status bar, or by selecting Tools ⇨ Page Editor Options.

Another handy shortcut offered by Code view is *code snippets*. SharePoint Designer includes snippets for such things as HTML document types, script blocks, and style sheet links. You can insert a snippet by pressing Ctrl+Enter and typing the snippet name/keyword, or by selecting the one you want from a list just like an IntelliSense parameter. If you find yourself frequently typing the same thing, maybe with minor variations, you can define your own code snippets to help you.

To define a snippet:

1. Copy the code you want to include in the snippet to the Clipboard.

2. Press Ctrl+Enter. Select the first item on the list (Customize List), which opens the Code Snippets tab (see Figure 1-19) of the Page Editor Options dialog. (You can also summon this dialog by selecting Tools ⇨ Page Editor Options, and picking the Code Snippets tab.)

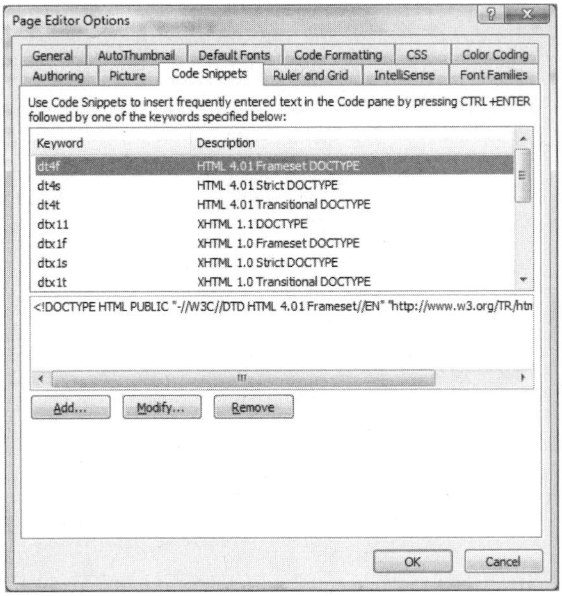

Figure 1-19

3. Click Add to summon the Add Code Snippet dialog (see Figure 1-20).

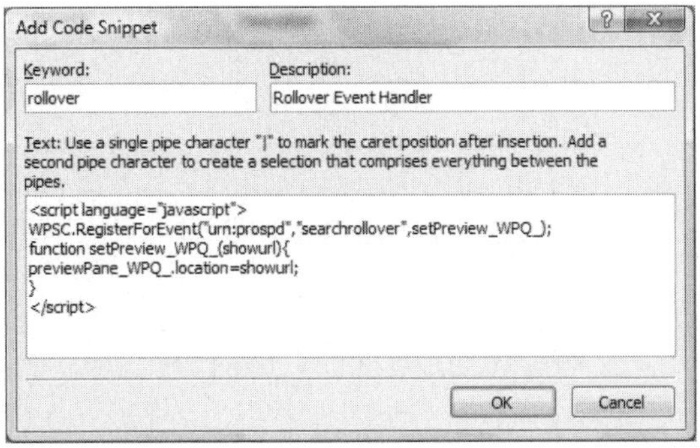

Figure 1-20

4. Enter appropriate information in the Keyword and Description fields.

5. Paste your code into the Text box. (Alternatively, you can manually enter any desired text, but using copy and paste from a known-good source is more reliable.)

6. Specify insertion points and/or selection by using the pipe character (|) if needed.

7. Click OK to save and close each dialog.

Visual Coding

In the past, you might have gone back and forth between an application's Design and Code views, depending on what you needed to change. For example, after editing a piece of script in Code view, you would return to Design view to set some text formatting. Otherwise, you would need to manually enter or edit the formatting tags in code. In SharePoint Designer, that kind of toggling is much less necessary. SharePoint Designer allows you to use many of the same techniques for formatting text in Code view as in Design view.

Figure 1-21 shows that the toolbar formatting (bold, italic, and underline) is available while you are editing in Code view. In fact, they are fully active and interactive with your HTML.

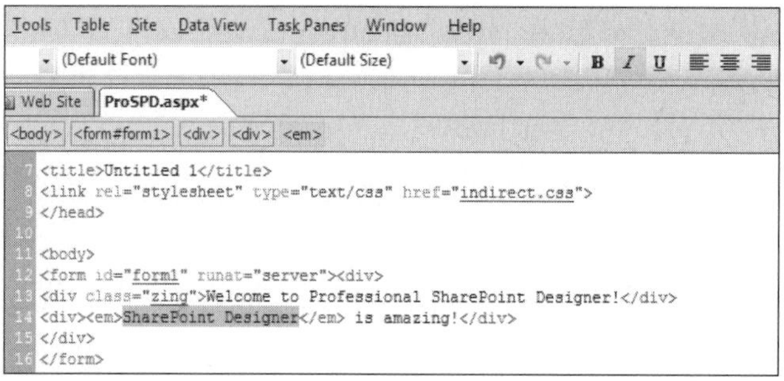

Figure 1-21

Just as in Design view, selecting a formatting command from the toolbar applies that format to (or removes it from) your selection. Unlike Design view, Code view does not show you the item in its formatted state. Instead, you see the HTML tags that are applied to make that format happen.

In addition, notice that the state of the toolbar icons follows the current HTML. In Figure1-21, the highlighted text is inside an <em> (emphasis) tag, which is rendered in italic on a web page. Also notice that the Quick Tag Selector for the emphasis tag is active.

The same holds true when adding elements to a page. You can easily drag an item from the Toolbox task pane into the Code view editing window. SharePoint Designer automatically creates and inserts the appropriate HTML, just as if you had dropped the item into position in Design view.

Script Editor

If you are familiar with development tools such as Visual Studio, you may have noticed something
missing in SharePoint Designer — a way to test your code. (Many IDEs use the F5 key as the command
to run the current program, often called the F5 experience.) Although Code view does provide
IntelliSense code completion for several scripting languages, scripts do not run within the context of
SharePoint Designer. To actually see scripts run, you need to shell out of the primary SharePoint
Designer environment.

There are two ways to do this. One, as you have seen, is to use the Preview in Browser tool.
The disadvantage of this option is that you must save your page and all changes before invoking the
preview. The other way is to use the Microsoft Script Editor (see Figure 1-22).

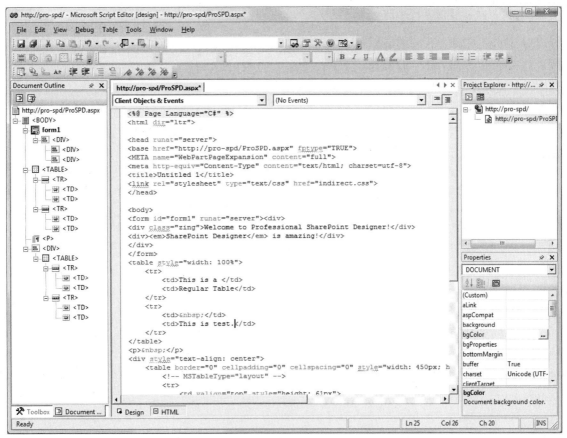

Figure 1-22

Microsoft Script Editor is essentially a lightweight IDE based on an older version of the Microsoft Visual Studio development environment. It was included and integrated with FrontPage for many versions, and is now carried through to SharePoint Designer.

Access the Script Editor by selecting Tools ⇨ Macro ⇨ Microsoft Script Editor or via the icon on the Code view toolbar. It is considered an optional component of SharePoint Designer, so upon first invocation you may see Setup run to install it.

The Script Editor starts with the current page from SharePoint Designer open in its HTML (code) view. A link is maintained between the two environments, so any change you make in the Script Editor is transferred to SharePoint Designer, and vice versa.

In the Script Editor, press F5 to launch Internet Explorer with the current state of your page, without first saving it. You can set breakpoints, debug variables, and do many of the other things you can do in other development environments.

Selecting which browser to use for preview in the Script Editor is independent of the configuration of the main SharePoint Designer application. To make multiple browsers available, you need to configure each via File ⇨ Browse With. The browser you set as the default is the one that F5 launches.

About the Script Editor

One reason the Script Editor is an optional component is that SharePoint Designer is focused toward editing SharePoint sites, and the editor does not work effectively on live SharePoint Web Part Pages. It remains extremely useful, however, for debugging client-side scripts before inserting them into a SharePoint page (chapter 13 provides some tips to this effect, as well as workarounds for Web Part Pages), and for working on non-SharePoint sites.

The online help for the Script Editor contains very useful references for JavaScript and VBScript languages.

Finally, the script editor can be used as the editing environment for InfoPath forms.

Split View

The Split view of the Page Editor provides all of the advantages of both Design and Code view. Each half of the view behaves exactly like its dedicated view. Code view, for example, gives you IntelliSense, while Design view maintains rulers and any page sizes you have set. In Figure 1-23 a table row has been selected from the Quick Tag Selector. Notice the highlighting in both the Code and Design panes of the Split view.

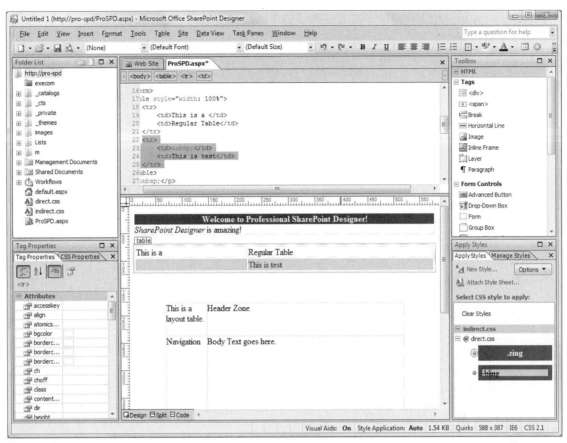

Figure 1-23

As you make changes in the Design pane, you can immediately see the effect on your code. The reverse is not true. Changes you make as you are editing code are not visible in the Design pane right away. You must act to indicate to SharePoint Designer that you are done with your edits, such as by clicking in the Design pane or saving your file, before the edits are reflected, because while you are editing in the Code pane, much of the time your markup may be in a transitional state that does not have a valid rendering. By waiting until you explicitly select the Design view, SharePoint Designer helps avoid the confusion that can result from page elements jumping all over the place as the rendering engine tries to make sense of the invalid markup.

Toolbars and Task Panes

SharePoint Designer is a versatile, powerful application. Helping you control that power and versatility is the province of the toolbars and task panes. SharePoint Designer proffers 11 toolbars (not counting the menu and any custom toolbars you may create), and no fewer than 24 task panes! Each toolbar or task pane controls a related set of functions. Earlier in the chapter, you were introduced to the Layout Tables task pane and the Common toolbar. The following sections briefly discuss these, as well as the other various toolbars and task panes, and how to manage them.

Managing Toolbars and Task Panes

With that many possible control elements in the application, showing them all at once is totally impractical. Assuming they fit at all, you'd have no room left on the screen for the Page Editor to perform any work. Fortunately, SharePoint Designer provides a great deal of flexibility in their display.

In many respects, toolbars and task panes behave similarly. They can be individually shown or hidden, docked or floating. The possible docking positions are the four edges of the SharePoint Designer window — above, below, right, and left of the design surface (which is always visible). Figure 1-24 shows toolbars and task panes in many of their possible visible states.

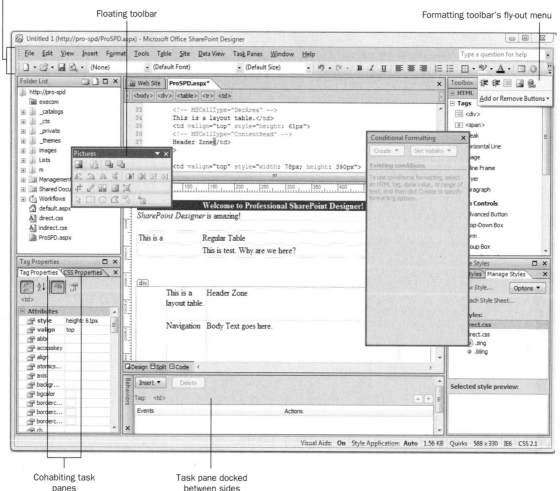

Figure 1-24

When both toolbars and task panes are docked to the same region, toolbars are always placed closest to the edge of the window. When docked to the top or bottom, toolbars fill the entire width of the window, while task panes — like the Behaviors task pane in Figure 1-24 — sit between anything docked at the sides.

Toolbars can be placed on multiple levels within a docking region, each level farther away from the docking edge. Multiple toolbars can occupy the same level. If a toolbar docked on a given level cannot fit in its allocated area, the items in the bar are hidden and added to a fly-out menu, as shown in the upper-right corner of Figure 1-24. Floating toolbars, such as the Pictures toolbar in the figure, always show all of their available items, but will rearrange them as needed to fit a resized window.

All task panes in a docking region are arrayed along the edge of the region, inside any toolbars. In addition, you can place multiple task panes in the same space. These cohabiting task panes are selectable via tabs in that space, as are the Tag Properties and CSS Properties task panes in the figure. You can maximize a task pane to take up its entire docking zone, and restore it to its former size.

After showing, hiding, and moving task panes around extensively, you may find it difficult to locate a particular item. SharePoint Designer offers a quick way to reset the task panes to a known state: Select Task Panes ⇨ Reset Workspace Layout. The task panes return to the state shown in Figure 1-25.

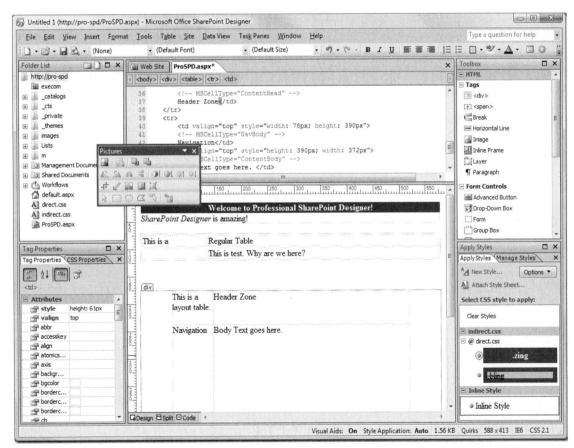

Figure 1-25

Notice that the Pictures toolbar remains floating as it was in Figure 1-24. The reset function only impacts task panes. You can show and hide individual toolbars either by right-clicking an existing toolbar, or by selecting from View ⇨ Toolbars. You can also show and hide individual task panes by selecting them from the Task Panes menu.

Toolbars

In general, toolbars provide quick access to functions that are also available in other places in SharePoint Designer, but may be buried deep in a menu tree or dialog box. By default, SharePoint Designer shows the Menu (which itself is a special toolbar) and the Common toolbar.

The following table briefly describes each of the toolbars that come with SharePoint Designer. The actual functions contained therein are described in detail, as appropriate, throughout the book.

Toolbar	Description
Standard	A basic toolbar containing an array of features, except formatting.
Formatting	Contains selectors for fonts, sizes, styles, and so on.
Code View	Assists with formatting items in SharePoint Designer's Code view.
Common	A single toolbar containing the most frequently used elements from both the Standard and Formatting toolbars; shown by default in SharePoint Designer.
Dynamic Web Template	For managing the editable regions of Dynamic Web Templates (DWT files).
Master Page	For managing the content regions of .NET Master Pages.
Pictures	For manipulating the properties of images included on a web page.
Positioning	For adjusting the positions of items with the absolute position style, such as layers.
Style	For managing the style of a selected item, or attaching a style sheet to a page.
Style Application	For controlling how styles are applied by SharePoint Designer.
Tables	Assists with table manipulation.

General-Purpose Task Panes

Most task panes in SharePoint Designer are useful in web editing, regardless of whether you are editing a SharePoint site. The following table briefly describes these general-purpose task panes.

Task Pane	Description
Folder List	A tree view of the files and folders in your site (shown by default).
Navigation *	Management of menu hierarchies.
Tag Properties	All parameters and properties available for the current HTML tag (shown by default).
CSS Properties	All the available CSS Properties for the current item (shown by default).
Layout Tables	Controls for configuring tables specially designed to help lay out web pages.
Apply Styles	The style classes currently defined and available — and tools to add more (shown by default).
Manage Styles	Defines new styles and arranges where they are stored (.css, which file, in page, and so on) (shown by default).
Behaviors	Sets actions to perform on events for various page elements.
Layers	Creates and manages layers.
Toolbox	Quick access to the elements that you can place on a page (shown by default).
Data Source Library *	Data sources available for use on pages.
Data Source Details	Shows the schema and data from a data source; allows drag and drop onto a page.
Conditional Formatting *	Changes the way data is presented based on conditions set by the page designer.
Find 1	Results from a find operation.
Find 2	Results from a find operation.
Accessibility	Reports on design issues that may cause problems for people with limited vision.
Compatibility	Reports on design issues that may cause problems with particular browsers and standards.
Hyperlinks	Reports on the status of hyperlinks used on the site.
CSS Reports	Shows styles in use, style sheet files, and references to styles that do not exist.
Clip Art **	Allows search and selection of images from various sources.
Clipboard **	Shows a history of items clipped in various Office applications.

*Although these task panes are available on non-SharePoint sites, on those sites they manipulate different objects behind the scenes than they would on a SharePoint site.

**The Clip Art and Clipboard task panes behave like toolbars in the way they dock. Only one of them may be visible at a time, and you can toggle between them with a menu in the task pane title bar.

SharePoint-Specific Task Panes

In addition to the general-purpose task panes, SharePoint Designer has some task panes that are used only when working on a SharePoint site. The following table briefly describes these panes:

Task Pane	Description
Find Data Source	Searches among the data sources defined in the current SharePoint site.
Web Parts	A gallery of the Web Parts available on the site.
Contributor *	For controlling access to SharePoint Designer functionality.

*This task pane is shared with the Clip Art and Clipboard panes, and behaves in the same fashion.

Web Site (Structural) Views

When you don't have a file open in the Page Editor, the design surface shows a variety of structural views of your web site. These are also available by clicking the Web Site tab in the design surface when you have files open.

Files and Folders

Like the Folder List task pane, the Folders web site view shows the files and folders currently in the web site. If the Folder List task pane is shown, the Folders view shows the contents of the currently selected folder in the task pane, as shown in Figure 1-26.

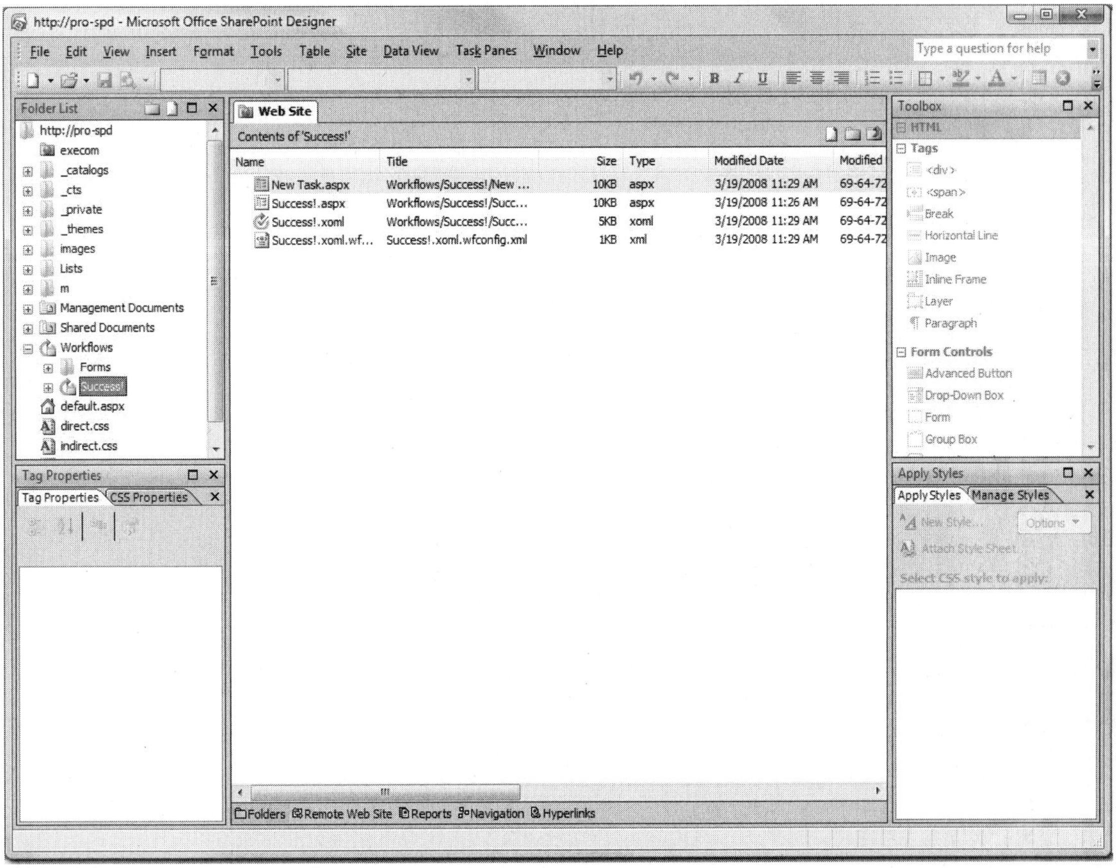

Figure 1-26

Remote Web Site

SharePoint Designer can be used to transfer files from one site to another. The Remote Web Site view, as shown in Figure 1-27, is used to control synchronization of the two sites.

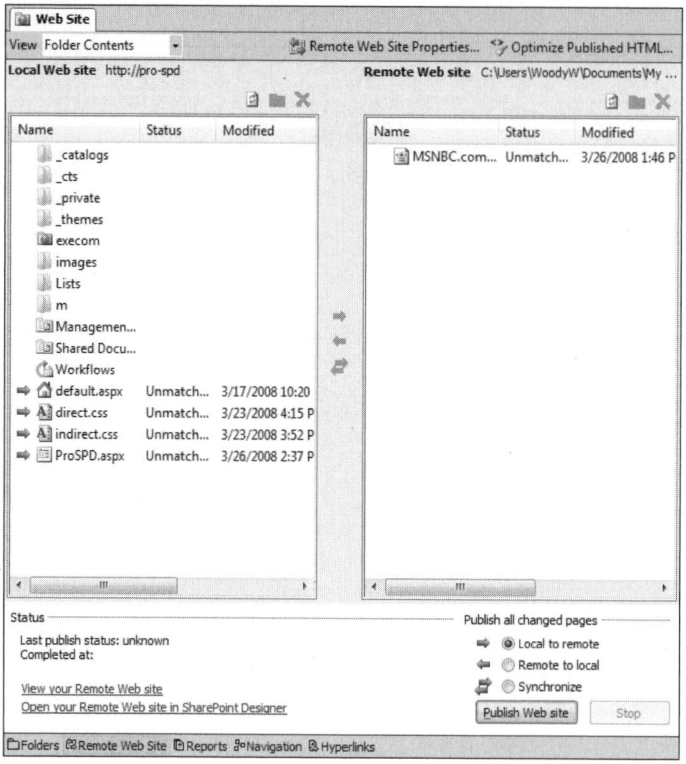

Figure 1-27

The site you are editing, regardless of whether it is on your current machine, is considered the local web site. The Remote Web Site is usually considered the target of the synchronization. However, you have the option of pulling information back from the remote site (essentially taking a snapshot of its current state), or performing a two-way synchronization. When there are conflicting changes, SharePoint Designer prompts you to decide which change takes precedence.

This function does not work for data stored in SharePoint Lists and Libraries.

Reporting Tools

In addition to the Accessibility, Compatibility, and CSS report task panes, SharePoint Designer offers a wide array of Web Site reports. Figure 1-28 Shows the Site Summary report, which itself offers links into many of the other reports available.

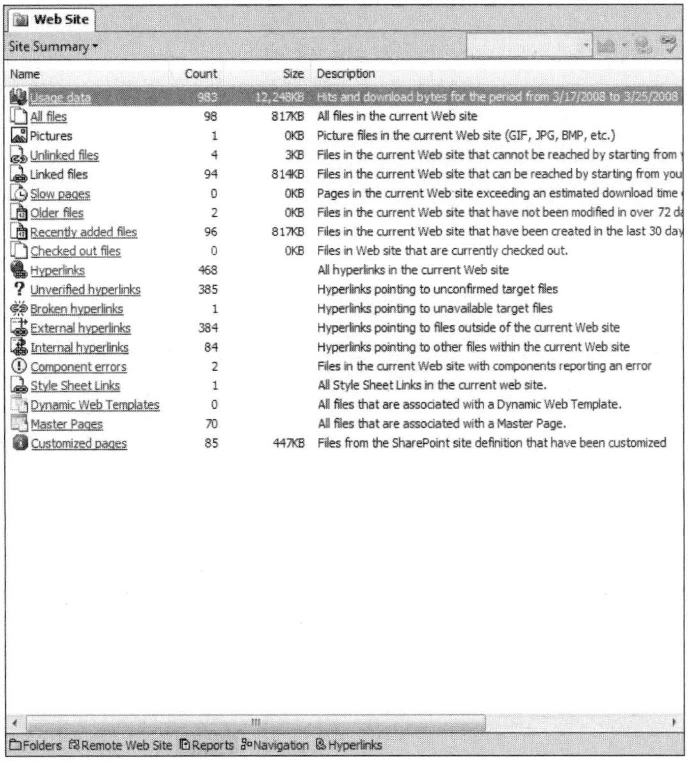

Figure 1-28

Several of these reports are useful to you as a designer. You can see at a glance which pages have broken hyperlinks, or might take an excessive amount of time to load for a typical user. You can use the Older Files report to check for potentially stale content.

See chapter 18 for more information on the administrative and usage reports, as well as reports available from within SharePoint itself.

Navigation and Hyperlinks

The Navigation Web Site view, Figure 1-29, shows the same tree as the Navigation task pane. In the case of a SharePoint site, they show the links used for the Quick Launch and Top-level tab menus.

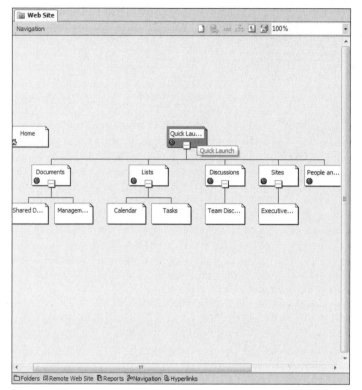

Figure 1-29

You can also create your own menu hierarchies, and insert them on pages using SharePoint Designer.

Generally speaking, on SharePoint sites, you should allow the standard SharePoint web interface tools to manage the navigation (see chapter 3).

Another way to look at how your users might navigate around your site is through the Web Site Hyperlinks view, as shown in Figure 1-30.

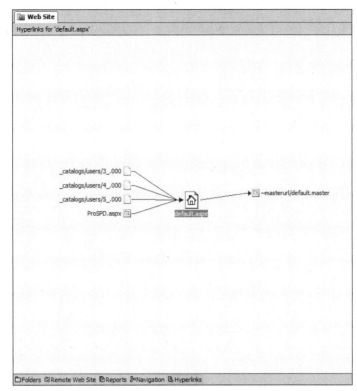

Figure 1-30

This view allows you to see the hyperlinks leading to, and exiting, the individual pages in your site. As with the Folders and Navigation views, you can directly open a particular page for editing, set its properties, or launch a browser preview. You can also select any page to be the center of attention, and view the link tree from that perspective.

> *The Hyperlinks view is based on links that are actually coded into your pages. On a SharePoint site, most links are generated by the server at run time and therefore they will not reflect in the Hyperlinks view. On non-SharePoint sites, changes to the navigation structure embed links directly into the pages at design time, and therefore do appear.*

Summary

This chapter gave you an overview of Microsoft Office SharePoint Designer 2007. You learned about the Page Editor, and how to get around its various views. You discovered:

❑ SharePoint Designer is not just for SharePoint. It incorporates a wide variety of features that make it an ideal all-around web design tool.

❑ SharePoint Designer's user interface is very flexible, and can be adapted to almost anyone's work style.

❑ How to access the Microsoft Script Editor, a powerful code-debugging environment.

The next few chapters take you on a walk through a SharePoint site as seen from several different perspectives: by a user through the web; by a site owner/administrator, both on the web and on the file server; and by you via SharePoint Designer. Along the way, you will pick up valuable insight and tips on what to change for your customizations (and how), as well as a few things that might be better left alone.

2

SharePoint from the User's Perspective

SharePoint Designer includes a broad array of features and functions that make it a powerful web design tool. Yet, one of the key purposes of SharePoint Designer is to enable you not only to "make it look less like SharePoint," but also to leverage and build upon a number of SharePoint's features. But what does that mean? What is SharePoint? It's important to remember that you (or your clients) are implementing SharePoint for a reason. In your efforts to customize its look, you need to be sure you retain its feel — its core capabilities.

In this chapter, you get a feel for what SharePoint is and what it offers the user. Most of the elements described from the user's perspective can be configured to some extent through the web interface. While you will have a much greater capability to customize them in SharePoint Designer, understanding the built-in functionality will give you a better foundation for your construction. This chapter introduces SharePoint's:

❑ Basic structure

❑ Lists and libraries

❑ Web Parts

A Default SharePoint Home Page

On the surface, SharePoint is a fully functional web application. Out-of-the-box, you get pages you can browse through, places you can put information, and lots of ways to get that information back out again. Figure 2-1 shows a basic SharePoint site.

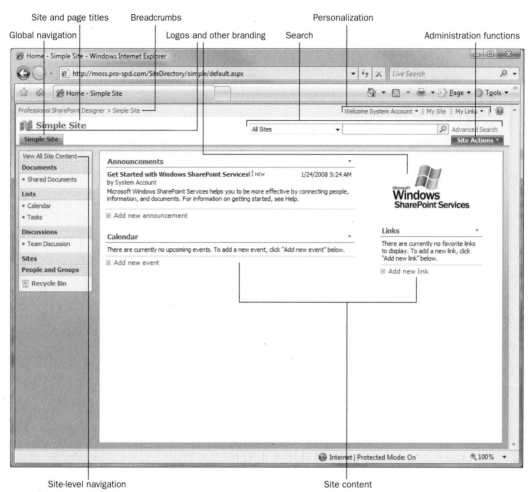

Figure 2-1

Scratch that surface, and you find a whole lot more, including the capability to define new forms of information, to pick and choose what gets displayed on a page, and to create new pages. It can all be done without programming or even leaving the friendly confines of your web browser.

Many web designers new to SharePoint create a site the way they always have, and then try to graft on bits and pieces of SharePoint functionality. While that can create sites that are functional, it often presents challenges for maintainability, future expansion, and consistency.

SharePoint provides a number of functions for you (see Figure 2-1):

❑   Global navigation

❑   Site-level navigation

- ❏ Breadcrumbs
- ❏ Personalization
- ❏ Site and page titles
- ❏ Logos and other branding
- ❏ Administrative functions
- ❏ Search
- ❏ Site content

These are all features needed by virtually every web site in one form or another. The default cosmetic aspects of these features may not be to your liking, but that doesn't mean you have to scrap them. This book shows you how to change those cosmetics without discarding and rebuilding the features themselves.

SharePoint Content: Lists, Libraries, and More

At its basic level, virtually everything that is displayed in a SharePoint site comes out of a list. A list is much like a database table, in that it is made up of rows of data, which in turn are composed of fields of different types. There are many types of lists predefined in SharePoint, but they fall into two main categories. One is simply called the list. The rows of a list are called items. The other category is the library. The fundamental difference is that a library's principal row element is a file, or document.

Almost any list can have a file as an attachment, but in those cases, the individual fields of the list are primary, and the attachment is just another piece of data in the list. In the case of the library, however, the file is considered the core element, and the fields are considered properties or metadata for that document.

> *Although it's convenient to think of lists and libraries as tables, for management and display purposes, their architectures are very different. This is described in more detail in chapter 3.*

Depending on the template or site definition used to create a SharePoint site, certain lists are automatically created. The home page displayed in Figure 2-1 shows four lists and libraries in the left navigation bar (also called the Quick Launch bar): Shared Documents, Calendar, Tasks, and Team Discussion. The Announcements and Links lists both have Web Parts placed on the page, as does the Calendar list, which has a navigation link as well.

Templates and Site Definitions

Templates and site definitions are two ways to expand the collection of SharePoint site types available for users to create.

Templates are customizations of existing SharePoint functionality. Almost any changes you make to a site through the web interface or SharePoint Designer can be saved into a template. These templates can be instantiated repeatedly on the same server, or easily exported from the site they were created on, and imported onto another SharePoint Server Farm. Templates can be saved with existing data intact, or with only the schema information. Lists, libraries, sites, or even site hierarchies can be saved as templates.

Site definitions are more foundational. They are created on the server file system as collections of SharePoint Features and are implemented through Features. Site definitions enable you to create a reusable site model that includes custom pages that access the SharePoint API directly, or require other server-side code to execute. Chapter 18 describes how to convert a site you have customized with SharePoint Designer into a site definition.

You are not stuck with the lists and libraries created by default in a site. New lists and libraries can be created and existing ones deleted at any time. In addition, you can display information from diverse sources both inside and outside of your enterprise with such features as data views and the MOSS Business Data Catalog (you'll see more about these in chapters 10 and 11). When creating a new list or library, you can choose from several standard and custom types.

List and Library Types

SharePoint provides a number of standard list types. New lists can be added to a site at any time by anyone with sufficient rights. The particular list types available depend on a number of factors, including the edition of SharePoint installed (WSS, Search Server, or MOSS Enterprise), the Features activated, and the template used for the site. Figure 2-2 shows the default list and library types available in the Team site template in MOSS.

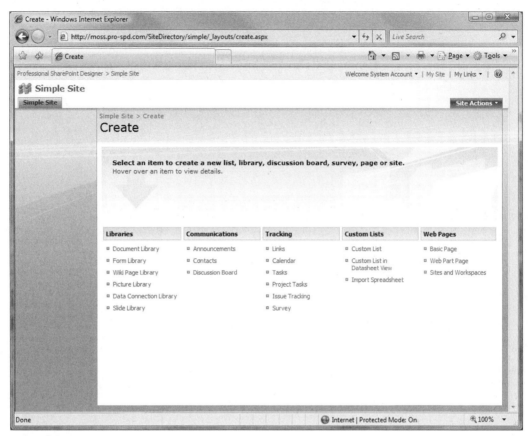

Figure 2-2

This page was accessed from Site Actions ⇨ Create. In addition to providing existing list and library templates, the Create page may allow you to make custom lists, site pages, or even child sites, depending upon the site template.

While there are many common elements, each list and library type has some unique characteristics — such as predefined fields, views, and custom actions that can be performed automatically on its items. For example, one of the most commonly used library types is the Document Library, which is primarily designed to contain documents, such as those produced by word-processing, spreadsheet, and presentation applications; or final-form files, such as Adobe PDF. It includes features suitable for that task, such as versioning, check-in, and check-out. The Shared Documents library in the default site shown earlier is a document library. The following table describes several of the common list and library types.

Type	Principal Characteristics
Document Library	Contains files such as Word Documents. It provides easy access to version control, folders, and check-out/in. This library can be email-enabled. Fields in this library can be derived from and written to embedded file metadata in supported formats.
Form Library	Designed to hold XML files, each file representing the data in a single instance of a form, such as InfoPath.
Wiki Page Library	Wiki libraries form the basis of SharePoint's Wiki functionality. They support pages, images, and automatic generation of new pages from Wiki links.
Picture Library	Picture libraries contain picture files, and contain predefined views, which include thumbnail images, slide shows, and bulk download options.
Slide Library	Slide libraries are unique to Microsoft Office SharePoint Server, and therefore not available in Windows SharePoint Services. They are used in conjunction with Microsoft PowerPoint to store individual slides for re-use.
Announcements	Announcements lists are designed to show time-critical information on the home page of a site. Announcement items can be set to expire. This list can be email-enabled.
Contacts	Contacts lists have predefined fields that are suitable for holding information about people. In addition, functions are provided for synchronizing contact information with SharePoint-compatible applications such as Microsoft Outlook.
Discussion Board	A discussion board provides the ability to host persistent communications on a SharePoint site. It includes facilities for thread management, post approval, and email enabling.
Links	Links lists automatically display their items as hyperlinks to the specified locations, rather than list items. While most lists can be sorted, items in links lists can also be ordered explicitly.
Calendar	Calendar lists have features convenient for maintaining schedules, and can be synchronized with SharePoint-aware applications such as Microsoft Outlook.
Tasks	Tasks lists include fields for due dates and status, and can be assigned to individual site users.
Project Tasks	Project tasks lists include all task functions above, plus Gantt chart views, and the ability to be opened in SharePoint-aware applications.
Issue Tracking	Issue tracking lists are similar to task lists, but also maintain a revision history to track changes to the issue's status.
Survey	Survey lists are designed for streamlined handling of large sets of response data.
Custom Lists	Custom lists can be defined to contain arbitrary information, and present it in various ways. They can be displayed as a static text table, or as an editable Datasheet, by default. You can also import the contents of simple Excel worksheets into a custom list, and have the fields defined automatically from the columns present in the workbook.

Other list and library types may be available in your particular installation of SharePoint.

Customizing Lists and Libraries

Once a list or library has been created, it contains a number of characteristics that can be customized. Figure 2-3 shows the Settings page for a document library.

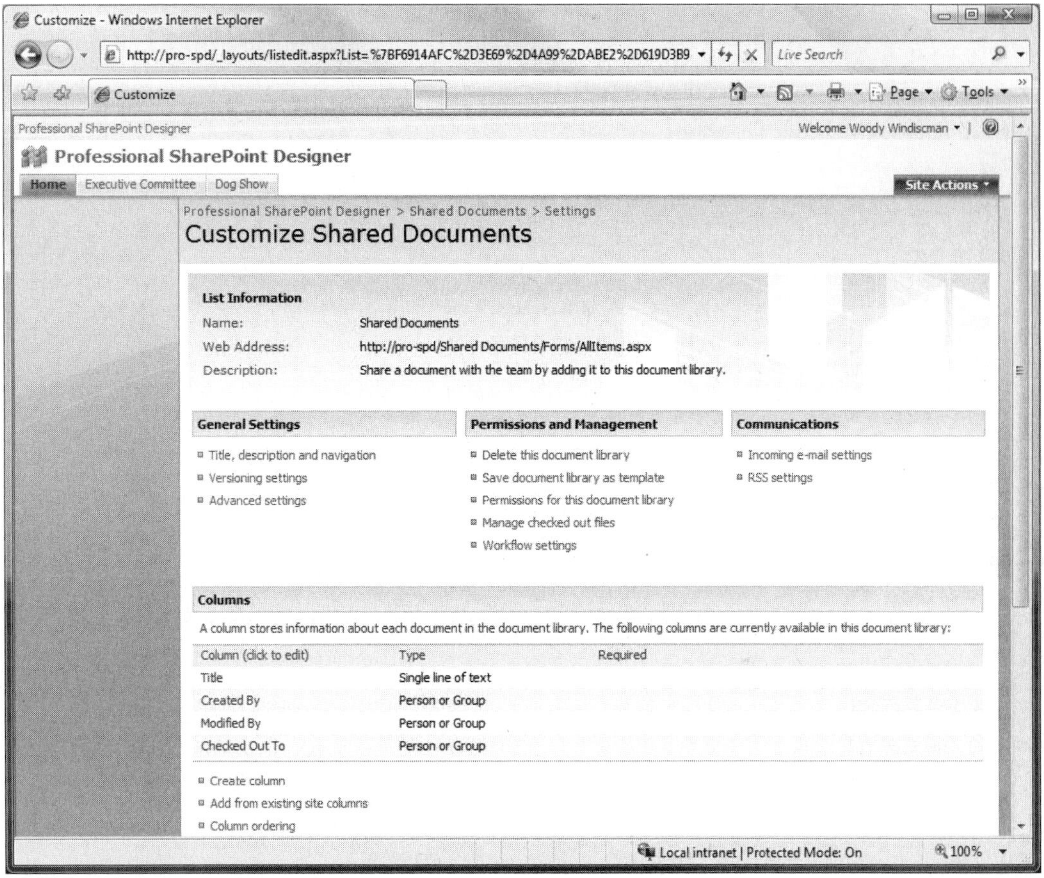

Figure 2-3

While much customization can be done through the web interface, there are certain settings, including hiding particular lists or libraries, that can be set only through SharePoint Designer. They are discussed in the next chapter. Some settings, such as permissions, can only be changed in the web interface. And some settings, such as creating views, can be changed in either place.

Columns (Fields)

Each list or library contains certain default columns. You are not limited to using them as is. Just as you can add and remove lists or libraries from a site, you can also easily add and remove most columns.

> *Key identity columns, such as ID and Title (Name in some lists), and administrative columns, such as Modified By, cannot be removed from a list or library.*

Columns can be added or removed via the web interface, but not through SharePoint Designer. Figure 2-4 shows some of the column types available out-of-the-box. Custom column types can be created and deployed server-side as SharePoint Features, but that process is beyond the scope of this book.

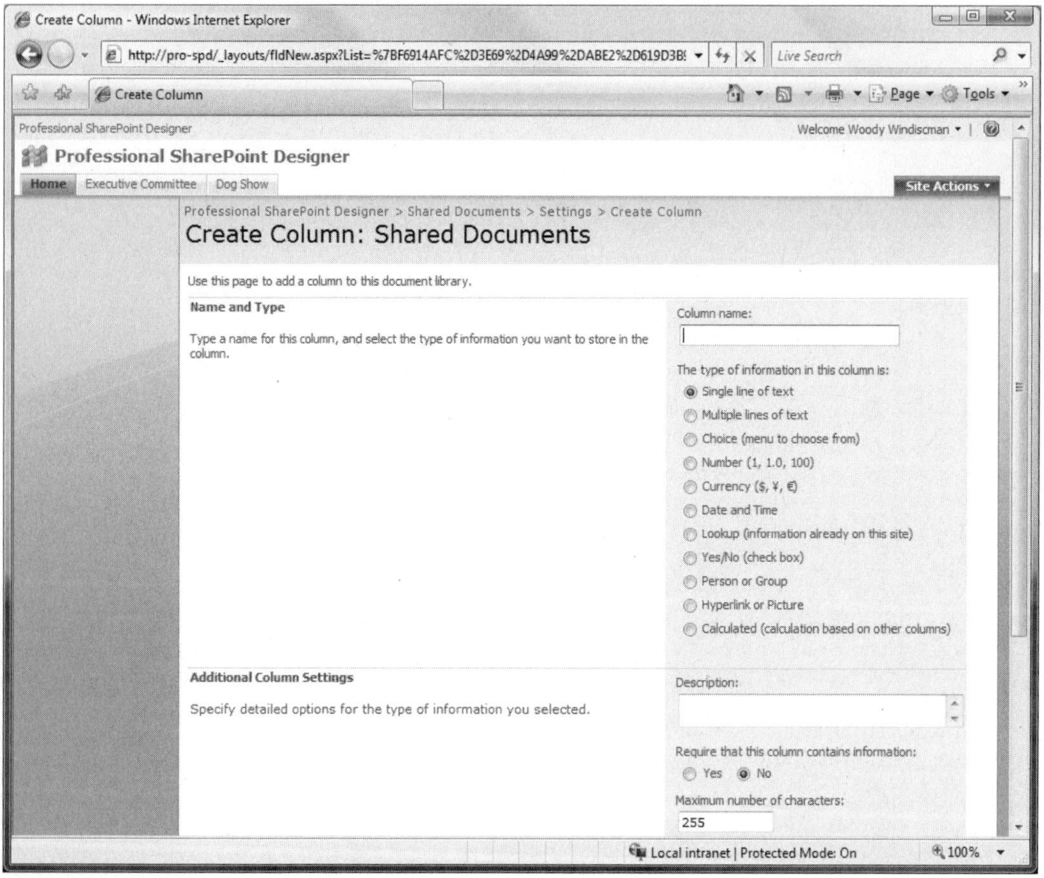

Figure 2-4

Content Types

In a database, each table is defined with a particular schema, or set of columns. If you want to store a different kind of information, you use a different table. In SharePoint, you can store information with more than one schema in a single list or library, through a mechanism called *content types*.

SharePoint content types enable you to define a schema for a particular type of object, such as a news article or a contact, and use it wherever it makes sense in your site. Consider an inventory application for a hardware store. You can create a single list for your stock that includes a content type for paint, which includes columns for latex and oil base, color, and interior or exterior application, while a content type for lumber might include the type of wood, dimensions, and so on.

Each content type can have its own entry forms and workflow associated with it. When you create or edit items with different content types, the appropriate form — with the fields defined for that type — is shown. You can also create custom forms for individual content types. Chapter 12 discusses forms in detail.

Content types are particularly important in MOSS Publishing sites. In a publishing site, your pages are stored in a single library, and you associate different layout pages with particular content types, such as press releases, executive biographies, and so on. This is described in more detail in chapter 8.

Understanding Views

Information from lists and libraries is typically presented in a *view*. A view consists of selected information from a list or library, presented in a particular way. You can choose a subset of columns, filter and group data, or even change the format of the information. Figures 2-5 and 2-6 show two very different views of the same data. There are several predefined view styles that can be applied to various lists. Almost any list with a date column, for example, can be presented as a calendar.

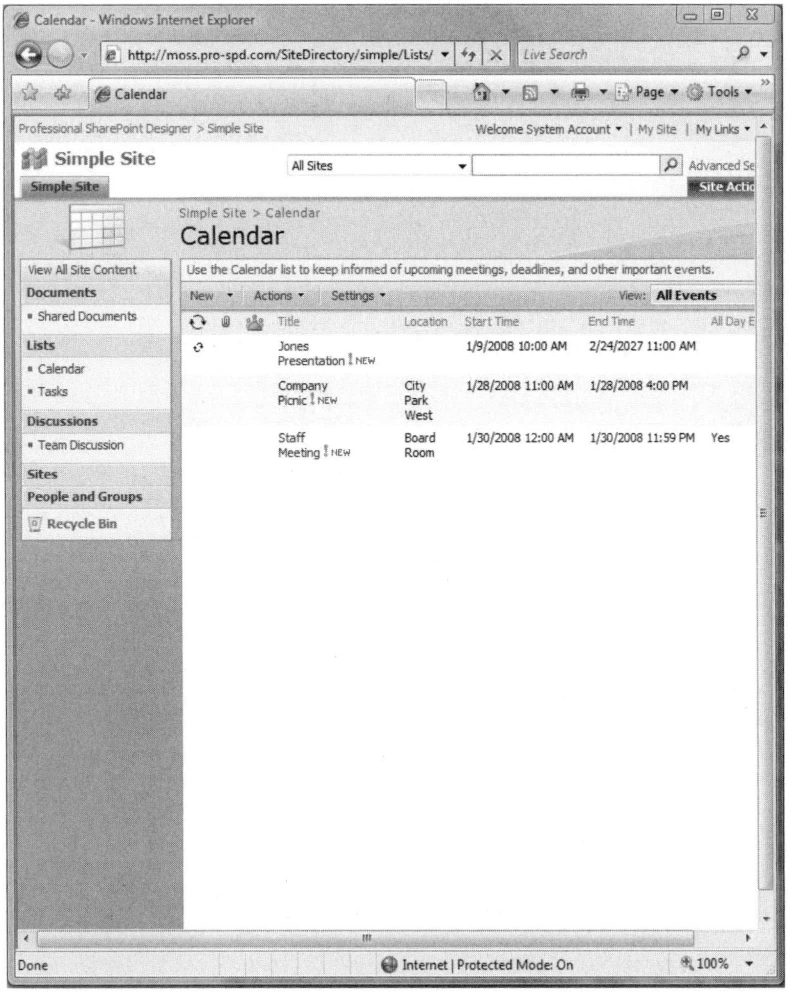

Figure 2-5

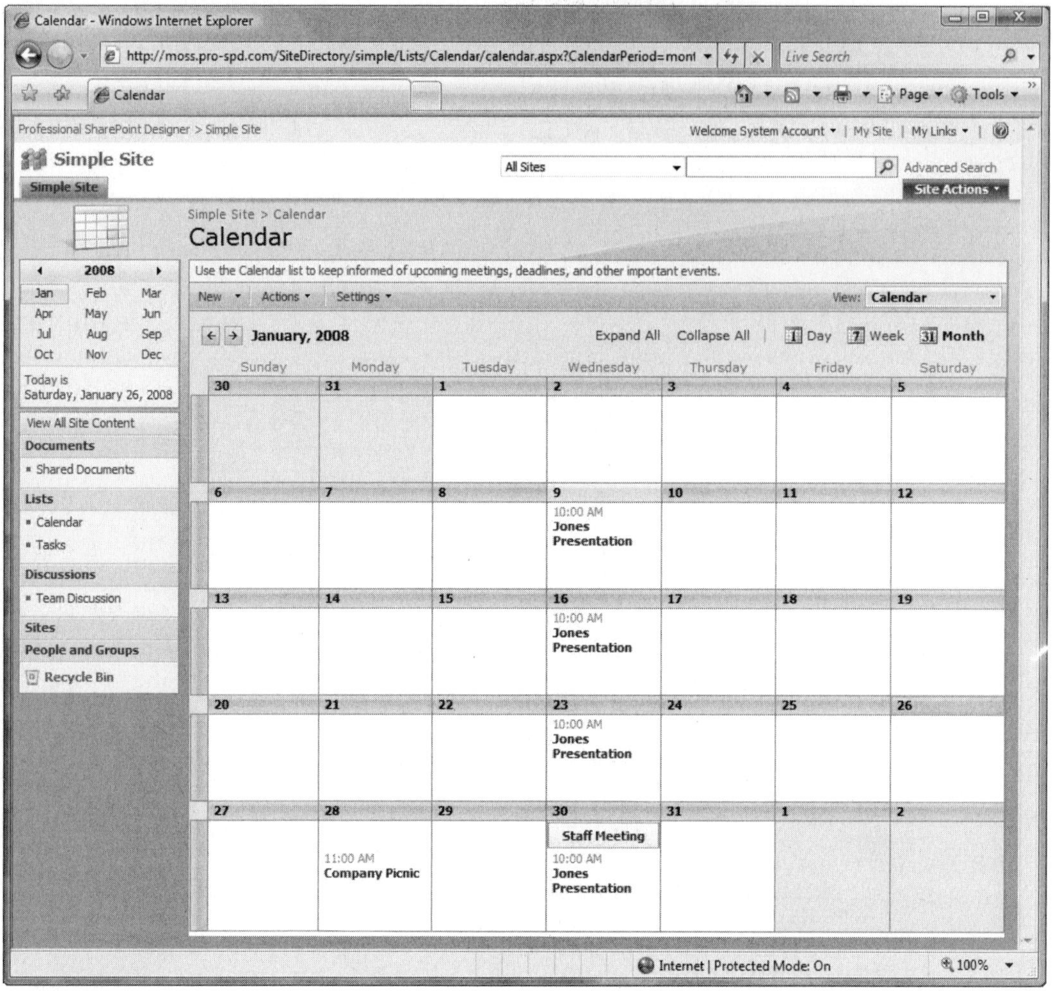

Figure 2-6

One of the powerful features of SharePoint is the capability to personalize the user experience. To that end, a user can create views to be either public or private. A sales manager, for example, might want to see information grouped by region and ordered by total sales, whereas an individual sales rep would need a view showing the details of her closings for the month, and would not be allowed to see the details for the other representatives.

Web Parts

Web Parts are one of the primary means by which content is displayed in SharePoint. MOSS Publishing Pages use a slightly different model, called Layout Pages, that is discussed in chapter 8. A Web Part may display static content, a view of a list or library, the interface for a business application, or virtually anything else.

In the Zone

A typical page in SharePoint consists of *Web Part Zones* into which a user may place any of the Web Parts available on the site. A page with Web Part Zones is called a *Web Part Page*. Several Web Part Page templates are provided with SharePoint, with varying sizes and positions of Web Part Zones. You may have noticed that the Create page (shown in Figure 2-2), which enables you to add lists and libraries to a site, also has an option to create a Web Part Page. Figure 2-7 shows the New Web Part Page page.

Figure 2-7

Notice from the layout thumbnail that Web Part Zones can be configured to arrange the parts they contain either vertically or horizontally. A zone can hold any number of Web Parts.

Even the home page of a team site is actually a Web Part Page. Figure 2-8 shows a page in edit mode.

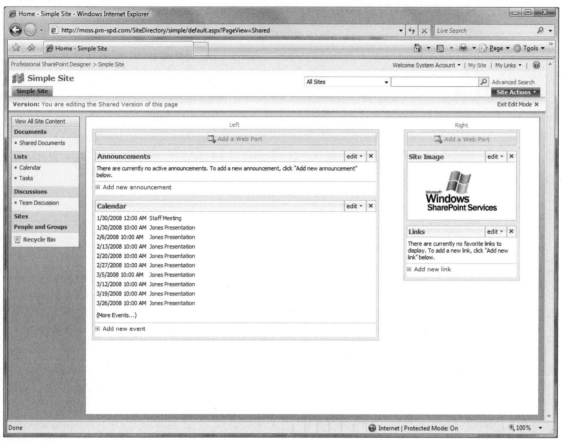

Figure 2-8

Like list views, most Web Part Pages can have a public and a personal view. The public view is edited by selecting Edit Page from the Site Actions menu. The personal view is edited by selecting Personalize this Page from the Welcome menu.

When you click the Add a Web Part caption in a Web Part Zone, an Add Web Parts dialog like the one shown in Figure 2-9 opens. The dialog first lists the Web Parts that are most likely to be appropriate for the zone selected, followed by the other Web Parts available on your site.

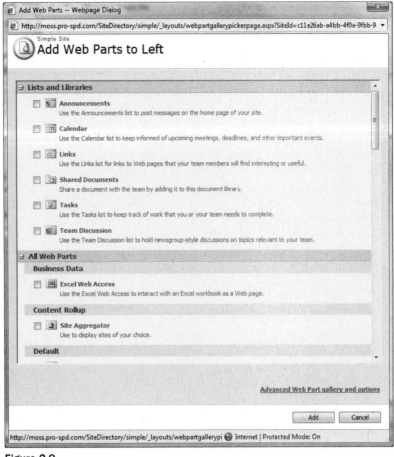

Figure 2-9

You can have multiple copies of the same Web Part on a page.

Once a Web Part is added to a Web Part Zone, you can change its properties by selecting Edit ⇨ Modify Shared (or My) Web Part. Figure 2-10 shows the Edit menu, as well as the Web Part properties pane.

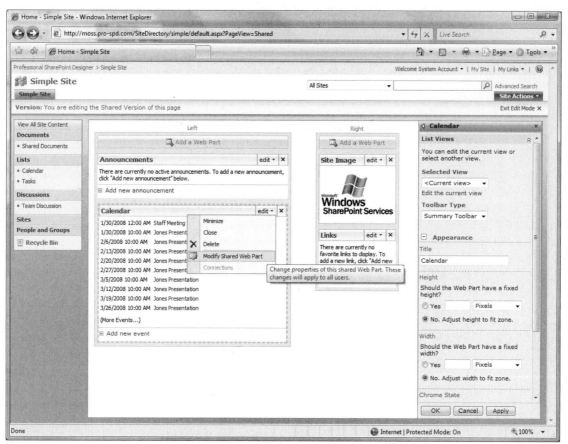

Figure 2-10

Depending upon the Web Part, some properties can be set only through the web interface, and others may only be available, or offer significantly easier control, when using SharePoint Designer. For example, the XML Web Part offers plain text editing of the XML data and XSL source in the web interface, but allows full WYSIWYG editing within SharePoint Designer. This is described in detail in chapters 10 and 11.

Some Standard Web Parts

All editions of SharePoint come with several key Web Parts built in. They give you features that range from displaying images and plain static text, to list views, working with external data, and information about users of the site.

> *Web Parts are one of the principal expansion points in SharePoint. MOSS and Search Server include a variety of parts far beyond those described in this book. Many third-party Web Parts are also available. Chapter 16 shows you how to create a simple Web Part in Visual Studio and package it for easy deployment to a SharePoint Server.*

Some of the key Web Parts are:

❑ **List View Web Part:** One of the most common SharePoint Web Parts, but it is almost never shown by this name. That's because when a new list or library is created, a List View Web Part with the same name is created to go with it. Most standard list types include a hidden summary view that the automatic Web Part uses by default. You can edit the properties of the current view, or you can replace it with any existing view of the list or library.

❑ **Image Web Part:** Enables you to display a picture on a page.

❑ **Page Viewer Web Part:** Enables you to easily add content from another location to a page. This can be another web page (or web application), a file share, or even an individual document. This content is typically displayed in an IFRAME on the current page.

If the content cannot be rendered in an IFRAME in the user's browser, a new window may be opened to display it.

❑ **Form Web Part:** Enables you to add HTML form field elements and other content to a page.

❑ **Content Editor Web Part:** Enables you to insert virtually any valid HTML into a page. While often used for static rich text, this Part also allows client-side scripts. You will learn how to take advantage of this in chapter 13.

❑ **XML Web Part:** Enables you to display and style XML data. Both the XML data and the XSL styling can be statically entered in the Part, or read from an external source. This allows for flexible presentation of many kinds of information.

❑ **Data View/Form Web Part:** Not available for insertion directly from the web interface. It can be added only through SharePoint Designer, and is one of the most powerful tools in your arsenal. Several chapters later in the book are dedicated to using the amazing Data View Web Part.

Making the Connection

Web Parts are more than just static display containers. In addition to the scripting alluded to earlier, many Web Parts support an interpart communications mechanism called *Web Part connections.* Web Part connections allow you to use the contents of one Web Part to affect the data displayed in another.

For example, selecting a client's name from a dropdown can filter lists of orders, contacts, and service calls. As long as all of the parts support connections, it does not matter what the source of the data is — SharePoint, XML, or your corporate Customer Relationship Management (CRM) system. This allows heterogeneous applications to be developed with little or no code. Some people refer to this kind of application development as a mashup.

When combined with the Data View Web Part and SharePoint Designer, Web Part connections provide an easy yet powerful way to provide rich functionality to your users.

Summary

This chapter explained how SharePoint is more than just another web server. SharePoint provides many features out-of-the-box that make it a full-fledged web application, including:

❑ Site navigation.

❑ Page layout templates.

❑ A flexible list structure that lets you mange many kinds of content.

❑ Web Parts to display content both from within and from outside the current site.

The next chapter provides a look at the administrative tools provided with SharePoint, and how information is actually stored on the server.

SharePoint from the Administrator's Perspective

One of the key benefits of SharePoint is its capability to push functions that used to be solely the province of web designers and server administrators down to more appropriate personnel. This chapter describes some of the elements that can be managed within the context of the web site, as well as aspects that require more direct contact with the server. As with the basic functionality described in chapter 2, by understanding the administrative tools SharePoint provides, you can avoid reinventing the wheel in your designs. This chapter explores:

❑   User management

❑   Site navigation

❑   SharePoint architecture

❑   Server-side tools

On the Site

In the previous chapter, you saw how easy it is to create and manipulate the content of a SharePoint site. There are many other elements of a site that can be managed by the designated owner without the assistance of a server administrator or web designer. Figure 3-1 shows the main settings page of a SharePoint site. The page with these functions is accessed through Site Actions ⇨ Site Settings. (On some site types, particularly MOSS collaboration and publishing portals, this item may be labeled Modify All Site Settings because certain common tasks are given their own menu items.)

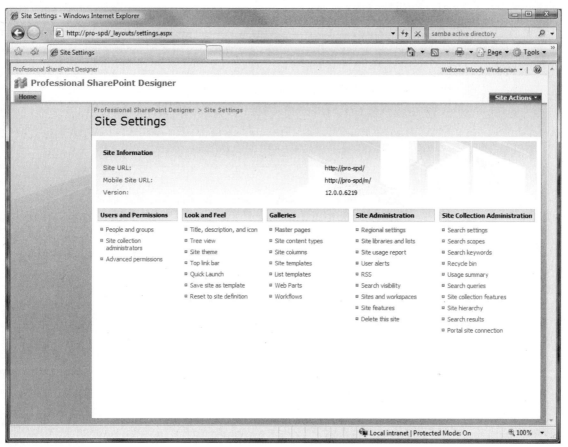

Figure 3-1

This is not a book about SharePoint administration, so you don't need to worry about all of the items on the list. Clearly, though, the user can manage many aspects of his site, from permissions to creating reports to determining the hierarchy of the sites in the collection. This section looks at how some of these administrative elements can (and should) play a crucial role in how you approach the design and customization of a SharePoint site. In particular, you'll see how you can simplify ongoing site maintenance by leveraging SharePoint's user management, navigation, and resource galleries.

Chapter 18 describes administrative functions that are more relevant post-design in more detail.

Users and Permissions

One of the most important functions that can be delegated to site owners is the management of permissions for their sites. Most functions in SharePoint feature *security trimming*. This means that user interface elements are hidden for users who do not have permission to access the underlying data or function. For example, a site owner can typically see everything on the site, including administration and control functions. An average user, on the other hand, might see a subset of the content, and no administration features. Figure 3-2 shows the site owner's view, while Figure 3-3 shows the same site as viewed by a visitor. You'll note that in Figure 3-3, the user has no access to the Site Actions menu, Management Documents, or the Executive Committee site.

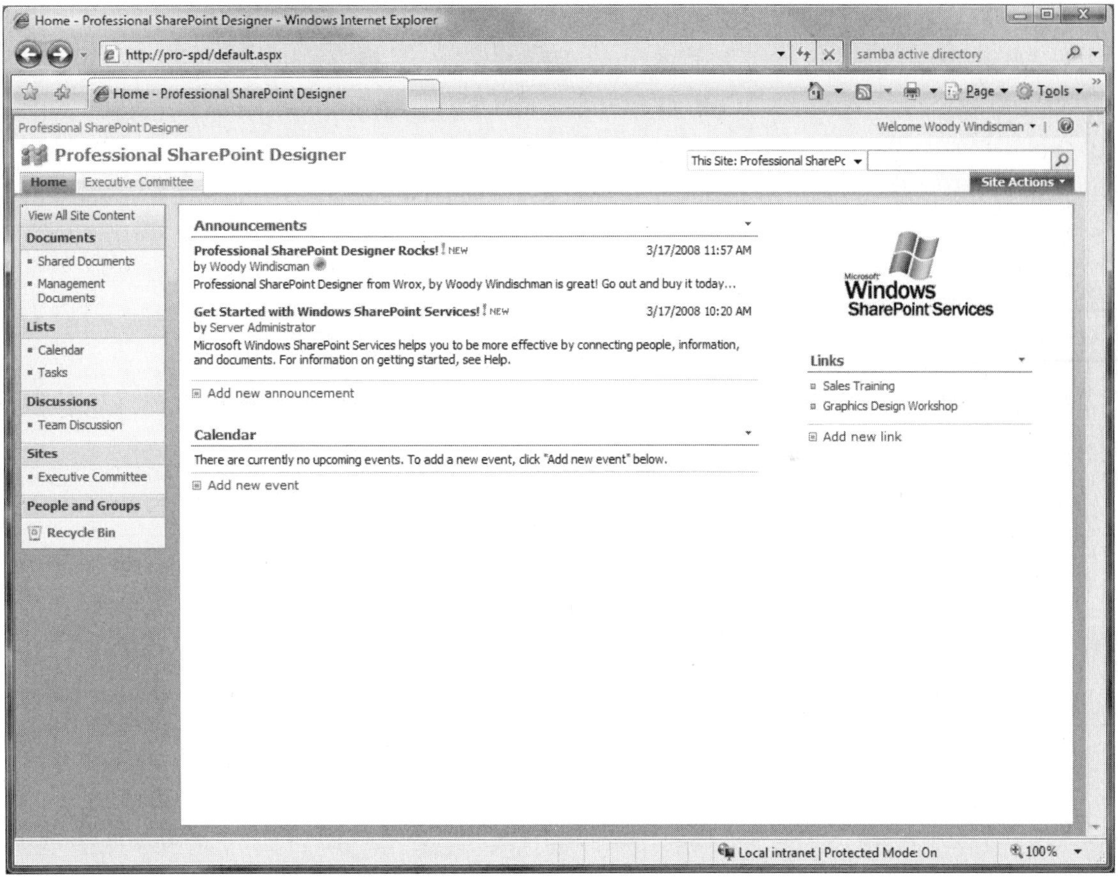

Figure 3-2

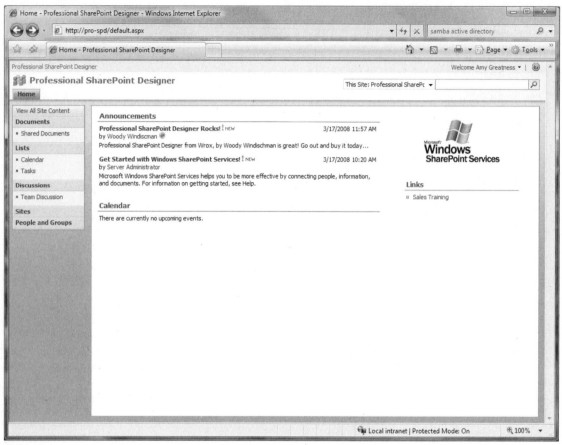

Figure 3-3

By making use of the standard SharePoint controls in your designs, you inherit this trimming, which makes site maintenance much easier in the long run, because you will not have to create separate pages for each user or role. chapter 5 shows you how to incorporate security trimming controls into your site designs.

Being a User

SharePoint can use any of the authentication methods supported by ASP.NET, including Windows integrated, Forms, and (in MOSS) LDAP. There are two ASP.NET providers involved in authentication:

❑   The membership provider

❑   The role provider

The membership provider provides the list of users, their credentials (e.g., ID and password), and at least some basic attributes (e.g., display name, email address). The role provider, if supplied, provides a way to manage groups of users. SharePoint itself also provides group management, described in the next section.

When SharePoint is installed, it is configured to use Windows integrated authentication — via NTLM, Basic (clear text), or Kerberos — as the default membership and role providers. Anonymous access is just a few clicks away. For companies that use Active Directory for their user base, this is sufficient for intranet use. Although Forms and other authentication mechanisms are supported, they require considerable effort to configure. Such configuration is beyond the scope of this book; however, be aware that each membership provider requires its own web application zone to be configured (that is, Windows authentication on `http://intranet`, Forms authentication on `http://intranet.pro-spd .com`). Each zone will serve the same content. Therefore, wherever possible, avoid hard-coding server names into your pages when linking to other pages in the same namespace. Instead, use *root relative* references (that is, use `"/sites/finance/default.aspx"` rather than `"http://intranetet/sites/ finance/default.aspx"`) in your links.

Regardless of the authentication method, permissions are assigned to users the same way. When assigning permissions to a resource, whether it is a list item or an entire site, you typically manually enter users' IDs into a web form, as shown in Figure 3-4. One of the many places you would see this form is accessed starting under Site Actions ⇨ Site Settings (click People and Groups, and click the New button in the list toolbar).

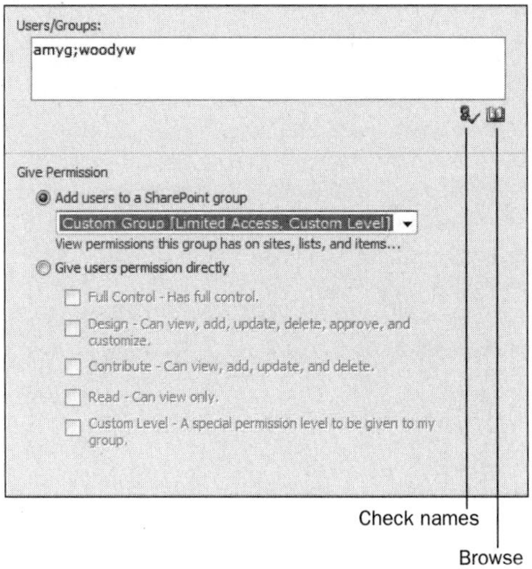

Figure 3-4

After you enter IDs, you can verify them against your membership providers by clicking the Check Names icon. If you are not sure of a user's ID, SharePoint provides a standard user browser, accessed by the Browse icon. Clicking that icon summons the People and Groups selector, which enables you to select users from whatever authentication providers may be installed, simply by entering a portion of the user's name. Figure 3-5 shows the People and Groups selector.

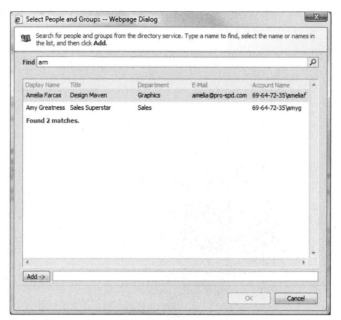

Figure 3-5

Group Think

The most convenient way to manage permissions on a SharePoint site is by assigning users to groups. These may be groups created in your role provider. You can also assign users and/or role provider groups to SharePoint groups, which are created within a SharePoint site and used to grant access to particular resources. For example, someone in a Site Members group might have permissions to modify the content of lists and libraries, but not to make any changes to their structure. The Site Visitors group might have read-only access to most of the site, but added permission to post to discussion boards.

Groups are each assigned *permission levels* — a set of default permissions constructed from a broad spectrum of rights that apply across the entire site, except where explicitly overridden.

> *SharePoint groups are distinct from any groups that may be defined in your ASP.NET membership and/ or role providers (e.g. Windows Domain Groups), but may contain such groups as members.*

When you create a SharePoint site, you have the option to also create certain groups and permission levels by default. The exact items created will depend upon the version of SharePoint and the type of site being provisioned. You can then add to, remove from, or edit the items on these lists. Figure 3-6 shows a selection of groups created by SharePoint for a typical team site.

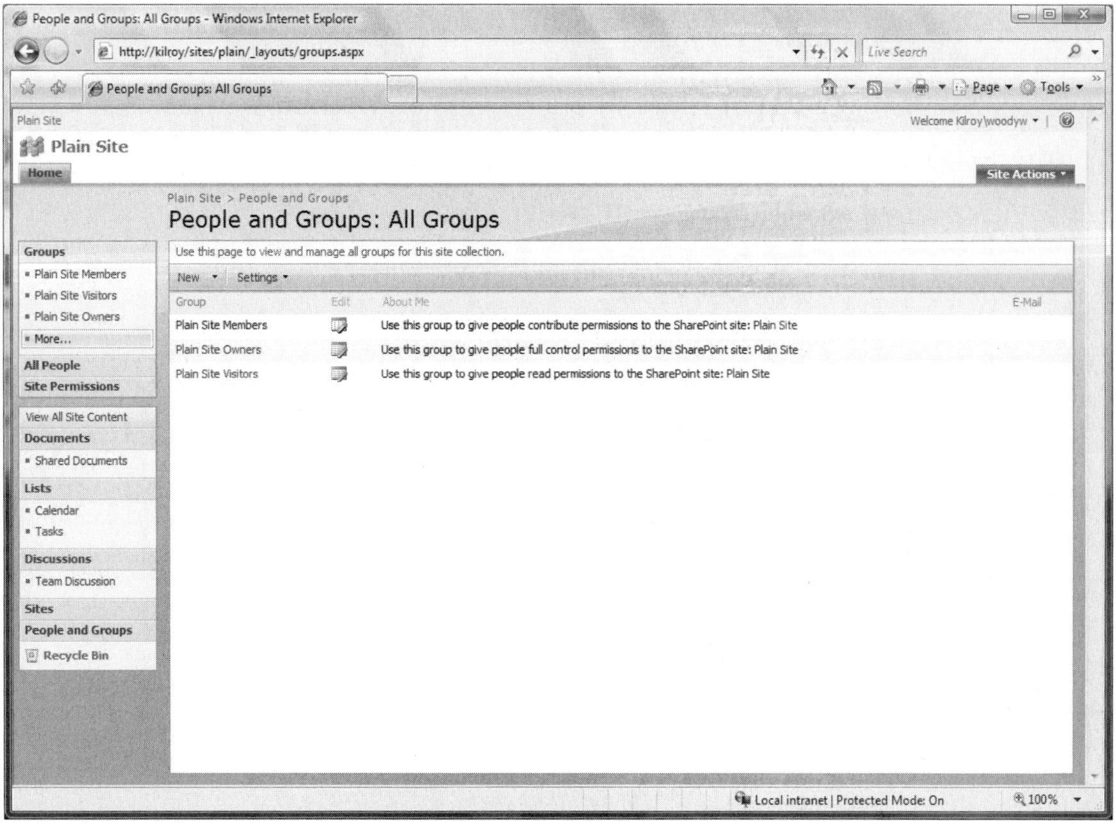

Figure 3-6

The default description shows the Permission Level associated with the group. You can see the groups available on your own site by starting from the Site Settings page, clicking the People and Groups link, and then clicking the Groups section header in the Quick Launch bar.

To change the permission levels associated with a group or to modify the permission levels available on your site, display the permissions screen shown in Figure 3-6, and then click the Permissions header in the Quick Launch bar. (You can also display this page by clicking the Advanced Permissions link on the Site Settings page.)

To create or modify a permission level, click the Settings link on the list toolbar, and select Permission Levels from the menu that appears to display the current list of permission levels. Click on a permission level, or click New in the list toolbar to open the appropriate form.

The permission levels Full Control and Limited Access are defined by SharePoint and cannot be edited; however, you can display their effective permissions.

Look and Feel — Navigational Elements and More

Almost all sites require navigation, and SharePoint provides two primary navigation hierarchies: a global navigation bar, represented by default as a tab strip below the site title; and local navigation, represented by the Quick Launch bar on the left of the page. SharePoint provides a built-in capability for site owners to modify the items and their order. Figure 3-7 shows the editor for the Quick Launch bar on a WSS Site. MOSS Publishing sites have a more extensive editing capability. In particular, Publishing sites support the easy editing of two-level navigation. This capability is described in more detail in chapter 5.

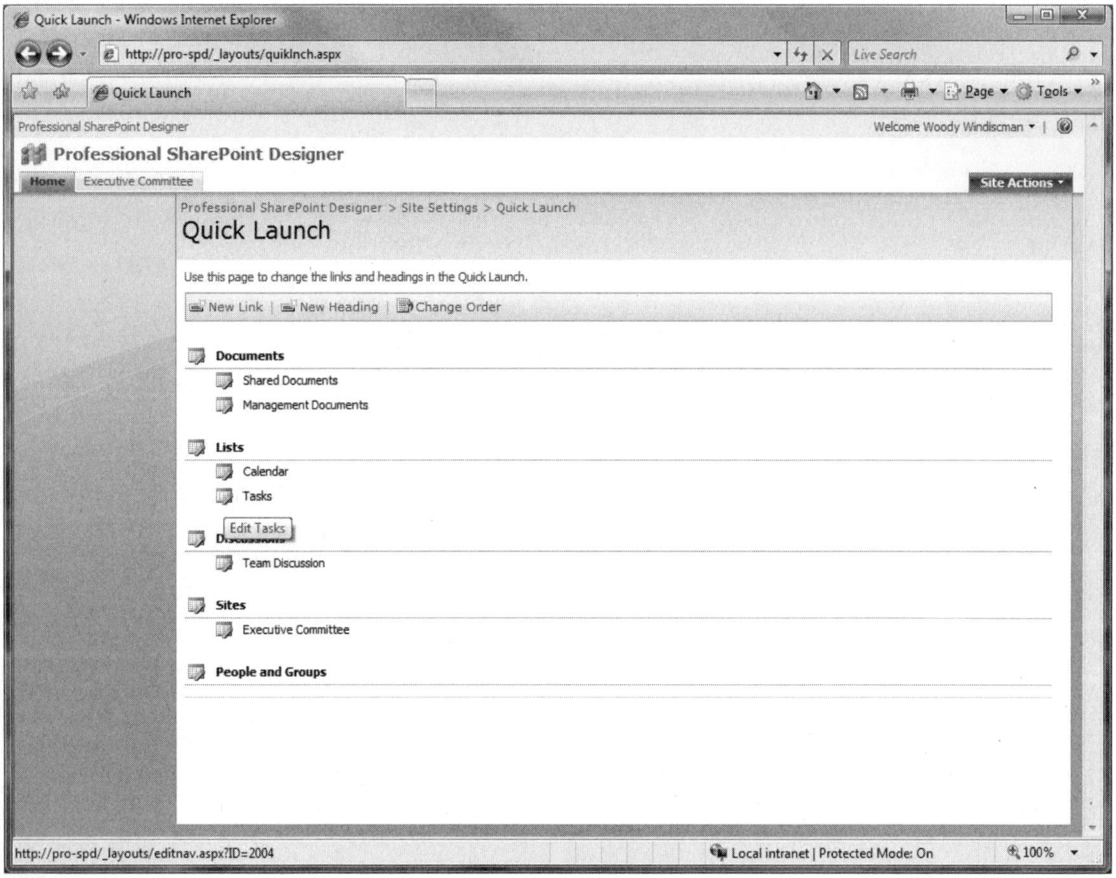

Figure 3-7

By retaining and styling these elements to match your vision, you can save yourself a lot of work when your customer comes back to you in six months saying, "I need to change 'Widget Construction' to 'Gizmo Assembly.'" In the case of navigation, this can simply be changed by the user in the navigation screens just described. On Publishing sites, you can also create reusable content, which, when edited, will propagate to all pages in which that content is used. In chapters 7 and 8, you will see how to customize the look of these standard menus, as well as techniques for building other easily maintainable navigation components.

The Site icon is the picture which (by default) appears to the left of the site title in the page header. Changing the image used is as simple as entering the URL of the preferred image in the Title, Description, and Icon form. Of course, the text of the site title is edited on the same form.

The final critical item to notice in this section is the Site Theme option. A SharePoint Theme is a collection of images and Cascading Style Sheets (CSS) files that can be applied to a site at any time. Figures 3-8 and 3-9 show the same site with two different Themes applied. Figure 3-8 uses the Theme Simple; Figure 3-9 uses Citrus.

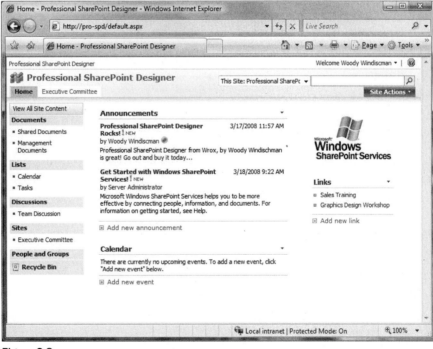

Figure 3-8

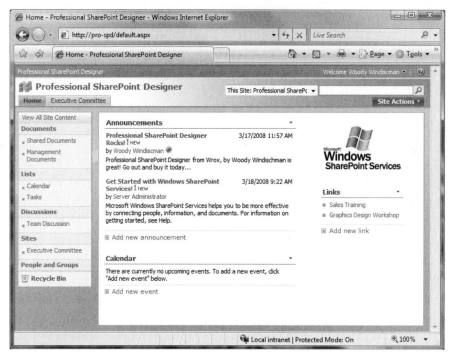

Figure 3-9

Themes can make both subtle and drastic changes to the *format* (font, size, color, etc.) of virtually any element on a page, as long as those changes can be implemented via CSS. While CSS offers powerful layout capability, by default SharePoint makes heavy use of tables for layout. Therefore most *position* changes usually need to be made by designing a custom *Master Page*. In chapters 5, 7, and 8, you will learn how to create and deploy custom CSS, Themes, and Master Pages.

Galleries

SharePoint galleries are lists or libraries of elements that are used throughout a site. Some galleries apply to an entire site collection, while others apply only to the current site and its children.

The first item in the galleries list is the Master Pages gallery. This gallery is essentially a specialized document library designed to hold — surprise! — Master Pages. Site owners can upload any number of customized Master Pages (and, in MOSS Publishing sites, layout pages), which can then be applied to the content of the site.

> ### MVP Workaround
>
> While the Site Settings page provides access to the Master Pages gallery on all SharePoint sites, only MOSS sites on which the Publishing features are activated allow you to apply a Master Page and alternative CSS file from the web interface. On all other sites, a Master Page must be selected through the site definition, the SharePoint API, or from within SharePoint Designer.
>
> This inconvenience in WSS and non-Publishing MOSS sites has been addressed by SharePoint MVP Renaud Comte through his Stramit SharePoint Master Picker Project on CodePlex (`http://codeplex.com/SPMasterPicker`).

The other galleries most relevant to users of SharePoint Designer are those for content types, site and list templates, and Web Parts. Workflows allow you to set up automated, multistep processes that act on SharePoint information. While you can create workflows in SharePoint Designer (the process for which is described in chapter 9), the workflow gallery primarily shows the status of built-in workflows on the site, rather than custom SharePoint Designer workflows. Site columns are available to be added to any list or content type in your site collection.

The Web Parts gallery contains the default configurations (in Web Part description files `*.dwp` or `*.webpart`) for the Web Parts available on your site. This gallery allows your users to preview a Web Part before adding it to a page.

After you make changes to a list or a site, whether through the web interface, or in SharePoint Designer, you can save your changes as a template, either with or without data (content). These templates automatically go into the site collection's list or site template gallery, as appropriate. Templates are stored as .STP files, which are essentially customized CAB files. You can export your .STP files to the file system and then upload them to other site collections, even on other servers, and create instances of your customized items. In addition, you can install site template files (although not list templates) onto your server at the root level, so they may be instantiated on any site.

> *Site and list templates are keyed to site definitions and Features. A site template can only be instantiated on a server that has the site definition upon which it is based installed. In addition, any additional Features used by the template must be installed and activated. A list template can only be installed on a site that has the features the list depends upon activated.*

On the Server

As you have seen, SharePoint presents a consistent, unified face to its users and site owners. That all changes when you get to the server; it is here that the long and varied history, described in Appendix A, surfaces in the many different methods used to perform individual tasks. While most common administration can be performed through the Central Administration web interface, other tasks can only be performed by editing configuration files manually, or using the SharePoint command-line tool STSADM.EXE. Still other tasks require some combination of these methods.

Again, it is not the purpose of this book to explain all of the nuances of SharePoint administration; however, you need to know certain things to make appropriate customization choices. This section presents an overview of a SharePoint Server farm. Details of particular configuration tasks are provided as needed throughout the rest of the book.

Central Administration

SharePoint Central Administration is the primary control panel for a SharePoint Server farm. Figure 3-10 shows the Central Administration home page. If you think it looks a lot like a SharePoint site, you're right!

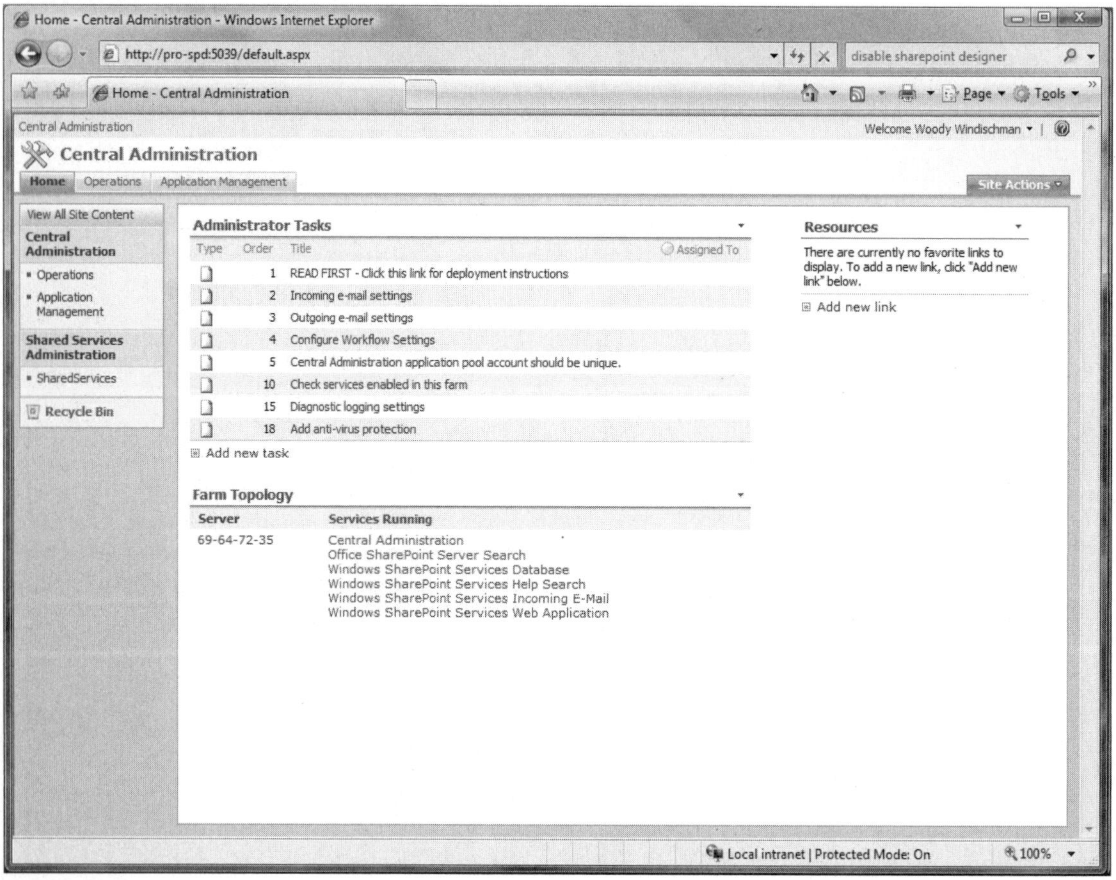

Figure 3-10

The Central Administration site is a custom SharePoint *web application*, created automatically with a random TCP port on the first server configured in your farm. It is called a farm because SharePoint's functions can be spread across multiple servers for performance and/or resilience.

Even if SharePoint is configured on a single server, that one system is still referred to as a farm.

While the exact functions available in Central Administration depend on which edition of SharePoint you have installed, every SharePoint farm has sections for Operations and Application Management. In a basic Windows SharePoint Services 3.0 installation, these will be the only choices available. MOSS 2007, Forms Server, and Search Server 2008 will also have a section for Shared Services.

The Operations section consists of a multitude of functions that impact a full server or operate across the entire farm. Most of these functions are not relevant to the use of SharePoint Designer. The two exceptions, Farm Features and Solution Management, are discussed in more detail in chapter 18.

The Application Management section contains many functions relevant to SharePoint site customization. In particular, it enables you to create and manage the Web applications and site collections that make up your SharePoint site. A Web application is the logical top-level container for SharePoint content. A SharePoint farm will host one or more Web applications. Each Web application will contain one or more site collections.

Site collections are the primary units of granularity in the overall scheme of SharePoint administration. A site collection has its own permission groups, template galleries, and navigation hierarchy. Site collections cannot be split across content databases. In addition, the site collection is the smallest unit that can be backed up or restored with full fidelity. And, most important, from the standpoint of this book, a site collection is the scope that can be browsed easily in SharePoint Designer.

Each site collection will contain one or more sites or webs. The site is the working unit of SharePoint, containing the pages, lists, and libraries used to present content to your users. The first site created in a site collection is called the root. This root web has certain unique properties. For example, the root web of a site collection is where the site and List Template galleries are stored. The root web may contain zero or more child webs, which in turn may be nested to an arbitrary level. Figure 3-11 illustrates the logical hierarchy of content in a SharePoint farm.

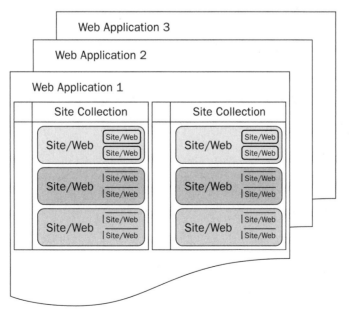

Figure 3-11

The File Structure

The physical layout of files on a SharePoint server bears no resemblance at all to the logical content hierarchy described in the previous section. In fact, files critical to the operation of SharePoint are stored in no less than four locations on the server, and that doesn't even count the databases! (The SharePoint databases are discussed later in this chapter.)

These four areas, in increasing order of relevance to the web designer, are:

❑ The SharePoint Installation directory. Typically C:\Program Files\Microsoft Office Servers\12.0.

❑ The Windows Global Assembly Cache (GAC). Typically C:\Windows\Assembly\.

❑ The SharePoint Web Site root. Typically C:\inetpub\wwwroot\wss\VirtualDirectories.

❑ The 12 Hive. Typically C:\Program Files\Common Files\Microsoft Shared\web server extensions\12.

It is a bit ironic that the path containing the files you most likely need to manipulate is the longest path. Even more, the 12 Hive itself contains very complicated folder structure, most of which resides in the .\12\TEMPLATE subtree.

Chapter 5 will describe in detail the hybrid nature of serving SharePoint files, with each page being assembled at service time from a combination of information stored on the file system and in the content database. The TEMPLATE subtree contains the portions that are served from the file system.

The key thing to remember at this time is to never open the files in the TEMPLATE subtree directly from the disk with SharePoint Designer. Many of these files contain tokens that only make sense to SharePoint Designer when opened in the context of a web site, as preprocessed by the SharePoint server. When they are opened outside of this context, SharePoint Designer attempts to treat them as if they were on a web site, and save them incorrectly, resulting in a corrupt template file.

The STSADM Command

One of the files in the BIN subfolder of 12 Hive is the STSADM.EXE command. The name is inherited from the original SharePoint Team Services, and originally meant SharePoint Team Services Administration. Although the name is still the same, the STSADM command today has grown to encompass virtually all aspects of SharePoint administration.

Not only can STSADM perform most of the functions exposed through the SharePoint Central Administration Web Site, there are many operations that only STSADM can perform. For example, if you wish to make the site templates you customize and create with SharePoint Designer available to all sites on a farm without manually copying the template to each site collection, you issue an STSADM command.

The STSADM.EXE command is actually a shell that passes the commands to appropriate modules in the SharePoint API to perform the requested function. This command can be expanded by writing and registering custom modules, which can then be invoked just like the native operations.

The SharePoint Databases

With all of the files and locations mentioned in the previous section, you might think that your content has to be in there someplace. Well, it isn't. At its heart, SharePoint is a database application, and it doesn't stop with just your content.

There are several types of databases used by SharePoint. The primary ones you need to recognize are:

❑ **Content databases:** These store all of your lists, documents, user details, and virtually everything else there is inside your sites.

❑ **Configuration database:** This contains most of the information related to the configuration of the SharePoint environment, as well as detailed information about your sites.

❑ **Search databases:** These contain information about searches, as well as metadata (properties) from index crawls. Search databases, while used internally by the WSS search engine, are only of significance to site designers in MOSS, MOSS for Search, and Microsoft Search Server 2008. Crawled properties are exposed as fields in search results, which can be manipulated as Data Views. (Data View Web Parts are described in chapter 11.)

These databases can be stored on virtually any available SQL server in your environment, as long as it is running at least SQL Server 2000 with the latest service pack. The many factors involved in the selection and configuration of a SQL Server environment are beyond the scope of this book.

Alternatively, SharePoint itself ships with limited versions of SQL Server — either WMSDE, or SQL Server Express — which are used in the case of a Basic or Single Server install. (The exact version of SQL varies depending upon the version of SharePoint being installed.) If this option is selected, the SQL databases for this edition are stored in a branch of the SharePoint Installation Directory.

The Configuration Database

The main things to remember about the configuration database are:

❑ There is only one configuration database per SharePoint Server farm, and it defines the farm.

❑ The configuration database is created when the farm is first installed, and cannot be changed, although it can be moved to a different server in most cases, with some effort.

❑ The configuration database can be backed up, but not restored under normal circumstances.

The Content Databases

All of the site-specific information that is presented to your users comes from the content databases. Although one content database per web application is created by default, more can be added at any time. At minimum, each content database in use contains the information for a complete site collection — including its root and any child webs that may be created. If multiple content databases are created for a web application, new site collections are allocated to content databases in an unpredictable order, until the configured maximum number of collections for a particular database is reached.

Chapter 2 discussed how SharePoint lists and libraries, to a large extent, behaved like database tables. While in SharePoint Team Services, each list and library was actually stored as a distinct table in a database, WSS 2.0 and SPS 2003 changed that, and the same mechanism, slightly expanded, is used in WSS 3.0 and MOSS 2007.

In current versions of SharePoint, all fields, from every list and library, in every site, are stored in a single table. This table, called AllUserData (just UserData in WSS 2.0/SPS 2003), is preconfigured with every possible column/field, which may be defined in a SharePoint list or library. In WSS 2.0/SPS 2003, this resulted in hard limits to the number of fields of any given type that could be created. In WSS 3.0/MOSS, the schema has been updated to use multiple AllUserData rows for each list or library item if more fields of a particular type than were predefined are required. Figure 3-12 shows the complete list of column fields in the SharePoint AllUserData table.

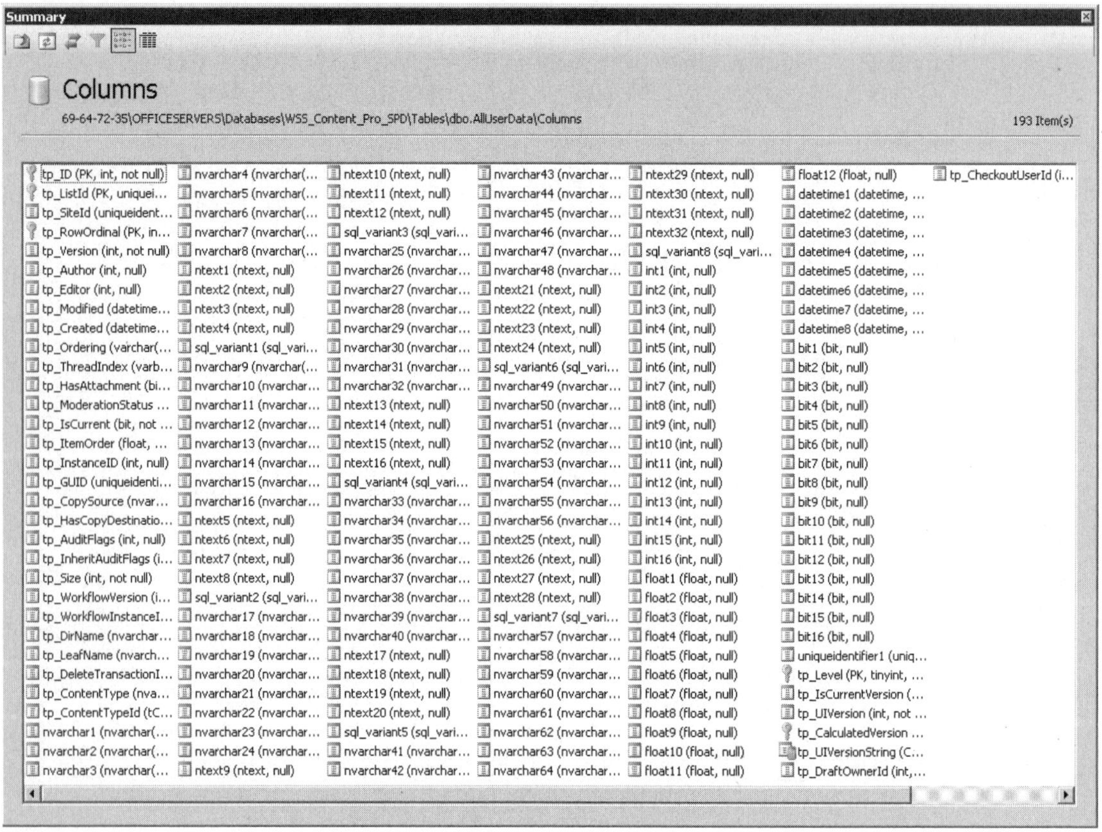

Figure 3-12

Because of this unusual, highly denormalized schema, direct user access to the database is problematic. In fact, direct access to any SharePoint database is considered unsupported by Microsoft in most cases, and is highly discouraged in the one case that is supportable (nonexclusive read-only queries).

One result of this architecture is of keen interest to web designers. There is a performance issue with the rendering (but not the querying) of large result sets. The commonly accepted rule is that any query that would result in the display of more than 2000 items in a single view will cause noticeable performance degradation to your users.

Some people call this "The 2000 Item Limit." This is a misnomer. Understand that this does not restrict how much information can be stored. It only influences how quickly results can be presented. When designing your sites, be conscious of this, but not a slave to it. Let it inform your choice of folder structures, or view filters. Also remember that performance falls off on a curve, not off of a cliff, and that a query or view with a few more than 2000 results is not going to bring your application to a halt.

Summary

This chapter showed you that SharePoint provides an array of tools to make many aspects of web administration much easier, and therefore possible even for people without server or network configuration experience. Once a SharePoint farm is initially configured, almost everything can be controlled through a web interface that is itself based upon SharePoint. You also learned:

❑ SharePoint provides built-in navigation controls, galleries for templates and Master Pages, and easy tools for site owners to customize them.

❑ There is a great difference between the way a final SharePoint site looks to a user and how it is actually assembled on the server.

❑ SharePoint databases need to be understood, but are nothing to be trifled with.

The next chapter shows you how all of these elements are brought together inside of SharePoint Designer, and gives you your first taste of actually modifying a SharePoint site.

SharePoint from a SharePoint Designer's Perspective

You already know that although a SharePoint site is presented to the user as a unified web browsing experience, behind the scenes things are a lot more complicated. This chapter shows you SharePoint Designer as the workshop where all of the raw materials are brought together in one place, ready for you to polish and assemble. It shows you how to:

❏   Find and recognize SharePoint elements within SharePoint Designer.

❏   Read and modify SharePoint site and object properties.

❏   Configure a site to restrict the features SharePoint Designer offers to users.

Navigating a SharePoint Site

Once you open a SharePoint site in SharePoint Designer, you'll see how SharePoint Designer features apply, including how lists, libraries, pages, and other components described in chapters 2 and 3 are represented.

Opening a SharePoint Site

SharePoint Designer is able to open most web sites in a number of different ways, from the file system, to FTP, to the FrontPage (and SharePoint) Server Extensions, to the WebDAV protocol (via http or https). While SharePoint allows both WebDAV and Server Extension–based access to SharePoint sites, SharePoint Designer accesses SharePoint only through the Server Extensions.

A Note about Protocols

WebDAV stands for *Web Distributed Authoring and Versioning*. It was originally designed for source-code control and content management systems. The Server Extensions protocol was originally developed for FrontPage (see Appendix A), and is maintained and enhanced for accessing SharePoint sites.

Although WebDAV and the Server Extensions are distinct, they perform similar functions. A complete technical description of these protocols is beyond the scope of this book, but think of them as extensions of the HTTP and HTTPS protocols that allow two-way communication between a client application and a Web server. They allow for such functions as check-in and check-out, permission management, and much more.

To open a SharePoint site in SharePoint Designer, select File ⇨ Open Site. Type in the URL of the site you want to open, as shown in Figure 4-1.

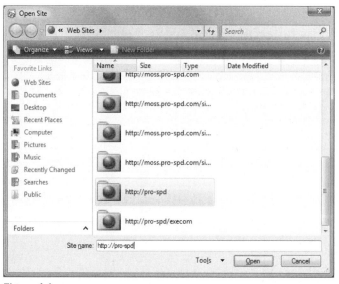

Figure 4-1

If you have opened other web sites in the past, they will be listed under the Web Sites section of the Favorite Links list. You may click the name to select it. Double-clicking a site name in the Open Site dialog drills you into that site and allows you to choose a child site to open (if any). Once you have selected a site to open by any of these methods, click the Open button to open the site in SharePoint Designer. You may be prompted to enter credentials for the web site, either upon drilling down, or after clicking the Open button. Until you close all instances of SharePoint Designer, any other site you open in the same URL domain will attempt to use the same credentials. You will be prompted again if the account used does not have sufficient permission to open the new site.

Successfully opening a site in SharePoint Designer does not guarantee you can perform all editing functions on that site. See the section "Contributor Settings" later in this chapter for details on how the usage of SharePoint Designer may be limited by site administrators.

SharePoint Designer can only have one site open within an application window. If you attempt to open another site while one is currently open, the new site opens in a new instance of SharePoint Designer.

By default, when you start SharePoint Designer, it attempts to open the most recently edited site. You can disable this behavior by selecting Tools ⇨ Application Options, and unchecking the option Open last Web site automatically when SharePoint Designer starts.

Identifying Components

Because SharePoint Designer accesses your site through a web-based protocol (HTTP/S and the Server Extensions), it sees the files and folders as assembled by the SharePoint server. This means the organization of a site within SharePoint Designer more closely reflects the URLs seen in a browser than the physical layout on the file server and in the content database.

All of a site's elements are presented as a hierarchy of files and folders. Many of the icons, such as the basic folder, may be familiar to users of Windows. Office documents that are stored on the site are shown with their normal icons as well. Many other icons, however, are customized to help you identify components of the site. The components they represent will be described in detail as needed throughout the remainder of this book. The following table shows the custom icons you will typically encounter when browsing files and folders in SharePoint Designer.

These are the icons you see in the Folder List task pane or web site Folders view. Other places inside and outside of SharePoint Designer (for example, the File Open dialog, or Windows Explorer) may use slightly different icons.

Icon	SharePoint Component
	Basic Folder
	Library Folder
	Workflows Folder
	List Folder (most lists, except surveys)
	Survey List Folder

(continued)

Icon	SharePoint Component
	Subweb/Site Folder
	HTML Page (.htm, .html)
	ASPX/Form/Layout Page (.aspx)
	Site Home Page (.aspx, .htm, .html)
	Master Page (.master)
	Cascading Style Sheet (.css)
	Customized/Unghosted File (displayed in addition to the regular file icon)
	Dynamic Web Template (.dwt)
	Script (.js)
	Plaintext File (.txt)
	File (of any type) Currently Open for Editing in the SharePoint Designer Workspace
	Workflow Definition (.xoml)
	XML Data file (.xml)
	Other Files

You cannot simply browse the files in a subsite through SharePoint Designer in the containing site. You must double-click the subsite folder to open the subsite in its own SharePoint Designer window.

Libraries, Lists, and Content Types

Although lists and libraries have much in common, a SharePoint list is mainly used to store data, while a library is primarily a file repository. Content types are predefined schemas (sets of fields) that can be used in multiple lists and libraries. As befits the difference in their usage, SharePoint's lists and libraries and content types have different representations in SharePoint Designer that extend far beyond the different icons representing them.

Libraries

Each library created on a SharePoint site shows up in SharePoint Designer as a folder at the root of the site. Figure 4-2 shows a document library and its contents. Each document in the library shows up as a file in SharePoint Designer.

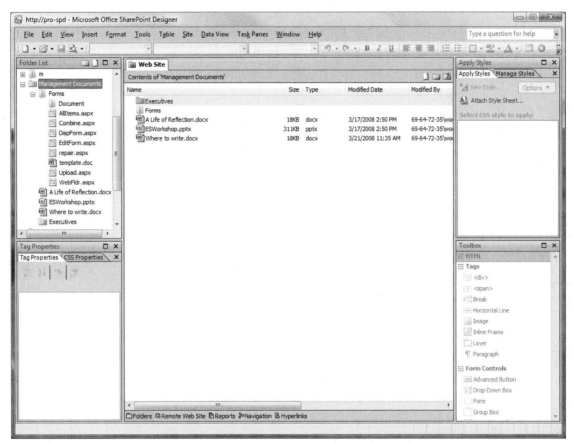

Figure 4-2

Notice the Forms folder. In addition to your files, every SharePoint library contains a collection of preconfigured Web Part Pages that are used for displaying and managing its content. At a minimum, a library contains forms for:

❑ Uploading and/or creating a new file (Upload.aspx or NewForm.aspx).

❑ Displaying a document's property fields (metadata) (ViewForm.aspx).

❑ Editing a document's metadata (EditForm.aspx).

❑ Listing the files in the library (AllItems.aspx).

In addition, each view created of the files in the library is stored as a page in the Forms folder. You can create your own views of a library through either the web interface or SharePoint Designer. A view lists the files in the library (or a subset thereof) with a particular subset of the metadata in a particular layout. For example, your library may have an added field to indicate the Project for which the document was created, and you could create a view that's prefiltered to just the documents that have a Project field that equals Universe Plaza.

Although each item in a library is represented as a file, not every library's files are quite what meets the eye. In a MOSS Publishing site, for example, site content is stored in a special library, called Pages. The files in this library cannot be directly edited in SharePoint Designer, however. Chapter 8 details the intricacies of customizing publishing pages in SharePoint Designer.

The other special case library is the Wiki library. While these pages can be edited in SharePoint Designer (unlike publishing pages), the actual wiki content can still only be edited through the browser. A SharePoint wiki page is essentially a Web Part Page that contains a view of a specific wiki content item. Editing Web Part Pages in general will be covered in detail in the next chapter.

Lists

Unlike document libraries, which are created as folders at the site root, all lists on a SharePoint site are created inside a separate Lists folder. Figure 4-3 shows the Lists folder, with an Announcements list fully expanded.

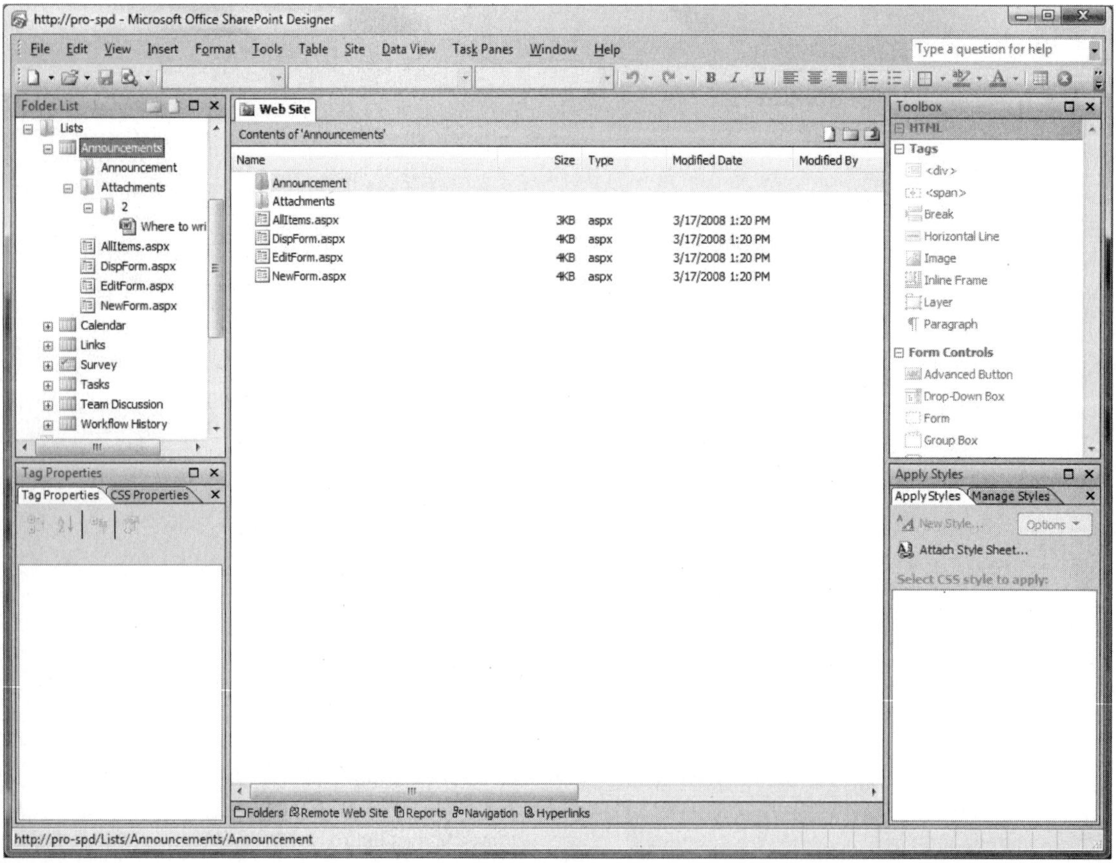

Figure 4-3

In many respects, a list's structure is the inverse of a library. The individual items stored in a list are not represented as files in SharePoint Designer. A list is primarily a tabular data store. Because there are not normally files to display, there is no need for a separate Forms folder. Instead, forms and view pages are stored at the root of the List folder. (Views work the same for lists as they do for libraries.)

That doesn't mean that files cannot be stored within a list. Most list types can be enabled for file attachments. When file storage is needed, these files are kept in an Attachments folder. In the Attachments folder, a separate folder is created for each list item that has attached files. This folder is named with the item ID of the item the files are associated with; thus, in the figure above, Announcements list item number 2 has a Word document attached to it.

By maintaining a separate folder for each list item, multiple attachments per list item can be supported. In addition, there is no need to worry about conflicts if multiple items have attachments of the same name.

Content Types

One thing lists and libraries have in common is their capability to support multiple content types. Content types allow you use a single list or library to contain items with multiple schemas. They do not inherently relate to file types such as `.doc`, `.pdf`, or `.zip`, although for document libraries you can create a content type that uses a particular file type as a template.

Content types are represented in SharePoint Designer as basic folders. Each list or library shows folders for the content types enabled in that list or library. Site content types (those available for use in any of the site's lists or libraries that have content type management enabled) are listed in the _cts folder at the root level of your site.

The types contained in the _cts folder vary depending on a number of factors, including the edition of SharePoint installed (WSS, MOSS, and so on), the site definition used, and the features active. In general, you have a content type for each list or library type available in the site (Contacts, Calendar, and document library, for instance).

In addition, there's the Dublin Core document content type, which is a set of properties commonly used in document management systems. Enabling and using this content type in your libraries can facilitate data interchange with other systems. Keep in mind, however, that users tend to be resistant to entering extra information about documents. If you decide to use Dublin Core, make certain that policies and procedures are in place to ensure that the users comply.

> *Although you can see this folder representation of content types, there is no provision within SharePoint Designer for editing the content types themselves. They must be edited through the web interface. When a site-level content type is modified, you can choose to have its changes propagated to the lists and libraries that make use of the content type.*

Galleries

In chapter 3, you learned about several galleries that may contain items and templates used throughout your SharePoint site. The Site Content Types gallery was described earlier (the _cts folder). Many of the remaining galleries available in SharePoint Designer are shown as lists and libraries in the _catalogs folder, as shown in Figure 4-4.

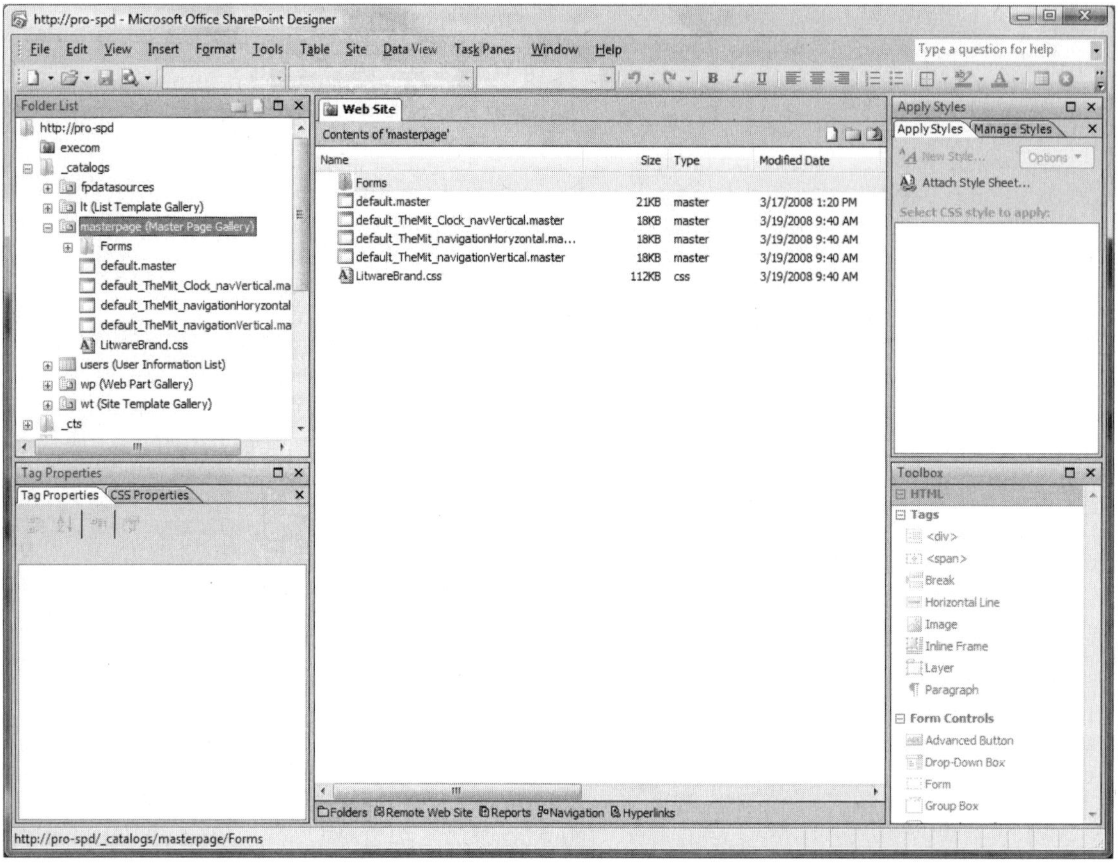

Figure 4-4

Most of the _catalogs galleries are in the form of libraries. The one exception is the users list, which maintains information about the users and groups in your site. Here are descriptions of these galleries:

Gallery	Description
fpdatasources library	The internal representation of the Data Source Library. It is the only gallery that is not surfaced in the web interface (the Forms folder is empty). This gallery holds XML definitions for any external data sources you configure for use on your SharePoint site. Those definitions are created and managed through the Data Source Library task pane. Chapters 11 and 12 describe the Data Source Library, its contents, and its usage in detail.
lt library	The storage behind the List Template gallery. This is where you will find any custom list templates that you have created in, or uploaded to, your site collection. Although you cannot directly edit list template files in SharePoint Designer, you can upload new templates and delete those that are not needed. You can also customize the forms used by the gallery's web interface.

Gallery	Description
Master Page library	A key repository both for SharePoint Designer (the application) and for you as a SharePoint designer. In most SharePoint sites, this gallery holds the Master Pages and CSS files that control the overall look of your site. In MOSS Publishing sites, this gallery also contains the layout files used to present particular types of content to your users. The creation and customizing of Master Pages is covered in detail in Part II of this book.
users list	Enables you to customize how certain user-related detail information is presented to your users.
wp library	The Web Part gallery. It does not contain any binary executable information. Rather, it contains XML definition files (either `.dwp` or `.webpart`) that describe the default properties of a Web Part when placed on a page, including such things as the Web Part title, its description, and even default content.
wt library	Contains the Site Template gallery. — template files for the creation of complete, precustomized SharePoint sites. Again, you cannot edit the template files directly through SharePoint Designer; however, any customizations you have made are saved as part of the template file when it is created through the web interface.

Workflows

Workflows in SharePoint allow you to monitor list items for conditions, and set sequences of actions to perform if those conditions are met. If you have any workflows defined on your site, you will see a Workflows folder that contains their definitions. Workflows, including the Workflows folder and its contents, are described in detail in chapters 9 and 17.

List and Library Properties

In addition to editing web pages navigating through your site, SharePoint Designer allows you to set many of the properties of key SharePoint Objects — particularly lists and libraries. You access the properties of a list or library either by selecting File ⇨ Properties or by right-clicking the list or library and choosing Properties.

You may need to wait a few seconds after clicking the list's or library's root folder before the options appropriate to that context are available. That's because SharePoint Designer needs to verify with the server the actual state of the item you are selecting.

The Document Library Properties dialog (see Figure 4-5) opens. This same basic dialog is used for lists and libraries, as well as for basic folders (for basic folders only the General tab is visible on a SharePoint site).

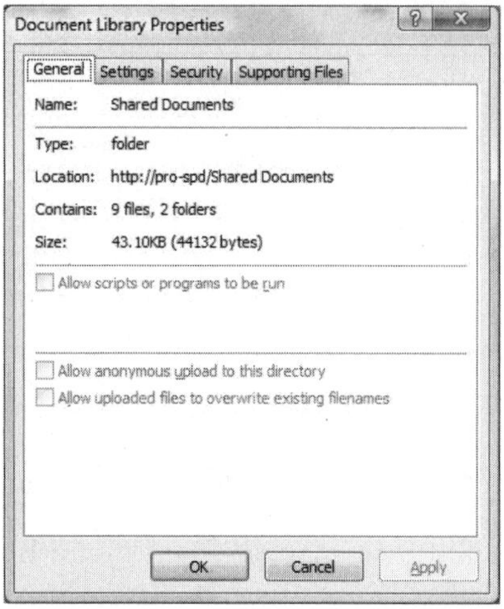

Figure 4-5

The disabled items on the General tab do not apply in most SharePoint sites, which are accessed using the newer SharePoint Server Extensions. These extensions are similar to the FrontPage Server Extensions in many respects, but certain functions have been deprecated and removed in newer versions of SharePoint. SharePoint Designer continues to support them on older sites, however. The scripting and upload options are supported by folders created in sites created using the FrontPage Server Extensions, or SharePoint Team Services 1.0.

The Settings Tab

The Settings tab will contain slightly different options, depending upon the particular library or list type selected. Figure 4-6 shows the settings for a document library.

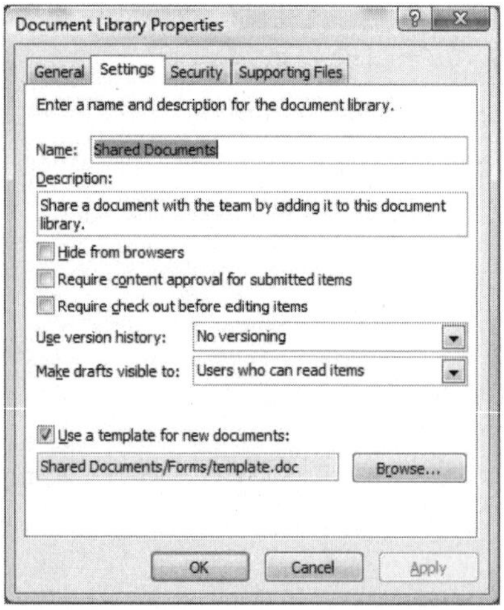

Figure 4-6

There are a few options that are available for all list and library types through the Settings tab. These include:

❑ Editing the name of the list or library.

❑ Editing the description.

❑ Hiding the list or library from browsers.

Most options in the Settings dialog are available both through SharePoint Designer and the web interface. However, one critical element — Hide From Browsers — is only accessible from SharePoint Designer.

The Hide From Browsers option is very useful if you have information — such as workflows, specific Data Views, or manual links — on the site that you want to make available to your users in a highly controlled way. The galleries described earlier in the chapter, for example, all have the Hide option set. Lists and libraries with the Hide option set do not appear in the Quick Launch menu, available Web Parts, or in the All Site Content page.

The Hide option is not a security feature. It simply prevents SharePoint from creating default navigation into the hidden object. It does not restrict access by any users who have permissions on the list or library if they know the URLs of the views or files. Nor does it hide the library from SharePoint Designer. If you need to prevent all access to the item, you should use the Security features of SharePoint, as described in the "Users and Permissions" section of chapter 3.

The Security Tab

For libraries, the Security tab simply provides a link to the web interface's security management pages. For lists, the security tab provides this link, but also directly controls a basic form of security — whether a user can view and edit all items in the list, none of them (edit only), or only their own. For Survey lists, you can select whether responses are anonymous or tagged with the user's login ID, and whether users can enter multiple responses to the survey (see Figure 4-7).

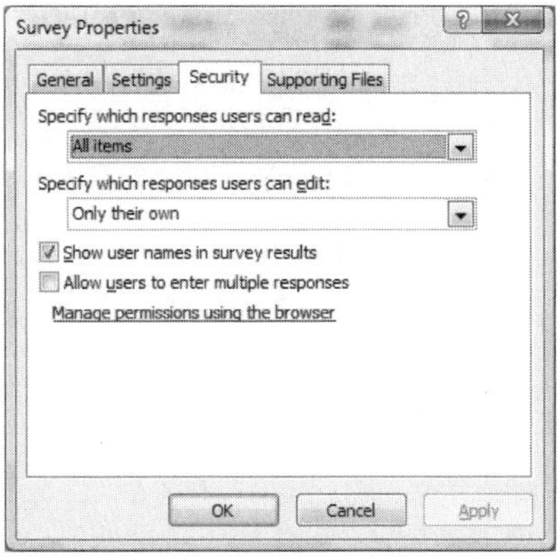

Figure 4-7

The items in the Security tab are all accessible via the web interface, as well as from within SharePoint Designer.

The Supporting Files Tab

Each list and library contains a set of files, each representing a different view or editing form. The List Properties dialog's Supporting Files tab in Figure 4-8 shows examples of these files. You can edit these files in SharePoint Designer, or you can create new, totally custom forms. (This process is shown in detail in chapters 10 and 12.)

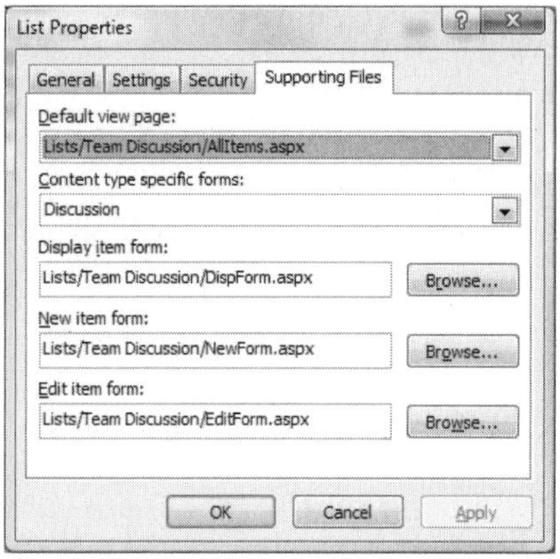

Figure 4-8

The Default view page can be set either through the web interface or via SharePoint Designer. The other files on this tab are only configurable in SharePoint Designer. Different lists or libraries may have different sets of forms. In addition, if you have enabled multiple content types in your list or library, you can set up different forms for each content type.

Contributor Settings

SharePoint Designer provides a great deal of customizing power to its users. In some environments, particularly in an enterprise, it may not be appropriate to give all users access to this level of power. To address this, SharePoint Designer allows you to configure different levels of Contributor Settings. These settings allow or prevent access to certain features by users of SharePoint Designer, based upon permission levels defined by the owner of the site.

Contributor Settings are applied at the individual site level. They are not inherited by child sites.

From the Site Menu, select Contributor Settings to display the Contributor Settings dialog, shown in Figure 4-9. This display is available only to site owners/administrators, and allows them to manage the settings for other users of the site.

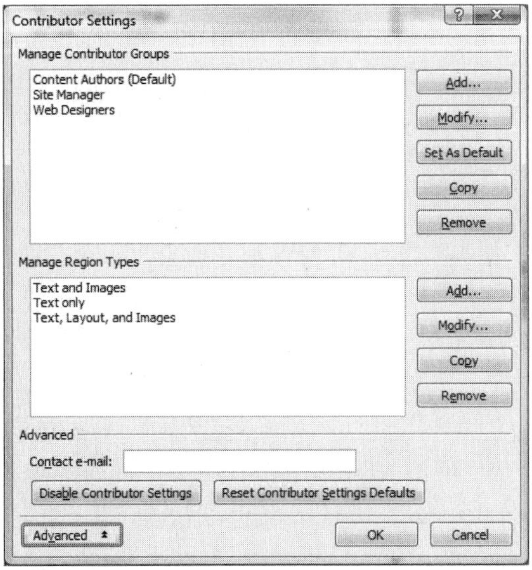

Figure 4-9

If Contributor Settings are enabled on a site and a nonadministrative user opens the site in SharePoint Designer, that user will get a limited view of the elements in the site, as appropriate, based on his or her settings. This view, as shown in Figure 4-10, may not have such features as the Web Site view in the workspace.

(1) Contributor Mode designation   (3) Contributor task pane

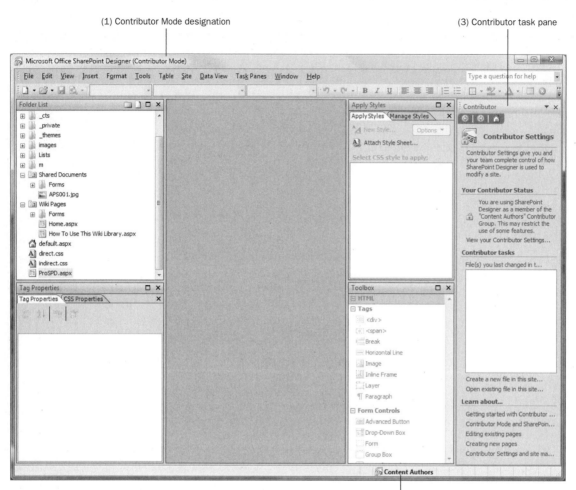

Figure 4-10

(2) Group to which current user belongs

Notice that the SharePoint Designer title bar shows "Contributor Mode" (1). The status bar will show which of multiple potential contributor groups the currently signed-in user belongs to. In this case, that group is Content Authors (2). Figure 4-10 also shows the Contributor task pane (3). This task pane provides certain useful information, such as recently modified files, quick access to appropriate help topics, and a link to view the exact contribution restrictions currently in effect.

Contributor Settings versus Permission Levels

One thing to understand about Contributor Settings is that they do not affect what a user is able to do through the SharePoint web interface. Contributor Settings only modify what users are allowed to do in SharePoint Designer itself. The reverse is not the case, as the Contributor Settings are *dependent upon* the SharePoint permission levels.

The site administrator links a Contributor group to a particular permission level within SharePoint Designer. In SharePoint, administrators assign a user or SharePoint group to a permission level. Then, when that user or members of that group open the site in SharePoint Designer, the permission level they are assigned to is used to select the Contributor group settings that are used.

Configuring Contributor Settings

There are two types of contributor settings that you can configure — Contributor groups and region types. Contributor groups enable you to set restrictions on who can make particular changes over the scope of the whole site or in particular folders. Region types give control over what can be changed on pages, regardless of the person doing it. When a restriction based on these features is in effect, the SharePoint Designer user interface options for that feature are disabled (grayed out) or suppressed (invisible).

Contributor Groups

By default, SharePoint Designer creates three Contributor groups. While these groups provide a flexible set of capability restrictions right out-of-the-box, you can modify the existing groups, or create new groups. New groups can be based on a copy of an existing group, or created from scratch. The default Contributor groups are as follows:

Contributor Group	Description
Content Authors	Content Authors are heavily restricted in what they can view and modify in SharePoint Designer. They are explicitly associated with the Contribute permission level. In addition, the settings of the Content Authors group are initially the Default Contributor Settings for any permission levels that are not explicitly associated with a different group.
Site Manager	The Site Manager group has unrestricted access to all SharePoint Designer functionality, and is associated with the Full Control permission level. While you can change this, it may create difficulties in site management down the road.
Web Designers	Web Designers also have unrestricted access to SharePoint Designer by default, although they may still be restricted in what they can do based on their SharePoint site permissions. Web Designers are associated with the Design permission level by default.

The following figures show the Properties of the Web Designer Contributor group. This is accessed by first opening the Contributor Settings dialog (Site ⇨ Contributor Settings), then selecting the Web Designers group, and clicking the Modify button. The accompanying discussion for each describes the functions covered.

On the General page (see Figure 4-11), the Allow unrestricted use Of SharePoint Designer box is unchecked to enable the other pages of the properties dialog to display. Allow use of Code View is checked to keep all functionality active. The ramifications of allowing Code view will become manifest with later figures.

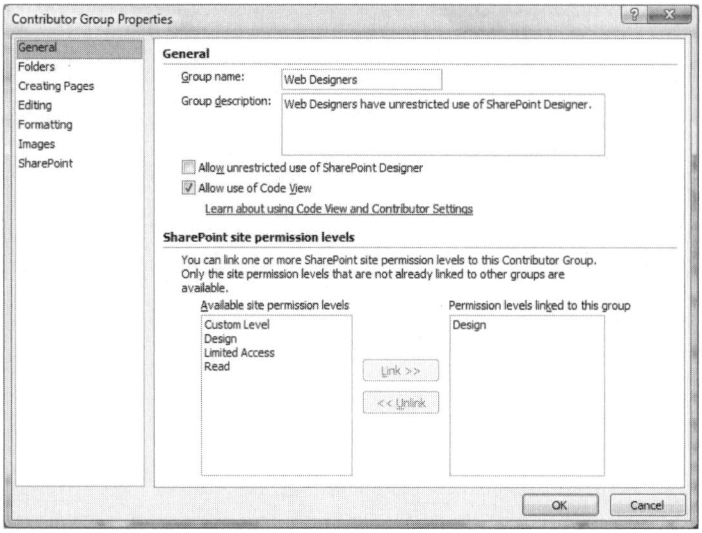

Figure 4-11

SharePoint Designer normally gives access to all folders on the site. You can configure specific folder access on the Folders page (see Figure 4-12), limiting your users to editing files only in particular folder trees. In addition, you can force all images and nonpage files to go into specified, standard locations.

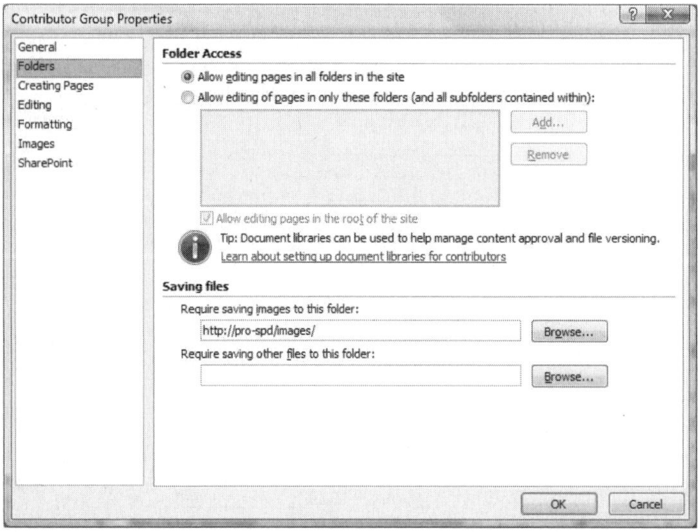

Figure 4-12

The Creating Pages page (see Figure 4-13) shows the options for restricting file creation and file system modification. These include:

❑ Restricting the types of files that can be created.

❑ Restricting the templates available for new pages (Master Pages and DWT).

❑ Restricting or permitting renaming of others' and/or the user's own files and folders.

❑ Restricting or permitting changes to existing templates.

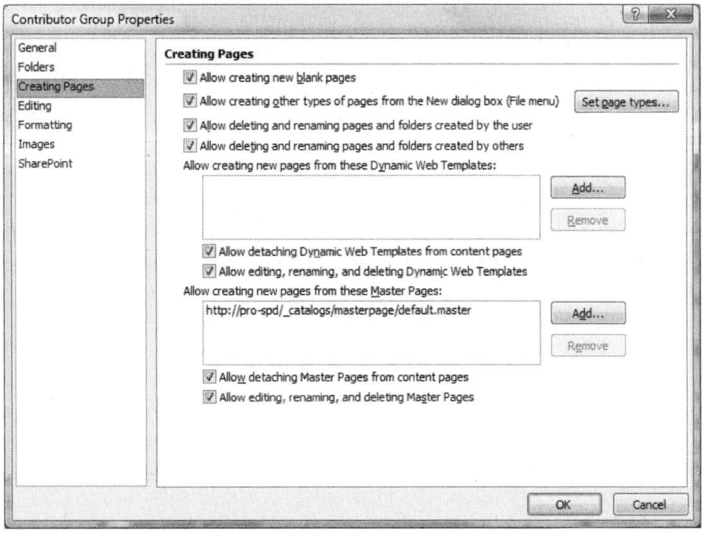

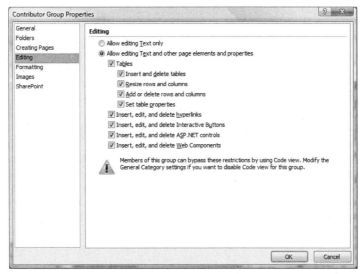

Figure 4-13

Use the Editing page, shown in Figure 4-14, to control what can be modified on a page in terms of content and layout. Note the warning about Code view. Contributor groups only affect the WYSIWYG design surface. If you know the appropriate markup, and have permission to use Code view, you can manually create virtually any element. That holds true for all other page-level Contributor restriction elements as well.

Figure 4-14

You can control the style of the text with the options on the Formatting page (see Figure 4-15). You can allow anything from full style flexibility to forcing simple text editing. Experts in HTML markup will have no problem overriding this if you allow them access to Code view.

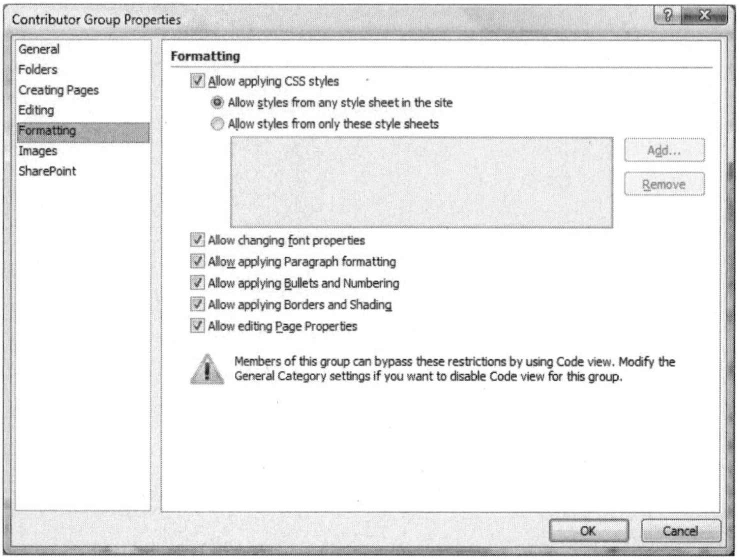

Figure 4-15

The most bandwidth-intensive aspects of any design are its graphics and other media elements. The Contributor Group Properties Images page, shown in Figure 4-16, enables you to restrict the media elements your users can insert on their pages. You can opt to control the source location, file sizes, and file types. The Code view warning appears in this page as well.

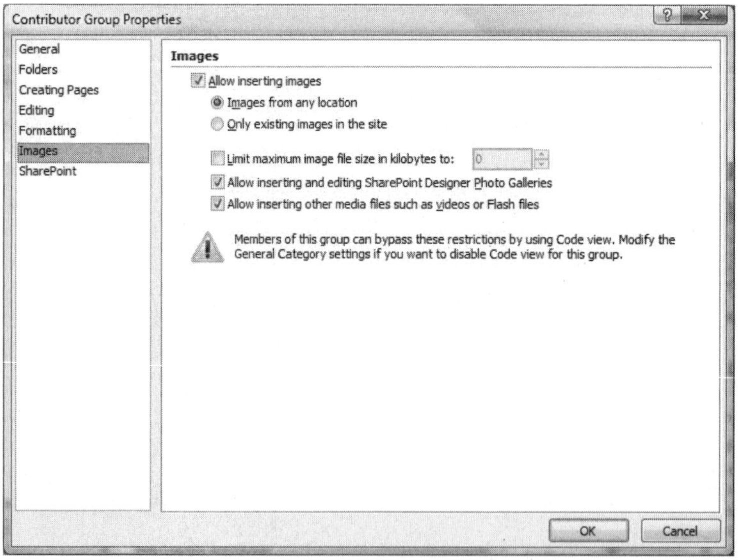

Figure 4-16

The SharePoint page (see Figure 4-17) allows you to restrict changes of certain SharePoint-specific functionality. The two groups on this page let you control site-level and page-level, functionality. One of the important site-level options is to permit overwriting pages from the site definition. This is also called customizing or unghosting a page. Again, note that the page-level restrictions can be overridden in Code view if the user knows the right markup.

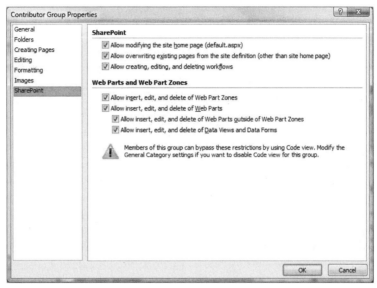

Figure 4-17

Region Types

In chapters 5 and 8, you will learn about creating and customizing Master Pages. One aspect of this customization is the creation of regions on the Master Page, into which content is placed. When using Contributor Settings on your site, you can assign region types to these content regions. You may then use the region type to control the kind of editing that can be done in that region.

You configure region types from the Contributor Settings dialog (Site ⇨ Contributor Settings). Click the Add button to define a new region type, or select an existing region type and click Modify. Region type settings apply to the portions of a page the regions represent; therefore, there are not as many options for their configuration as for contributor groups. These options are those appropriate for use at the page, rather than site, level.

The key benefit of region types, however, is that the settings of a region type can override the user's Contributor group settings within that region. This override can affect all or only certain groups, as shown in Figure 4-18.

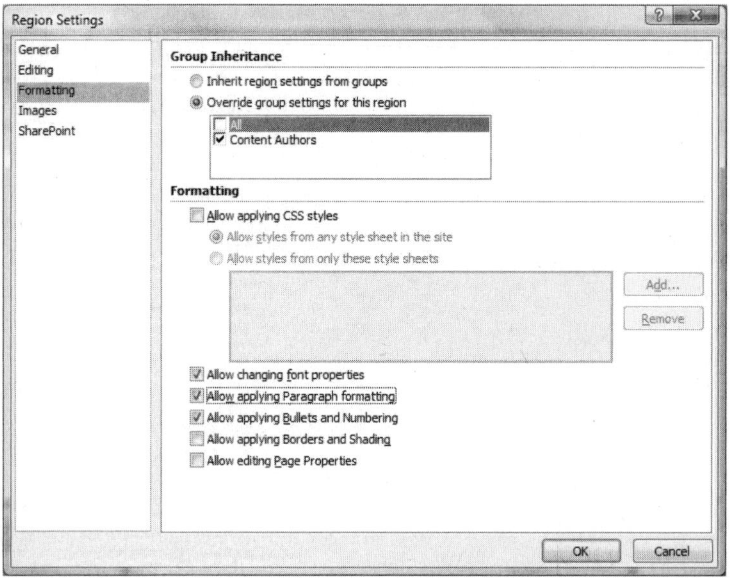

Figure 4-18

Like the Contributor groups, only Site Owners/Administrators have access to the region type configuration options.

Summary

In this chapter, you learned how many of the components of a SharePoint site are represented in SharePoint Designer. You also learned that you can restrict access to certain SharePoint Designer functionality through the use of Contributor Settings and region types. Key points include:

❑ Almost everything is manifest in a file/folder structure.

❑ Galleries are special cases of lists and libraries.

❑ Lists and libraries can be hidden from most elements of the web interface navigation.

In Part II, you look at how to pull it all together, edit pages, and customize your site's look and feel.

Part II

Customizing the SharePoint Look and Feel

The Anatomy of a SharePoint Page

In Part I, you learned about the basic functions of SharePoint Designer, some of the capabilities of SharePoint itself, and how various SharePoint Features were represented in SharePoint Designer. In Part II, you discover how to use SharePoint Designer to customize the look and feel of your site.

Muscle and blood, skin and bones make up the body of a person. This chapter takes you deep inside a SharePoint Page to show you the parts and processes that make up the structure (body). You will learn about:

❑   The page assembly process.

❑   What it means to customize a page.

❑   The roles of styles and Web Parts.

❑   How to build the skeleton of your site with Master Pages.

Bits and Pieces

Web pages have always been a bit like a jigsaw puzzle. The page name a user enters into a browser's address bar rarely contains everything that will be displayed in the window by the time the rendering process is completed. Images, scripts, and style sheets are simply stated by reference, and loaded by the browser.

CGI (Common Gateway Interface) and other server-side programming systems like ASP (Active Server Pages), PHP, and ASP.NET made the rendering of Internet sites even less direct. They automate the generation of the HTML, which is used to assemble the pieces for the final page rendering. While these systems have often been used to present information stored in databases, rarely has the combination of database, application code, and physical files been as balanced as that used by SharePoint.

Here, There, and Everywhere

Leaving aside the client-side final assembly by the browser, a SharePoint server normally combines information from a number of locations to create a page.

The first stage is the configuration database. Based upon the URL entered, SharePoint determines which web application and site collection are being requested, and which content database contains files for that site collection. The server then looks up which row in the AllUserData table of that database represents the page in question.

This is where things start to get interesting. Most pages on a SharePoint site are assembled from a combination of a file-based template and instance information from the content database. While this instance information may tell the server to retrieve even more data from other places (such as a SharePoint list), the core structure of the page will still be served from the site definition on the web server's file system. In earlier versions of SharePoint, this two-part file service was called ghosting (a term still used by many people) because the instance information stored in the content database was just a "ghost" — the real page was on the web front-end server.

That is, unless a page had been customized in a tool such as SharePoint Designer. Because SharePoint Designer accesses the file through a web protocol, it has no capability to modify the files on a server directly. (This is a good thing, because if your change were saved to the template file, it could impact every page on every site served by the server.) Instead, after you customize a page and save it, SharePoint breaks the link to the file system, and stores the entire page in the content database. SharePoint gives the warning shown in Figure 5-1 before breaking this link. Because the page being pulled from the database is now real, it was called unghosted.

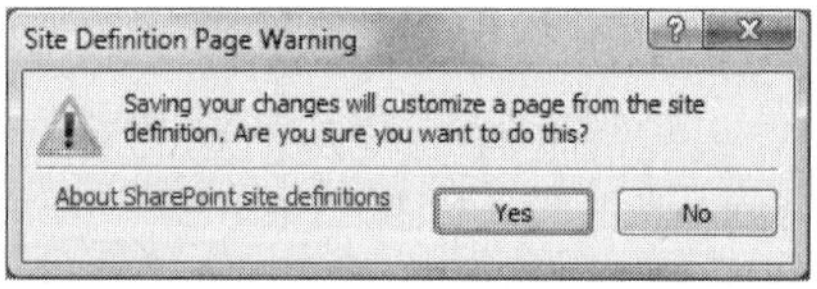

Figure 5-1

No Longer Seeing Ghosts

For Windows SharePoint Services 3.0 and Microsoft Office SharePoint Server 2007, the terminology in the official documentation changed from the prior versions. Ghosted pages are now referred to as *uncustomized*, and unghosted pages are now simply *customized*. Throughout most of this book, the new terms are preferred, though occasionally both may be used where needed for clarity.

Figure 5-2 shows the process by which a page is assembled by a SharePoint server.

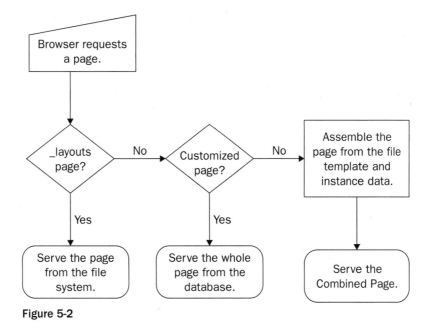

Figure 5-2

Ramifications and Reversion

Naturally, changing the way your page is assembled has a number of ramifications. Most of them are minor, and most are far outweighed by the flexibility you gain from the customizations you make in SharePoint Designer. Nevertheless, there are two key impacts you should understand so that you can make informed choices about when (and when not) to customize pages:

❑　Lost ties to the underlying site definition.

❑　Potential impacts to performance.

The sections below explain the ramifications of these changes, and show you how to return a page to its uncustomized state.

Lost Ties

The biggest impact from customizing a page is the loss of the link to the template page in the site definition. Once you customize a page, any changes made to the template file will not be reflected in the customized pages.

While, in theory, this could be considered a major loss, in practice it usually is not. There are two main reasons:

1. It is generally considered bad practice to directly modify the template files of the default site definitions. These files are potentially subject to being overwritten by patches and upgrades. Any changes you made to these files would, in those cases, be lost, and you would need to recreate them.

2. Modifying any site definition (default or custom), after sites based on it have been deployed, is not officially supported by Microsoft. The preferred method for changing sites based on existing definitions is to create and activate stapled features. A *stapled* feature is one that is linked to a preexisting site definition. Although not the easiest process, features can be changed/updated at a later date. See the SharePoint SDKs for further information on features and feature staples.

Of course, that doesn't prevent people from making those kinds of changes. In some cases, they can be an expedient way of enforcing company standards across the entire environment. Nevertheless, if you are seriously concerned that you may need to change these server files, you might wish to avoid customizing pages based on them.

Performance

It is a fact of life that retrieving information directly from a local hard disk will be faster than pulling it from a (possibly remote) database. Because customizing a page forces the entire page to be read from the database, there is indeed a small performance penalty for customized files. How small? That depends upon a number of factors, so there is no way to give a definite percentage, but the impact truly is minor. Consider this — whether the whole page is in the database, or just the ghost, *you still need to read the database to find out!* It isn't as if you don't read the database at all when the file is not customized, so the difference is minimal.

In addition, SharePoint is designed with built-in caching mechanisms to ensure that as few database hits as possible are performed under any circumstances. Under all but the most demanding conditions, you don't need to worry about the relative performance of customized and uncustomized pages.

Back to the Future

So, what happens if you have made changes to a page in SharePoint Designer, and for whatever reason, decide you need to get back to the original disk files? Fortunately, there is an easy process for that. Figure 5-3 shows a customized file (note the extra "i," or customized, icon) upon which the right-click context menu has been summoned. Choosing Reset to Site Definition will make a backup copy of the existing page, and change the entry in the content database so that it is once again served from the file system.

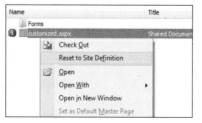

Figure 5-3

Pages created completely from scratch in SharePoint Designer (i.e., not based on one of the SharePoint Page templates) will not have the file-system template to pull from, and therefore are always served from the content database. The Reset to Site Definition option is not available on these files, nor are they flagged with the "customized" icon.

Restoring a page's link to its site definition does not delete the instance information for the page. It remains in the content database, and continues to inform the rendering of the page. This means, for example, that the page title, and any Web Parts you have placed in Web Part Zones on the page, will remain intact.

The Special Case of the _layouts Folder

There is a set of pages to which the above service process does not apply. In fact, they are not held in the content database at all. These are the files that are served from the *_layouts* folder of a site. The _layouts folder is the location for various system pages, such as Site Settings, that access the administrative APIs, or perform other tasks at a very deep level in SharePoint. While most _layouts files are administrative in nature, and therefore not seen by a typical site user, there are some that may bleed through. The All Site Content Page (./_layouts/viewlsts.aspx) is a prime example.

The _layouts folder is a *virtualization* of a folder from the 12 Hive, typically `C:\program files\ common files\microsoft shared\web server extensions\12\template\layouts\`. Every SharePoint site in the farm serves _layouts files directly from this physical path. Layouts files are not assembled from the database, and do not use the local site's Master Page (discussed below). This folder is read-only from the web sites, and does not appear in folder lists generated via the SharePoint Web API.

Because SharePoint Designer reads and saves SharePoint files via the Web API, you will notice that the _layouts folder does not appear when you open a site in SharePoint Designer. You are not able to access or make changes to _layouts files. This also means that most changes you make to an individual site will not be reflected in files served from the _layouts folder.

There is only one exception. Files served from the _layouts folder will respect the local site's Theme, or a globally applied CSS style sheet. By ensuring that as much of your site's branding as possible is achieved through the Theme or CSS, you will minimize the discontinuity between those _layouts files that are seen and the rest of your site. Use of CSS and Themes in SharePoint will be discussed in detail in chapter 7.

Thinking outside the Box

One of the approved locations to install custom web-based applications (not to be confused with SharePoint Web Applications) which make use of the SharePoint binary API is 12 Hive's `.\template\layouts` directory.

Files in the _layouts folder are served directly from the web front-end server, without going through SharePoint's safety mechanisms. While this allows great power in deploying an application that is then available to all sites in your SharePoint farm, it is accompanied by corresponding risks. Be very certain of the source and quality of any applications deployed in `.\template\layouts`.

Web Part Pages

You can create many types of pages and files with SharePoint Designer, and use most of them on a SharePoint site. You can even display SharePoint content on some of them (general .ASPX pages, for example); however, in most cases, you need to manually generate many of your own user interface components. While there may be times this is exactly what you want or need to do (and this book assumes you have the fundamental web design skills to do so), most of the time you will be better served by using SharePoint Web Part Pages.

Virtually all of the pages you see in SharePoint are forms of the Web Part Page. Technically, a Web Part Page is any .ASPX page inheriting from the `Microsoft.SharePoint.WebPartPages.WebPartPage` assembly. In practice, most SharePoint Web Part Pages have the following key characteristics:

❑ They are .ASPX (ASP.NET) form pages.

❑ They use a .NET Master Page that contains SharePoint-related placeholders (including the requisite `WebPartPage` inheritance just mentioned).

❑ The content area contains one or more *Web Part Zones*.

There are a number of Web Part Page templates provided with SharePoint, which can be instantiated in a document library by end users. Users can then add and connect Web Parts through the web interface. You can add and connect Web Parts through SharePoint Designer as well. In addition, with SharePoint Designer, you can fully customize the content area of these pages.

Although you can edit pages based on these templates from within SharePoint Designer, you cannot directly create instances of them.

There are also several specialty page types. These specialty types, while still fundamentally Web Part Pages, are not usually referred to as such. In particular, MOSS Publishing pages have another layer to their architecture, which will be described more fully in chapter 8.

Files served from the _layouts folder, though they may contain Web Parts, are not Web Part Pages. They cannot contain a Web Part Zone, and therefore cannot have Web Parts added dynamically at run time.

Master of Their Own Destiny

To fully take advantage of the functionality ASP.NET has to offer, all SharePoint-generated pages are derived from Master Pages. A Master Page is essentially a template, which provides elements that are common across a number of pages. These elements can range from navigation to style sheet links, to placeholders for the users' content. The pages that use a Master Page are called *Content Pages*, described in the next section.

As shown in Figure 5-4, you can easily create new Master Page–derived pages as well.

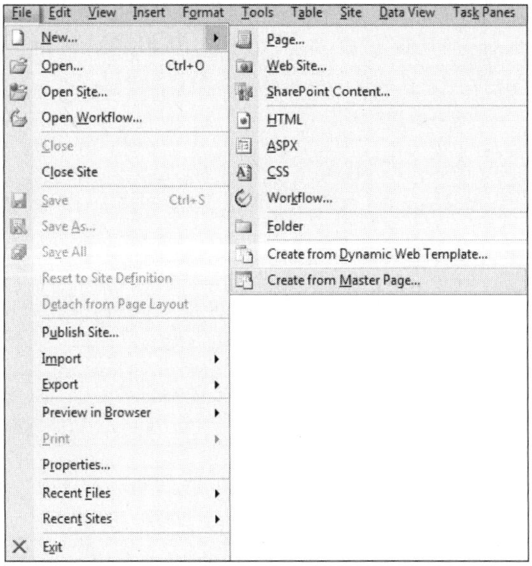

Figure 5-4

The SharePoint server manages several Master Pages, over two of which you have control in SharePoint Designer. You can also create arbitrary Master Pages of your own, and derive new Content Pages from them. Figure 5-5 shows the Master Page selector that results from choosing File ⇨ New ⇨ Create from Master Page.

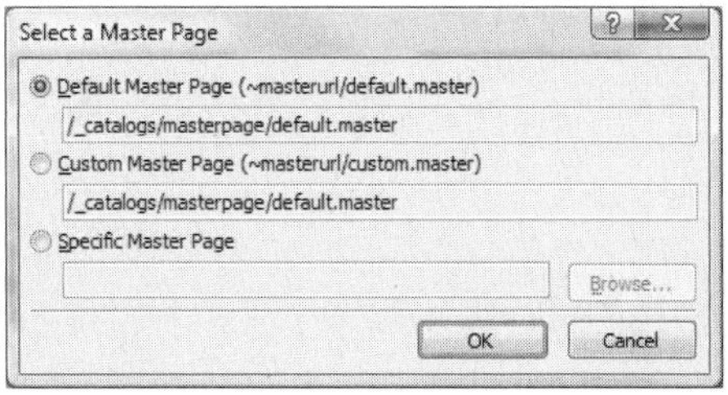

Figure 5-5

The Default Master is used by `default.aspx` and most other pages in WSS. The Custom Master is not used as often in WSS, but figures prominently in MOSS Publishing sites. There is no requirement that these point to different Master Pages; they simply give you the option to do so for different sets of pages. You will get an extensive look inside a Master Page later in this chapter.

A Few Words about Dynamic Web Templates

Users of Dreamweaver or FrontPage may have recognized the .DWT extension in earlier figures. DWT stands for either Dynamic Web Template or Dreamweaver Web Template — the file format is the same, though the name is different in the two products. Like Master Pages, .DWT provides a way for web designers to create a common page design, with regions for Content Editors to fill in with the actual page information.

Although it is possible for you to create .DWT files and pages based on .DWT in a SharePoint site, you should *not* use them for creating SharePoint pages: .DWT is provided primarily for working with types of sites other than SharePoint.

Inside a Content Page

Figure 5-6 shows a freshly created Content Page, NewSPPage.aspx, which is based upon (or *inherits*) the site's Default.master. The Split view lets you see the full "chrome" typical of a SharePoint site in the Design pane, whereas the Code pane on top shows the entire functional code of the page.

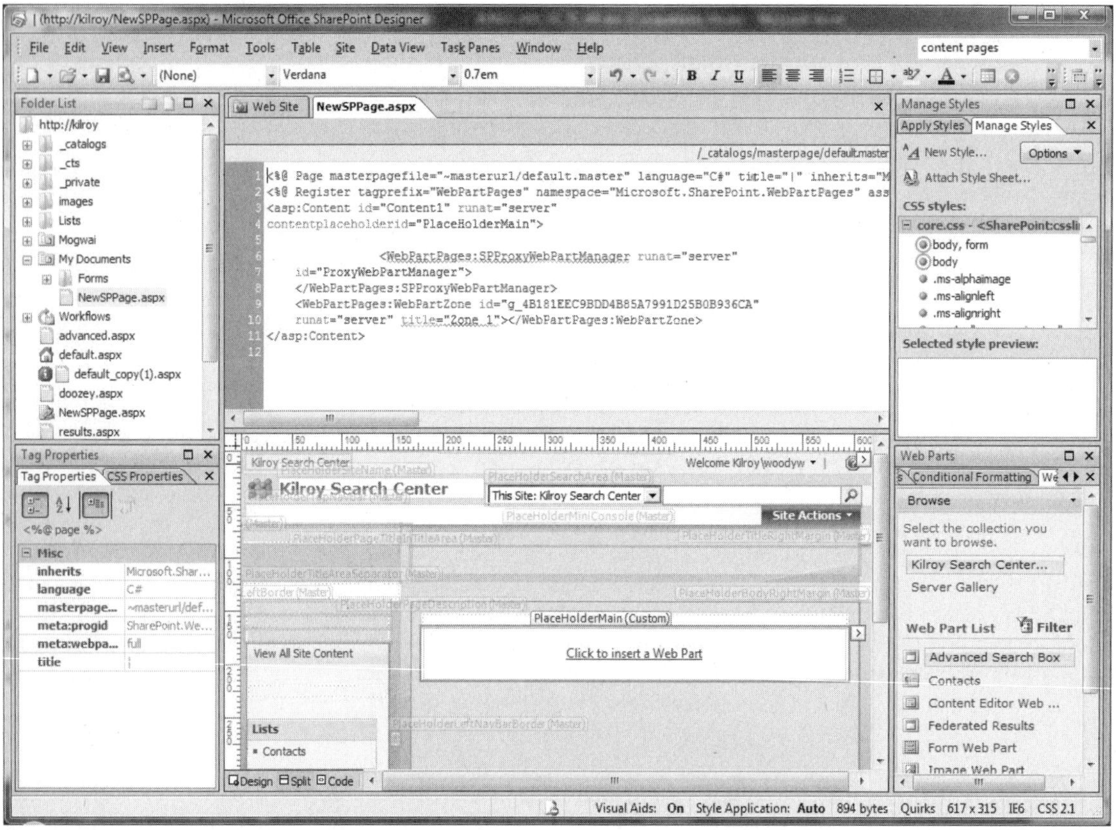

Figure 5-6

There are only ten lines of active code on this page.

Lines 1 and 2 define the Master Page to be used, and declare the page a WebPartPage. The Master Page is usually declared with one of two *tokens*: `~masterurl/default.master` or `~masterurl/custom` `.master`. This will force the page to use either the site's default or Custom Master Page, as selected previously in Figure 5-5. This is distinct from the page actually named default.master.

```
<%@ Page masterpagefile="~masterurl/default.master" language="C#" %>
title="|" inherits="Microsoft.SharePoint.WebPartPages.WebPartPage, %>
Microsoft.SharePoint, Version=12.0.0.0, Culture=neutral, %>
PublicKeyToken=71e9bce111e9429c" meta:webpartpageexpansion="full" %>
meta:progid="SharePoint.WebPartPage.Document" %>
<%@ Register tagprefix="WebPartPages" %>
namespace="Microsoft.SharePoint.WebPartPages" %>
assembly="Microsoft.SharePoint, Version=12.0.0.0, Culture=neutral, %>
PublicKeyToken=71e9bce111e9429c" %>
```

Lines 3 and 5 are empty placeholders for additional page header information.

Lines 6 through 13 define the main content of the page, which in this case consists of a single Web Part Zone, and the Web Part support module. This is held in an `<asp:Content>` tag, and will substitute in the Master Page for the corresponding `"PlaceHolderMain"` `<asp:ContentPlaceHolder>`.

```
<asp:Content id="Content2" runat="server" %>
contentplaceholderid="PlaceHolderMain">

                <WebPartPages:SPProxyWebPartManager runat="server" %>
id="ProxyWebPartManager">
                </WebPartPages:SPProxyWebPartManager>
                <WebPartPages:WebPartZone %>
id="g_D519CCB8D15C4984807064C581F37CC3" runat="server" title="Zone 1">
                </WebPartPages:WebPartZone>

</asp:Content>
```

When working with content placeholders in Code view, you may see elements underlined by the red squiggles that IntelliSense uses to indicate a potential problem. If you hover over the element, the details will appear to explain how the code is invalid for a particular browser. This is because the editor is interpreting these as client-side elements, when in actuality they will be rendered by the server. You can safely ignore these "errors."

Other than the Web Part Zone, everything that produces the rendering seen in the Design pane comes from the Master Page. Just above the Code pane, on the right-hand edge, SharePoint Designer shows you the address of the Master Page actually in use (expanded from the token above).

On SharePoint sites, you rarely edit Content Pages with SharePoint Designer, unless you are using a **Data View** *Web Part (see chapter 9). Most of your changes will be to the site's Master Pages, style sheets, and layout pages.*

List and Library View Pages

In chapter 4, you saw the folder structure of SharePoint lists and libraries. In the root of each list, and the Forms folder of each library, is a collection of pages used for entering and displaying the information in that list. These are called view pages, and are also Web Part Pages.

End users can create view pages through the web interface, but unlike the generic Web Part Pages mentioned above, view pages can be both edited *and created* in SharePoint Designer. When creating a new page, select the List View Pages section, as shown in Figure 5-7.

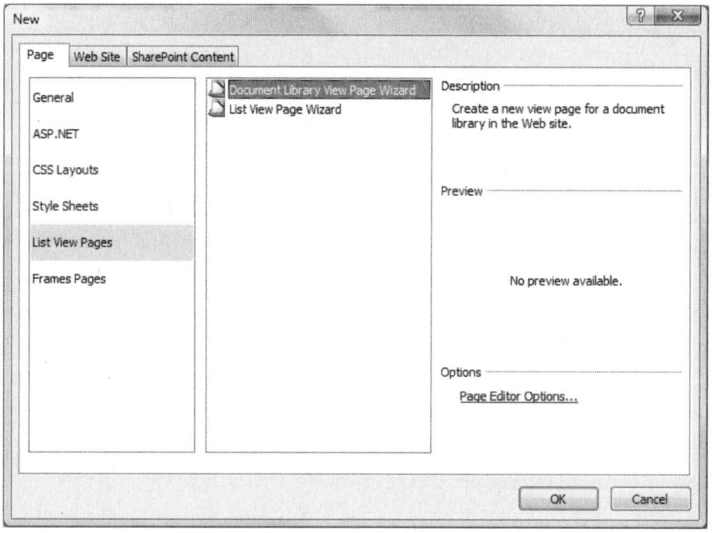

Figure 5-7

Notice that the create options refer to List and Library View Page *Wizards*. As wizards go, these are pretty simple. Figure 5-8 shows the whole wizard. You are asked only to select the (existing) list or library the form will be used for, and to enter the name you want to give the page.

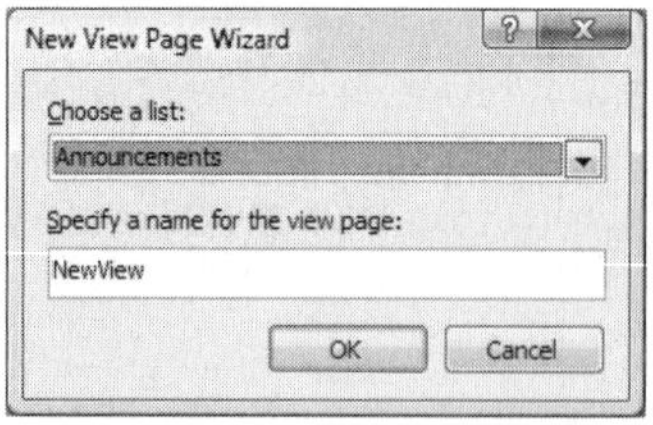

Figure 5-8

The result of the wizard is a Web Part Page in the view folder (either the root of the list, or the `./forms` subfolder of a library, as seen in chapter 4) of the list or library selected in the wizard. This page contains a single Web Part Zone (like the example above), which by default is populated with a Web Part for the default view of the list or library in question. When creating custom view forms in SharePoint Designer, you will almost always discard the default view part, and make extensive use of Data View Web Parts.

SharePoint Master Pages — A Deep Dive

Master Pages are used throughout SharePoint to provide common navigation and apply a consistent look and feel. As stated earlier, a Master Page is a combination of common elements and replaceable *content regions*.

Content regions are represented by `<asp:ContentPlaceHolder>` tags. These tags are assigned various properties and default content. The default content in a region can be replaced on the individual pages based on this Master. You can use the Region Types feature discussed in chapter 4 to restrict the kinds of changes made to content regions in SharePoint Designer.

In addition to the content region placeholders, a SharePoint Master Page contains tags that aren't replaced by content, but rather control page layout, set fonts, or invoke or render a particular piece of SharePoint functionality.

The Default Style Sheets

The default.master Master Page provided in SharePoint is over 400 lines long. Most of these lines are typical HTML tags defining the placement and style of various elements, defining the standard SharePoint look and feel. All of the styles used are defined in a style sheet called `core.css`. The following lines of code load the core.css style sheet, and any Theme that may be applied to the site.

```
<SharePoint:CssLink runat="server"/>
<SharePoint:Theme runat="server"/>
```

In Figure 5-9, these two lines have been removed, and default.master is saved as nostyle.master. The remainder of the Master Page is unchanged. Nostyle.master was then applied as the Default Master Page of the same site you have seen before.

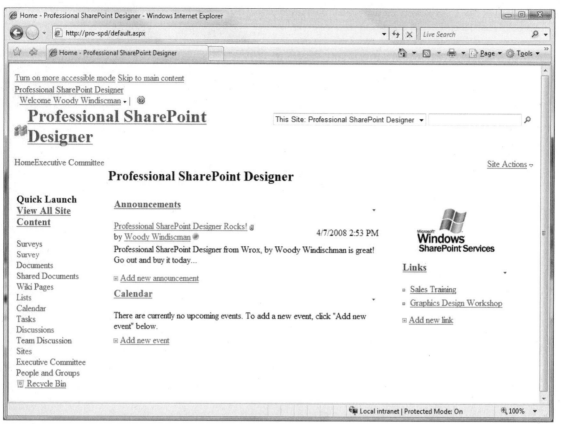

Figure 5-9

Everything still works. Most things are pretty close to the same location as well. This is because default .master uses tables to lay out most of the elements on the page. Different tables, cells, and other elements are assigned CSS classes, which are defined in core.css, and can be overridden by styles in a Theme., or as defined and invoked by you.

In many situations, you can satisfy the branding needs of a client purely with CSS and associated images, and leave all SharePoint's functionality intact. The styles used in Themes and core.css, and the default.master elements they apply to, will be covered in detail in chapter 7.

The Bare Necessities

The remainder of this chapter will focus on the content regions and functional elements that are necessary to the operation of SharePoint. In the process, you will see how to create a pure function or minimal Master Page, which you can then further customize with the branding and other look and feel elements you need.

> Remember that such a Master Page will not apply to pages served from the _layouts folder.

Content Regions

SharePoint's default.master contains the 31 content regions listed in the following table. These will be described in detail, and in the order they normally appear in the page, later in this section, along with the default content they contain.

Placeholder Name	Default Content/Function
PlaceHolderAdditionalPageHead	Placeholder used for any extra markup you may need between the `<head>` tags on a particular page.
PlaceHolderBodyAreaClass	Extra styles injected at the bottom of a page rendering, thus ensuring they take priority.
PlaceHolderBodyLeftBorder	Element left of the page body.
PlaceHolderBodyRightMargin	Element right of the page body.
PlaceHolderCalendarNavigator	Calendar View Date Navigator/Picker.
PlaceHolderFormDigest	Contains encrypted information when using Forms and Digest authentication.
PlaceHolderGlobalNavigation	Breadcrumb at the top of the page (usually to the portal site, if any).
PlaceHolderHorizontalNav	The tab site navigation element.
PlaceHolderLeftActions	Bottom of the left navigation area.
PlaceHolderLeftNavBar	Container for the Quick Launch bar.
PlaceHolderLeftNavBarBorder	Right side element on the left navigation bar.
PlaceHolderLeftNavBarDataSource	Data source for the Quick Launch menu.
PlaceHolderLeftNavBarTop	Top of the left navigation area
PlaceHolderMain	The main content of the page.
PlaceHolderMiniConsole	Certain commands appropriate to a particular page, such as Wiki editing.
PlaceHolderNavSpacer	Sets the width of the left navigation area.
PlaceHolderPageDescription	Description text from the page's definition.
PlaceHolderPageImage	Icon in the page title area.
PlaceHolderPageTitle	The title that is shown in the browser's title bar (within the `<title>` tag).

(continued)

Placeholder Name	Default Content/Function
PlaceHolderSearchArea	Holds the Search box control.
PlaceHolderSiteName	The site name as set in Site Settings.
PlaceHolderTitleAreaClass	Extra styles injected at the bottom of a page rendering, thus ensuring they take priority.
PlaceHolderTitleAreaSeparator	Below the title area.
PlaceHolderTitleBreadcrumb	Breadcrumb in the page title area.
PlaceHolderTitleInTitleArea	Page title (shown immediately below the breadcrumb in default.master).
PlaceHolderTitleLeftBorder	Element left of the title area.
PlaceHolderTitleRightMargin	Element right of the title area.
PlaceHolderTopNavBar	Top navigation area including the tabs and Site Settings menu.
PlaceHolderUtilityContent	Extra content that needs to be at the bottom of the page.
SPNavigation	Empty by default in Windows SharePoint Services; can be used for additional page-editing controls.
WSSDesignConsole	The page-editing controls when the page is in Edit Page mode (after clicking Site Actions, then Edit Page).

What if you don't want to show all of these regions on your site? Can you just delete the placeholders and their contents? In most cases, the answer is no. This is because of the way a Master-based .ASPX page is built at run time.

Many of the content placeholders contain default content, and many do not. Those that start out empty rely on the Content Page to provide information to inject into them if needed. Placeholders that are not empty will render the default content unless the Content Page provides its own content for that placeholder. In that case, the Content Page's content will override (be substituted for) the default content. While there is no requirement that a Content Page fill all of the potential slots in a Master, the reverse is not the case. A Master Page must have a corresponding placeholder for every element a Content Page tries to inject. If it does not, the ASP.NET engine will generate an error; however, your users will not be subjected to the raw ASP.NET error message. Instead, SharePoint captures the error and produces a page similar to Figure 5-10.

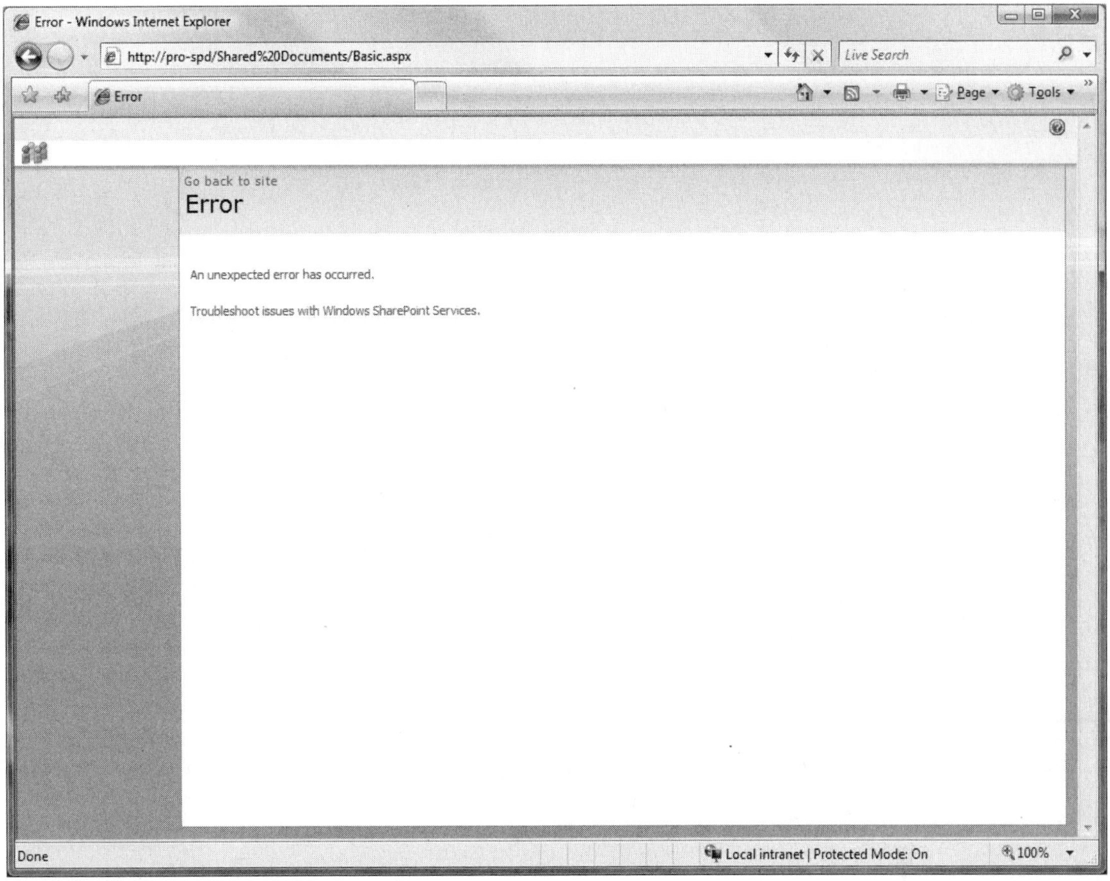

Figure 5-10

One way to suppress display of the content regions you aren't planning to use, but still allow the page to work, is to include empty versions of the placeholders in an <asp:panel> control, with the visible property set to false, as shown below.

```
<asp:Panel visible="false" runat="server">
<%-- The ContentPlaceHolders in this group are required to %>
exist (although they don't have to be visible) in any master %>
used by a SharePoint page. --%>
<asp:ContentPlaceHolder id="PlaceHolderAdditionalPageHead" runat="server" />
<asp:ContentPlaceHolder id="PlaceHolderPageTitle" runat="server" />
<asp:ContentPlaceHolder id="PlaceHolderSearchArea" runat="server"/>
<asp:ContentPlaceHolder id="PlaceHolderTitleBreadcrumb" runat="server"/>
<asp:ContentPlaceHolder id="PlaceHolderPageTitleInTitleArea" %>
 runat="server"/>
<asp:ContentPlaceHolder id="PlaceHolderLeftNavBar" runat="server"/>
<asp:ContentPlaceHolder ID="PlaceHolderPageImage" runat="server"/>
<asp:ContentPlaceHolder ID="PlaceHolderBodyLeftBorder" runat="server"/>
<asp:ContentPlaceHolder ID="PlaceHolderNavSpacer" runat="server"/>
```

```
<asp:ContentPlaceHolder ID="PlaceHolderTitleLeftBorder" runat="server"/>
<asp:ContentPlaceHolder ID="PlaceHolderTitleAreaSeparator" runat="server"/>
<asp:ContentPlaceHolder ID="PlaceHolderMiniConsole" runat="server"/>
<asp:ContentPlaceHolder id="PlaceHolderCalendarNavigator" runat ="server" />
<asp:ContentPlaceHolder id="PlaceHolderLeftActions" runat ="server"/>
<asp:ContentPlaceHolder id="PlaceHolderPageDescription" runat ="server"/>
<asp:ContentPlaceHolder id="PlaceHolderBodyAreaClass" runat ="server"/>
<asp:ContentPlaceHolder id="PlaceHolderTitleAreaClass" runat ="server"/>
<asp:ContentPlaceHolder id="PlaceHolderBodyRightMargin" runat="server" />
</asp:Panel>
```

The `ContentPlaceHolder` highlighted below is not absolutely required for MOSS Publishing pages; however, it is used by various other SharePoint pages (e.g., library instantiated Web Part Pages). You should include it on any general-purpose Master for use in Team Collaboration sites.

```
<asp:ContentPlaceHolder id="PlaceHolderBodyRightMargin" runat="server" />
<asp:ContentPlaceHolder ID="PlaceHolderTitleRightMargin" runat="server" />
</asp:Panel>
```

The items in this final group of `ContentPlaceHolders` are not required in every case, but encapsulate certain pieces of SharePoint functionality that may be useful in your environment. If you do not use this functionality, you may totally remove them from your Master Page, or just include the elements you need.

```
<asp:ContentPlaceHolder id="PlaceHolderFormDigest" runat="server">
<asp:ContentPlaceHolder id="PlaceHolderGlobalNavigation" runat="server">
<asp:ContentPlaceHolder id="PlaceHolderHorizontalNav" runat="server">
<asp:ContentPlaceHolder id="PlaceHolderLeftNavBarBorder" runat="server">
<asp:ContentPlaceHolder id="PlaceHolderLeftNavBarDataSource" %>
runat="server" />
<asp:ContentPlaceHolder id="PlaceHolderLeftNavBarTop" runat="server"/>
<asp:ContentPlaceHolder id="PlaceHolderTopNavBar" runat="server">
<asp:ContentPlaceHolder id="PlaceHolderUtilityContent" runat="server"/>
<asp:ContentPlaceHolder ID="SPNavigation" runat="server">
<asp:ContentPlaceHolder ID="WSSDesignConsole" runat="server">
<asp:ContentPlaceHolder id=PlaceHolderPageTitle runat="server"/>
</asp:Panel>
```

Thinking outside the Box

If you don't want to modify the Master Pages on your own, there are a number of alternative SharePoint Master Pages available.

❑ Microsoft has made a variety of Custom Master Pages for Windows SharePoint Services, along with accompanying CSS style sheets, available for you to download. Although these were designed primarily to accompany the Fab 40 custom application templates, they are applicable to any WSS-based site. An interesting characteristic of these Masters is that, when applied, they appear to be mild variations on the WSS default.master, but in actuality they completely reformulate the layout to use <DIV> tags and CSS instead of tables.

> ❑ Several people have published their own interpretations of minimal Master Pages. Most of these are designed for MOSS, though they can be adapted to WSS. Those posted by SharePoint MVP Heather Solomon are particularly popular, and can be accessed at the following site:
>
> http://www.heathersolomon.com/blog/articles/BaseMasterPages .aspx

The Very Least You Can Do

The following listing is a Master Page called wssminimum.master. It provides a bare shell around `PlaceHolderMain`, which is the primary content placeholder in SharePoint. It does not include the default style sheet, site navigation, utility JavaScript, or any kind of "chrome" around the content area. Nor does it provide any way to log in if you have enabled anonymous access. However, if you manually navigate to any standard SharePoint Content Page, this Master Page will render it without an error.

The first group of lines are directives to identify this page as a Master Page, and to register the various assemblies and namespaces required to implement SharePoint functionality.

```
<%@Master language="C#"%>
<%@ Register Tagprefix="SharePoint" %>
Namespace="Microsoft.SharePoint.WebControls" %>
Assembly="Microsoft.SharePoint, Version=12.0.0.0, Culture=neutral, %>
PublicKeyToken=71e9bce111e9429c" %>
<%@ Register Tagprefix="Utilities" %>
Namespace="Microsoft.SharePoint.Utilities" %>
Assembly="Microsoft.SharePoint, Version=12.0.0.0, Culture=neutral, %>
PublicKeyToken=71e9bce111e9429c" %>
<%@ Import Namespace="Microsoft.SharePoint" %>
<%@ Import Namespace="Microsoft.SharePoint.ApplicationPages" %>
<%@ Register Tagprefix="WebPartPages" Namespace="Microsoft.SharePoint.WebPartPages"
Assembly="Microsoft.SharePoint, Version=12.0.0.0, Culture=neutral,
PublicKeyToken=71e9bce111e9429c" %>
```

Next comes the HTML itself. The HTML head section includes a mandatory tag to prevent the SharePoint search engine from crawling the code on SharePoint Content Pages. The page body includes a Web Part management component, and the placeholder for the actual page content. Finally, the panel control described earlier is included, and the HTML is closed.

```
<html dir="ltr">
 <head runat="server">
  <SharePoint:RobotsMetaTag runat="server"/>
 </head>
<BODY onload="javascript:if (typeof(_spBodyOnLoadWrapper) != 'undefined')%>
_spBodyOnLoadWrapper();">
<WebPartPages:SPWebPartManager runat="server"/>
<form runat="server" onsubmit="return _spFormOnSubmitWrapper();">
  <asp:ContentPlaceHolder id="PlaceHolderMain" runat="server" />
<asp:Panel visible="false" runat="server">
<asp:ContentPlaceHolder id="PlaceHolderAdditionalPageHead" runat="server" />
<asp:ContentPlaceHolder id="PlaceHolderPageTitle" runat="server" />
<asp:ContentPlaceHolder id="PlaceHolderSearchArea" runat="server"/>
<asp:ContentPlaceHolder id="PlaceHolderTitleBreadcrumb" runat="server"/>
<asp:ContentPlaceHolder id="PlaceHolderPageTitleInTitleArea"  %>
runat="server"/>
<asp:ContentPlaceHolder id="PlaceHolderLeftNavBar" runat="server"/>
<asp:ContentPlaceHolder ID="PlaceHolderPageImage" runat="server"/>
<asp:ContentPlaceHolder ID="PlaceHolderBodyLeftBorder" runat="server"/>
<asp:ContentPlaceHolder ID="PlaceHolderNavSpacer" runat="server"/>
<asp:ContentPlaceHolder ID="PlaceHolderTitleLeftBorder" runat="server"/>
<asp:ContentPlaceHolder ID="PlaceHolderTitleAreaSeparator" runat="server"/>
<asp:ContentPlaceHolder ID="PlaceHolderMiniConsole" runat="server"/>
<asp:ContentPlaceHolder id="PlaceHolderCalendarNavigator" runat ="server" />
<asp:ContentPlaceHolder id="PlaceHolderLeftActions" runat ="server"/>
<asp:ContentPlaceHolder id="PlaceHolderPageDescription" runat ="server"/>
<asp:ContentPlaceHolder id="PlaceHolderBodyAreaClass" runat ="server"/>
<asp:ContentPlaceHolder id="PlaceHolderTitleAreaClass" runat ="server"/>
<asp:ContentPlaceHolder id="PlaceHolderBodyRightMargin" runat="server" />
<asp:ContentPlaceHolder ID="PlaceHolderTitleRightMargin" runat="server" />
</asp:Panel>
</form>
</body>
</html>
```

Figure 5-11 shows the home page with wssminimum.master applied. This provides a clean slate for you to build virtually your entire user interface from scratch.

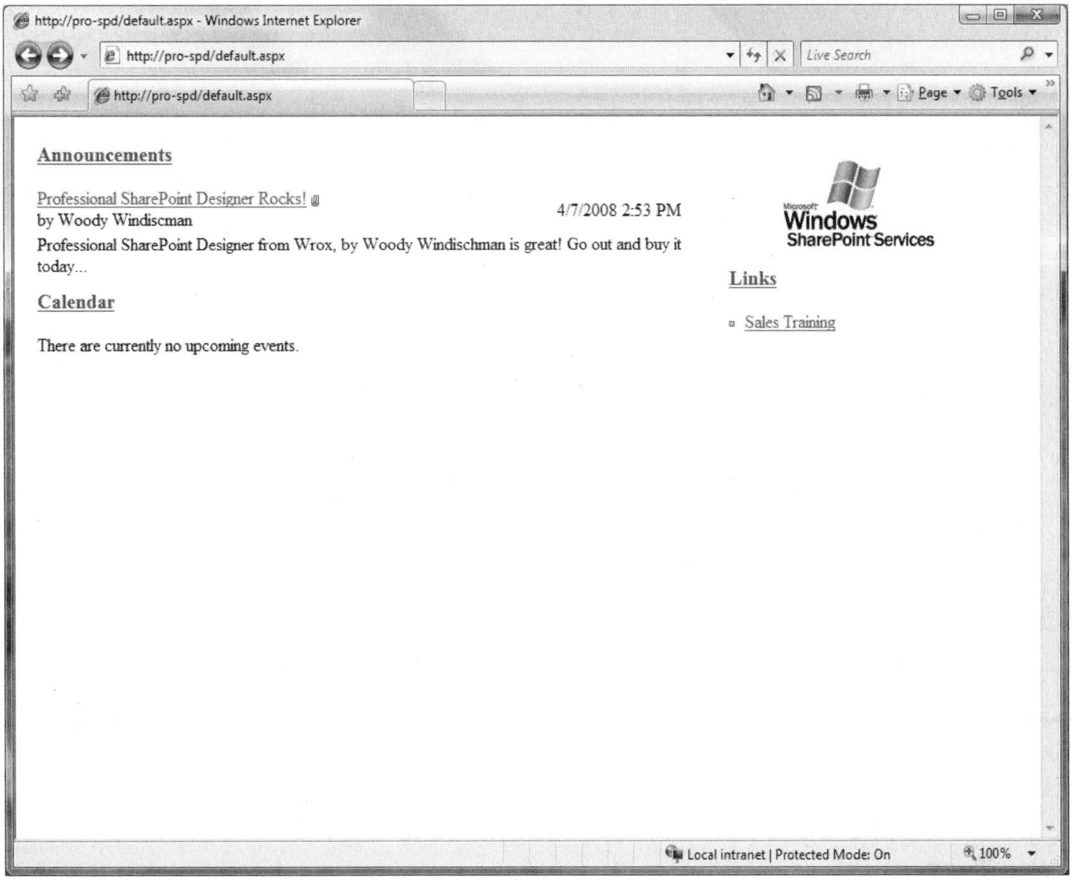

Figure 5-11

The downside of such a minimal Master Page is that you *must* build your entire user interface from scratch. The SharePoint content placeholders and web controls described later provide a rich toolbox that can help you provide a consistent user experience.

MOSS Publishing Pages require several additional directives in their Master Pages, which should not be used unless MOSS is installed. These are detailed in chapter 8.

SharePoint: Functional Stuff

In addition to, and often within, the content regions are a number of tags that invoke or include particular pieces of SharePoint functionality on a page. These tags are generally in the form `<SharePoint:somefunction>`, and invoke SharePoint Web Controls (the SharePoint tag prefix is defined in one of the directives at the top of the page). You have already seen the two simple SharePoint: controls that load the style sheets used on a typical SharePoint page.

Unlike the content region placeholders, which either stand alone or wrap default content, `<SharePoint:` tags are not always simple. Because they are instantiating real controls, they will often

include an array of parameters appropriate to the function being invoked. The default.master includes 38 SharePoint Web Controls.

A Not-So-Minimal Master, from Head to Toe

There is a lot of ground between the wssminimum.master described above and the default.master provided with SharePoint. This section will walk you through a page called purefunction.master. This Master Page contains all of the functionality provided in default.master, but, for ease of reading, strips out all of the tables used to create the layout.

Some of the removed table components have classes and names that are styled by core.css, and contribute styles to the retained elements. This can cause the rendering of the child elements to be suboptimal.

Naturally, unless you want your site to look like Figure 5-12, you will never use this Master Page as is. Rather, you will either use the actual default.master, or wrap your own layout markup around the components described later. Any further screenshots in this section will assume this to be the case, and show the components in an appropriate context.

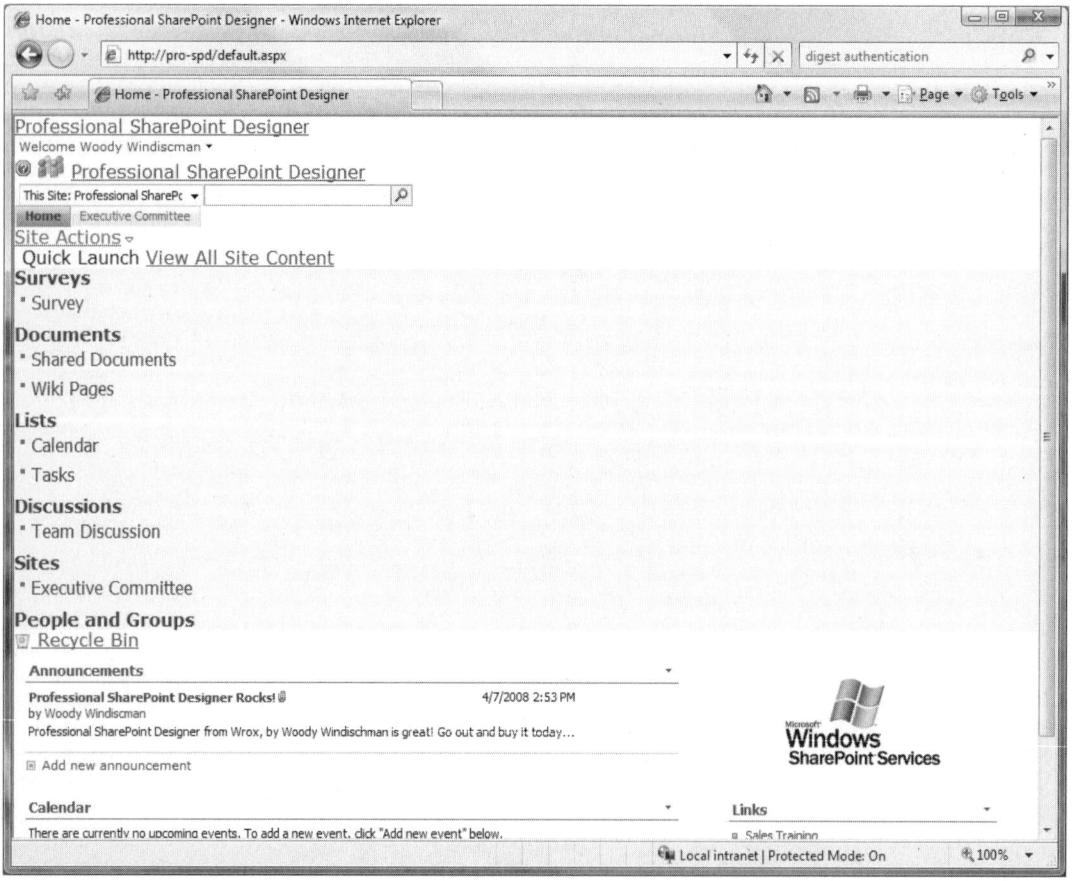

Figure 5-12

Unlike the empty placeholders in the minimal Master Page, the placeholders and web control definitions in this Master Page often span many lines. You may want to save any of these components you find useful as code snippets in SharePoint Designer.

Just as a Content Page could use a token to select a shared Master Page, the Master Page itself uses tokens to access certain controls. As you look through the code, note the presence of the tilde (~) in paths. This indicates that the control being referenced may be substituted dynamically based upon the particular site and configuration options.

Sight Unseen

Many of the lines at the top of this Master Page file are the same as those you saw in the minimal Master Page. These are two sections of content that are not actually seen by your user:

❑   The declarations and directives, which appear before any "normal" HTML.

❑   The <head> section of the HTML.

The new directives are `TagPrefix` registrations for two `wssuc` components — the `Welcome.ascx` token and the `DesignModeConsole` token. These tokens provide references to controls that exist in both MOSS and WSS, but are implemented differently. This tokenization allows the same Master Page to be used in both environments, and rendered appropriately in context.

An element that is used throughout the Master Page, but which makes its first appearance in this code block, is the *resource reference*. For example, in the <HTML tag, you see the segment <%$Resources:wss,multipages_direction_dir_value%>. The resources are stored in RESX files on the web server's file system. A .resx file is an XML listing of resource name/value pairs. If you have multiple language resources installed, a resource reference will pull the name's associated value from the file appropriate to the site's language. This allows you to avoid hard-coding common strings into your Master Page. The RESX files are generally kept in the Web Root folder for the web application.

In the head section are several SharePoint Web controls. The `CssLink`, `Theme`, and `RobotsMetaTag` controls you have already seen. There are also two script-loading controls. Just as the style controls load default and custom styles respectively, the first script link control loads the primary script file for SharePoint (core.js), and the second is there to allow the loading of any custom scripts that need to be common to every page.

The `ContentPlaceHolders` in this section implement the page tile as seen in the browser's title bar, and allow for the addition of custom page headers if needed.

```
<%@Master language="C#"%>
<%@ Register Tagprefix="SharePoint" %>
Namespace="Microsoft.SharePoint.WebControls" %>
Assembly="Microsoft.SharePoint, Version=12.0.0.0, Culture=neutral, %>
PublicKeyToken=71e9bce111e9429c" %>
<%@ Register Tagprefix="Utilities" %>
Namespace="Microsoft.SharePoint.Utilities" %>
Assembly="Microsoft.SharePoint, Version=12.0.0.0, Culture=neutral, %>
PublicKeyToken=71e9bce111e9429c" %>
<%@ Import Namespace="Microsoft.SharePoint" %>
```

```
<%@ Import Namespace="Microsoft.SharePoint.ApplicationPages" %>
<%@ Register Tagprefix="WebPartPages" %>
Namespace="Microsoft.SharePoint.WebPartPages" %>
Assembly="Microsoft.SharePoint, Version=12.0.0.0, Culture=neutral, %>
PublicKeyToken=71e9bce111e9429c" %>
<%@ Register TagPrefix="wssuc" TagName="Welcome" %>
src="~/_controltemplates/Welcome.ascx" %>
<%@ Register TagPrefix="wssuc" TagName="DesignModeConsole" %>
src="~/_controltemplates/DesignModeConsole.ascx" %>
<HTML dir="<%$Resources:wss,multipages_direction_dir_value%>" %>
runat="server" xmlns:o="urn:schemas-microsoft-com:office:office" %>
__expr-val-dir="ltr">
<HEAD runat="server">
 <META Name="GENERATOR" Content="Microsoft SharePoint">
 <META Name="progid" Content="SharePoint.WebPartPage.Document">
 <META HTTP-EQUIV="Content-Type" CONTENT="text/html; charset=utf-8">
 <META HTTP-EQUIV="Expires" content="0">
 <SharePoint:RobotsMetaTag runat="server"/>
 <Title ID=onetidTitle><asp:ContentPlaceHolder id=PlaceHolderPageTitle %>
runat="server"/></Title>
 <SharePoint:CssLink runat="server"/>
 <SharePoint:Theme runat="server"/>
 <SharePoint:ScriptLink language="javascript" name="core.js" %>
Defer="true" runat="server"/>
 <SharePoint:CustomJSUrl runat="server"/>
 <SharePoint:SoapDiscoveryLink runat="server"/>
 <asp:ContentPlaceHolder id="PlaceHolderAdditionalPageHead" runat="server"/>
 <SharePoint:DelegateControl runat="server" %>
ControlId="AdditionalPageHead" AllowMultipleControls="true"/>
 </HEAD>
```

The Global Navigation Bar

This code block includes the start of the body, which begins the .ASPX form and instantiates the SPWebPartManager control. This is followed by the PlaceHolderGlobalNavigation placeholder. This placeholder is filled with default content, including:

- ❑ Some hidden links to control accessibility.
- ❑ The Global breadcrumb.
- ❑ The Welcome menu.
- ❑ The SharePoint Help link.

As shown in Figure 5-13, the accessibility controls are normally not visible on the page.

Professional SharePoint Designer   Welcome Woody Windiscman ▼ |

Figure 5-13

```
<BODY scroll="yes" onload="javascript:if %>
 (typeof(_spBodyOnLoadWrapper) != 'undefined') _spBodyOnLoadWrapper();">
 <form runat="server" onsubmit="return _spFormOnSubmitWrapper();">
 <WebPartPages:SPWebPartManager id="m" runat="Server"/>
 <asp:ContentPlaceHolder id="PlaceHolderGlobalNavigation" runat="server">
  <span id="TurnOnAccessibility" style="display:none">
   <a href="#" class="ms-skip" %>
onclick="SetIsAccessibilityFeatureEnabled(true);UpdateAccessibilityUI();%>
return false;">
    <SharePoint:EncodedLiteral runat="server" %>
text="<%$Resources:wss,master_turnonaccessibility%>" %>
EncodeMethod="HtmlEncode"/></a>
   </span>
   <A href="javascript:;" onclick="javascript:this.href='#mainContent';" %>
class="ms-skip" AccessKey="<%$Resources:wss,maincontent_accesskey%>" %>
runat="server">
   <SharePoint:EncodedLiteral runat="server" %>
text="<%$Resources:wss,mainContentLink%>" EncodeMethod="HtmlEncode"/></A>
   <span id="TurnOffAccessibility" style="display:none">
    <a href="#" class="ms-acclink" %>
onclick="SetIsAccessibilityFeatureEnabled(false); %>
UpdateAccessibilityUI();return false;">
     <SharePoint:EncodedLiteral runat="server" %>
text="<%$Resources:wss,master_turnoffaccessibility%>" %>
EncodeMethod="HtmlEncode"/></a>
   </span>
```

The left breadcrumb is implemented as the default content of the PlaceHolderGlobalNavigationSiteMap content placeholder. This is a standard ASP.NET breadcrumb control, connected to SharePoint's Site Map data source. It will show either one or two levels, depending on whether or not a portal site connection is configured in the site collection administration page. If a portal site is configured, the leftmost link will be to that site, and the right link will be to the root of the current site collection. If no portal connection is specified, only the site collection root link is shown.

Notice the CSS class designator, NodeStyle-CssClass="ms-sitemapdirectional". The class being assigned, like all of the classes you will see throughout this listing, is defined in core.css. Some SharePoint controls have hard-coded style references, while others allow you to specify their style in the Master Page. Generally, you want to retain the core.css class reference, and use your own Theme or CSS file to override the default styling, but this is not required.

There are four delegate controls on the right side of the global navigation bar, only one of which is normally visible in WSS — the Welcome control mentioned above.

Finally, there is a link to the help system. This is built up with JavaScript and several resource strings, as it needs to be available in many languages, and opens into its own customized window.

```
    <asp:ContentPlaceHolder id="PlaceHolderGlobalNavigationSiteMap" %>
runat="server">
      <asp:SiteMapPath SiteMapProvider="SPSiteMapProvider" %>
id="GlobalNavigationSiteMap" RenderCurrentNodeAsLink="true" %>
SkipLinkText="" NodeStyle-CssClass="ms-sitemapdirectional" runat="server"/>
    </asp:ContentPlaceHolder>
    <SharePoint:DelegateControl runat="server" ControlId="GlobalSiteLink0"/>
    <wssuc:Welcome id="IdWelcome" runat="server" EnableViewState="false">
    </wssuc:Welcome>
    <SharePoint:DelegateControl ControlId="GlobalSiteLink1" Scope="Farm" %>
runat="server"/>
    <SharePoint:DelegateControl ControlId="GlobalSiteLink2" Scope="Farm" %>
runat="server"/>
    <a href="javascript:TopHelpButtonClick('NavBarHelpHome')" %>
AccessKey="<%$Resources:wss,multipages_helplink_accesskey%>" %>
id="TopHelpLink" title="<%$Resources:wss,multipages_helplinkalt_text%>" %>
runat="server"><img align='absmiddle' border=0 %>
src="/_layouts/images/helpicon.gif" %>
alt="<%$Resources:wss,multipages_helplinkalt_text%>" runat="server"></a>
    </asp:ContentPlaceHolder>
```

Site (Global) Title Area

The site title area, Figure 5-14, contains three primary elements:

❑ The `SiteLogoImage` web control, which defaults to the pawn icon, will instead render the image defined on the Site Settings Title, Description, and Icon page if it is set.

❑ The `PlaceHolderSiteName` content placeholder, whose default content consists of the Site Title itself, linked to the home page of the site. The title is set at creation time, and can be edited through the same settings page as the `SiteLogoImage`.

❑ The `PlaceHolderSearchArea` content placeholder. This defaults to the `SmallSearchInputBox` delegated web control, which is configured based upon the version of SharePoint and the site administrator's option choices.

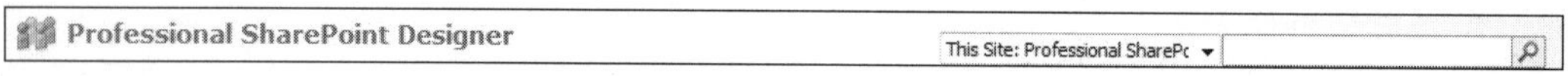

Professional SharePoint Designer

This Site: Professional SharePc ▾

Figure 5-14

```
<SharePoint:SiteLogoImage id="onetidHeadbnnr0" %>
LogoImageUrl="/_layouts/images/titlegraphic.gif" runat="server"/></td>
  <asp:ContentPlaceHolder id="PlaceHolderSiteName" runat="server">
    <SharePoint:SPLinkButton runat="server" NavigateUrl="~site/" %>
id="onetidProjectPropertyTitle">
    <SharePoint:ProjectProperty Property="Title" runat="server" />
    </SharePoint:SPLinkButton>
  </asp:ContentPlaceHolder>
  <asp:ContentPlaceHolder id="PlaceHolderSearchArea" runat="server">
    <SharePoint:DelegateControl runat="server" %>
ControlId="SmallSearchInputBox"/>
  </asp:ContentPlaceHolder>
```

Top (Tab) Navigation Area

The top navigation area is defined by the `PlaceHolderTopNavBar` content placeholder, and contains two menus. Although (by default) they share a content placeholder and a tablike inactive state, these menus are very different from one another, both operationally and in how they are generated.

The TopNavigationMenu (Tab Bar)

The top tab menu is based on two controls — the `SharePoint:AspMenu` and a delegate data source control. You can see from the many parameters that you have a great deal of control over how this menu is presented. Again, many of the styles used are drawn from the core.css and applied Theme or custom .CSS files.

This is one of the two standard menus your site administrator can control the elements in. The delegate data source control is populated differently in MOSS Publishing sites and WSS collaboration sites, in that MOSS allows a full multilevel hierarchy for navigation elements, whereas WSS is limited to a single level for the top menu.

Notice the `StaticDisplayLevels` and `MaximumDynamicDisplayLevels` parameters in the `AspMenu` control. You can determine how many levels are presented directly versus as dropdowns. In fact, the control offers full flexibility to provide vertical or horizontal menus, as may be appropriate in your design. By leveraging this control (and its Quick Launch counterpart described later), you can both control the look and feel, and keep administrative overhead to a minimum.

You can leverage SharePoint's AspMenu control with other data sources as well, although without the built-in Administrative UI.

```
<asp:ContentPlaceHolder id="PlaceHolderTopNavBar" runat="server">
 <asp:ContentPlaceHolder id="PlaceHolderHorizontalNav" runat="server">
  <SharePoint:AspMenu
    ID="TopNavigationMenu"
    Runat="server"
    DataSourceID="topSiteMap"
    EnableViewState="false"
    AccessKey="<%$Resources:wss,navigation_accesskey%>"
    Orientation="Horizontal"
    StaticDisplayLevels="2"
    MaximumDynamicDisplayLevels="1"
    DynamicHorizontalOffset="0"
    StaticPopoutImageUrl="/_layouts/images/menudark.gif"
    StaticPopoutImageTextFormatString=""
    DynamicHoverStyle-BackColor="#CBE3F0"
    SkipLinkText=""
    StaticSubMenuIndent="0"
    CssClass="ms-topNavContainer">
  <StaticMenuStyle/>
  <StaticMenuItemStyle CssClass="ms-topnav" ItemSpacing="0px"/>
  <StaticSelectedStyle CssClass="ms-topnavselected" />
  <StaticHoverStyle CssClass="ms-topNavHover" />
  <DynamicMenuStyle  BackColor="#F2F3F4" BorderColor="#A7B4CE" %>
BorderWidth="1px"/>
```

```
      <DynamicMenuItemStyle CssClass="ms-topNavFlyOuts"/>
      <DynamicHoverStyle CssClass="ms-topNavFlyOutsHover"/>
      <DynamicSelectedStyle CssClass="ms-topNavFlyOutsSelected"/>
    </SharePoint:AspMenu>
    <SharePoint:DelegateControl runat="server" %>
  ControlId="TopNavigationDataSource">
      <Template_Controls>
       <asp:SiteMapDataSource
         ShowStartingNode="False"
         SiteMapProvider="SPNavigationProvider"
         id="topSiteMap"
         runat="server"
         StartingNodeUrl="sid:1002"/>
      </Template_Controls>
    </SharePoint:DelegateControl>
  </asp:ContentPlaceHolder>
```

The Site Actions Menu

The other menu in the top menu bar is the Site Actions dropdown, shown in Figure 5-15. There are several things to notice about this menu:

❑   Site Actions is not enclosed in its own placeholder (though it is within the `PlaceholderTopNavBar` placeholder along with the horizontal tab bar).

❑   The items in the menu are defined explicitly, meaning you can easily add your own arbitrary items to the menu.

❑   The menu uses a verbose display format, including icons and descriptions.

❑   There is a `PermissionsString` parameter, allowing you to trim the menu to users with particular rights on the site.

Figure 5-15

The order in which the elements are rendered is not based upon their order in the code. Rather the `MenuGroupId` and `Sequence` parameters are used. Items within the same menu group are ordered by the Sequence. The groups are ordered by their `MenuGroupID` and separated by a bar. Both orderings are smallest to largest.

```
<SharePoint:SiteActions runat="server"%>
 AccessKey="<%$Resources:wss,tb_SiteActions_AK%>" id="SiteActionsMenuMain"
  PrefixHtml="&lt;div&gt;&lt;div&gt;"
  SuffixHtml="&lt;/div&gt;&lt;/div&gt;"
  MenuNotVisibleHtml=" ">
  <CustomTemplate>
   <SharePoint:FeatureMenuTemplate runat="server"
    FeatureScope="Site"
    Location="Microsoft.SharePoint.StandardMenu"
    GroupId="SiteActions"
    UseShortId="true"
   >
   <SharePoint:MenuItemTemplate runat="server" id="MenuItem_Create"
    Text="<%$Resources:wss,viewlsts_pagetitle_create%>"
    Description="<%$Resources:wss,siteactions_createdescription%>"
    ImageUrl="/_layouts/images/Actionscreate.gif"
    MenuGroupId="100"
    Sequence="100"
    UseShortId="true"
    ClientOnClickNavigateUrl="~site/_layouts/create.aspx"
    PermissionsString="ManageLists, ManageSubwebs"
    PermissionMode="Any" />
   <SharePoint:MenuItemTemplate runat="server" id="MenuItem_EditPage"
    Text="<%$Resources:wss,siteactions_editpage%>"
    Description="<%$Resources:wss,siteactions_editpagedescription%>"
    ImageUrl="/_layouts/images/ActionsEditPage.gif"
    MenuGroupId="100"
    Sequence="200"
    ClientOnClickNavigateUrl="javascript:MSOLayout_ChangeLayoutMode(false);"
   />
   <SharePoint:MenuItemTemplate runat="server" id="MenuItem_Settings"
    Text="<%$Resources:wss,settings_pagetitle%>"
    Description="<%$Resources:wss,siteactions_sitesettingsdescription%>"
    ImageUrl="/_layouts/images/ActionsSettings.gif"
    MenuGroupId="100"
    Sequence="300"
    UseShortId="true"
    ClientOnClickNavigateUrl="~site/_layouts/settings.aspx"
PermissionsString="EnumeratePermissions,ManageWeb,ManageSubwebs,%>
AddAndCustomizePages,ApplyThemeAndBorder,ManageAlerts,ManageLists,%>
ViewUsageData"
    PermissionMode="Any" />
   </SharePoint:FeatureMenuTemplate>
  </CustomTemplate>
 </SharePoint:SiteActions>
 </asp:ContentPlaceHolder>
```

Page Edit Bar

The Page Edit Bar (`DesignModeConsole` and `PublishingConsole`) is visible in the browser when you are editing the content area of a page. On WSS pages (Figure 5-16) the bar is very simple — little more than a status line and close box. As shown in Figure 5-17, however, MOSS Publishing pages have a variety of tools for content management in their edit bar.

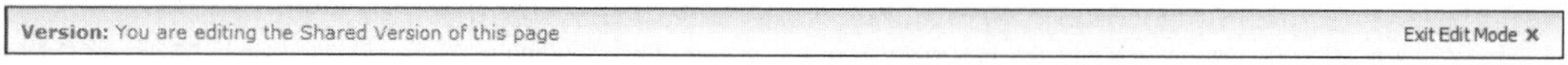

Figure 5-16

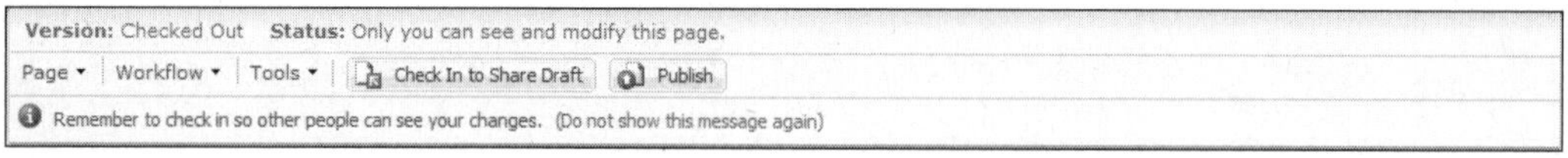

Figure 5-17

The WSSDesignConsole *is still present, but it is overlaid by the* PublishingConsole. *Removing the* PublishingConsole *delegate control allows the simple WSS bar to show through.*

```
<asp:ContentPlaceHolder ID="WSSDesignConsole" runat="server">
 <wssuc:DesignModeConsole id="IdDesignModeConsole" runat="server"/>
</asp:ContentPlaceHolder>
<asp:ContentPlaceHolder ID="SPNavigation" runat="server">
 <SharePoint:DelegateControl runat="server" ControlId="PublishingConsole"
  PrefixHtml="&lt;tr&gt;&lt;td colspan=&quot;4&quot; %>
id=&quot;mpdmconsole&quot; class=&quot;ms-consolemptablerow&quot;&gt;"
  SuffixHtml="&lt;/td&gt;&lt;/tr&gt;">
 </SharePoint:DelegateControl>
</asp:ContentPlaceHolder>
```

Page Title Area

The title area spans the width of the page, and contains elements for both content and layout. The four functional components, as shown in Figure 5-18, are:

❑ The Page Image.

❑ The primary site breadcrumb.

❑ The PageTitleInTitleArea version of the Page Title.

❑ The mini console.

Figure 5-18

The layout elements are used to help keep the title area consistent in style and alignment with the left navigation and page body sections below it. In particular, the Page Image aligns with the left navigation. The breadcrumb and title align with the body area. The mini console is rendered at run time in a relatively positioned <div>, and normally aligned to the upper-right corner of the main body element below it.

```
<asp:ContentPlaceHolder id="PlaceHolderPageImage" runat="server"/>
<asp:ContentPlaceHolder id="PlaceHolderTitleLeftBorder" runat="server">
</asp:ContentPlaceHolder>
<asp:ContentPlaceHolder id="PlaceHolderTitleBreadcrumb" runat="server">
<asp:SiteMapPath SiteMapProvider="SPContentMapProvider" id="ContentMap" %>
SkipLinkText="" NodeStyle-CssClass="ms-sitemapdirectional" %>
runat="server"/>  
</asp:ContentPlaceHolder>
<asp:ContentPlaceHolder id="PlaceHolderPageTitleInTitleArea" %>
runat="server" />
<asp:ContentPlaceHolder id="PlaceHolderMiniConsole" runat="server"/>
<asp:ContentPlaceHolder id="PlaceHolderTitleRightMargin" runat="server">
</asp:ContentPlaceHolder>
<asp:ContentPlaceHolder id="PlaceHolderTitleAreaSeparator" runat="server"/>
```

Left Navigation Bar

The left navigation bar contains placeholders and controls for a variety of navigation elements. Not all of these elements are available at all times.

Navigation Data Source and Calendar Control

The first control is not a visible element. It is a placeholder for an alternate data source for the left Quick Launch navigation bar.

The second control is the placeholder for the calendar navigator, shown in Figure 5-19. This date picker is only injected into this placeholder on Calendar view pages. If the parent calendar is in month view, it displays the 12 months (as shown), otherwise it shows the days in the current month for day and week views.

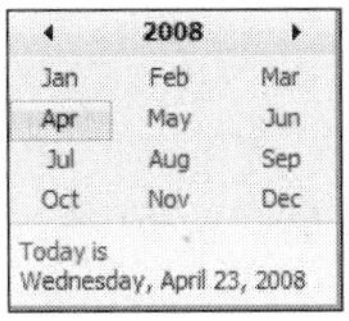

Figure 5-19

```
<asp:ContentPlaceHolder id="PlaceHolderLeftNavBarDataSource" %>
runat="server" />
<asp:ContentPlaceHolder id="PlaceHolderCalendarNavigator" runat="server" />
```

Quick Launch

The Quick Launch bar is assembled from several components:

❑   The Quick Launch title label (hidden in default.master).

❑   The View All Site Content link.

❑   The Quick Launch menu itself.

❑   The Quick Launch data source delegate control.

Notice the `SPSecurityTrimmedControl` wrapper around the View All Site Content link. This wrapper class can be useful any time you have content you wish to restrict to users with a particular right. In this case, the link is only displayed to users who have the `ViewFormPages` right.

Like the `TopNavigationMenu`, the Quick Launch is an `ASPMenu` fed by a data source maintained by SharePoint, and customizable by the site owner. Unlike the top menu, this data source is hierarchical in WSS as well as MOSS — for example, the data source has multiple levels. In the case of WSS, this is two levels (listed as link and heading), but MOSS is more flexible in defining site hierarchies.

You can take advantage of this by changing the values for `StaticDisplayLevels` and `MaximumDynamicDisplayLevels` from their defaults of 2 and 0 to create fly-out menus such as that shown in Figure 5-20.

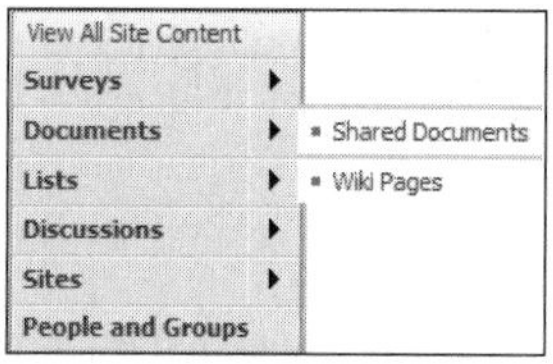

Figure 5-20

Just as in the top menu, you have full flexibility both in setting the style classes used by the menu elements and, of course, in setting the values of those classes.

```
<asp:ContentPlaceHolder id="PlaceHolderLeftNavBarTop" runat="server"/>
<asp:ContentPlaceHolder id="PlaceHolderLeftNavBar" runat="server">
 <SharePoint:EncodedLiteral runat="server" %>
text="<%$Resources:wss,quiklnch_pagetitle%>" EncodeMethod="HtmlEncode"/>
 <Sharepoint:SPSecurityTrimmedControl runat="server" %>
PermissionsString="ViewFormPages">
 <SharePoint:SPLinkButton id="idNavLinkViewAll" runat="server" %>
NavigateUrl="~site/_layouts/viewlsts.aspx" %>
Text="<%$Resources:wss,quiklnch_allcontent%>" %>
AccessKey="<%$Resources:wss,quiklnch_allcontent_AK%>"/>
 </SharePoint:SPSecurityTrimmedControl>
 <Sharepoint:SPNavigationManager
  id="QuickLaunchNavigationManager"
  runat="server"
  QuickLaunchControlId="QuickLaunchMenu"
  ContainedControl="QuickLaunch"
  EnableViewState="false">
<div>
 <SharePoint:DelegateControl runat="server"
  ControlId="QuickLaunchDataSource">
  <Template_Controls>
   <asp:SiteMapDataSource
```

```
        SiteMapProvider="SPNavigationProvider"
        ShowStartingNode="False"
        id="QuickLaunchSiteMap"
        StartingNodeUrl="sid:1025"
        runat="server"
        />
     </Template_Controls>
   </SharePoint:DelegateControl>
   <SharePoint:AspMenu
    id="QuickLaunchMenu"
    DataSourceId="QuickLaunchSiteMap"
    runat="server"
    Orientation="Vertical"
    StaticDisplayLevels="2"
    ItemWrap="true"
    MaximumDynamicDisplayLevels="0"
    StaticSubMenuIndent="0"
    SkipLinkText=""
   >
   <LevelMenuItemStyles>
    <asp:MenuItemStyle CssClass="ms-navheader"/>
    <asp:MenuItemStyle CssClass="ms-navitem"/>
   </LevelMenuItemStyles>
   <LevelSubMenuStyles>
    <asp:SubMenuStyle CssClass="ms-navSubMenu1"/>
    <asp:SubMenuStyle CssClass="ms-navSubMenu2"/>
   </LevelSubMenuStyles>
   <LevelSelectedStyles>
    <asp:MenuItemStyle CssClass="ms-selectednavheader"/>
    <asp:MenuItemStyle CssClass="ms-selectednav"/>
   </LevelSelectedStyles>
   </SharePoint:AspMenu>
  </div>
  </Sharepoint:SPNavigationManager>
```

Site Hierarchy (Tree View)

In addition to (or instead of) the traditional Quick Launch view of a site, site administrators can select a full tree view. This view allows the user to browse and navigate to any site, list, or library (or even folders within them) in the site collection, as shown in Figure 5-21.

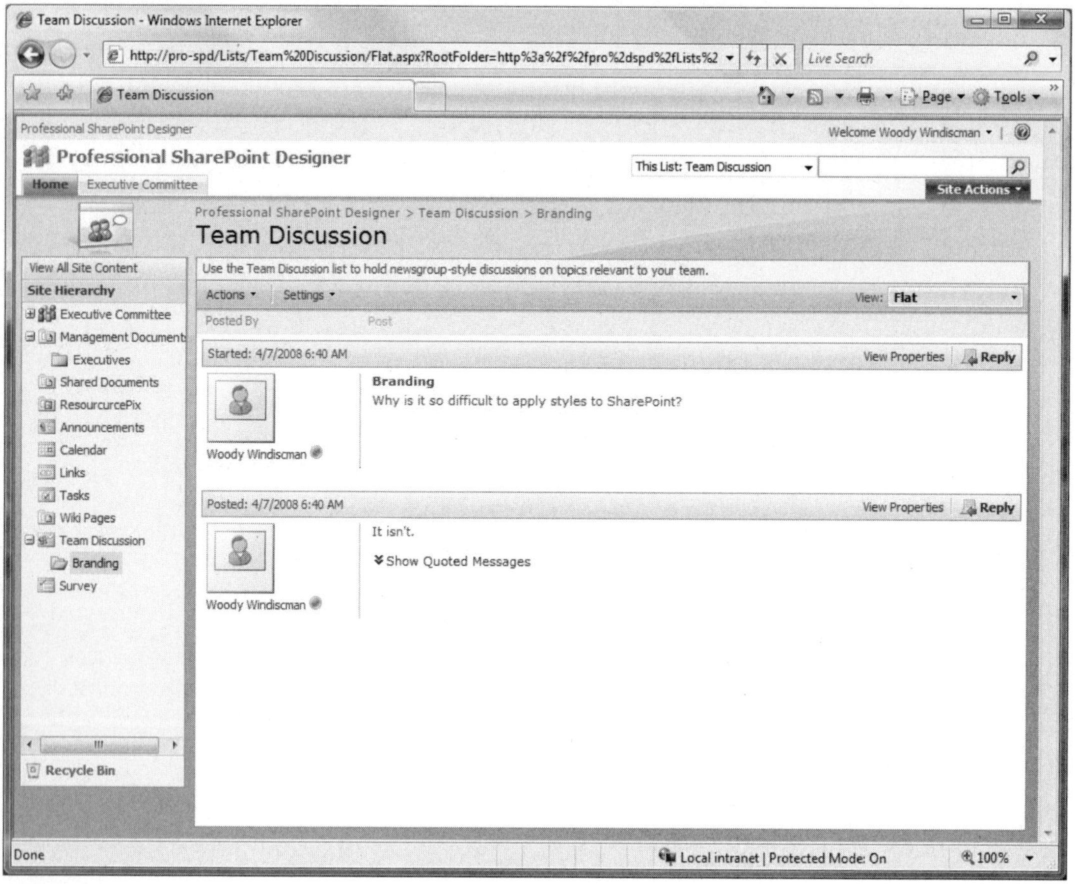

Figure 5-21

As with all of the SharePoint navigation controls, you can define many aspects of the control's look through its parameters, from the styles used for the text to the specific images used for the navigation icons.

```
<Sharepoint:SPNavigationManager
 id="TreeViewNavigationManager"
 runat="server"
 ContainedControl="TreeView">
<SharePoint:SPLinkButton runat="server" %>
NavigateUrl="~site/_layouts/viewlsts.aspx" id="idNavLinkSiteHierarchy" %>
Text="<%$Resources:wss,treeview_header%>" %>
AccessKey="<%$Resources:wss,quiklnch_allcontent_AK%>"/>
<SharePoint:SPHierarchyDataSourceControl
 runat="server"
 id="TreeViewDataSource"
 RootContextObject="Web"
 IncludeDiscussionFolders="true"
/>
```

```
<SharePoint:SPRememberScroll runat="server" id="TreeViewRememberScroll" %>
onscroll="javascript:_spRecordScrollPositions(this);" Style="overflow: %>
auto;height: 400px;width: 150px; ">
<Sharepoint:SPTreeView
 id="WebTreeView"
 runat="server"
 ShowLines="false"
 DataSourceId="TreeViewDataSource"
 ExpandDepth="0"
 SelectedNodeStyle-CssClass="ms-tvselected"
 NodeStyle-CssClass="ms-navitem"
 NodeStyle-HorizontalPadding="2"
 SkipLinkText=""
 NodeIndent="12"
 ExpandImageUrl="/_layouts/images/tvplus.gif"
 CollapseImageUrl="/_layouts/images/tvminus.gif"
 NoExpandImageUrl="/_layouts/images/tvblank.gif"
 >
</Sharepoint:SPTreeView>
</Sharepoint:SPRememberScroll>
</Sharepoint:SPNavigationManager>
```

Recycle Bin and Left Actions

Access to the Recycle bin is implemented via a SPLinkButton element. This implementation is slightly different from the View All Site Content link above, and leverages more of the SPLinkButton's native functionality. Notice that it allows an image to be associated, as well as providing for its own security trimming, without the SPSecurityTrimmedControl wrapper.

The PlaceHolderLeftActions placeholder is used primarily by Wiki pages to display the recent items menu.

```
<SharePoint:SPLinkButton runat="server" %>
NavigateUrl="~site/_layouts/recyclebin.aspx" id="idNavLinkRecycleBin" %>
ImageUrl="/_layouts/images/recyclebin.gif" %>
Text="<%$Resources:wss,StsDefault_RecycleBin%>" %>
PermissionsString="DeleteListItems"/>
</asp:ContentPlaceHolder>
<asp:ContentPlaceHolder id="PlaceHolderLeftActions" %>
runat="server"></asp:ContentPlaceHolder>
<asp:ContentPlaceHolder id="PlaceHolderNavSpacer" runat="server">%>
<IMG SRC="/_layouts/images/blank.gif" width=138 height=1 alt="">%>
</asp:ContentPlaceHolder>
<asp:ContentPlaceHolder id="PlaceHolderLeftNavBarBorder"
runat="server"></asp:ContentPlaceHolder>
```

Main Body Area

There are only two functional placeholders in this block. The first is a placeholder for the page description, if any, for the current page. The other is the actual content of the page. PlaceHolderMain is required to display any SharePoint content, and is substituted as appropriate for each page.

```
<asp:ContentPlaceHolder id="PlaceHolderBodyLeftBorder" runat="server">
<IMG SRC="/_layouts/images/blank.gif" width=10 height=1 alt="">
</asp:ContentPlaceHolder>
<PlaceHolder id="MSO_ContentDiv" runat="server">
<A name="mainContent"></A>
<asp:ContentPlaceHolder id="PlaceHolderPageDescription" runat="server"/>
<asp:ContentPlaceHolder id="PlaceHolderMain" runat="server">
</asp:ContentPlaceHolder>
</PlaceHolder>
<asp:ContentPlaceHolder id="PlaceHolderBodyRightMargin" runat="server">
</asp:ContentPlaceHolder>
```

More No-See-Ums

At the end of the page are several more placeholders for items that are not normally visible. The `FormDigest` is used in extranet and Internet scenarios to store encrypted ID information when you are using forms and digest authentication. Utility content is a place for extra things you may need to put at the bottom of a page, such as script, or a company footer/disclaimer. The two `Class` placeholders are for CSS that may need to guarantee it is loaded last in order to override any other style sheets used on the page.

```
<asp:ContentPlaceHolder id="PlaceHolderFormDigest" runat="server">
<SharePoint:FormDigest runat=server/>
</asp:ContentPlaceHolder>
<input type="text" name="__spDummyText1" style="display:none;" size=1/>
<input type="text" name="__spDummyText2" style="display:none;" size=1/>
</form>
<asp:ContentPlaceHolder id="PlaceHolderUtilityContent" runat="server"/>
<asp:ContentPlaceHolder id="PlaceHolderBodyAreaClass" runat="server"/>
<asp:ContentPlaceHolder id="PlaceHolderTitleAreaClass" runat="server"/>
</BODY>
</HTML>
```

Summary

This chapter explained how a typical SharePoint Page is constructed. You saw the power of Master Pages, and discovered many of the building blocks available to you to change the overall feel of your site. You also found out:

❑ SharePoint Pages are built up from elements retrieved from many locations.

❑ You are not stuck with the layout or structure provided out-of-the-box.

❑ SharePoint Designer cannot directly reach into the server's file system.

❑ Even the canned navigational elements provided by SharePoint allow for significant customization.

This chapter touched briefly on the importance of CSS styles in SharePoint. The next two chapters will introduce you to SharePoint Designer's powerful Style Sheet Editor, and how CSS is used by SharePoint's Theme mechanism, giving you full control over the look, to make it go along with the feel of your site.

Using SharePoint Designer's CSS Editing Tools

A whole book can be written — and many good ones have been — about Cascading Style Sheets (CSS). This is not one of those books, but this chapter describes how the power of CSS is used in SharePoint through the use of the powerful tool known as Microsoft Office SharePoint Designer.

After a brief introduction to CSS, this chapter shows you:

❑   How CSS is used in SharePoint.

❑   Tools available in SharePoint Designer to manage CSS in SharePoint.

❑   How to create your own CSS styles.

What Are Cascading Style Sheets?

On the World Wide Web and in any intranet site, content is key for any web page. Cascading Style Sheets (CSS) describe the presentation of that content. CSS is used to define aspects such as colors, fonts, background styles, layout of elements, and more. The CSS declaration (often referred to as a rule) contains two parts: the selector and the declaration (containing one or more properties and their values). The selector indicates what to style, and the declaration specifies how to style it. The following shows the parts of the CSS statement:

```
Selector {property: value;}
```

Styling versus Formatting Objects

As the Internet grew more and more popular, browsers such as Netscape and Microsoft's Internet Explorer continued to introduce new HTML tags and attributes to format content. These tags served the purpose, but they made the content look very cluttered. In addition, because Microsoft,

Netscape, and others were competing for the same market share and introducing tags that worked with their browser, not all formatting tags worked uniformly in all browsers. CSS was envisioned and produced by the World Wide Web Consortium (W3C) to resolve those issues. You can find more info on that at `http://w3.org/Style/CSS`. Styling the objects separates the content from the markup that produces the final presentation layer, thus reducing the inline code required to format the objects. This makes the management of the content and style an easier task. The many advantages of separating content from style include:

❑ The design elements encompassed in one CSS file can be reused to style multiple elements on one or more web pages.

❑ Making updates to the style entails updating the central repository of styles, instead of having to change code on multiple pages.

❑ Content managers can be tasked with changing the content files, while designers are responsible for managing the style sheets.

An Analogy for the Developer in You

The separation of presentation from formatting markup is similar to the enhancements that classic Active Server Pages (ASP) received. ASP.NET introduced a way to separate the presentation layer from the logic layer, improving the manageability and readability of code.

CSS Code Placement

CSS code can be referenced inline, placed within the `<head>` tag of the web page, or stored in a separate file altogether. The following table shows how each of these is configured:

Style Placement	Example
Inline	`<table style="background-color: yellow; font-style: italic">`
`<head>` tag	```<head> <style> table { background-color: yellow; font-style: italic; } </style> </head>```
External file	```Within custom.css - table { background-color: yellow; font-style: italic; }```

Referencing styles inline means that each HTML tag has to be tagged separately and uniquely. There is no reuse of the styles, and the end result seems very similar to HTML formatting tags. This technique should not be used if a set of styles needs to be used in multiple places.

Grouping styles in the <head> tag in a web page facilitates reuse of those styles. In the example in the table, all tables in the page get the background color of yellow, and font style will be set to italic.

Storing styles in an external file provides the benefit of truly separating the styles from the content and is usually the preferred way to go. Another benefit of using styles this way is that the style sheet can be centrally located and referenced by multiple web pages, as illustrated in Figure 6-1.

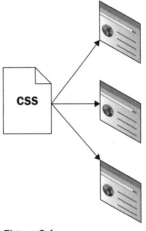

Figure 6-1

Riding the Cascade: Inheritance and Overrides

Unlike life, in the CSS world, the last declaration of a property value wins. That is where *cascading* comes into play. If a style is specified in a linked external file declaring, for example, the background color to be red and the font style to be bold, and then the same style is declared again inline (side by side) with the content, but this time declaring the background color to be yellow, the inline style will prevail, overriding the earlier background color declaration. The final outcome is: background color: yellow, and font style: bold (bold was not overwritten by the inline styles).

> *Think of the cascading nature of styles as an amendment made to an existing law. If certain parts of the law are not mentioned in the amendment, then they stand as is. The ones that need to be overridden have to be stated clearly and then overridden with the new set of rules.*

A Touch of Class

The selector in a CSS statement can be an HTML element, a class specified for the element, or an ID of the element. Classes are generally used as the selector because the same class can be assigned to multiple elements. An element is specified as a selector when all instances of that element need to be styled the same way. An element's ID can be used if a class is being used in multiple places and a specific element needs to be singled out and styled differently. Having said that, it is recommended that an element's ID on a page be unique, just like any other control ID on the page.

Selector	Example

Element	`p {`
	`font-family: Tahoma`
	`}`

Class	`.my-class`
	`{`
	`font-family: Tahoma`
	`}`

Id	`#elementID`
	`{`
	`font-family: Tahoma`
	`}`

As shown in the preceding table, a class is declared with a dot (.), while an ID is signified with a pound sign (#).

Another way to identify a specific selector is by using Contextual Selectors. What you are basically doing is narrowing down a specific selector by specifying its lineage. Here's an example:

```
div p a
{
Font-family: Tahoma;
}
```

Here you apply some styles to a link tag a, but not just any link tag a — the tag that is encompassed under a paragraph p tag, which in turn resides under a div. It's like saying: "I'm looking for John who lives in Chicago in the state of Illinois."

There are more powerful CSS concepts that can help you simplify your CSS statements or make them very selective in nature. For a tutorial of CSS syntax, check out `http://w3schools.com/css`.

CSS in SharePoint

Building a brand and a good functional user interface facilitates attracting users to your site. CSS is a great way to brand SharePoint, in addition to other technologies. The power of CSS should not be taken lightly because it is a major component used for branding SharePoint. SharePoint Themes (chapter 7) as well as Master Pages (chapter 8) rely on style sheets to format fonts and tables, declare color schemes, change backgrounds, insert images, and more.

When a custom user interface is required (fonts, colors, images, and so forth) but the guts of the site do not need to be restructured, using style sheets alone and/or within Themes works just fine. If you do need to significantly change the look and feel of the page and the placement of components on the page, then you may require a new Master Page that would in turn point to one or more style sheets. In other words, when you are working with new Master Pages, you are styling your newly created classes and components within that Master Page. When you are working with just style sheets or SharePoint Themes, you are overriding the existing classes that come as part of SharePoint.

Preexisting CSS Files in SharePoint Server

SharePoint Server comes with quite a lot of CSS files. There are 26 files altogether. Yes, 26 of them! (WSS only deployments have a smaller number of files.) Now don't be alarmed, because many of the modifications you make do not include modifying most of these files. Usually, you end up modifying just a handful of them, even when making major branding modifications.

The CSS files are stored in the following locations:

No. of Files	Location
13	<root>\Program Files\Common Files\Microsoft Shared\Web Server Extensions\ 12\Template\Layouts\1033\Styles.
5	Root of Style Library (document library located at the root site in the site collection).
8	en-us folder in the Style Library.

The number 1033 in the first path stands for the English language. Other language packs installed with SharePoint place similar style files in a different numbered directory. Similarly, the en-us folder signifies "English – US". An additional folder would be created if another language were being used.

The styles on the web server in the . . . \layouts\1033\styles directory are available to all sites deployed on that server. However, the styles in the Style Library are stored in the database. Therefore, those sets of files are only available to the site collection in which the Style Library is located.

Don't Mess with the Existing CSS

It is best not to edit existing CSS files in SharePoint. That's true when you are working with CSS files just as it's true when you are working with existing site definitions, list definitions, Theme packages, site templates, and of course the database schema. Why? Well, when you think about it, SharePoint is a Microsoft product (OK, it's truly a platform), the internals of which have been made available to build solutions upon. If you modify the existing product's internals, then it's not really Microsoft's product anymore — it's your customized copy, and those edits are not really supported by Microsoft. This scenario works fine until a service pack or upgrade needs to be applied to your environment, which, potentially, can override your customizations. On the other hand, if you copy and rename an existing component and build additional functionality on top of that, you can rest assured that at least your additions will not be overridden by any future updates.

SharePoint Themes can add additional CSS files to the mix. Themes are built from a collection of style sheets and images and can be applied by a designer of the site through the web browser. Depending on which Theme is applied to a site, the _theme folder, which appears when you open a site in SharePoint Designer, contains additional CSS files with the unique styles for that Theme. Chapter 7 focuses exclusively on SharePoint Themes.

Style Sheets Can Be Stored in Multiple Locations

The style sheets you create for SharePoint can be stored either on the web server or in the content database. There is no right choice in this matter, as long as you understand that the styles stored on the web server are available to all web applications that reside on that server, while the styles stored in the content database are available only to the site collection in which they are stored. Following are a few additional points to consider when deciding where to place your custom styles.

Styles in the Content Database

Storing the styles in the content database does not mean you crank up SQL Server Management Studio and stick your style sheets directly in there. It means that you store the styles as part of a SharePoint site somewhere. Because SharePoint's entire user-created site content goes into the database, your styles end up there as well. Style sheets can be dumped directly into the root of a site using SharePoint Designer. However, for a more functional (and clean looking) structure, it is recommended that you store your styles in a document library. If you are working in a Microsoft Office SharePoint Server (MOSS) environment, and you have access to the parent site of the site collection as a designer, store your styles in the site collection's Style Library (located at the parent site of the site collection). If you are a site admin and don't have access to the parent site of the site collection, store the style sheet in a local document library on the site, and call the document library by an easily recognizable name such as Styles or *your site name* Styles (example: HR Styles).

Styles stored in the content database are accessible to the designers of the site, who would not usually have access to them if they were stored on the web server. A side benefit of storing styles in the database is that they get backed up as part of your backup solution for the content database.

Alternate CSS Feature in MOSS

The Alternate CSS feature lets you override any previously declared style sheet by applying an alternate style sheet through the Site Master Page settings page. This option is only available through sites created using the Publishing Sites template that comes as part of the MOSS licensing. The Alternate CSS feature can be used if creating a new Master Page is not necessary, and you just want to apply your own custom style sheet to the site and all of its subsites. The alternate style sheet is usually stored in the Style Library of the parent site of the site collection. The Alternate CSS feature is covered more thoroughly in chapter 8.

Styles on the Web Server

When the style sheets are stored on the web server, usually the server administrator is the only one who has access to the web server's file structure. A designer can request access to the server, or at least access to the location of the styles directory where the style sheets are stored. All web applications on the server have access to the styles located on this directory.

```
C:\Program Files\Common Files\Microsoft Shared\Web Server
Extensions\12\Template\Layouts\1033\Styles
```

This can be a very good thing because the styles can be reused by multiple web applications. It can also be a challenging situation because changing shared styles in this directory potentially affects another web application that depends on these styles.

To keep a uniform central location of all styles on the web server, it is recommended that custom style sheets be stored in a Custom folder that's created side-by-side with the other style sheets on the server:

```
C:\Program Files\Common Files\Microsoft Shared\Web Server
Extensions\12\Template\Layouts\1033\Styles\Custom
```

The style sheets in the Custom folder will then be available to all web applications on the server.

Saving Styles to an External Location

Styles can be stored in a separate site collection or outside of SharePoint altogether. The @Import statement lets you import that external file into your SharePoint web page or another CSS file. For example, consider the following statement:

```
@import "ExternalStylesheet.css";
```

If this statement is placed in a web page, it imports the styles in ExternalStylesheet.css within that web page. Similarly, if this import statement is called out from another style sheet, the styles from ExternalStylesheet.css will be embedded in that style sheet.

In practice, the import directive is generally used from within a style sheet that's being linked to from a web page, to summon other style sheets; these import styles become child styles underneath the main style sheet. To learn more about the @import statement, refer to the following resource: http://webdesign.about.com/cs/css/qt/tipcssatimport.htm. You'll learn more about the @Import statement in chapter 7.

Working with Style in SharePoint Designer

SharePoint Designer is *the* customization editor for SharePoint. It provides powerful tools for discovering, configuring, and creating new styles. It's an awesome way to navigate around the seemingly complex web of SharePoint's style sheets. This section shows which tools SharePoint Designer provides and how these tools are used to work effectively with styles in SharePoint.

> **While SharePoint styles are used for the examples in this chapter, the tools and concepts in this chapter apply fully to any web site.**

Page-Editing Options

Before starting to use the CSS tools in SharePoint Designer, it is beneficial to browse through the page-editing options in the Page Editor Options dialog box. Open the dialog by selecting Tools ⇨ Page Editor Options. There is much that can be configured in this dialog box. However, the only options of interest at this time are the ones that deal with styles, so it's the Authoring, IntelliSense, and CSS tabs that you should look through.

On the Authoring tab (see Figure 6-2), you should see the default version, CSS 2.1, selected in the CSS Schema section. If you do, good! Keep it that way. If not, change it to that setting. CSS version 2.1 is the latest CSS specification revision, building on CSS 2.0. If you keep this setting, you will be provided with the schema options for CSS 2.1 when using CSS IntelliSense (more on using CSS IntelliSense later in this chapter).

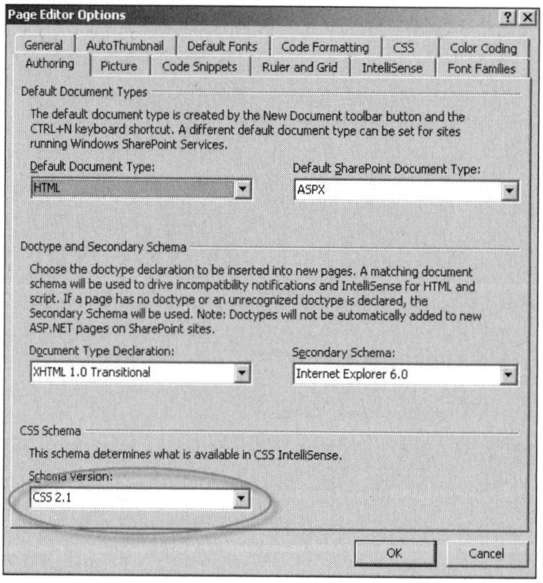

Figure 6-2

Now click on the IntelliSense tab. IntelliSense is truly an awesome feature for typing in any type of code. No one can be expected to remember all of the tags and attributes available in a particular programming or scripting language. Refer to chapter 1 for more information on this tab. You only need to make sure here that the CSS options are checked as indicated in Figure 6-3.

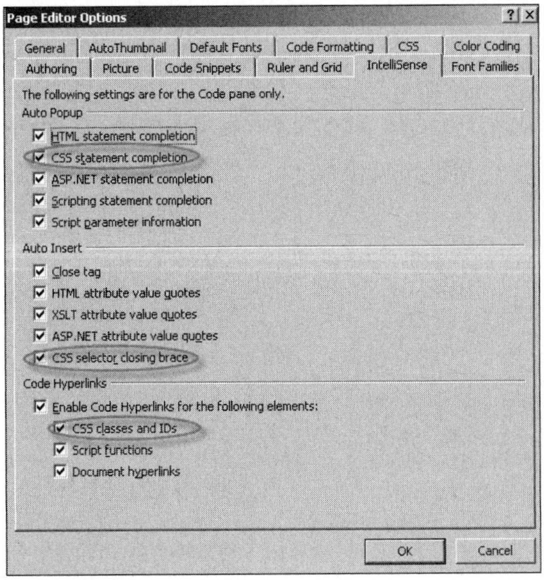

Figure 6-3

When you ask SharePoint Designer to automatically generate and apply styles for you, the rules listed on the CSS tab are the ones it will use by default to designate styles inline or within a class. Figure 6-4 shows the default selected options for this tab.

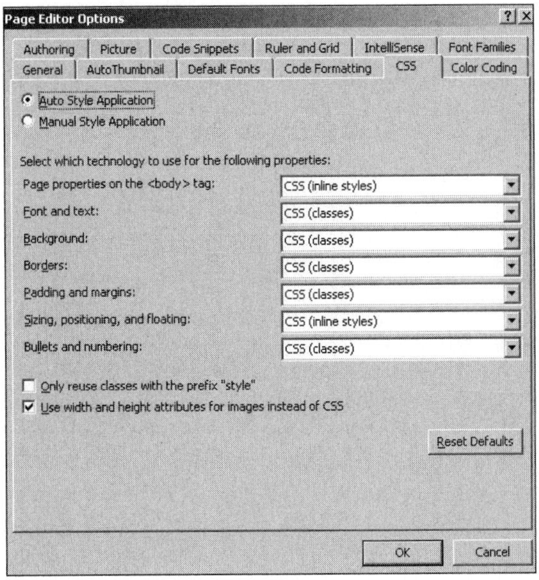

Figure 6-4

There is no reason to change any of these settings, unless your company standards require that certain elements use inline styles and that others be specified in classes, and those standards don't match what's shown in Figure 6-4. For instance, if you want the styles for the background of elements to always be defined inline, go ahead and change the Background selection to CSS (inline styles). The same goes for other elements identified here. If no such requirements exist or none have been defined yet by your company, leave the settings as they are, because you can always go ahead and change the location of the styles after the fact, if needed.

Other tabs in the Page Editor Options dialog box also have a few CSS-related settings, but you've now configured the most important ones. Close this dialog box by clicking OK.

SharePoint Designer's Task Panes and Toolbars

SharePoint Designer provides an abundance of functionality in its arsenal. These functionalities are tucked away in a variety of task panes. Finding the appropriate task pane to use in the predecessor of SharePoint Designer (FrontPage 2003) was a task in itself. As a result of all the feedback Microsoft received about that product, one of the things that thankfully changed was the creation of a new menu item called Task Panes. It is now very easy to open and close a task pane. Feel free to fool around with the positioning of the task panes, and try to configure them so that your workspace has the most comfortable setting for you. Rest assured, you can reset the task panes layout to the default at any time by selecting Task Panes ➪ Reset Workspace Layout. The default view when all the task panes have been reset looks similar to Figure 6-5.

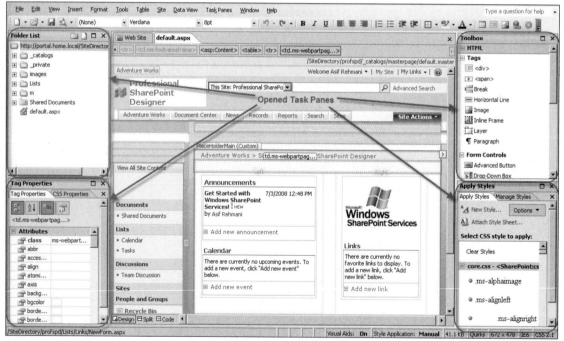

Figure 6-5

If you are following along while working in a SharePoint Designer environment, start by resetting the workspace layout. That will make it easier to follow the concepts being presented. SharePoint Designer comes with a set of very useful task panes to let you work with styles in SharePoint sites. You use them to identify, modify, create, and delete styles.

Identify Your Style

Half the battle of defining a style for a page or site is actually finding it. If you can identify which styles to change and where they are located, you are well on your way to defining your own style. The other half of the battle is creating new, or modifying existing, styles and placing them in the appropriate location for processing. SharePoint Designer provides you with task panes that ease the task of identifying these styles. The use of the CSS Properties task pane together with the Manage Styles task pane (see Figure 6-6) makes this an almost painless task.

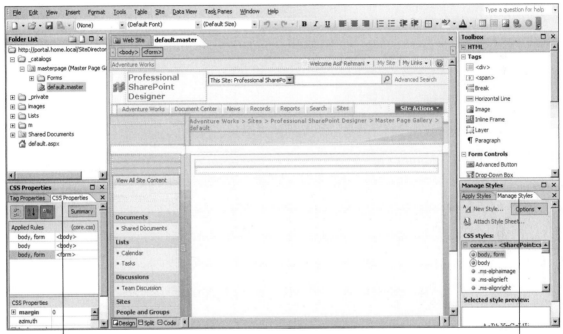

CSS Properties task pane   Manage Styles task pane

Figure 6-6

To explore the functionality in these task panes, open a `default.master` Master Page (to read more about Master Pages, please refer to chapter 8) in a site created using the Team site template. To refresh your memory, the `default.master` Master Page is located in the _catalogs folder when a site is opened in SharePoint Designer.

To identify the styles being applied to an element, start by selecting that element on the page. For example, click on the site navigation breadcrumb that appears directly below the global navigation toolbar (see Figure 6-7).

Figure 6-7

Notice that the information in the CSS Properties task pane is context-specific and changes to show you the styles being applied to the selected element (in this case, the site navigation breadcrumb). You can see that the CSS Properties tab of the CSS Properties task pane is split into two sections: Applied Rules at the top and CSS Properties at the bottom. Clicking on a rule in the Applied Rules section displays the name of the style sheet in which it is defined (see Figure 6-8), and shows its properties in the CSS Properties section.

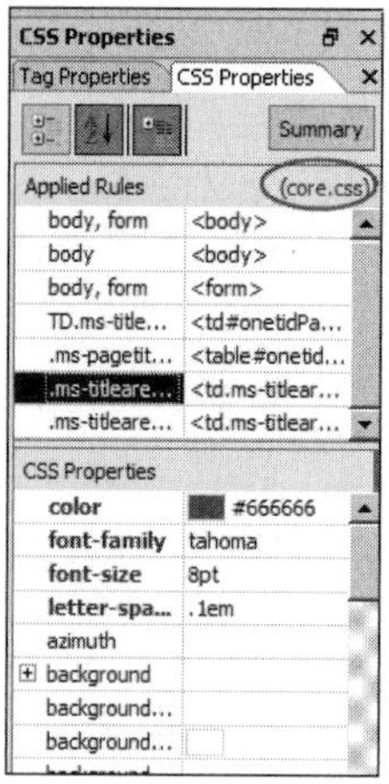

Figure 6-8

The properties that appear in bold blue letters (`color`, `font-family`, `font-size`, and `letter-spa...` in the figure) are the only ones being altered by the selected rule.

There are seven rules being applied to the site navigation breadcrumb, but not all of them stick to it. The Applied Rules section shows you the cascading nature of the styles as they are being applied. The breadcrumb is styled according to the last property that was applied to it, so the most recent attribute defined within a rule is the one that prevails. To show which properties do ultimately stick to the selected element, the CSS Properties task pane has a special button called Summary (see Figure 6-9) that can be toggled to show how the properties are applied. It is highly recommended you use this button to get a big-picture view of your styling.

Figure 6-9

The `color` and `font-family` properties are both shown twice in the CSS Properties section. The first instance of each has a red line through it. The red strikethrough line signifies that this style was identified higher in the cascading tree and is now being overridden. Both of them have been applied in multiple rules, and the most current rule has prevailed. So how can you tell which rule defines each of them? Click on the color value #000000. In the Applied Rule section, a rectangle appears around `body` — the second rule that's being applied. Now click on the color value #666666; a rectangle appears around `.ms-titlearea, .ms-mwstitlearea`, which is the rule that has overridden the color attribute defined in `<body>`.

It's time to now drill into the code a bit. You already know from the CSS Properties task pane that the `.ms-titlearea, .ms-mwstitlearea` rule is defined in `core.css`. There is a very easy way to navigate to the exact location where this rule is defined: Double-click on the rule, and the `core.css` style sheet opens with the cursor blinking at the exact location of that rule. Earlier in this chapter, it was stated that IntelliSense for CSS is made available by specifying it in the Page Editor Options dialog box (refer to Figure 6-3). The Code view for CSS is where that IntelliSense comes in handy. Once you start declaring a new property for your rule, IntelliSense shows you a list of properties you can choose from. Likewise, when you have chosen a property to declare, IntelliSense presents you with appropriate value options for that property, as shown in Figure 6-10.

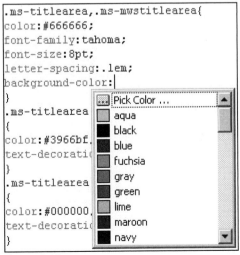

Figure 6-10

In the `core.css` Code view, the Manage Styles task pane, which appears on the right of the screen, comes in very handy. As Figure 6-11 shows, the rule you selected in the CSS Properties task pane (`.ms-titlearea, .ms-mwstitlearea` in this example) is selected automatically in the Manage Styles task pane. A preview of the selected style is shown at the bottom of the task pane.

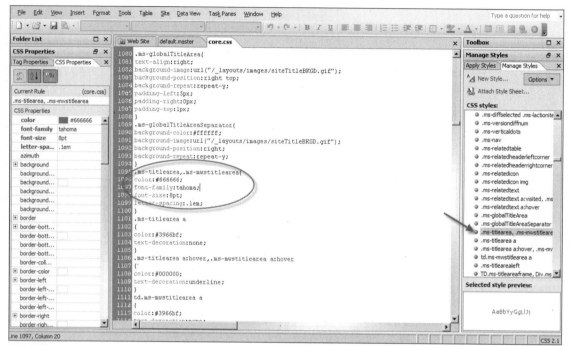

Figure 6-11

Hovering over a style in the Manage Styles task pane displays a ToolTip that shows all properties declared in that style.

In this view, the Manage Styles task pane shows all element-based (identified by a blue ball icon), id-based (red ball), and class-based (green ball) styles that are defined in `core.css`. Styles used within the current web page are marked by a green ball surrounded by a circle, and imported style sheets show an @ symbol.

The styles listed in the Manage Styles task pane are in the same exact order as they are listed in the opened style sheet. For instance, `.ms-titlearea, .ms-mwstitlearea` is followed by `.ms-titlearea` both in the style sheet Code view and in the Manage Styles task pane. You can easily rearrange the order of these styles by simply dragging a style up or down in the task pane list. Similarly, if more than one style sheet (internal or external, it doesn't matter) is displayed in this task pane, each style can be moved from one style sheet to another just by dragging it to the location you want to move it to. Now that's cool! The Manage Styles task pane can do a whole lot more, some of which you'll see in the next section.

Create Your Own Style

With the help of SharePoint Designer's toolset, you can create new web pages, define layouts of those pages, and format the content in a very short amount of time. A new web page can be directly based on one of the many built-in CSS layout styles. To see all of the CSS layouts available, choose File ⇨ New and then select the CSS Layouts section, as shown in Figure 6-12.

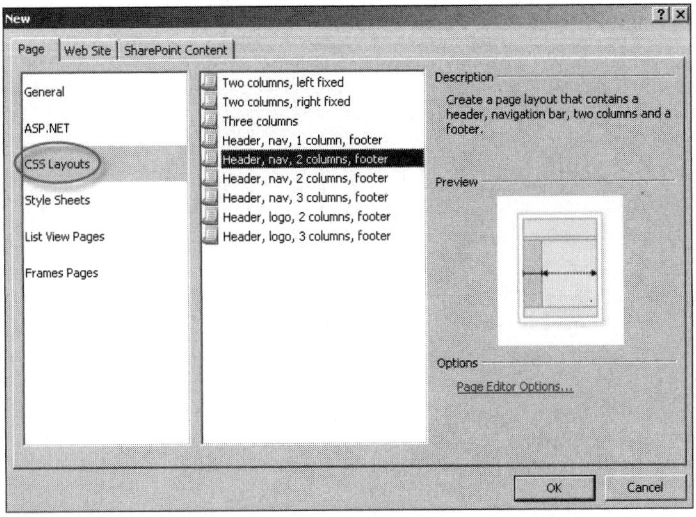

Figure 6-12

Choose a CSS layout, click OK, and SharePoint Designer creates an `.htm` file and a `.css` file. The `.css` file is linked to the `.htm` file. Notice there are no tables at all in the `.htm` file; it's created completely with `<div>` tags. The `.css` file defines the layout styles of the div id tags in the `.htm` file.

```
/* CSS layout */
#masthead {
}

#top_nav {
}

#container {
    position: relative;
    width: 100%;
}

#left_col {
    width: 200px;
    position: absolute;
    left: 0px;
```

```
    top: 0px;
    font-size: x-small;
}

#page_content {
    margin-left: 200px;
}

#footer {
}
```

Tables are still used in a variety of places in SharePoint. In fact, unless you override its default behavior, many server controls (such as the navigation controls) create tables when they render the HTML.

You need to save the .htm and .css files created by this process. You can save them directly at the root of the site or, better yet, save them in their own distinct document libraries. For instance, you can create a document library called Web Pages and store the .htm file there, renaming it to something like MyContentPage.aspx (chances are that the file will at some point have content that needs to be processed at the server level, which requires the .aspx extension). Create another document library and call it Styles. Store the .css file there, renaming it Layout.css because it formats the layout of the Content Page.

The Content Page MyContentPage.aspx is not ready for prime time just yet. Aside from the basic layout created by Layout.css, it has no chrome or branding applied to it. Quickly apply the Default Master Page of the site to a Content Page by selecting Format ⇨ Master Page ⇨ Attach Master Page. Accept the defaults in the two dialog boxes that pop up in succession, and you have the look and feel of the rest of the site applied to this page, as shown in Figure 6-13.

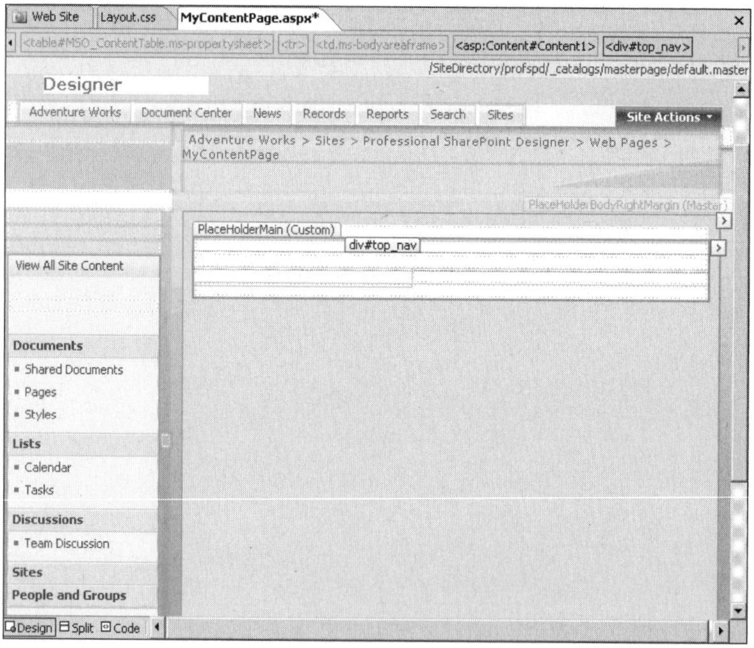

Figure 6-13

The <head> tag of default.master contains server controls that declare the order in which the style sheets are applied, which is described in the following table:

Order	Style Sheets	Description	Server Control
1	Core	Core.css and Master Page style sheets.	<SharePoint:CssLink>
2	Theme-related	Theme CSS files taken from web server.	<SharePoint:Theme>
3	Page-specific	Styles declared within the Content Page.	<asp:ContentPlaceHolder id="PlaceHolderAdditionalPageHead">

The following code appears in the <head> tag of default.master:

```
<HEAD runat="server">
    <META Name="GENERATOR" Content="Microsoft SharePoint">
    <META Name="progid" Content="SharePoint.WebPartPage.Document">
    <META HTTP-EQUIV="Content-Type" CONTENT="text/html; charset=utf-8">
    <META HTTP-EQUIV="Expires" content="0">
    <SharePoint:RobotsMetaTag runat="server"/>
<Title ID=onetidTitle><asp:ContentPlaceHolder id=PlaceHolderPageTitle
runat="server"/></Title>
    <SharePoint:CssLink runat="server"/>
    <SharePoint:Theme runat="server"/>
<SharePoint:ScriptLink language="javascript" name="core.js" Defer="true" runat="server"/>
    <SharePoint:CustomJSUrl runat="server"/>
    <SharePoint:SoapDiscoveryLink runat="server"/>
<asp:ContentPlaceHolder id="PlaceHolderAdditionalPageHead" runat="server"/>
<SharePoint:DelegateControl runat="server" ControlId="AdditionalPageHead"
AllowMultipleControls="true"/>
</HEAD>
```

The PlaceHolderAdditionalPageHead content placeholder in default.master places a matching content region in any Content Page to which this Master Page is attached. So in this example, MyContentPage.aspx also has this content region present. Any custom style sheets referenced in this region propagate to the location of the content placeholder in the Master Page. Because the content placeholder is applied after the core and Theme-related style sheets, any styles placed in your custom style sheet override any previous declaration instances of those styles.

Once you have identified the rule you want to override, navigate to the original declaration of that rule so you can copy it. SharePoint Designer provides a very easy way to navigate to the rules in the linked style sheets: just hold the Ctrl key down and click on an underlined style to be taken to the declaration of that style (see Figure 6-14).

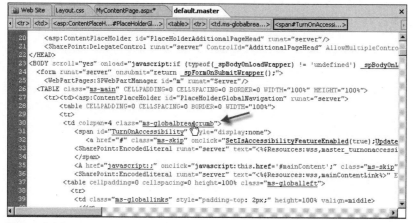

Figure 6-14

Once you are at the declaration of the rule in the CSS file, the Manage Style task pane on the right shows that rule as well. Right-click on the rule and select New Style Copy (see Figure 6-15).

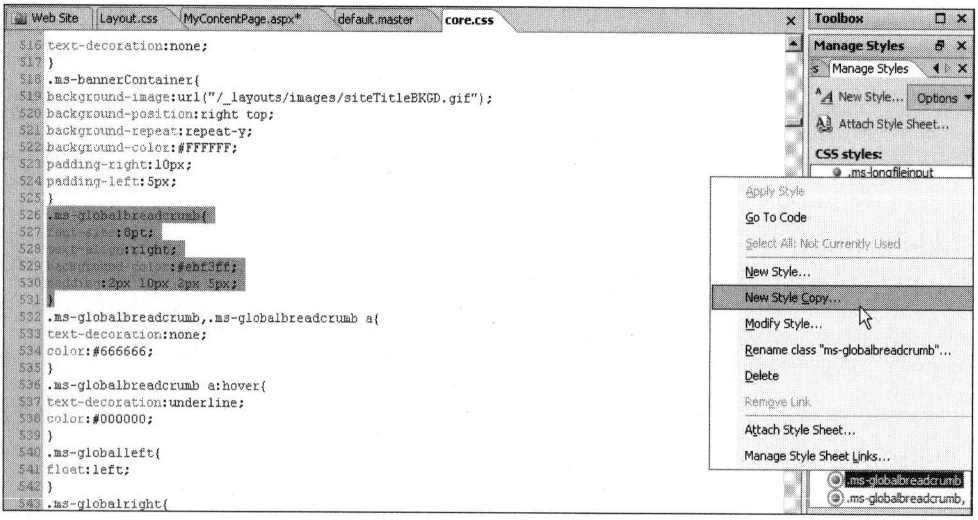

Figure 6-15

SharePoint Designer appends the word Copy at the end of the name of the rule and opens the New Style dialog box (see Figure 6-16) for you to modify the rule.

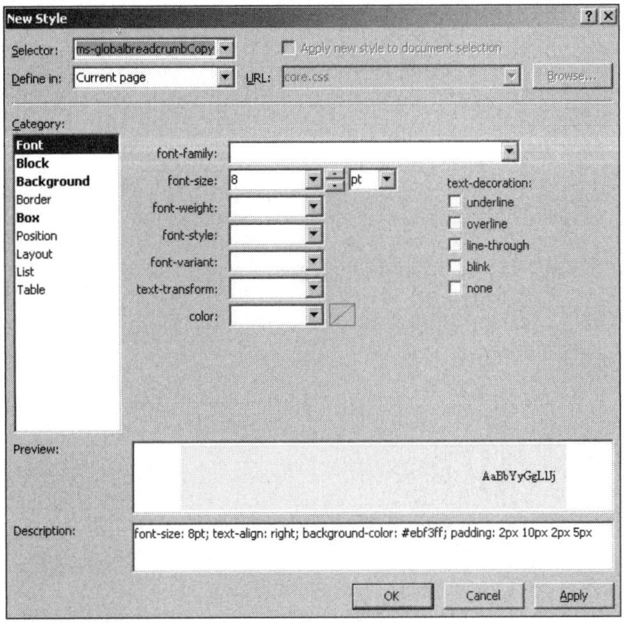

Figure 6-16

It is not very obvious, but after you make modifications to this copy of the rule and click OK in the dialog box, SharePoint Designer places the rule at the bottom of the CSS file (in this case, the `core.css` file). This copy of the rule is created in this manner so that it can be copied out of the `core.css` file and placed into a new custom style sheet.

> **Do not save and overwrite the `core.css` file with that new rule! When `core.css` is directly modified in an opened site, a local copy of `core.css` is made and saved in the _styles directory. This places the new style in the database and breaks the link to the original `core.css` on the web server. That is not recommended, since any later changes to the original `core.css` style sheet will not be reflected on this site**

Create a new style sheet by clicking the New Style link in the Apply Styles task pane to open the New Style dialog box. In the Define in dropdown near the top of the dialog, select New Style Sheet, as shown in Figure 6-17.

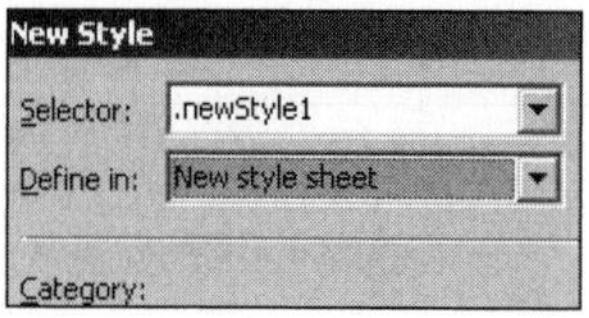

New Style

Selector:	.newStyle1
Define in:	New style sheet
Category:	

Figure 6-17

Because you need just an empty style sheet for now, click OK without changing any styles, and then click Yes when a dialog box pops up asking if you want to attach the style sheet for this new style. This style sheet has now been linked to from the Content Page. The PlaceHolderAdditionalPageHead content region is where this link appears (see Figure 6-18). As described earlier, any style sheets referenced from this location are applied after the core style sheets. The new style sheet is referred to as `Untitled_1.css` and the location is shown as `unsaved:///`. This is expected behavior because it has not been saved yet. Save the style sheet in the Styles document library, and the link in the Content Page automatically reflects the new name and location.

```
17 <asp:Content id="Content2" runat="server" contentplaceholderid="PlaceHolderAdditionalPageHead">
18
19    <link rel="stylesheet" type="text/css" href="../Styles/Layout.css">
20    <link rel="stylesheet" type="text/css" href="unsaved:///Untitled_1.css">
21 </asp:Content>
```

Figure 6-18

The rule copied earlier can now be cut out of the bottom of the `core.css` file and placed in the new style sheet. Remove the word Copy from the end of the rule's name, save the style sheet, and it's now ready to override the rules in `core.css`.

Making CSS Changes with the Style Application Toolbar

To change styles already applied in your custom style sheet, use the functionality provided in the Style Application toolbar to quickly target a rule and apply changes to it without even navigating to the style sheet. To bring up the Style Application toolbar (see Figure 6-19), select View ⇨ Toolbars ⇨ Style Application.

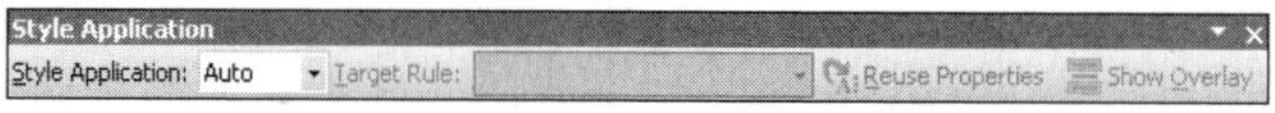

Style Application

| Style Application: Auto | Target Rule: | Reuse Properties | Show Overlay |

Figure 6-19

There are two modes in the toolbar: Auto and Manual. Both of them allow you to make style changes to the elements on your Content Page. When you make a formatting change to an element in Auto mode, the new style defined for that element is declared inline with your code. Generally, you'd prefer that the change be made in the linked style sheet. For that, change the mode to Manual. Then when you select an element to change its style, the Target Rule field shows the rule to which the change will be made. For example, Figure 6-20 shows that #page_content is the Target Rule to be changed. In Manual mode, all changes are made in the linked style sheet instead of to the Content Page.

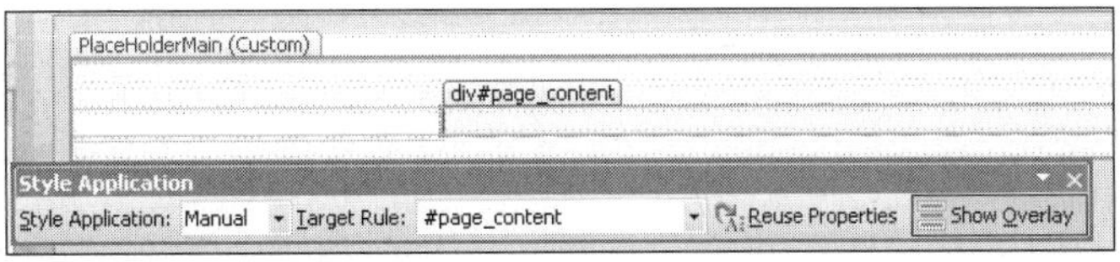

Figure 6-20

Quickly Apply Styles with the Style Toolbar

SharePoint Designer's Style toolbar (see Figure 6-21) also comes in handy. Access it by selecting View ⇨ Toolbars ⇨ Style.

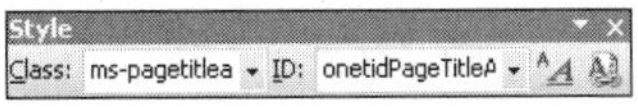

Figure 6-21

It's a very simple toolbar with only four components: Class and ID fields and New Style and Attach Style Sheet buttons. The buttons have the same functionality as the New Style and Attach Style Sheet links in both the Apply Styles and Manage Styles task panes. Use the Class and ID fields to quickly apply an ID or a class to any selected element. The fields are populated with the available IDs and classes in the currently displayed page and any linked pages (such as style sheets). For example, Figure 6-22 shows a Class dropdown list populated with all the styles from Layout.css and Style.css.

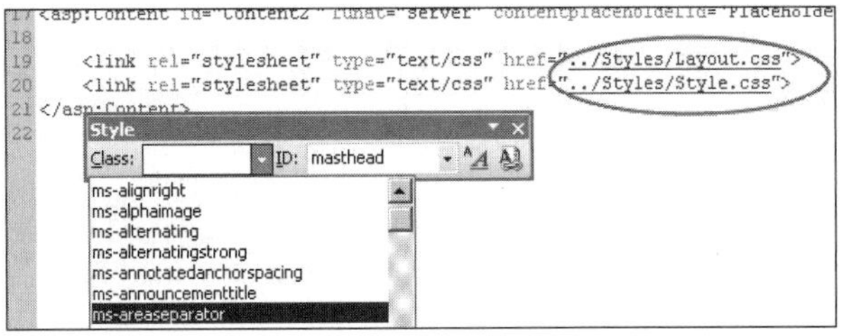

Figure 6-22

To apply any of the classes in the Class dropdown list to an existing element, just select an element on the page and then select the class you want to apply (Figure 6-23).

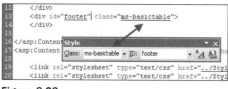

Figure 6-23

Checking Your Work

It's always good to be able to check your work for any errors in your code. Developers have been doing it for years by debugging their code, and designers can do the same by running reports on their Content Pages and CSS files. SharePoint Designer provides the CSS Reports task pane for designers to check their work for errors, as well as run reports to analyze how and where the styles are being used. To run a report on a Content Page or a Master Page, choose Tools ⇨ CSS Reports. Figure 6-24 shows the CSS Reports dialog box that appears.

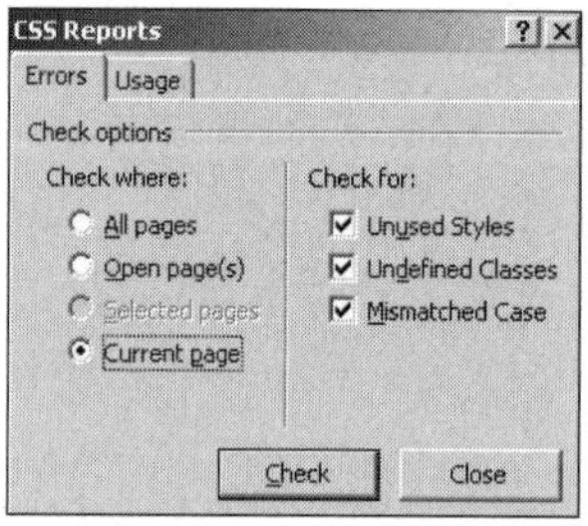

Figure 6-24

After selecting the appropriate options for the report you want produced, click the Check button, and the CSS Reports task pane opens up with the findings.

Discover Errors in Your Code

The Errors tab (see Figure 6-24) in the CSS Reports dialog box reports on things such as classes defined in the page but not declared in any associated style sheet. It also tells you which styles have been defined but are not being used. These should not be classified as errors in your code because, for instance, there are times when you might want to leave a style undeclared until a later time when you need it. Figure 6-25 shows the result of running the CSS Reports for errors on a `default.master` page.

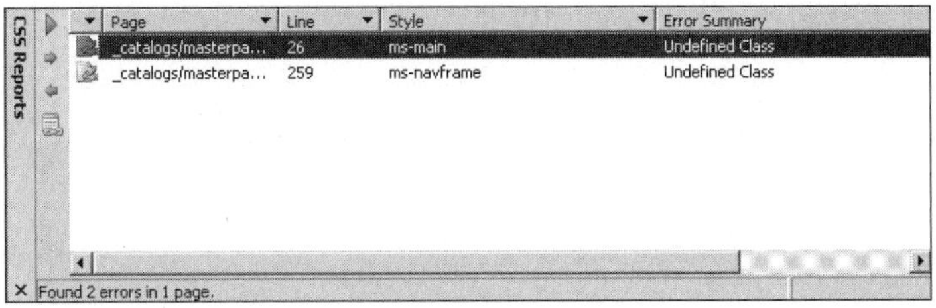

Figure 6-25

The .ms-main and .ms-navframe classes have not been declared in the core.css style sheet. These rules can be declared easily in a custom style sheet to have a big impact on the look and feel of all of your pages that use default.master.

Usage Report on Your Style Elements

A multitude of elements, classes, and IDs are used in a web page. The CSS selectors are then used to identify and style these components. To answer questions such as "How many times on a page is a certain class being used?" and "Where exactly in the CSS file is a particular class being declared?" a CSS usage report can be run on a page. The Usage tab of the CSS Reports dialog box is used to generate a report that provides you with this information and more. Figure 6-26 shows the CSS usage report from a default.master page.

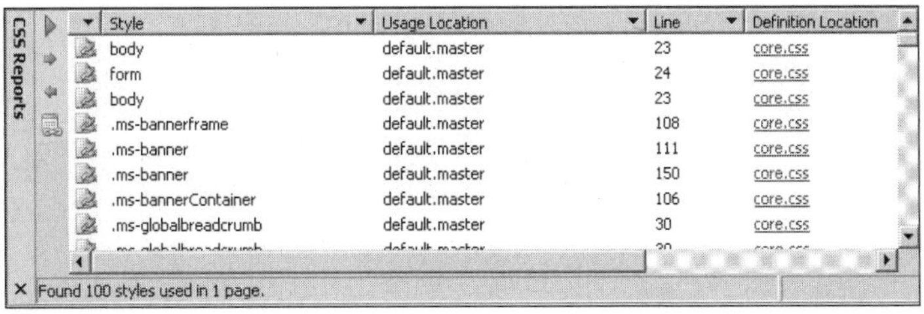

Figure 6-26

In addition to the SharePoint Designer utilities described here, you can validate your code using CSS validator tools available on the web. One free validator tool is available at http://validator.w3.org/.

You can use this tool to point to your style sheet, upload your style sheet, or just directly input the styles from your style sheet on this site. In return, it produces a report that displays an error report for the styles.

Summary

This chapter gave a brief overview of some of the concepts in CSS. Then you saw how styles are used in SharePoint, and the benefits of using SharePoint Designer to manage and create styles in a web site were discussed. The main takeaways from this chapter are:

❑   CSS is a major part of branding SharePoint sites.

❑   SharePoint provides you with several out-of-the-box style sheets in which all of the SharePoint styles are defined.

❑   Style sheets can be stored either on the web server or within the database (depending on your needs).

❑   SharePoint Designer provides you with a variety of task panes and toolbars that allow you to easily discover existing styles and create new ones.

The next chapter focuses exclusively on SharePoint Themes. You'll see why Themes are necessary and how Themes and CSS team together to change the look and feel of SharePoint sites.

7

The Anatomy of a Theme

Chapter 6 showed how powerful Cascading Style Sheets (CSS) are in terms of branding your SharePoint sites. SharePoint Themes take advantage of the power of CSS to package a set of styles and images to be applied to any SharePoint site. This chapter focuses on the internals of Themes, how they operate within the SharePoint framework, and how to generate a new Theme and publish it back to the web server. You will:

❑   See how SharePoint Themes work.

❑   Explore Themes that come with SharePoint.

❑   Create a customized Theme using SharePoint Designer and publish it back to the web server.

❑   Examine the main styles of a sample Theme.

What Are SharePoint Themes?

A Theme is a collection of style sheets and images packaged together. Themes are used as a lightweight mechanism to brand Windows SharePoint Services (WSS)–based sites after they have been provisioned. The styles sheets in a Theme override the styles in the default Theme originally applied to the site. Once the Theme is applied, it takes over the look and feel of all the pages within a site. New pages that are created after a Theme is applied inherit the styles in the Theme. There are 18 Themes that come with WSS. An end user with the designer or higher privilege on a site can effortlessly apply a SharePoint Theme using the browser. More information is presented on the Themes that come with WSS and how to apply them in the upcoming sections.

Master Pages (covered in chapters 5 and 8) can be used in tandem with style sheets to change the look and feel of a site. So why are Themes needed? Master Pages are very powerful and can change more than the look and feel of a site. They can change, among other things, positioning of the elements on a page, such as the navigation component, header, and footer of a site. You can define your own new classes in a Master Page and use style sheets to brand them. Check out these

Internet sites based on Microsoft Office SharePoint Server (MOSS) that make use of Master Pages to drastically change the layout of their pages:

❑ **Hawaiian Airlines:** www.hawaiianair.com

❑ **Paul Mitchell:** www.paulmitchell.com

❑ **Energizer:** www.energizer.com

Comparing the listed sites to a default installation of MOSS (Figure 7-1), you can see that these sites have been gutted and rebranded completely. This functionality is powerful enough that Master Pages can prove to be overkill for some branding needs. If the branding calls for changing fonts, images, and colors on a site, you can get away with using the more lightweight Themes instead of restructuring the site using Master Pages. Just as you do not need a hammer for a thumbtack, you do not need to implement Master Pages for simple changes to the user interface. Now, keep in mind that Master Pages and Themes are not mutually exclusive. It is definitely possible for you to create a layout using a Master Page for your site and then style it with a custom Theme.

Figure 7-1

Themes depend highly on CSS, and the better you are with CSS, the more you can do with a Theme. Themes work by overriding styles for existing elements, classes, and IDs. You need to figure out what styles are provided with SharePoint before you can override those styles. There is no way to create new elements by using Themes. You need Master Pages for that. Consider this analogy: You are redecorating your office space. All you plan to do is paint the walls and hang new pictures on the existing hooks. In the SharePoint world, these types of changes can be implemented by using just Themes. On the other hand, if the redecoration of your office space requires expansion by tearing down a wall and creating a new one, putting up new hooks for pictures, and rearranging the furniture in the room . . . well, translating this into the SharePoint world means there is a whole lot of gutting that needs to be done to the site. That's when you need to create a new Master Page.

Themes are applied on a per-site basis. They cannot be inherited, nor can they be pushed down from a parent site. So a subsite cannot inherit its parents site's Theme, and a parent site cannot push a Theme down to its child site. However, there is a way around this limitation. You can use the techniques described in this chapter to create a custom CSS file and then apply the file using the Alternate CSS URL option which can be accessed through the Site Master Page settings page. Unlike Master Pages, Themes can be used to affect the look and feel of the _layouts pages. The _layouts folder includes pages such as the Site Settings, View All Site Content, and Create pages.

> *The _layouts folder is located at <Program_Files_Directory>\Common Files\Microsoft Shared\ web server extensions\12\TEMPLATE\LAYOUTS.*

It would be beneficial to apply a Theme in tandem with a Master Page if the look and feel of the _layouts pages need to be altered.

To sum up, here's a decision matrix of which technology should be used in a certain situation:

Themes	Master Pages
Changing colors, fonts, and images on a site.	Changing layout of elements, the top link bar, quick launch navigation, header and footer of the site.
Altering the look of a collection of sites — each with its own unique branding.	Subsites need to inherit the look and feel of the Parent site (MOSS-only functionality).
Branding the _layouts pages.	

SharePoint's Themes

In the SharePoint 2003 world, there was a set of Themes available as part of FrontPage 2003, and another set of Themes that resided on the SharePoint web server. With the demise of FrontPage 2003, the Themes that came with it are gone. There are no Themes available as part of SharePoint Designer.

> *FrontPage Themes were implemented through the FrontPage Server Extensions, which Microsoft no longer actively develops. Some interesting posts on life after FrontPage Server Extensions can be found on this blog:* http://blogs.msdn.com/robert_mcmurray/archive/2008/ 04/17/life-after-fpse-part-1.aspx.

The Themes that reside on the SharePoint front-end web servers are the only ones that now come with SharePoint. Any user with designer rights or above can apply Themes to a SharePoint site by navigating to Site Settings ⇨ Site Theme (under the Look and Feel section), as shown in Figure 7-2.

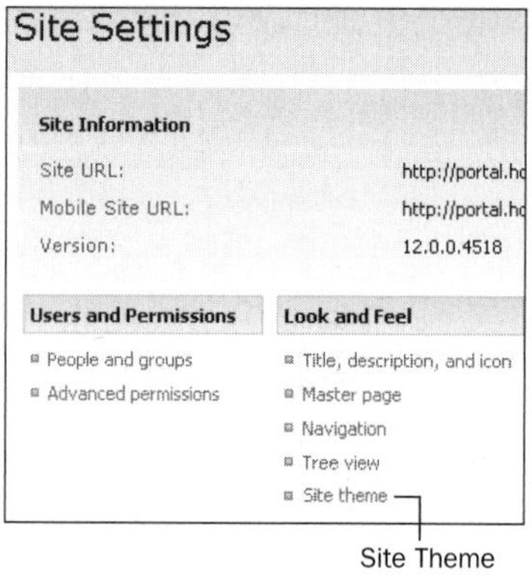

Figure 7-2

On the Site Theme page, any of the 18 SharePoint Themes (including the Default Theme) can be applied to the site. Select a Theme from the list on the right and see a preview of it on the left (see Figure 7-3).

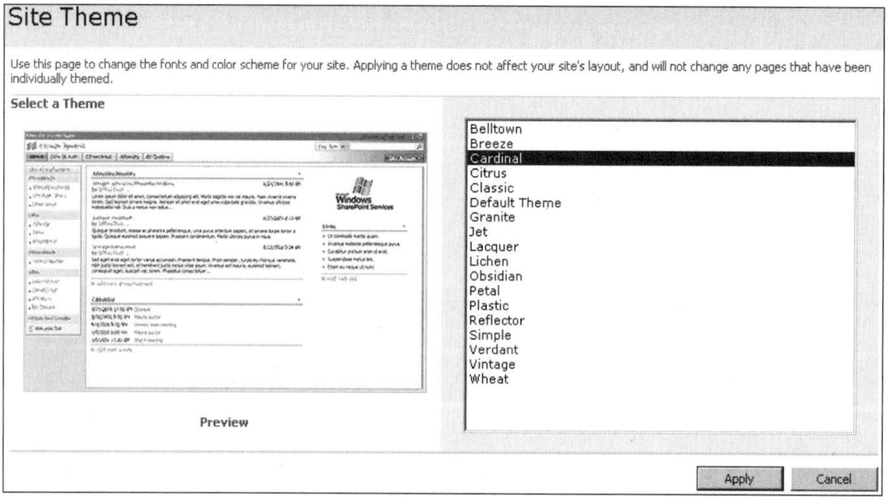

Figure 7-3

Where Themes Live — The 12 Hive

When SharePoint is installed on a web server, it creates a special folder hierarchy at the following location:

```
<Program_Files_Directory>\Common Files\Microsoft Shared\web server extensions\12
```

The 12 folder (also referred to widely in the SharePoint world as the 12 hive) contains site definitions, Features (a way to add various types of functionality to sites), style sheets, administration utilities,

Themes, and more (the 12 hive is discussed in more detail in chapter 3). The folder that contains all the built-in Themes is at:

```
<Program_Files_Directory>\Common Files\Microsoft Shared\
web server extensions\12\TEMPLATE\THEMES
```

There are 22 subfolders (if you have a WSS-only installation, you will see 21 subfolders — the SHAREDSERVICES subfolder is present only in a MOSS installation) under the Themes folder (see Figure 7-4). Each of them represents a Theme.

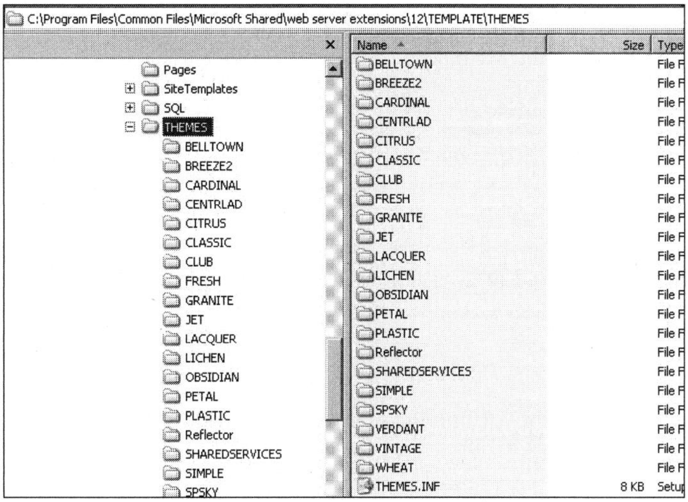

Figure 7-4

Not all of these Themes are visible to a designer when applying a Theme to a site. The 18 that represent Themes that are available to be applied to a site are:

BELLTOWN	JET	Reflector
BREEZE2	LACQUER	SIMPLE
CARDINAL	LICHEN	SPSKY (the Default Theme)
CITRUS	OBSIDIAN	VERDANT
CLASSIC	PETAL	VINTAGE
GRANITE	PLASTIC	WHEAT

The other folders — CENTRALD, CLUB, FRESH, and SHAREDSERVICES — are internally used system Themes that are applied to sites such as Central Administration and Shared Services.

The preview images for each of the 22 Themes are located in the following folder:

```
<Program_Files_Directory>\Common Files\Microsoft Shared\
web server extensions\12\TEMPLATE\IMAGES
```

Each of the image names starts with a th prefix. For example, the image for the OBSIDIAN Theme in the IMAGES folder is thObsidian.gif.

A Look Inside a Theme Folder

Each existing Theme folder consists of one .inf file, one or two .css files, and multiple image files (with either .gif or .jpg extension).

This statement refers to the contents of the existing Theme folders. In a custom-designed Theme folder (steps for which are described later in the chapter), you can have as many .css files as you want. Also, the image files can have any valid image extension that's viewable in an Internet browser. You are not limited to .gif and .jpg extensions.

The .inf file contains the metadata information about each Theme. Here's what the file for the BELLTOWN theme looks like:

```
[info]
title=Belltown
codepage=65001
version=3.00
format=3.00
readonly=true
refcount=0

[titles]
1031=Belltown
1036=Belltown
1040=Belltown
3082=Belltown
1043=Belltown
1046=Belltown
1053=Belltown
1044=Belltown
1030=Belltown
1035=Belltown
1041=Belltown
1042=Belltown
1028=Belltown
2052=Belltown
1029=Belltown
1045=Belltown
1032=Belltown
1038=Belltown
1049=Belltown
1055=Belltown
2070=Belltown
1025=Belltown
1037=Belltown
1054=Belltown
```

The two things to note in the .inf file are the code page designation and the title of the Theme. The codepage=65001 line is present because the code page is 65001 in Windows (more information on code page can be found at http://en.wikipedia.org/wiki/Code_page_65001). The default entry for title at the top of the file represents the title that would be shown by default in an English installation of SharePoint. The [titles] section shows how the title of the Theme would appear if another language pack were being utilized in the SharePoint installation. For example, 1041 stands for Japanese, while

German is represented by 1031 (a table of Language IDs can be found at http://technet.microsoft.com/en-us/library/cc824907.aspx). By default, the title is the same for all languages. However, it can be changed pretty easily by modifying the appropriate language title in this file.

The .css files in the folder are the style sheets for the Theme. Every Theme folder contains a theme.css file. If you have MOSS installed on the server as well, then you see an additional .css file called mossExtension. When a Theme is applied to a site, the theme.css and mossExtension.css files are merged (in that order) to create a new file at run time; that's the file that ultimately is applied to the site. There's more information about this later in this chapter. Also, keep in mind that you can't put an arbitrarily named .css file in the folder (ThirdStyleSheet.css, for example) and expect it to be merged with the other two as well. SharePoint is looking for specific named files to merge, and it will ignore your file.

The images files in the folder are the ones that are applied to a site when a particular Theme is selected. The style sheets reference this unique set of images and designate their placement on the site.

How to Declare Themes

Each of the 18 Themes that can be applied by a designer to a site is declared in a file called SPTHEMES.xml. This file is located in the following folder on the web server:

```
<Program_Files_Directory>\Common Files\Microsoft Shared\
web server extensions\12\TEMPLATE\LAYOUTS\1033
```

The number 1033 in this path stands for the English language. Other language packs installed with SharePoint place the style sheets in a different numbered directory.

The following is part of the SPTHEMES.xml file (the rest was truncated for brevity):

```
<SPThemes xmlns="http://tempuri.org/SPThemes.xsd">
    <Templates>
        <TemplateID>simple</TemplateID>
        <DisplayName>Simple</DisplayName>
        <Description>Simple has a white background with minimal blue
         highlights.</Description>
        <Thumbnail>images/thsimple.gif</Thumbnail>
        <Preview>images/thsimple.gif</Preview>
    </Templates>
```

Each Theme is declared within a separate <Templates> section in the file. There are five XML nodes within each section:

❑ The <TemplateID> node lists the system name of the Theme. This name *must* be exactly the same as the folder name in which this Theme file resides. Otherwise, the theme is not recognized by the system.

❑ The <DisplayName> and <Description> nodes are where a user-friendly name and description for the Theme are placed. This is the information that a designer sees in the Site Theme page when deciding which Theme to apply to the site.

❑ The <Thumbnail> and <Preview> nodes list the location of the Theme's preview image in the IMAGES folder.

153

If a new Theme is created, this file is edited, and a new `<Templates>` section must be created with the information about that new Theme. You'll see an example of how that's done later in this chapter.

Use SharePoint Designer to Explore and Customize Themes

As described earlier in this chapter, applying a Theme to a SharePoint site is a simple process. Any site user who has the designer or higher permissions can apply a Theme to a site by navigating to Site Settings ⇨ Site Theme (under the Look and Feel section). To customize the Theme further after it has been applied to a site, however, you need to understand what is happening under the hood.

Exploring a Theme Once It's Applied to a Site

To start exploring a Theme, open a SharePoint site using SharePoint Designer. (In SharePoint Designer, select File ⇨ Open Site, type the site address into the Open Site dialog box, and click Open.)

The site opens up in SharePoint Designer to show all the files and folders that make up the site. The Folder List task pane shows a tree view of all top-level folders and files. A SharePoint site to which a Theme has been applied shows a _themes folder in the folder tree. When that folder is expanded, the name of the applied Theme appears as a subfolder. That name comes directly from the `title` attribute in the Theme's `.inf` file. Once this subfolder is expanded, all the files that make up the Theme are presented, as shown in Figure 7-5.

Figure 7-5

When a designer selects and applies a Theme to a site, a couple of things happen:

1. A copy is made, from the web server, of the chosen Theme folder and all of the files (`.inf`, `.css`, and images) in that folder.

2. The copy of the folder and the files are placed in the content database with an association to the site.

In addition to all the files from the chosen Theme's folder, the `Theme.css` and the `mossExtension.css` (if it exists) files are merged (in that order) to create a new file that is also stored in the content database. This file is named `xxxx1011-65001.css`, where the xxxx is the first four letters of the name of the Theme being applied. For example, if the Obsidian Theme is being applied, the file created will be named `Obsi1011-65001.css`.

> *The 65001 number comes from the code page number within the `.inf` file, as mentioned earlier in this chapter.*

The `xxxx1011-65001.css` style sheet is the only CSS file that's applied to the site by this Theme. It is applied right after the `core.css` style sheet is applied by the `default.master` Master Page. Because of the cascading nature of the style sheets, any core styles that are redefined in this Theme's style sheet prevail.

> *You can open the `default.master` Master Page in SharePoint Designer by navigating to the _catalogs/masterpage folder that appears in the Folder List task pane. The `default.master` Master Page lists the following lines in the header of the page, which show the order in which the style sheets are applied to a site:*

```
<SharePoint:CssLink runat="server"/> - Server control linking to Master
    Page core styles
<SharePoint:Theme runat="server"/> - Server control linking to Theme
    related styles
```

The order of the applied style sheets can be verified by examining the source of the page after it is rendered in the browser. The following code block shows the source of a page to which the Vintage Theme is applied. You can clearly see that the `core.css` style sheet is applied first, followed by the customized `Prof1011-65001.css` style sheet (the creation of which is explained later in the chapter) for the Vintage Theme. The code is truncated to focus only on the relevant area of the source.

```
<HTML xmlns:o="urn:schemas-microsoft-com:office:office" dir="ltr">
<HEAD><meta name="GENERATOR" content="Microsoft SharePoint" /><meta name="progid"
content="SharePoint.WebPartPage.Document" /><meta HTTP-EQUIV="Content-Type"
content="text/html; charset=utf-8" /><meta HTTP-EQUIV="Expires" content="0" /><title>
    Home - Vintage
</title>
<link rel="stylesheet" type="text/css"
href="/_layouts/1033/styles/core.css?rev=5msmprmeONfN6lJ3wtbAlA%3D%3D"/>
<link rel="stylesheet" type="text/css" id="onetidThemeCSS"
href="/SiteDirectory/vintage/_themes/ProfSPD/Prof1011-65001.css?rev=12%2E0%2E0%2E4518"/>
<script type="text/javascript" language="javascript"
src="/_layouts/1033/init.js?rev=VhAxGc3rkK79RM90tibDzw%3D%3D"></script>
```

If another Theme is later applied to the site, the same process takes place as when the first Theme was applied, replacing the Theme subfolder and all of the files for the first Theme with the second Theme's.

Run CSS Report to Pinpoint Usage of the Styles

To dissect the Theme further, you can run the CSS report on the Master Page of the site to which the Theme has been applied. (This utility was explained in chapter 6.) To run the utility on a site's Master Page file, select the `.master` file in the folder tree (the Master Page can be found under `_catalogs\masterpage`). Then navigate to Tools ⇨ CSS Reports. Click on the Usage tab, and then, in the Check where list, choose Selected pages, and in the Check for list, choose all three options (Class Selectors, ID Selectors, and Element Selectors), as shown in Figure 7-6.

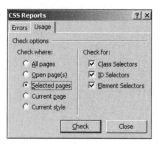

Figure 7-6

Clicking on the Check button runs the report and displays the findings in the CSS Reports task pane, as shown in Figure 7-7.

Style	Usage Location	Line	Definition Location
.ms-banner	default.master	111	core.css
.ms-bannerContainer	default.master	106	core.css
.ms-bannerframe	default.master	108	core.css
.ms-bodyareacell	default.master	388	core.css
.ms-bodyareaframe	default.master	392	core.css
.ms-bodyareaframe	default.master	392	core.css
.ms-bodyareapagemargin	default.master	409	core.css
.ms-bodyareapagemargin	default.master	409	Vint1011-65001.css
.ms-globalTitleArea	default.master	82	core.css
.ms-globalbreadcrumb	default.master	30	Vint1011-65001.css
.ms-globalbreadcrumb	default.master	30	Vint1011-65001.css
.ms-globalbreadcrumb	default.master	30	core.css
.ms-globalbreadcrumb	default.master	30	core.css

Figure 7-7

The report shows all of the style selectors declared in the file. It lists the exact line(s) in the Master Page where the style is declared. Double-clicking on a style opens the exact location of that style in the Code view of the Master Page (see Figure 7-8). To also see the visual of where the style is being applied, open the Split view of the page.

Figure 7-8

In addition, the definition location of each style is linked to the appropriate style sheet as well. Clicking the link opens that style sheet and places the cursor on the exact location where the style is defined within that style sheet, as shown in Figure 7-9.

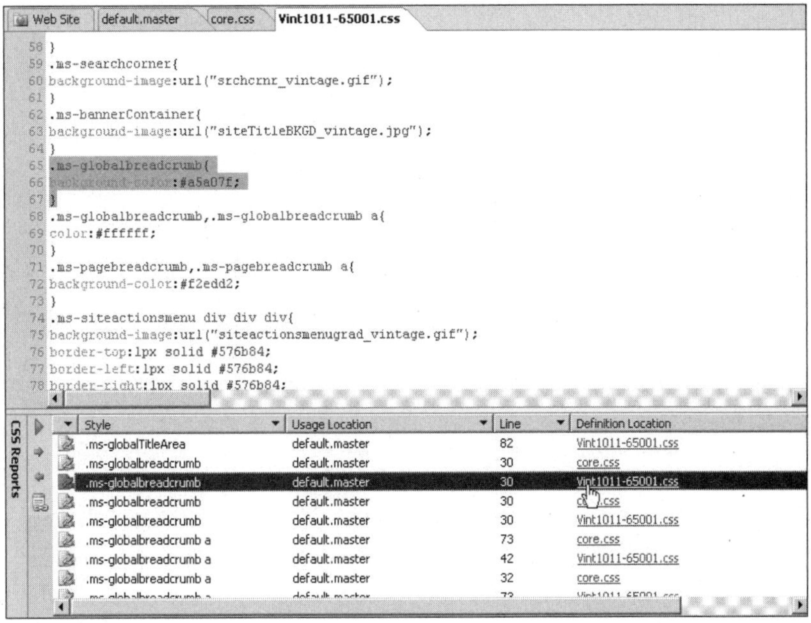

Figure 7-9

Customize the Theme

Once you have decided that using SharePoint Themes is the best route to take for your branding needs, take the following steps to implement a unique Theme for your site:

1. Select an existing Theme that closely resembles your target Theme.

2. Apply that built-in Theme to a site, and open the site in SharePoint Designer.

3. Modify the Theme's `.inf` file, the styles, and the images to finalize your target Theme.

4. Publish the modified Theme back to the web server, and make it available side by side with the other existing Themes.

To modify a Theme, all the style changes need to take place in the `xxxx1011-65001.css` file. This is the style sheet that is applied last, and the only one that matters when overriding any styles. The CSS Reports functionality, as you've seen, is a very powerful tool to discover how and where styles are currently being used. Once you know the location of the style declaration, the existing styles can be changed, or new ones can be created. In addition to the CSS Reports, the task panes and toolbars described in chapter 6 can also be used to ease the task of discovering and applying styles to the site. The following examples utilize these tools in SharePoint Designer to modify some of the elements in the Vintage Theme.

Change the Global Breadcrumb Background Color

The global breadcrumb area is topmost on the page. It's the area in which you see links such as Welcome, My Site, and My Links. To change the background color of that area using the Style Application toolbar, follow these steps:

1. Open `default.master` for the site and bring up the Style Application toolbar by selecting View ⇨ Toolbars ⇨ Style Application.

2. Change the Style Application setting in the toolbar to Manual. Doing this ensures that the style changes you make are all implemented in the linked style sheet (this behavior was further explained in chapter 6).

3. Click in the middle of the global breadcrumb area. The Style Application toolbar shows the Target Rule. Open the Target Rule dropdown and select the `.ms-globalbreadcrumb` that shows the current background color of the global breadcrumb (see Figure 7-10).

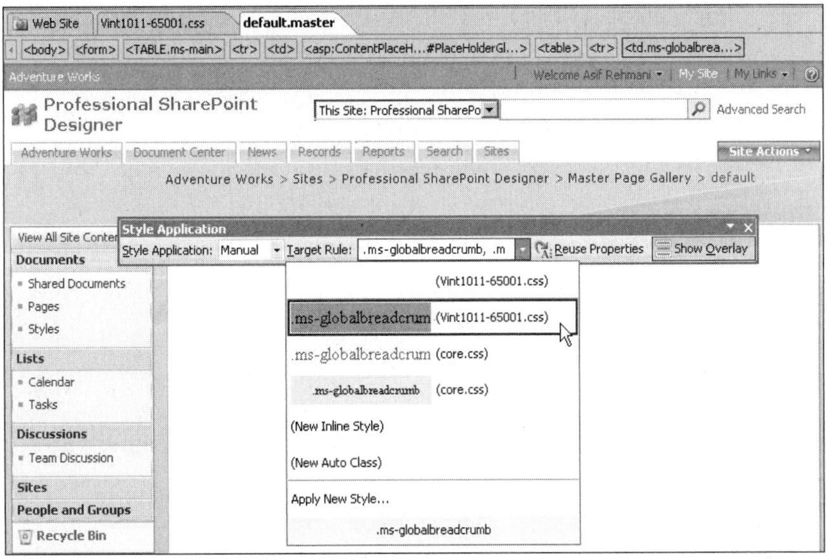

Figure 7-10

4. Click the Highlight button in the toolbar, and then click More Colors (see Figure 7-11).

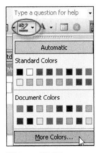

Figure 7-11

5. In the More Colors dialog box, click the Select button. A color selector in the shape of an eyedropper is now available to you, to point to any color on the page. Once a color is selected using the eyedropper tool, the Hex value for that color is displayed in the Value text box. Click OK to make the color change. Figure 7-12 shows the eyedropper tool, as well as the Hex value for the selected color.

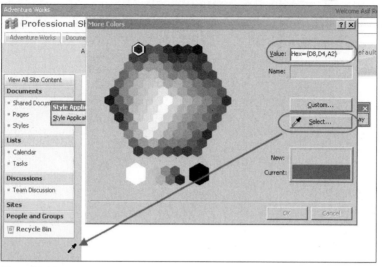

Figure 7-12

The change is made in the .ms-globalbreadcrumb section of the Vint1011-65001.css file as follows:

Before:

```
.ms-globalbreadcrumb {
background-color:#a5a07f;
}
```

After:

```
.ms-globalbreadcrumb {
background-color:#D8D4A2;
}
```

The default.master and all other files in the site are untouched. Save Vint101165001.css and then view the change in the browser.

Change Font Color of Global Links

By default, the Vintage Theme shows the link for the name of the Portal and the link for My Site in white text. The following steps utilize the CSS Properties and the Manage Styles task panes to discover the style selector that controls the color for that text and then change it.

1. Open default.master for the site and click on the global navigation breadcrumb link in the upper-left corner of the page. The rules that are applied to this text are displayed in the CSS Properties task pane. The .ms-globallinks, .ms-globallinks a rule, which resides in core.css, appears as the last one applied to this text (see Figure 7-13).

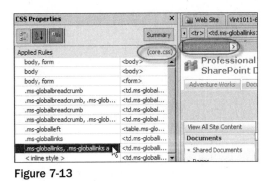

Figure 7-13

2. Click on the `.ms-globallinks`, `.ms-globallinks` a rule in CSS Properties to display that rule in the Manage Styles task pane.

3. Right-click on the `.ms-globallinks`, `.ms-globallinks` a rule in the Manage Styles task pane and select New Style Copy (see Figure 7-14).

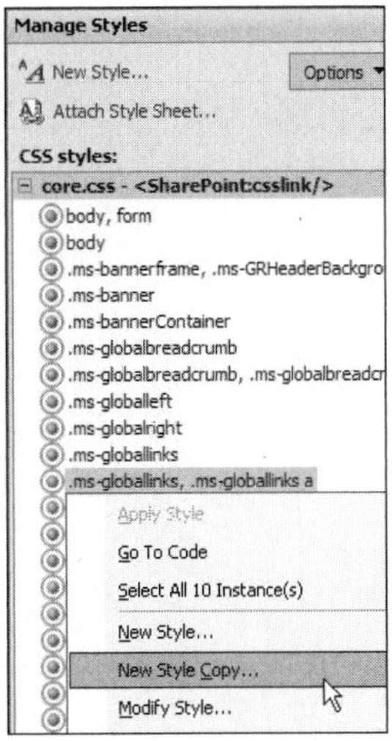

Figure 7-14

4. The New Style dialog box opens, with the rule and its current style declarations in the `core.css` file. This rule needs to be declared anew in the `Vint1011-65001.css` file, so choose that style sheet in the URL dropdown list (Figure 7-15).

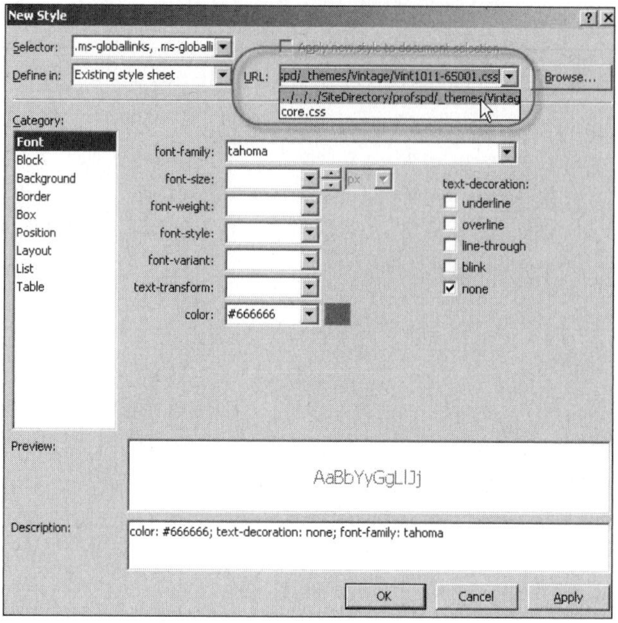

Figure 7-15

5. Use the color dropdown list to bring up the More Colors dialog box. As in the last section, use the eyedropper color selection tool to choose the color of the My Links link (see Figure 7-16). Click OK to commit the change.

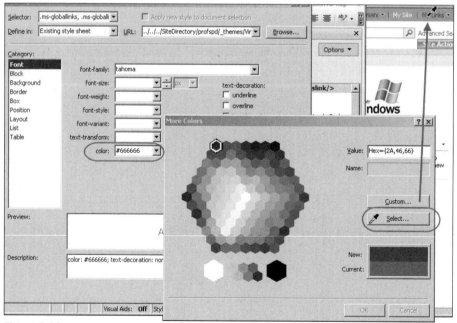

Figure 7-16

6. Verify that the rule for `.ms-globallinks`, `.ms-globallinks a` now appears at the bottom of the `Vint1011-65001.css` file as follows:

```
.ms-globallinks,.ms-globallinks a{
    color: #2A4666;
    text-decoration: none;
    font-family: tahoma;
}
```

7. Save the `Vint1011-65001.css` file now, and test your changes in the browser.

The preceding examples demonstrate a couple of ways in which you can use tools in SharePoint Designer to modify or create new styles in a Theme's `xxxx1011-65001.css` style sheet.

Publishing the Modified Theme

When you are satisfied with all the changes you have made in the `Vint1011-65001.css` file, you can package your changes in a new Theme folder and publish it back to the web server. That makes the Theme available to be applied on any SharePoint site using just the browser.

Adding a new Theme to the web server is a relatively easy process, but it requires write access to the web server files. As stated at the beginning of this chapter, all of the Themes reside in:

```
<Program_Files_Directory>\Common Files\Microsoft Shared\
web server extensions\12\TEMPLATE\THEMES
```

The new Theme is created at that location as well. Follow these steps to create the new Theme. Once again, the starter Theme is assumed to be Vintage in this example.

1. Navigate to the THEMES folder and make a copy of the entire Vintage Theme folder.

2. Give the new folder a unique name that the system will use to identify it internally. For this example, the new Theme folder is named PROFSPD, as shown in Figure 7-17.

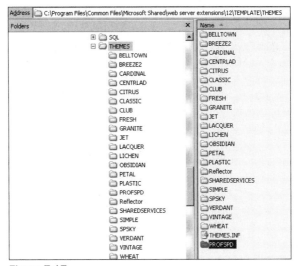

Figure 7-17

Again as stated earlier, a Theme folder is composed of one `.inf` file, one or two `.css` files, and multiple image files. These are the files that need to be changed to configure the new Theme. Here's what to do:

1. Change the name of the `.inf` file from `VINTAGE.INF` to `PROFSPD.INF`.

2. Open the `.inf` file and change all instances of Vintage to ProfSPD. Save this file.

3. Delete the `mossExtension.css` file (you will only see this file if you are running a MOSS installation). There is no use for this file when creating your own customized Theme package.

4. Open the `theme.css` file in SharePoint Designer, and replace its contents with all of the text from your modified `Vint1011-65001.css` file.

5. Delete any image files in the Theme folder that are no longer referenced by the new `theme.css` style sheet. Also, add any new image files that are referenced by the new `.css` file. (The example that you are following here does not require this action. However, in your future projects, if you add or remove image references in your CSS file, you must make sure the images in the Theme folder are complete and accurate.)

The PROFSPD packaging is now complete. The next thing to do is create a preview image for the new Theme that will appear on the Site Theme page when a designer is deciding which Theme to apply to a site. The dimensions for this image are recommended by Microsoft to be 375 px wide by 231 px high. (A simple resize tool on the web, such as the one at `http://resizr.com`, can be used to size your image to these dimensions.) When creating the image, make sure to show the browser and the colors of the Theme. Crop out the menus, toolbars, and status bars in the browser. Any image utility (Microsoft Paint, which comes with the Windows operating system, for example) can be used to create the preview image. Name this image `thPROFSPD.gif` and store it along with other preview images at:

```
<Program_Files_Directory>\Common Files\Microsoft Shared\web server
extensions\12\TEMPLATE\IMAGES
```

An example image is shown in Figure 7-18.

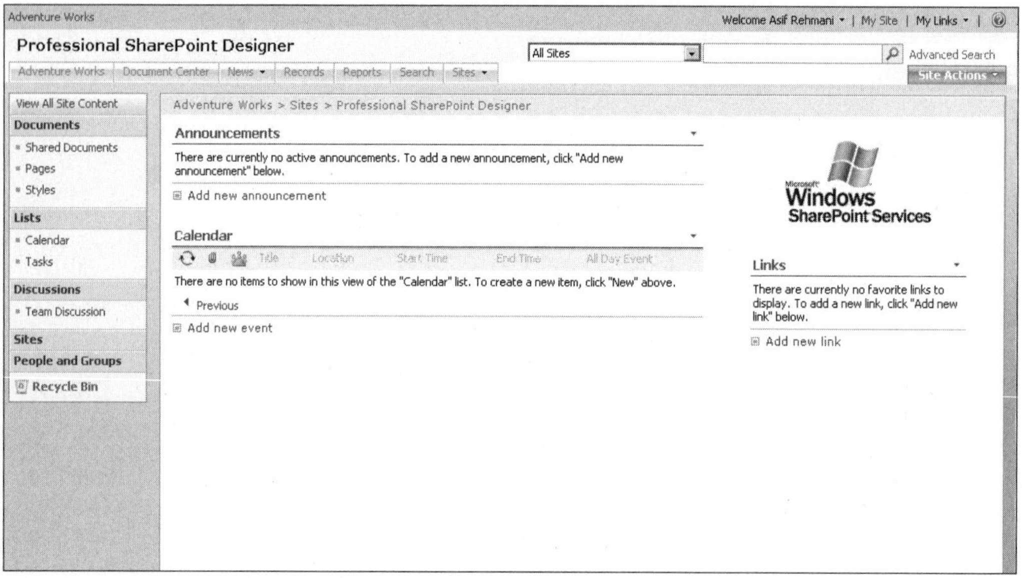

Figure 7-18

The next step is to configure the SPTHEMES.xml file, which declares all available SharePoint Themes. This file, whose contents were explained earlier in the chapter, is located at:

```
<Program_Files_Directory>\Common Files\Microsoft Shared\web server
extensions\12\TEMPLATE\LAYOUTS\1033
```

A new <Templates> section needs to be inserted in this file to declare the PROFSPD Theme, as follows.

```
<Templates>
    <TemplateID>ProfSPD</TemplateID>
    <DisplayName>Professional SharePoint Designer</DisplayName>
    <Description>Sample Theme created for the SharePoint Designer
    book</Description>
    <Thumbnail>images/thProfSPD.gif</Thumbnail>
    <Preview>images/thProfSPD.gif</Preview>
</Templates>
```

The new <Templates> node declares the internal name of the PROFSPD Theme, gives it a friendly display name, provides the Theme's description, and points to the location of the Theme's preview image file.

The last step is to reset Internet Information Services (IIS) by typing **iisreset** at the command prompt of the web server, so the declaration of the new theme is recognized by the server. Keep in mind that while this step is executed, all your web applications on the server are momentarily unavailable.

That's it! The Theme is now published to the web server. To test out the Theme, apply it to an existing SharePoint site by selecting Site Actions ⇨ Site Settings and then clicking on Site Theme under Look and Feel. The Professional SharePoint Designer Theme should appear in the list of Themes, as shown in Figure 7-19.

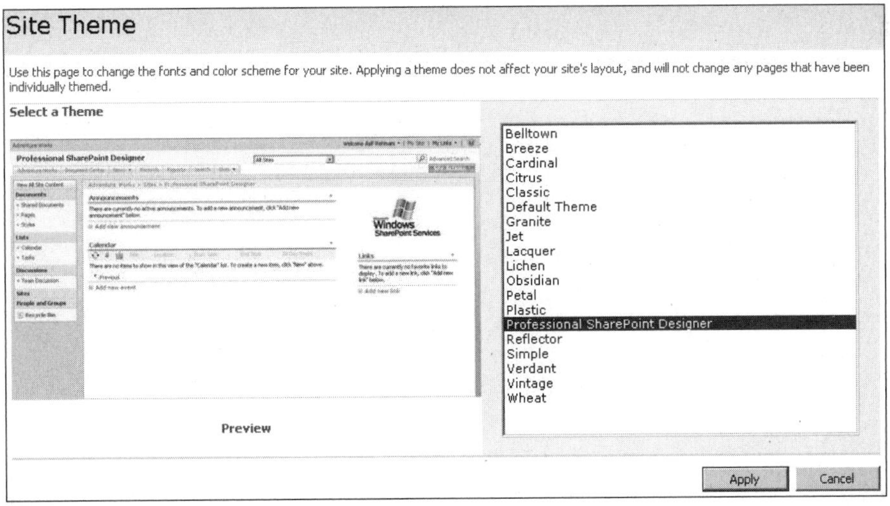

Figure 7-19

A Customized Theme, from Head to Toe

There are lots and lots of components in the `default.master` page that can be styled by Themes. The following section walks through a simplified custom Theme that is designed to point out the major styles in a Theme and also to point out the section(s) of the Master Page that the styles impact.

The simplified Theme file (`ProfSPDTheme.css`) is included in the download code for this chapter. The style sheet is not meant to be used as is (unless you want your final site to look like Figure 7-20), but serves as a reference when you are creating your own custom Theme. The styles in this file have been grouped together in order of the section of the page they impact, for ease of reading.

Page Banner and Background

The `ms-main` element in the `default.master` page handles the look and feel for the entire main portal table. It is declared as follows in the Master Page:

```
<TABLE class="ms-main" CELLPADDING=0 CELLSPACING=0 BORDER=0 WIDTH="100%" ↵
HEIGHT="100%">
```

The style for `ms-main` is not defined in the `core.css` file or anywhere else. It can be easily defined in a custom style sheet to implement a banner image or apply background color to the entire portal area. For example, the following code in the custom Theme declares the background color for the banner on top of the page:

```
.ms-main {
    background-color: #FFFBD8;
}
```

And here's the code that removes the white background image that appears by default on the right side of the banner, as shown in Figure 7-20:

```
.ms-globalTitleArea {
    text-align: right;
    background-image: none;
    background-position: right top;
    background-repeat: repeat-y;
    padding-left: 5px;
    padding-right: 0px;
    padding-top: 1px;
}
```

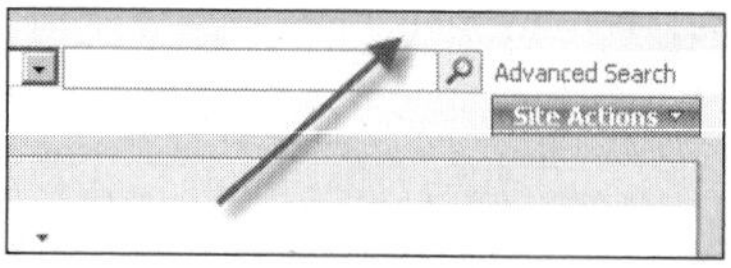

Figure 7-20

Global Breadcrumb and My Site Link

The global breadcrumb navigation at the left of the navigation bar and the My Site link on the right of the navigation bar, shown in Figure 7-21, are styled together.

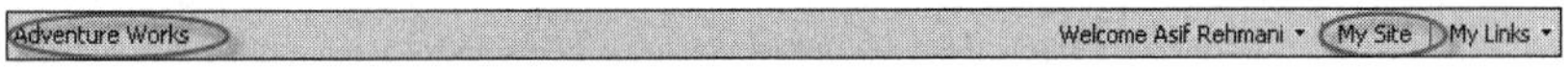

Figure 7-21

The `ms-globalbreadcrumb` and the `ms-globallinks` classes in the Master Page mainly deal with styling these components:

```css
/* Global breadcrumb navigation and My Site link */
.ms-globalbreadcrumb {
    font-size: 8pt;
    text-align: right;
    background-color: #D8D4A3;
    padding: 2px 10px 2px 5px;
}
.ms-globalbreadcrumb, .ms-globalbreadcrumb a {
    text-decoration: none;
    color: #000000;
}
.ms-globalbreadcrumb a:hover {
    text-decoration: underline;
    color: #808000;
}
.ms-globallinks,.ms-globallinks a{
    color: #2A4666;
    text-decoration: none;
    font-family: tahoma;
}
```

Global Links — Welcome and My Links

The navigation bar of the Master Page also contains the Welcome and the My Links controls (see Figure 7-22).

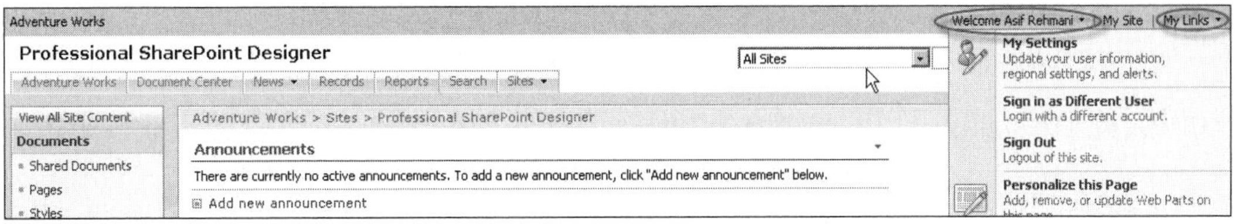

Figure 7-22

These controls are styled mainly with the msSPLink class. Because these are dropdown controls, unlike the global breadcrumb and My Site links, the styles for these controls also control the look and feel of the dropdown menu colors:

```
/* Global Links - Welcome and My Links */
.ms-SPLink {
    font-family: Tahoma;
    font-size: 8pt;
    color: #000000;
}
.ms-SPLink A:link, .ms-SPLink A:visited {
    color: #000000;
    text-decoration: none;
}
.ms-HoverCellActive, .ms-SpLinkButtonActive {
    border: #6f9dd9 1px solid;
    background-image: url("/_layouts/images/trans.gif");
}
/* Global Links hover state */
.ms-HoverCellActive, .ms-SpLinkButtonActive {
    border: #e8e3b7 1px solid;
    vertical-align: top;
    background-color: #FF9900;
    background-image: url("menubuttonhover_vintage.gif");
}
```

Site Logo

Figure 7-23 shows the default logo of a site.

Figure 7-23

The custom Theme calls for hiding the site logo with the following code:

```
/* Hide site logo */
IMG#ctl00_onetidheadbnnr0 {
    display: none;
}
```

Site Title

The title of a site appears directly under the global navigation bar (see Figure 7-24).

Adventure Works

Professional SharePoint Designer ◄———

All Sit

Adventure Works | Document Center | News ▾ | Records | Reports | Search | Sites ▾

Figure 7-24

The text and the background color of the site title are styled by the ms-sitetitle class:

```
/* Site title */
.ms-sitetitle a {
    font: 11pt verdana;
    font-weight: bold;
    color: #000000;
    background-color: transparent;
    text-decoration: none;
}
.ms-sitetitle a:hover {
    text-decoration: underline;
}
```

Search Controls

The search controls appear on the top right of the page, below the navigation bar, as shown in Figure 7-25. The main class controlling the style for these controls is the ms-sbtable.

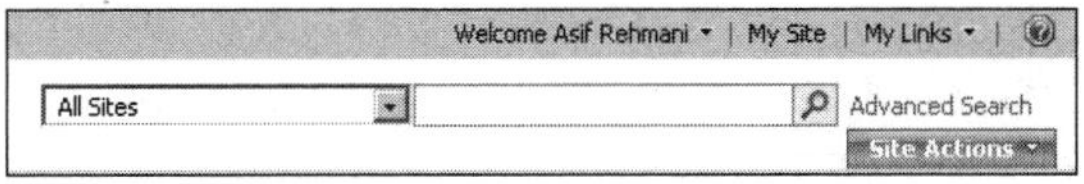

Figure 7-25

Here's the code for the search controls:

```
/* Search box */
.ms-sbtable {
    background-color: #FFFFFF;
    color: #000000;
    font-family: Verdana;
    font-size: 0.7em;
    font-style: normal;
    font-weight: normal;
}
```

Global Navigation

The look and feel of the global navigation of the site (see Figure 7-26) is controlled by the following class selectors.

Figure 7-26

```
/* Global Navigation */
.ms-topnavContainer {
    border-left: solid 1px #a2b9d6;
}
.ms-topnav {
    border: solid 1px #a2b9d6;
    border-left: solid 1px #ffffff;
    border-bottom-width: 0px;
    background: #e1eaf4 url("topnavunselected_vintage.gif");
    color: #7c7c7c;
}
.ms-topnavselected {
    background: url("topnavselected_vintage.gif");
    border: solid 1px #8099b7;
    border-left: solid 1px #f7f3cd;
    border-bottom-width: 0px;
    background-color: #e8e3b7;
}
.ms-topNavHover {
    background-image: url("topnavhover_vintage.gif");
    background-color: #ffe59d;
    border: solid 1px #758ead;
    border-left: solid 1px #ffffff;
    border-bottom-width: 0px;
}
.ms-topNavFlyOutsContainer {
    border: solid 1px #a2b9d6;
}
.ms-topNavFlyOuts {
    background-color: #fffbd8 !important;
}
.ms-topNavFlyOutsHover {
    background-color: #ffe6a0 !important;
}
```

Site Actions Menu

The following classes style the Site Actions menu (see Figure 7-27) that appears directly below the search controls.

Figure 7-27

```
/* Site Actions Menu */
.ms-siteactionsmenu div div div {
    background-image: url("siteactionsmenugrad_vintage.gif");
    border-top: 1px solid #576b84;
    border-left: 1px solid #576b84;
    border-right: 1px solid #576b84;
    background-color: #8b99aa;
}
.ms-siteactionsmenu div div div.ms-siteactionsmenuhover {
    background-image: url("siteactionsmenuhovergrad_vintage.gif");
    background-color: #db9a59;
}
```

Page Navigation Breadcrumb

The page navigation breadcrumb appears at the top of the Content Page and below the global navigation of the site, as shown in Figure 7-28.

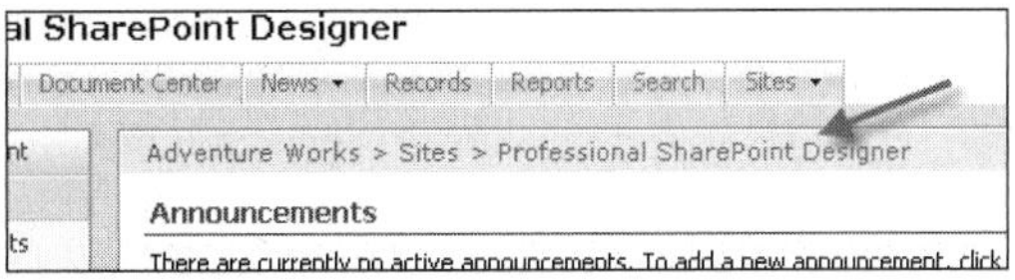

Figure 7-28

Here's the code that styles the page navigation breadcrumb:

```
/* Page navigation breadcrumb */
.ms-pagebreadcrumb, .ms-pagebreadcrumb a {
    background-color: #f2edd2;
}
```

Quick Launch Navigation Area

The quick launch navigation area (see Figure 7-29) is also referred to as the Current Navigation.

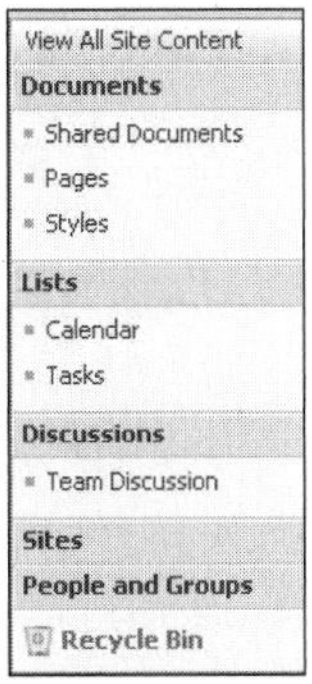

Figure 7-29

The following style selectors style the quick launch:

```
/* Quick Launch */
.ms-quickLaunch {
    border: solid 1px #949172;
    background-color: #fffbd8;
}
.ms-quicklaunchheader {
    background-image: url("quickLaunchHeader_vintage.gif");
    background-color: #e8e3b7;
    border-left: solid 1px #fffbd8;
}
.ms-quicklaunch table td {
    border-top: 1px solid #ccc6a5;
}
.ms-quicklaunch table.ms-navheader td, .ms-navheader2 td, .ms-quicklaunch span.ms-
navheader {
    background-color: #e8e3b7;
    border-top: solid 1px #fffbd8;
    border-left: solid 1px #fffbd8;
}
.ms-quicklaunch span.ms-navheader {
    background-color: #e8e3b7;
    border-left: solid 1px #fffbd8;
    border-bottom: 1px solid #efebc2;
}
.ms-quicklaunch table.ms-selectednav {
    border: solid 1px #8099b7;
    background-image: url("selectednav_vintage.gif");
    background-color: #fffbd5;
}
.ms-quicklaunch table.ms-selectednav td {
    background: transparent url("selectednavbullet_vintage.gif") no-repeat;
}
.ms-quicklaunch table.ms-selectednavheader td {
    background-color: #fffbd5;
    background-image: url("selectednav_vintage.gif");
}
table.ms-navitem td, span.ms-navitem {
    background: #fffbd8 url("navBullet_vintage.gif") no-repeat;
}
.ms-pagemargin {
    /* area to the right of the quick launch */
    background-image: url("navshape_vintage.jpg");
    background-position: -143px 0px;
    background-color: #d8d4a4;
}
.ms-navsubmenu1 {
    background-color: #fffbd8;
}
.ms-navsubmenu2 {
    background-color: #fffbd8;
}
table.ms-navselected, span.ms-navselected {
```

```
        background-image: url("SELECTEDNAV_vintage.GIF");
        background-color: #FFFBD5;
        background-repeat: repeat-x;
}
table.ms-navselected td {
        background-image: url("navBullet_vintage.gif");
        background-repeat: no-repeat;
}
.ms-quicklaunchouter {
        border-bottom: solid 1px #d8d4a2;
        border-right: solid 1px #d8d4a2;
}
table.ms-recyclebin td {
        background-color: #fffbd8;
        border-top: solid 1px #ffffff;
        border-left: solid 1px #ffffff;
}
```

Tree View Pane

The tree view pane (see Figure 7-30) can be used in addition to or instead of the quick launch navigation area.

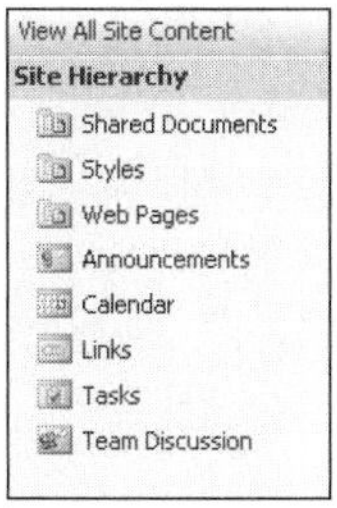

Figure 7-30

It's styled by the following selectors:

```
/* Tree View Pane */
div.ms-treeviewouter div {
    border-top: solid 1px #efebc2;
}
.ms-treeviewouter td.ms-navitem {
    border: none;
    padding: 0px 4px;
}
.ms-tvselected {
    background-color: #8ba3c1;
}
```

Web Parts

Web Parts (see Figure 7-31) are styled using the following styling rules.

Figure 7-31

```
/* Web Parts */
/* Separating line under web part and above Action links (such as "Add New
Announcements") */
.ms-partline {
    background-color: #A2B9D6;
}
.ms-WPTitle {
    font-weight: bold;
    font-family: tahoma,sans-serif;
    color: #4c4c4c;
    font-size: 10pt;
}
.ms-WPTitle A:link, .ms-WPTitle A:visited {
    color: #4c4c4c;
    text-decoration: none;
    cursor: pointer;
}
.ms-WPTitle A:hover {
    color: #000000;
    text-decoration: underline;
    cursor: pointer;
}
.ms-WPHeader TD {
    /* line right below Web Part name */
    border-bottom: 1px solid #0000FF;
}
.ms-WPBorder, .ms-WPBorderBorderOnly {
    /* border around web part (when border is made visible) */
    border-color: #0000FF;
}
```

List or Library Description Text

When you navigate to a list or a library, the text describing the purpose of that list or library is placed directly under its title, as shown in Figure 7-32.

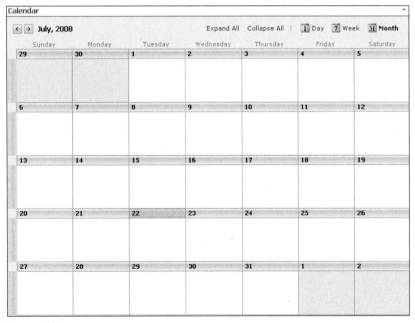

Figure 7-32

The following styles are used in the custom Theme file to style this text.

```
/* Style to alter description text of a list or library */
.ms-listdescription {
    color: #4c4c4c;
    font-family: tahoma;
    background: #F1F0DB;
    padding: 2px 6px 4px 6px;
    border-bottom: 1px solid #f8f8f8;
}
```

Calendar List

The styles for a calendar (see Figure 7-33) are not declared in the `core.css` file. Instead, they exist in the `calendar.css` file (located in the same directory on the web server as `core.css`).

Figure 7-33

Calendar styles govern how the calendar is rendered in the Calendar List View and also when displayed through a Web Part:

```
/* Calendar styles from calendar.css */
.ms-calheader {
    background-color: #f7f3cd;
}
.ms-cal-weekempty, .ms-cal-weekemptyRTL {
    background-color: #f7f3cd;
}
.ms-cal-weekname {
    background-color: #f7f3cd;
}
.ms-cal-weekday {
    background-color: #f7f3cd;
}
.ms-cal-week, .ms-cal-weekB, .ms-cal-weekRTL, .ms-cal-weekRTLB {
    background-image: url("weekbox_vintage.gif");
    background-color: #efebc2;
    border: 1px solid #e8e3b7;
}
.ms-cal-weekselected, .ms-cal-weekselectedRTL {
    border: 1px solid #e8e3b7;
    background-color: #f7f3cd;
}
.ms-cal-topday, .ms-cal-topdayL, .ms-cal-wtopdayL, .ms-cal-wtopday {
    background-image: url("calnumBttn_vintage.gif");
    background-repeat: repeat-x;
    background-color: #f5f1cb;
    border: solid 1px #a5a07f;
}
.ms-cal-topdayRTL, .ms-cal-topdayRTLL, .ms-cal-wtopdayRTL, .ms-cal-wtopdayRTLL {
    background-image: url("calnumBttn_vintage.gif");
    background-repeat: repeat-x;
    background-color: #f5f1cb;
    border: solid 1px #a5a07f;
}
.ms-cal-wtopday {
    border-right: none;
}
.ms-cal-wtopdayRTL {
    border-left: none;
}
.ms-cal-topdayfocus, .ms-cal-topdayfocusL, .ms-cal-topdayfocusRTL, .ms-cal-
topdayfocusRTLL, .ms-cal-wtopdayfocus, .ms-cal-wtopdayfocusL, .ms-cal-wtopdayfocusRTL,
.ms-cal-wtopdayfocusRTLL {
    background-image: url("calnumBttnfocus_vintage.gif");
    background-repeat: repeat-x;
    background-color: #e7e2b6;
    border: solid 1px #a5a07f;
}
```

```
}
.ms-cal-topday-todayover, .ms-cal-wtopday-todayover, .ms-cal-topday-todayoverRTL, .ms-
cal-wtopday-todayRTLover {
    background-image: none;
    background-color: #fff;
    border: solid 1px #a5a07f;
}
```

Bottom Area of the Master Page

The bottom area of the Master Page (see Figure 7-34) is controlled by the following classes.

Figure 7-34

```
/* bottom of master page */
.ms-pagebottommarginright {
    background: #D8D4A4;
}
.ms-pagebottommarginleft {
    background: #D8D4A4;
}
.ms-pagebottommargin {
    background: #D8D4A4;
}
.ms-bodyareapagemargin {
    background: #D8D4A4;
    border-top: 1px solid #D8D4A4;
}
```

Title Area of a Web Part Page

When a new Web Part Page is created, the title area (see Figure 7-35) of that Web Part Page is styled with the following code.

Figure 7-35

```
/* Title area of a web part page */
.ms-titlearea a {
    /* page breadcrumb navigation font */
    color: #003399;
}
.ms-titlearealeft {
    background-color: #003399;
}
TD.ms-titleareaframe, Div.ms-titleareaframe, .ms-pagetitleareaframe, .ms-
mwspagetitleareaframe, .ms-consoletitleareaframe {
    background-image: url("pageTitleBKGD_vintage.gif");
    background-color: #e8e3b7;
}
.ms-pagetitleareaframe table {
    background-image: url("topshape_vintage.jpg");
}
.ms-nav {
    background: #d8d4a4 url("navshape_vintage.jpg") no-repeat;
}
```

New Items Toolbar

The following are the styles for the toolbar that's displayed when new items are being created in a list (see Figure 7-36).

Figure 7-36

```
/* Toolbar that appears when creating new items or editing existing in a list */
.ms-toolbar, .ms-viewtoolbar, .ms-formtoolbar, .ms-toolbarContainer {
    font-family: verdana;
    font-size: 8pt;
    text-decoration: none;
    color: #003399;
}
table.ms-toolbar, table.ms-viewtoolbar, .ms-toolbarContainer {
    background-image: url("toolgrad_vintage.gif");
    background-color: #d0dded;
}
table.ms-toolbar, .ms-toolbarContainer {
    border: 1px solid #96aecc;
}
```

Form Field Background

When a new item is being created or an existing item is edited, the background color of form fields (see Figure 7-37) is controlled by the style selector .ms-formbody:

```
/* Background for cells with form fields */
.ms-formbody {
    background: #efebc2;
}
```

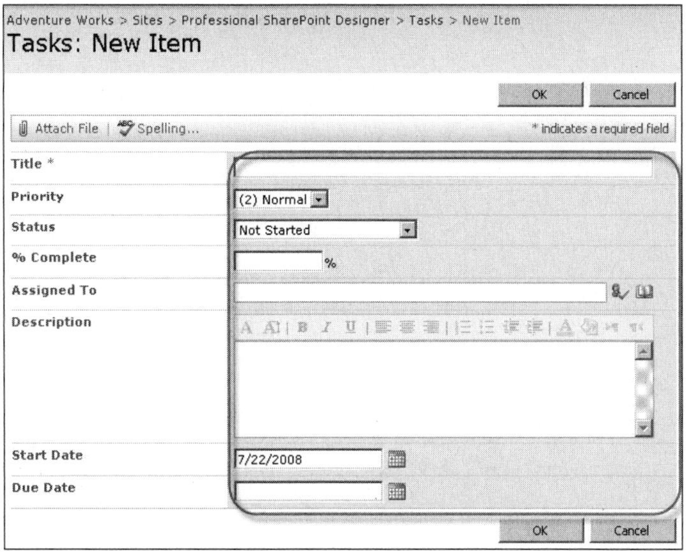

Figure 7-37

Toolbar for Lists and Libraries

The toolbar that appears when you are in a list or library view shows items such as New, Actions (Fig. 7-38), and Settings (see Figure 7-38).

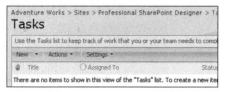

Figure 7-38

The styles for this toolbar are as follows:

```
/* Toolbar menu for Lists and Libraries */
.ms-menutoolbar {
    border-bottom: 1px solid #8099b7;
    border-top: 1px solid #8099b7;
    background: #cbd9eb url("listheadergrad_vintage.gif") repeat-x;
}
.ms-menutoolbar td {
    border-top: solid 1px #e1eaf4;
    border-bottom: solid 1px #e1eaf4;
}
td.ms-menutoolbarheader {
    color: #d8d4a2;
}
.ms-menutoolbar td td.ms-viewselector, .ms-menutoolbar td td.ms-viewselectorhover,
.ms-
toolbar td td.ms-viewselector, .ms-toolbar td td.ms-viewselectorhover, .ms-
authoringcontrols td td.ms-viewselector, .ms-authoringcontrols td td.ms-
viewselectorhover, td.ms-viewselector {
    border: solid 1px #6b84a3;
    background-image: url("selectednav_vintage.gif");
    background-color: #fffbd5;
}
```

Summary

This chapter focused exclusively on SharePoint Themes, showing why Themes are important, and in which situations they should be used. A comparison of Themes and Master Pages explained the need for each of these technologies to be used within SharePoint.

You looked at the Themes that come with SharePoint and saw how an existing Theme can be modified using the tools provided within SharePoint Designer. Lastly, a new Theme was produced and published back to the web server for re-use.

The main takeaways from this chapter are:

❑ Themes serve a unique branding need within SharePoint. They can change colors, fonts, images, and more within a site.

❑ Several out-of-the-box SharePoint Themes are available that a designer of the site can apply directly by using the browser.

❑ Styles within a Theme can be easily discovered and changed, and new ones can be created using the tools provided within SharePoint Designer.

❑ A new Theme can be easily created and published back to the web server.

Master Pages and Layouts

You can use SharePoint Designer, together with the SharePoint site management functions accessible through the browser, to create publishing pages that take advantage of web content management (WCM) concepts in SharePoint to streamline management of content. This chapter shows you how to incorporate the WCM features in SharePoint Server 2007. In particular, this chapter examines:

❑   What WCM provides in SharePoint.

❑   The components needed to build publishing pages.

❑   Creating Master Pages.

❑   Building page layouts and the underlying content type.

❑   Constructing publishing pages.

Web Content Management in SharePoint

In the previous versions of SharePoint Server (SharePoint Portal Server 2001 and SharePoint Portal Server 2003), SharePoint technologies were focused on how to build a portal for the intranet and the extranet. A few brave companies had forayed into creating their public-facing Internet sites using the SharePoint server, but because SharePoint lacked web content management features, the server product was not considered the best solution for the Internet or even large intranets that required a robust content management solution.

Critical to the success of any web site — internal or external — is the content creation and management of its pages to keep the site content fresh and relevant. Of course, the content management process is not as simple as it may sound. You have to consider many aspects of the process. Who will have access to create new content and manage existing content? Does the content have to be approved by a person or a group of people before it becomes live on the site? What if some published content on a page needs to be rolled back to its previous version?

How will you restrict the look and feel and the layout of the type of pages that can be created on the site, to keep it consistent with the rest of the site?

Because of the complexity of the whole process, the publishing infrastructure usually falls into the laps of the folks in the IT department. To avoid letting IT become the bottleneck for all content creation and management, and to empower the knowledge workers and the content managers in the company with a highly dynamic page creation and content management model, you need to implement robust content management tools. Microsoft Office SharePoint Server (MOSS) 2007 comes bundled with the web content management components that can help accomplish this goal.

MOSS has already been used to create hundreds of Internet sites, a list of which has been compiled by SharePoint MVP Ian Morrish at `http://wssdemo.com/Pages/websites.aspx`.

When SPS Met CMS

Before MOSS entered the picture in late 2006, the recommended Microsoft product for creating Internet sites was Content Management Server (CMS) 2002, which included robust WCM features. SharePoint Portal Server (SPS) 2003 was well suited to create intranet and extranet sites. SPS used Windows SharePoint Services (WSS) as its core foundation of services, such as site and list creation, user management, document libraries with check-in/check-out and versioning features, site columns, content types, and much more.

With the introduction of MOSS, WCM features have been integrated with SharePoint server technologies. CMS is no longer a separate product offered by Microsoft. Even the CMS team in Redmond, Washington, has been merged into the SharePoint team. A MOSS standard license is required to get access to the WCM set of tools. WCM features, like the rest of the MOSS features set, are built on top of the WSS platform, which provides the plumbing and the infrastructure.

Publishing Sites: The Key to WCM

There are many site templates that come with MOSS. The publishing site templateis the one that utilizes the WCM features of SharePoint. Publishing sites are content-centric web sites. They are informative in nature, which means that there are few contributors and many consumers of the information on the site. This usually applies to large intranets as well as Internet sites. In a typical scenario, a group of users, controlled by the SharePoint security mechanisms, is designated to create new and manage existing content, while another group of users is tasked with approving the content. Once the content is approved by all approvers, it can be set up to be automatically published to the live site, at which point the content becomes viewable to the visitors of the site. A visitor on an intranet site is typically an employee of the company, while a visitor on an Internet site is anyone anonymously browsing the site on the web.

The WCM capabilities in a publishing site are activated by the Publishing feature (see Figure 8-1).

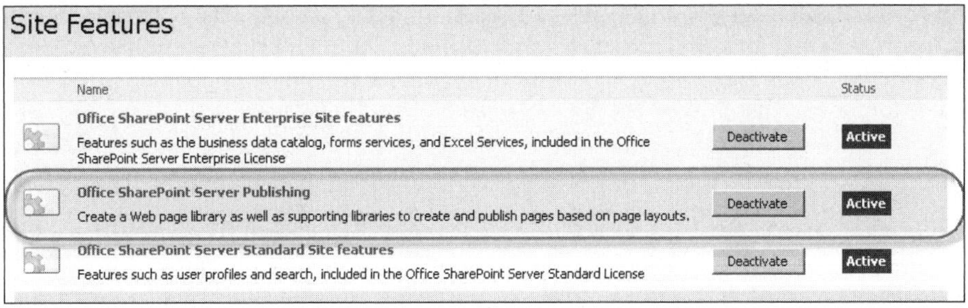

Figure 8-1

You can get to the Site Features screen shown in Figure 8-1 by clicking the Site Features link on the Site Settings page for the site.

> *Features in SharePoint let you package functionality and easily deploy it at the site, site collection, web application, or the whole farm level. Read more about the SharePoint feature called Features at* http://msdn.microsoft.com/en-us/library/ms460318.aspx.

The Publishing feature enables three supporting libraries on the site. They're described in the following table.

Library Name	Description
Documents	Contains the documents used on pages in this site.
Images	Stores the images displayed on pages in this site.
Pages	Contains the publishing pages of this site, including the home page `default.aspx`.

The Pages library is by far the most important one on the site because it stores all of the site's publishing pages. A publishing page is made up of a Master Page and page layout. A Master Page provides the branding and page structure, while the page layout is what makes up the body of the page.

The remainder of this chapter shows how Master Pages and page layouts are built to facilitate creation of publishing pages.

Master Pages Revisited

Master Pages were covered initially in chapter 5, where you saw how Master Page content regions worked and how they applied in the context of a collaborative site. This section builds on that knowledge and shows how Master Pages tie in with page layouts to render pages in publishing sites.

In a publishing site, Master Pages have the same type of task that they do in nonpublishing sites. They provide a consistent look and feel by defining the layout and design for that site. A site's chrome (global navigation, quick launch, and so forth) is made up of the elements defined in the Master Page. Master Pages use content placeholders to define areas within the layout of the page that can be replaced by content provided by a Content Page. Content placeholders are wrapped in a `table`, `div`, or `span` tag. Here's a typical content placeholder tag defined within the Master Page:

```
<asp:ContentPlaceHolder id="MainPlaceholder" runat="server" />
```

In publishing sites, the Master Pages must live in the Master Page gallery. The Master Page gallery exists in the root site of a site collection, as shown in Figure 8-2. It's accessible through the site collection's Site Settings page.

Adventure Works > Site Settings

Site Settings

Site Information

Site URL:	http://portal.home.local/
Mobile Site URL:	http://portal.home.local/_layouts/mobile/default.aspx
Version:	12.0.0.4518

Users and Permissions	Look and Feel	Galleries	Site Administration	Site Collection Administration
▫ People and groups	▫ Master page	▫ Site content types	▫ Regional settings	▫ Search settings
▫ Site collection administrators	▫ Title, description, and icon	▫ Site columns	▫ Site libraries and lists	▫ Search scopes
▫ Advanced permissions	▫ Navigation	▫ Site templates	▫ Site usage reports	▫ Search keywords
	▫ Page layouts and site templates	▫ List templates	▫ User alerts	▫ Recycle bin
	▫ Welcome page	▫ Web Parts	▫ RSS	▫ Site directory settings
	▫ Tree view	▫ Workflows	▫ Search visibility	▫ Site collection usage reports
	▫ Site theme	▫ Master pages and page layouts	▫ Sites and workspaces	▫ Site collection features
			▫ Site features	▫ Site hierarchy

Figure 8-2

This gallery is built using the document library template, so it has all of the features of a document library. Its default configuration facilitates creation and management of Master Pages and page layouts (page layouts are discussed thoroughly later in this chapter):

❑ The security of the library is configured to allow only users with design permissions and higher to create new files and manage existing ones.

❑ Major and minor versioning is turned on, and draft item security is enabled so that only users who can edit items can see and work with the draft (minor versions) of the items.

❑ Content approval is required for newly created or changed items in the library.

❑ Documents are required to be checked out before they can be edited.

What You Get with the Default Installation of MOSS

When a site collection is created, using either the collaboration portal template (recommended for creating intranets) or the publishing portal template (recommended when creating an Internet or extranet), nine different Master Pages are placed in the Master Page gallery: `BlackBand.master`,

`BlackSingleLevel.master`, `BlackVertical.master`, `BlueBand.master`, `BlueGlassBand.master`, `BlueTabs.master`, `BlueVertical.master`, `default.master`, and `OrangeSingleLevel.master`. Each of these Master Pages can be used to change the look and feel of the site. They can be applied directly to the portal using the browser. A designer or administrator of a publishing site can navigate to Site Settings ⇨ Master Page (under the Look and Feel section) to get to the Site Master Page settings page (see Figure 8-3), which allows assignment of a Master Page to a site.

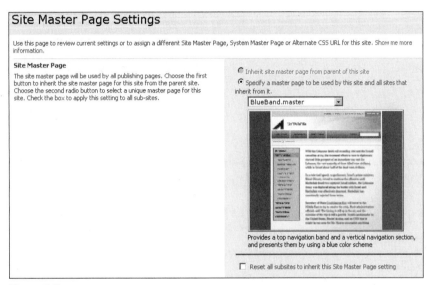

Figure 8-3

The `default.master` Master Page contains 32 content placeholders that are used by content and layout pages throughout SharePoint sites. The other eight Master Pages contain 21 of the total 32 content placeholders, plus an extra one (OSSConsole), as shown in the following list:

PlaceHolderAdditionalPageHead	PlaceHolderPageDescription
PlaceHolderBodyAreaClass	PlaceHolderPageImage
PlaceHolderBodyLeftBorder	PlaceHolderPageTitle
PlaceHolderBodyRightMargin	PlaceHolderPageTitleInTitleArea
PlaceHolderCalendarNavigator	PlaceHolderSearchArea
PlaceHolderLeftActions	PlaceHolderTitleAreaClass
PlaceHolderLeftNavBar	PlaceHolderTitleAreaSeparator
PlaceHolderLeftNavBarTop	PlaceHolderTitleBreadcrumb
PlaceHolderMain	PlaceHolderTitleLeftBorder
PlaceHolderMiniConsole	PlaceHolderTitleRightMargin
PlaceHolderNavSpacer	OSSConsole

The content placeholders are provided so the Content Pages that attach to the Master Page can fill in the content as needed. However, many of these content placeholders are not even rendered in these Master Pages. For example, `BlackVertical.master` contains the following code to render some select placeholders invisible:

```
<asp:panel visible="false" runat="server">
    <asp:ContentPlaceHolder ID="PlaceHolderPageImage" runat="server" />
    <asp:ContentPlaceHolder ID="PlaceHolderBodyLeftBorder" runat="server" />
    <asp:ContentPlaceHolder ID="PlaceHolderTitleLeftBorder" runat="server" />
    <asp:ContentPlaceHolder ID="PlaceHolderTitleAreaSeparator" runat="server" />
    <asp:ContentPlaceHolder ID="OSSConsole" runat="server" />
    <asp:ContentPlaceHolder ID="PlaceHolderTitleRightMargin" runat="server" />
    <asp:ContentPlaceHolder id="PlaceHolderPageDescription" runat ="server" />
    <asp:ContentPlaceHolder id="PlaceHolderBodyAreaClass" runat ="server" />
    <asp:ContentPlaceHolder id="PlaceHolderTitleAreaClass" runat ="server" />
    <asp:ContentPlaceHolder id="PlaceHolderBodyRightMargin" runat="server" />
</asp:panel>
```

Some placeholders are a necessity for the Master Page to remain operational and not be deemed malformed by the ASP.NET engine. (Chapter 5 showed you a Master Page that contains the minimal number of placeholders necessary for any Master Page to remain functional.)

Creating a Master Page for a Publishing Site Using SharePoint Designer

You are by no means limited to the Master Pages that come with SharePoint Server. New Master Pages can be easily created by a designer or a developer. A designer will typically choose SharePoint Designer to create the new Master Pages, while a developer might lean more toward Visual Studio for Master Page creation. Both are viable solutions, and both have their pros and cons.

Using Visual Studio, Master Page files can be created and packaged as Features and Solution Packages. Deploying Master Pages in this manner provides for easy source control and portability of the files, because all the files are created physically on the web server. However, this method calls for a developer with programming knowledge and familiarity with Visual Studio to create and then maintain the Master Pages.

When a Master Page is created using SharePoint Designer, it ends up directly in the content database and is exposed through the Master Page gallery. It is much easier to create Master Pages using SharePoint Designer, and no programming knowledge is required to create or maintain the pages. However, because the file is created in the database, there is no physical file available on the web server to route through the development, integration testing, staging, and production cycle. On the other hand, the Master Page gallery is configured to create versions of all files, so subsequent versions of the Master Page will not overwrite the original version, which will still be available if it needs to be restored.

This section deals only with creating Master Pages using SharePoint Designer. For a good example of how Master Pages can be created using Visual Studio, check out Andrew Connell's book *Professional SharePoint 2007 Web Content Management Development* (Wrox).

Create the .master File

A publishing site is created by using the publishing site template when provisioning a new site using the browser. Once you have a publishing site at your disposal, start SharePoint Designer and then select File ⇨ Open Site. In the Open Site dialog box, enter the address to your site, and then click the Open button. The folder structure for the site should appear. To create a new Master Page using SharePoint Designer, first select File ⇨ New. The New dialog box appears. Select Master Page, as shown in Figure 8-4, and then click OK to create the Master Page.

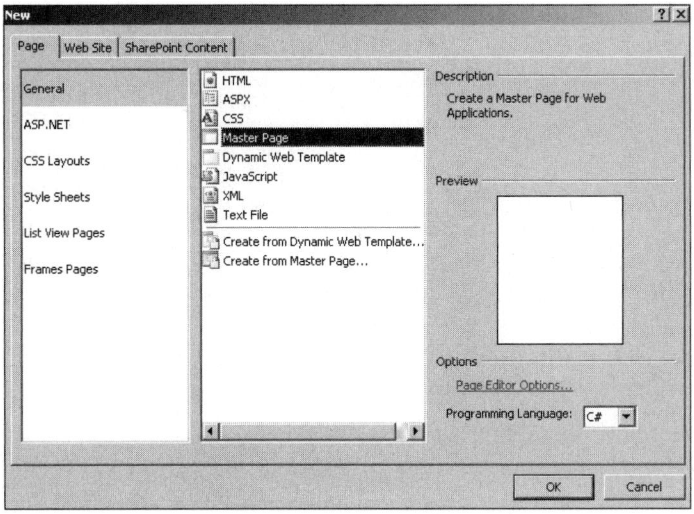

Figure 8-4

Exploring the Code view of this Master Page, notice that only a couple of content placeholders have been placed in it, and no other tags exist yet.

```
<%@ Master Language="C#" %>
<html dir="ltr">

<head runat="server">
<meta http-equiv="Content-Type" content="text/html; charset=utf-8">
<title>Untitled 1</title>
<asp:ContentPlaceHolder id="head" runat="server">
</asp:ContentPlaceHolder>
</head>

<body>
<form id="form1" runat="server">
    <asp:ContentPlaceHolder id="ContentPlaceHolder1" runat="server">
    </asp:ContentPlaceHolder>
</form>
</body>

</html>
```

This Master Page now must be saved in the Master Page gallery, where all other Master Pages reside. Select File ⇨ Save, and then browse to the _catalogs\masterpage folder. Name the file minimal.master and then click Save. At this point, a SharePoint Designer dialog box appears, stating that SharePoint Services recommends including a SharePoint Web Part Manager on all Master Pages and asking if you want it to be automatically included. Treat this as more than a recommendation. The SharePoint Web Part Manager manages all Web Part controls, functionality, and events that occur on a web page, and is thus a necessity for all Master Pages. Click the Yes button to include it.

Doing that adds some code to the Master Page. The top of the page gets the following Register directive:

```
<%@ Register tagprefix="WebPartPages" namespace="Microsoft.SharePoint.WebPartPages"
assembly="Microsoft.SharePoint, Version=12.0.0.0, Culture=neutral,
PublicKeyToken=71e9bce111e9429c" %>
```

And the following is embedded within the form tags in the body section:

```
<WebPartPages:SPWebPartManager runat="server" id="WebPartManager">
</WebPartPages:SPWebPartManager>
```

A second dialog box appears, stating that SharePoint Services requires including a SharePoint Robots Meta Tag control on Master Pages to secure search indexing on web sites that use fine-grained permissions, and asking if you want it to automatically include this control. This is a pretty straightforward scenario. It is a required control and must be included on all Master Pages, so click Yes to include it.

Now the top of the page gets the following Register directive:

```
<%@ Register tagprefix="SharePoint" namespace="Microsoft.SharePoint.WebControls"
assembly="Microsoft.SharePoint, Version=12.0.0.0, Culture=neutral,
PublicKeyToken=71e9bce111e9429c" %>
```

And the following is embedded within the head section of the page:

```
<SharePoint:RobotsMetaTag runat="server"></SharePoint:RobotsMetaTag>
```

Finally, SharePoint Designer saves the new Master Page in the Master Page gallery. At this point, you can start building the Master Page by adding the additional necessary SharePoint server controls and content placeholders that are required for the Master Page to be considered well-formed by SharePoint. Which controls and placeholders are required, you ask? Well, that's not an easy question to answer, because there are a lot of them. A sample Master Page named mossminimum.master is provided in this chapter's download folder. It has the minimum amount of code required for the Master Page to be rendered. Style sheets and formatting code have been stripped, and most content placeholders have been hidden. Do not use it as is, unless you want your site to look like the portal home page shown in Figure 8-5.

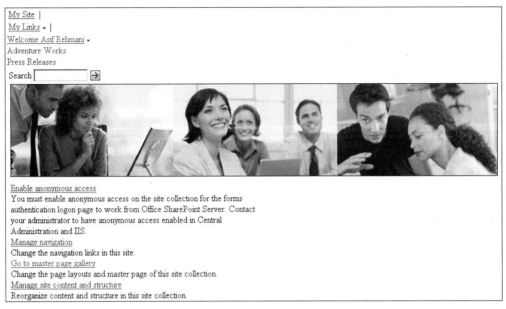

Figure 8-5

You can use the `mossminimum.master` Master Page as a starting point to build out your own page structure and then use your own style sheets to apply your unique brand to the site.

Master Page Corruption

Aside from all the cool things that SharePoint Designer can do, there is an uncool thing that it does, of which you should be aware. If you download `mossminimum.master`, then open it directly from the file system, some key symbols that are required for the page to work are stripped off. The Register tag on top of the file that has the reference `~/_controltemplates` is changed automatically to `_controltemplates`. The tilde and the front slash (`~/`) are stripped off. If this Master Page is now used in SharePoint, you receive a File Not Found error. This corruption issue was briefly mentioned back in chapter 3. The workaround for this is to first upload the `mossminimum.master` file to the Master Page Gallery then point SharePoint Designer to open the file from that gallery.

Building the Master Page's Preview Image

A preview image is provided for each Master Page. The images reside in the Master Page Gallery\en-us\Preview Images folder. Each image is 216 px × 160 px and is displayed to a designer when a Master Page selection is being made at the following page: Site Settings ⇨ Modify All Site Settings ⇨ Master Page. Any image utility (for example, Microsoft Paint, which comes with the Windows operating system) can be used to create the preview image. Crop out the menus, toolbars, and status bar in the browser to show as much of the actual page as possible. The new preview image can then be uploaded to the Preview Images folder where the other images reside.

Unfortunately, the functionality to associate a preview image with a Master Page file is not provided in SharePoint Designer. Navigate to the Master Page gallery to accomplish this task. Hover over your Master Page file and click the downward arrow that appears to open its context menu. Select Edit Properties from the menu options. In the Preview Image section of the next screen, enter the web address of the location of your image file in the Preview Image folder, as shown in Figure 8-6, and then click OK.

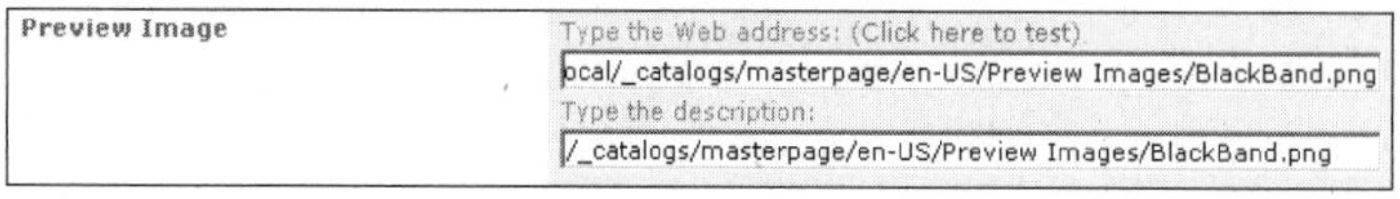

Figure 8-6

Publishing the Master Page

A Master Page in the production site's Master Page gallery needs to be checked in, published, and approved. Master Pages are attached to Content Pages, so even when a Content Page is in published format, the viewer of the site receives an error if the Master Page associated with the Content Page is not checked in.

In SharePoint Designer, right-click on your Master Page and click Check In. The Check In window (see Figure 8-7) appears.

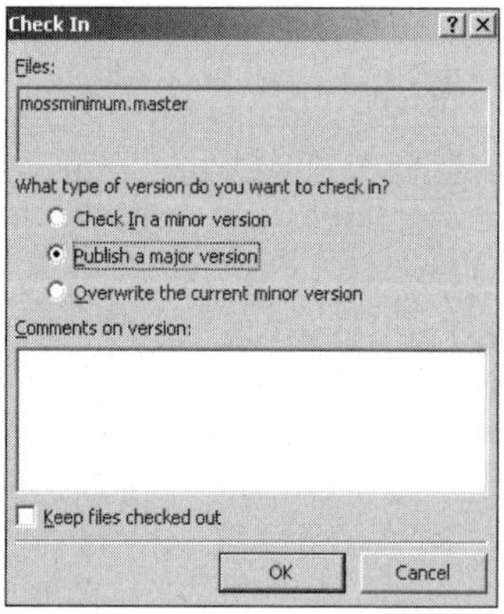

Figure 8-7

Choose Publish A Major Version, and then click OK. A dialog box appears, stating that content approval is needed for this item and asking if you want to modify its approval status. Clicking Yes in this dialog box takes you to the Master Page Gallery's My Submissions view, as shown in Figure 8-8.

Figure 8-8

Hover over the item that you want to approve, and click on the downward arrow that appears, to open its context menu. Select Approve/reject from the menu options. On the next screen, choose the Approved option, and then click OK. The Master Page's status should now show as Approved.

Apply the Master Page to the Site

Master Pages are applied at the site level. A Default Master Page applied to the site can be used by all pages on the site. A Custom Master Page can also be declared at the site level.

It is a common misconception that the Default Master Page property must always be set to the `default.master` *page. In fact, the Default Master Page property can be pointed to any existing or newly created Master Page.*

By default, all Content Pages in a WSS site are configured to use the Default Master Page. On the other hand, all of the page layouts in a publishing site are set to use the Custom Master Page property. A Master Page can be designated as the Default or Custom Master Page for the site by right-clicking on the page in SharePoint Designer and choosing the proper option, as shown in Figure 8-9.

Figure 8-9

A Master Page can also be declared a default or Custom Master Page through the browser. Navigate to Site Settings ⇨ Modify All Site Settings ⇨ Master Page. You'll see sections — Site Master Page and System Master Page — on the Site Master Page settings page, as shown in Figure 8-10.

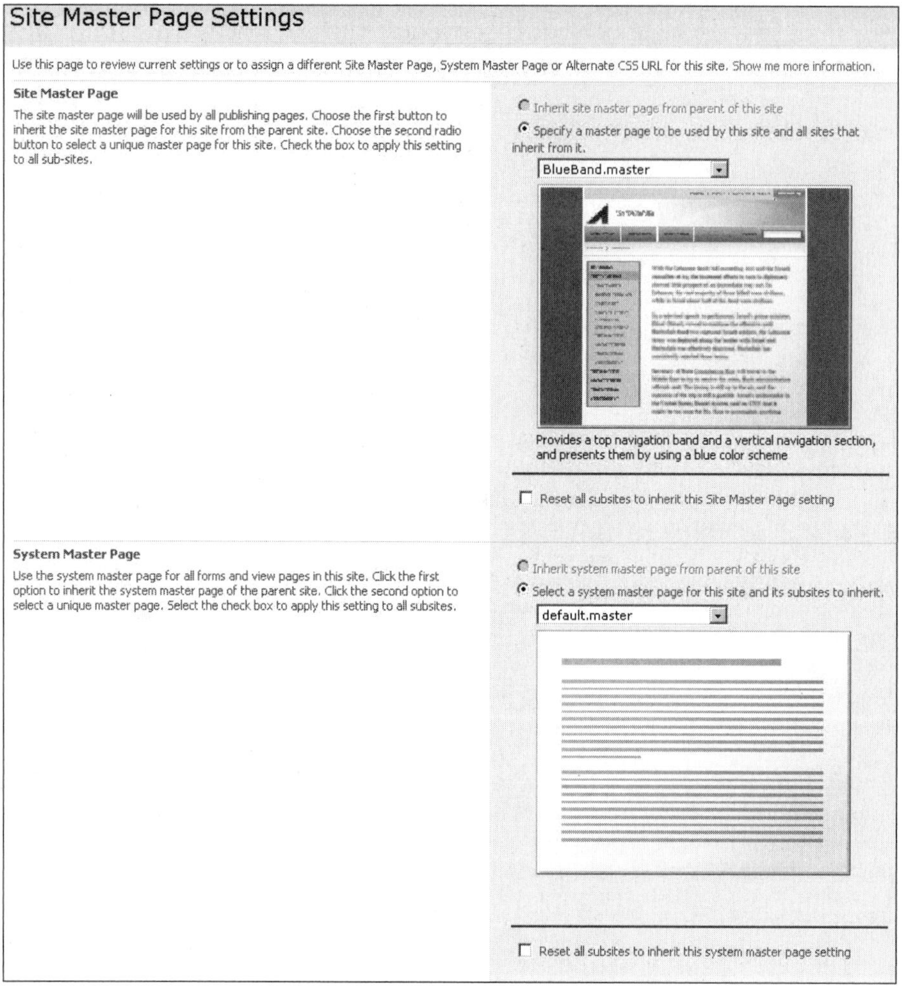

Figure 8-10

All of the Master Pages in the Master Page gallery of this site collection are listed in the dropdown lists of the Site and System Master Page sections. Selecting a Master Page in the Site Master Page section is equivalent to designating it as a Custom Master Page through SharePoint Designer. All publishing pages that exist in the Pages library of the site are affected by this selection. Vice versa, selecting a Master Page in the System Master Page section is equivalent to designating it as a Default Master Page through SharePoint Designer. All forms and view pages in the site are affected by this selection.

The Site Master Page settings page has a section at the bottom of the page labeled Alternate CSS URL. The address to a custom CSS file stored either in the content database or the web server can be placed in this section. This style sheet is applied last on the site, which means that any of the styles applied earlier to the site can be overridden in this file.

Lay Out Your Page Layout

The Content Pages in a publishing site reside in the Pages library. Each page uses a preconfigured page layout for its visual rendering. Page layout pages reside in the Master Pages gallery and are sometimes referred to as page templates, since that is their function — to serve as templates of publishing pages being created by the content authors of the site.

Page Layouts That Come with SharePoint Server

Several page layout pages are provided, depending on which site template is chosen to create the site. All of them reside in the Master Page gallery (Site Settings ⇨ Modify All Site Settings ⇨ Master Pages and Page Layouts) with the extension `.aspx,` as shown in Figure 8-11.

Figure 8-11

By default, a content author can use any of the available page layouts to create a new page in the Pages library. However, a site collection designer or administrator can decide to make available only certain page layouts to the content creators. That's done using the Page Layout and Site Template Settings page, which can be accessed through Site Settings ⇨ Page Layouts and Site Templates under the Look and Feel section. Figure 8-12 shows a snapshot of this page.

Page Layouts

Specify the page layouts preferred for new pages in this site.

○ Pages inherit preferred layouts from parent site
○ Pages in this site can use any layout
● Pages in this site can only use the following layouts:

(Article Page) Article page with image on left
(Article Page) Article page with image on right
(Article Page) Article page with summary links
(Redirect Page) Redirect Page
(Welcome Page) Welcome page with table of c
(Welcome Page) Welcome splash page

Add >

< Remove

(Article Page) Article page with body only
(Welcome Page) Welcome page with summary
(Welcome Page) Blank Web Part Page

☐ Reset all subsites to inherit these preferred page layout settings

The article page with links contains an image field and summary links.

Figure 8-12

New page layouts can be created by users with Designers permissions or above. This process is detailed starting in the next section.

Content Types — At the Heart of It All

A publishing page layout provides the visual representation of the content on the page. However, the type of content that can be contained in the page layout is defined by the underlying content type.

Content types are a new feature introduced with SharePoint 2007. Simply put, they can manage the settings and behavior of a document or item type in a centralized and reusable manner. A detailed introduction to content types can be found at `http://msdn.microsoft.com/en-us/library/ms472236.aspx`. In the context of publishing sites, content types are a set of columns and settings that define the structure of a content-centric page. They are defined at a site level and reside in the Content Type gallery of a site. Content types defined at a site are inherited by all of its subsites. So if a content type is meant to be used throughout the site collection, it should be defined at the parent site of a site collection.

Each page layout is paired with one content type. Conversely, a content type can be used for multiple page layouts. There is a one-to-many relationship between content types and page layouts.

The Master Page gallery shows which content type a page layout is associated with (see Figure 8-13).

Type	Name	Modified	Modified By	Checked Out To	Approval Status	Contact	Hidden Page	Associated Content Type
📁	Editing Menu	8/8/2008 2:42 PM	HOME\Administrator		Approved			
📁	en-us	8/8/2008 2:42 PM	HOME\Administrator		Approved			
📁	Preview Images	8/8/2008 2:42 PM	HOME\Administrator		Approved			
📄	ArticleLeft.aspx	8/8/2008 2:43 PM	HOME\Administrator		Approved			Article Page
📄	ArticleLinks.aspx	8/8/2008 2:59 PM	HOME\Administrator	Asif Rehmani	Draft			Article Page
📄	ArticleRight.aspx	8/8/2008 2:43 PM	HOME\Administrator		Approved			Article Page
📄	BlackBand.master	8/9/2008 11:33 AM	HOME\Administrator	Asif Rehmani	Draft			
📄	BlackSingleLevel.master	8/8/2008 2:43 PM	HOME\Administrator		Approved			
📄	BlackVertical.master	8/8/2008 2:43 PM	HOME\Administrator		Approved			
📄	BlankWebPartPage.aspx	8/8/2008 2:43 PM	HOME\Administrator		Approved			Welcome Page
📄	BlueBand.master	8/8/2008 2:43 PM	HOME\Administrator		Approved			
📄	BlueGlassBand.master	8/8/2008 4:11 PM	HOME\Administrator	Asif Rehmani	Draft			
📄	BlueTabs.master	8/8/2008 2:43 PM	HOME\Administrator		Approved			
📄	BlueVertical.master	8/8/2008 2:43 PM	HOME\Administrator		Approved			
📄	default.master	8/8/2008 2:42 PM	HOME\Administrator		Approved			
📄	mossminimum.master	8/9/2008 11:30 AM	Asif Rehmani	Asif Rehmani	Draft			
📄	OrangeSingleLevel.master	8/8/2008 2:43 PM	HOME\Administrator		Approved			
📄	PageFromDocLayout.aspx	8/8/2008 2:43 PM	HOME\Administrator		Approved			Article Page

Figure 8-13

In the figure, the Article Page content type is associated with multiple page layouts. Each of these page layouts is restricted to the rules and settings for the type of content it can contain, as defined in the Article Page content type.

As mentioned earlier, content types do not control the look and feel aspects of the page. When a page layout is created, it must be based on a particular content type. The designer then lays out the page presentation using the fields exposed by the content type.

Creating a Content Type for a Page Layout

Content types can be created by anyone with Designers permission or higher on the site, using just the browser. Navigate to the Site Content Type gallery by selecting Site Settings ➪ Modify All Site Settings ➪ Site Content Types in the Galleries section. This gallery shows all the available content types by default. For the purpose of this chapter, focus only on the Page Layout Content Types and the Publishing Content Types, as shown in Figure 8-14.

Page Layout Content Types		
Article Page	Page	Adventure Works
Redirect Page	Page	Adventure Works
Welcome Page	Page	Adventure Works
Publishing Content Types		
Page	System Page	Adventure Works
Page Layout	System Page Layout	Adventure Works
Publishing Master Page	System Master Page	Adventure Works

Parent Content Type

Figure 8-14

When a content type is being created to be used in a page layout, it must be based upon the Page parent content type that resides in the Publishing Content Types group. As shown in Figure 8-14, the Article Page, Redirect Page, and Welcome Page content types all are based on the Page parent content type.

Create a new content type using the Create link located at the top of the Site Content Type gallery page. Clicking this link opens the New Site Content Type page, where you can define the following properties about the content type: Name, Description, Parent Content Type, Content Type Group. For example, create a new content type called Product Specification, base it on the Page Parent Content Type, and save it in the Page Layout Content Types group, as Figure 8-15 shows.

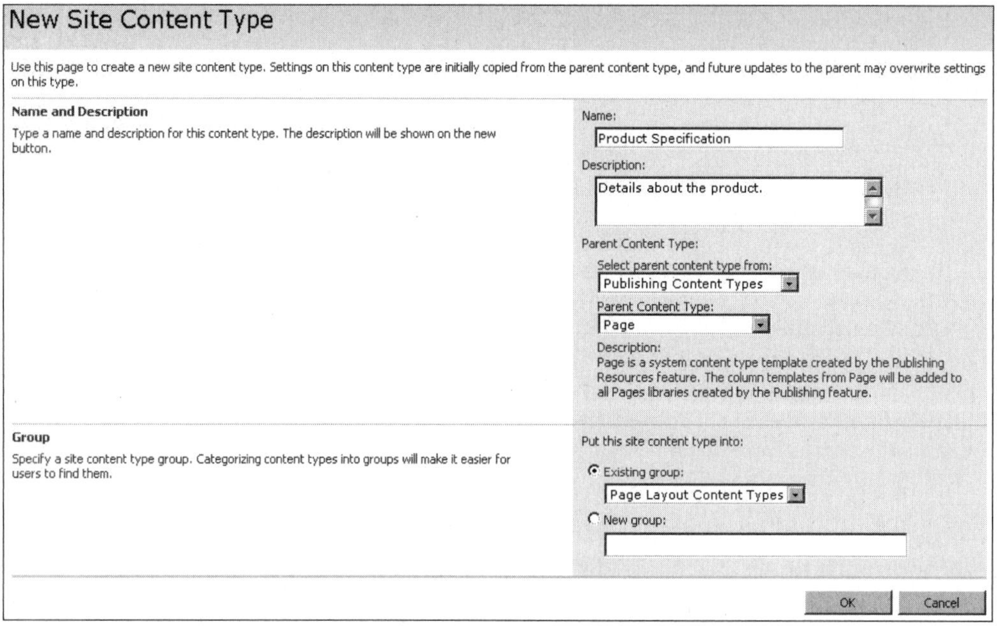

New Site Content Type

Use this page to create a new site content type. Settings on this content type are initially copied from the parent content type, and future updates to the parent may overwrite settings on this type.

Name and Description

Type a name and description for this content type. The description will be shown on the new button.

Name:

Product Specification

Description:

Details about the product.

Parent Content Type:

Select parent content type from:

Publishing Content Types

Parent Content Type:

Page

Description:
Page is a system content type template created by the Publishing Resources feature. The column templates from Page will be added to all Pages libraries created by the Publishing feature.

Group

Specify a site content type group. Categorizing content types into groups will make it easier for users to find them.

Put this site content type into:

⊙ Existing group:

Page Layout Content Types

○ New group:

OK   Cancel

Figure 8-15

Then click OK. The newly created content type's settings page opens. This settings page is where you declare the associated document/item type, set up a workflow, create an information management policy, define columns, and more. The only thing of interest in this scenario is to set up columns for this content type. Columns declared in a content type are used as fields in the associated page layout. The columns referenced here are of a special type called site columns. Site columns (also sometimes referred to as column templates) are saved definitions of columns that can be reused in multiple content types, lists, or libraries. The only caveat is that the site column being used in a content type must be defined within the same site or inherited from a parent site. More information about site columns is available at http://msdn.microsoft.com/en-us/library/ms450825.aspx.

Notice that there are already several site columns (see Figure 8-16) present for the Product Specification content type. Because Product Specification content type is based on the Page content type, it inherits all of the site columns from the Page content type.

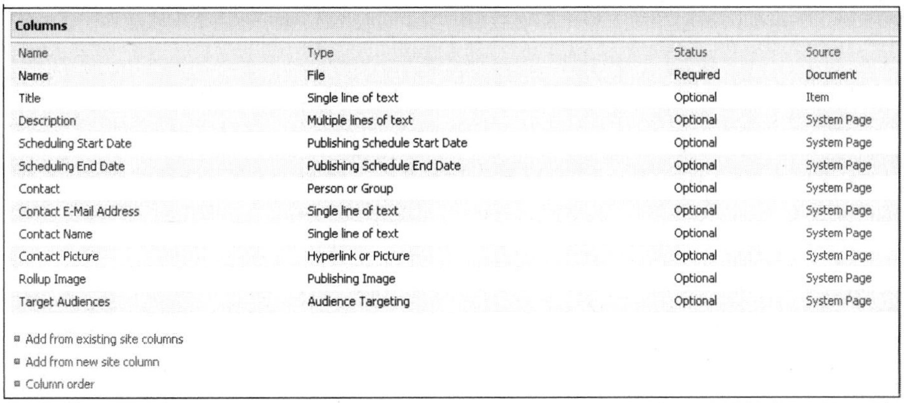

Columns

Name	Type	Status	Source
Name	File	Required	Document
Title	Single line of text	Optional	Item
Description	Multiple lines of text	Optional	System Page
Scheduling Start Date	Publishing Schedule Start Date	Optional	System Page
Scheduling End Date	Publishing Schedule End Date	Optional	System Page
Contact	Person or Group	Optional	System Page
Contact E-Mail Address	Single line of text	Optional	System Page
Contact Name	Single line of text	Optional	System Page
Contact Picture	Hyperlink or Picture	Optional	System Page
Rollup Image	Publishing Image	Optional	System Page
Target Audiences	Audience Targeting	Optional	System Page

- Add from existing site columns
- Add from new site column
- Column order

Figure 8-16

For the Product Specification content type, define a new site column by clicking the Add from new site column link near the bottom of the page (this link is visible in Figure 8-16), naming the column, selecting its type, and then clicking OK. Do that for three new columns, using the following information:

New Column	Name	Type
1	Product Image	Image with formatting and constraints for publishing.
2	Product Launch Date	Date and Time.
3	Product Summary	Full HTML content with formatting and constraints for publishing.

The content type is now ready to be consumed by a page layout.

Create Page Layouts Using SharePoint Designer

Page layouts can be created using the browser, SharePoint Designer, or Visual Studio. Using Visual Studio, the page layout is created as a Feature that stores the page layout files on the web server. (Connell's *Professional SharePoint 2007 Web Content Management Development* has a good explanation about how to accomplish this.) Creating the page layout using the browser or SharePoint Designer places it in the Master Page gallery of a site collection that stores all its content in the content database. To create a page layout using a browser, navigate to the Master Page gallery, click the New dropdown, and select the page layout content type. That brings up the screen shown in Figure 8-17.

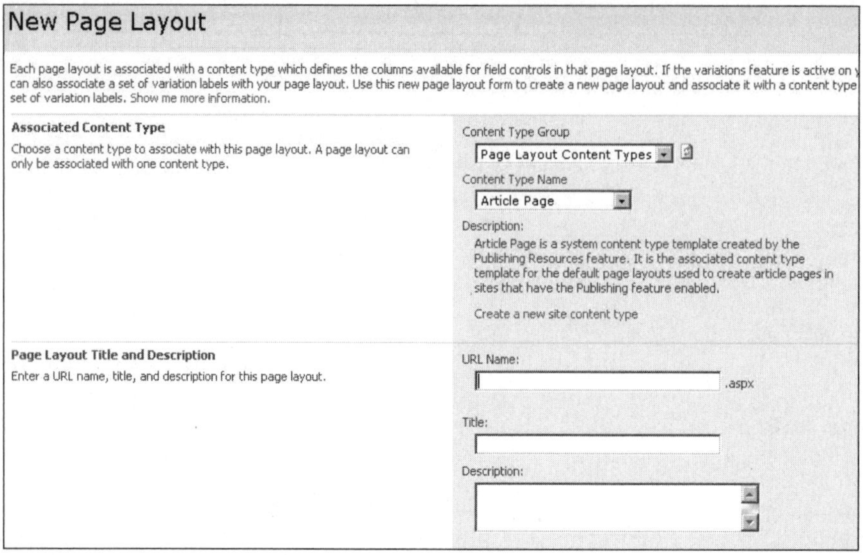

New Page Layout

Each page layout is associated with a content type which defines the columns available for field controls in that page layout. If the variations feature is active on y can also associate a set of variation labels with your page layout. Use this new page layout form to create a new page layout and associate it with a content type set of variation labels. Show me more information.

Associated Content Type

Choose a content type to associate with this page layout. A page layout can only be associated with one content type.

Content Type Group

Page Layout Content Types

Content Type Name

Article Page

Description:

Article Page is a system content type template created by the Publishing Resources feature. It is the associated content type template for the default page layouts used to create article pages in sites that have the Publishing feature enabled.

Create a new site content type

Page Layout Title and Description

Enter a URL name, title, and description for this page layout.

URL Name:

.aspx

Title:

Description:

Figure 8-17

However, this method only facilitates the creation of a layout page based on a content type, not the design of it. You still need to open SharePoint Designer to lay out the fields on the page. This section walks you through the steps of creating and configuring/designing the page layout in SharePoint Designer.

In SharePoint Designer, open the site in which the content type was created in the previous section. Select File ➪ New. On the New dialog box's SharePoint Content tab, select SharePoint Publishing and then Page Layout. In the Options section on the right, set the following values:

Option	Value
Content Type Group	Page Layout Content Types.
Content Type Name	Product Specification.
URL Name	ProductSpecLeft.
Title	Product Specification with image on left.

Click OK. All of these settings are shown in Figure 8-18.

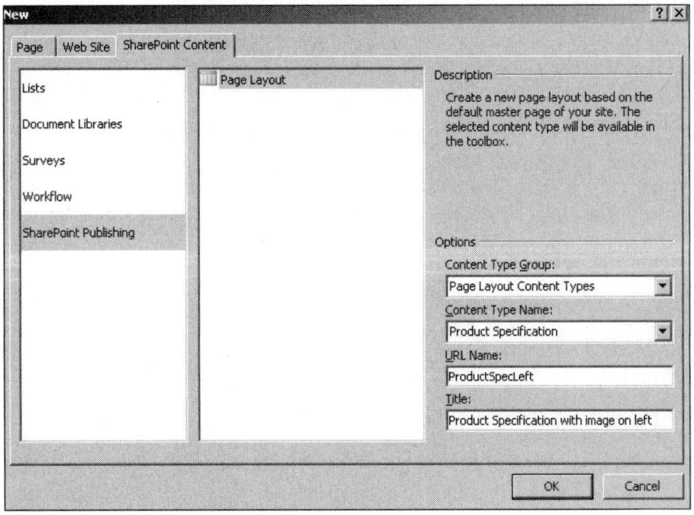

Figure 8-18

The new layout page, `ProductSpecLeft.aspx`, is displayed on the screen. It has been created as a draft file in the Master Page gallery. Open the Split view of the page (see Figure 8-19) in SharePoint Designer. Notice that there are many design elements present in the Design view part of the pane, but only a few lines of code appear in the Code view part of the page. The reason is that the majority of this page structure is coming from the attached Master Page (the attached Master Page — `BlueBand.master` in this case — is shown on the top right of the Split View screen).

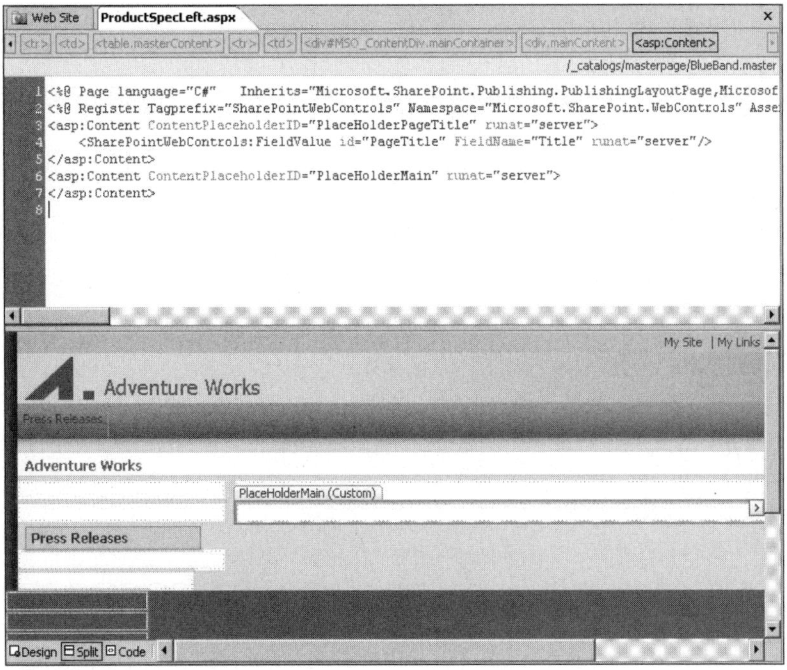

Figure 8-19

A couple of ContentPlaceHolderID sections are present in the Code view; they hook back into the matching ContentPlaceHolder tags in the Master Page. The first section, PlaceHolderPageTitle, encompasses the field control PageTitle. The content of this control will come from the name of the publishing page that will eventually be built based on this page layout. The second section, PlaceHolderMain, is empty to start with. This is the body of the page that can be designed to contain any of the available field controls or Web Parts (both of these are discussed in the next section). Additional ContentPlaceHolderID sections can also be placed anywhere in this page layout. Keep in mind that each content placeholder ID section declared here must match a content placeholder section in the attached Master Page (for a list of content placeholders, refer to the Master Page section of this chapter).

Now comes the time to lay out the controls on this page. Two types of controls can be placed on a Page Layout: field controls and Web Parts. The next two sections explain each of them in detail.

Field Controls

Field controls are content areas that correspond to columns defined in the underlying content type of the page layout. Unlike Web Parts in a Web Part Zone, these controls cannot be moved by a person editing the page using the browser. Field controls are great for putting content in a fixed location on the page to create a consistent look and feel. Also, the content in a field control is versioned along with the page.

To explore which field controls are available for this page layout, select Task Panes ⇨ Toolbox. The Toolbox task pane should now be visible. Scroll all the way down to the SharePoint Controls section. Two sections of fields — Page Fields and Content Fields — are available, as shown in Figure 8-20.

Figure 8-20

The Page Fields section exposes all of the fields from the Page parent content type. The Content Fields section exposes the fields defined in the Product Specification content type created earlier in this chapter. Any of these fields can be dragged onto the page layout. However, table, div, or span tags are generally used first to create the structural layout of the page before the controls are placed within it.

In Design view, click the PlaceHolderMain content placeholder ID, and then select Table ⇨ Insert Table. Accept the defaults and click OK. Now you have a table that you can style and populate with field controls. Select Task Panes ⇨ Apply Styles. The Apply Styles task pane shows all of the styles from all linked style sheets. You can apply any of these styles by clicking on it. Additional style sheets can also be linked from this layout page. In the Folder List task pane, navigate to Style Library ⇨ en-us ⇨ Core Styles. Drag PageLayouts.css from the Core Styles folder to the PlaceHolderMain section, as shown in Figure 8-21.

Figure 8-21

Switch to Code view of the ProductSpecLeft.aspx page layout and notice that the following piece of code has been placed at the end of the file to make the link to the style sheet:

```
<asp:Content id="Content1" runat="server"
contentplaceholderid="PlaceHolderAdditionalPageHead">
<link rel="stylesheet" type="text/css" href="../../Style%20Library/en-us/
Core%20Styles/PageLayouts.css">
</asp:Content>
```

The matching PlaceHolderAdditionalPageHead content placeholder appears in the Master Page. It is applied after the core and any Theme-related style sheets. Any styles placed in this way override any previous declaration instances of those styles (see chapter 6 for further discussion of cascading styles).

In the Apply Styles task pane, the PageLayouts.css section now appears with all the defined styles displayed underneath it, as shown in Figure 8-22.

Figure 8-22

In the Code view of the page, place the cursor in the `<table>` tag and click on the `.floatLeft` style under `PageLayouts.css` to apply that style to the table. The final table tag should look like this:

```
<table style="width: 100%" class="floatleft">
```

Switch to Design view. Now you can place field controls in the table. Click and drag the Product Image field control, found under Content Fields in the Toolbox task pane, to the first cell of the table. To view properties of this control, select Task Panes ➪ Tag Properties. The Tag Properties task pane displays all the properties (such as `FieldName` and `ID`) of the Product Image field control (see Figure 8-23). 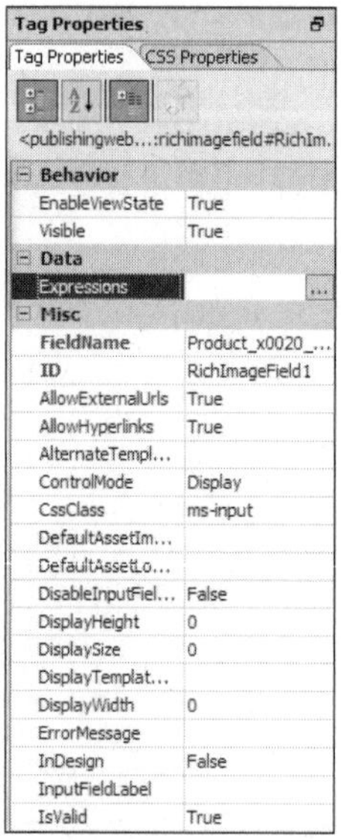

Figure 8-23

Click and drag the Product Launch Date field control to the second column of the table. Subsequently, place the Product Summary field control in the first cell of the second row. Notice the Tag Properties task pane is now showing the properties of this field control. Set `AllowImages` and `AllowTables` properties to `False`, as shown in Figure 8-24. Now images and tables cannot be placed in the product summary field control. An example of this is shown in the next section, when a publishing page is created using this page layout.

Figure 8-24

Web Part Zones

Web Parts and Web Part Zones can be added to the page layout as well. Unlike field controls, Web Part Zones allow the user to move around the Web Parts within the zone or to a different zone. The content of the Web Part is not versioned. For example, if you placed a Content Editor Web Part in a Web Part Zone with some text in it, that text would not be versioned along with the page.

Click on the second row of the second column in the table (the same table you were working with in the previous section). Now select Insert ⇨ SharePoint Controls ⇨ Web Part Zone. A Web Part Zone is added to the table cell. Double-click on the Web Part Zone. The Web Part Zone properties dialog appears. You can use this dialog box to configure Web Part Zone properties such as its title, the orientation of Web Parts that will reside in this zone, and allowing or denying the user to move Web Parts around within the zone. For this example, just change the title to `Bottom Zone`, as shown in Figure 8-25, and click OK.

Figure 8-25

Building the Page Layout's Preview Image

A preview image is provided for each of the page layouts. The images reside in the Master Page gallery \en-us\Preview Images folder. Each image is 216 px × 160 px in dimension and is displayed to a content manager when a new publishing page is being created. The image is usually just a graphical rendering of the components on the page layout. When you create a new preview image, you can upload it to the same Preview Images folder.

The functionality to associate a preview image with a page layout file is not provided in SharePoint Designer. Just like associating a preview image for a Master Page (described earlier in the chapter), the association of a preview page for a page layout has to be done using the browser. Use your browser to navigate to the Master Page gallery. Hover over the `ProductSpecLeft.aspx` file and click on the downward arrow that appears, to open its context menu. Select Edit Properties from the menu options. In the Preview Image section of the next screen, enter the web address to the location of your image file in the Preview Images folder, as shown in Figure 8-26, and then click OK. (In this example, an existing image, `ArticleLeft.png`, located at: `http://<YourServerName>/_catalogs/masterpage/en-us/Preview%20Images/ArticleLeft.png` is being used.)

Preview Image	Type the Web address: (Click here to test)
	/_catalogs/masterpage/en-us/Preview%20Images/ArticleLeft.png
	Type the description:
	/_catalogs/masterpage/en-us/Preview%20Images/ArticleLeft.png

Figure 8-26

Save the Layout Page

The `ProductSpecLeft.aspx` page layout now has to be checked in and published so content authors can create publishing pages based on the layout. In SharePoint Designer, navigate to `ProductSpecLeft.aspx` under _catalogs/masterpage. The file should have a green check mark beside it, signifying that it's currently checked out. Right-click on the file and select Check In from the resulting context menu. The Check In dialog box appears. Select the radio button for Publish A Major Version, and then click OK. A dialog box appears, stating that content approval is needed for this item and asking if you want to modify its approval status. Click Yes, and the Master Page Gallery's My Submissions view opens, as shown in Figure 8-27.

Adventure Works > Master Page Gallery

Master Page Gallery

Use the master page gallery to store master pages. The master pages in this gallery are available to this site and any sites underneath it.

New ▼   Upload ▼   Actions ▼   Settings ▼   View: **My submissions** ▼

Type	Name	Modified	Modified By	Approval Status	Approver Comments
Approval Status : Draft (1)					
	SampleArticleLayout	8/8/2008 2:39 PM	Asif Rehmani	Draft	
Approval Status : Pending (1)					
	ProductSpecLeft	8/21/2008 8:47 PM	Asif Rehmani	Pending	
Approval Status : Approved (1)					
	mossminimum	8/9/2008 9:18 AM	Asif Rehmani	Approved	

Figure 8-27

Hover over the item `ProductSpecLeft.aspx`, click the downward arrow that appears, to open its context menu, and select Approve/Reject from the menu options. In the next screen that appears, click the Approved option and then click OK. The layout page's status should now show as Approved.

Create Publishing Pages Based on Page Layouts

Publishing pages in publishing sites are always created based on existing page layouts and reside in the Pages library. Navigate to the Pages library by selecting Site Actions ⇨ View All Site Content ⇨ Pages. Only the `default.aspx` file is there initially, and a column called Page Layout shows that this page is based on the page layout called "Welcome page with Web Part zones." You can also configure this library to show the underlying content type on which this page layout is based. Click on the All Documents view dropdown, and then click on Modify This View. Once the view is displayed, select the checkbox for Content Type in the Columns section. Click OK at the top of the page. The Pages library now shows the Content Type column with the name of the appropriate content type, as shown in Figure 8-28.

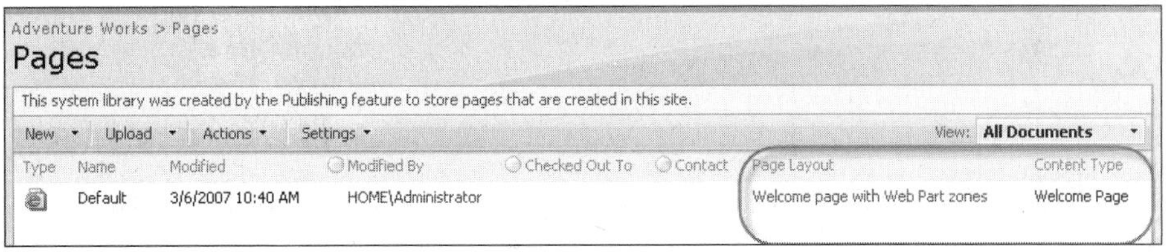

Figure 8-28

A content author can start the creation of a new publishing page by selecting Site Actions ⇨ Create Page from a publishing site or by clicking the New button while at the Pages library. The Create Page screen shows all of the available page layouts and the content type on which each page layout is based, as shown in Figure 8-29.

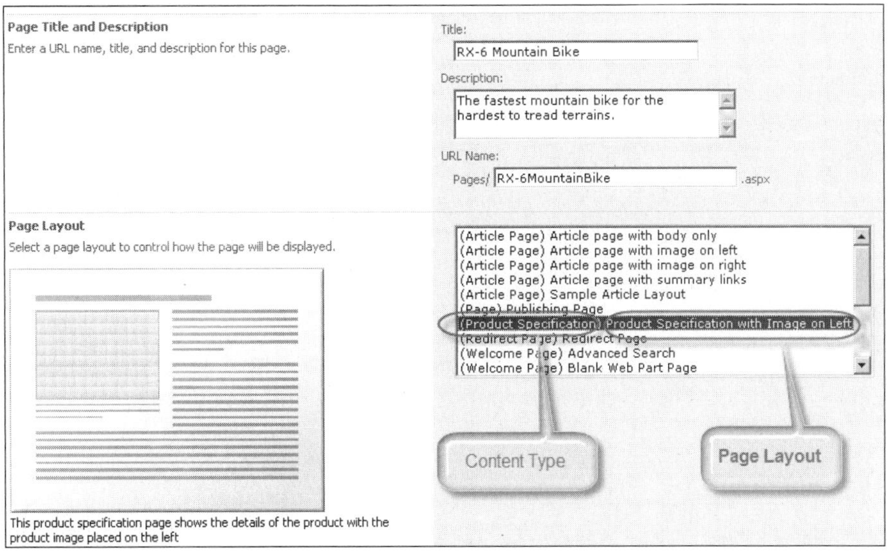

Figure 8-29

The newly created "(Product Specification) Product Specification with Image on Left" page layout appears in this list. Select that layout and fill out the Title, Description, and URL Name parameters as shown in Figure 8-29. Click the Create button at the bottom of the page to create the page. The new published page appears in edit mode, as shown in Figure 8-30.

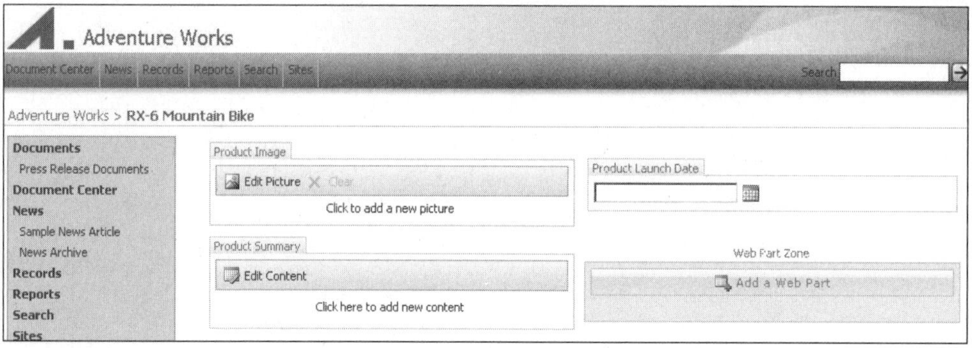

Figure 8-30

The structure of this new published page shows three field controls and one Web Part Zone. The content creator can now fill in the contents of those field controls, but cannot move the field controls around on the page. They are in an absolute fixed location designed by the page layout designer. The Web Part Zone, however, can be populated with Web Parts that can be shifted around in the Web Part Zone any way the content creator wants.

Click the Click To Add A New Picture link in the Product Image field control. The Edit Image Properties dialog opens (see Figure 8-31).

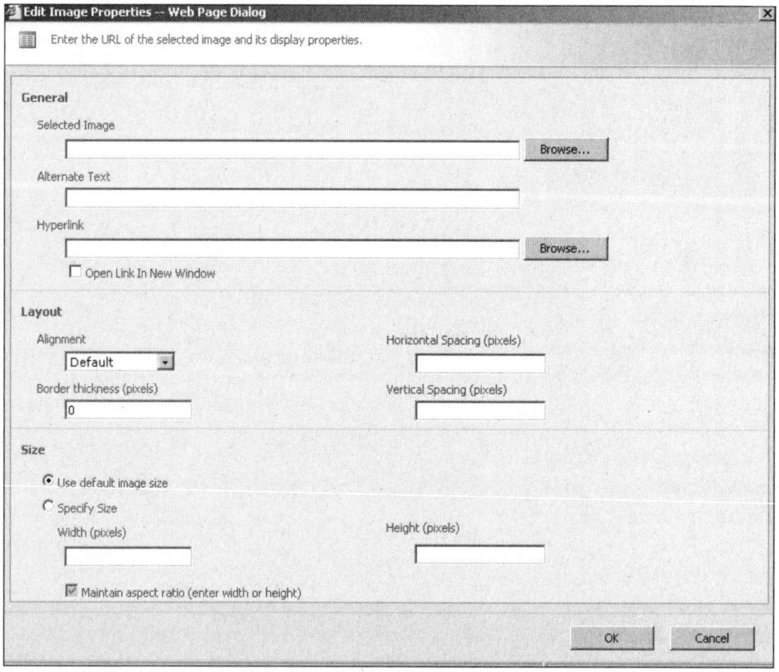

Figure 8-31

You can use this window to browse and point to any image in an existing Images library on the site. Other properties here let you do things such as declare a hyperlink that this picture can point to, define the layout of the picture, and change the dimensions. Select a picture, adjust the properties as you prefer, and click OK.

The next field control to populate is the Product Launch Date. Because it is defined as a Date and Time column in the underlying content type, it shows a calendar icon next to it. Click on the calendar icon and pick a date to populate the date in the Product Launch Date text box.

Next, click the Click Here To Add New Content link in the Product Summary field control. A rich text editing toolbar appears above the field control. The toolbar is used to format the text that's placed in the field control. Notice that the Insert Image button and the table-related buttons are all grayed out in the toolbar, as shown in Figure 8-32. That's because two properties of the Product Image field control — `AllowImages` and `AllowTables` — were both set to `False` when the page layout was designed, in the previous section of this chapter. The content author is restricted from inserting tables or images in this field control. Fill in some text in this control.

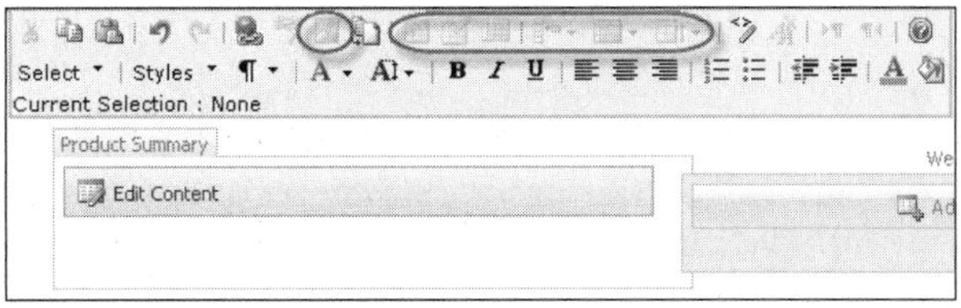

Figure 8-32

A Web Part Zone can have Web Part(s) inserted into it by clicking Add a Web Part and selecting one or more Web Parts in the resulting Add Web Parts page dialog. For this example, a Web Part that shows the Links list on the site is added. The Web Part is named Relevant Links, and a link is created within it. Once the content author is finished modifying content on this page, an approval process can be executed. The workflow can be set up to publish the page after it has been approved.

Chapter 9 delves deeply into how to create really powerful workflows using the Workflow Designer utility provided within SharePoint Designer.

Click the Publish button that appears on the top of the page. The published page should now look similar to Figure 8-33.

Figure 8-33

Decoupling a Page from a Page Layout

The structure of the earlier created published page called RX-6 Mountain Bike is dependent on and tied to the underlying page layout, which in turn is based on the content type on which the page layout is based. Double-clicking on this page to try to open it in SharePoint Designer produces the dialog box shown in Figure 8-34.

Figure 8-34

The dialog indicates that SharePoint Designer is unable to open published pages directly. It presents you with the options to open the underlying page layout in SharePoint Designer to make structural changes or to open the published page in the browser to edit its content.

There is a way to decouple this page from the page layout. Decoupling a page means that no future changes to the underlying page layout or the content type will affect this page. A person with Designers' rights or higher can right-click on the published page in SharePoint Designer and select Detach from Page Layout. A dialog box appears warning the designer that performing this step will copy the page layout's markup into the published page, and break the page's link to the layout page. Any future changes made to the page layout will not affect this published page. Click Yes to detach the page. After performing this step, the published page can be opened in SharePoint Designer, and changes to it can be made directly.

The published page keeps a reference to the page layout from which it was detached. The reference, which appears in the Page Layout column in the Pages library (see Figure 8-35), shows the absolute location of the page layout from which the page was detached. When a page is not detached, this column shows the name of the page layout.

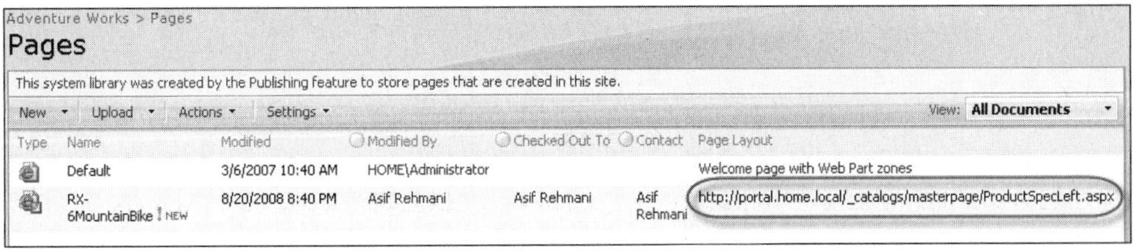

Figure 8-35

The published page can be reattached to the page layout from which it was detached (and only that page layout). This can be done in SharePoint Designer by right-clicking on the page and selecting Reattach to Page Layout. A warning dialog box pops up letting you know that doing this will delete the markup on this published page, and it will revert to the shared markup in the page layout. Click Yes to reattach the page. Performing this step changes the status of this page back to what it was before it was detached.

Summary

This chapter focused on using SharePoint's web content management facilities to build publishing pages. The combination of Master Page and page layout is used to build the layout of the final publishing page, which a content author uses to create and present content. SharePoint Designer and the browser are used to create these components.

The main takeaways from this chapter are:

❏ The addition of Content Management Server 2002 to SharePoint Products and Technologies has created a robust content management solution.

❏ Publishing sites provide web content management features in SharePoint.

❏ Master Pages can be created using SharePoint Designer. A default and a Custom Master Page can be declared for each site.

❏ Page layouts, also created using SharePoint Designer, display the body elements of a page such as field controls and Web Parts.

❏ Publishing pages are created by content authors and are always based on an existing page layout.

Part III
Applications without Programming

Building Your Own Workflows

In the preceding chapter, you saw how to use a built-in workflow to control the approval of content in a MOSS site. This chapter shows you how to use SharePoint Designer's Workflow tools to perform much more sophisticated tasks. You will learn about:

❑   How to use the Workflow Designer.

❑   Using conditions to control actions in a workflow.

❑   How to send email to users via a workflow.

❑   The difference between workflow variables and initiation parameters.

❑   Things to keep in mind when designing workflows.

Introducing the Workflow Designer

SharePoint provides many automated processes out-of-the-box, such as email alerts and a basic tri-state workflow. A tri-state workflow enables you to track the state of a process as it moves from an initiated condition to an in-process state to its concluded state (New order entered, Order Shipped, Payment Received, for instance). This is very useful, but, as its name implies, it can only handle three states and notifications about changes in those states.

Often, you might want to perform a task based on a value entered by your user, such as creating a new item in a different list, or escalating an issue after a certain amount of time has passed and an action has not been taken. While SharePoint's workflow engine is capable of such things, there is no web interface for creating these more sophisticated functions.

That's where the SharePoint Designer Workflow Designer comes in. The Workflow Designer is a tool that enables you to create a sequence of steps that need to be taken when certain conditions are met for a document or list item. The tool resembles an email inbox rules wizard, making it easy for people without a procedural programming background to produce sophisticated workflow applications.

Creating a New Workflow

There are several components in a SharePoint Designer workflow:

❑ **Start options:** Define the situations in which the workflow can be initiated.

❑ **Initiation parameters:** Information required to start the workflow.

❑ **Variables:** Temporary storage used within the workflow.

❑ **Steps:** Major groups of conditions and actions.

❑ **Conditions:** Enable you to choose whether or when to execute certain actions.

❑ **Actions:** The actual functional elements in the workflow.

You begin the process of creating a workflow by selecting File ➪ New ➪ Workflow or by selecting Workflow ➪ Blank Workflow from the SharePoint Content tab of the New dialog box. In either case, the result is the first step of the Workflow Designer wizard, shown in Figure 9-1. Here you set the workflow's name, associate it with a list or library, and define the situations in which the workflow can be started. You can also define initiation parameters and variables by clicking the buttons at the bottom of the window.

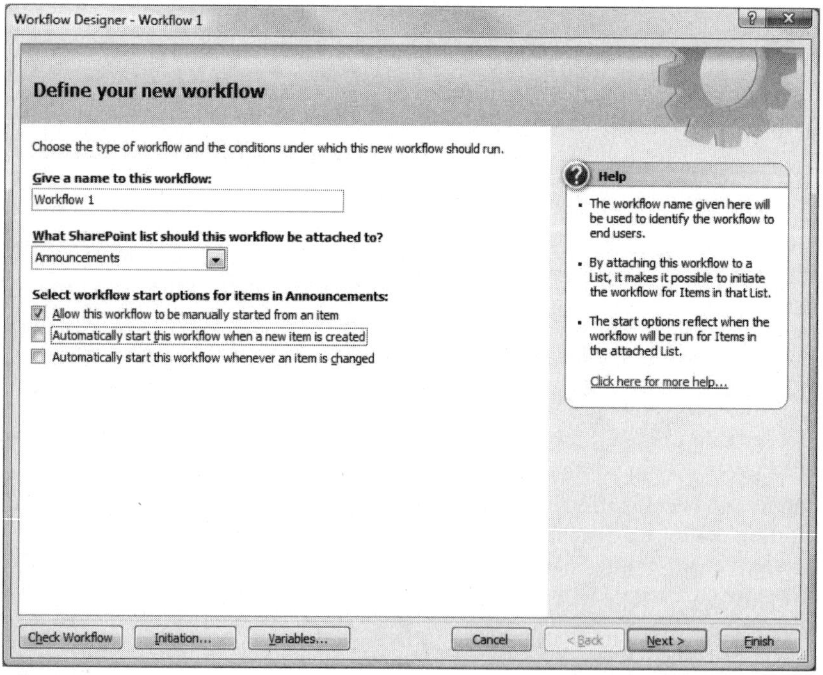

Figure 9-1

Once you have the initial information defined, click Next. The wizard displays the page where you can define the steps, conditions, and actions that execute in the workflow (Figure 9-2).

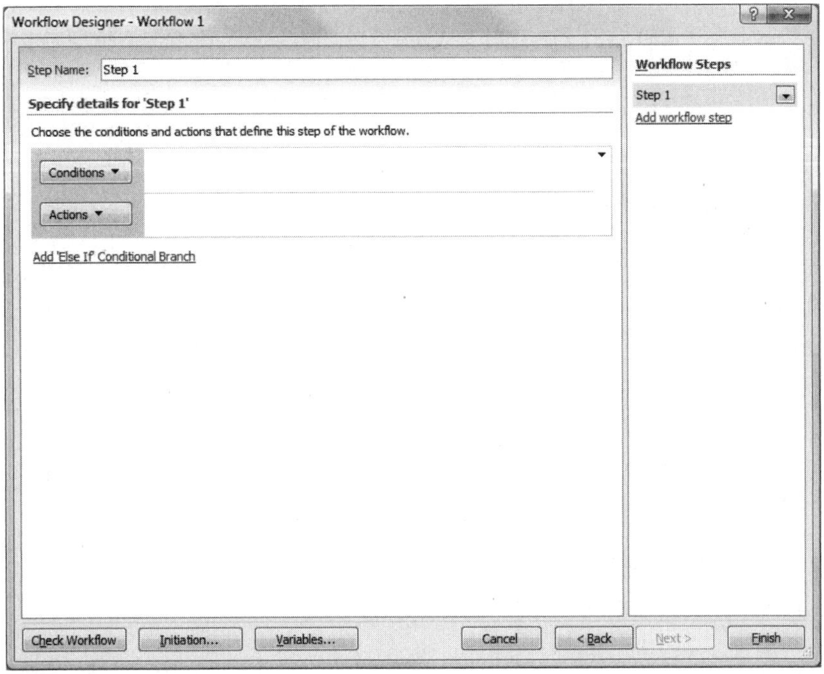

Figure 9-2

Example Workflow

The Workflow Designer is a complicated dialog, with lots of moving parts. This section introduces you to the components of the Workflow Designer by creating a simple workflow. The next section shows you how to change an existing workflow. Later in the chapter, you learn more about the elements that can go into a workflow itself.

Most Microsoft Office documents contain a title field in their metadata. A title is often much more descriptive, and therefore more useful to a user, than the filename. Document libraries, therefore, have a title field in addition to the filename. When you upload a document, any title present is promoted into the title field of the document library.

Using the title is ideal if you want to use a document library for a lookup on your site. Unfortunately, files other than Office documents may not have a Title property to promote when uploaded. In addition, not everyone fills in the title field, so even an Office title may be blank. Unless the title field is populated, the document represented will not appear in the lookup.

The proposed solution is to create a workflow that will check the title field in an uploaded document. If it is blank, the filename will be copied into the title field.

Here's what to do:

1. Start a new empty workflow by selecting File ⇨ New ⇨ Workflow.

2. Enter the name Ensure Title.

3. Select the Shared Documents library.

4. Check the option to Automatically Start This Workflow When A New Item Is Created.

5. Click Next.

Although they look like buttons, the objects labeled Conditions and Actions on the Step details page are actually menus, as shown in Figure 9-3.

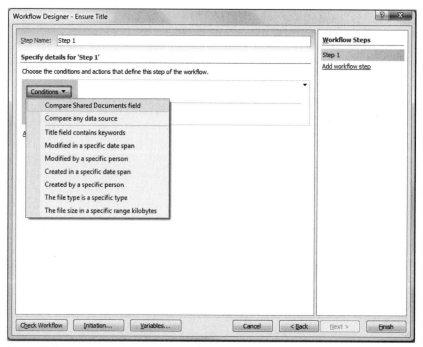

Figure 9-3

6. Select Conditions ⇨ Compare Shared Documents field. This inserts the stub shown in Figure 9-4.

Figure 9-4

7. Click `field` and select `Title` from the combo box.

8. Click `equals` and select `is empty`.

> **Conditions are optional in a workflow. If there are actions you want to perform every time the workflow is executed, you can leave the Conditions section blank, and every action in the step will be performed.**

9. Select Actions ⇨ Set Field in Current Item.

10. Click `field` and select `Title`.

11. Click `value`. This changes the placeholder to an editable field, as shown in Figure 9-5.

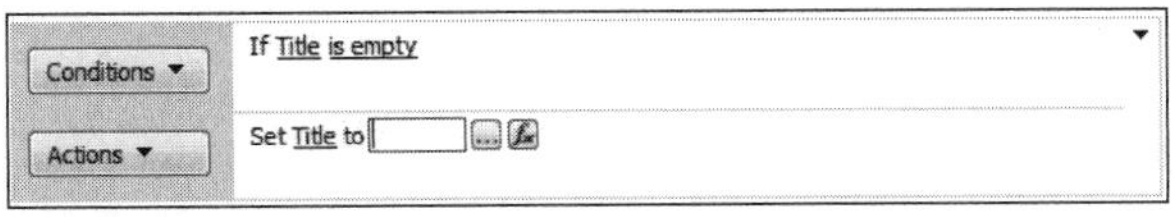

Figure 9-5

Field-level entry forms such as this are used throughout the Workflow Designer. The controls and subcontrols available depend upon the element being configured.

12. Click the formula (*fx*) icon beside the editable field. This launches the Define Workflow Lookup dialog.

13. Current Item should be the default Source. Select Name, as shown in Figure 9-6, and click OK.

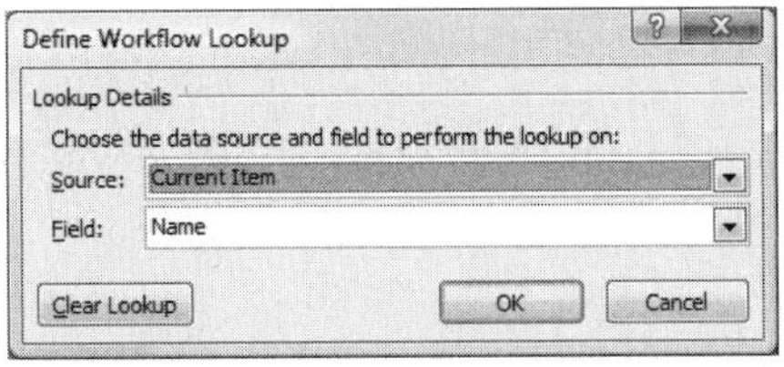

Figure 9-6

By default, the actions in a branch are set to run in sequence (one after another, waiting for one to finish before the next begins). You can change this by selecting Run All Actions in Parallel from the branch menu (shown in Figure 9-7). If you select this option, all actions in the block run at the same time. (Do not select this option at this time.)

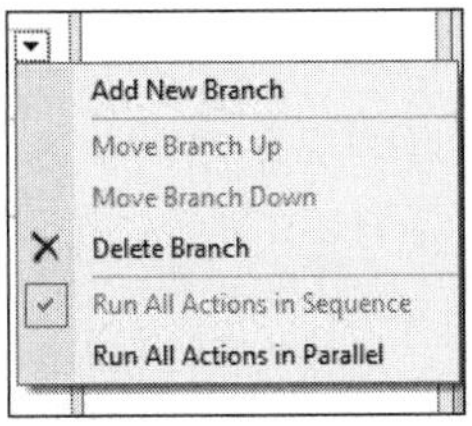

Figure 9-7

Running actions in parallel is only possible if you have multiple actions to run. If you try to configure parallel execution with only one action, the Workflow Designer displays an error message when you run a check (as described in the next step). Also note that "at the same time" in this case simply means that the actions don't wait for each other. They may start or finish at slightly different times.

14. Click Check Workflow. If there is no missing or incorrect information in your definition, you get a confirmation, as shown in Figure 9-8. Otherwise, items that need to be addressed are highlighted in the workflow display.

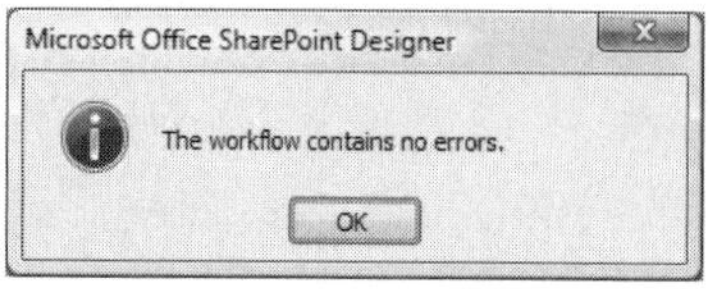

Figure 9-8

15. Click Finish. While SharePoint Designer processes the steps you defined in the workflow, it displays the status window in Figure 9-9.

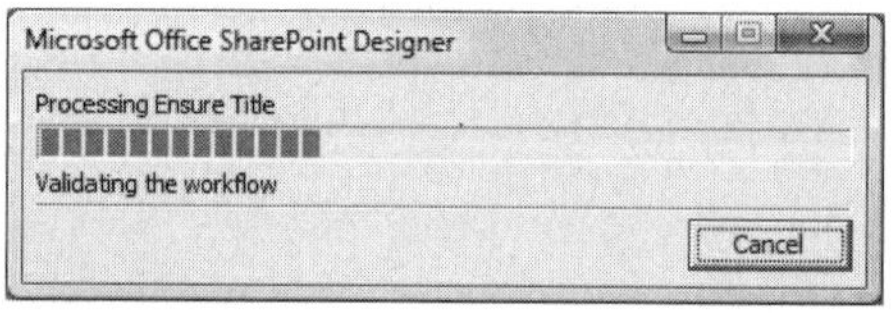

Figure 9-9

The processing described in step 15 is not a binary compilation. SharePoint Designer is converting your wizard input into a collection of markup files.

Congratulations! You have just created a workflow. The markup files and any default forms are stored in a folder in the Workflows library, as shown in Figure 9-10.

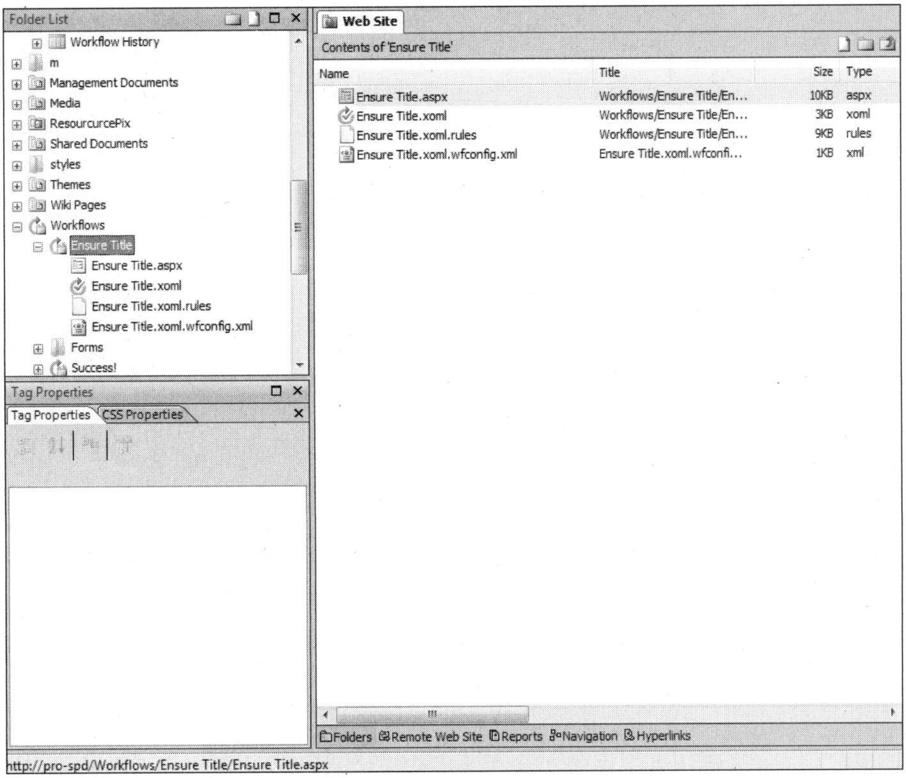

Figure 9-10

Because this was a simple workflow, only a few files were created:

❑ **Initiation form** (`Ensure Title.aspx`): A page to collect initiation parameter values from the user when the workflow is started manually.

❑ **Workflow definition file** (`Ensure Title.xoml`): The actual steps defined for your workflow.

❑ **Workflow rules file** (`Ensure Title.xoml.rules`): Used in evaluating the conditions defined in your workflow.

❑ **Workflow configuration file** (`Ensure Title.xoml.wfconfig.xml`): Used to define the connection between the workflow and SharePoint.

Workflows with lots of user interaction may contain many more files — typically ASPX forms, one for each action that requests user input. The initiation and other forms are described in more detail later in this chapter. See chapters 15 and 17 for more information about workflow definition, rules, and configuration files.

Editing an Existing Workflow

Like any design endeavor, workflows are subject to change. Your user's needs might change over time, or you might have forgotten something, or even made a mistake. Fortunately, you can easily modify a SharePoint Designer workflow after it has been created.

There are two ways to open an existing workflow for editing:

❑   Browse to it through the folder list, and double-click the workflow's XOML file.

❑   Select File ➩ Open Workflow, and select from a list of the workflows on the site.

In either case, the Workflow Designer opens on the first step in your workflow. You can then make any change you want to the workflow. For example, what if the users of the Ensure Title workflow complain because the title field is being set without their knowledge? They want to be notified, so they have an opportunity to change the title themselves to something that makes sense.

That is easily accomplished:

1.   Open the Ensure Title workflow.

2.   Select Actions ➩ Send an Email.

3.   Summon the Define E-mail Message dialog by clicking This Message.

4.   Click the Address Book icon to the right of the To field.

5.   Select User who Created Current Item, and click the Add >> button.

6.   Enter `Blank title replaced with filename` in the Subject Line.

     Notice the *fx* button next to the Subject line. As with the editable field described earlier, you can use lookups to populate the fields of the message with information from many places within SharePoint. If you were adding a lookup for the To, CC, or Subject line, it would be the only content for the entire field. This restriction is not the case when editing the body of an email, as shown in the next steps.

7.   Enter the following text:

```
You recently uploaded the file: to the Shared Documents library. This file did not
have a Title field, therefore we have automatically assigned the name of the file
to the title. If you wish to change the title to something easier for users to
understand, please edit the properties of the document.

Thank you.
```

8. Place the entry cursor after the colon (:), and click the Add Lookup to Body button. The Define Workflow Lookup dialog opens.

9. Leave the source at Current Item, and select Name for the Field. Click OK. The Define E-mail Message dialog should now look like Figure 9-11.

Figure 9-11

10. Click OK, and then click Finish and wait for the Workflow to process.

SharePoint Designer workflows take advantage of SharePoint's versioning capability. If you edit a workflow while instances of it are executing, those instances will continue to run under the version of the workflow that was current when they were initiated. You can navigate into the Workflow Settings of the list or library, see how many instances of each workflow version are running, and delete any versions that are no longer needed.

To get to the Workflow Settings, Open your document library, and select Settings ⇨ Document Library Settings from the library toolbar. In the Permissions and Management section, click Workflow Settings. Figure 9-12 shows a Remove Workflows page.

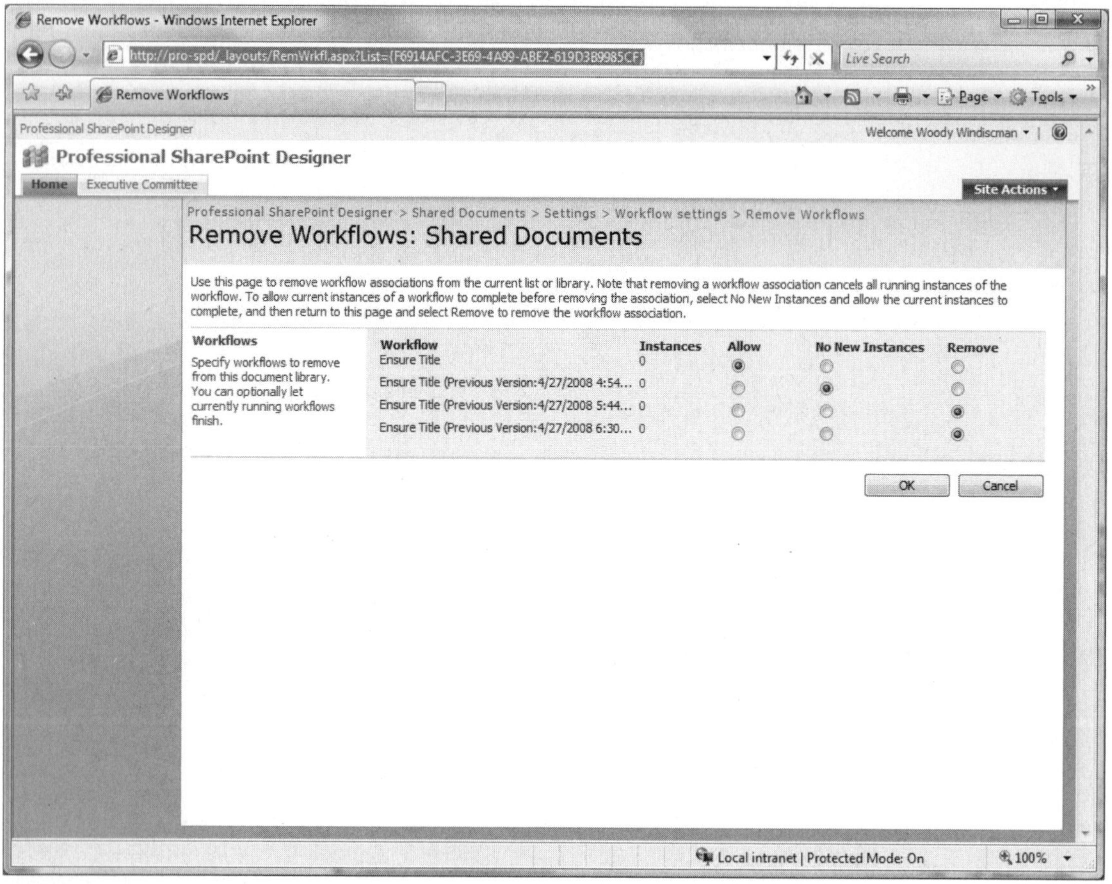

Figure 9-12

Workflow Elements in Detail

The example in the previous section provided a simple situation and a simple solution. Workflows you create with SharePoint Designer can perform much more sophisticated tasks as well. This section explores the elements available for your workflows.

Start Options

There are three ways to start running a SharePoint Designer workflow:

❑ Allow your user to start the workflow manually (selected by default).

❑ Start the workflow automatically when a new item is created.

❑ Start the workflow automatically when an item is edited.

When the workflow is automatically started, no workflow interface is presented — execution simply proceeds to the first step. By default, there are two ways for a user to manually invoke a workflow:

❑　A Workflows command on the item's action menu, as shown in Figure 9-13.

❑　The Workflows command on the item's Properties page toolbar.

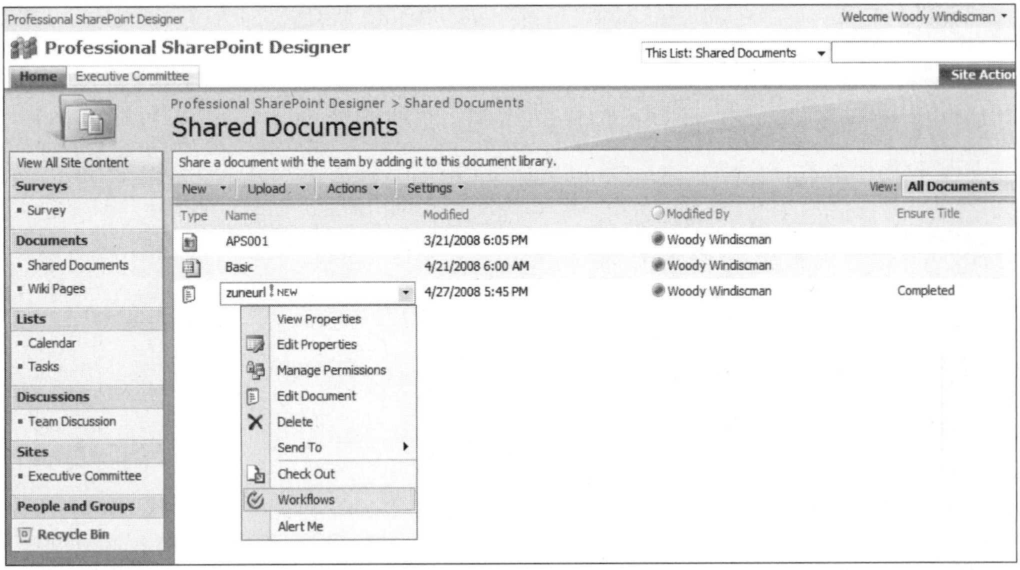

Figure 9-13

In either case, the user is presented with a page showing a list of workflows available to items in the list or library, and the status of any workflows currently associated with the item, as shown in Figure 9-14.

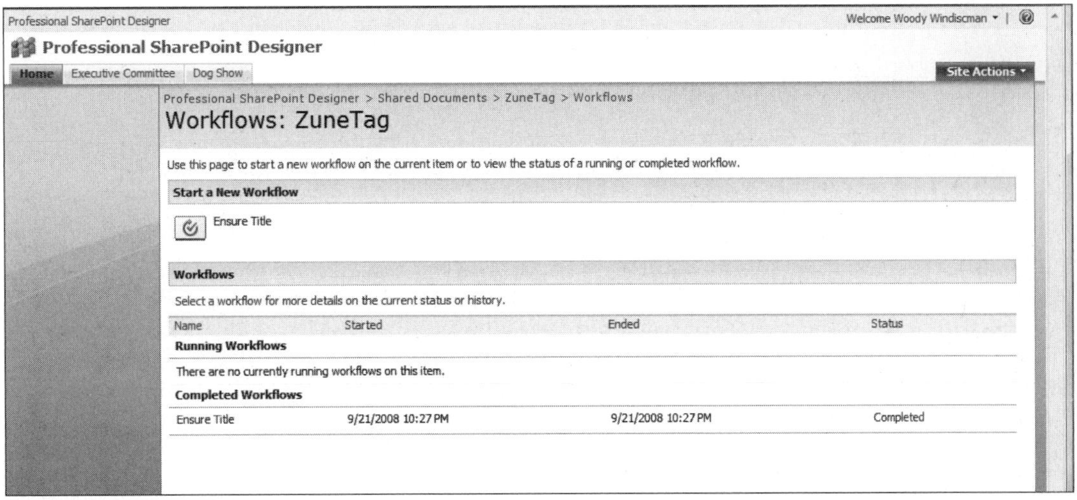

Figure 9-14

Initiation Parameters

Occasionally, you may want to start your workflow with information that isn't already in SharePoint. Workflow initiation parameters enable you to provide (or request) that information. When you define a parameter, you give it a name and a data type. Initiation parameters are accessed in the Workflow Designer by clicking the Initiation button at the bottom of the wizard.

When you click the Initiation button, you are presented with the Workflow Initiation Parameters dialog, as shown in Figure 9-15.

Figure 9-15

From the parameters list, you can add or remove parameters, and change the order in which they will appear on the initiation form. Click the Add button to open the Add Field wizard (see Figure 9-16).

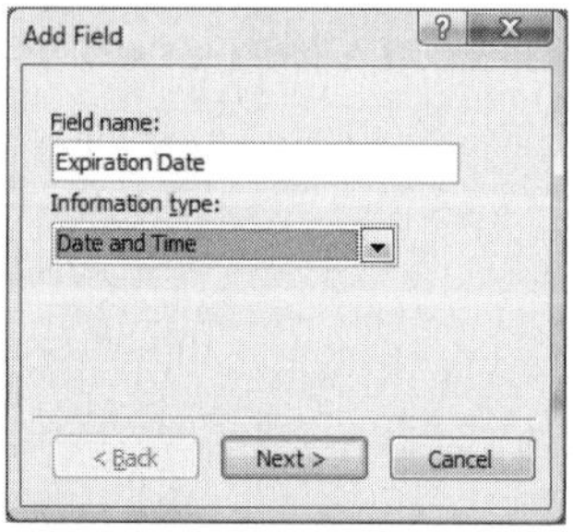

Figure 9-16

The Add Field wizard first asks for the name of the field, and provides a dropdown for the type of data. Click Next and you are shown a form appropriate for selecting a default value for your field. This is provided because the initiation form is not displayed if the workflow is started automatically. Figure 9-17 shows the Default value entry form for a Date and Time field.

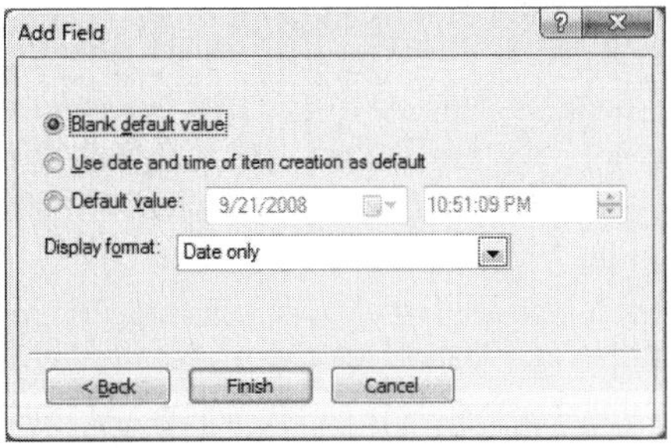

Figure 9-17

Initiation parameters can each be any of the following types:

- ❑ Single line of text.
- ❑ Multiple lines of text.
- ❑ Number.
- ❑ Date and time.
- ❑ Choice (a list of preset values to choose from).
- ❑ Yes/No (a Boolean/check box).

Initiation Form

An initiation form is created automatically by the Workflow Designer when you save your workflow. It is used to allow the user to enter the initiation parameters you have defined (if any), as well as to verify that the user actually wants to start processing a workflow that was initiated manually. An example initiation form is shown in Figure 9-18.

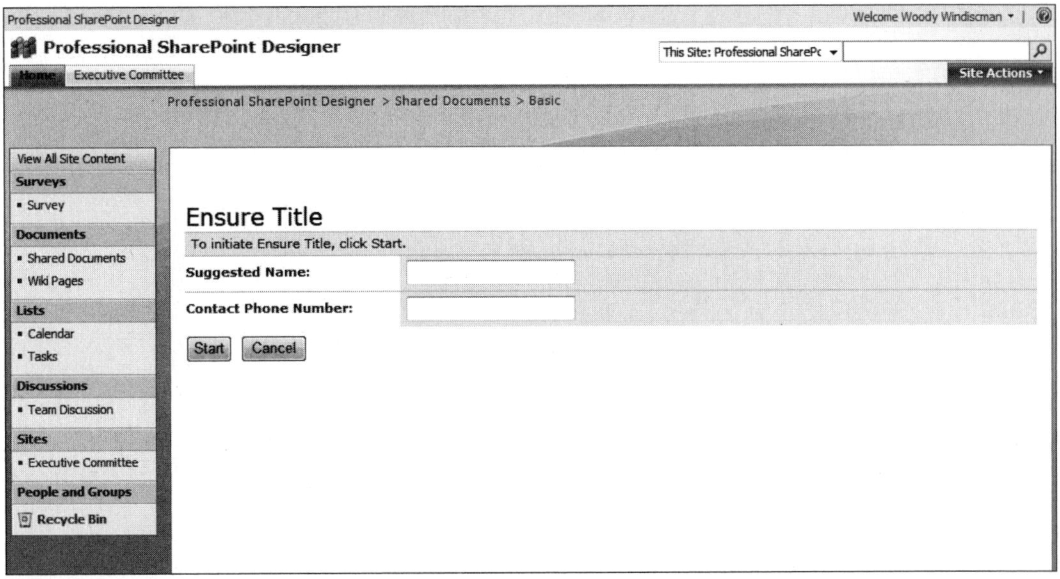

Figure 9-18

The initiation form is a SharePoint ASPX page. It contains a static Data Form Web Part (not a Web Part Zone) to support the entry of the initiation information. This form is highly customizable. The customization of Data Form Web Parts is described in detail in chapter 12.

Variables

Variables in a workflow give you a place to store values, such as for storing information between steps, holding interim calculation results, or just about anything else. In the workflow, information held in variables and initiation parameters is accessed in the same way. The key difference is that users have the opportunity to directly interact with initiation parameters, while variables are used only within your workflow.

You can create variables by clicking the Variables button at the bottom of the Workflow Designer dialog, or when configuring an action that can use a variable as an information target. Although there are similarities between variables and initiation parameters, there are also some significant differences.

Like an initiation parameter, a variable has a name (otherwise you couldn't refer to it) and a data type. Your workflow can read variables' current values in conditions, and set their values as actions. Unlike initiation parameters, variables do not have a default value, nor is a data entry form automatically generated for them. As Figure 9-19 shows, this results in simpler forms for managing (left) and creating (right) variables.

Figure 9-19

There are also slight differences in the data types available. The variable data types are:

❑ Boolean

❑ Date/Time

❑ List Item ID

❑ Number

❑ String

Because users do not enter variables directly, and no form is generated to represent them, there is a single String data type instead of the Choice, Single line of text, and Multiple lines of text types seen in initiation parameters.

Steps

Steps are the major blocks of instructions for a workflow. They contain the conditions and actions that are executed to perform the workflow's functions.

A workflow always has at least one step. For simple workflows, that may be all that is needed. Steps can be given friendly names, so that your users can easily understand where they are in your process.

Each step is executed in sequence, unless a Stop Workflow action is executed.

Conditions

Workflow conditions enable you to control the execution of the actions in your workflow. Earlier, you saw how a single condition determined whether a simple series of actions was performed. Much more complicated conditions are possible, such as the following:

❑ You can add multiple conditions to a single branch (If the Title is empty and created by a specific person, for instance).

❑ You can add alternative actions if the conditions specified are false (this is called an `Else If` clause). The Else If clause may have its own set of conditions. While the words `"Else if"` are not displayed in the block unless you specify conditions, it is still considered an `Else If` branch.

❑ You can have several of these `Else If` branches in a single step.

> *Each branch (including the initial Conditions and Actions block) is also known as a Rule.*

Using the Ensure Title workflow created in the earlier exercises, consider the case where your users create their document based on a template that already has a title (Proposal Sample). Other templates in your organization also contain the words "Template" or "Example" in their titles. While titles like those meet the requirement that a document have a title, they still aren't particularly useful. You can enhance the workflow further by checking for this template text and asking the user to enter something better. The following steps show one way to do that:

1. Open the Ensure Title workflow.

2. Click the link Add "Else If" Conditional Branch link.

3. Select Conditions ⇨ Compare Shared Documents field.

4. Click the `field` link, and select Title.

5. The default comparison is equals. Do not change this.

6. Click the `value` link, and enter `Proposal Sample`.

7. Select Conditions ⇨ Title Field Contains Keywords.

8. Click the `and` link (it will change to `or`).

9. Click the `keywords` link and enter `Template, Example`.

10. Select Actions ⇨ Send an Email.

11. Click the `this message` link.

12. Click the Address Book icon to the right of the To field.

13. Select User Who Created Current Item, click the Add >> button, and then click OK.

14. In the Subject field, enter `Template title not changed`.

15. Enter the following text:

```
You recently uploaded the file: to the Shared Documents library. This file's title
does not appear to have been changed from the template used to create the file. If
you wish to change the title to something easier for users to understand, please
edit the properties of the document.

Thank you.
```

16. Place the entry cursor after the colon (:), and click the Add Lookup to Body button. The Define Workflow Lookup dialog opens.

17. Leave the source at Current Item, and select Name for the Field. Click OK.

18. Click OK. The Workflow Designer dialog should now look like Figure 9-20.

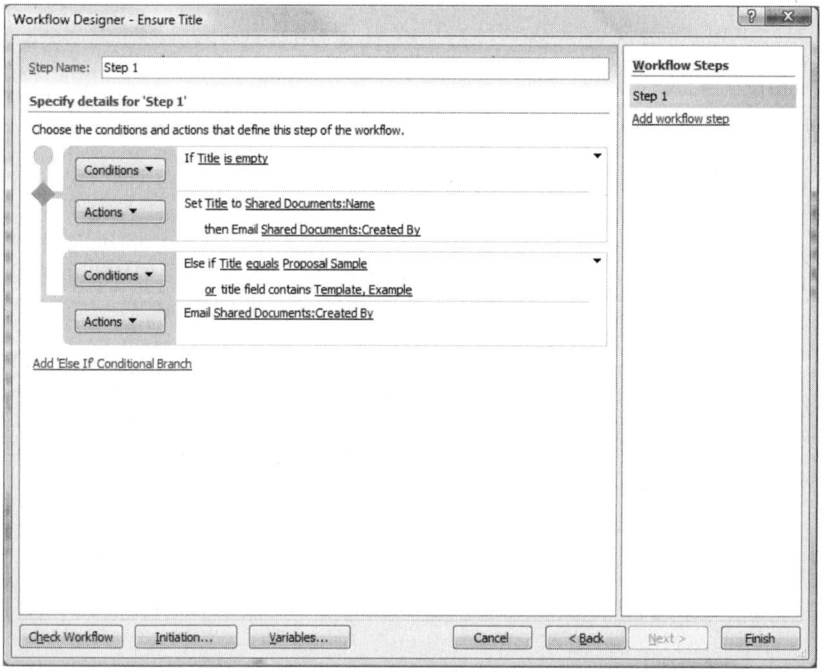

Figure 9-20

19. Click Finish to save your updated workflow.

You now have a workflow that can give your users appropriate instructions, depending on the nature of the file they have uploaded.

The types of conditions you can set in a workflow include:

❏ Comparisons to fields in the current list or library.

❏ Comparisons between any two data sources internal to the site (including lists, libraries, workflow variables, or initiation parameters, but not external data sources like XML files and web services).

❏ Checking the title field for specific keywords.

❏ Checking whether the file was created or modified, either by a specific person or within a specific date range.

❏ Checking the file type.

❏ Checking the size of the file.

Notice that several of these conditions could be interpreted as subsets of others. In those cases, the selection user interface is streamlined and tailored specifically to the comparison at hand. For example, comparisons between "any" data sources require you to choose not only the data sources, but the values for each side of the comparison. While you could certainly have built a comparison between the title field and a list of keyword values in the preceding exercise, that would have taken several steps, and opened up the chance of selecting the wrong field or value. On the other hand, because you used the Title Field Contains Keywords condition, the current document's title field was assumed, and the only thing you needed to enter was the keywords themselves.

Actions

Actions are the key elements of a workflow. Although every workflow has at least one step, and conditions are optional, nothing happens unless an action is defined.

The default actions provided with SharePoint fall into three categories:

❏ **Core actions:** These revolve around manipulating a particular piece of information (a variable or list field, for instance), or control overall workflow execution.

❏ **List actions:** These work on an entire list item at one time.

❏ **Task actions:** These manipulate the Tasks list, and pause the workflow until completed.

In many conditions and actions, you have the capability to look up or update information in other lists or libraries on the site. To access an item in another list or library, you need to provide some query information to determine the particular item you want to read or modify. Such a lookup is shown in Figure 9-21.

Figure 9-21

Note that if the parameter you enter results in more than one list or library item being returned, only the first result is used for the action.

Core Actions

Core actions let you set values, send emails, pause, or even prematurely end the workflow. They're described in the following table.

When configuring an action that allows you to assign a value to a variable, you are also given the option to create a new variable.

Core Action	Description
Add Time to Date	Enables you to perform date arithmetic. You can add a specified amount of time to an existing date/time element, and store the results in a workflow variable. Adding a negative unit of time results in subtracting time. You can add Minutes, Hours, Days, Months, and Years.
Build Dynamic String	A dynamic string is a combination of static text and lookup values, resolved at the workflow's run time. Figure 9-22 shows how the lookups appear in the flow of the text. Lookups cannot be edited once they are inserted. To change an existing lookup, delete it, and then create it anew. The results of the dynamic string are stored in a workflow variable.
Do Calculation	Performs a simple arithmetic operation (add, subtract, multiply, divide, or mod/remainder) on two values, and stores the result in a workflow variable.
Log to History List	Enables you to write an item to the hidden list that stores workflow history information.
Pause For Duration	One of the timer actions. It causes the workflow to wait a specified amount of time before proceeding to the next action in the workflow.

Core Action	Description
Pause Until Date	Causes the workflow to wait until a specified date and time before continuing to the next action. The date may be hard-coded into the workflow, or it may be a lookup value.
Send an Email	Enables you to send an email to a user or a set of users. The body of the email uses the same user interface as the Build Dynamic String action. You used this action in the exercises earlier in the chapter.
Set Content Approval Status	When content approval is turned on for the list, this action enables you to directly change the status of the current item and set the approval comment. The comment may be static text or a lookup value.
Set Field in Current Item	Sets the specified field to either a static or lookup value.
Set Time Portion of Date/ Time Field	Overrides the current time in a date/time lookup value, leaving the date intact. It then stores the new date/time value into a date/time variable.
Set Workflow Variable	Although several other actions set the values of workflow variables with their results, this one enables you to directly set the value of a variable or Initiation Form field. You can set it to either a static value or a lookup.
Stop Workflow	Stops the execution of the workflow immediately and logs a specified message into the Workflow History list. No further steps or actions are performed.
Wait for Field Change in Current Item	Pauses the workflow until a field matches a particular condition.

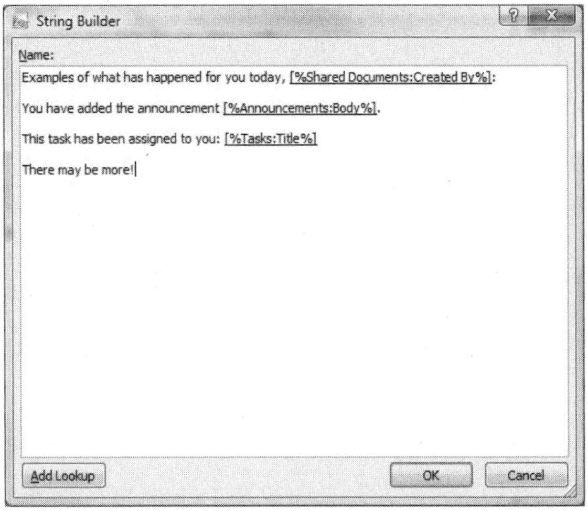

Figure 9-22

List Actions

The List actions let you perform such tasks as checking items in or out; creating new ones; and copying, editing, or deleting items. Many of these actions default to acting on the current item (the one for which the workflow was initiated), although in most cases you can specify a different item — even one in a different list. If you want to act on an item other than the current item, you are presented with the Choose List Item dialog shown in Figure 9-23.

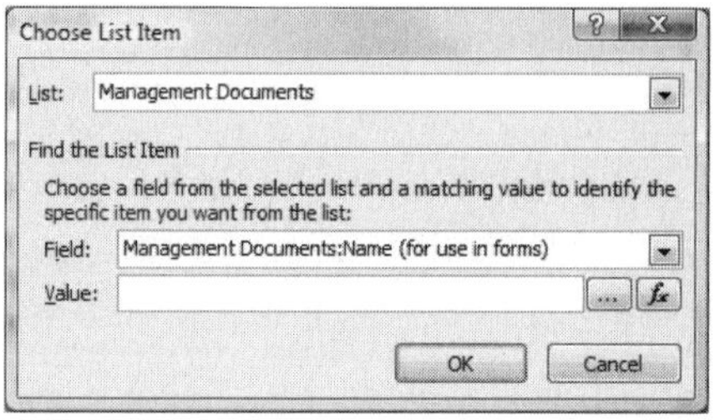

Figure 9-23

The Value field will be compared to the field selected. You can use a lookup, or enter a specific value to compare. If multiple items match your query, the action will take place on the first matching item, so try to ensure that your queries will return a single item. Otherwise you could end up deleting the wrong document, for instance.

Here are descriptions of List actions:

List Action	Description
Check In Item	Checks in the specified item and sets the check-in comment appropriately.
Check Out Item	Locks an item so that only the person who has it checked out can make changes. There is no comment on a check-out.
Copy List Item	Copies items between almost any two lists on the site. The lists must be of compatible types (both must be document libraries, for instance) or allow mixed content types. The default source is the current list item.
Create List Item	Enables you to create a new item in any list. Figure 9-24 shows the Create New List Item action configuration dialog. Each field in the list may be populated from a different source. The ID code of the item created is returned to a workflow variable.
Delete Item	Removes the specified item from the list.
Discard Check Out Item	Undoes any changes made since the item was checked out and removes the change lock.
Update List Item	Enables you to change the fields of an existing item. The interface for setting the field values is the same as that used in the Create List Item action.

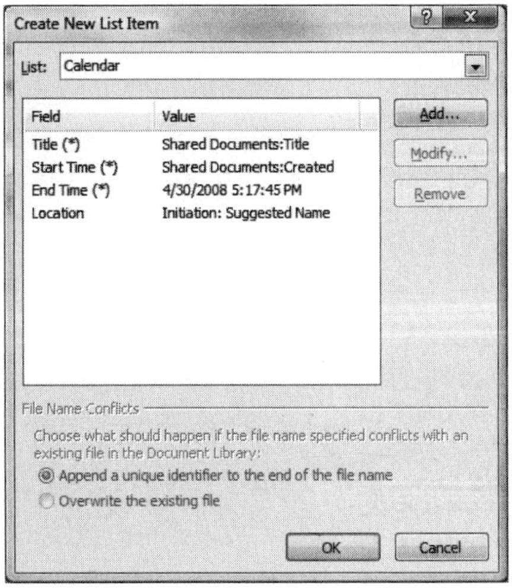

Figure 9-24

Task Actions

Task actions enable you to pause a workflow for more user input. The kind of input, and who must provide it, varies from action to action.

Because these tasks pause your workflow, you cannot use the current workflow to set the task fields dynamically on initiation. You can, however, create a separate workflow on the Tasks list which is invoked by the creation of the task item by this action. This is called a secondary workflow. The ramifications of secondary workflows are discussed later in the "SharePoint Designer Workflow Considerations" section.

Task actions are described in the following table:

Task Action	Description
Assign a Form to a Group	Enables you to create a survey that everyone in a group needs to complete, in order for the workflow to continue to the next action. The results are stored as items in the task list.
Assign a To-do Item	Creates a standard task that must be marked as Complete before the workflow will continue. The Custom Task Wizard shows the same initiation form as for the Group form, but does not call for the addition of any fields.
Collect Data from a User	Similar to the Assign a Form to a Group action. The primary differences are that the survey form is targeted to a single user, rather than a group, and that because there is only one instance of the form created, its ID is available to be assigned to a workflow variable.

Users who are assigned a task receive an email similar to the one shown in Figure 9-25.

Figure 9-25

They need to click the Edit this task link to see any instructions or fill in any requested information. This takes them to the edit form defined for the task. In the case of Assign a To-do Item, it is simply the standard edit form for the Tasks list. For the Assign a Form to a Group or Collect Data from a User actions, you create a custom form for the user to fill in.

If you click the A Custom Form link (for the Group action) or the Data link (for the User action) in the action definition window, the Custom Task Wizard launches. That's where you define your form. The first page of the wizard describes how the form you are about to create is used. Click Next to actually begin entering information.

The first real step of the Custom Task Wizard (see Figure 9-26) enables you to provide some descriptive information about the form for your users.

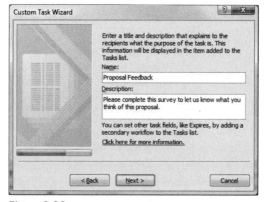

Figure 9-26

After clicking Next, you add the fields/questions to which you want your users to respond. This operates just like selecting Initiation form fields, except that you can provide additional descriptive text for each field. The following field types are available:

- ❑ Single line of text
- ❑ Multiple lines of text
- ❑ Number
- ❑ Currency
- ❑ Date and Time
- ❑ Choice
- ❑ Lookup
- ❑ Yes/No
- ❑ User
- ❑ Hyperlink or Picture
- ❑ Calculated

> *The information type selector also offers the option of choosing a Page Separator or Extended Field field type. These choices are artifacts of a different use for this dialog (on legacy FrontPage Server Extensions–based sites, which are not covered in this book), and are not valid for workflow forms. Attempting to select them results in an alert asking you to make another selection.*

The field types available (including the invalid choices) are the same for the actions Assign a Form to a Group and Collect Data from a User.

Changing a Workflow

This exercise walks you through changing the Ensure Title workflow to allow the user, who simply leaves the template title in place, to enter a real title without needing to manually edit the document's properties. It assumes you have performed all of the Ensure Title exercises to this point.

1. Open the Ensure Title workflow.

2. Select Delete Action from the item menu for the Email Shared Documents:Created By in the *second* branch.

3. Select Actions ⇨ Collect Data from a User.

4. Click the Data link, and click Next to get to the first entry page of the Custom Task Wizard.

5. Enter `Update Document Title` in the Name: field.

6. Enter the following text into the description field, and then click Next:

```
You recently uploaded a file to the Shared Documents library. This file's title
does not appear to have been changed from the template used to create the file. This
task allows you to enter a more descriptive title.
```

7. Click the Add button.

8. Enter `Descriptive Title` for the Field Name.

9. Enter the following text into the Description: field:

`Please enter a title which will make sense to the users of your document.`

10. Set the Information Type to Single Line Of Text (if it is not already).

11. Click Next.

12. Leave the default value blank, but uncheck Allow Blank Values?

13. Click Finish to complete creating the field, and then click Finish in the Custom Task Wizard.

14. Click the This User link, and select the User Who Created Current Item, as in previous examples.

15. Click the Variable: link, and select Create New Variable (it may already have a default value, but you want something understandable).

16. Enter `TitleTask` in the Name: field. Leave the type as List Item ID. Click OK.

17. Select Actions ⇨ Update List Item.

18. Click the This List link to open the Update List Item dialog.

19. Click the Add button.

20. For Set This Field, select Title.

21. Click the *fx* button for the To this value: field.

22. Select the Tasks list for the Source.

23. Select Descriptive Title for the Field in the Lookup Details section. (You defined this field in steps 8–13.)

24. In the Find List Item section, select Tasks:ID for the field.

25. Click the *fx* button. Another Define Workflow Lookup dialog appears.

26. Select Workflow Data for the source.

27. Select Variable: TitleTask for the field. (You defined this variable in steps 15 and 16.)

28. Click OK in each of the open dialogs until you get back to the main Workflow Designer window.

29. Click Finish.

The workflow will be processed, and a new file (`Update Document Title.aspx`) will be created in the Ensure Title workflow folder. This is the form the user will see when he or she clicks the Edit This Task link in the notification email. Figure 9-27 shows the form.

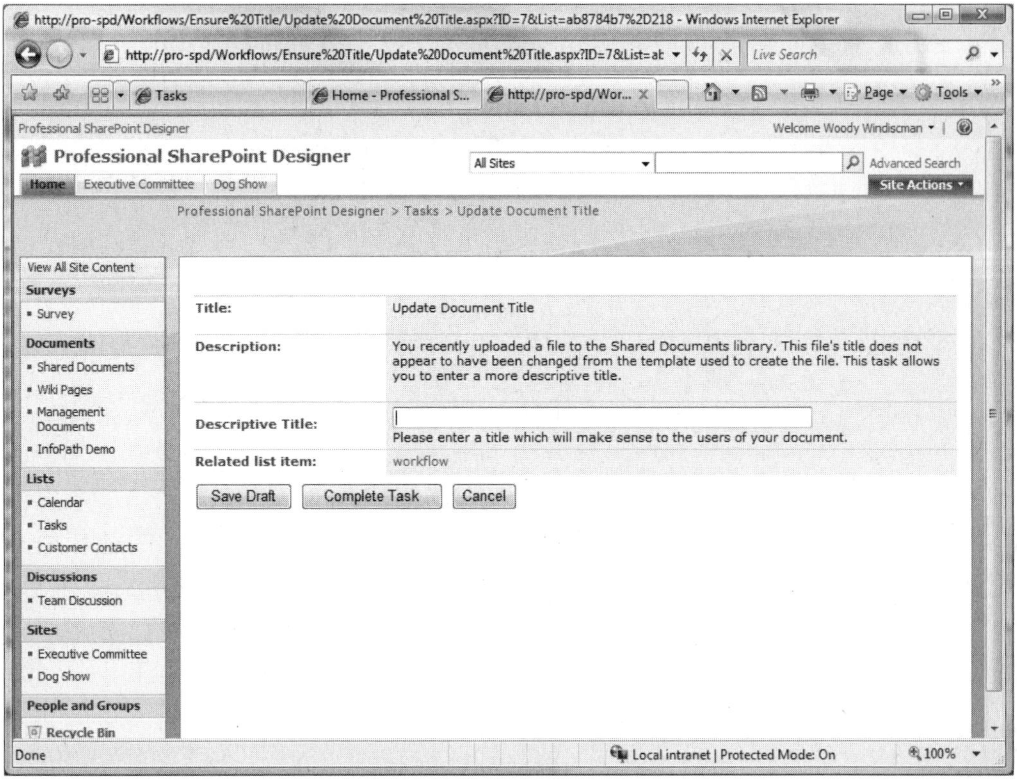

Figure 9-27

Like the initiation form, it is a standard SharePoint page with a static Data Form Web Part for the user's information entry. Chapter 12 shows you how to customize Data Forms.

SharePoint Designer Workflow Considerations

As you have seen, SharePoint Designer workflows provide many powerful actions for manipulating the information in your site. There are limits to this functionality, however, and some areas where you should be cautious of the ramifications of your choices.

Limitations

One of the key limitations to SharePoint Designer workflows is that they are bound strictly to the list on which they are created. You cannot directly move a SharePoint Designer workflow to a different list. However, if you create a template based on a site containing a SharePoint Designer workflow, then, when you create a new instance of the site, an appropriate workflow for the new location is created.

SharePoint Designer creates workflows that can execute actions either in sequence or in parallel. While SharePoint's built-in workflows offer a state-based execution flow, SharePoint Designer workflows do not. There is no built-in looping or iteration mechanism. For example, you cannot create a SharePoint Designer workflow that automatically performs an action on every item in a list.

SharePoint Designer workflows use a tasks list to coordinate their functions. This list is always the list called Tasks. If that list doesn't exist, the first workflow you create automatically creates a Tasks list as well.

If you have multiple workflows defined on a list or library, and you invoke a workflow on an item in that list (whether manually or automatically), you cannot invoke a second workflow on the same item until the first completes.

> *Workflows in SharePoint are based on the Windows Workflow Foundation (WWF). While many powerful actions are available to you in SharePoint Designer, these are but a sampling of the kinds of functions the WWF can be programmed to perform. By using Microsoft Visual Studio, you can create custom workflows that can be associated with any list or library. You can also build your own custom conditions and actions, and make them available for use within SharePoint Designer. These options are covered in chapter 15.*

Ramifications and Cautions

As you have seen, a SharePoint Designer workflow can make changes to information anywhere on a site. Some of the items a workflow can change may themselves have automatically starting workflows associated with them. If a SharePoint Designer workflow makes a change to such a list, the workflow that is triggered is considered a *secondary workflow* to the workflow that triggered it.

Secondary workflows can be a powerful tool. For example, although the Task actions described earlier in this chapter will stop executing until their associated tasks have been completed, you can place a workflow on the Tasks list that will pick up where the primary workflow leaves off. Such a workflow might set an expiration date on the task, thus allowing the original workflow to continue if the task is never acted upon by the user.

This brings up an important point about workflows: Your users may not always behave in the way you expect. Whenever you implement a workflow that requires user input, test it thoroughly to see how it behaves if the user inserts incorrect or invalid data, or if the user completely ignores it. Otherwise, you may find your system littered with partially executed workflows. On a busy site, and a list with frequent additions and changes, this could potentially cause performance issues, as the lists used to control workflows grow to thousands of active and unresolved items.

Another potential issue is the circular reference, which can lead to an infinite loop. A circular reference occurs when an item refers to another, which in turn refers back to the original item. It may be a direct reference, as just described, or the reference may pass through several other items, but it always gets back to the item that originally started the chain, which then starts the chain all over again. If these references trigger actions and there are no mechanisms set up to stop them (a passage of time, for instance, or a comparison to some maximum or minimum value that is incremented or decremented by the chain itself), the result is never-ending activity — the infinite loop.

Consider the case where a workflow makes a change to a list that triggers an automatic workflow. That secondary workflow makes a change to the original list, triggering the workflow that changes the secondary list again. If you do not detect this condition and stop the workflows, it can quickly result in thousands of workflow instances, absorbing system resources and ultimately leading to a system crash — and a nightmare to clean up.

One way to build in some control over runaway workflows is to create a list with a known item in it for your workflow. The item should contain a number field to use as a counter. When you create a workflow that you believe has the potential to run away, the first action should test the list item for the current value of the counter. If it is not over some reasonable value (which only you can determine, based upon your environment), the next action increments the counter, and you then proceed with the workflow. The last action of any step that terminates the workflow should decrement that counter. If the initial comparison is greater than your threshold, end the workflow immediately. (You may opt to send an email notice of the termination to the site owner, but that may be problematic if the runaway process is not controlled by your workflow.)

> You learned earlier that SharePoint Designer workflows do not have a built-in mechanism for loops or state-based control flow. If you build appropriate logic into your workflows, and are careful to avoid infinite loops, circular references and secondary workflows can be used to work around this limit. You can deliberately create loops to execute a certain number of times, or until other desired conditions are met.

Summary

This chapter examined how to use SharePoint Designer to create workflows that add powerful application logic to your site. It described the conditions and actions used within a workflow, and how to add user interaction. You also discovered some of the limits to workflows created with SharePoint Designer.

Other points to take from this chapter:

❑ Workflows can modify information throughout the SharePoint site.

❑ SharePoint Designer workflows do not have built-in looping or iteration capability.

❑ SharePoint Designer workflows use SharePoint lists and libraries to manage their operation.

Chapter 10 tackles the Data View (also known as the Data Form) Web Part. Later chapters show how to use SharePoint Designer to bring workflows and Data Views together to create sophisticated applications — from data collection to application logic to presentation — all without programming.

10

Working with SharePoint Data

SharePoint lists and libraries provide flexible storage for many kinds of information. The List View Web Part affords an easy way for users to control the presentation of that information both from within the browser and SharePoint Designer. Yet this control is limited. SharePoint Designer also provides a tool that gives you very fine control over the presentation of data — the Data View Web Part.

This chapter shows you how to customize both List View and Data View Web Parts. It explores:

❑ The flexibility and limits of List View Web Parts.

❑ Comparing List View and Data View Web Parts.

❑ The Data Source Catalog.

❑ XSLT basics.

❑ Visually editing XSLT in SharePoint Designer.

❑ The XPath Expression Builder.

List View Revisited

In chapter 2, you learned about list and library views, and that a List View Web Part is automatically defined for any list or library you create. The List View Web Part can be used on any Web Part Page to display the contents of the associated list or library. To add the predefined default List View Web Part to a page through SharePoint Designer:

1. Open the Web Parts task pane (shown in Figure 10-1).

Figure 10-1

2. Select the Web Part for the desired list or library.

3. Drag the Web Part onto the page.

The Web Parts task pane also allows you to insert a new Web Part Zone, if needed. In addition, you can reduce paging through the Web Part list by filtering the view to specific types of Web Parts.

Once placed on a page, the List View Web Part can be set to use any defined view of the list. In addition, it can be further customized as appropriate for the context of that particular page. How this is accomplished is very different in the web interface and SharePoint Designer.

The following figures show the properties of the Announcements list in each environment. Figure 10-2 shows the task pane summoned in the web interface (select Edit ⇨ Modify Shared Web Part).

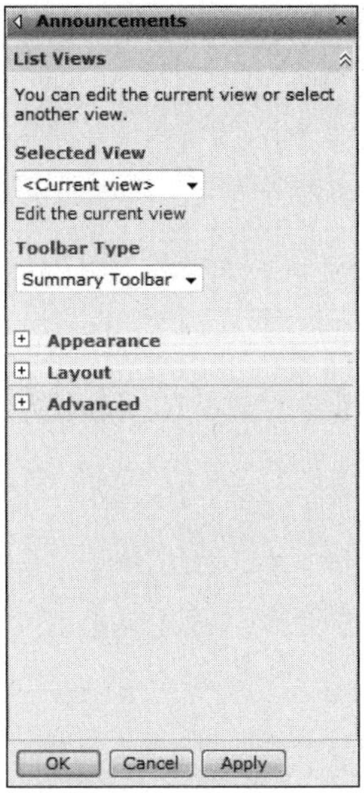

Figure 10-2

Figure 10-3 shows the Web Part properties pop-up dialog for the same part, accessed in SharePoint Designer by right-clicking the part and selecting Web Part Properties from the context menu. Notice that SharePoint Designer defaults to the Appearance section and does not offer control over the Selected View or Toolbar.

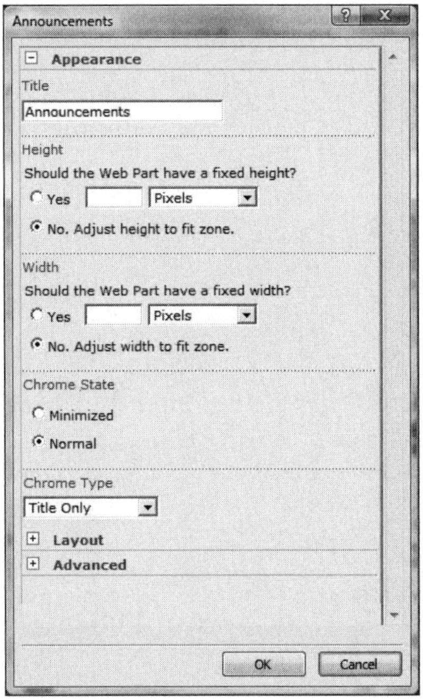

Figure 10-3

List View Control Menu

Rather than use the web-based properties dialog for modifying the data shown by a List View, SharePoint Designer offers a much richer user interface. When you select a List View Web Part, an icon appears in its upper-left corner. This icon summons the List View control menu, as shown for an Announcements Web Part in Figure 10-4.

Figure 10-4

The first four options in this menu — Fields, Change Layout, Sort and Group, and Filter — give access to most of the controls provided by the SharePoint interface when you use the Edit the Current View link; they are displayed in one page. In SharePoint Designer, each of the options has its own dialog appropriate to the task. These four List View control menu options are discussed in greater detail in the following sections.

Web Part Properties summons the same dialog shown earlier, in Figure 10-3. Web Part Zone Properties summons the dialog shown in Figure 10-5. Like Web Part Properties, this dialog is also available from the right-click context menu of the Web Part.

Figure 10-5

While most of the options in this dialog are self-explanatory, and apply to the zone itself, the Frame style dropdown applies to the Web Parts contained in the zone. This configures the default state of the chrome for Web Parts — whether a title bar, a border, both, or neither is displayed for each Web Part. This can be overridden for the individual Web Parts in the zone.

There are two aspects of a List View Web Part you cannot control through SharePoint Designer. First, while you can make extensive changes to the currently displayed view, you cannot select a different custom view that may have been defined for the list. Second, in SharePoint Designer, you cannot select or make changes to a Calendar view.

Fields

When you select Fields from the control menu, the Displayed Fields dialog (see Figure 10-6) opens.

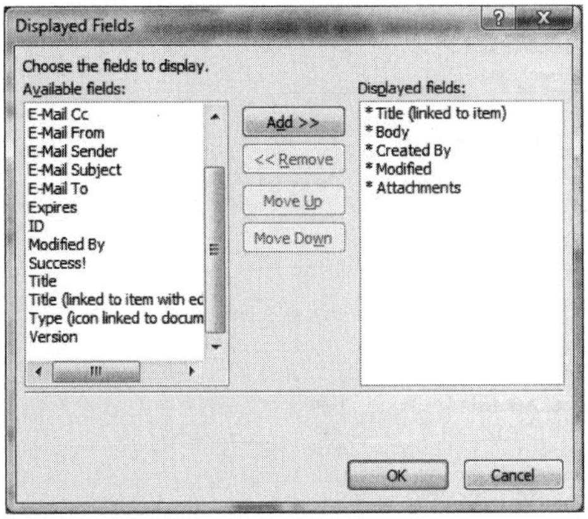

Figure 10-6

The list of Available fields is on the left, and the currently selected fields are on the right. The fields indicated with an asterisk (*) are required for the base List View selected. To create a view without those fields, either select a different view in the web interface and reopen the page in SharePoint Designer, or delete and replace the view. You can add a default List View as described earlier in this chapter, or use a Data View as described later in this chapter. You can change the order of field presentation by selecting a field and then clicking the Move Up or Move Down button.

To start with a view that has already been customized through the SharePoint web interface, you need to also use that interface to select the new view. Otherwise, starting with a SharePoint Designer–created view provides the greatest customization flexibility.

You can usually add each field to a List View only one time. Notice, however, that some fields (such as Title) are listed as available several times, but with different suboptions. This gives you choices for providing item control in your view. For example, to allow access to the Item menu from this view, you'd select Title (Linked To Item With Edit Menu), rather than simply Title. In certain view formats, you can take advantage of this to show the title in multiple contexts.

Change Layout

The Change Layout option gives you several display controls, which are presented in the multi-tab List View Options dialog. Figure 10-7 shows the General tab, which allows you to pick the toolbar you want to display for the List View Web Part. You can also uncheck the Show Toolbar With Options For check box, to hide the toolbar. In addition, the General tab enables you to make modifications to the Header and Footer sections of the List View.

Figure 10-7

The Layout tab (see Figure 10-8) allows you to control how each list or library item is displayed.

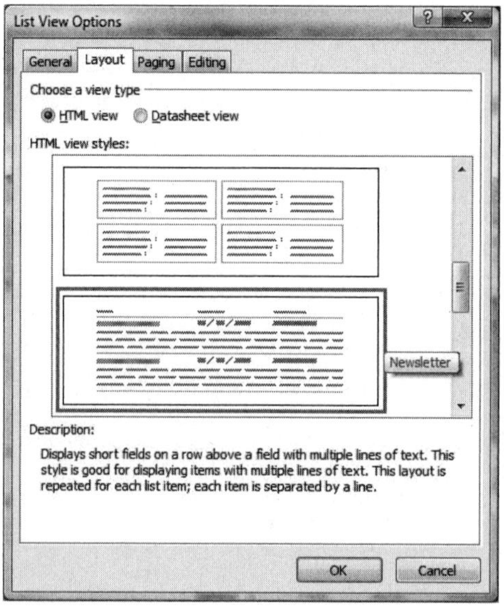

Figure 10-8

There are many useful basic display options on the Layout tab, from a simple tabular presentation to multicolumn boxed layouts. Hover the mouse over one of the style options to see its name; click on an option to see a detailed description.

One interesting layout available for most List Views is the preview pane layout. The preview pane lists the titles of the items on the left, and dynamically shows the details of the item on the right as you pass the mouse pointer over the title.

The Paging tab allows you to control how many items are shown at one time in the view. You can also determine whether you want the user to be able to scroll through all of the list or library or to see only the first group.

The Editing tab is not used by the List View Web Part. It is used in Data Views and is explained later in this chapter.

Sort and Group

The Sort and Group menu option opens a dialog with the same name that allows you to control the display order of the items in your view. Figure 10-9 shows the field chooser. It is similar to the one used to select the fields to be included in the view, but also includes the Sort Properties and Group Properties options. Instead of Displayed Fields, the second list column of this dialog indicates the selected sorting and grouping options.

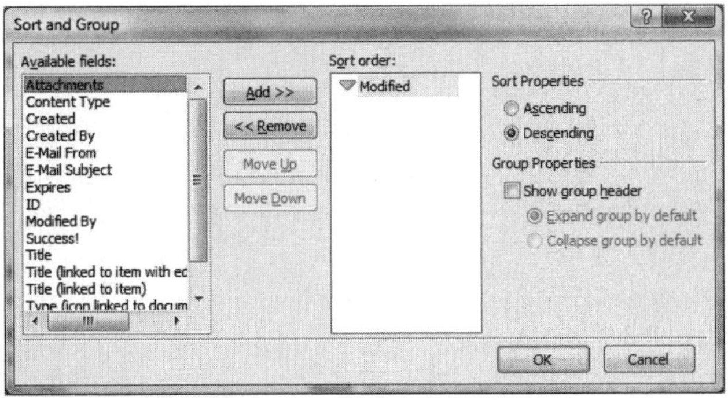

Figure 10-9

Sorting

The order in which the fields appear in the Sort order list controls the order that SharePoint uses to sort the items. This means that SharePoint first sorts the included items by the field indicated (ascending or descending). Fields sorted in ascending order are indicated with a triangle with the small end up, descending with the small end down. Items sharing the same value for the first sort field are then sorted by the next field. The process continues for each field specified in the sort order list.

Grouping

Once the items are sorted, you can create visual groups of items that share a field value by highlighting the field and checking the Show Group Header box. This creates an extra row for each unique value of the field selected, and collects the rows for the items that share that value underneath it. The group header row displays only the field used for that grouping, a count of how many items match that value, and a control for expanding and collapsing that group (to show or hide the matching items). Figure 10-10 shows a grouped List View.

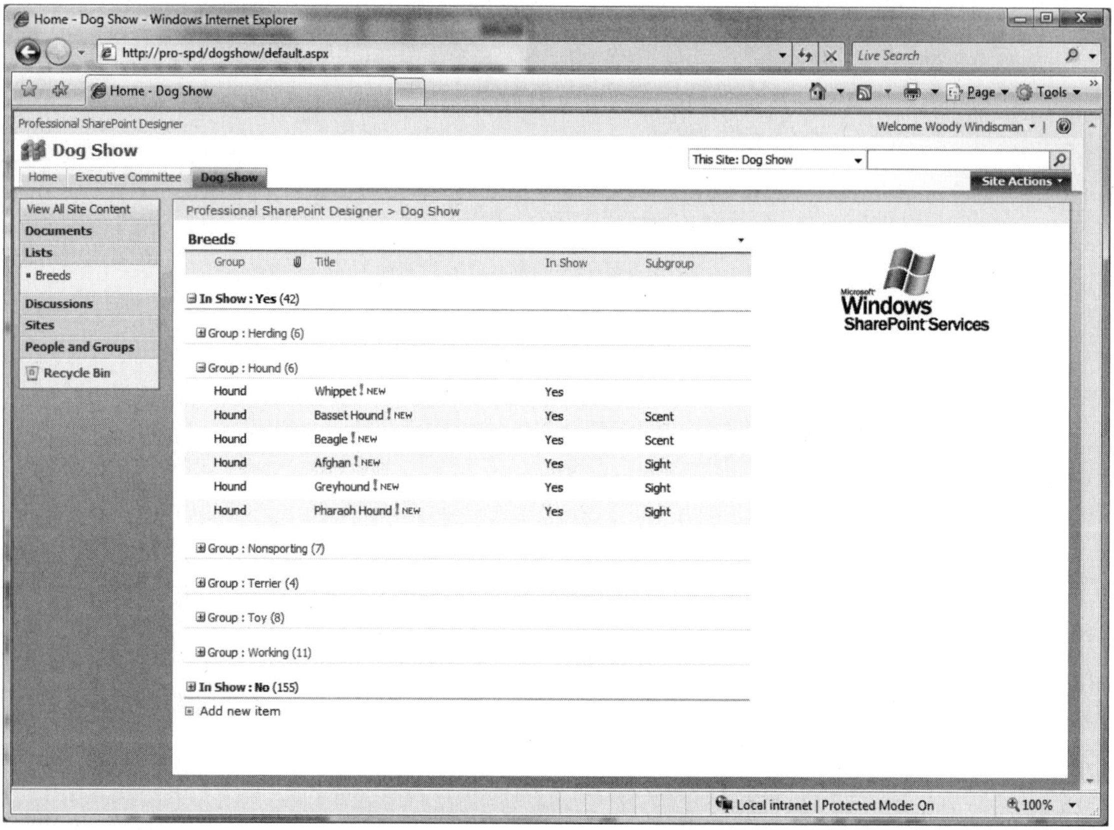

Figure 10-10

Due to the hierarchical nature of a grouped display, grouped fields are automatically moved to the top of your sort order when you save the Sort and Group settings. List views are limited to displaying two levels of grouping. If you attempt to create a third grouping level, the alert shown in Figure 10-11 pops up, advising you to convert the view to an XSLT Data View.

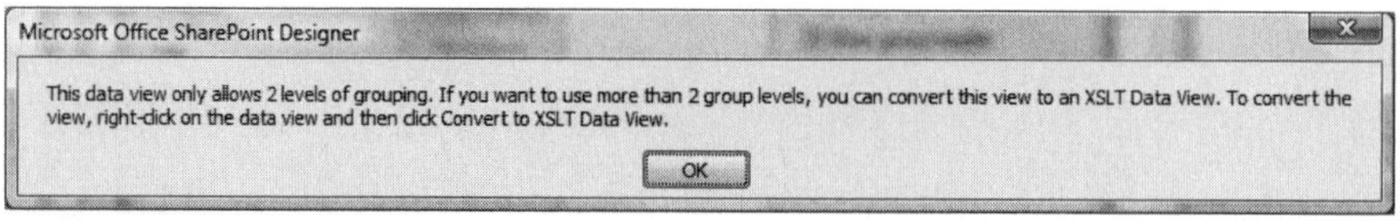

Figure 10-11

The process and results of converting a List View to an XSLT Data View are covered later in this chapter.

Not all layouts can be displayed well when grouped. Grouping is best restricted to generally tabular layouts.

Filter

Choose Filter to select a subset of the possible list items for display. The Filter Criteria dialog (see Figure 10-12) opens, and you specify the conditions you want.

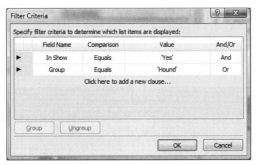

Figure 10-12

Each criterion consists of a field, the type of comparison you want to perform, and the value to which you are comparing the field's value. The types of comparison available and the available values vary based on the type of field. For example, a text field allows you to compare whether it begins with or contains the value. Such a comparison is irrelevant for a date field, so it is not available.

If you insert additional criteria lines, you may also define whether all of the criteria must be met (an And operation), or if any match allows the item to be displayed (Or).

Filter grouping specifies that certain filter conditions are processed before other conditions are applied. There is an implicit grouping among consecutive And criteria. In other words, consecutive And options are processed before any Or selections. You cannot explicitly set filter grouping in List View Web Parts, so the Group and Ungroup buttons are disabled. (They are available in Data View Web Parts.)

Introducing the XSLT Data View

The standard List View Web Part provides many options for displaying SharePoint information, yet there are also many restrictions, such as the limit of two sort groups. In addition, you are restricted to formatting the view in accordance with a handful of predefined layouts, and you have no control over how individual fields are presented.

Fortunately, SharePoint Designer provides a way to get around those limits: the XSLT Data View, also called the Data Form or simply the Data View Web Part. The XSLT Data View provides a powerful way to interact with the XML data returned by SharePoint when querying lists and libraries. As its full name implies, it uses eXtensible Stylesheet Language Transforms as the markup language to format the data.

Converting a List View

Most List View Web Parts can be converted to Data Views. To do so, right-click a List View, and then select Convert to XSLT Data View in the context menu, as shown in Figure 10-13.

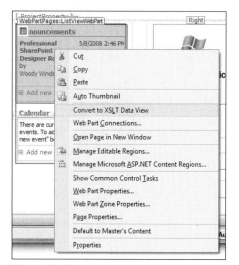

Figure 10-13

Certain List View styles cannot be converted to Data Views. In particular, the Calendar and Preview Pane views are only available as standard List Views.

Once you have converted to a Data View, on the surface very little changes. The conversion process matches the style of the new Data View as closely as possible to the state the List View was in. For most purposes, an end user sees no difference between the new view and the original when browsing your site. Scratch the surface, however, and the differences become apparent.

> **Changing a List View Web Part into a Data View (or vice versa, as described later) breaks any existing Web Part connections. They will need to be reestablished manually following the conversion.**

Changes for the User

So, what is different? The most obvious change is that the Data View cannot be easily edited through the web interface. All elements for controlling field selection, layout, and so forth are absorbed into an underlying XML data source and XSL Template code. While this code is accessible through the web interface, it is shown simply as raw text.

The other visible difference is the appearance of Web Part connections. When you make a connection between standard List Views, the view that provides data is modified to add a radio button that indicates which item is being used to provide data to the target Web Part(s). On connected Data Views, instead of a radio button, a selected key field is typically turned into a hyperlink.

While this describes the difference in the appearance of Web Part connections in the two types of Web Parts, connections are not carried over if you convert between them. You will only see these changes once you reestablish the connection. Web Part connections are described later in this chapter.

These changes are the result of the intrinsic difference between Data View and List View Web Parts. After converting, you are free to make many other kinds of changes, as described later in the chapter.

> It is much harder for users without SharePoint Designer to make changes once a Web Part has been converted to a Data View. Therefore, it is advisable to allow them to customize the part to be as close as possible to its desired configuration prior to the conversion.

Changes in SharePoint Designer

The changes within SharePoint Designer are a bit more noticeable. First, unlike the List View Web Part, which was only selectable as a block, each element of the Data View Web Part is available for modification individually. This brings the full WYSIWYG, drag-and-drop, formatting, and layout power of SharePoint Designer's design surface to bear. Using these features on Data View Web Parts is covered in more detail later in the chapter.

Notice that the control menu that was in the upper-left corner of the List View Web Part is gone. Instead, fly-out menus are available to the right of the different elements as they are highlighted. At the top level of the Data View is the Common Data View Tasks menu shown in Figure 10-14. Many of the features that were a part of the List View control menu are available here in an expanded form. These extended options as well as the options for formatting individual data elements are described later in the chapter.

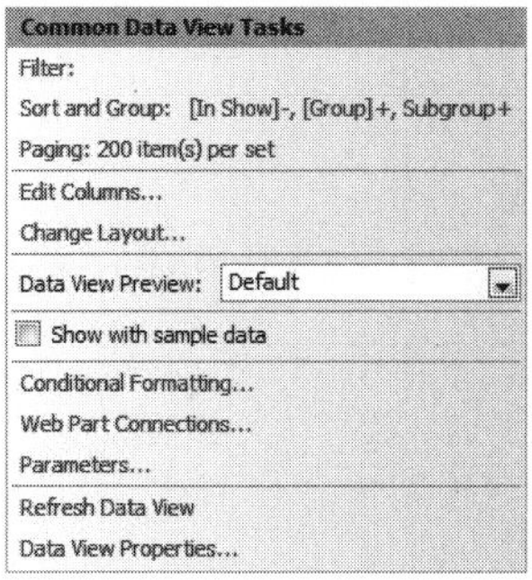

Figure 10-14

Reverting

Data views created by converting a List View Web Part can be reverted back to List Views. This is done by right-clicking the Web Part and selecting Revert to SharePoint List View. Again, you are warned that any Web Part connections will be lost. In addition, the formatting changes you made to the part while it was a Data View will be gone.

The reversion does not necessarily return the part to the state it was in before being converted to a Data View. The part is converted into a standard tabular view with a full toolbar. If that's not the view you want, you need to do one of the following:

❑ Go back to the web interface and reselect the original view.

❑ Recreate all of the view settings from scratch, as described in the first part of this chapter.

The Data Source Library

Data View Web Parts can also be created without first instantiating a List View, by way of the *Data Source Library*. The Data Source Library is a special hidden document library, `fpdatasources`, which is maintained by SharePoint Designer in the _catalogs folder. Interaction with it, however, is normally through the Data Source Library task pane (see Figure 10-15).

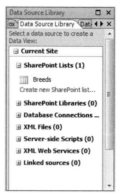

Figure 10-15

By default, the Data Source Library contains an entry for each list and library in the current SharePoint web, except for certain system lists such as the Web Part Catalog or the Data Source Library itself. SharePoint Designer also automatically includes any XML files it finds in the current web. In addition, you can add entries for many other kinds of data sources, which are described more fully in the next chapter.

Automatically detected/generated data sources, such as SharePoint lists and local XML files, do not appear in the_catalogs/fpdatasources folder.

Creating a Data View from the Data Source Library

There are several ways to add a Data View to a page within SharePoint Designer. If the Data Source Library is open, the easiest way is to open a Web Part Page and drag the data source onto your page. This creates a Data View Web Part containing the first few fields defined in the data source (typically Title, Modified, and Modified By). Figure 10-16 shows a default Data View Web Part.

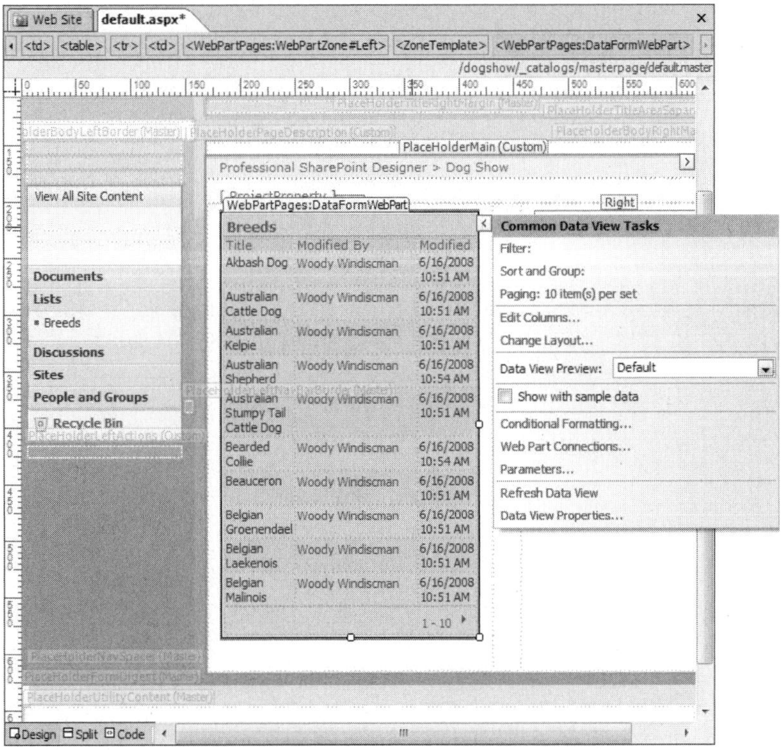

Figure 10-16

You do not need to place a Web Part into a Web Part Zone. Placing a Web Part outside of a Web Part Zone results in a static instance of the Web Part. Web Parts within a Web Part Zone are called dynamic Web Parts. Although the normal user interaction with the Web Part is not affected, the configuration properties of a static part cannot be modified by the end user through the web interface like those of dynamic Web Parts.

Although simple, this method does not offer much control over the initial state of the Web Part. You may not want to use the default fields, for example. Although you can easily change this after the fact, it would be better to be able to select the desired fields before placing the part on the page. Fortunately, you can!

To insert a Data View with full manual control:

1. Place your cursor where you want the Data View to appear.

2. Select Data ⇨ Insert Data View. This creates an empty Data View, as shown in Figure 10-17.

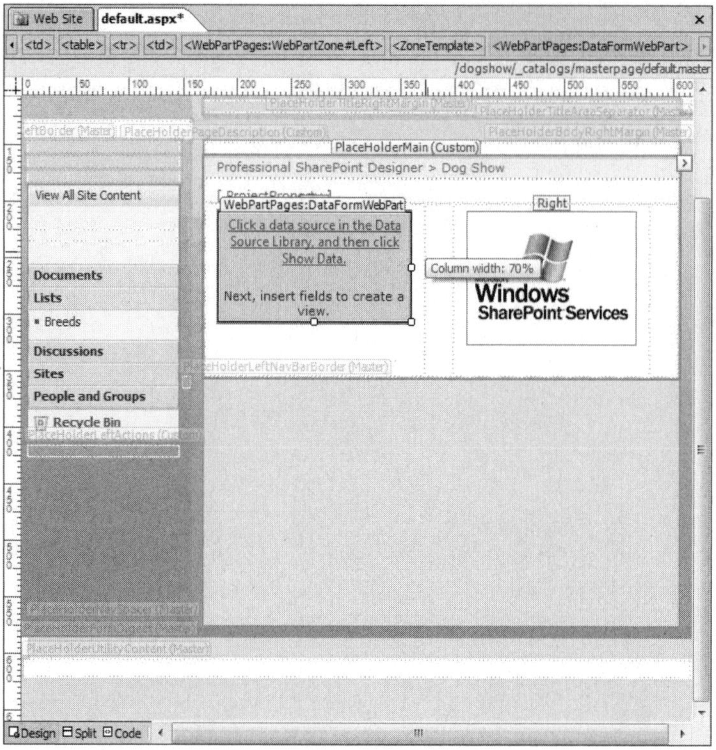

Figure 10-17

3. In the Data Source Library task pane, click on the data source you want to display in the Web Part, and select Show Data from the menu that appears. The Data Source Details pane appears.

4. Highlight the fields you want to include in the Data Source Details pane. Use Ctrl+click to select discontinuous fields, or Shift+click to select a block.

5. Click Insert Selected Fields As at the top of the field list. The menu shown in Figure 10-18 appears. (There may be different choices, depending on the particular data source.)

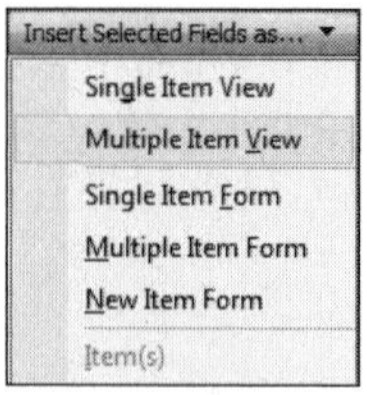

Figure 10-18

6. Select the base format you want to use for the Data View.

Notice that you may have been able to select Form options when creating the initial insertion. Those choices enable you to create an always-editable Data View. This means the data is always displayed as edit fields. If you want to have a *modal* view — normally plain read-only text with an option to place a particular item into edit mode — insert the fields as a single- or multiple-item view, rather than as a form.

Making Connections

One of the most powerful capabilities of SharePoint is *Web Part connections*, which enable you to configure one Web Part to influence the happenings in others. List views, Data Views, and many other Web Parts support the Web Part connection interface.

What Is a Web Part Connection?

With Web Part connections, you go beyond displaying information from multiple sources to creating composite applications drawing from (and potentially updating) information from all over your organization, and beyond. Web Part connections can be created both from the web interface and from within SharePoint Designer.

> Some Web Parts, such as MOSS filter parts, only implement the provider interface, meaning they can only send information to other parts. Some parts, like the Image Web Part, only implement the receiver function. Others, such as most list and Data Views, provide both.

Connections can be made between any two Web Parts that support the provider and receiver interfaces. You can, for instance, create a master/detail display, a form to provide query parameters to a report, or almost any other type of (potentially heterogeneous) web display.

Be careful, however, that you draw from the provider the type of information the receiver expects. Otherwise, the results can be unexpected (the GIGO — Garbage In, Garbage Out — principle). For example, the Image Web Part expects a connection to contain the URL of the image it is to display. If you map it to a plaintext field, the information may or may not resolve into an image, and the Image Web Part could display a missing image icon.

Creating a Web Part Connection

As with many multistep processes, Web Part connections are created with a wizard. You can launch the wizard from a Web Part's context menu. Right-click a Web Part that supports connections, and select Web Part Connections, as shown in Figure 10-19. This is also available in the Web Part control menu, and the Common Data View Tasks menu, as appropriate to the Web Part.

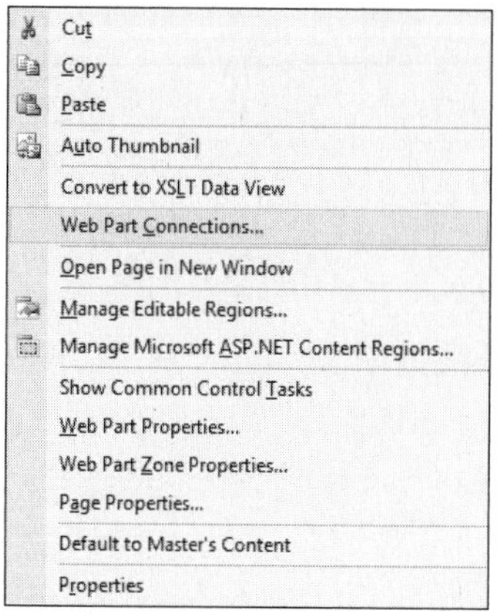

Figure 10-19

If there are no existing connections on this Web Part, you automatically enter the wizard. If there are already connections associated with the Web Part, you have the option of deleting or modifying an existing connection or creating a new one. Choosing to modify or add a connection opens the wizard, pre-populating the steps if modifying an existing connection.

The choices available in the first step depend upon whether the Web Part supports the provider interface, the receiver, or both. If this Web Part is to provide data to another, select one of the Send options. To use data from another Web Part to control the current part, select one of the Get options.

The Send and Get options available depend on both the interfaces supported by the Web Part you have selected and the interfaces supported by other parts on the target page. Send options may be listed as Send or Provide, depending upon the Web Part.

The Send Options

Send options may include:

❑ Provide Row of Data To.

❑ Provide Data To.

❑ Provide Form Values To.

Most of the time, you will use the Provide (or Send) Row of Data To option. When your user invokes the connection, the data associated with that row is provided to the target Web Part, and the action you indicated when defining the connection is performed.

The Provide (or Send) Data To choice provides the entire contents of a data set to the target part. None of the Web Parts provided with SharePoint supports receiving from this interface; however, you may see it if you have installed custom Web Parts from a third party (or written your own Web Parts) that do handle that interface.

Provide Form Values To is typically used by the Form Web Part. You will see an example of its use in chapter 11.

The Get Options

The target Web Part accepts either the row or block of data provided by the source Web Part. Your choices here may include:

- ❑ Get Sort/Filter From.
- ❑ Get Filter Values From.
- ❑ Get Parameters From.
- ❑ Get Data From.
- ❑ Get Image From.

The most commonly used selection is Get Filter (or Filter Values) From, which limits (or filters) the display of the data set to rows that match the values in the source Web Part. This does not change the query to the data source itself. It only filters the rendering of the view.

Unlike filter values, which influence the rendering of information by removing it after the query process is completed, parameters are used by the query itself. The Get Parameters From option is used to provide values to the query that generates the data rendered by the Data View. This can be very useful if the target Web Part performs calculations, or generates reports based on the information provided by the connection.

> *Parameters are only applicable if the query underlying the Data View supports them. In addition, not all queries that accept parameters use them to restrict the results returned.*

As with sending, the Get Data From option is not visible with the standard SharePoint Web Parts, but may be implemented by custom parts.

Get Image From is used by the Image Web Part, and expects the source data to be the URL of an image file.

Selecting a Target

Once you have chosen your action, the next step in the connection wizard is to choose the location of the target Web Part. This can be another Web Part on the current page, or (in the case of the Send options) a Web Part on another page in the same web. If you choose to connect to another page, the interface to select the target page is enabled.

Next you select the other end for the connection. You are presented with a list of the parts that support the appropriate response actions to the one you selected in the first stage of the wizard (that is, if you selected a Send action, suitable Get actions for the selected target part are listed).

Mapping Source and Target Entities

Now that you have indicated which parts to connect, you need to define exactly what information is to be passed between them. Figure 10-20 shows the field/parameter mapping selector for List Views. When using two List View Web Parts, a single column from each view can be selected for the connection.

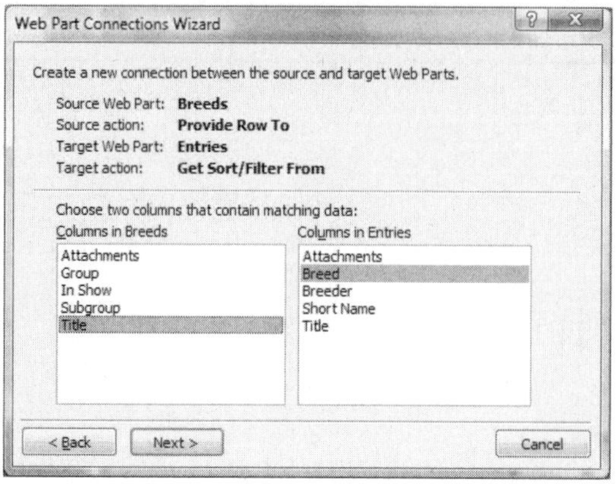

Figure 10-20

For Data View Web Parts, multiple fields may be mapped as appropriate to your particular connection. Each row of the selector can show the source and target fields for one join. There is no need for the names of the fields to match in both the source and destination; however, the data types for each row must be at least nominally compatible (that is, both source and target fields must be dates, numbers, or string representations). Figure 10-21 shows the field mapper for Data Views.

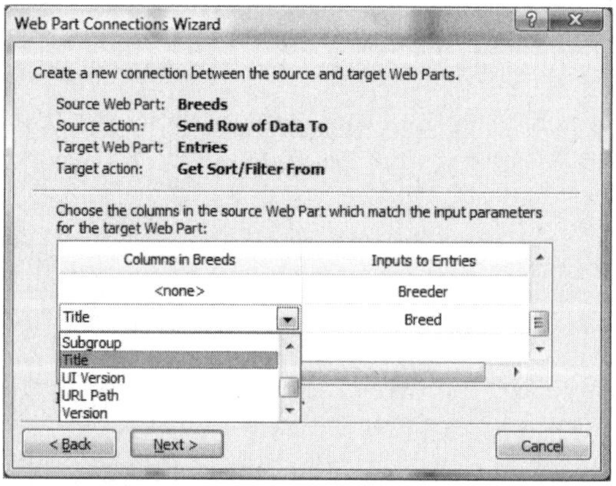

Figure 10-21

Not every field of your view is available for mapping in a connection. Availability depends on the type of Web Part, the nature of the connection, and the kind of data the parts can provide and receive, respectively. For example, most List Views can connect only on fields that are included in the view itself, while a Data View can connect on almost any of the fields defined in the data source.

Defining the Trigger

The trigger is the element in the source Web Part the user clicks to cause the connection to fire, prompting the desired change in the target part. For List View sources, the trigger is always a radio button that is added to each item in the List View.

For a Data View, the trigger is created as a hyperlink on some element of the displayed item. You have the option of choosing one of the displayed fields or [Current selection]. Current selection is very useful if you enter some static text or a graphic element/icon that appears in each row, and select it with the mouse before starting the connection wizard.

When you're done, you click the Finish button, and you have a functioning connection.

Data View Editing Basics

As mentioned earlier, a Data View enables you to use the full WYSIWYG power of SharePoint Designer's design surface. Although your actions within SharePoint Designer are similar to those you take when editing normal web page elements, there are some differences in the effect those actions have on the underlying page code.

The main thing to keep in mind is that what is rendered behind the scenes is not standard HTML. Rather it is XSL, keyed to the data source defined when you created the Data View. This means that when you look at the page in Code view, you do not see the actual information that is shown in the design surface. Instead, you see the XSL code with references to fields (@title, for instance).

Table for One (One Row, That Is . . .)

Data Views are presented as a table — but not quite a standard table. You do not explicitly state the number of rows it displays, for example, because that is managed by the data definition.

The Data View table functions as a repeating data grid in XSL, so whatever changes you make in one row of the table apply to every data row. This includes which data fields are used, formatting options, and any other change. Outside of the data rows, there are also header and footer rows, which are each formatted separately.

Other than those considerations, you can use most of the standard SharePoint Designer table manipulation functions to control its format, such as border formats, cells within a row, and so on. You can control how each field is rendered by applying typical formatting (CSS styles).

You can enter static display items such as field labels, images, or even intra-row layout elements into a Data View. If these are entered into a data row, they will be repeated in every data row.

Conditional Formatting

As nice as these basic formatting capabilities are, having every row of data look the same can get pretty monotonous, or even hard to read. Fortunately, you aren't stuck with that. Data Views offer the powerful capability of *conditional formatting*. Conditional formatting allows you to base formatting decisions *within* any given row on the data it contains.

Consider a Data View showing a list of sales representatives and their sales for the month. With conditional formatting, you could have the background behind the name of a representative turn red if his sales are below a target level.

The Conditional Formatting task pane (see Figure 10-22) is summoned in SharePoint Designer by selecting Data View ⇨ Conditional Formatting, or from the Common Data View Tasks context menu.

Figure 10-22

You use it to define display conditions.

Conditional Formatting Actions

Formatting actions apply to the element(s) selected in the Data View when you open the Create menu. (Remember, all rows look alike to the Data View, so you can select the data in any visible row.) The Create menu gives you three choices:

❑   Show Content

❑   Hide Content

❑   Apply Formatting

The Show and Hide Content choices are the inverse of each other. Use a Show Content condition when you want the highlighted item(s) to be displayed *only if* the specified condition is true. Use a Hide Content condition if you want the highlighted item(s) to be displayed *unless* the specified condition is true.

Apply Formatting allows you to change the style of the highlighted items if the specified conditions are met. You can highlight an entire row, or any portion thereof that is selectable. The formats available are the same as those you saw for creating CSS style sheets in chapter 6. Anything from fonts to colors, backgrounds, or even position settings can be changed. A typical use might be to set the background color of values over some threshold to yellow.

When applied to an entire data row, the Show and Hide Content options have a similar visible effect to applying a filter to the data source, with a significant difference: The underlying data remains and is used in any summary calculations in the Data View. In addition, like the Apply Formatting option, Show and Hide can be used on individual elements within a row.

Setting the Condition(s)

Regardless of which format action you choose, the Condition Criteria dialog (see Figure 10-23) appears.

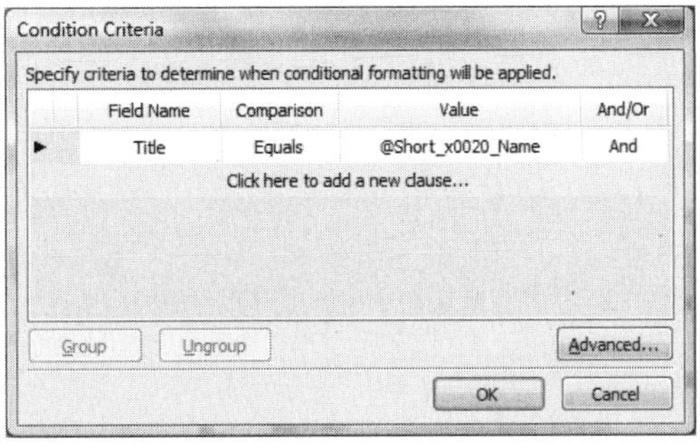

Figure 10-23

The basic Condition Criteria dialog looks and behaves much like the filter dialog described earlier for List Views, except that Data View conditions activate the Advanced criteria option. That summons the XPath editor, which is described in detail later in this chapter.

Modifying the Data View Properties

All of the tools described earlier in this chapter for modifying a List View (sorting, grouping, and so on) are also available for Data Views. Some of these tools provide enhanced functionality. For example, the Sort and Group tab allows more than two levels of grouping.

Other tabs enable more or different controls. Compare the Data View Properties' General tab (right side of Figure 10-24) to the List View Options corresponding tab (left side of Figure 10-24), which was discussed earlier in this chapter.

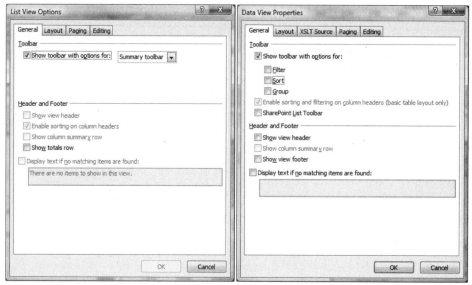

Figure 10-24

Instead of simply a full and summary toolbar, the Data View Properties dialog offers you the granularity to pick the individual functions you want to display. You also can explicitly set the text to display when there are no items visible with the current filter conditions.

Also notice that the Data View Properties dialog contains an XSLT Source tab. It can be used to specify an external file to store the XSL for the Data View (described in the next section).

XSLT in Brief

When you select a data source for a Data View, SharePoint queries that source and returns the results in XML. Although XML is a text-based format, it can be very difficult for human beings to read, so XML is usually processed through an eXtensible Stylesheet Language Transform (XSLT). XSLT is used to transform XML data from one format (or schema) into another. This transformation is based on templates created in the eXtensible Stylesheet Language (XSL), which is itself an implementation of XML.

> *This section describes how XSLT is managed in SharePoint Designer. While some aspects of XSL are introduced as needed in passing, this is not intended to be a full tutorial on the nuances of XSL itself.*

In many ways, XSLT is a programming language — it consists of instructions on how to render the incoming XML data. Like most languages, it has syntax, contains keywords, can abstract data in variables, and has control structures to allow different renderings based on conditions in the data. The XSLT markup generated by SharePoint Designer intersperses static HTML markup with the dynamic data from the XML source.

Although SharePoint Designer uses XSLT to transform XML data into browser-readable HTML, the language itself can be used to transform XML data into virtually any other text format, including a different pure XML schema.

Because XSL is a markup-based language, each command or statement in XSL is a bracket (<>) tag set. Because it is an XML implementation, every opening tag (<) has a corresponding close tag (/>). The following code fragment shows the XSL to call one template (i.e., function) from within another.

```
<xsl:call-template name="dvt_1.body">
    <xsl:with-param name="ParentPath" />
    <xsl:with-param name="Rows" select="$Rows" />
    <xsl:with-param name="FirstRow" select="1" />
    <xsl:with-param name="LastRow" select="$LastRow - $FirstRow + 1" />
</xsl:call-template>
```

Within the XSL language is the XPath language, which is used to select and render data elements and attributes from the source XML. The `select` attributes in several rows of the preceding example are XPath expressions.

Location, Location, Location...

Like CSS styles, XSL templates can be stored inline (within the page), or imported for a Data View from external XSL files. Unlike CSS, XSL does not cascade through the Web Part. If you attach an external XSL file to a Data View, that file is used to the exclusion of any XSL defined within the Web Part itself.

Using an XSL file allows you to re-use the same transform template for multiple Data Views. An external XSL file opened directly in SharePoint Designer is treated as XML for editing purposes and is only displayed in Code view. However, if you have attached the XSL file to a Data View, formatting changes to the Data View in WYSIWYG mode are saved back into the external file.

When you create a Data View, a default XSL template is created inline with the Web Part. The inline XSL is accessible directly through the XSL property of the Web Part, or in Code view. You can use that XSL as the starting point for an external XSL template, ensuring that the initial XSL contains all of the elements needed to support the current Data View.

To create the initial XSL template file, follow these steps:

1. Select a Data View Web Part.

2. Right-click the Data View, and select Web Part Properties.

3. In the Data View Properties section is a small XSL Editor window containing the XSL code and an ellipsis (. . .) button. Click the button.

4. Click within the source window that pops up, press Ctrl+A to select all of the text, and then press Ctrl+C to copy it to the Clipboard.

5. Close the editor window and Data View properties.

6. Select File ⇨ New.

7. From the General section, select XML, and click OK. A new XML document opens.

8. Delete the XML header that appears by default in the document.

9. Press Ctrl+V to paste the XSL code copied in step 4 into the document.

10. Select File ⇨ Save As, give the new file an appropriate name, such as `entries.xsl`, and click Save.

11. Switch back to your page. (You can close the XSL file at this time if you want, but it is not required.)

12. Choose Common Data View Tasks ⇨ Data View Properties, and select the XSLT Source tab.

13. Browse to, or enter the name of, the XSL file you saved in step 10, as shown in Figure 10-25.

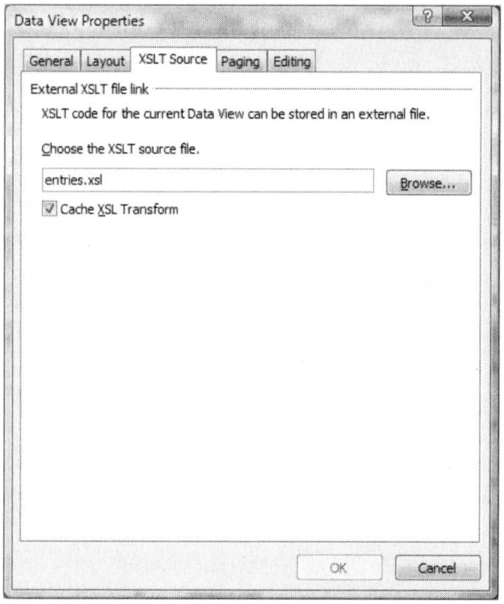

Figure 10-25

14. Click OK.

All WYSIWYG changes made in the Data View will now be made to the external XSL file, and not to the default embedded XSLT.

By saving your XSL to an external file, you make it very easy to see the effect different changes to your Web Part have on the underlying code, making it an excellent learning tool. If you did not close the file in step 11, you can toggle back and forth between the displayed page and the source to observe the changes, almost in real time.

The XPath Expression Builder

The XPath (XML Path) language is a formulaic language similar to that used by a spreadsheet cell. It contains constructs for pattern matching, and other ways to specify a particular data element in an XML file. Specifically, XPath supports a path notation, much like the path to a file or URL, to get from the root of an XML data source to an atom node, or any point in between. In addition, it contains functions for numeric calculation, date arithmetic, string manipulation, and Boolean comparison. This can result in very complicated expressions.

The SharePoint Designer XPath Expression Builder provides an easy way to construct XPath expressions. XPath expressions are used throughout XSL to select the XML data used in the rendering of a Data View Web Part. When you're editing a Data View in SharePoint Designer, you can invoke the XPath Expression Builder from a number of locations:

❑   The Advanced condition button in Conditional Formatting.

❑   XSLT Filtering.

❑   Advanced Sorting (Edit Sort Expression).

❑   Creating a Formula Column.

The title bar of the XPath Expression Builder may vary, depending upon the calling function.

Figure 10-26 shows the XPath Expression Builder.

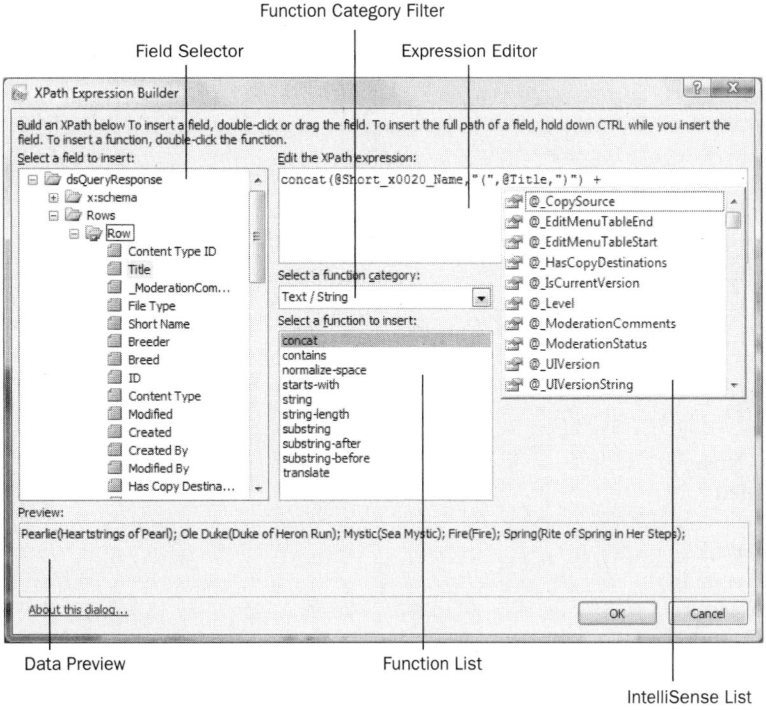

Figure 10-26

It consists of five primary regions:

❑ Field selector.

❑ Expression editor.

❑ Function list (including a category filter).

❑ Function description (area is overlaid by the IntelliSense list in Figure 10-26; see Figure 10-27).

❑ Data preview.

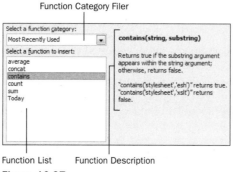

Figure Category Filer

Figure 10-27

The field selector shows the elements of the data source. This includes not only the data elements available, but the schema elements as well.

The expression editor itself shows the current XPath formula. It is fully enabled with IntelliSense, meaning your syntax is checked, and you are provided with lists of appropriate elements when editing the text.

The function list enables you to filter the functions by category, or view all available functions. Available function categories include:

❑ Math / Number.

❑ Text / String.

❑ Field / Node (for accessing XML data from other rows).

❑ Date / Time.

❑ Boolean.

❑ Parameters (for global Web Part settings).

❑ XPath Axes (more XML data access functions).

❑ Operators (numeric and Boolean).

❑ XSLT (for accessing XSL context information).

Once you have started using the XPath Expression Builder, the category will default to Most Recently Used functions when you open the dialog. If the function you want is not in that list, you need to select a different category.

When you highlight a function in the list, a description of that function appears next to the list.

The preview window shows the output of the current XPath expression as applied to your data source, so you can tell right away if you are going to get the expected results in your Data View.

Summary

This chapter explored the display and manipulation of SharePoint data on a page using SharePoint Designer, and introduced you to the XSLT Data View Web Part. It also discussed:

❑   SharePoint lists and libraries that can be rendered on a page in a number of ways.

❑   How to add a Web Part to a page with SharePoint Designer, and place it outside of a Web Part Zone.

❑   How SharePoint lists and libraries exposed as data sources can be used by the Data View Web Part.

❑   That the XSL transform for a Data View can be inline or in a separate file.

❑   How the XPath editor makes it easy to build complicated XML data expressions.

The next chapter explains how to take the Data View to a whole new level by accessing data from outside of the current SharePoint web, and directly editing the XSL transforms.

11

Advanced Data Access: External Data and More

Now that you know how easy it is to modify SharePoint list and library views, and how to convert them to the much more flexible Data View Web Part, you're ready to move ahead. This chapter builds on your experience with the Data View and Data Source Library to reach beyond SharePoint and build truly heterogeneous applications and mashups. You will learn about:

❑   Types of data sources.

❑   Displaying external data in SharePoint.

❑   Using SharePoint data in multiple sites.

❑   Displaying images in XSL in Data Views.

❑   Exporting Data Views.

The Data Source Library in Detail

In the previous chapter, you saw how SharePoint lists and libraries are reflected in the Data Source Library task pane. You probably noticed several other sections. SharePoint Designer enables you to connect to and manage many different types of information.

All of the formatting and display capabilities of Data Views described in chapter 10 can be used with any data source defined in the Data Source Library, including conditional formatting, Web Part connections, and custom XSL.

The Data Source Types

The Data Source Library task pane is divided into a number of sections that group similar types of data, helping you keep track of where the information displayed in your site is coming from. The following table describes those sections:

Section	Description
SharePoint Lists and Libraries	Lists and libraries are intrinsic data sources in SharePoint. Whenever you create a list or library — whether through the web interface or SharePoint Designer — it automatically becomes available in the appropriate section.
Database Connections	Database connections enable you to define a source to connect to an arbitrary database on your network. SharePoint Designer supports creating data sources for SQL Server and Oracle, as well as virtually any database for which an OLE DB or ODBC connection is available, such as MySQL.
XML Files	All data sources are converted to XML before a Data View Web Part can render them. It's no surprise, then, that you can provide XML directly to the part as a file. SharePoint Designer automatically detects any `.xml` files that may be stored in your site and lists them in the XML Files section. In addition, you can define connections to XML files that reside in other locations on your network.
Server-Side Scripts	Server-side scripts are web pages that return (usually dynamically generated) XML data in response to a request. This differs from a web service in that the required form of the request, and the resultant XML, do not necessarily follow published standards for interprocess communication.
XML Web Services	XML Web Services typically follow a standardized set of rules — usually Simple Object Access Protocol (SOAP). This allows a client process to learn about the functions available, query the parameter formats required, and learn result formats provided by the service.
Business Data Catalog	If you open a Microsoft Office SharePoint Server 2007 Enterprise Edition site with SharePoint Designer, you will also see a Business Data Catalog (BDC) section in the Data Source Library task pane. The BDC enables the SharePoint administrator to define connections — not only to databases, but to enterprise applications such as SAP — and make their information available for use in various locations throughout SharePoint.
Linked Sources	Linked sources are made up of combinations of other sources in the Data Source Library.

Adding and Modifying Data Sources

Within each section of the Data Source Library, you will see a link to enable you to add a new data source of that type. After filling in the definition forms (except for lists and libraries), an XML file defining the data source will be saved in the /_catalogs/fpdatasources library.

> *XML definition files are not grouped within the fpdatasources library folder to match the grouping in the Data Source Library task pane. They are all simply stored at the root level.*

Each type of data source has slightly different configuration requirements and therefore different forms for filling in the details. Nevertheless, there is certain information that is similar for any data source, and that information is entered on the General tab, as shown in Figure 11-1.

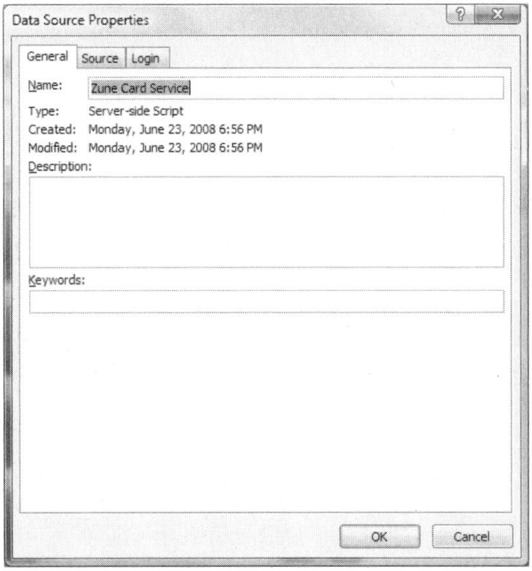

Figure 11-1

To enter or edit any of this information, switch to the General tab (when you create a new data source, the Source tab opens by default). You are not required to enter any information on the General tab; however, if you do not enter a friendly name, an arbitrary generic name such as NewDataSource1 is created when you save the data source for the first time.

> *Although the forms for adding and modifying a data source are the same, be aware that changes made to a data source after Data Views based on it have been created do not flow through to the existing Web Part. In essence, once created, each Data View retains its own independent instance of the data source definition.*

Each data source in the task pane has a menu that provides you with several options. Figure 11-2 shows the menu for the Announcements list.

Figure 11-2

SharePoint Lists and Libraries

SharePoint lists and libraries are automatically added to the Data Source Library task pane when they are created. You do not need to manually create entries for them. In addition, unlike most data source definitions, these automatic entries have direct links to the underlying list or library, and therefore are not normally listed in the fpdatasources folder. You have the option to create new lists or libraries from the appropriate sections. Remember, however, that SharePoint Designer does not offer the capability to add or remove list or library fields directly.

Because the data source is tied directly to the list or library, unlike most data sources, lists and libraries do not show a query editor by default. The Data Source Library does give you a way to limit the available fields or rows when creating Data View Web Parts, though, and that is through the Copy and Modify option in the item's menu. This overrides the normal direct connection to the list, and opens the query editor shown in Figure 11-3.

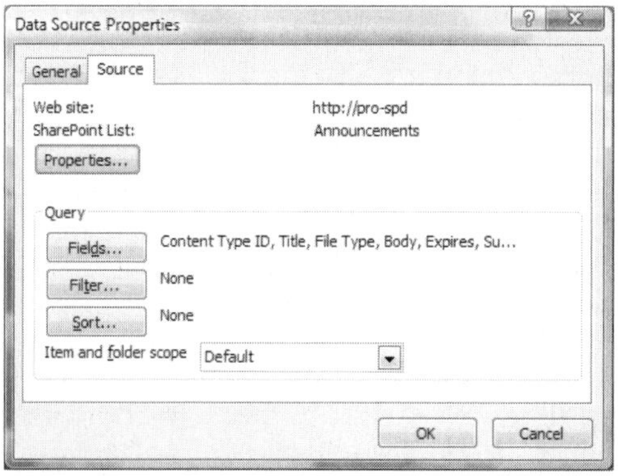

Figure 11-3

The query editor is normally readily available when defining other types of data sources.

From here you can simplify the list's data display, prefilter results down to a subset, or create XPath calculated fields for direct selection when creating Data View Web Parts. When you click OK, SharePoint Designer saves a copy, and it appears as a new source in the list or library section of the Data Source

Library task pane. In addition, unlike its parent list, this entry has an .xml definition file in the fpdatasources library, just like any other data source.

An HTMLEncoded version of the CAML query you define with the query editor is embedded in the XML definition file.

Database Connections

Creating a database connection is a two-stage process. First, clicking the "Connect to a database . . . " link produces a very simple dialog containing the General tab described previously and a Source tab with a single button (Configure Database Connection). Clicking this launches the second stage — the Database Connection Wizard.

There are several steps to creating a database connection. The first step (see Figure 11-4) defines the type and location of the database, and provides any needed access credentials.

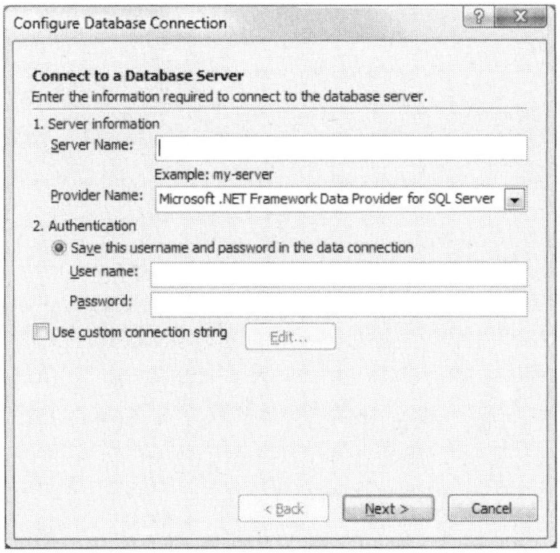

Figure 11-4

If you wish to connect to a database other than Microsoft SQL Server (for example, Oracle or MySQL), you can check the Use custom connection string box and provide an appropriate connection string directly.

> It is important that both the SharePoint server(s) and the client running SharePoint Designer have access to the database server for this process to succeed. This includes both network access and appropriate client drivers. Visitors to the site will not need client drivers. They may require appropriate credentials if common credentials or anonymous access to the database is not provided.

When you click Next, connection to the database is verified, and you are presented with a form to define the record set you want to use. You can select a table, view, or stored procedure, or indicate that you wish to enter a SQL query directly. If your SharePoint Server administrator has enabled update query support, you may also define the statements required for writing information back to your data set. Figure 11-5 shows the Database and Table (etc.) selection page of the Database Connection Wizard.

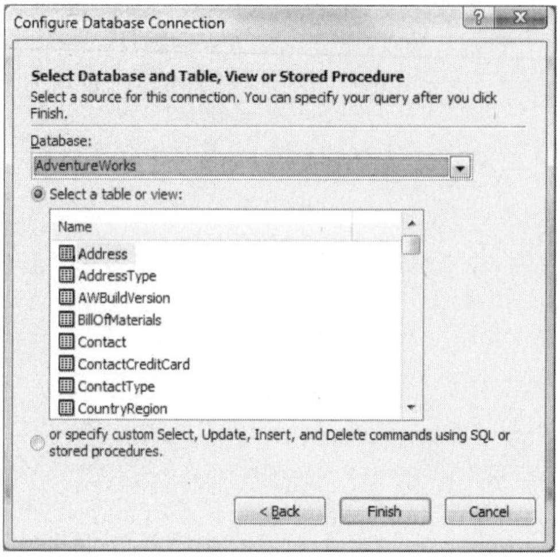

Figure 11-5

If you select the option to specify custom queries, when you click Finish, this dialog will be followed by a form for building your queries.

After completing the wizard and saving your database connection, viewing the properties displays the Query options panel in the Source tab, allowing you to easily define or fine-tune subsets of your primary data source query.

XML Files

Creating a new XML reference is very straightforward. You can either import an XML file into your SharePoint site, or if the XML file is stored online, simply create a link to it. An online XML file does not need to be within a SharePoint site, but it does need to be accessible via either http or https.

If the server containing the file does not allow anonymous access, you can provide login information on the Login tab of the data source definition, shown in Figure 11-6.

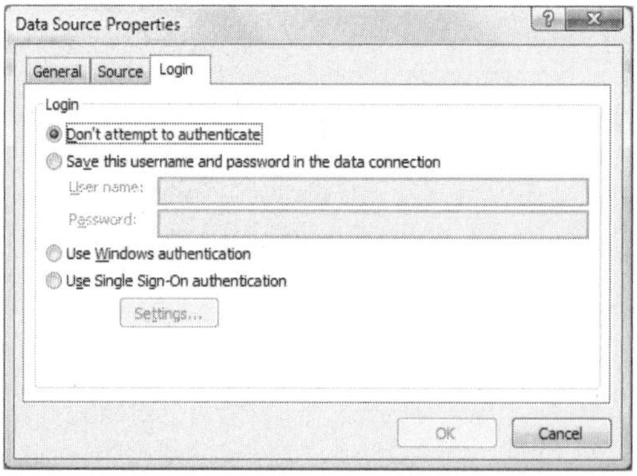

Figure 11-6

The Login tab is the same for most data sources other than databases, the BDC, and SharePoint lists and libraries.

Server-Side Scripts

Most server-side scripts, such as traditional .asp, .php, and Cold Fusion (.cfm), are designed to accept parameters from a form page. If the script can return results in XML format, you can create a connection to that script that provides the input parameters it expects, and returns the XML to SharePoint. Figure 11-7 shows the Source tab of a server-side script data source.

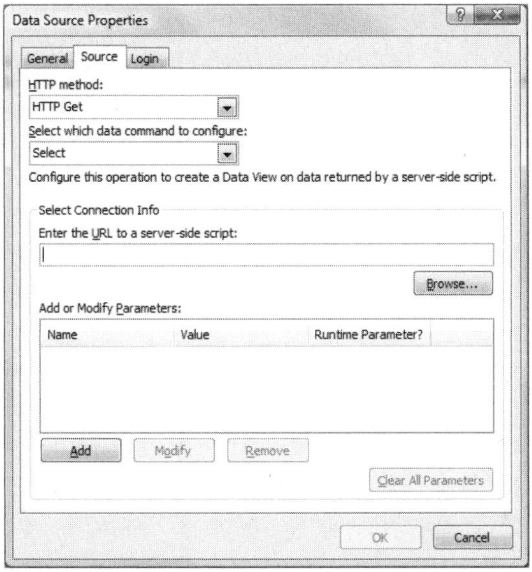

Figure 11-7

At a minimum, you need to provide the URL of the script. If the script does not require any parameters, you do not need to enter any other information. If you need (or want) to provide extra information for the script, there is further work to do.

HTTP Method

Web forms can be submitted in two ways: HTTP Get and HTTP Post. The method you choose depends on the server-side script. Some scripts are independent of the method, but most require one or the other.

A script that uses the HTTP Get method is easy to recognize because parameters are passed as part of the URL. Such a URL might look like this:

```
http://www.example.com/inventory/products.asp?CompanyID=25&InStock=true
```

The parameters in this case are `CompanyID` and `InStock`.

When accessing a script that requires the HTTP `Post` method, the parameters are passed within the HTTP request header itself and are not normally visible to a user. To use this method, you need to find out from the application designer what parameters are expected by the script.

A few, very rare scripts depend on certain parameters to be submitted with each method. SharePoint Designer cannot configure connections for scripts that require parameters from both methods simultaneously.

Data Command

Most of the time, you only want to read and display (that is, Select) information from your external data source, so you simply leave the default Select option chosen. In addition to querying, however, some scripts allow you to insert, update, or delete the underlying data. To implement those functions in your Data View or forms, select the appropriate command from the Data Command dropdown. Each of the functions has its own set of parameters defined.

Parameters

Once you determine the HTTP method and Data Command, you can add any required parameters to the parameter table. In the parameter dialog, you can specify both the name and a default value for each parameter. In addition, you can designate a parameter as run time by checking the box for The value of this parameter can be set via a Web Part connection. Figure 11-8 shows the dialog to add or modify a parameter.

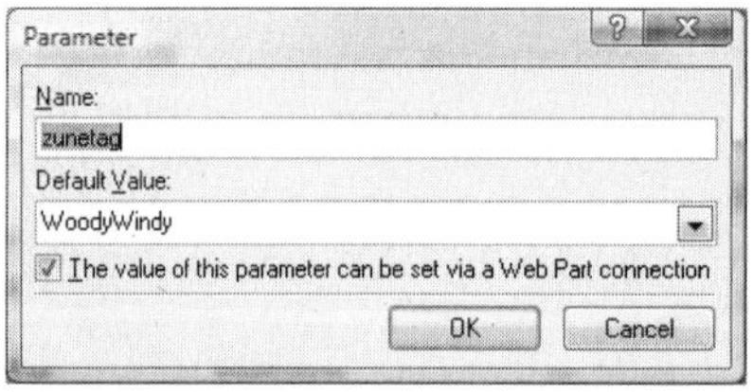

Figure 11-8

XML Web Services

XML Web Services are like an enhancement of server-side scripts, with a major exception — most server-side scripts are meant to be called from other pages within the same application. Web services, on the other hand, are designed specifically to be called by other applications, so there are some key differences between setting up a server-side script data source and setting up an XML Web Service data source. Figure 11-9 shows the Source configuration screen for an XML Web Service.

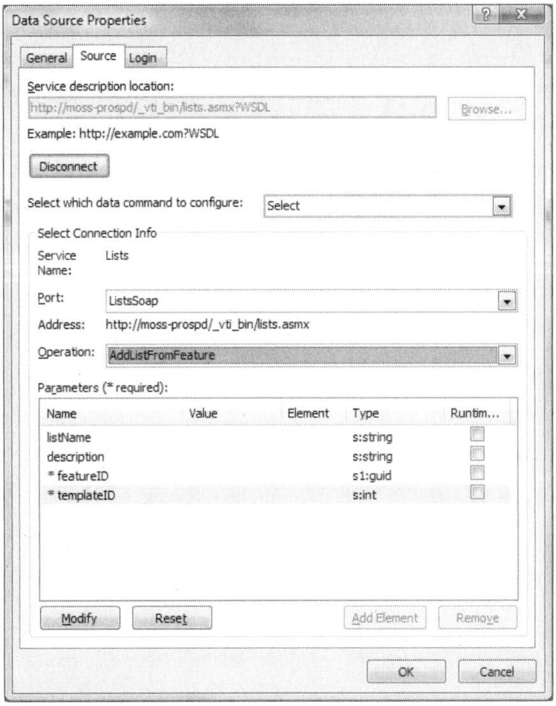

Figure 11-9

Service Description Location

As you did for the server-side script, you need to provide a URL to access a web service. For a web service, however, the URL you enter here typically will include the specific parameter `?WSDL`, which means Web Services Description Language, or Web Service Definition Language. This parameter instructs the web service to return information about how it is used in a standardized XML form. SharePoint Designer then uses that information to provide the options for the remainder of the configuration.

Data Command

Again, as with the server-side script, you configure `Select`, `Insert`, `Update`, and `Delete` commands independently. Most of the time, you only configure a `Select` command. If the web service provides operations for the other commands, and you want your Data View Web Part to implement them, simply configure the remaining sections appropriately for each command.

Port

If a web service supports multiple interfaces, the Port option allows you to specify which interface to use. You typically use the first option provided, unless the web service provider gives specific instruction to the contrary.

Operation

Upon connecting to the WSDL file, SharePoint Designer populates the Operation dropdown with the supported functions of the web service. Select the operation you want to perform to implement the current command.

Parameters

After you select an operation, SharePoint Designer populates the Parameters table. This is much simpler than discovering the parameters for a server-side script because you do not have to guess or dig through possibly unobtainable documentation to determine what the functions expect.

Parameters to a web service may be optional or required. Required parameters are indicated by an asterisk (*). As with server-side script parameters, you may predefine a default value for a parameter and also make it configurable at run time (through a Web Part connection, for instance). Unlike server-side script parameters, these values can be complex entities that contain many elements, such as arrays, and have data types that can be enforced. For complex data types, each element can have a default value and/or runtime source specified.

You cannot add parameters to or remove parameters from a web service data source, because they are predefined in the WSDL. For optional parameters, just leave the configuration elements blank if you are not going to use them.

Business Data Catalog

Unlike other intrinsic SharePoint components, Business Data Catalog (BDC) objects are not automatically included in the Data Source Library. When you open a MOSS site, you need to add them individually to the available data sources. Figure 11-10 shows the BDC data source configuration screen.

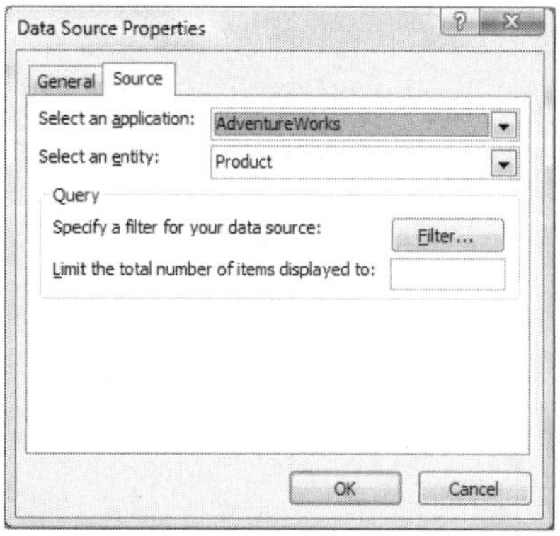

Figure 11-10

Each BDC data source represents one entity type from one application. BDC applications and entities are defined farm-wide, and invoked where needed. Most parameters of a BDC list are set centrally, but you can apply basic filters to your data source to avoid returning the potentially millions of records in an enterprise application with a single query. In addition, when creating a Data View, you still have the option of selecting specific data columns and applying additional filters.

Connecting to Other Libraries

SharePoint Designer also allows you to connect to Data Source Libraries in other SharePoint sites and to leverage some or all of the data sources defined therein. The exact sources available through the connection will depend on the relationship (if any) between the current site and the site of the library to which you are connecting.

To connect to another site, open the Data Source Library task bar, and click the Connect To Another Library link at the bottom of that pane. This opens the Manage Library dialog, which lists the external libraries that are currently connected (see Figure 11-11).

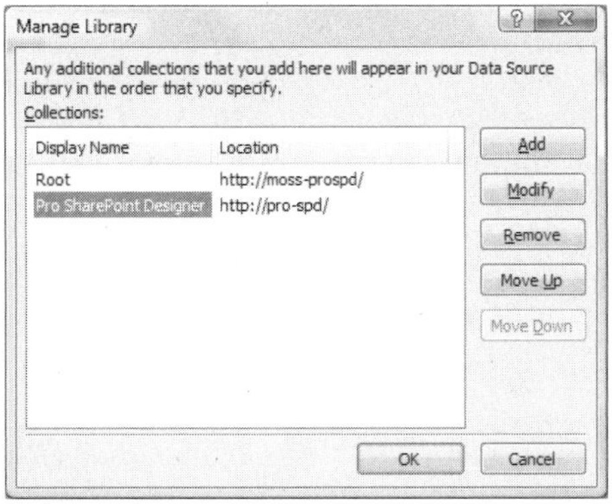

Figure 11-11

Click the Add button to enter a descriptive name and the URL of the library you want to add. Click the Browse button to navigate to a particular SharePoint site, and click the Open button in the browse dialog to insert the selected site into the Location field. Alternatively, you can manually enter a URL in the field. In either case, once you have selected the site, click OK to establish the connection.

If the site you have selected is not available, or does not have a sharable Data Source Library, you will get an error message, and the library will not be added to the list.

> **Once you have opened another site's Data Source Library, you are not working on a local copy of the data source. Any changes you make in the connected library are reflected back to the original source! Verify which portion of the Data Source Library you are working with before making changes.**

Sites in the Same Site Collection

Connect to another site in the same site collection, and you have access to all of the data sources defined within the site, including the site's lists and libraries, and any external data sources. If you are using a MOSS server, you also have access to the BDC sources defined in the target site. Linked data sources are available, but may not function as expected if any of the constituent data sources require permissions not possessed by users of the connecting site.

Sites in a Different Site Collection

When you connect to sites in a different site collection — whether on the same server or on a different SharePoint server — you only get access to the user-defined data sources and XML files. You cannot access the target site's lists and libraries. If the target site is a MOSS site, you do not have direct access to any Business Data Catalog entries.

All linked data sources from the selected Data Source Library will be listed. Linked data sources made up of elements that can cross site collections will function normally. If a linked data source is composed with any elements that are not available as described above, however, that data source will not function.

Linking Data Sources

In the previous chapter, you saw how you could use SharePoint and SharePoint Designer to relate Web Parts through Web Part connections. Another way to blend the display of heterogeneous data is through *linked data sources*. A linked data source enables you to define a relationship between two or more existing data sources and present them in a single Data View.

To select elements for a linked data source, click the Create A New Linked Source link, or select Edit from the data source context menu. The Data Source Properties dialog shown in Figure 11-12 appears. It is initially unpopulated.

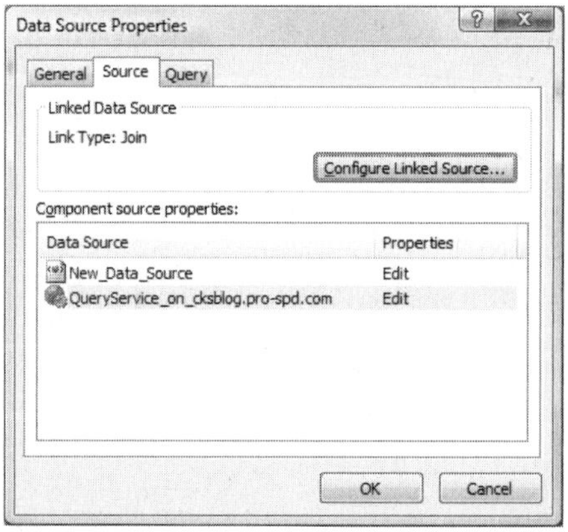

Figure 11-12

Click the Configure Linked Source button to launch the Link Data Source Wizard. The first page, shown in Figure 11-13, lists all of the data sources in each of the Data Source Libraries you currently have connected.

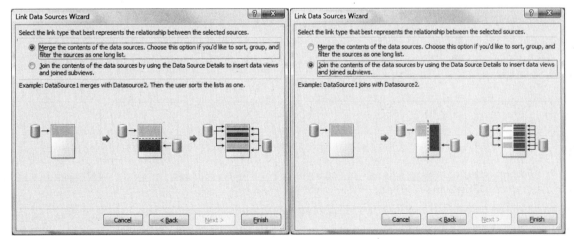

Figure 11-13

Select and order the data sources you want, and then click Next. Select the type of link you want to create: merge or join.

A *merged* data source (see the left side of the Link Data Source Wizard example in Figure 11-14) is useful if the information in the component sources can be considered components in a single list. For example, you may want to roll up list information from multiple sites in your collection for a single view on the home page.

Figure 11-14

A *joined* data source (see the right side of the wizard example in Figure 11-14) is most useful when there is a hierarchical or one-to-many relationship between the elements in the component data sources. A SharePoint list of client contacts, joined to the Orders table of a financial system (connected through the BDC), for instance, might make a very useful linked data source.

> When creating a linked data source, ensure that your intended users have permission to at least read all of the constituent data sources. Otherwise, any Data View Web Parts using that source will display only an error message for users who do not have such permission, even if they have permission to read some of the data.

Working with Hierarchical Data

Until now, the discussion of data display has been about working with data in the relatively simple tabular form. Many kinds of information, however, do not naturally lend themselves to a simple tabular organization. The joined mode linked data source described previously is just one of many possible sources of hierarchical, or *nested*, information.

XML, with its capability to have nodes within nodes within nodes, is designed to easily represent such multidimensional data. Because the Data View Web Part is at its core an XML display tool, its usefulness would be quite limited if it were not capable of handling hierarchical data as well as tabular information. Fortunately, it handles it quite easily.

For this example, you will connect SharePoint to Microsoft's Zune Social Web site. Zune Social is an online community closely associated with the Microsoft Zune digital media player. It allows Zune users to register and share information about their entertainment preferences with other users.

This sharing is done through what is known as a Zune Card. Zune Cards are used throughout the Zune Social site. They can also be shared and displayed on other web sites, usually rendered through an Adobe Flash applet. The information the Zune Card applet uses can be retrieved as hierarchical XML through a server-side script. You will use this as the data source in the following exercise.

The exercise walks you through creating a Data View Web Part that shows the playlists of a Zune Card, along with the album cover art. In it, you create a Web Part connection to allow you to choose the user whose playlist information you want to display. In the process, you will leverage many of the capabilities of the SharePoint Designer Data Views you have learned about in this and the preceding chapter, as well as several methods for selecting and inserting fields for a Data View.

This exercise assumes you have created a Web Part page to contain the Web Parts, and have it open in SharePoint Designer. (A Header, Left Column, Body page layout is suggested.) Save your page after the second and each subsequent module.

Create the Data Source

In this module, you create an external data source, and set up a parameter to be used later for a Web Part connection.

1. In the Data Source Library, open the Server-side scripts section.

2. Click the Connect To Script Or RSS Feed link.

3. Enter the following URL for the script:

```
http://zcards.zune.net/zcard/usercardservice.ashx?src=external&zunetag=WoodyWindy
```

4. Click the Add button to register the existing parameters. (Cancel the Parameter pop-up.)

5. Select the `src` parameter and click Modify.

6. Uncheck the box for The Value Of This Parameter, and click OK.

   a. *Optional:* Change the default value of the zunetag parameter to your own Zune tag.

7. Click on the General tab and enter `Zune Card Service` into the Name field.

8. Click OK.

9. Select Show Data from the Zune Card Service context menu. The Data Source Details window shown in Figure 11-15 will appear. Notice that there are many nested folders, containing many kinds of data.

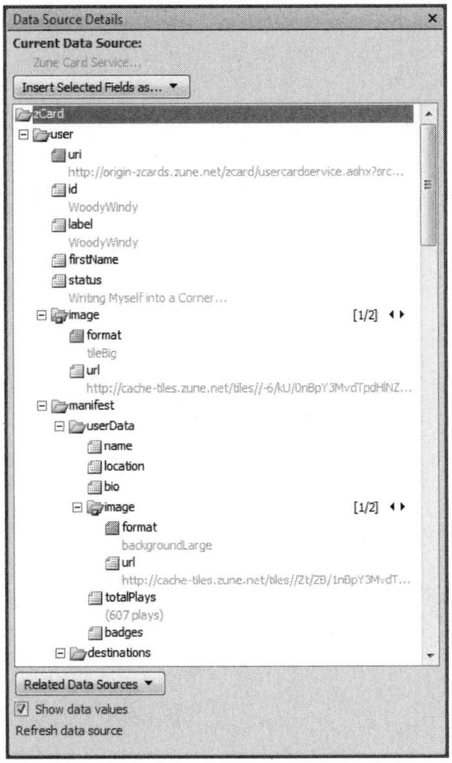

Figure 11-15

Insert the Web Part

In this module, you create a Data View Web Part based on the data source created in the first module. Because the primary iterating level of this view is the playlist, that is the first data segment to be inserted. You will set the header of the view to include some of the Zune user's general information.

1. If the page you want to create this Web Part on is not already open, open a Web Part Page.

2. Highlight the Web Part Zone in which you want to insert the Web Part (typically the Body).

3. Select Data View ⇨ Insert Data View.

4. Select Show Data from the Zune Card Service context menu.

5. Scroll down the list of fields, and select the object /zCard/user/manifest/playlists/playlist/label, opening any folders that may be closed. Figure 11-16 shows the expanded data source with the correct element highlighted.

Figure 11-16

6. Click Insert Selected Fields as and select Multiple Item View. A basic list formatted Web Part similar to the one shown in the center of Figure 11-17 should be inserted.

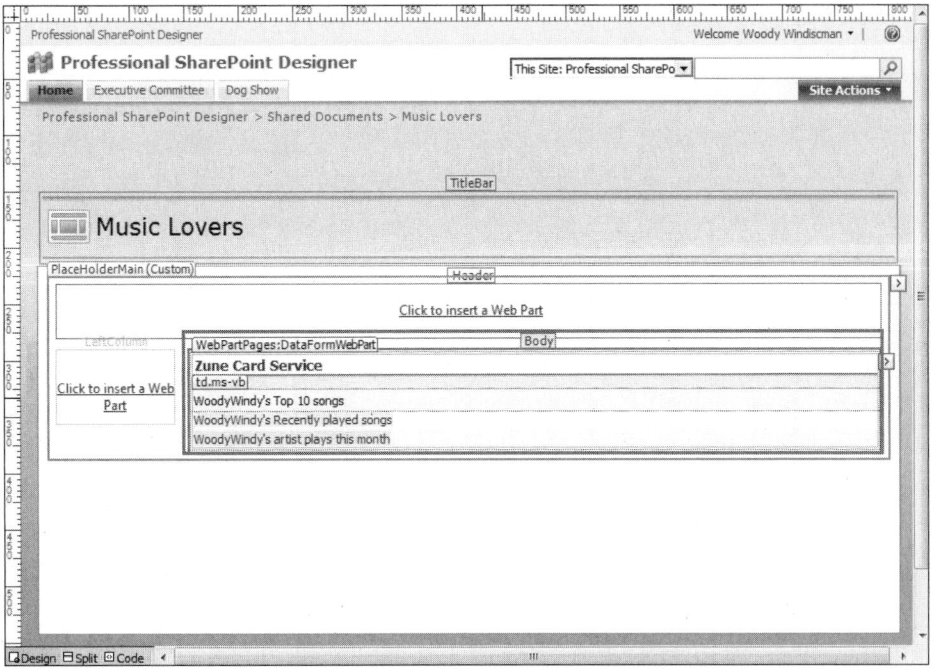

Figure 11-17

7. Select Common Data View Tasks ⇨ Change Layout.

8. Select the view described as The Two-Column Repeating Form.

9. Click the General tab, and check the Show View Header check box.

10. Click OK. The View should now look like Figure 11-18 (with callouts added to indicate some of the following steps).

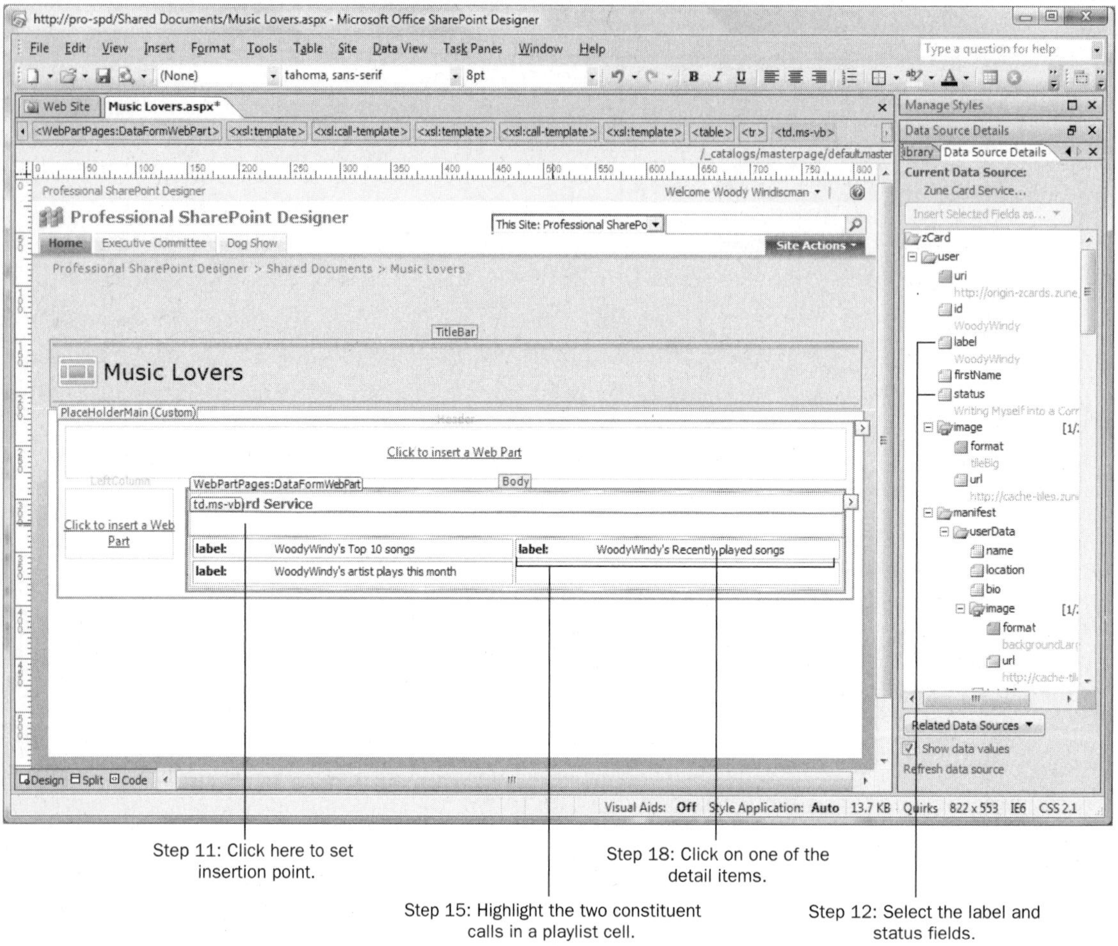

Step 11: Click here to set
insertion point.

Step 18: Click on one of the
detail items.

Step 15: Highlight the two constituent
calls in a playlist cell.

Step 12: Select the label and
status fields.

Figure 11-18

11. Click in the blank area above the playlist grid to set the insertion point.

12. From the user node in the data source, select the label and status fields.

13. Click Insert Selected Fields as, and select Item(s).

14. Click to set the text insertion point between the newly inserted fields, and type a colon (:) and a space, to separate the items.

15. In one of the playlist cells, highlight the two constituent cells.

16. Right-click the selected cells, and select Modify ⇨ Merge Cells.

17. Switch to Split view.

18. Click on one of the detail items. The Code pane should show a line that reads:

```
<b>label:</b><xsl:value-of select="label" /></td>
```

19. Click in the Code pane, and edit that line so that it reads:

```
<b><xsl:value-of select="label" /></b></td>
```

20. Click back in the Design pane, and the Web Part will now look like Figure 11-19. Notice that the user's Zune tag and status are displayed above the grid, and the word "label" is gone from the playlist cells.

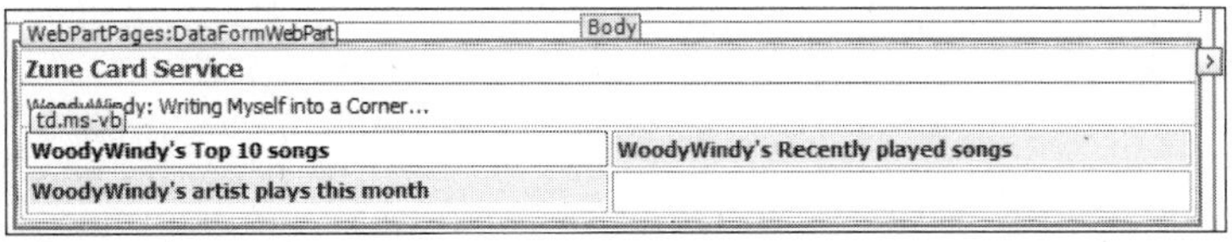

WebPartPages:DataFormWebPart	Body	
Zune Card Service		▸
WoodyWindy: Writing Myself into a Corner... td.ms-vb		
WoodyWindy's Top 10 songs	**WoodyWindy's Recently played songs**	
WoodyWindy's artist plays this month		

Figure 11-19

Insert and Customize the Subview

In this module, you add the playlist details and customize their display to show a small image of the album cover for each song.

1. Click in the Design pane to place the insertion point at the end of the Top 10 Songs label.

2. Right-click in the Data view, and select Data Source Details. (This may be required any time you restart SharePoint Designer or open the page, to ensure that the correct instance of the data source is displayed.)

3. In the Data Source Details task pane, scroll down to the track folder (/zCard/user/manifest/playlists/playlist/track).

4. Open the track folder (if required), and select the first label field.

5. Drag the label field and drop it when the insertion point is at the end of the Top 10 Songs label. The display should look like Figure 11-20.

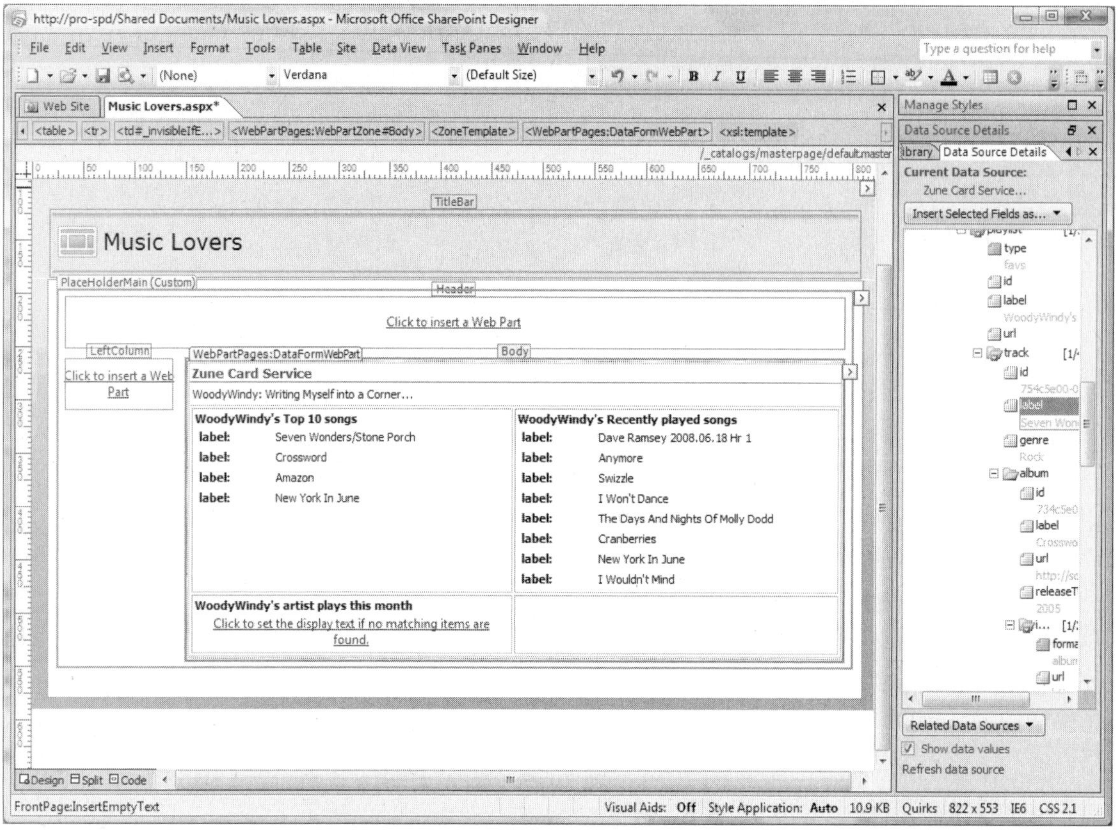

Figure 11-20

6. Highlight the text `label:` in any cell.

7. In the Data Source details pane, drill into the ./album/image folder, and select `url`.

8. Right-click `url` and select Insert As Picture. You may be warned that images from untrusted data sources can be dangerous. If so, click OK. You should now see album cover images in your Data View.

9. Right-click an album image, and select Picture Properties from the context menu.

10. In the Picture Properties dialog, check the Alternate Text, and enter the text **{album/label}**. This will show the title of the album when your user hovers over the image.

11. In the artist folder, drag the label field into the text area, beside the song title.

12. Place the text entry cursor between the title and artist name, and press Enter to put the artist's name on its own line.

13. Save your page, and click the Preview in the Browser icon. Your completed Zune Card Web Part should resemble Figure 11-21.

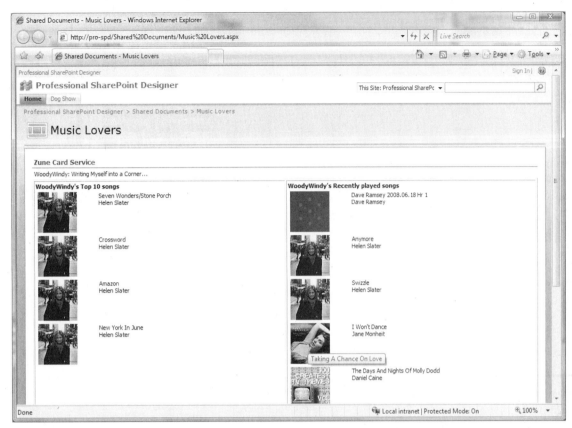

Figure 11-21

Get Connected

The final module in the exercise shows how you can use the Data View you created to display any Zune Card you want. In the process, it introduces a very simple Form Web Part. (Forms will be treated in detail in the next chapter.)

1. Display the Web Parts task pane.

2. Drag a Form Web Part on the page. (If you're using the suggested Web Part page template, drag it into the LeftColumn Web Part Zone.) Notice that the form has a text box and a Go button.

3. Right-click the form, and select Web Part Connections from the context menu.

4. The default action is Provide Form Values To. That is correct, so click Next.

5. Ensure that Connect To A Web Part On This Page is selected, and click Next.

6. Select your Zune Card Web Part, and select Get Parameters From as the Target Action. Click Next.

7. Figure 11-22 shows the Parameter matching page of the Web Part Connections Wizard. In the Columns in Form Web Part column, select T1 (the default name for the text box) on the zunetag line.

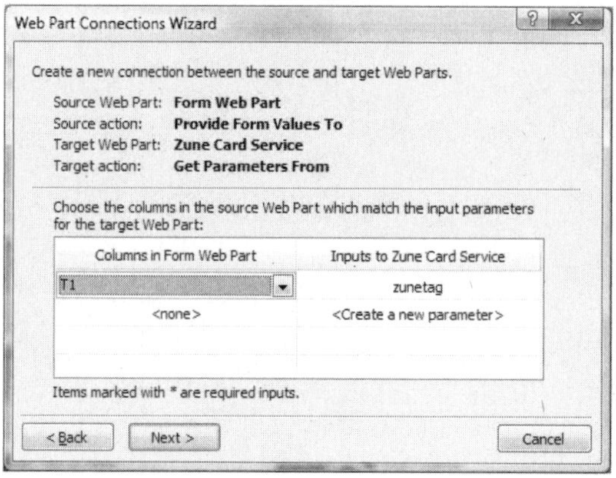

Web Part Connections Wizard

Create a new connection between the source and target Web Parts.

Source Web Part: **Form Web Part**
Source action: **Provide Form Values To**
Target Web Part: **Zune Card Service**
Target action: **Get Parameters From**

Choose the columns in the source Web Part which match the input parameters for the target Web Part:

Columns in Form Web Part	Inputs to Zune Card Service
T1	zunetag
<none>	<Create a new parameter>

Items marked with * are required inputs.

< Back   Next >   Cancel

Figure 11-22

8. Click Next.

9. Click the Finish button.

10. Save your page, and view it in the web browser.

11. Enter various values in the Form Web Part, and click Go to see the associated Zune Cards.

Exploring Further

This exercise walked you through creating a powerful data query and display application without writing any code. There is almost no limit to the kinds of things you can do with the Data View. Here are some possible ways to extend this exercise:

❑ Add a zunetag field to a list on your site, and use a view of that list to feed the Web Part connection.

❑ Play around with the formatting and the many other fields available.

❑ Add the Zune user's picture to the view.

❑ Use the URL fields to create hyperlinks into the Zune Social site to see more information about the songs and albums in the playlists.

❑ Add another Web Part connection to filter the display to a single type of playlist.

❑ Create a data source based on a public RSS feed, and build your own targeted news page.

More about the Business Data Catalog

As previously mentioned, the Business Data Catalog (BDC) allows Enterprise data to be surfaced in various places within Microsoft Office SharePoint Server, Enterprise Edition. Earlier in this chapter, you saw how the BDC could be surfaced as a data source for Data View Web Parts. There is another kind of Web Part that is designed specifically for displaying information from BDC: the Business Data Web Part.

Business Data Web Parts are available through the web interface, and allow your end users to easily display BDC elements on their sites. There are limits to the flexibility of these parts, however. Specifically, when a user inserts a Web Part for a particular entity, the Web Part will display all of the fields for that entity. There is no easy way for the end user to select and display a subset of the fields, or select a layout other than the single record or basic table.

SharePoint Designer recognizes and supports Business Data Web Parts. While there are some extra controls specific to the BDC, the primary display elements of these parts are treated just like any other Data View Web Part. You can modify fields, create conditional formatting, or apply any other XSL Data View formatting.

In this respect, SharePoint Designer can give you the best of both worlds — your users can select the BDC elements they want to display through the web interface, and then you can use SharePoint Designer to customize them to your exact needs.

Data Views on the Move

Although you use SharePoint Designer to create Data View Web Parts, once they are placed on a page they can be exported to files through the web user interface. Exported Data Views retain not only the formatting XSL, but also the connection information required to access the data source. This can be very useful because it allows you to easily re-use a Data View in other environments.

An exported Data View Web Part is stored as an XML file with the extension `.webpart`. If you import it onto another SharePoint page and that server has access to the data source defined within the Web Part, the Web Part will work perfectly in its new home. The access rules for exported Data Views are similar to those for making connections to other Data Source Libraries in SharePoint Designer:

❑ Used on another page within a site collection, almost all Data Views function correctly. There is a limit to this: Data Views of a SharePoint list cannot be built from the default list connection in the site that hosts the list. You must build the Data View from a connected library.

❑ Used on another site collection, list-based Data Views do not work. BDC views do not work on sites other than those on the MOSS Enterprise farm containing the BDC entities referenced.

Summary

This chapter explored the Data Source Library, and showed how to use the Data View Web Part to produce powerful displays of those data items. It explained:

❑　How to add data sources to SharePoint Designer.

❑　XML and Data Views can represent and display complex hierarchies of data.

❑　External data is just as easy to connect as internal SharePoint lists.

❑　There are many ways to insert specific fields or other elements into a Data View.

❑　The BDC is surfaced in many different ways.

❑　Data View Web Parts can be exported for use on other pages, potentially even on other sites and servers.

The next chapter introduces you to the many different kinds of Forms you can work with in SharePoint Designer.

12

Working with Forms

Chapters 10 and 11 showed you a number of ways to show information on a page from various sources, both from within SharePoint and from the outside world. Yet, data display — however sophisticated — is only half of the story. You still need a way to collect information from your users, whether it is data to store, or a set of query parameters for a report. In the digital realm, as in the paper, that way is typically a form. In this chapter, you will learn about working with forms in SharePoint Designer, including:

❑ Types of forms supported.

❑ Testing non-SharePoint forms with the ASP.NET Development Server.

❑ How SharePoint Data Forms relate to Data View Web Parts.

SharePoint Designer's Form Tools

Since the inception of the World Wide Web and Hypertext Markup Language, forms have been an important part of Internet technologies. Broadly speaking, any web page that accepts user input for processing by the server is a form. Basic HTML forms, list and library forms, and forms that request input to a workflow (whether InfoPath-based or ASP.NET) all look alike to the user. Yet, in practice, these are very different kinds of entities, and each requires its own techniques.

SharePoint Designer and InfoPath Forms

Although SharePoint Designer supports several different implementations of Web Forms, there are many circumstances where common forms need to be completed, both on the web and off. Microsoft's tool for working with such forms is called Microsoft InfoPath. InfoPath maintains its own mechanisms for supporting workflow, notification, and data validation.

(continued)

All editions of SharePoint support a Forms Library, which is designed specifically to hold the XML results of InfoPath forms, whether created with the InfoPath Client or Forms Server. In addition, Microsoft Office SharePoint Server 2007 Enterprise Edition and Microsoft Office Forms Server 2007 support web-based forms created using InfoPath.

Other than through Data Views into XML Form libraries, which operate as described in the previous chapters, SharePoint Designer 2007 is not an appropriate tool for manipulating InfoPath forms.

In the previous chapter's exercise, you were given a glimpse of a SharePoint Form Web Part. This Web Part is used primarily as a connection source, this is, for passing user input to other SharePoint Web Parts through Web Part connections.

SharePoint Designer also supports the Data Form Web Part. A data form is essentially a Data View Web Part, but with the capability to input as well as display data. Custom list and library forms and input to SharePoint workflows are provided via the data form as well.

When working with forms, you will make extensive use of the Toolbox task pane. You may find it helpful to maximize it, as shown in Figure 12-1.

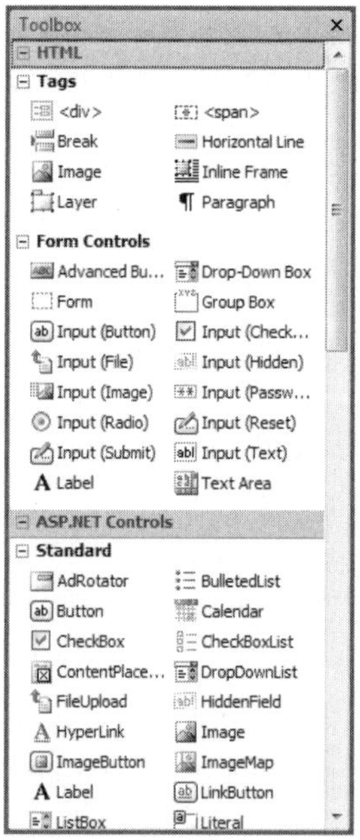

Figure 12-1

The Toolbox has sections for classic HTML components, general ASP.NET components, and SharePoint-specific components. These are not limited to forms. Almost any object that you can place on a page (other than a SharePoint Web Part) can be found in the Toolbox.

HTML elements can be added to any page by selecting them from the Toolbox task pane. However, the type of page you are working on may influence where you can place the controls. For example, when editing a page based on a Master Page or Dynamic Web Template, you can only place objects in designated content areas. (You have full control over object placement when editing the Master Pages or DWTs themselves.)

There are two ways to add an element from the Toolbox:

❑ Drag the control from the Toolbox to the position where you desire it on the page.

❑ Set the insertion cursor to the position in the document where you want the control, then either double-click the control in the Toolbox, or right-click the Toolbox control and select Insert from the context menu.

The next section discusses how to use SharePoint Designer to create and manipulate forms in environments other than SharePoint.

Traditional Web Forms

SharePoint Designer supports the creation of traditional HTML-based forms, which can be used both within and outside of SharePoint sites. When on a non-SharePoint server that supports ASP.NET, you can also create standard ASP.NET (ASPX) applications, which have full database interactivity.

HTML Forms and Legacy FrontPage Webbots

Traditional HTML forms are simple client-side constructs. While you can use JavaScript for validation prior to submission, generally speaking, the forms themselves are not active components. Information appropriate to the defined field types is collected from the user and passed on to the server for processing.

You can always create static HTML pages, no matter what kind of site you are working on.

Creating an HTML Form

To create an HTML form, do the following:

1. Select File ➪ New ➪ HTML to open a new blank HTML page.

2. From the Form Controls section of the Toolbox, drag a form control onto the page.

3. Drag an Input (Text) control into the form area.

HTML form controls do not need to be placed within a form, although unscripted processing is only possible if they are.

When you select a form element from the Toolbox and place it on a page outside of an existing form, by default, SharePoint Designer automatically creates a form to contain the control. You can control whether this occurs by selecting Tools ⇨ Page Editor Options, and then checking or unchecking the Automatically enclose form fields within a form check box on the General tab, as shown in Figure 12-2.

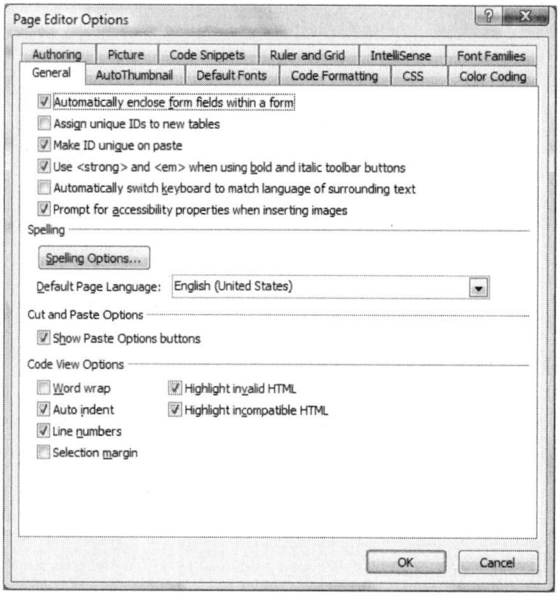

Figure 12-2

4. Drag an Input (Submit) control into the form area.

You now have a complete, if simple, form.

In the real world, forms often have many fields, of many different types. Typically, you will want to use tables or CSS layout to control the positioning of your fields. You have total freedom to lay out your form however you choose. You can add descriptive text, images, field labels, and so on. When the form is submitted, only the contents of form field objects are passed to the handling process.

When you add a form control, SharePoint Designer assigns it a generic name based upon the type of control it is, such as Text1. This name is assigned to the name property of the control. The name property of each control is passed to the processing action along with the associated value. Most back-end scripts expect specific input field names, so rename the control to whatever name the back-end process is expecting. Figure 12-3 shows a classic Guest Book form, laid out with a table, appropriate labels, and the form fields renamed.

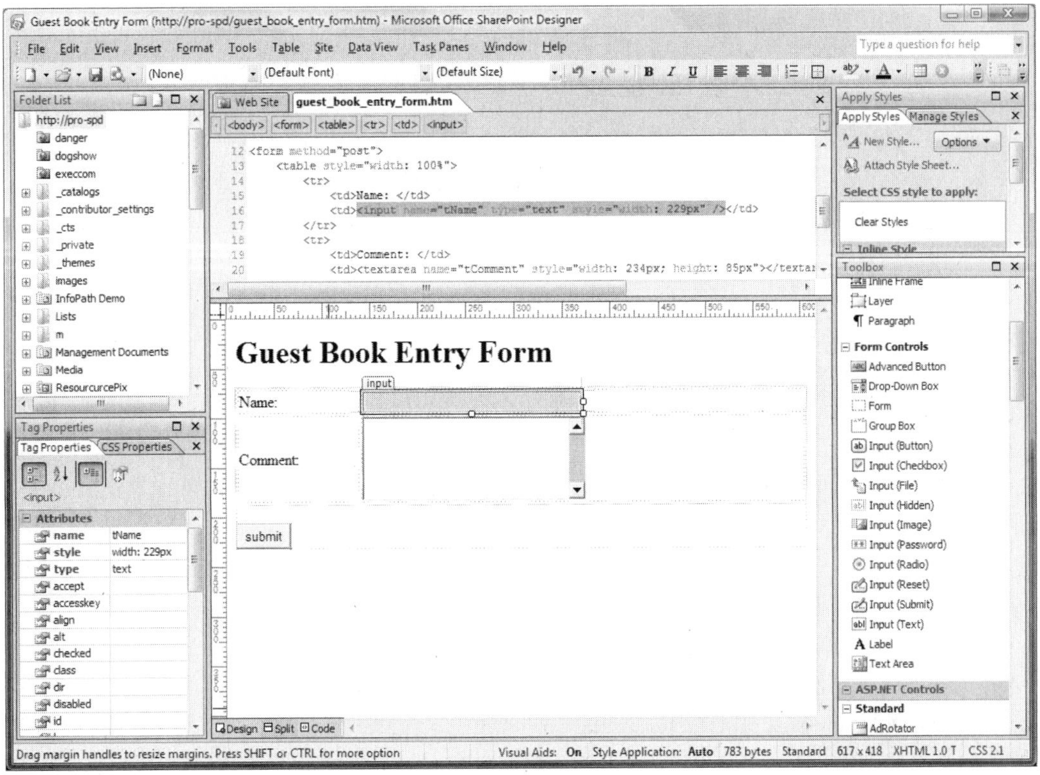

Figure 12-3

You may plan to write page script to preprocess the form control contents prior to submission, such as for input validation. If so, assign appropriate ID properties to the controls as well.

Assigning a Back-End Processing Action

An HTML form doesn't do anything on its own. To give it purpose, you must assign an action to the form. To assign an action, right-click on the form and select Form Properties from the context menu. The dialog shown in Figure 12-4 appears.

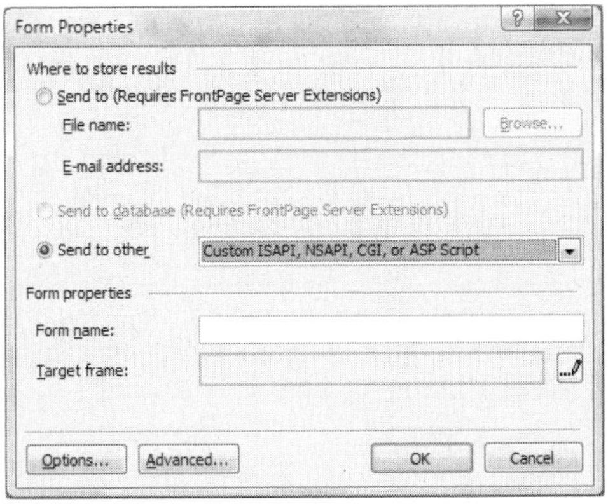

Figure 12-4

From this dialog, you can select among alternative actions, set various processing options, or give the form a name. The actions available and the default action vary, depending upon the type of site being edited. On a SharePoint site (WSS 2.0 or higher), the default is to Send To Other, with "other" being a classic web form–processing engine such as a CGI or ASP script. Sending to a database is not available on a SharePoint server.

You can have multiple HTML forms on a single page. Each form will typically be named, and have its own Submit button. When a Submit button is clicked, the field names and values are read and provided to the back-end processing application. Only the field contents of the form in which the Submit button resides are processed. Each form can use a different back-end processing option.

The Advanced button gives you a convenient way to add hidden fields to a form. You can directly add, remove, and edit Name/Value pairs. This function is equivalent to manually selecting Input (Hidden) from the Toolbox and manually editing the properties for each hidden field.

The Options button accesses different choices, depending on which back-end processing option is chosen. The most basic set of options, as set for CGI, ASP, and so forth, includes:

❑   **Action:** The URL of the page that will accept the input from the form. If blank, the page will post to itself.

❑   **Method:** HTTP `Post`, or HTTP `Get`. `Post` uses the host header to pass parameters. `Get` uses the connection string (`/formprocessor.aspx?field1=this&field2=that` for example).

❑   **Encoding type:** Provides handling instructions to the form processor. Typical values are blank, text/plain, and multipart/form-data.

A typical Options configuration for a Custom Form Handler is shown in Figure 12-5.

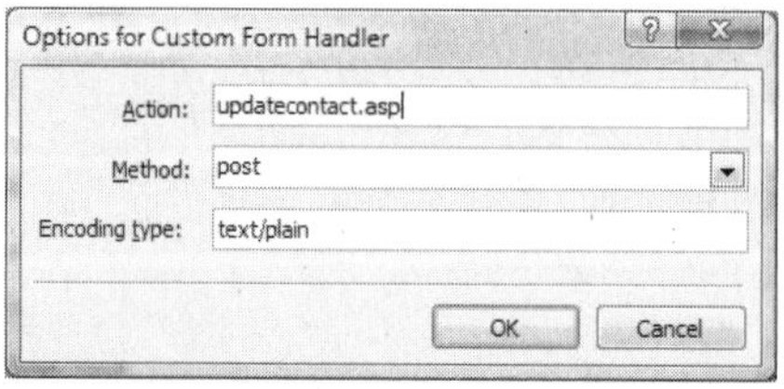

Figure 12-5

Send To Other also supports legacy FrontPage Server Extension registration and discussion form handlers. These are not supported on SharePoint servers, and are not discussed here.

RPC Interface

SharePoint provides a Remote Procedure Call (RPC) Protocol programming interface that is exposed through URLs. Although documentation of the functions of this interface is beyond the scope of this book, it is thoroughly covered in the WSS SDK. Forms such as those described in this section can be an ideal way of interacting with this API.

Classic FrontPage Processing — The SaveResults Webbot

SharePoint servers support a number of classic FrontPage extension functions. When you select the Send to (Requires FrontPage Server Extensions) option in the Form Properties dialog, you are given two immediate fields to populate: File name and File format. This doesn't begin to cover the flexibility of this form processor.

Clicking the Options button opens the four-page Saving Results dialog shown in Figure 12-6.

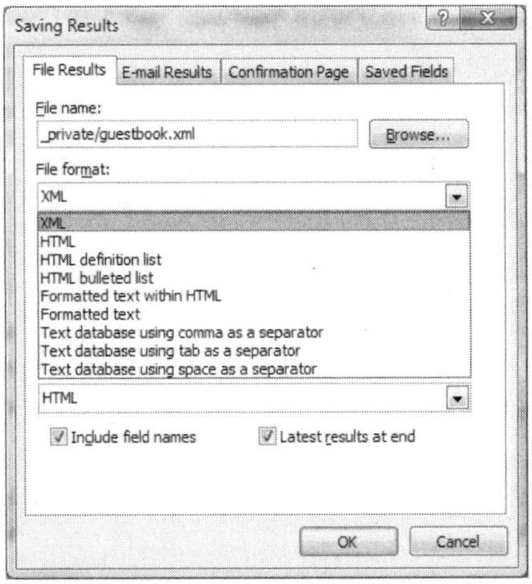

Figure 12-6

The SaveResults bot stores form entries in a file on your web server. The Saving Results dialog offers you the choice of several formats, from HTML to comma-separated text to XML. Using XML for results is particularly useful because you can then integrate the results of the form with your SharePoint content via Data Views.

Notice in Figure 12-6 that the File name is being stored in the _private folder. While you are not required to save form results in this folder, there are special benefits of doing so. In particular, files in the _private folder are accessible only to server-side processes, and are not served directly via the URL. This gives you complete control over how the information stored is presented.

The two scenarios just described are mutually exclusive. XML Data Views read the data into the web browser via the URL, and therefore cannot access the _private folder.

Other key features of the SaveResults component are as follows:

❑   You can save data into two files, each of which may be a different format.

❑   On the E-mail Results tab, you can configure the email subject and return address, which may themselves be derived from submitted fields. The email body can be formatted with any of the options available for results storage.

❏ You may designate a confirmation page. After the form is submitted, this page is displayed. The submitted data is available for use on the page through the use of Confirmation Fields — select Insert ⇨ Web Component ⇨ Advanced Controls ⇨ Confirmation Field.

❏ On the Saved Fields tab, in addition to specifying all (or any subset) of the fields available in the form, you may also submit the date and time, user name, remote computer, and/or web browser information.

The FrontPage SaveResults and Confirmation webbots are only valid on HTML pages. You are not prevented from inserting the components on ASPX pages, but they will not function.

ASP.NET Data Forms

When you are working on a site that is not SharePoint-based, or working outside of a Managed Path (a folder under SharePoint's control) on a SharePoint server, you can create normal ASP.NET applications from within SharePoint Designer. Although teaching ASP.NET itself is beyond the scope of this book, SharePoint Designer provides several tools to assist you in creating ASP.NET applications.

Working Locally

SharePoint Designer includes the ASP.NET Development Server. This allows you to build a site in a local folder on your hard disk, but still run ASP.NET code. To create a local web site, do the following:

1. Select File ⇨ New.

2. On the New dialog's Web Site tab, select a site option from the General or Templates subsections. The One Page Web Site option is sufficient for this example.

3. Enter the local path for the web site.

   If there is already information in the folder specified, it will be deleted unless you check the Add To Current Web Site box.

4. Click OK.

A web site based upon the selected template is created at the specified location, and opened in SharePoint Designer.

Enabling the ASP.NET Development Server

The ASP.NET Development Server is controlled through the Site Settings dialog (Site ⇨ Site Settings). Figure 12-7 shows the dialog's Preview tab.

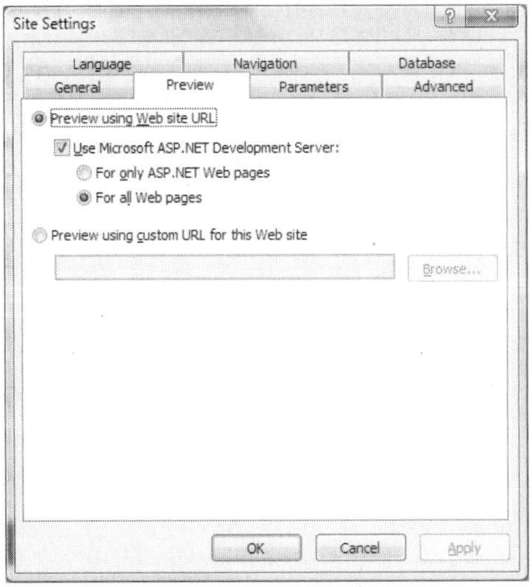

Figure 12-7

On the Preview tab, you select whether to let SharePoint Designer control the rendering, or use another web service. To let SharePoint Designer control the rendering, select Preview using Web site URL. If Use Microsoft ASP.NET Development Server is not checked, SharePoint Designer will preview files by opening a browser directly on the file system. This does not allow any server-side ASP.NET code to run. To run server-side code, check the box. That enables SharePoint Designer to launch the ASP.NET Development Server. This server will be assigned to a random port each time it is initialized. It supports ASP.NET, but not traditional ASP or FrontPage Server Extensions. You have the option to run either all pages, or only ASP.NET pages from the Development Server.

While the Development Server is running, an icon is displayed in your computer's system tray. Upon initial invocation, it identifies itself with the pop-up shown in Figure 12-8.

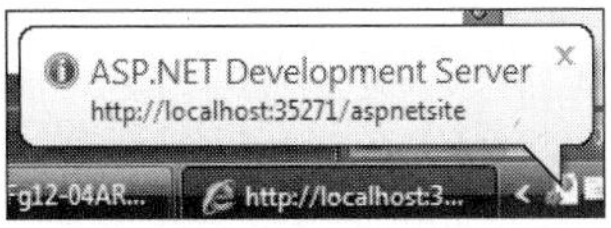

Figure 12-8

Right-click the icon to perform any of the following tasks:

❑ Browse to the site.

❑ Stop the instance.

❑ View configuration details, as shown in Figure 12-9.

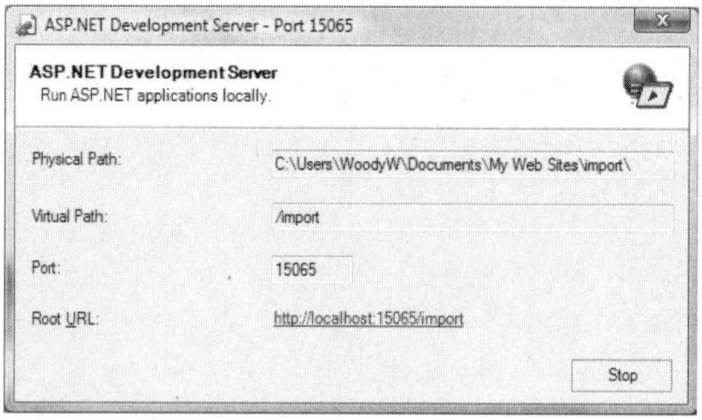

Figure 12-9

Multiple instances of the Development Server can be running concurrently, each on its own port. Each instance also has its own system tray icon.

The Preview Using Custom URL For This Web Site option lets you view your site through IIS or another web server. When you select one of SharePoint Designer's preview options, it uses the base URL specified instead of the local folder. This option assumes that your web server is mapped to the working location specified when you created/opened the site.

The remaining exercises in this section assume you have access to a test or training database environment.

Configuring a Database Connection

Just as when working with SharePoint sites, you use the Data Source Library task pane to manage connections to various databases. The sources available and management techniques are different, however. You can connect to XML files and ASP.NET-compatible database sources.

To connect to a database, perform the following steps:

1. Display the Data Source Library task pane.

2. Click New ASP.NET connection.

3. Select the type of database from the options, as shown in Figure 12-10. The list may vary, depending upon the sources and drivers you have installed.

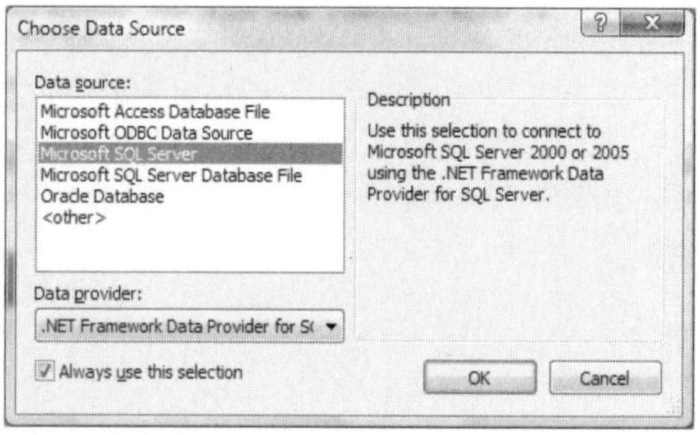

Figure 12-10

A configuration dialog appropriate to your selected database, like the SQL Server configuration dialog shown in Figure 12-11, opens.

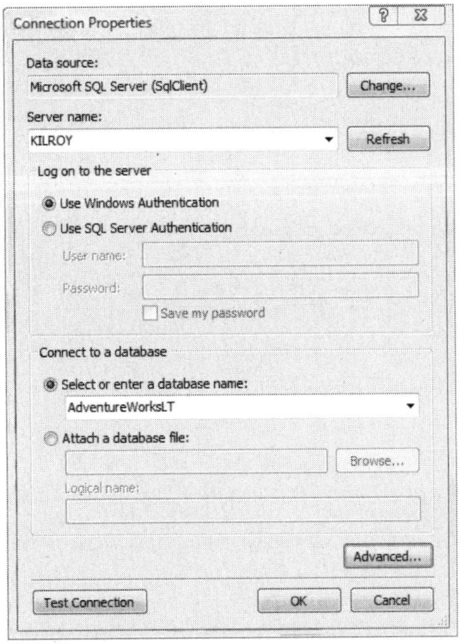

Figure 12-11

4. Set the connection for your selected database type.

5. If needed, click the Advanced button to enter the Advanced Properties dialog (see Figure 12-12) and set more properties. When you finish, click OK to return to the configuration dialog.

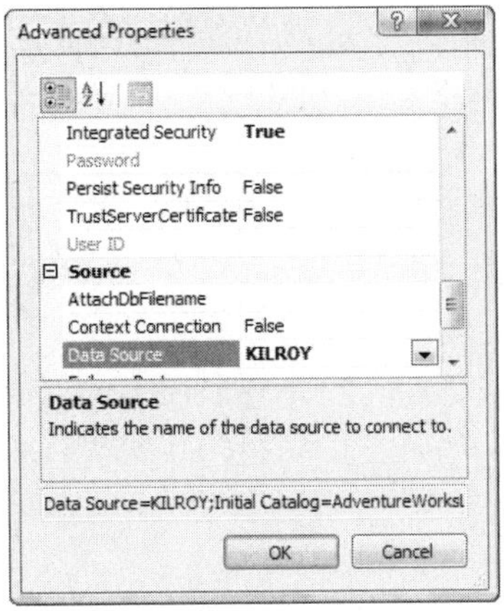

Figure 12-12

6. Test the connection with the Test Connection button.

7. If the test is successful, click OK.

8. Enter a name for the connection, and click OK.

Connecting Controls to a Data Source

You've seen how to create a connection to a database. Controls on the page require another component — the *data source*. Although the database connection was defined in the Data Source Library, this simply establishes the parameters needed to see the database. A page data source provides the connection to the specific table, query, or stored procedure that is usable by the data-bound controls on the page.

There are two ways to create a page data source.

❑ Insert a data source template onto the page from the Toolbox.

❑ Insert a data-bound control onto the page, and create a data source from the control options.

In either case, once the data source is inserted on the page, you need to configure it.

This exercise walks you through creating an ASP.NET page, adding a form control, and connecting it to a data source. It assumes an existing site and a database connection that has already been created.

1. Select File ⇨ New ⇨ ASPX.

2. From the ASP.NET controls Data section of the Toolbox task pane, insert a Details View control.

3. From the Common Details View Tasks fly-out, select New Data Source from the Choose Data Source dropdown. The Data Source Configuration Wizard appears.

4. Choose Database on the Choose Database Type page, and click OK.

5. Select a database connection, and click Next. (Notice that you can also create a new database connection at this point.)

6. Configure the query for the data source. Figure 12-13 shows all fields from the Buyer table selected.

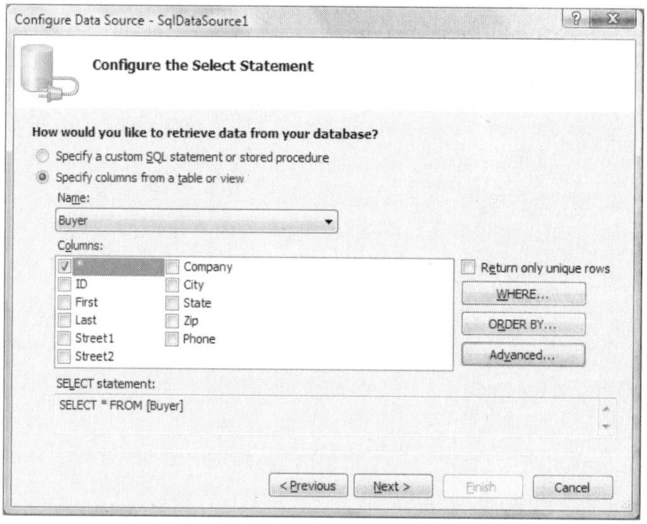

Figure 12-13

7. Click the Advanced button.

8. Check the Generate INSERT, UPDATE, and DELETE Statements option, and click OK.

   This option is only available if you have a primary key field in the table you are connecting to, and it is incorporated into the query you have selected.

9. Click Next.

10. Test your query. If it returns the expected results, click Finish.

    The form should now display the fields selected in your query. In addition, the Common tasks menu should now show options appropriate to the query you generated, such as Enable Inserting and Enable Editing (see Figure 12-14).

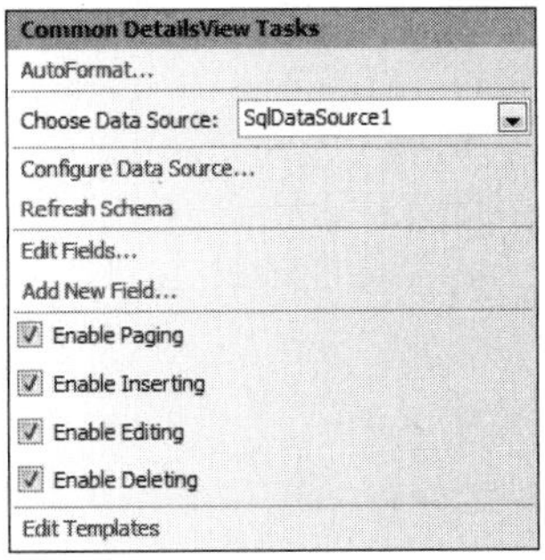

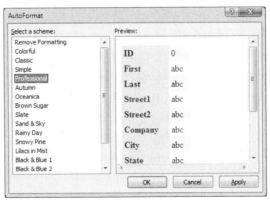

Figure 12-14

11. Check the options you want on your form. Click the AutoFormat link. Select Professional from the list of styles available, as shown in Figure 12-15.

Figure 12-15

12. Save your page, and click the Preview in Browser button.

If you enabled the options for Editing or Inserting, notice that the form is automatically generated and styled to match the AutoFormat scheme you selected, as shown in Figure 12-16.

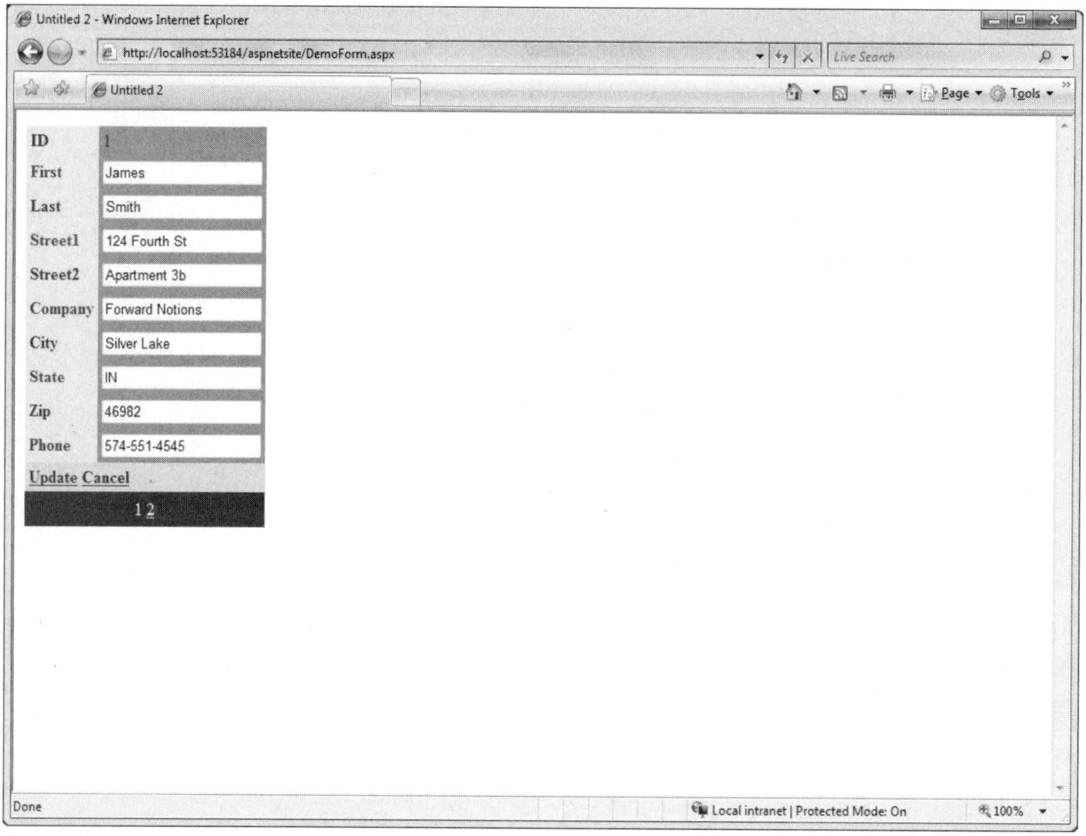

Figure 12-16

SharePoint Data Forms

Back in the SharePoint world, you know from chapters 10 and 11 that SharePoint Designer gives you great control over the display of data through the Data View Web Part. You have now also seen that it is capable of creating data entry forms outside of the SharePoint context. Fortunately, you have the capability to create forms within SharePoint as well. Just as the ASP.NET data form control could both display and enter data, the Data View Web Part can also be used for entry. In fact, the Data View Web Part is also known as the Data Form Web Part.

Multimode Data Views

When inserting Data Views, you may have noticed options for single- and multiple-item forms. These allow you to insert views that have editing enabled by default. Figure 12-17 shows the same data source inserted as a multiple-item view, and as a multiple-item form.

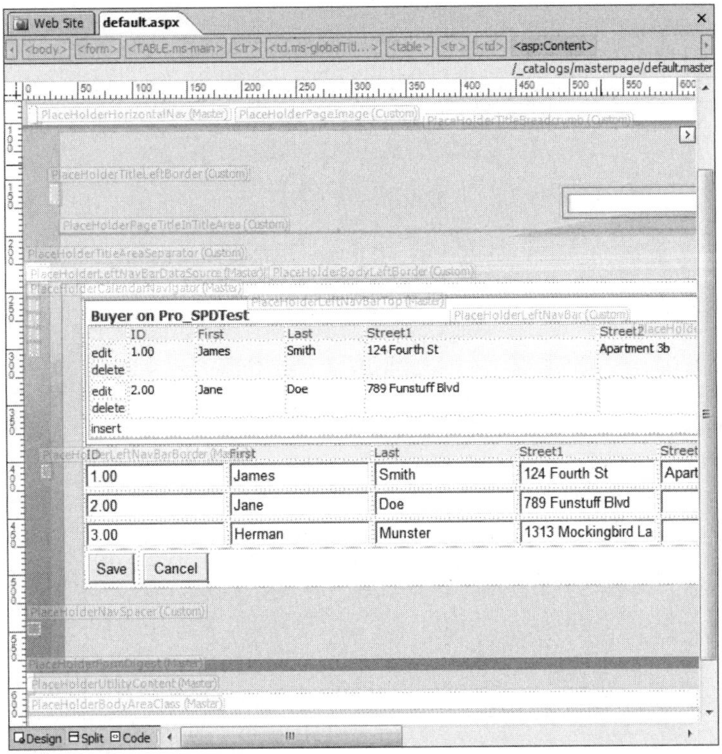

Figure 12-17

Single-item versions are also available. In addition, a single-item form type called the *new item form* allows you to have a distinct view for adding items to your data source.

To have usable data forms, the data source must support update-type queries. SharePoint Lists, XML, and SQL data sources support updates by default. Some external data sources (OLEDB) only support insert and update queries if they are enabled in Central Administration.

As mentioned in chapter 3, Central Administration is a special SharePoint web site. You may need to get the URL from your server administrator to complete these steps in your environment.

To enable update queries for all supported data types, perform the following steps in Central Administration:

1. Navigate to the Operations tab.

2. Select Data Retrieval Service under the Data Configuration section.

3. Check the Enable Update Query Support box.

4. Click OK.

Data retrieval service options are set globally, but may be overridden on a per-web-application basis.

You can also enable editing on regular Data View Web Parts, either single or multiple items. Open the Data View Properties dialog and navigate to the Editing tab; you will see options similar to those in Figure 12-18. Depending on the type of data source, some options may be disabled or not shown.

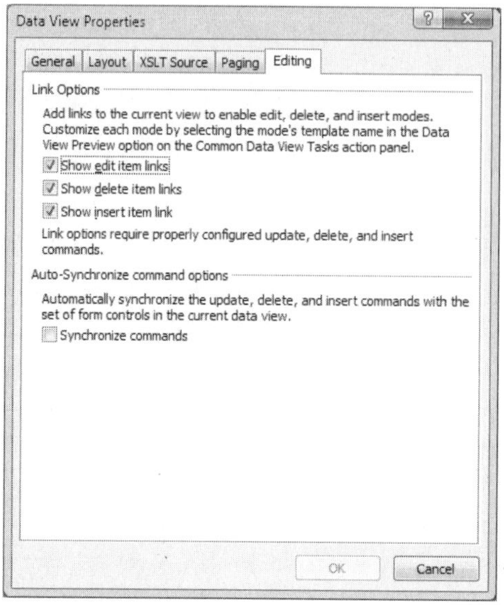

Figure 12-18

Enabling the Edit option for a form view converts it to a regular Data View, with an edit link for each item displayed.

Just as with the ASP.NET data form controls, SharePoint Data Views provide templates for each mode selected. To edit a particular template, select it from the Data View Preview dropdown in the Common Data View Tasks fly-out, shown in Figure 12-19.

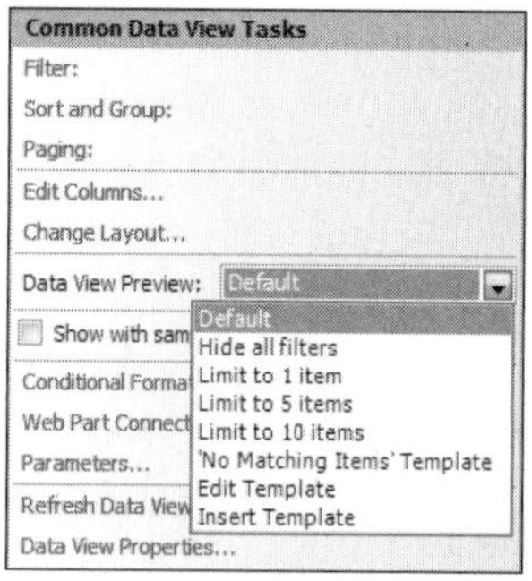

Figure 12-19

Notice that in addition to the edit, view, and insert modes, you can also design the template to display that there is no data that matches the view's conditions.

You can control the display format of each field in the form. You may want to do this, for example, when a field is a data type that lends itself to a particular presentation, such as a check box for a Boolean value, or a simple text label if a field is read-only or system-controlled (that is, ID or Modified Date).

To set the display type of a field on any SharePoint Data Form Web Part, do the following:

1. Click the field.

2. Click the fly-out indicator.

3. Select an appropriate value from Format as, as shown in Figure 12-20.

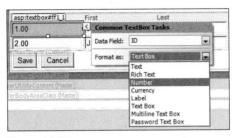

Figure 12-20

4. If needed, enter detailed format information, as shown in Figure 12-21.

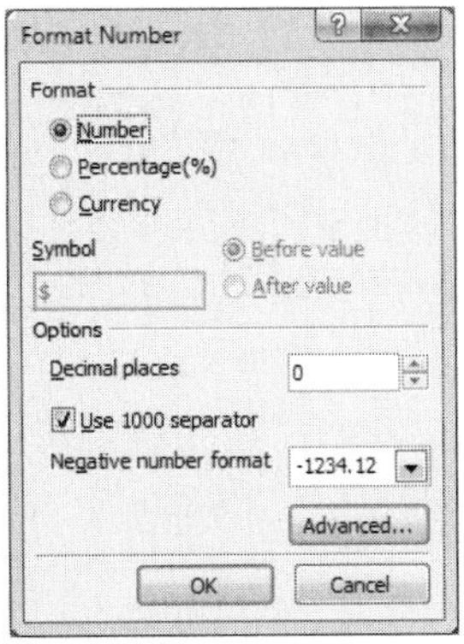

Figure 12-21

Custom List and Library Forms

Custom list and library views and forms can be placed on any Web Part Page. Sometimes, however, you may want to use custom forms as the primary mode of interaction with a list or library. SharePoint Designer allows you to designate customized forms as the defaults for this interaction.

When you create a list or library, a set of forms is created by default (the set may vary, depending on the particular list). Because list and library view forms are simply Web Part Pages, all of the editing power described up to this point can be brought to bear on list and library forms. For example, you can create a new item form that contains only a subset of the fields available in the list (provided all required fields are included). You can then create an Edit Item form that has those fields set to be displayed as plaintext labels, while the rest of the fields are available to be filled in.

Although you can edit the default forms directly, it is a better practice to create new view pages, and add a Data View or data form, and edit that.

Creating a New List or Library Form

You can easily create a new form of the type you want by copying an existing form. You can also create a new view page by right-clicking the list or library name, and selecting New ⇨ List View Page (or Library View Page) from the context menu, as shown in Figure 12-22.

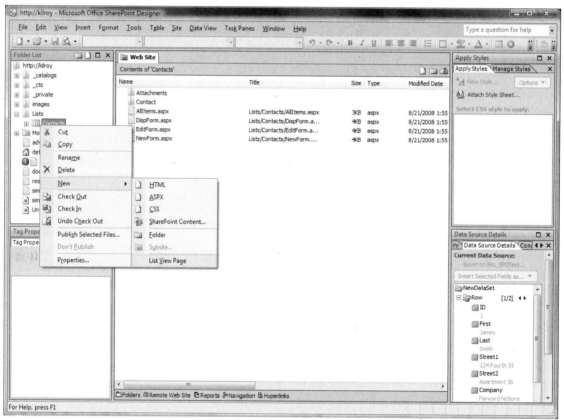

Figure 12-22

You are prompted for the name you want to give the view page. When you create the view from the menu, it is automatically opened in SharePoint Designer.

A new view page typically has a List View Web Part comparable to All Items included by default. If you copy an existing page, the default view will be that of the page you copied.

Once you have the page, customization is slightly different, depending upon which type of form you want to create. In either case, you should hide, close, or delete the default view. Hiding and closing the view retains it, and its attendant support code, on the page, but does not display it to the end user. This makes it easy to recover the default form functionality if needed. Deleting the default view gives you a clean slate for your own view.

New Item Form

Because they do not require information about existing items, *new item* forms are the simplest to create. To create a basic new item form, do the following:

1. Create a new view page as described earlier.

2. Highlight the Web Part Zone.

3. Select Insert Data View from the Data menu.

4. Select your list or library data source, and pick Show Data.

5. Select the fields you want to include on the initial entry form. (Use Ctrl+Click to select noncontiguous fields.) Make sure that you include all fields defined as Required.

6. From the Insert Selected Fields As button, select New Item Form.

7. Save the page.

At this point, you have a functional new item form. You can navigate to the page, enter, and save data. You can also edit the page to rearrange fields, add descriptive text, set formatting, and perform any other customization you can make to Data Views and data forms.

Display and Edit Forms

Display and edit forms are a little more complicated. You need to determine which item the user wants to view and/or modify. Fortunately, SharePoint makes it easy by always passing the item ID of the desired item in the URL query string. You need to configure your Data View/form to display the selected item, and to suppress navigation.

The first five steps to create a display or edit form are the same as for the new item form:

1. Create a new view page as described earlier.

2. Highlight the Web Part Zone.

3. Select Data View ⇨ Insert Data View.

4. Select your list or library data source, and pick Show Data.

5. Select the fields you want to include.

Required fields are not required for display forms.

The next step, inserting the selected fields, varies depending upon whether you are creating a Display or an Edit form.

If you are creating a display form:

6. Click the Insert Selected Fields As button, and select Single Item View.

If you are creating an edit form:

7. Click the Insert Selected Fields As button, and select Single Item Form.

From this point, the handling for each is the same, as follows:

8. From the Common Data View Tasks fly-out, pick Filter.

9. In the criteria dialog, set the following:

Field Name: ID

Comparison: Equals

10. Under Value, select Create A New Parameter.

11. The Data View Parameters dialog opens. Enter values to match those shown in Figure 12-23 for ItemID.

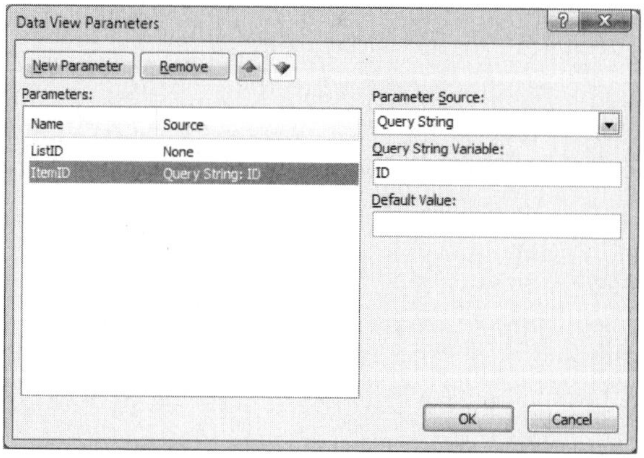

Figure 12-23

You will need to set the name of the new parameter to ItemID.

12. Click OK.

13. From the Common Data View Tasks fly-out, check the Show With Sample Data box.

14. Save the page.

Again, you now have a fully functional display or edit form, which you can customize to your liking. When viewing the page in a browser, you can manually add ID values to the URL (&ID=3, for instance) to test the filter.

Although it is not required for a functional page, you should edit the Data View properties' Paging tab to limit the display to a single item. This will prevent your users from scrolling to previous or next items, and is the typically expected behavior for such pages.

Using Your Form(s)

Once you have created and tested your forms, you can access them in a number of ways. One option is to manually create links from other pages. Typically, however, you will connect the forms to your list as the defaults for the relevant actions.

You can connect the forms to your list or document library as follows:

1. In the Folders view, right-click the list or library root folder, and select Properties.

2. Select the Supporting Files tab.

3. Enter or browse to the paths for the forms you have created, as shown in Figure 12-24.

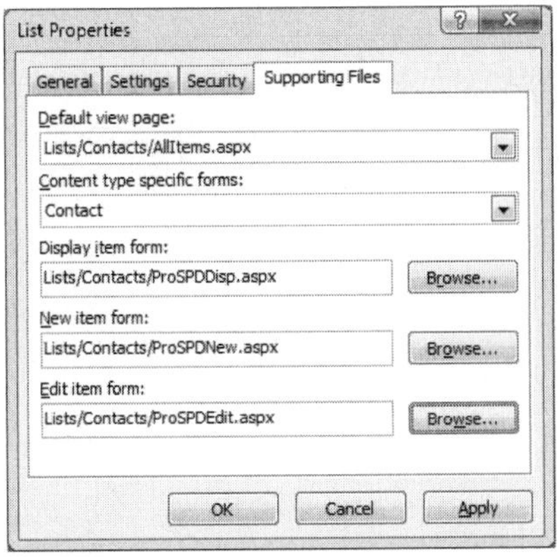

Figure 12-24

4. Click OK.

Now, when someone selects the SharePoint-created links for new, view, or edit, your forms are shown by default for that list.

This change takes immediate effect on the live site.

Although these forms are now the default, users with appropriate permissions are still able to create other views of the list or library. In addition, this does not affect non–form-based methods of accessing the data. This means that you cannot use custom forms as a way to simulate field-level security. Any user with update permissions may still find a way to update fields that you have made display-only (or even hidden completely) on the new or edit forms.

Return to Sender

One final element you may want to implement in your custom list or library form is an option to return to the page that called your form. When SharePoint invokes one of the default forms, in addition to the Item ID you saw earlier, the URL of the calling page is also passed as a connect string parameter.

This parameter is called Source, and you can configure your Data View to look for and use it. The following steps show you how to add the parameter and use it for the Cancel button on a new or edit item form.

1. Open your custom page in SharePoint Designer.

2. From the Common Data View Tasks fly-out, choose Parameters.

3. Click New Parameter.

4. Name the new parameter PageSource.

5. From the Parameter Source dropdown, select Query String.

6. Enter Source for the Query String Variable.

7. Your configuration should resemble the dialog shown in Figure 12-25. Click OK.

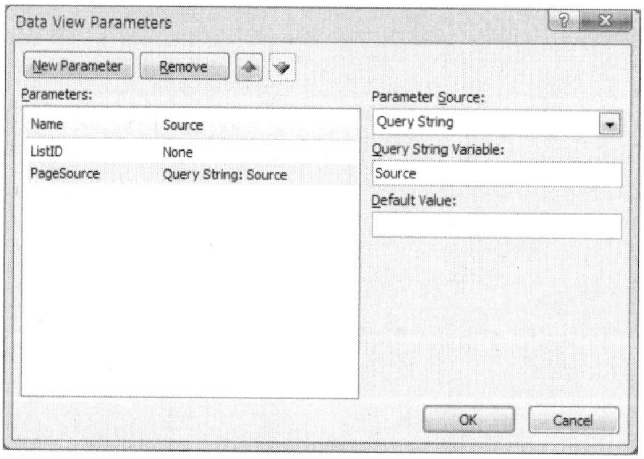

Figure 12-25

8. Highlight the Cancel button in your form.

9. In the Tag Properties task pane's Events section, select the onclick event (see Figure 12-26).

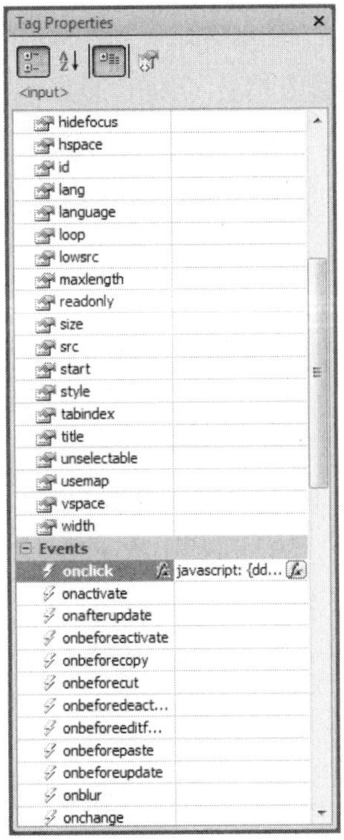

Figure 12-26

10. Edit the existing script, which should resemble:

```
javascript: {ddwrt:GenFireServerEvent('__cancel')}
```

by appending:

```
;STSNavigate('{$PageSource}')
```

Do not invoke the XPath Editor (by clicking the fx button) to make this change.

11. Save the page.

Now when you click Cancel on the form, you are returned to the calling page.

Once you have completed all of the edits you have made to the form, if you have not made any changes outside of your Data View, or the form itself, other than adding more Web Parts, you may reset the page to its site definition, and your changes will remain intact.

Summary

In this chapter, you have seen some of the many ways you can work with forms in SharePoint Designer. In particular, you have learned:

❑ SharePoint Designer supports everything from HTML through ASP.NET and SharePoint Data Forms.

❑ You can use SharePoint Designer's WYSIWYG editing functions not only to decorate forms, but to control how the data itself is presented.

❑ You can replace the standard SharePoint forms with those of your own design.

Throughout Part III of the book, you have seen how to create powerful, data-driven applications without using any code. In Part IV, you will see how SharePoint Designer goes beyond visual design to give you a programming environment for even more client-side flexibility.

Part IV

Programming on the Client Side

13

The Content Editor Web Part

There are two powerful tools for programmatically interacting with a SharePoint page: the Content Editor Web Part (CEWP) and the Web Part Page Services Component (WPSC). You'll tackle them in this chapter and the next.

The Content Editor Web Part is basically a box into which you can place the content of your choice. A simple concept, yet it's a key that unlocks a vast and powerful world to the knowledgeable designer and developer. This chapter explores:

- ❑ The basics of the Content Editor Web Part.
- ❑ Embedding client-side script on a SharePoint Page.
- ❑ SharePoint tools for client-side scripts.
- ❑ Tips to make using the CEWP easier.

What Is the Content Editor Web Part?

Good things come in simple packages. That's been the case since the beginning of time, and it is still true today. In SharePoint terms, a package doesn't get much simpler than the Content Editor Web Part.

The web interface to SharePoint provides a structured environment for content to be rendered. The borders and navigation are fixed, and while you have great flexibility in adding Web Parts to a page, the user is generally at the mercy of the kinds of content provided in the existing Web Parts.

The Content Editor Web Part is designed to alleviate that problem. By providing a "page within a page," the CEWP allows site owners to add arbitrary text and images to their pages. In addition, you can have some control over that content's layout by overriding existing formatting, or even use JavaScript to enhance page functionality. One use of the CEWP would be to place a brief description or instructions on the home page of a site. The "About this Site" sidebar shown in Figure 13-1, for instance, is a Content Editor Web Part.

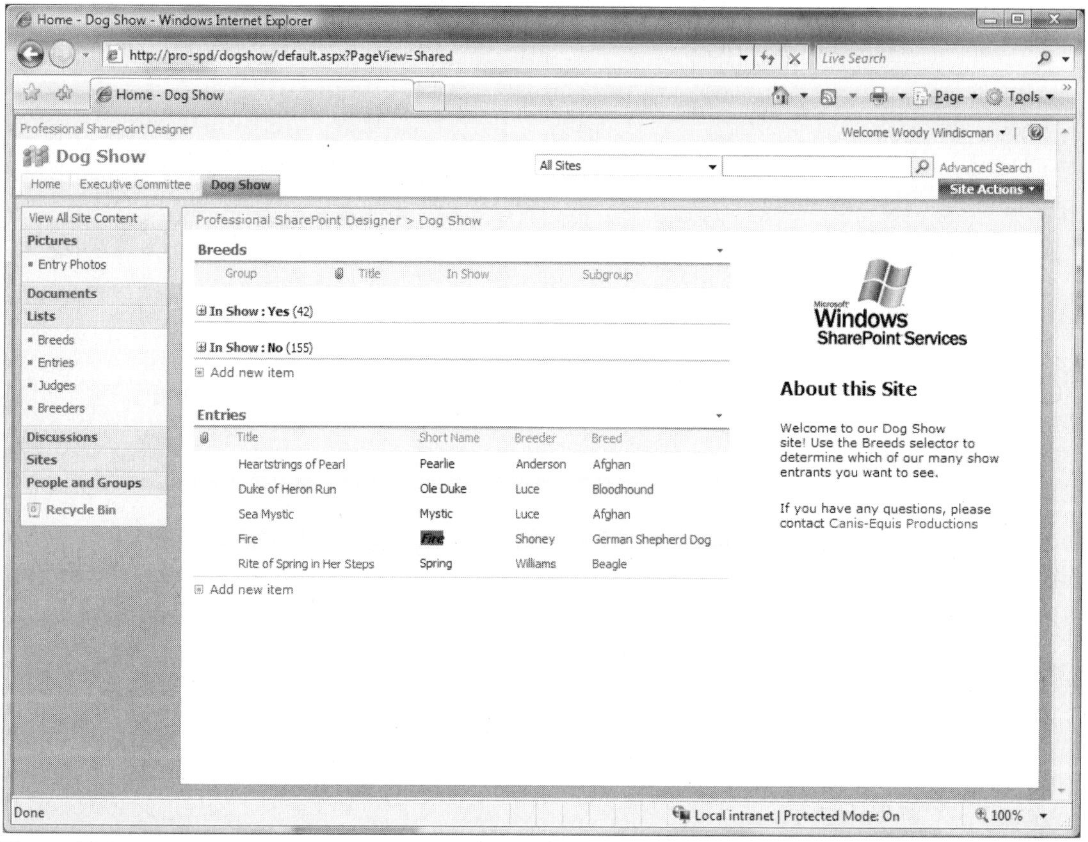

Figure 13-1

The CEWP provides two editing options for web browsers:

❑   Rich text editor

❑   Source editor

These are available in the Web Part Tool Pane, which is accessed by selecting Modify Shared Web Part from the Web Part menu. Figure 13-2 shows the Web Part menu and Editor buttons on the tool pane for a Content Editor Web Part.

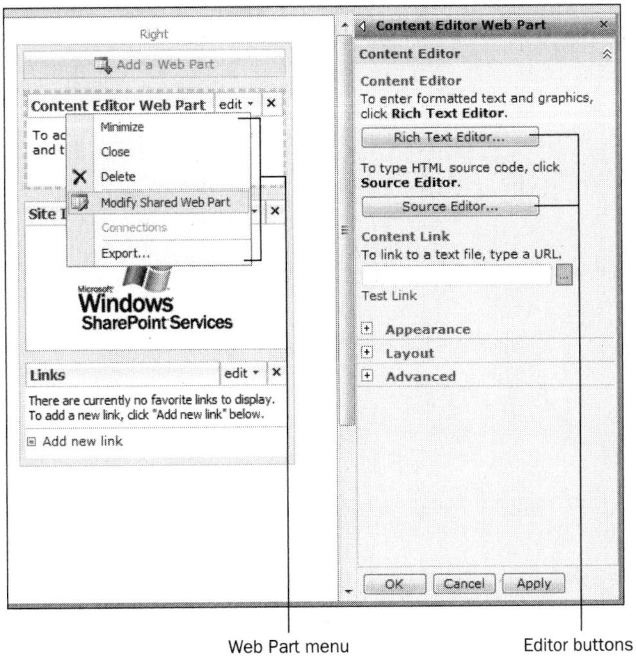

Web Part menu   Editor buttons

Figure 13-2

If the Web Part title bar is not accessible, you may need to view the page in Edit mode (Site Actions ⇨ Edit Page).

Rich Text Editor

The browser-based rich text editor provides a simple, WYSIWYG environment for adding content to pages. It enables you to control the text format and layouts. You can insert tables, images, and hyperlinks into the page. Figure 13-3 shows the Web Part from Figure 13-1, as seen by the rich text editor.

Figure 13-3

The rich text editor is your basic design tool.

Source Editor

The browser-based source editor is little more than a plaintext box. The source editor uses a fixed-width font, and displays the HTML code that makes up the information to be displayed in the Web Part. Figure 13-4 shows the web content from the previous figures as it looks in the source editor.

Figure 13-4

While simple, the source editor is the first key to unlocking the Content Editor's power. The rich text editor is limited in the number of features supported. For example, it has no way to set the thickness of table borders. In the source editor, on the other hand, you can enter virtually any HTML, and when saved, it is rendered on your SharePoint page.

That "any" includes such things as form fields (but not `<form>` tags), CSS style definitions, and even client-side script. Unlike the Code view in SharePoint Designer, however, there is no IntelliSense or other design-time validation of the text you enter. SharePoint does validate the HTML against the `<form>` restriction after the text is submitted, and may show an error in the Web Part's display area if the illegal tag is found. Incorrect and invalid code is not removed from the entered content.

The text entry dialog is used throughout the web interface of SharePoint. Validation of the contents is done by the calling function, not the dialog itself. Other parts or properties entered using this dialog may not allow the same content as the CEWP, and may strip invalid code.

External Content

The Content Editor Web Part is not limited to information that is entered directly by a user. The properties of the CEWP include an External Content Link option. Much as the Data view allows you to specify an external .XSL file, the Content Link property enables you to specify a file that contains the content to be displayed.

When an external file is specified, SharePoint reads the file and uses its contents in place of any content that may be defined in the rich text or source editors. If the external file is not available, the content defined in the part itself is used.

For files within the site of the SharePoint page containing the Web Part, the content is read directly from the site, without being processed by SharePoint. For files outside of the SharePoint context, the page is read the same way a browser would, so server-side processing (if any) takes place, and the processed results are used for rendering.

Rendering

Regardless of whether the content is specified via the rich text editor, the source editor, or an external file, it is rendered through the same process. The content is read by the server, parsed, and fed into the page stream as an integral part of the page. The result of this rendering process is HTML within the current page's context. The content of the Web Part is not set apart in an IFrame, or processed independently by the .NET framework on the server. This means that server-side scripts and control tags are ignored or generate an invalid content error. However, any client-side script is incorporated and will run in the page's context. This gives you access to any of the objects on the page, including text, site navigation, and the Web Part Services Component (detailed in the next chapter).

A Simple Example

Besides the basic content display already mentioned, a common use for the CEWP is to make a design change to a specific page. Frequently a designer is asked to suppress a standard element. Rather than customizing the page, breaking its links to the site definition, or possibly creating a whole new Master Page, a Content Editor with a small piece of CSS code can be used to reformat or even completely suppress an element.

The examples in this chapter make use of Search Web Parts which are not part of WSS. These parts are available though MOSS, or through Microsoft Search Server 2008. A free Express edition of Search Server is available for download from Microsoft, and can be installed on its own, or as an upgrade to WSS.

Preparation

Suppose you want to add an Advanced Search Box Web Part to the home page of your intranet. Follow these steps:

1. Select Site Actions ⇨ Edit Page.

2. In the header of the left Web Part Zone, click Add a Web Part to open an Add Web Parts dialog similar to the one shown in Figure 13-5. (Listed parts may vary, depending on your environment.)

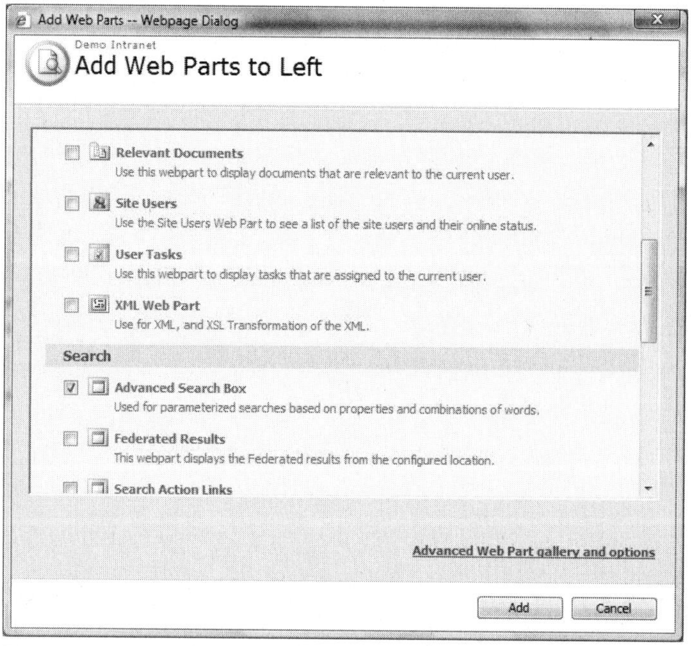

Figure 13-5

3. Select the Advanced Search Box Web Part, and click the Add button.

4. Exit edit mode (if editing a MOSS Publishing site, you also may need to check in your page).

You now have an Advanced Search function on your home page, as shown in Figure 13-6.

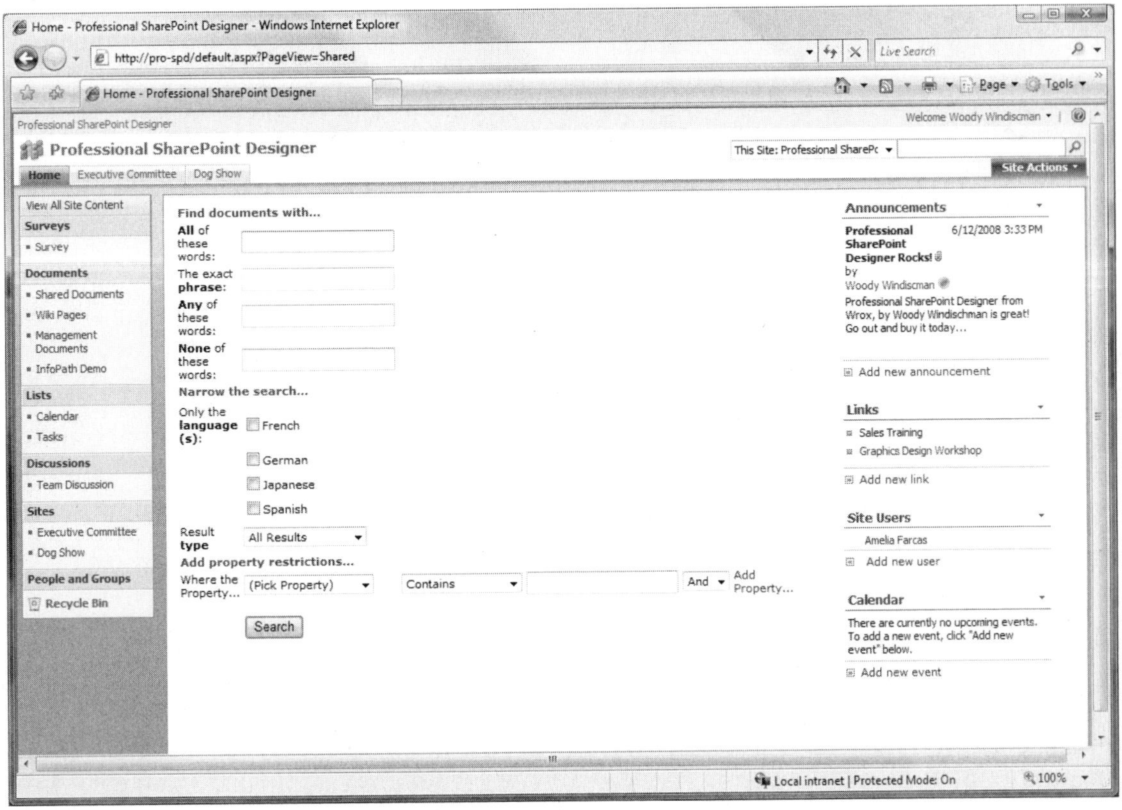

Figure 13-6

The Change

Now management decides that the regular search box in the upper-right corner is redundant on this page, and wants it removed, to avoid the possibility of confusing the users.

The search box in the corner is defined as a placeholder in the Master Page for the site. To truly remove it would require a new Master Page. Changing the Master Page normally affects all pages on the site, and would remove the box from other pages where you may want to retain it.

Fortunately, most standard SharePoint objects are assigned a CSS class. These classes are given default styles by `core.css`, which are easily overridden in a Theme.

In the case of the standard corner search control, the relevant standard class is `ms-sbtable`. This class is applied to the subtable containing all of the elements that make up the search control. While each of these elements also has its own CSS class, you want to use the class of the outermost stylable container for this operation. Doing so allows you to suppress the display of the entire group with a single statement. To suppress its display on a page:

1. Add a Content Editor Web Part to the page.

2. Set the Chrome type to None (in the Appearance section of the Web Part Tool pane).

3. Set the Title to `Suppress Default Search Box`.

4. Open the source editor.

5. Enter the following code. Because the Web Part will be loaded after `core.css` and any Theme you have applied, this will be the last style defined and will therefore override the existing styles of the same name.

```
<style>
.ms-sbtable {
display: none;
}
</style>
```

6. Click the Save button in the source editor and, in the Properties task pane, click Apply.

7. Exit page edit mode. (If you're on a MOSS Publishing site, you may also need to check in your changed page.)

The default search box is now hidden. Unlike the changes made to the core or to the page itself, the search box can be restored simply by removing the CEWP from the page. You can remove the part temporarily by selecting Close from the Web Part menu, or you can remove it permanently by selecting Delete from the Web Part menu.

The Content Editor in SharePoint Designer

The Content Editor Web Part provides a flexible tool for adding content to pages for web browser users. Yet the power afforded is limited to some extent by the web interface itself. Opening a page containing a CEWP in SharePoint Designer brings the full power of SPD's design surface to bear, as well as the additional capabilities of the Code view, such as IntelliSense.

Design View: The Page within a Page

In SharePoint Designer, the Design view simply treats the content area of the CEWP as a container such as a <DIV> or table cell. If there is no content, SharePoint Designer displays a message indicating that you can directly edit the contents of the Web Part. Figure 13-7 shows the default, empty CEWP in SharePoint Designer.

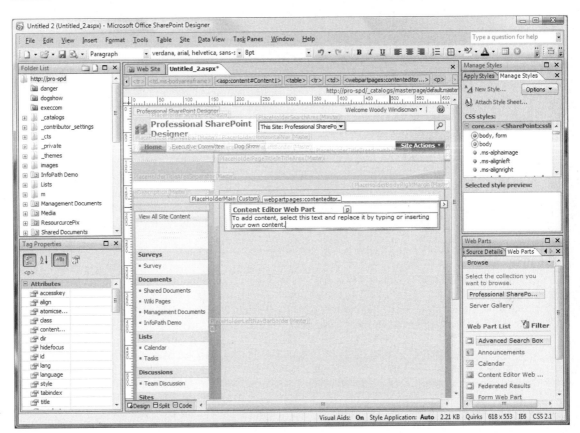

Figure 13-7

Notice that the empty CEWP is relatively small. The part expands as you add content to it, just like any other container. You may find it convenient, however, to set the height and width properties of the part to a more workable size prior to inserting any highly formatted content, such as a table or IFrame. You can find these properties by right-clicking the Web Part and selecting Web Part Properties from the context menu.

While the CEWP is capable of supporting virtually any client-side functionality, the SPD Design view is aware of the nature of the CEWP, and the restrictions placed upon it by SharePoint. Such things as ASP.NET user controls, Web Part Zones, and other Web Parts all represent server-side functionality. If you attempt to add a server-side control to a CEWP, SharePoint Designer will remind you of these limits with the alert shown in Figure 13-8.

Figure 13-8

Code View: XML Strikes Back

While SharePoint Designer provides an excellent and easy-to-use visual experience for Content Editor Web Parts in the Design view, the story in Code view is not quite as pretty. When you look at a Web Part in Code view, you are presented with the full XML-based definition, just as though you had opened the DWP or WEBPART file.

In Code view, the content of the CEWP is just another property — Content property. The content itself, however, is not likely to be well-formed XML. For that reason, and to prevent accidental parsing of the content, the content of the Web Part is contained in a CDATA (Complex Data) element.

The following code is how the Content Editor Web Part used earlier for suppressing the search box appears in Code view within SharePoint Designer. The highlighted text shows the content region itself.

```
<WebPartPages:ContentEditorWebPart runat="server" __MarkupType="xmlmarkup" 
WebPart="true" __WebPartId="{663AA85A-F907-4316-8234-239ADDA32B68}" >
<WebPart xmlns:xsi="http://www.w3.org/2001/XMLSchema-instance" 
xmlsn:xsd="http://www.w3.org/2001/XMLSchema" 
xmlsn="http://schemas.microsoft.com/WebPart/v2">
  <Title>Suppress Default Search Box</Title>
  <FrameType>None</FrameType>
  <Description>Use for formatted text, tables, and images.</Description>
  <IsIncluded>true</IsIncluded>
  <PartOrder>1</PartOrder>
  <FrameState>Normal</FrameState>
  <Height />
  <Width />
  <AllowRemove>true</AllowRemove>
  <AllowZoneChange>true</AllowZoneChange>
  <AllowMinimize>true</AllowMinimize>
  <AllowConnect>true</AllowConnect>
  <AllowEdit>true</AllowEdit>
  <AllowHide>true</AllowHide>
  <IsVisible>true</IsVisible>
  <DetailLink />
  <HelpLink />
  <HelpMode>Modeless</HelpMode>
  <Dir>Default</Dir>
  <PartImageSmall />
```

```
<MissingAssembly>Cannot import this Web Part.</MissingAssembly>
<PartImageLarge>/_layouts/images/mscontl.gif</PartImageLarge>
<IsIncludedFilter />
<ExportControlledProperties>true</ExportControlledProperties>
<ConnectionID>00000000-0000-0000-0000-000000000000</ConnectionID>
<ID>g_663aa85a_f907_4316_8234_239adda32b68</ID>
<ContentLink xmlns="http://schemas.microsoft.com/WebPart/v2/ContentEditor" />
  <Content ↵
xmlsn="http://schemas.microsoft.com/WebPart/v2/ContentEditor"><![CDATA[<style>
.ms-sbtable {
display: none;
}
</style>]]></Content>
  <PartStorage xmlns="http://schemas.microsoft.com/WebPart/v2/ContentEditor" />
</WebPart>
</WebPartPages:ContentEditorWebPart>
```

Because the contents are considered a data element within the Web Part, they are not given the same color coding as other code in Code view. Most other functions of Code view remain available. IntelliSense still operates, allowing tag completion, and flagging potential compatibility problems with the HTML being entered.

Customized Search Results: A Complete Page Example

For this exercise, the manager who wanted you to hide the default search box in the earlier example now wants a customized results page. The goal? As the user hovers over the title of each result, show a preview of the result in another Web Part. The exercise touches on most of the aspects of SharePoint Designer covered in the book up to this point. There are five major parts to the exercise:

❑   Create the page.

❑   Add the Web Parts.

❑   Prepare the Content Editor.

❑   Modify the core results.

❑   Attach the results to the Query Web Part.

Create the Page

Select File ⇨ New, Page, and then follow these steps:

1. From either the General or ASP.NET section of the Page tab, select Create from Master Page. The Select a Master Page dialog, shown in Figure 13-9, is displayed.

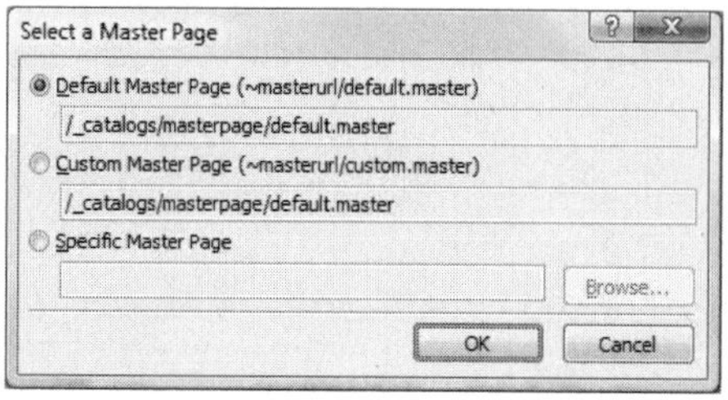

Select a Master Page

⦿ Default Master Page (~masterurl/default.master)
  /_catalogs/masterpage/default.master
○ Custom Master Page (~masterurl/custom.master)
  /_catalogs/masterpage/default.master
○ Specific Master Page

                                        Browse...

              OK   Cancel

Figure 13-9

2. Use the Default Master Page. Click OK.

   In this dialog, "Default" means the Master Page defined as the site's default. This may or may not be the out-of-the-box Default Master Page. See chapters 5 and 8 for more information on customizing Master Pages.

3. A new page opens, displaying the Master Page's common elements. Select the PlaceHolderMain placeholder. (You may need to set Visual Aids to On.)

4. From the Common Content Tasks side menu, select Create Custom Content, as shown in Figure 13-10.

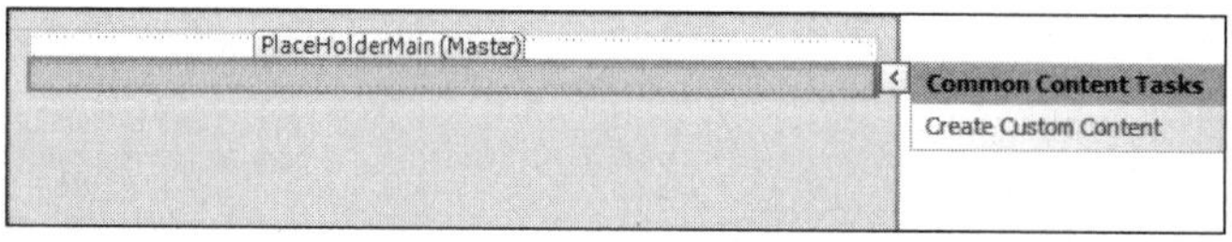

PlaceHolderMain (Master)

Common Content Tasks
Create Custom Content

Figure 13-10

5. Click within the placeholder and insert a 1 row × 2 cell table into the placeholder.

6. Select both cells. Right-click and select Cell Properties from the context menu.

7. Set the vertical alignment to Top, and click OK.

8. Select File ⇨ Save As, and name the file `previewresults.aspx`. Save this page in the root of your site. Leave the file open.

Add the Web Parts

As the Project continues, you insert Web Part Zones into the table cells:

9.   Click in the left cell. Select Insert ⇨ SharePoint Controls ⇨ Web Part Zone (see Figure 13-11).

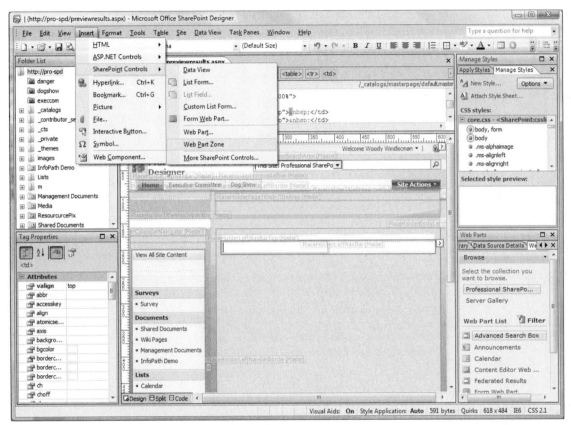

Figure 13-11

10.   Repeat step 9 for the right cell.

11.   In the left zone, click the link Click To Insert A Web Part, to summon the Web Parts task pane (shown maximized in Figure 13-12).

Web Parts task pane

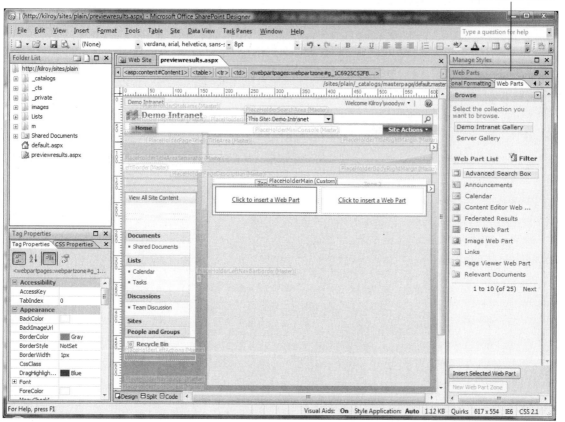

Figure 13-12

12. From the Web Parts task pane, select the Search Core Results Web Part. (You may need to page through the parts list.) Click the Insert Selected Web Part button.

Notice that SharePoint Designer treats the Core Results Web Part as a Data View, with an example result element displayed.

13. From the Quick Tag Selector, select the Web Part Zone element.

14. From the Web Parts task pane, select the Search Paging Web Part, and click the Insert Selected Web Part button.

15. Select the Content Editor Web Part from the Web Parts task pane. Use the mouse to drag it into the right Web Part Zone.

16. Save your page. The Design view should resemble the one shown in Figure 13-13.

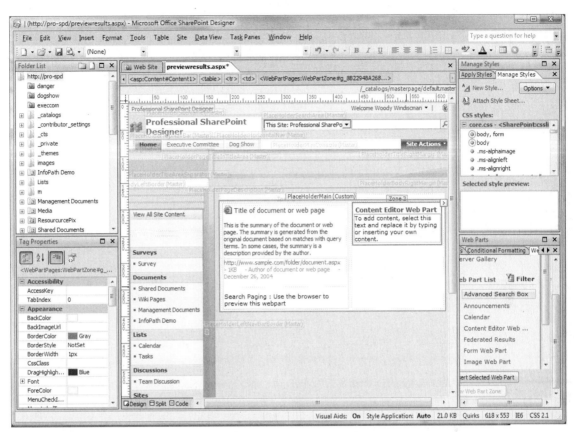

Figure 13-13

Prepare the Content Editor

The Content Editor Web Part is where the preview will be displayed. The following steps add an IFrame to hold the preview, and a script to set the source file for the IFrame.

17. Select the text within the Content Editor.

18. Choose Insert ⇨ HTML ⇨ Inline Frame.

19. In Inline Frame, click the New Page button.

20. In the blank content area for the new page, type **Roll over the title of a search result to preview the page here.**

21. Click Save to open the Save As dialog. This is for the new page you created within the IFrame. You can leave the name as is, or change it to something shorter, such as `blankresults.htm`. Save the page.

22. Click the title of the Content Editor to select the Web Part instead of the IFrame contents.

23. Switch to Code view. The code for the Content Editor Web Part will be selected.

24. Find the IFrame tag. It looks like this:

```
<iframe name="I1" id="I1" src="blankresults.htm">
```

25. Change the `name` and `id` values from `"I1"` to "previewPane", resulting in the tag looking like this:

```
<iframe name="previewPane" id="previewPane" src="blankresults.htm">
```

26. Within the CDATA element, before the IFrame, there is a paragraph tag (`<p>`). Click to place the insertion point before that tag, and press Enter twice.

27. Starting on the blank line you created, enter the following code. This function will replace the display contents of the IFrame with the URL provided.

```
<script language="javascript">
function setPreview(showurl){
previewPane.location=showurl;
}
</script>
```

Notice the IntelliSense auto-completion when entering the script tag.

Although the script tag is auto-completed, elements defined within the content tag are not.

28. Save the page.

Modify the Core Results

In the Core Results Web Part, you will modify the XSL to add an `onmouseover` event to the title of a search result to call the `setPreview` function you defined in the previous segment.

29. Set the page view to Split mode.

30. In the core results part, click the example title. The title is contained in a Span tag. In the Quick Tag Selector, click the `<span.srch-Title>` element. (You may need to click twice to highlight the tag.) The code for the span will be highlighted in the Code pane, as shown in Figure 13-14.

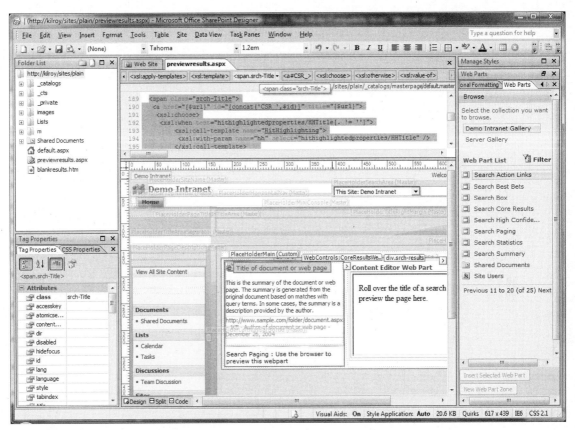

Figure 13-14

31. Find the line opening the Span. It looks like this:

```
<span class="srch-Title">
```

32. Edit the line to add an `onmouseover` parameter that calls the `setPreview` function, passing the XPATH {url} value. After editing, it looks like this:

```
<span class="srch-Title" onmouseover="setPreview('{url}');">
```

Notice that IntelliSense is fully functional, providing color coding as well as function and XPATH lookups.

33. Save the page.

34. Click the Preview in Browser icon (which is next to the Save button). The web browser will open, showing the page.

35. In the address bar, add a ?k=XXXX parameter to the URL of your page, where XXXX is a keyword that will return results in your environment. (If you are in a clean environment with no content, try the word "home.")

36. If you get results, roll over the title. The target page should appear in your preview pane, as shown in Figure 13-15.

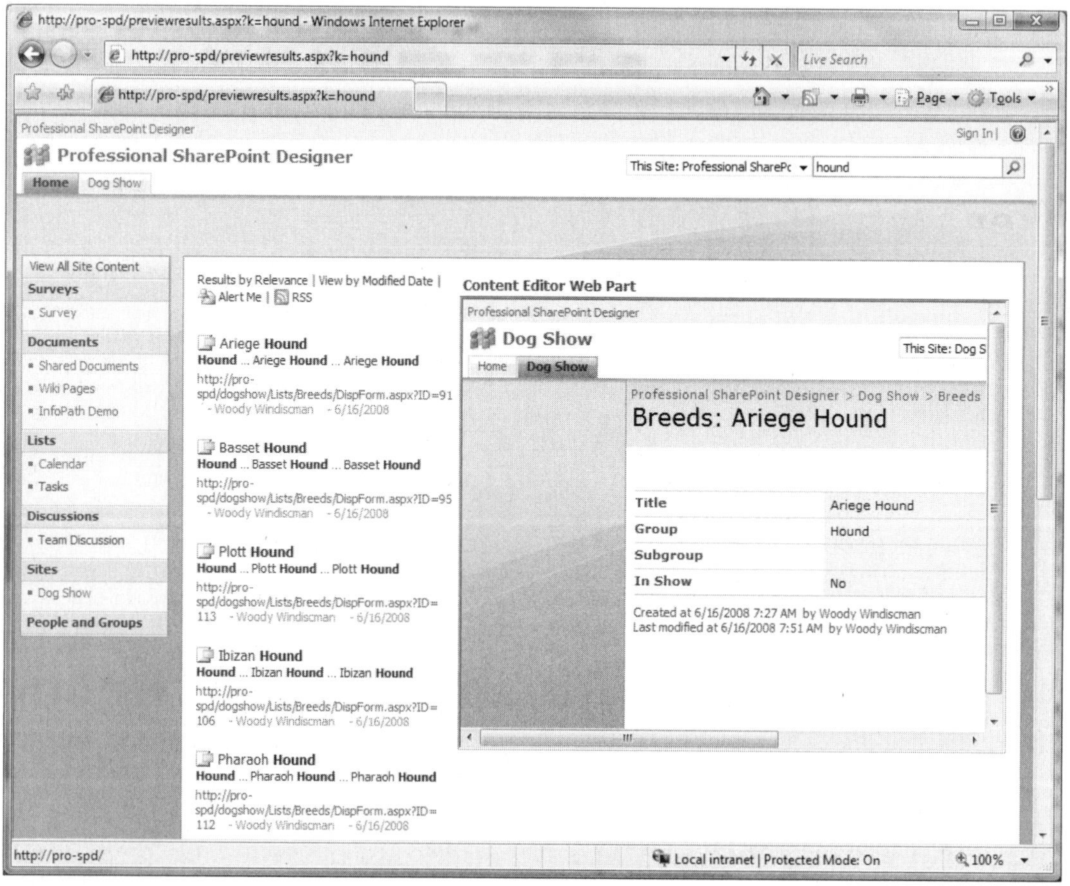

Figure 13-15

Attach the Results to the Query Web Part

While you now have a functional results page, you still need to tell the query page about it. These instructions assume you have a page containing an Advanced Search Web Part.

1. Open the page you created in the Preparation section of this chapter.

2. Right-click the Advanced Query Web Part, and select Web Part Properties.

3. Expand the Miscellaneous section.

4. Enter the root-relative URL of the results page you created (such as ./previewresults.aspx) into the Results URL box.

5. Click OK.

6. Save the page.

The Results URL setting can also be accessed through the web interface, via the Modify Shared Web Part option.

Now when you perform a query with the Advanced Search box, your customized results page will be displayed.

Tokens of Affection

Although largely self-contained, Web Parts do not operate in a vacuum. They are part of a larger framework that includes Web Part Zones, Web Part Pages, and ultimately, SharePoint itself. Many aspects of Web Part development are of interest only to server-side programmers. Some, however, revolve around client presentation, and allow Web Parts to interact with each other.

The most important of these, the Web Part Services Component (WPSC), is discussed in the next chapter. Other aspects can be useful to you even without the WPSC. In particular, the Web Part Page framework offers several *tokens* you can use in your Content Editor Web Part to ascertain things about the environment in which your part exists. Tokens are essentially placeholders. They are strings of text that are replaced at run time with appropriate real information.

There are four tokens, and each token is delimited by an underscore (_) character both before and after the token name:

❑ `_WPQ_`

❑ `_LogonUser_`

❑ `_WPID_`

❑ `_WPR_`

When a Web Part is rendered, SharePoint looks for occurrences of these tokens in the content, and replaces them with values appropriate to that Web Part's context. Token names are case sensitive.

Token replacement occurs for all Web Parts that use the framework's render method, not just Content Editors.

The _WPQ_ Token

One of the great things about using a modular development framework like Web Parts is the capability to place components on pages as needed. Users can add and remove Web Parts at will. This often leads to multiple instances of the same basic Web Part being on a page at the same time. Because there's usually no way to know at design time what other Web Parts will share the page, or even where on a page a given Web Part will be placed, each Web Part is given a unique identifier, the *Web Part Qualifier*, at run time.

The _WPQ_ token allows a Web Part to take advantage of this unique identifier without knowing in advance what it will be. This is critical in cases where a part containing script may be instantiated multiple times. By incorporating the token into your variable and function names, you can be certain that they will be unique on the page, and there will be no naming conflicts with other Web Parts.

The following two code fragments show the IFrame and its population function from the search results example edited to use the _WPQ_ token. The first fragment shows how the code looks at design time, while the second, highlighted, fragment shows the function as it is actually rendered to the page.

```
<script language="javascript">
function setPreview_WPQ_(showurl){
previewPane_WPQ_.location=showurl;
}
</script>
<p>
<iframe name="previewPane_WPQ_" id="previewPane_WPQ_" src="preresult.htm" ↵
width="100%" height="600px">
Your browser does not support inline frames or is currently configured ↵
not to display inline frames.
</iframe>
</p>
```

```
<script language="javascript">
function setPreviewWPQ2(pvURL){
previewPaneWPQ2.location=pvURL;
}
</script>
<iframe name="previewPaneWPQ2" id="previewPaneWPQ2" src="preresult.htm" ↵
align="top">
Your browser does not support inline frames or is currently configured ↵
not to display inline frames.
</iframe>
```

It is best practice to use the _WPQ_ token in script that will be rendered in a Web Part. Even if you do not believe your part will be instantiated multiple times, using the token prevents possible naming conflicts with scripts in Web Parts you did not design.

Using the _WPQ_ token in your function names will result in the inability to call that function directly from other Web Parts. The next chapter introduces the Web Part Page event model, which facilitates interpart communication.

The _LogonUser_ Token

For developers of server-side code, it has always been easy to determine the identity of the current user. Not so for the client-side script user. Users may be logged in to their home PCs, for example, with a default ID, while logged in to SharePoint with their work credentials. Yet, the scripts on the page need to know a user's network ID to properly call web services.

SharePoint resolves this problem for Web Part developers by providing the _LogonUser_ token. This token is resolved to the identity currently logged in to the SharePoint site. Note that this is the User ID, not the "friendly" name. In the case of a Windows authentication, for example, the _LogonUser_ token is resolved and returned in the form DOMAIN\UserID.

The _WPID_ Token

In addition to the Web Part Qualifier, each Web Part on a page is assigned a GUID. The _WPID_ token makes the GUID available to the client side. Although binary Web Parts have access to APIs that make use of the GUID, it is not typically needed or used in Content Editor script. This token is listed for completeness only.

The _WPR_ Token

CompiledWeb Parts, described in chapter 16, have the option of specifying a resource folder on the server's file system. The _WPR_ token provides the URL for the Web Part resource folder. Content Editor Web Parts do not have a resource folder; therefore, this token is listed for completeness only.

A Few Tips and Tricks

Even with the normal editing power of SharePoint Designer, sometimes things aren't as easy or straightforward as you might like. This section provides a few suggestions or workarounds to help you get the most out of the CEWP.

Keep It Simple

For self-contained Projects, you may want to keep the script in its own file. If the functionality you are implementing does not depend on the fact that you are running in SharePoint, coding around the overhead of a Web Part page can be a pain. In these instances, you may find yourself better off taking advantage of the capability to define an external source file for the CEWP.

Use the Script Editor

SharePoint Designer's design surface does not have the capability to execute a script in real time. The default method for testing a script is to save the page and preview it in the browser. For complicated scripts, this can be a very inefficient debugging workflow.

The SharePoint Designer Script Editor allows you to run your scripts in the browser without first saving them to your SharePoint site. You can toggle back and forth between the Script Editor and the main SPD environment, and changes you make in one are automatically reflected in the other.

Create a Shell Page

SharePoint Designer does a great job of rendering previews of the information contained in Web Parts. When you are creating script to interact with SharePoint Page objects, however, sometimes you need to test with the real thing. In addition, most SharePoint objects are not rendered when you try running a page from the Script Editor.

To ensure you have access to the real objects, you can create a prerendered page to use when you design your scripts. To create this shell:

1. Set up the page with all of the Web Parts with which you plan to interact, as well as a Content Editor that just contains some dummy text. (The text will make the CEWP easy to find in the source code.)

2. Save the page, and preview it in Internet Explorer.

3. In Internet Explorer, right-click on the rendered page and select View Source to see the complete HTML for the output in Notepad.

4. In Notepad, right-click the text and choose Select All.

5. Press Ctrl+C to copy the source code to the Clipboard.

6. In SharePoint Designer, select File ⇨ New.

7. On the Page tab, in the General section, select HTML. Click OK.

8. Switch to Code view on the new page.

9. Press Ctrl+A to select all of the existing code, and then press Ctrl+V to paste your prerendered source code into the window, replacing what was there.

10. Save the page to your site with a useful name (`scriptshell.htm`, for instance).

You now have a page that contains all of the elements that will exist when your script executes. In addition, it will be rendered correctly when shelled from the Script Editor. When you write your code, locate and replace the dummy text with your actual script functions.

After you have written and tested your script in this context, you can copy and paste it back into your original Content Editor Web Part on the real SharePoint page.

While this is not a perfect solution, it is the best workable option with current tools. Keep in mind that this page will have been rendered with the tokens expanded or replaced. These values may not be the same at run time. In addition, any list, library, or Data View Web Parts contain only a snapshot of data, which will probably change by the time your script gets to run.

Keep CEWPs Portable

Most Web Parts have an `Export` function available from the Web Part menu in the web browser (your page may need to be in Edit mode if the Web Part title bar is not shown). This saves the full XML definition of the Web Part, including any script you have written, in a DWP file. That file can then be imported into virtually any other SharePoint site, on any server.

Naturally, the full extent of this portability depends upon what you have created. Simple text, HTML content, and script that does not depend upon SharePoint Page objects (Document Object Model, or DOM) can all transfer without any changes. If you have written a script that calls other parts, or makes use of elements in the SharePoint DOM, you are still OK as long as equivalent objects with the same names exist in your target site.

However, you may run into trouble if you have Web Parts try to call other Web Parts directly, but have not transferred those parts into the new environment. You can avoid trouble by thinking of your Content Editor Web Parts as modules of an application and allowing any scripts you write to degrade gracefully if their desired objects are not present.

Summary

This chapter explored the Content Editor Web Part, and explained how it can be used to easily extend the power of SharePoint without writing server-side code. You saw how to use it both from the web interface and within SharePoint Designer.

The chapter also showed you that:

❑   Content Editors allow client-side script.

❑   IntelliSense works in Code view, even though the code is just a parameter of the Web Part.

❑   The Script Editor allows you to test your code without first saving the page.

Chapter 14 presents the Web Part Services Component, which allows you to leverage even more of the SharePoint client-side object model from within your scripts.

The SharePoint Client-Side Object Model

SharePoint provides a number of objects you can access from your scripts. Key among them is the Web Part Page Services Component (WPSC). Through its object model, it provides the glue that connects the pieces of the page to each other and to the SharePoint server.

This chapter explains what the Web Part Page Services Component is and then examines:

❑ Services and events.

❑ Web Part storage.

❑ Other client-side SharePoint objects.

What Is the Web Part Page Services Component?

A SharePoint Web Part Page is a complicated beast. It must support the loading and display of components from a variety of sources. In addition, it must be able to adapt to the changes as users add and remove Web Parts (and connections between them) at run time. Coordinating all of this is the job of the Web Part Page Services Component (WPSC).

In code, the component's object ID is WPSC. The rest of this chapter uses WPSC for all references to the component in the text as well.

The functions of the WPSC fall into two general categories:

❑ Page initialization

❑ Page services

Page Initialization

SharePoint detects which browser is being used, and takes slightly different actions based on what it finds. A variety of JavaScript objects, typically including the WPSC, are instantiated at run time by including the file IE50UP.JS, IE55UP.JS, or NON_IE.JS, depending upon what functions the user's browser supports.

As implied by their titles, IE55UP.JS is used for IE 5.5 or higher browsers, while IE50UP.JS is used for down-level versions of IE, and NON_IE.JS is for other browsers. This allows calls made to the WPSC to degrade gracefully on older versions of Internet Explorer. The WPSC is not implemented in NONIE.JS. As always, test your code on multiple browsers.

As a Web Part Page loads, the WPSC receives information about the Web Parts on the page, and performs various housekeeping tasks. Among other things, the WPSC is responsible for:

❑   Building the Parts collection.

❑   Registering Web Part connections.

❑   Creating a varPart_WPQ_ variable for each Web Part in the parts collection, based upon the Web Part Qualifiers (WPQ) assigned by SharePoint.

Once the page is initialized and rendered, you will have access to this framework in your own client-side code as Page Services.

Page Services

For the developer and page designer, the WPSC object is the primary entry point for client-side interaction between Web Parts. The WPSC provides a number of services. These are not services in the traditional sense of constantly running applications, nor are they web services called via HTTP. Rather, WPSC page services are simply the properties and methods of the WPSC object.

Microsoft groups these services into three broad categories:

❑   Discovery

❑   Notification

❑   State management

These groupings are logical only. There is no discovery property or method, for example. You simply access the Parts property (a collection) of the WebPartPage object, and enumerate the collection's members if you want to know what other Web Parts are on the page. (See the code example in the next section.)

WPSC Child Objects

Discovery services are generally the properties of the WPSC and its child objects. Figure 14-1 shows the primary objects defined within the WPSC.

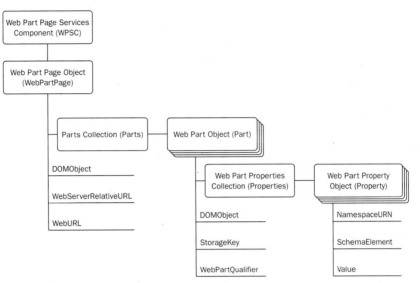

Figure 14-1

WebPartPage Object

The WPSC defines a single WebPartPage object to represent the core functionality of the Web Part Page. The WebPartPage object defines three simple public properties and the Parts collection. The properties are:

- ❑ DOMObject
- ❑ WebServerRelativeURL
- ❑ WebURL

The DOMObject property gives you access to the HTML Document Object Model for the Web Part Page. It enables you to write script, relatively independently of the browser version, that accesses the various visible elements of the page that are not contained in the Parts collection.

The WebServerRelativeURL and WebURL properties allow your script to quickly determine the SharePoint subweb the page resides on. This is useful because your page could be in the root of a subweb, a document library, or even a subfolder within a library. Simply using the browser's DOM to find the location of your page cannot reliably determine which it is.

WPSC Collections

There are two public collections in the WPSC: the Parts property of the WebPartPage object and the Properties property of the Part object. These collections are not intrinsic language objects; rather, they are JavaScript constructs.

Two public properties are implemented: Count and Item. Count returns the number of items (parts or properties) in the collection. The Item function returns the appropriate object.

You must use the `Item` property to retrieve an item from the collection. Items may be accessed by their numeric index, or by a text key value. You cannot access an item by simply applying the index or key to the `Parts` or `Properties` collection. Here are some examples of valid and invalid code:

Valid usage

```
var myPart = WPSC.WebPartPage.Parts.Item(0);
var yourPart = WPSC.WebPartPage.Parts.Item("WPQ3");
myPropertyValue = myPart.Properties.Item
("http://schemas.microsoft.com/WebPart/v2#Title").Value;
```

Invalid usage

```
var myPart = WPSC.WebPartPage.Parts["WPQ3"];
var myProperty = myPart.Properties(5);
```

The makeup of the text key varies for the `Parts` and `Properties` collections, and is explained in their respective descriptions.

Parts Collection and Part Object

Most of the individual Web Parts on a page are registered with the `Parts` collection of the WebPartPage object. At the time of this writing, the Windows SharePoint Services Software Development Kit (WSS SDK) documentation is incomplete in this regard. It simply states that the Parts collection "Contains the set of Web Parts on a Web Part Page." In practice, not every Web Part on the page is fully represented.

Standard List and Library View Web Parts are not included in the `Parts` collection. Data Views of lists and libraries are included, however. Static Web Parts (those not in a Web Part Zone), which are not standard lists or libraries, will be listed in the `Parts` collection; however, static parts do not have a run time–accessible `Properties` collection.

> The HTML Document Object Model (DOM) of List and Library Views, as well as that of static Web Parts, can be accessed directly if you know the Web Part Qualifier, but such access is not achieved through the WPSC object. This is discussed briefly later in the chapter.

A Web Part has three simple properties and the `Properties` collection. The Properties collection is described in the next section. The simple properties are:

❑ `DOMObject`

❑ `StorageKey`

❑ `WebPartQualifier`

As with the WebPartPage object, the `DOMObject` property of a Web Part gives a handle to the HTML code that makes up the rendered part's content area. In the case of a Web Part, the handle is to the outermost (root) `<DIV>` below the title bar of that Web Part.

The `StorageKey` property is used by the SharePoint API to store and retrieve properties from the content database. For dynamic Web Parts, a GUID is assigned to the part when it is registered on the page. For static Web Parts, the StorageKey is always `00000000-0000-0000-0000-000000000000`. (The properties of static Web Parts are hard-coded into the page, and therefore a unique identifier is not needed.)

The `WebPartQualifier` property stores the unique identifier provided to the Web Part at run time via the _WPQ_ token. Because each Web Part is assigned to an object variable when the page loads, you can access the properties of the current Web Part by using `varPart_WPQ_` in your code. The following line assigns the current part's Qualifier to a variable. The `WebPartQualifier` also acts as the text key for accessing a specific part through the `Parts` collection.

```
var myQualifier = varPart_WPQ_.WebPartQualifier;
```

The following code displays a list of the Web Parts in the `Parts` collection. Notice that for local variables declared inside a function, no _WPQ_ token is required to keep them distinct. The function name itself however, as well as the ID of the `<div>` that it references, is potentially visible outside of the scope of the Web Part, and is therefore tokenized to prevent conflicts.

To run this script, create a Content Editor Web Part on a Web Part Page that also contains a variety of other Web Parts. Include standard List Views, Data Views, and some nonlist Web Parts such as an Image Web Part and other Content Editor Web Parts on your test page. Enter the following code into the CDATA element, as described in chapter 13 (or use the source editor in the web interface).

```javascript
<script language="javascript">
function listParts_WPQ_() {
// Create a reference to the Parts collection, and a variable
// to hold the display text.
var objParts=WPSC.WebPartPage.Parts;
var partsList;
// Tell the user how many total parts there are
// (standard list and library views excepted)
partsList = '<b>There are ' + objParts.Count + ⏎
' parts on this page.</b><br />';
// Iterate through the parts to display their names.
for (var i=0; i<objParts.Count;i++){
try {
// create a reference to the current part
p=objParts.Item(i);
// WPQ1 is reserved - typically contains the "standard"
// search box in the page banner.
if (p.WebPartQualifier=="WPQ1")
{
partsList += '<i>WPQ1 is reserved for SharePoint.</i><br />';
// You can't get the properties, so on to the next part.
continue;
}
// Otherwise, add it to the display list.
partsList+=p.WebPartQualifier + ': ' + ⏎
p.Properties.Item(p.Properties.Item(1).NamespaceURN+"#Title").Value ⏎
+ '<br />';
}
catch(err)
{
// If you have any static, non-list/library, Web Parts, you can't read
// their "real" properties, but you know they exist.
// Let the user know at least that the part is there.
```

```
partsList+='Cannot get properties for '+p.WebPartQualifier+' due to: '
  + err.description;
}
}
// Display the part.
divList_WPQ_.innerHTML=partsList;
}
</script>
<!-- Invoke your function with a button press,
place the results inside a DIV tag. -->

<Input type="button" onclick="listParts_WPQ_();"
value="List Web Parts"><br />
<div id="divList_WPQ_" name="divList_WPQ_"></div>
```

Figure 14-2 shows the results of this Web Part. (Your results will vary, depending upon the Web Parts on your actual page.)

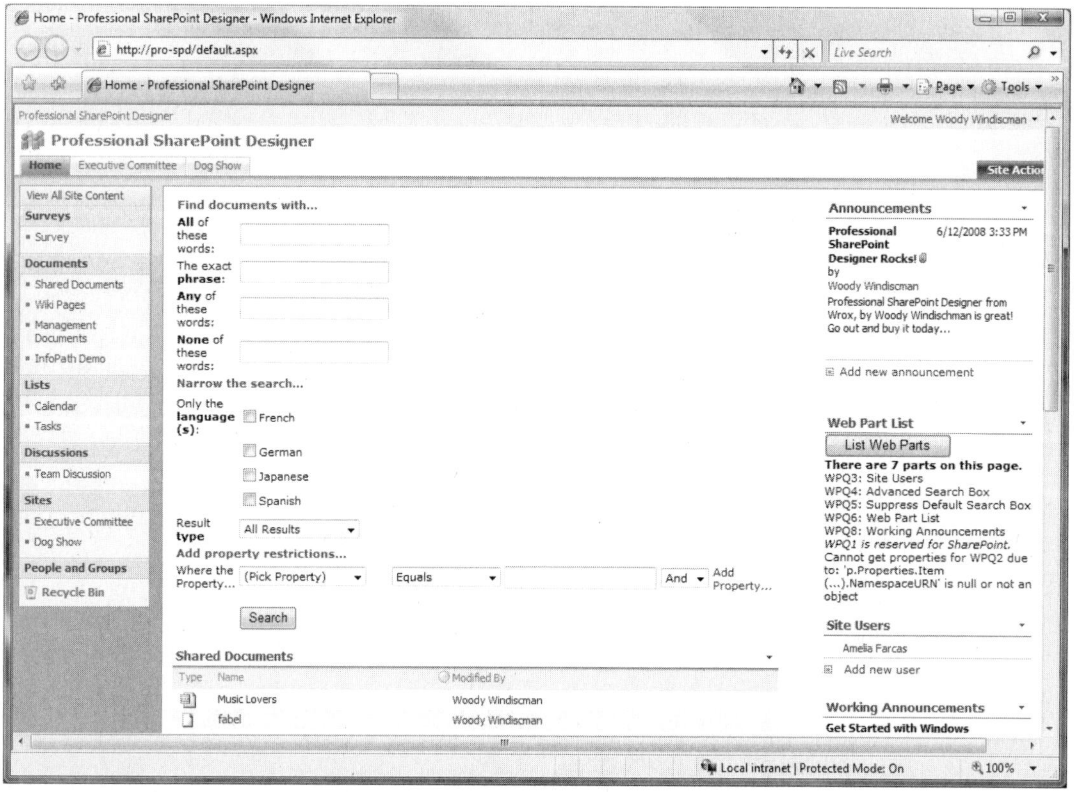

Figure 14-2

There are several things to notice from these results.

❏ You are invoking this script from a button. While it is possible to run script in a Web Part without its being in a function, the Parts collection is not initialized until the page is loaded. Therefore, the Web Parts are not registered or available for the script until page load completes. Most Web Part scripts (other than initializations) will be triggered by user interaction. Later in this chapter, you see how to trigger scripts based on page events.

❏ Announcements and Shared Documents are normal List/Library Views, and therefore not listed, while Working Announcements is a Data View of the Announcements list and appears in the list.

❏ WPQ2 is a static Web Part. When running the script, there will be an error alert. Displaying the error code shows you that the static part does not have fully populated properties.

❏ The Web Part Qualifiers in the `Parts` collection are not ordered based upon the visible position on the page, nor are they necessarily contiguous or sequential.

❏ The gap in numbers (7 is missing here) is due to either the Announcements or Shared Documents having been assigned WPQ7. The other will be WPQ9.

❏ The `Parts.Count()` property/method returns the number of Web Parts in the `Parts` collection, not the number of Web Parts on the page.

Properties Collection and Property Object

In the preceding code example, you saw the line:

```
partsList+=p.WebPartQualifier + ': ' + ↵
p.Properties.Item(p.Properties.Item(1).NamespaceURN + "#Title").Value ↵
+ '<br />';
```

This line accessed two different kinds of properties of the Part object: a simple property, `WebPartQualifier`, and a property from the `Properties` collection. In fact, the Properties collection was referenced twice. Each property in the `Properties` collection actually has three properties of its own:

❏ `NamespaceURN`

❏ `SchemaElement`

❏ `Value`

The `NamespaceURN` property specifies the schema that is used to interpret the remainder of the Property's properties. Notice that each property carries a copy of the NamespaceURN. This implies that it possible to create a Web Part with properties based upon multiple namespaces, and that is the case. In practice, however, most properties of a given Web Part are usually based on the same namespace.

A Web Part's developer may define his own namespace(s) for the Web Part. However, there are certain core properties possessed by every Web Part. These are usually the first items listed in the `Properties` collection. The example makes use of that assumption to get the namespace from the first property of the Web Part, and uses that namespace to get the Web Part's `Title`. A more robust, though less efficient, method would be to iterate through all of the items and look for `Title` in the `SchemaElement`.

The `SchemaElement` property is the name of the property being referenced.

The `Value` property is the actual value of the property.

Be aware that the `Value` property of a property item is named with an uppercase V. Because the `value` properties of form objects are named with a lowercase v, this can cause confusion. Also, using a lowercase v for this property does *not* cause an error in your script, so troubleshooting a case-related issue can be tricky.

`Value` *is a read/write property; however there are special considerations for writing property values, which will be discussed in a later section.*

When accessing an item from the `Properties` collection, you can either use a numeric index or a text key. Unlike the `Parts` collection, which used the single Web Part Qualifier value as its text key, the `Properties` collection uses a compound key. A `NamespaceURN` and `SchemaElement` must be combined, delimited by a hash character (#), to create the key to a specific property (for instance, `urn:myNamespace#myElement` or `http://schemas.microsoft.com/WebPart/v2#Title`).

The following code example builds upon the earlier Parts list to add the capability to display all of the properties from a particular Web Part. The highlighted code should be entered after the `listParts_WPQ_` function, and before the closing `</script>` tag. (Nonhighlighted lines are shown for context only.)

```
// Display the part.
divList_WPQ_.innerHTML=partsList;
}
function listProps_WPQ_(thisWPQ) {
// You are passed a WebPartQualifier. Get the associated Web Part.
var myPart=WPSC.WebPartPage.Parts.Item(thisWPQ);
// A variable to hold the current property as you iterate through the collection.
var thisProp;
// A variable to accumulate the properties to be displayed.
var propsList='<hr /><b>Web Part Properties</b><br />'
try {
// First, gather the simple properties for the Web Part.
propsList+='<b>WebPartQualifier:</b> ' + myPart.WebPartQualifier + '<br />';
propsList+='<b>StorageKey:</b> '+myPart.StorageKey + '<br />';
// Note: Because the DOMObject is a handle to a <DIV> object, you
// can't just display it. Get its ID instead.
propsList+='<b>DOMObject:</b> '+myPart.DOMObject.id + '<br />';
// Build a nice header for your property list. Because some of the
// "Value" property values can be pretty long, put the Property properties
// in a table.
propsList+='<b>Properties Collection:</b> (Contains '↵
+myPart.Properties.Count()+' properties)<br />';
propsList+='<table border="1"><tr bgcolor="Gainsboro"><td>Index</td>↵
<td>NamespaceURN</td><td>SchemaElement</td><td>Value</td></tr>';
// Iterate through the Properties collection.
for (var i=0;i<myPart.Properties.Count();i++){
thisProp = myPart.Properties.Item(i);
propsList +='<tr><td valign="top">'+i+'</td><td valign="top">'↵
```

```
+thisProp.NamespaceURN+'</td><td valign="top">'↩
+thisProp.SchemaElement +'</td><td valign="top">'
// For the actual value, you don't want it to render directly in case it
// contains valid HTML, so encode it. Borrow the existing URLEncode
// function from ie55up.js.
propsList+=URLEncode(thisProp.Value)+'</td></tr>';
}
}
catch(err){
// If there is a problem reading a property, display the error
propsList +='<tr><td colspan="4">Error reading properties: '↩
+err.description+'</td></tr>';
}
// Complete the table, and fill the target <DIV>.
propsList +="</table>";
divProps_WPQ_.innerHTML = propsList;
}
</script>
```

Next, insert the following highlighted lines between the `<div>` for the Parts list, and the closing line of the `<Content>` block.

```
<div id="divList_WPQ_" name="divList_WPQ_"></div>
<!-- A DIV to hold the Properties. -->
<div id="divProps_WPQ_" name="divProps_WPQ_"></div>
]]></Content>
```

Finally, give your user a link to view the properties for each Web Part. In the original `listParts_WPQ_` function, edit this line:

```
partsList+=p.WebPartQualifier + ': ' + ↩
p.Properties.Item(p.Properties.Item(1).NamespaceURN+"#Title").Value ↩
+ '<br />';
```

To read:

```
partsList+='<a href=javascript:listProps_WPQ_("'+p.WebPartQualifier+'")>'↩
+p.WebPartQualifier + '</a>: ' + ↩
p.Properties.Item(p.Properties.Item(1).NamespaceURN+"#Title").Value + ↩
'<br />';
```

Figure 14-3 shows the completed Part List with Properties Web Part after listing the parts, and clicking on the Site Users.

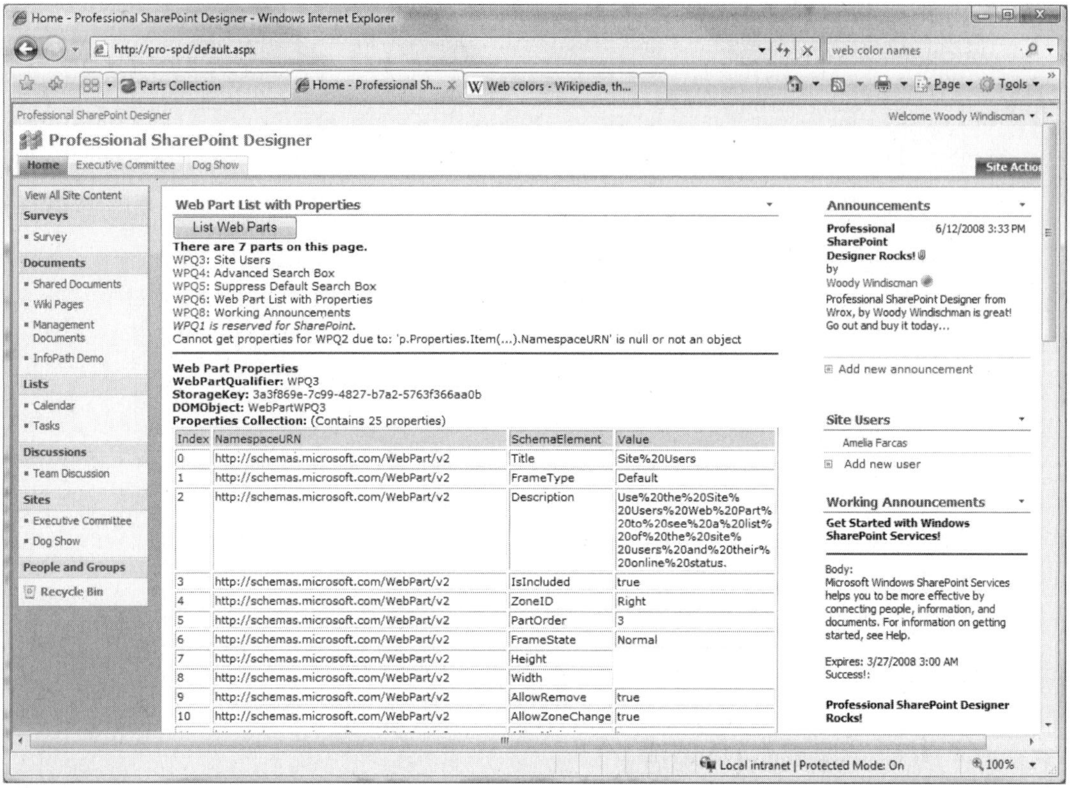

Figure 14-3

Notice the encoding in the Value properties. This sample used the URLEncode function of the SharePoint JavaScript library. The properties of a Web Part may contain renderable HTML code, such as the JavaScript code of a Content Editor or the HTML elements of the XSL property of a Data View. If, as an experiment, you want to see the actual values, you can temporarily remove the URLEncode function wrapper from the Value property.

Running code without its normal context can produce unpredictable results, and is not recommended.

The Web Part Page Event Model

WPSC notification services are embodied by the SharePoint Web Part Page event model. An *event* is something that happens that might be interesting to the components on a page. Letting the WPSC know that this has happened is called *raising* the event.

There are many different events that can be raised on a page. Some are generated by the system; others can be generated by user interaction, or even by your own code. Whatever the source, you can write code to respond to the events. If you want to respond to an event in your code, you *register* for it with the WPSC.

How does this help? In the search example in chapter 13, you saw how a script in one Web Part could directly call a function that resided in a different part. While convenient, this direct-access model is fraught with difficulties:

❑ You need to know the exact name of the function you are trying to call.

❑ If a part containing that function is not on the page, your script generates an error.

❑ If you need to make changes in multiple Web Parts, you must call all of the relevant part-specific functions.

❑ You need to be concerned that you do not have naming conflicts between the various functions.

With the event model, all of these problems go away. Raising an event provides benefits for the calling function, and registering for the event benefits the functions being called:

❑ Interfaces (namespaces and event names, and optionally a parameter) can be set early, without regard to the actual implementation function name.

❑ Web Parts can be added to the page in any order. Raising an event for which no part has registered does not generate an error.

❑ Multiple Web Parts can register for an event without needing to change the code in the raising Web Part.

❑ The use of a `NamespaceURN` prevents conflicts between similar event names.

Registering for an Event

If you want your Web Part to respond to an event, you *register* for that event using the `RegisterForEvent` method of the WPSC. This tells the WPSC that your Web Part has a function in it that should be called when an event is raised.

`RegisterForEvent` has three usable parameters:

❑ `NamespaceURN`

❑ `EventName`

❑ `Function`

The form of the call is generally:

```
WPSC.RegisterForEvent("urn:SomeNamespaceURN","SomeEventName",Function_WPQ_);
```

The `NamespaceURN` parameter allows you to set the context for the event. For example, you may have Web Parts from multiple vendors on your page, and each can raise an `Update` event. If each vendor sets a distinct `NamespaceURN`, it allows you to register for and respond appropriately to only the events you really need.

The `EventName` parameter specifies the name of the event within the namespace you are waiting for.

The `Function` parameter is a reference to the function you want to perform when the event occurs. Such a designated function is also known as an *event handler*. Because events are page-wide, the function can be stored within the Web Part or elsewhere on the page.

A fourth parameter, `UniqueQualifier`, is optional and not generally used.

When an event is raised, all Web Parts that have registered for that event will have the registered function called.

System Events

For users of Microsoft Internet Explorer 5.5 or higher, several system events are predefined in `ie55up` `.js`. You can register for any of these events and provide enhanced functionality for your users. By registering for these events, rather than attempting to access them directly through the page DOM, you can reduce the possibility of conflicts.

The system events are:

- ❏ `onafterprint`
- ❏ `onbeforeprint`
- ❏ `onbeforeunload`
- ❏ `onblur`
- ❏ `onclick`
- ❏ `onfocus`
- ❏ `onhelp`
- ❏ `onload`
- ❏ `onresize`
- ❏ `onunload`

The `NamespaceURN` for the system events is `urn:schemas-microsoft-com:dhtml`.

The following example makes use of the `onbeforeprint` and `onafterprint` events to allow you to block the direct printing of a page containing confidential information. It makes use of the page DOMObject to hide the content, and brings it back after warning the user. The function tags both the attempted print and the browser's title with the user's ID. The `<div>` section simply informs the user of the page's confidentiality.

Insert this code into a Content Editor Web Part, as shown in prior examples:

```
<script language="javascript">
   WPSC.RegisterForEvent("urn:schemas-microsoft-com:dhtml",↵
"onbeforeprint",hidePage_WPQ_);
   WPSC.RegisterForEvent("urn:schemas-microsoft-com:dhtml",↵
"onafterprint",restorePage_WPQ_);
   function hidePage_WPQ_() {
```

```
    WPSC.WebPartPage.DOMObject.body.style.display="none";
    WPSC.WebPartPage.DOMObject.title=↵
"_LogonUser_ attempted to print confidential page: "+document.title;
    alert('Printing of this page is prohibited. A nearly blank page ↵
with your UserID on it will be printed instead.');
    }
    function restorePage_WPQ_() {
    WPSC.WebPartPage.DOMObject.body.style.display="inline";
    }
    </script>
    <div id="HideIt_WPQ_" name="HideIt_WPQ_">
    Information on this page is confidential, and should not be printed.
    </div>
```

This affects only printing the page through Internet Explorer, and does not prevent the user from capturing the information in other ways, such as screen scraping or copy and paste.

Figure 14-4 shows what the user sees if he or she attempts to print a page with this Web Part on it. Notice that the URL hasn't changed, but the title reflects the User ID.

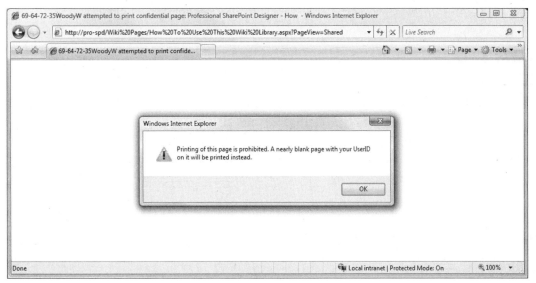

Figure 14-4

To apply this function to all pages in the site, add it as a static Web Part in your Master Page. Here's how:

1. Open your Master Page in SharePoint Designer.

2. Insert a Content Editor Web Part where you want the confidentiality notice to appear.

3. Add the preceding example code to the Web Part.

4. Save your Master Page.

You may also add the script directly to your Master Page without it being in a Content Editor Web Part; however, the _LogonUser_ token will not be expanded. In that case, you'd need to substitute the text A user for the token in the lines that change the page title and alert the user.

Some other possible uses for these events include:

❑ Use `onresize` to change your content to something more suitable for the new window dimensions.

❑ Use `onhelp` to display a window telling users about your site, or any special functions you have provided.

❑ Use `onbeforeprint` and `onafterprint` to hide the chrome of a regular page for a cleaner printing version. (You may want to customize the Master Page to provide conveniently named containers, allowing you to hide or show multiple objects with a single command.)

Raising Your Own Events

In addition to responding to events, you can raise your own events. Like the `RegisterForEvents` method described in the previous section, the `RaiseEvent` method takes three parameters. Two of these parameters are the same as in the register function:

❑ `NamespaceURN`

❑ `EventName`

The third parameter is optional. It is a variant value that, if present, is passed as a parameter to any functions registered for the event. The full form of the method is:

```
WPSC.RaiseEvent("urn:SomeNamespaceURN","SomeEventName",Parameter);
```

This example is based on the search results page example from chapter 13. You will modify the two Web Parts to use the WPSC event framework instead of a direct function call to display the result preview. Please complete that exercise and have the resulting page open in SharePoint Designer before proceeding.

Changing the Preview Web Part

The changes to the preview Web Part are straightforward, as shown in the following highlighted code lines. Add a line to register for an event. In this case, we are using `urn:prospd` as the `NamespaceURN`, and `searchrollover` for the `EventName`. In addition, now that you understand about naming conflicts, add the _WPQ_ token to the function name and iFrame. When you are finished, the code should look like this:

```
<script language="javascript">
WPSC.RegisterForEvent("urn:prospd","searchrollover",setPreview_WPQ_);
function setPreview_WPQ_(showurl){
previewPane_WPQ_.location=showurl;
}
```

```
</script>
<p><iframe name="previewPane_WPQ_" id="previewPane_WPQ_" width="500" ⏎
height="400" src="blankresults.htm">
Your browser does not support inline frames or is currently
configured not to display inline frames.
</iframe></p>
```

Once you have made these changes, clicking the results link in the other Web Part prompts an error until you complete the next section. You aren't using the event model there yet.

Changing the Results XSL

Changing the results Web Part to raise the event is even easier. As you did in the chapter 13 example, select the title of a result, and select the `srch-Title` span from the Quick Tag Selector. Locate the `onmouseover` event for the `srch-Title` span. Replace the existing direct function call:

```
setPreview('{url}');
```

with the raise event method here:

```
WPSC.RaiseEvent('urn:prospd','searchrollover','{url}');
```

You can make this change either through Code view, or in the Properties task pane.

Save your page, and run a search. You will find the new method works just as well as the old.

Special Event Functions

There are two special event types that each has its own set of WPSC methods.

❑   Connection events

❑   Prompted save

Connection Events

Connection events are the client-side manifestation of SharePoint's connected Web Part framework. The two events in this group, `RaiseConnectionEvent` and `RaiseConnectionEventSpecial`, are only usable in Web Parts that implement Web Part connection interfaces. The Content Editor Web Part does not support this interface.

Prompted Save

Many Web Parts request user input and either save the information or use it in other ways. Frequently, users will attempt to navigate away from a page before saving their work or completing whatever processing they were performing.

If all of the multiple interactive parts on a web page were to register for the `onunload` system event, each could prompt the user to save his or her data. This could result in a very confusing and frustrating user experience. The prompted save event resolves this problem by prompting the user once, and then raising itself for each Web Part that registers for the event.

`RegisterForPromptedSave` has a slightly different syntax than the typical `RegisterForEvent` method. It again takes up to three parameters. These are:

❏ `IsDirtyCallbackFunction`

❏ `SaveCallbackFunction`

❏ `Param` (optional)

Two of these parameters are callback functions. `Param` is an optional parameter that, if present, is passed to both callback functions. Typical syntax for this method would be:

```
WPSC.RegisterForPromptedSave(checkUpdated_WPQ_, saveState_WPQ_, "PageExit");
```

Saving data to a server is a notoriously expensive operation in terms of time and resources. Best practice, therefore, calls for avoiding it whenever it is not really necessary.

To aid you in this endeavor, when a prompted save event occurs, it first calls the `IsDirtyCallbackFunction` specified in the event registration. That function checks the state of the data, and returns either True if there has been a change to the data that needs to be updated, or False if the data does not need to be saved.

Do not execute the save process itself within `IsDirtyCallbackFunction`.

Only if the `IsDirtyCallbackFunction` returns True is the `SaveCallbackFunction` actually called. If called, it is the responsibility of the `SaveCallbackFunction` to take whatever steps are needed to save the data. You will see how to use this function later in the chapter.

Web Part Storage

As you know, a SharePoint page is served partially from the content database and (potentially) partially from the file system. Customized pages are served entirely from the database. In the case of dynamic Web Parts (those in Web Part Zones), all instance information is always served from the database, regardless of whether the page itself is customized. Although this information is kept in the content database, it can be thought of as a distinct repository, which is known as *Web Part storage*.

Web Part storage primarily contains the current values of each dynamic Web Part's properties. This is also known as the *state* of the Web Part. The retrieval of state information from Web Part storage was called a discovery service, but the updating of this information is called the state management service.

The Properties Collection

As noted earlier in this chapter, database access — especially updating — is an expensive operation. To make access as efficient as possible, the `Properties` collection of a Web Part is not retrieved from Web Part storage until a property is requested by the client.

When a property is requested, the WPSC checks to see if the properties have already been loaded from storage. If not, the entire `Properties` collection for that Web Part is retrieved and cached locally. All access to the properties thereafter, whether reading or writing, is made against the cache.

Into the Ether: Saving Changes, Or Not

So, what if you make a change to one of these properties? As described earlier, if the properties have not been read from storage, they are read into the page cache. Then, the value you are saving is written to the cache. If you change the value of a visible property, such as the Web Part title, the change may not be seen by the user until or unless the page is refreshed. Therein lies a problem.

Once the value is in the cache, as far as the client scripting model is concerned, the property has the new value. However, if the page is closed or refreshed, any changes you have made are lost. To make the change permanent, you have to commit it by using the Save method of the Web Part. Save has the following form:

```
varPart_WPQ_.Save(Async, CallBackFunction);
```

Both parameters are optional; however, if you specify one, you must specify both. Async is a Boolean value that tells the Save method whether to wait for the server to complete processing before calling the CallBackFunction. If true, the function is called immediately; if false, the callback is synchronous and is not performed until the server has completed processing.

The CallBackFunction parameter is a reference to the function called when the save is complete. Write the callback to take two parameters in the following order:

1. A Boolean value that reports the success (true) or failure (false) of the operation.

2. A string containing a description of any error that may have occurred. If there is no error, or the server does not pass an exception message, the string is returned empty.

It might help to think of a Web Part's state as an open transaction. You can read the values at any time. You can even make changes. But, until the part is saved, you can abort the changes and roll back simply by leaving the page.

Unfortunately, you rarely have the control over when a page is refreshed — or, more specifically, when it is *not* refreshed. This would be a good time to register for that prompted save event discussed earlier.

A Simple Property Update Example

This example demonstrates how to write to a Web Part property and save the Web Part's state. In this case, the property is the title of a Content Editor Web Part. The Title property is accessed with the URN: http://schemas.microsoft.com/WebPart/v2#Title. This consists of the NamespaceURN http://schemas.microsoft.com/WebPart/v2, which is the generic NamespaceURN for SharePoint Web Parts that do not require SharePoint 3.0 functionality. This is followed by the # separator and the field identifier Title.

The code following contains two functions: UpdateTitle_WPQ_ and checkUpdated_WPQ_. UpdateTitle_WPQ_ reads the value from the Text1 text box, assigns it to the Title property of the Web Part, and saves the state of the Web Part (remember, property changes are discarded if the state is not saved). It is called if the user clicks the Update Title button, or if the user responds OK to the Prompted Save dialog. checkUpdated_WPQ_ is called by the Prompted Save event and checks to see if the user has made a change to the text box but has not clicked the Update Title button.

As with the previous example, start by adding a Content Editor Web Part to a page. Find the CDATA element, and add the following code:

```
<script language="javascript" type="text/javascript">
// Define the function to update the title. Reads the value of
// the Text1 textbox and assigns it to the Web Part's title property.
// The state of the Web Part is then saved.
function UpdateTitle_WPQ_(){
    varPart_WPQ_.Properties.Item("http://schemas.microsoft.com/↵
WebPart/v2#Title").Value = document.all('Text1').value;
    varPart_WPQ_.Save();
}
// Define the function to see if the current value of the text field matches
// the title. Returns false if they are different, and the textbox is not
// blank.
function checkUpdated_WPQ_(){
    if ((varPart_WPQ_.Properties.Item("http://schemas.microsoft.com/↵
WebPart/v2#Title").Value != document.all('Text1').value)↵
 & (document.all('Text1').value != '')) {
    return(true);
    }
    else {
    return(false);
    }
}
// Register for the Prompted Save event.
WPSC.RegisterForPromptedSave(checkUpdated_WPQ_, UpdateTitle_WPQ_);
</script>
```

You also need two form controls in the Web Part: a text box and a Submit button. The Submit button will be used to explicitly call the UpdateTitle_WPQ_ function. You can add them via the Tools task pane, or you can directly enter the following code immediately after the script you have already entered. If you enter the controls via the task pane, you will need to edit them to match the values here:

```
<p><input name="Text1" id="Text1" type="text">↵
<input name="Update" type="button" value="Update Title"↵
onclick="UpdateTitle_WPQ_();"></p>
```

Because you're registering for the prompted save function in your code, a user will get the dialog shown in Figure 14-5 if he or she navigates away from the page after entering a value but before saving it.

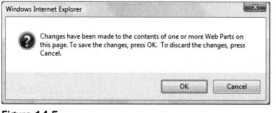

Figure 14-5

You will not see the results of the Title change until the next refresh of your page.

PartStorage: Your Very Own Property

The properties in the `Properties` collection of a Web Part are defined partially by SharePoint (`Title`, for instance) and partially by the developer of the Web Part. Although you can update the values of these items, you cannot add or delete Property items at run time. So, what do you do when you want to create all of this great script in a Content Editor, and need a place to maintain your own configuration information?

Fortunately, the designers of the Content Editor understood this need, and added a property just for you: the `PartStorage` property. `PartStorage` is a string into which you can place any information you want. While it is just one single property, there is nothing preventing you from formatting your string as XML (for example), and storing complex data. You can then parse it as needed when you read the property back in.

To access the `PartStorage` property, you need to use the `NamespaceURN http://schemas .microsoft.com/WebPart/v2/ContentEditor`. Notice that this NamespaceURN appends `/ ContentEditor` to the generic NamespaceURN used in the previous example. The `PartStorage` property is specific to the Content Editor Web Part, so the generic namespace was extended to cover it.

You will use PartStorage in the "Using Client-Side Objects" walk-through later in this chapter.

One for All?

In addition to being customizable in SharePoint Designer, Web Part Pages have the capability to be personalized for an individual user. A personalized version of a page starts with the shared state of the page, and creates a copy of that state in the content database.

> *All client-side access to information about Web Parts on the page depends upon the current mode.*

When the page is in *shared mode*, any changes and updates apply to all users who have not personalized their page. If a user who has a personalized view changes back to shared view, she will see the new state of the page, and, depending upon her permissions, may lose any customizations she has made.

If a page is in *personal mode*, changes to Web Part properties only impact the current user's page. If personal mode is available, it can be invoked from the system menu under the user's name, as shown in Figure 14-6. Once a page is in personal mode, it can be returned to shared mode through the same menu.

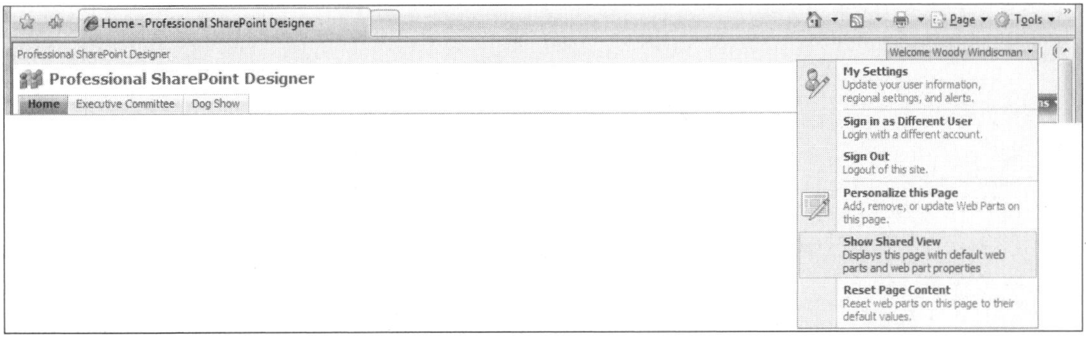

Figure 14-6

Notice the `?PageView=Personal` parameter in the URL of the page in the figure. It is present only if explicitly entered, or if the user has recently personalized the page. If a personalized version of a page exists, SharePoint displays it by default.

Access to personal views is controlled via Permission Levels, as described in chapter 3.

Although there are only two modes, the page state for each user's personal view is stored separately in the content database.

Beyond the WPSC

The Web Part Page Services Component provides a powerful and convenient framework for you to use when creating client-side scripts. But it is not the only way to interact with SharePoint from the browser client. This section gives you a few ideas for further exploration.

Accessing Page Components via the DOM

Earlier in the chapter, you saw how to use the `DOMObject` property of the WebPartPage to hide and redisplay the contents of a page. This object is actually a direct link to the document browser object. That means you have access to any component within the page for your scripts. Similarly, the `DOMObject` property of a Part object gives you a handle into that Web Part's displayed components.

While this is great, you also saw that some Web Parts, like List and Library Views, may not be exposed directly. To manipulate these — dynamically changing the contents in the dropdown of a choice field, for instance — you have no choice but to view the source of the web page and determine the `id` values of the controls you want to change. With that information, you can access those objects directly at run time, and override SharePoint's default behavior.

Other Client-Side Objects

SharePoint offers access to several client-side ActiveX controls that can provide enhanced functionality. Generally, you can assume that these controls require Internet Explorer 5.5 or higher, and most are only installed with versions of Microsoft Office. The exact version of Office installed may determine the features available.

The following table describes the controls you are likely to have available if you are using Internet Explorer 5.5 or higher and Microsoft Office Professional Plus 2007.

Control	Description
ListNet	When you configure a list in Datasheet view, this control is used to manage the user experience.
NameCtrl	Provides a UI for detecting and displaying presence information. If you render user information in your Web Parts, use this control to provide the same inline functions as shown in lists (like presence pawns and action menus). (See the example in the next section.)

Control	Description
OISClientLauncher	Enables you to launch the Microsoft Office Picture Manager (if installed). It has one method, LaunchOIS(cmdLine), which passes the provided command-line string to Picture Manager.
OpenDocuments	Provides several methods for creating, viewing, and editing documents on the client. Depending upon the operation, you can specify the source template or document path, default save locations, and even the application to use for the operation.
OpenXMLDocuments	SharePoint provides a special document library type for holding XML form data. The OpenXMLDocuments control enables you to create new XML form documents from a template, or invoke a locally installed form editor, such as Microsoft InfoPath.
SpreadsheetLauncher	Provides functions to enable the bulk import of data into SharePoint from spreadsheet workbooks and other tabular sources, such as address books. One of its key methods allows the page to check whether an import-compatible application is installed on the user's PC.
StssyncHandler	Allows your script to determine which application performs any data synchronization with SharePoint list data, such as appointments and contacts. This is typically Microsoft Outlook.
UploadCtl	Provides a mechanism for selecting multiple files to upload to a SharePoint library in a single operation.
DiagramLauncher	Gives control over creating a Visio diagram from a template. This control is installed with Visio 2007.

Full documentation for these components can be found in the Windows SharePoint Services SDK. The next section makes use of NameCtrl in a practical example.

Using Client-Side Objects — A Web Part Walk-Through

SharePoint offers Web Parts for listing the registered users of a site. The list lets you see the connection status of the listed users. While that's convenient, it does not provide a way to see the status of people who are not members of your SharePoint site. For this example, assume that your users would like to see the online status of their customer contacts. Ideally, they would like to be able to have the list tailored to the individual user.

This example walks you through creating a Web Part that allows your users to show the online status of their Windows Live Messenger and/or Microsoft Office Communicator contacts. It makes use of the Content Editor, form fields, the NameCtrl control, and WPSC Web Part storage to keep each user's configuration.

> **Web Part Personalization must be enabled for users to store individual contact lists. All users using the shared mode view will see the same set of contacts.**

Each of the following subsections describes a task required or function used in the Web Part you will create. Although you will build the visible elements first, you typically insert the script above the display code.

Unlike previous Content Editor Web Part–based examples, where you inserted your code directly into the Web Part, this example takes advantage of the Content Editor Web Part's capability to use a specified external file for its content.

Create an HTML Page and Insert the Visible Elements

To begin, select File ➪ New ➪ HTML to create an empty page. Add three `<div>` elements to the page. These will form the user interface. You can add them in Design view from the Toolbox, or enter the following source code directly between the `<body>` tags in the Code view. If you use Design view to add the `<div>` elements, you must edit their properties to match the provided code. Name your `<div>` elements:

- ❑ `ShowControls_WPQ_`: To provide a link to show the editing user interface.

- ❑ `Controls_WPQ_`: To contain a text box (the `<textarea>` tag) in which your users will enter their list of friends. It will also display some brief instructions, and buttons to either save the changes or hide the box. (You can enter the text through Design or Code view.)

- ❑ `Friends_WPQ_`: To contain the actual Friends list. The Friends list itself will be generated through code, and populated later. Because initial rendering can take a few seconds, add the message `Getting Data`, which will be displayed by default.

```
<div id="ShowControls_WPQ_" name="ShowControls_WPQ_" ↵
onclick="ShowEdit_WPQ_();">
    Edit Friends List</div>
<div id="Controls_WPQ_" name="Controls_WPQ_" style="display:none">
Please list your friends in the form &quot;Friend
Name,email@address&quot;. Separate friend entries with a semicolon
(;). <br>
 <textarea name="MyFriends_WPQ_" cols="20" rows="2"></textarea><br>
<input type="button" value="Save" onclick="saveFriends_WPQ_();">↵
<input type="button" value="Cancel" ↵
onclick="Controls_WPQ_.style.display='none';"></div>
<div id="Friends_WPQ_" name="Friends_WPQ_">Getting Data...</div>
```

> The remainder of the code in this example will be entered in Code view. Insert the first segment immediately after the opening `<body>` tag, and before the first `<div>` element. Each subsequent segment should immediately follow the segment just completed.

Initialize

The first block of code sets up your Web Part:

```
<script language="javascript">
NameCtrl_WPQ_ = new ActiveXObject("Name.NameCtrl.1");
WPSC.RegisterForEvent("urn:schemas-microsoft-com:dhtml","onload",setText_WPQ_);
function setText_WPQ_() {
```

```
var StartValue=varPart_WPQ_.Properties.Item(↵
"http://schemas.microsoft.com/WebPart/v2/ContentEditor#PartStorage").Value;
document.all("MyFriends_WPQ_").value = StartValue;
UpdateList_WPQ_();
NameCtrl_WPQ_.OnStatusChange = UpdateStatus_WPQ_;
}
```

In this section are the only two executable lines that are not contained within a function. This means they will be executed as the page is loading, without waiting for other things to happen. The first instantiates the `NameCtrl` control, and assigns it to `NameCtrl_WPQ_`. The second registers for the `onload` system event, and sets the `setText_WPQ_` as the designated event handler.

Several initializations cannot take place until the page is fully rendered:

❑ Any existing Friends list is read from Web Part storage, and loaded into a local variable.

❑ The current list is assigned to the `MyFriends_WPQ_` text box so that it is ready both for editing and to be used to render the initial list display.

❑ The `UpdateList_WPQ_` function is called to render the Friends status list for the first time.

❑ `NameCtrl` enables you to register for an event (`OnStatusChange`) that allows you to update your status display when a friend comes online or changes his status. The `UpdateStatus_WPQ_` function (described later) is your event handler.

These are invoked in the `setText_WPQ_` function.

Save the Friends List

After the user edits the text box and clicks Save, the `saveFriends_WPQ_` function is called:

```
function saveFriends_WPQ_(){
varPart_WPQ_.Properties.Item("http://schemas.microsoft.com/WebPart/v2/↵
ContentEditor#PartStorage").Value = document.all("MyFriends_WPQ_").value;
varPart_WPQ_.Save();
UpdateList_WPQ_();
Controls_WPQ_.style.display="none";
}
```

Here's what happens:

1. The current contents of the text box are assigned to the `PartStorage` property of your Web Part.

2. The change is committed to the database with the `Save` method.

3. The friend status table is regenerated.

4. The edit box is rehidden.

Build the Friend Display Table

This function builds the table that displays the list of friends and their presence status. There are three main blocks in this function: an initialization section and two loops. The Friends table is built in two passes. The first pass assembles the structure of the table, and the second populates the initial status of each friend.

Remember, each block of code immediately follows the previous segment.

Initialization

The initialization section reads the Friends list and sets up the variables that will be used throughout the rest of the function:

```
function UpdateList_WPQ_() {
var newList=document.all("MyFriends_WPQ_").value;
var Friends_Array=newList.split(";");
var Friends_Table="<table width=100%>";
var Friend_Data;
var Div_ID;
var i;
```

Here's what it does:

1. newList is assigned the raw text of the Friends list from the MyFriends_WPQ_ text box.

2. The raw list uses semicolons (;) to delimit each friend. Friends_Array is populated by using the JavaScript string split function.

3. Friends_Table is the string that will hold the list as it is constructed. It is initialized with a table header.

4. Friend_Data and Div_ID are used to hold temporary values in the loops. i is a simple loop counter.

Pass 1: Table Structure

Two passes are made over the elements in the Friends_Array. In the first pass, the physical structure of the Friends_Table is constructed. Each row of the table consists of two cells, one to hold the friend's name, and the other to indicate the friend's presence status. Each element in the Friends_Array is a two-part value, delimited by a comma (,). Each iteration in the loop again uses the JavaScript string split function to break the element into the Friend name and email address. Here's the code:

```
// Build Friend Table
for (i=0;i<Friends_Array.length;i++){
Friend_Data=Friends_Array[i].split(",");
Div_ID="Friend_WPQ__"+i;
Friends_Table+="<tr><td align='right'><div>"+Friend_Data[0]+"</div></td>"
Friends_Table+="<td align='left' width='100%'><div id='"+Div_ID↵
+"' onmouseover='NameCtrl_WPQ_.ShowOOUI("
Friends_Table+='"'+Friend_Data[1]+'"'+",0,MSOLayout_GetRealOffset("↵
```

```
+Div_ID+',"Left")'+",MSOLayout_GetRealOffset("
Friends_Table+=Div_ID+',"Top")-document.body.scrollTop'+");' ↵
onmouseout='NameCtrl_WPQ_.HideOOUI();'  style='padding-left: ↵
30px'> </div></td></tr>";
}
Friends_Table+="</table>";
Friends_WPQ_.innerHTML=Friends_Table;
```

There are several items of note in this pass:

❑   Part of this structure involves setting `mouseover` and `mouseout` events to show and hide a pawn, called the On-Object User Interface, or OOUI. The OOUI is generated by the `NameCtrl_WPQ_` object, and grants access to a menu of communications actions for a person.

❑   The `ShowOOUI` method of the `NameCtrl_WPQ_` object, which will be called by the `mouseover` event, requires three parameters: the ID (not the name) of the person whose presence is being monitored, and window-absolute Top and Left pixel positions. To fulfill the absolute position requirement, this function borrows a function from `IE55UP.JS` that can return the appropriate offset values for a DOM object.

❑   `Div_ID` is the ID value given to the `<div>`, which is used to hold both the current status and the OOUI when it is displayed. The ID is based on the loop iteration, concatenated with the string `Friend_WPQ__`.

> There are two underscore (_) characters at the end of `Friend_WPQ__`. The first completes the token; the other becomes part of the ID string.

❑   Although this is being generated within a function, the resulting objects are visible in the page DOM, so the `_WPQ_` token is used in all object names to prevent conflicts.

❑   Once the `for` loop is completed, the `<table>` tag is closed, and the completed table is injected into the Friends_WPQ_ `<div>`.

Pass 2: Set Initial Friend Status

The second pass of the `Friends_Array` is much simpler. It reads the Friends' email addresses from the second element (`[1]`) of the friend record, and uses it as a parameter when it manually calls the `UpdateStatus_WPQ_` function. Here's the code:

```
// update Friend Status
for (i=0;i<Friends_Array.length;i++){
Friend_Data=Friends_Array[i].split(",");
UpdateStatus_WPQ_(Friend_Data[1],NameCtrl_WPQ_.GetStatus(Friend_Data[1],"Friend_
WPQ__"+i),"Friend_WPQ__"+i);
}
}
```

Display the Editing Panel

The ShowEdit_WPQ_ function simply shows the editing panel:

```
function ShowEdit_WPQ_() {
Controls_WPQ_.style.display="inline";
}
```

While the display setting could have been directly incorporated into the onclick event of the ShowControls_WPQ_ <div>, leaving the function independent can make it easier to adapt to other user interfaces in the future.

Update a Contact's Status

The UpdateStatus_WPQ_ function is called in two contexts. It is called directly by the second pass of the Friends table generator, and it is called as an event handler for the NameCtrl_WPQ_ object. The function takes three parameters:

❑   userName: Typically the user's email address. The main requirement is that the host communication product (such as Windows Live Messenger or Microsoft Office Communicator) recognizes and can associate the ID with a user of that messaging system.

❑   newStatus: The new status to be displayed for that contact.

❑   show_id: The ID of the <div> tag which will hold the status indicator.

Here's the code:

```
function UpdateStatus_WPQ_(userName, newStatus, show_id) {
if (userName!=''){
switch(newStatus) {
case 0:
document.all(show_id).innerText="Online";
break;
case 1:
document.all(show_id).innerText="Offline";
break;
case 2:
document.all(show_id).innerText="Away";
break;
case 3:
document.all(show_id).innerText="Busy";
break;
case 4:
document.all(show_id).innerText="Be Right Back";
break;
case 5:
```

```
document.all(show_id).innerText="On the Phone";
break;
case 6:
document.all(show_id).innerText="Out to Lunch";
break;
default:
document.all(show_id).innerText="Unknown";
}
}
}
</script>
```

The remainder of the function simply maps the numeric status code parameter to an appropriate representation. For purposes of this example, the function uses a text description of the status. You may want to expand upon it later by substituting color-coded graphics or any other presentation changes that may be appropriate in your environment.

This page is now complete. Save it as `friends_list.htm`. The next section shows you how to use it in a Content Editor Web Part.

Using the Page

The page you created in the preceding steps will not be opened directly. Instead, it is used as the source for a Content Editor Web Part. To do this:

1. Create a Content Editor Web Part on a page.

2. Display the Web Part Properties.

3. Set the Content Link property to `friends_list.htm`.

4. Click OK to save the change.

5. Save your page.

In SharePoint Designer, the Web Part now displays this text: The content is provided by the URL in the Content Link property.

Once you have completed the Web Part, it automatically works if you have Messenger or Communicator installed. Third-party messenger systems may also make components compatible with the `NameCtrl` interface. Figure 14-7 shows the Web Part on a page with both the list editor and the contact action menu displayed.

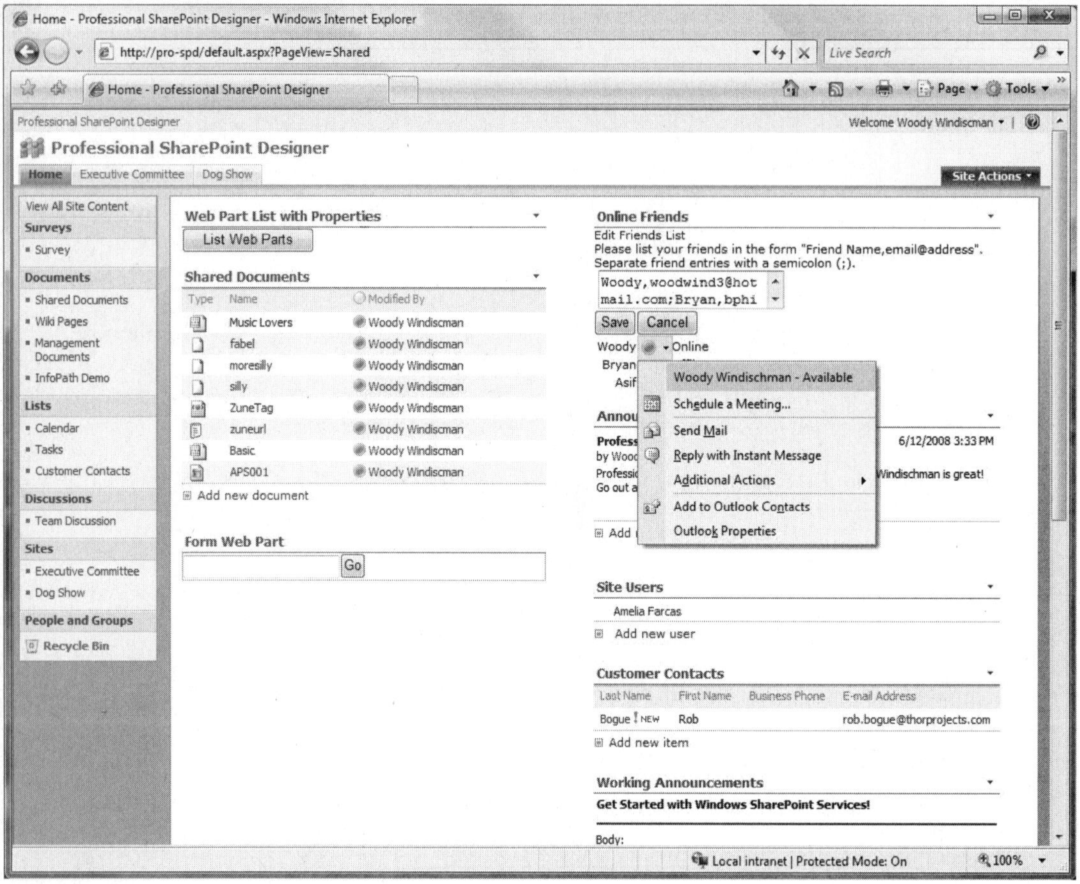

Figure 14-7

Summary

This chapter showed you how to take your SharePoint client-side programming to the next level with the Web Part Page Services Component. You learned about the communications framework, and how to find some of the buried goodies in the SharePoint system. Here are some key points to take away:

❑ The WPSC features are loosely organized into a set of services.

❑ Web Part properties are kept in the SharePoint content database.

❑ Changes you make to the `Properties` collection are not permanent until you use the `save` method.

The next few chapters take you outside the box of SharePoint Designer, and introduce some of the ways you can use Visual Studio to enhance not only SharePoint Designer through add-ins and workflow elements, but SharePoint itself with completely custom Web Parts.

Part V

Beyond SharePoint Designer

Creating Workflow Elements in Visual Studio

Chapter 9 demonstrated how to use the Workflow Designer in SharePoint Designer to create custom workflows using the default actions delivered with SharePoint. This chapter shows you how to take your workflows to the next level by creating custom actions in Visual Studio and configuring them to work inside SharePoint Designer.

Specifically, this chapter examines how to:

❑   Create custom actions.

❑   Deploy custom actions.

❑   Configure custom actions.

❑   Test your custom actions.

What You Need to Get Started

Before you jump in to create new actions, ensure that you have the correct tools. These tools include:

❑   Microsoft Visual Studio 2008 (not Visual Studio Express).

❑   Windows SharePoint Services 3.0 SDK
    (`http://www.microsoft.com/downloads/`
    `details.aspx?FamilyID=05e0dd12-8394-402b-8936-a07fe8afaffd&DisplayLang=en`)
    or Microsoft Office SharePoint Server 2007 SDK (`http://www.microsoft.com/downloads/`
    `details.aspx?FamilyID=6D94E307-67D9-41AC-B2D6-0074D6286FA9&displaylang=en`).

❑   Windows XP or Windows Vista. (I used Windows Vista.).

I chose General Development Settings when configuring Visual Studio 2008 for the first time. If you chose different settings, your screens may differ from the screenshots in this chapter.

If you want to reset your Visual Studio 2008 settings, select Tools ⇨ Import and Export Settings, and use the wizard to reset your settings. In the wizard, you have the option of backing up your existing settings if you want to revert to them later on.

Introduction to Custom Actions

The built-in actions in SharePoint are a good starting point for functionality to your workflows, but if you need functionality that these actions do not provide, you have to create a custom action. Once you have deployed a custom action to SharePoint and configured it to run, it appears in the SharePoint Workflow Designer. This section provides an example in which you build a custom action to create child sites that can be called as a part of a SharePoint Designer workflow.

Creating a Custom Action

Begin the process of creating a custom action by opening Visual Studio and selecting File ⇨ New ⇨ Project. The result is the New Project dialog, as shown in Figures 15-1 (Visual Basic) and 15-2 (C#). Ensure that .NET Framework 3.0 has been chosen from the dropdown list in the upper-right corner of the dialog. Do *not* choose .NET Framework 3.5 unless your SharePoint farm has been configured to support .NET Framework 3.5.

In the Project Types list on the left, expand either the Visual Basic or Visual C# node, depending on the language you want to use, and then click on Workflow in that node. (This example uses Visual Basic.)

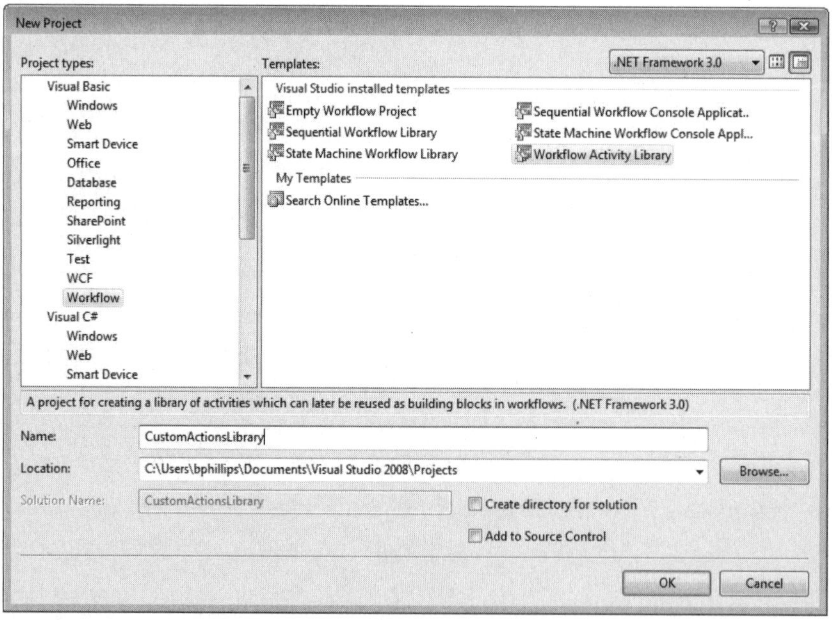

Figure 15-1

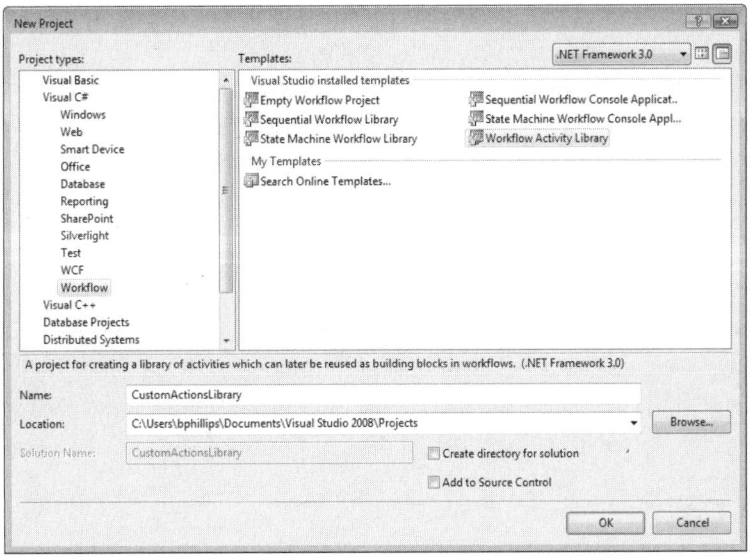

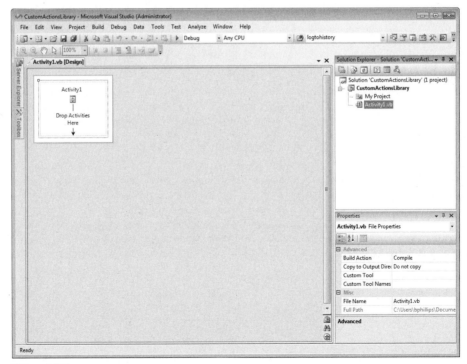

Figure 15-2

A list of Project templates will be displayed on the right. Choose the Workflow Activity Library template, and then enter a name (CustomActionsLibrary for this example) and location for the Project in the lower section of the dialog. Click OK, and the Project to contain your custom action is created, as shown in Figures 15-3 (VB) and 15-4 (C#).

Figure 15-3

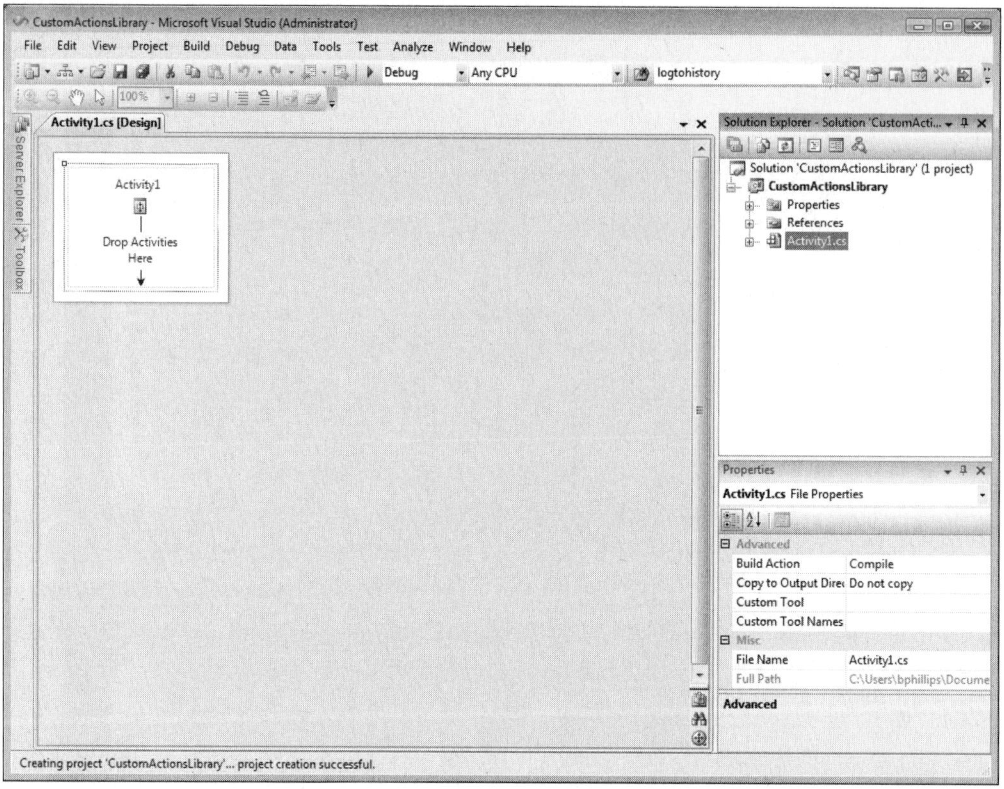

Figure 15-4

By default, Visual Studio automatically creates a file named `Activity1.vb` or `Activity1.cs` which you do not need. Remove the file by right-clicking `Activity1.vb` or `Activity1.cs` in the Solution Explorer window and selecting Delete from the context menu. A confirmation dialog appears. Click OK to confirm the deletion.

Assemblies that contain custom actions must be strong-named to run inside SharePoint. A strong name ensures that your assembly will not be mistaken for another assembly, even if both have the same name. To learn more about strong names, read the "Strong-Named Assemblies" article on MSDN (http://msdn.microsoft.com/en-us/library/wd40t7ad.aspx).

To configure the Project to have a strong name, right-click CustomActionsLibrary in the Solution Explorer window and select Properties to open the Project properties screen, as shown in Figures 15-5 (VB) and 15-6 (C#).

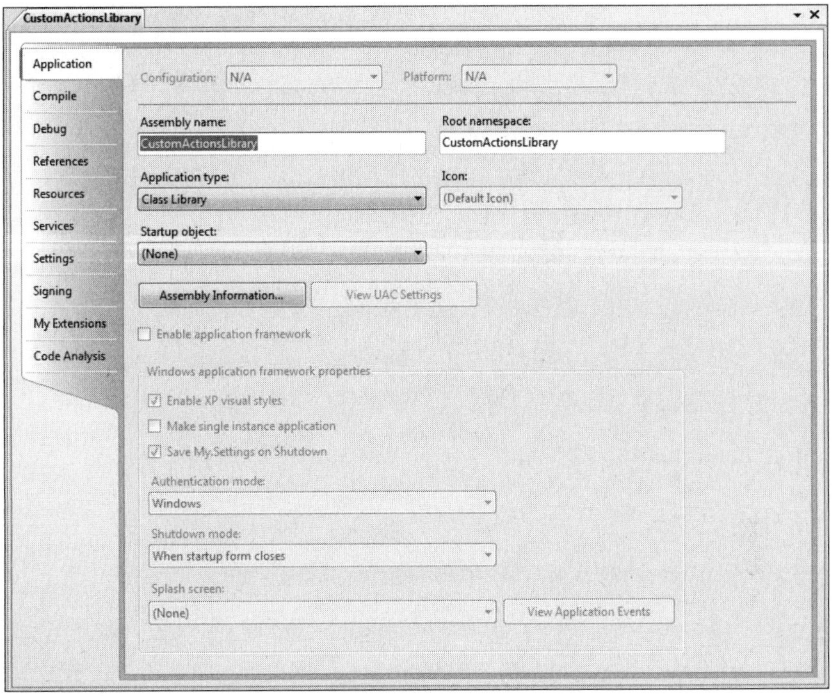

CustomActionsLibrary

Application	Configuration: N/A	Platform: N/A
Compile		
Debug	Assembly name:	Root namespace:
References	CustomActionsLibrary	CustomActionsLibrary
Resources	Application type:	Icon:
Services	Class Library	(Default Icon)
Settings	Startup object:	
Signing	(None)	
My Extensions		
Code Analysis		

Assembly Information...   View UAC Settings

☐ Enable application framework

Windows application framework properties

☑ Enable XP visual styles

☐ Make single instance application

☑ Save My.Settings on Shutdown

Authentication mode:
Windows

Shutdown mode:
When startup form closes

Splash screen:
(None)   View Application Events

Figure 15-5

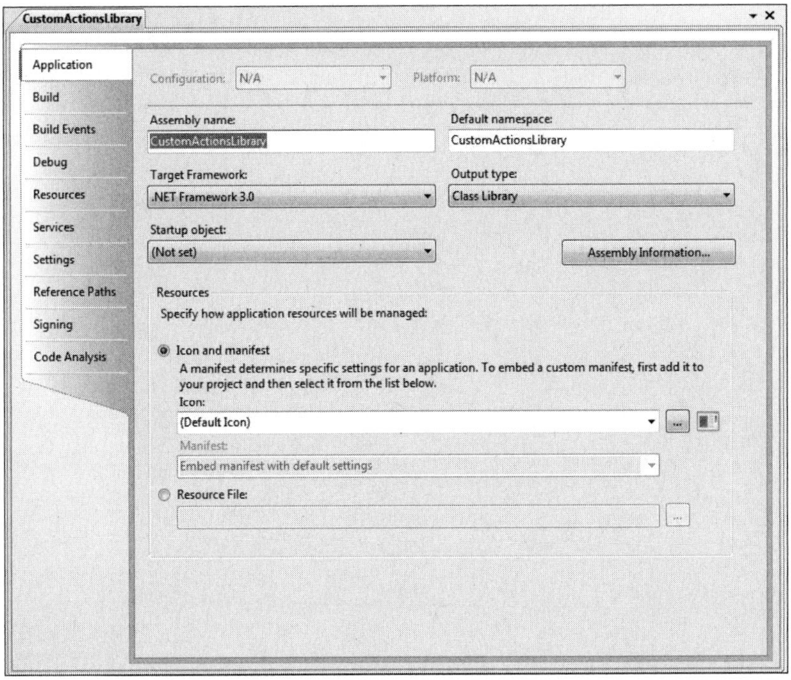

CustomActionsLibrary

Application	Configuration: N/A	Platform: N/A
Build		
Build Events	Assembly name:	Default namespace:
Debug	CustomActionsLibrary	CustomActionsLibrary
Resources	Target Framework:	Output type:
Services	.NET Framework 3.0	Class Library
Settings	Startup object:	
Reference Paths	(Not set)	Assembly Information...
Signing		
Code Analysis		

Resources
Specify how application resources will be managed:

◉ Icon and manifest
A manifest determines specific settings for an application. To embed a custom manifest, first add it to your project and then select it from the list below.
Icon:
(Default Icon)
Manifest:
Embed manifest with default settings

◯ Resource File:

Figure 15-6

Click the Signing tab, and click the Sign The Assembly check box. Select New from the Choose a strong name key file dropdown list to open the Create Strong Name Key dialog (see Figure 15-7). Enter Key.snk in the Key file name text box, uncheck the Protect my key file with a password check box, and click OK. Click the Save icon on the toolbar and close the Project properties screen.

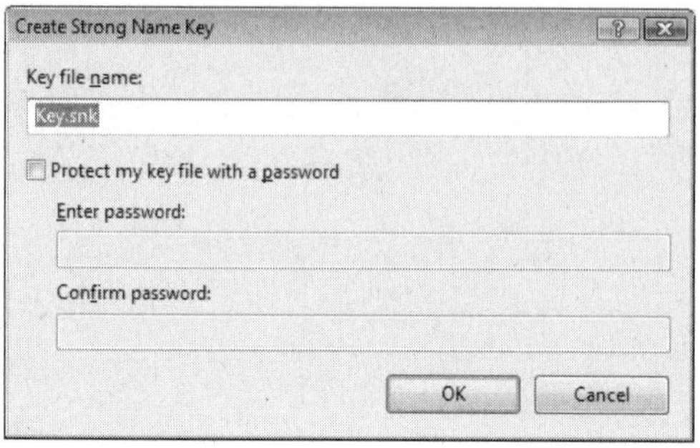

Create Strong Name Key

Key file name:

Key.snk

☐ Protect my key file with a password

Enter password:

Confirm password:

OK   Cancel

Figure 15-7

Before you add your custom action, you must add references to the SharePoint assemblies (DLLs) that will allow your custom action to participate in SharePoint workflows. Right-click CustomActionsLibrary in the Solution Explorer window, and select Add Reference. In the Add Reference dialog (see Figure 15-8), select the SharePoint assemblies by holding the Ctrl key down and clicking these items in the list box:

❑   Windows SharePoint Services

❑   Windows SharePoint Services Security

❑   Windows SharePoint Services Workflow Actions

Release the Ctrl key, and click OK.

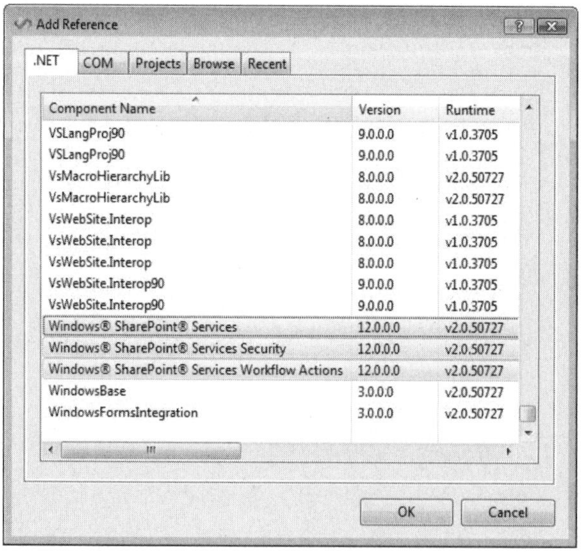

Add Reference

.NET | COM | Projects | Browse | Recent

Component Name	Version	Runtime
VSLangProj90	9.0.0.0	v1.0.3705
VSLangProj90	9.0.0.0	v1.0.3705
VsMacroHierarchyLib	8.0.0.0	v2.0.50727
VsMacroHierarchyLib	8.0.0.0	v2.0.50727
VsWebSite.Interop	8.0.0.0	v1.0.3705
VsWebSite.Interop	8.0.0.0	v1.0.3705
VsWebSite.Interop	8.0.0.0	v1.0.3705
VsWebSite.Interop90	9.0.0.0	v1.0.3705
VsWebSite.Interop90	9.0.0.0	v1.0.3705
Windows® SharePoint® Services	12.0.0.0	v2.0.50727
Windows® SharePoint® Services Security	12.0.0.0	v2.0.50727
Windows® SharePoint® Services Workflow Actions	12.0.0.0	v2.0.50727
WindowsBase	3.0.0.0	v2.0.50727
WindowsFormsIntegration	3.0.0.0	v2.0.50727

OK   Cancel

Figure 15-8

To create your first custom action, you must add an activity to the Project. Right-click CustomActionsLibrary in the Solution Explorer window, and select Add ⇨ New Item from the context menu. The Add New Item dialog opens (see Figure 15-9). Choose Workflow from the Categories on the left, and select the Activity template from the list on the right, enter a suitable name for the action, and click OK. For this example, name your custom action CreateSiteAction.

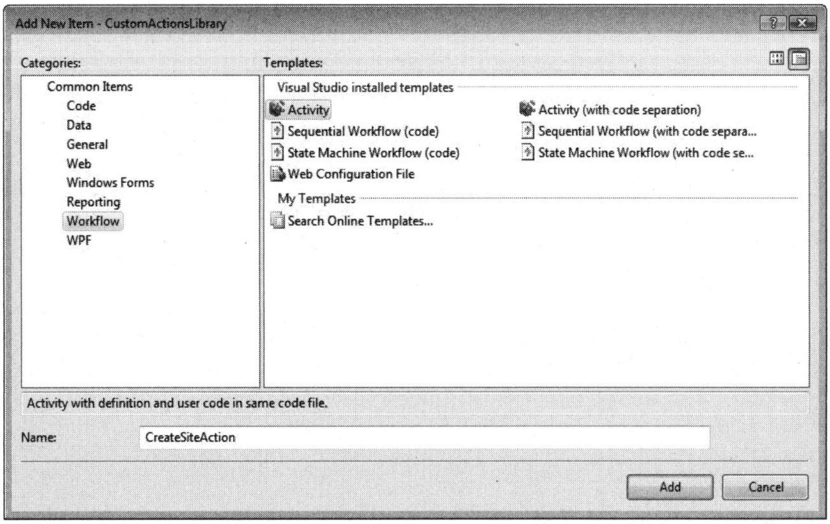

Figure 15-9

Visual Studio adds an empty action to the Project to hold the functionality you will create. After the action is created, Visual Studio automatically opens it in Design view. Close this view by selecting File ⇨ Close. Bring up the Code view for your custom action by right-clicking CreateSiteAction.vb, and selecting View Code. This chapter provides code in both VB.NET and C#. The following code is displayed:

VB.NET

```
Public class CreateSiteAction
    Inherits SequenceActivity
End Class
```

C#

```
using System;
using System.ComponentModel;
using System.ComponentModel.Design;
using System.Collections;
using System.Drawing;
using System.Workflow.ComponentModel;
using System.Workflow.ComponentModel.Design;
using System.Workflow.ComponentModel.Compiler;
using System.Workflow.ComponentModel.Serialization;
```

```
using System.Workflow.Runtime;
using System.Workflow.Activities;
using System.Workflow.Activities.Rules;

namespace CustomActionsLibrary
{
    public partial class CreateSiteAction: SequenceActivity
    {
        public CreateSiteAction()
        {
            InitializeComponent();
        }
    }
}
```

Now, you can start modifying this code to provide a mechanism that allows SharePoint Designer to provide values for your custom action before you add your custom functionality. This mechanism is called a property and is explained in detail in the next section.

To make it easier to use the classes in SharePoint and Windows Workflow Foundation, add these statements to the top of the file:

VB.NET

```
Imports Microsoft.SharePoint
Imports Microsoft.SharePoint.WebControls
Imports Microsoft.SharePoint.WorkflowActions
Imports System.ComponentModel
Imports System.Web
Imports System.Workflow.ComponentModel
```

C#

```
using Microsoft.SharePoint;
using Microsoft.SharePoint.WebControls;
using Microsoft.SharePoint.WorkflowActions;
using System.Web;
```

Creating Properties for Your Custom Action

To allow SharePoint Designer to pass values to your custom action when the workflow runs, you must create public properties inside your custom action. In this example, you will create a custom action that will create a new site within SharePoint whenever executed inside a SharePoint Designer workflow. To create a new site, SharePoint will need values for the following:

❑   SiteUrl: Where the site will be located.

❑   SiteTitle: Title for the new site.

❑   SiteDescription: Description for the new site.

❑   SiteTemplate: Template to use to create the new site.

❑   InheritPermissions: True, if the new site will inherit permissions from its parent site.

For each field, you create a property in your custom action to allow the users to specify these values when designing their workflow in SharePoint Designer. When creating properties for a custom action, you create the property itself and a matching DependencyProperty. The DependencyProperty class allows SharePoint Designer to bind the property to the UI in the workflow wizard, where the user specifies the values of these properties in the workflow being created. Later in the chapter, you will create an ACTIONS file to define the UI to display to the user configuring the custom action and to define how the controls in that UI will bind to the properties of the custom action. Inside the class, add the following code to create a property and DependencyProperty for SiteUrl:

VB.NET

```
Public Shared SiteUrlProperty As DependencyProperty = _
    DependencyProperty.Register("SiteUrl",
        GetType(String), _
        GetType(CreateSiteAction))

Public Property SiteUrl() As String
    Get
        Return CType(Me.GetValue(SiteUrlProperty), String)
    End Get
    Set(ByVal value As String)
        Me.SetValue(SiteUrlProperty, value)
    End Set
End Property
```

C#

```
public static DependencyProperty SiteUrlProperty =
    DependencyProperty.Register("SiteUrl", typeof(string),
    typeof(CreateSiteAction));

public string SiteUrl {
    get { return this.GetValue(SiteUrlProperty).ToString(); }
    set { this.SetValue(SiteUrlProperty, value); }
}
```

To be able to access the workflow's context to get a reference to the current SharePoint site, add this property:

VB.NET

```
Public Shared __ContextProperty As DependencyProperty = _
    DependencyProperty.Register("__Context", GetType(WorkflowContext), _
    GetType(CreateSiteAction))

Public Property __Context() As WorkflowContext
    Get
        Return CType(Me.GetValue(__ContextProperty), WorkflowContext)
    End Get
    Set(ByVal value As WorkflowContext)
        Me.SetValue(__ContextProperty, value)
    End Set
End Property
```

C#

```
public static DependencyProperty __ContextProperty =
    DependencyProperty.Register("__Context", typeof(WorkflowContext),
    typeof(CreateSiteAction));

public WorkflowContext __Context {
    get { return (WorkflowContext) this.GetValue(__ContextProperty); }
    set { this.SetValue(__ContextProperty, value); }
}
```

Copy and paste the code again for each new property, replacing `SiteUrl` with the name of the new property. The resulting class should look like this:

VB.NET

```
Imports Microsoft.SharePoint
Imports Microsoft.SharePoint.WebControls
Imports System.ComponentModel
Imports System.Web
Imports System.Workflow.ComponentModel

Public Class CreateSiteAction
    Inherits SequenceActivity

    Public Shared SiteUrlProperty As DependencyProperty = _
        DependencyProperty.Register("SiteUrl", GetType(String), _
        GetType(CreateSiteAction))

    Public Property SiteUrl() As String
        Get
            Return CType(Me.GetValue(SiteUrlProperty), String)
        End Get
        Set(ByVal value As String)
            Me.SetValue(SiteUrlProperty, value)
        End Set
    End Property

    Public Shared SiteTitleProperty As DependencyProperty = _
        DependencyProperty.Register("SiteTitle", GetType(String), _
        GetType(CreateSiteAction))

    Public Property SiteTitle() As String
        Get
            Return CType(Me.GetValue(SiteTitleProperty), String)
        End Get
        Set(ByVal value As String)
            Me.SetValue(SiteTitleProperty, value)
        End Set
    End Property

    Public Shared SiteDescriptionProperty As DependencyProperty = _
```

```vbnet
        DependencyProperty.Register("SiteDescription", GetType(String), _
        GetType(CreateSiteAction))

    Public Property SiteDescription() As String
        Get
            Return CType(Me.GetValue(SiteDescriptionProperty), String)
        End Get
        Set(ByVal value As String)
            Me.SetValue(SiteDescriptionProperty, value)
        End Set
    End Property

    Public Shared SiteTemplateProperty As DependencyProperty = _
        DependencyProperty.Register("SiteTemplate", GetType(String), _
        GetType(CreateSiteAction))

    Public Property SiteTemplate() As String
        Get
            Return CType(Me.GetValue(SiteTemplateProperty), String)
        End Get
        Set(ByVal value As String)
            Me.SetValue(SiteTemplateProperty, value)
        End Set
    End Property

    Public Shared InheritPermissionsProperty As DependencyProperty = _
        DependencyProperty.Register("InheritPermissions", GetType(Boolean), _
        GetType(CreateSiteAction))

    Public Property InheritPermissions() As Boolean
        Get
            Return CType(Me.GetValue(InheritPermissionsProperty), Boolean)
        End Get
        Set(ByVal value As Boolean)
            Me.SetValue(InheritPermissionsProperty, value)
        End Set
    End Property

    Public Shared __ContextProperty As DependencyProperty = _
        DependencyProperty.Register("__Context", GetType(WorkflowContext), _
        GetType(CreateSiteAction))

    Public Property __Context() As WorkflowContext
        Get
            Return CType(Me.GetValue(__ContextProperty), WorkflowContext)
        End Get
        Set(ByVal value As WorkflowContext)
            Me.SetValue(__ContextProperty, value)
        End Set
    End Property

End Class
```

C#

```csharp
using Microsoft.SharePoint;
using Microsoft.SharePoint.WebControls;
using Microsoft.SharePoint.Workflow;
using Microsoft.SharePoint.WorkflowActions;
using System;
using System.ComponentModel;
using System.Web;
using System.Workflow.Activities;
using System.Workflow.ComponentModel;
namespace CustomActionsLibrary {
    public class CreateSiteAction : SequenceActivity {
        public static DependencyProperty SiteUrlProperty =
            DependencyProperty.Register("SiteUrl", typeof(string),
            typeof(CreateSiteAction));

        public string SiteUrl {
            get { return this.GetValue(SiteUrlProperty).ToString(); }
            set { this.SetValue(SiteUrlProperty, value); }
        }

        public static DependencyProperty SiteTitleProperty =
            DependencyProperty.Register("SiteTitle", typeof(string),
            typeof(CreateSiteAction));

        public string SiteTitle {
            get { return this.GetValue(SiteTitleProperty).ToString(); }
            set { this.SetValue(SiteTitleProperty, value); }
        }

        public static DependencyProperty SiteDescriptionProperty =
            DependencyProperty.Register("SiteDescription", typeof(string),
            typeof(CreateSiteAction));

        public string SiteDescription {
            get { return this.GetValue(SiteDescriptionProperty).ToString(); }
            set { this.SetValue(SiteDescriptionProperty, value); }
        }

        public static DependencyProperty SiteTemplateProperty =
            DependencyProperty.Register("SiteTemplate", typeof(string),
            typeof(CreateSiteAction));

        public string SiteTemplate {
            get { return this.GetValue(SiteTemplateProperty).ToString(); }
            set { this.SetValue(SiteTemplateProperty, value); }
        }

        public static DependencyProperty InheritPermissionsProperty =
            DependencyProperty.Register("InheritPermissions", typeof(bool),
            typeof(CreateSiteAction));

        public bool InheritPermissions {
            get { return (bool) this.GetValue(InheritPermissionsProperty); }
            set { this.SetValue(InheritPermissionsProperty, value); }
```

```
        }

        public static DependencyProperty __ContextProperty =
            DependencyProperty.Register("__Context", typeof(WorkflowContext),
            typeof(CreateSiteAction));

        public WorkflowContext __Context {
            get { return (WorkflowContext) this.GetValue(__ContextProperty); }
            set { this.SetValue(__ContextProperty, value); }
        }

    }
```

Adding Functionality to Your Action

The final step in creating a custom action is to add the functionality itself. Each custom action has an `Execute` function that is called by SharePoint whenever that activity is reached in the workflow. To add the `Execute` method, put the following code before the `End Class` line:

VB.NET

```
Protected Overrides Function Execute(ByVal executionContext As _
        ActivityExecutionContext) As ActivityExecutionStatus

    Try

    Catch ex As Exception

    End Try

End Function
```

C#

```
protected override ActivityExecutionStatus Execute(ActivityExecutionContext
    executionContext) {

    try {

    } catch (Exception ex) {

    }

}
```

Now you can place your functionality inside the `Execute` function.

Before you can create a new site, you need to get a reference to the current site. Add this line to the `Try` block to get the current site:

VB.NET

```
Dim site As SPWeb = Me.__Context.Web
```

C#

```
SPWeb site = this.__Context.Web;
```

387

Later in the chapter, you will create a list to test this custom action. The list will include a choice column for choosing the site template. The following code will convert the user's choice into the site template ID required by the Webs.Add function:

VB.NET

```
Dim templateId As String

Select Case Me.SiteTemplate
    Case "Team Site"
        templateId = "STS#0"
    Case "Blank Site"
        templateId = "STS#1"
    Case "Document Workspace"
        templateId = "STS#2"
    Case "Wiki Site"
        templateId = "WIKI#0"
    Case Else
        templateId = "BLOG#0"
End Select
```

C#

```
string templateId;

switch (this.SiteTemplate) {
    case "Team Site":
        templateId = "STS#0";
        break;
    case "Blank Site":
        templateId = "STS#1";
        break;
    case "Document Workspace":
        templateId = "STS#2";
        break;
    case "Wiki Site":
        templateId = "WIKI#0";
        break;
    default:
        templateId = "BLOG#0";
        break;
}
```

Now you can use the properties you created to call the Webs.Add function to create a new subsite. Just add this line:

VB.NET

```
site.Webs.Add(Me.SiteUrl, Me.SiteTitle, Me.SiteDescription, 1033, _
    templateId, Not Me.InheritPermissions, False)
```

C#

```
site.Webs.Add(this.SiteUrl, this.SiteTitle, this.SiteDescription, 1033,
    templateId, !this.InheritPermissions, false);
```

Then, you need to tell SharePoint that the activity is finished by adding the following line to the end of the Execute function below the Try-Catch block:

VB.NET

```
Return ActivityExecutionStatus.Closed
```

C#

```
return ActivityExecutionStatus.Closed;
```

Finally, you need to add code to the Try-Catch block to write to the workflow's history list in case an exception occurs. Additionally, you need to tell SharePoint that the activity failed by returning ActivityExecutionStatus.Faulting to the calling function. To do so, add the following code just after the Catch line:

VB.NET

```
Dim service As ISharePointService = CType(executionContext.GetService( _
    GetType(ISharePointService)), ISharePointService)

If service Is Nothing Then
    Throw
End If

service.LogToHistoryList(Me.WorkflowInstanceId, _
    SPWorkflowHistoryEventType.WorkflowError, 0, TimeSpan.Zero, _
    "Error Occurred", ex.Message, String.Empty)

Return ActivityExecutionStatus.Faulting
```

C#

```
ISharePointService service = ←
(ISharePointService)executionContext.GetService(
    typeof(ISharePointService));

if (service==null) {
    throw;
}

service.LogToHistoryList(this.WorkflowInstanceId,
    SPWorkflowHistoryEventType.WorkflowError, 0, TimeSpan.Zero,
    "Error Occurred", ex.Message, string.Empty);

return ActivityExecutionStatus.Faulting;
```

Your custom action is now complete. Select Build ➪ Build Solution, and fix any compilation errors that appear. The only thing that remains is to create an ACTIONS file that tells SharePoint Designer what to display in the workflow wizard when the user configures your action. The next section describes this process.

Custom Actions and ACTIONS Files

An ACTIONS file is an XML file that is used by SharePoint Designer's workflow wizard to provide a user-friendly experience for configuring actions. Every action must be configured in an ACTIONS file before it can be used in SharePoint Designer. By default, there is only one ACTIONS file, located at C:\Program Files\Common Files\Microsoft Shared\Web Server Extensions\12\TEMPLATE\1033\ Workflow\WSS.ACTIONS, and it contains an entry for each of the built-in actions in SharePoint. The following snippet and Figure 15-10 show the relationship between the workflow wizard screen and its entry in the ACTIONS file for the Log to History List action:

```
<Action Name="Log to History List"
    ClassName="Microsoft.SharePoint.WorkflowActions.LogToHistoryListActivity"
    Assembly="Microsoft.SharePoint.WorkflowActions, Version=12.0.0.0,
        Culture=neutral, PublicKeyToken=71e9bce111e9429c"
    AppliesTo="all"
    Category="Core Actions">
    <RuleDesigner Sentence="Log %1 to the workflow history list">
        <FieldBind
            Field="HistoryDescription"
            Text="this message"
            Id="1"
            DesignerType="TextArea"/>
    </RuleDesigner>
    <Parameters>
        <Parameter
            Name="HistoryDescription" Type="System.String, mscorlib" ↵
Direction="In" />
    </Parameters>
</Action>
```

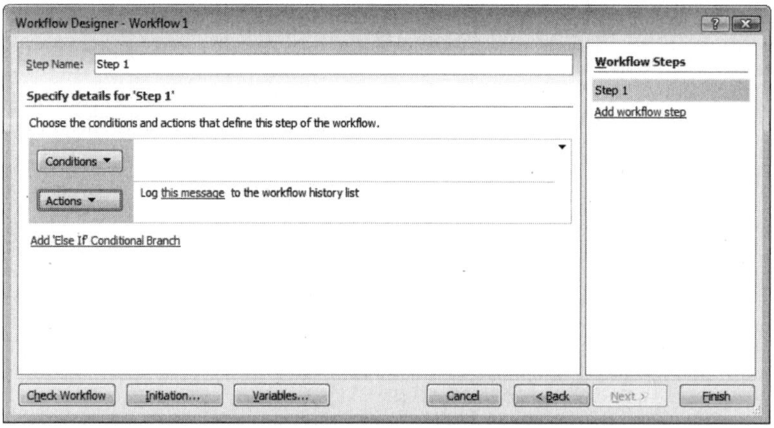

Figure 15-10

In the code snippet, the Sentence attribute of the RuleDesigner element is displayed by SharePoint Designer to provide the user a UI to specify values of parameters. The sentence contains a placeholder, indicated by the percent sign and the number 1. This number matches the Id attribute of the FieldBind element whose Text attribute is displayed in place of the placeholder in the UI. The Field attribute of the FieldBind element matches the Name attribute of the Parameter element, which represents the HistoryDescription property of the LogToHistoryActivity class. The relationships between these elements will be explained further later in the chapter.

The preceding code snippet may look complex, but it can be broken down into four simple parts:

❑ The Action element.

❑ The RuleDesigner element.

❑ Zero or more FieldBind elements.

❑ Zero or more Parameter elements.

Action Element

The Action element contains the location of the custom action, the name to display in the workflow wizard, and a category name that is used for filtering actions in the Workflow Actions dialog (see Figure 15-11). The Workflow Actions dialog is displayed when the user selects Actions ➪ More Actions on the step configuration screen of the workflow wizard.

Figure 15-11

RuleDesigner Element

The RuleDesigner element contains the sentence to display to the user and the replacement variables that will be bound to the action's properties. Replacement variables begin with a percent sign and are numbered starting with 1. In the preceding snippet, the sentence Log %1 to the workflow history list contains one replacement variable.

FieldBind Element

The FieldBind element indicates the text to display in place of the replacement variable in the workflow wizard, the type of designer used to specify the value for the replacement variable, and the name of the Parameter element that will receive or store the value from the replacement variable. There will be one FieldBind element for every replacement variable.

When the workflow wizard displays the Log to History Action, it will replace %1 with the value of the Text attribute of the FieldBind element, whose Id attribute has the value of 1. In this case, %1 will be replaced with this message since the FieldBind element has its Text attribute set to "this message" (refer to Figure 15-10).

Parameter Element

The Parameter element indicates which properties of the custom action will be configurable in the workflow wizard. For each FieldBind element, a Parameter element must be created so that its Name attribute matches the value of the Field attribute in the FieldBind element.

Creating a Custom ACTIONS File

It may be tempting to edit the WSS.ACTIONS file directly, but don't. If you edit the ACTIONS file incorrectly, no built-in actions will work in SharePoint Designer. Rather than modifying this file directly, you can create a new ACTIONS file to contain the information for your custom actions. This file is not required to be a part of the Visual Studio Project, but you can use Visual Studio or another XML editor to create it. This example uses Visual Studio.

To create a custom ACTIONS file, open Visual Studio and choose File ⇨ New ⇨ File. The New File dialog opens (see Figure 15-12). From this screen, choose General from the Categories on the left and select the XML File template from the list on the right.

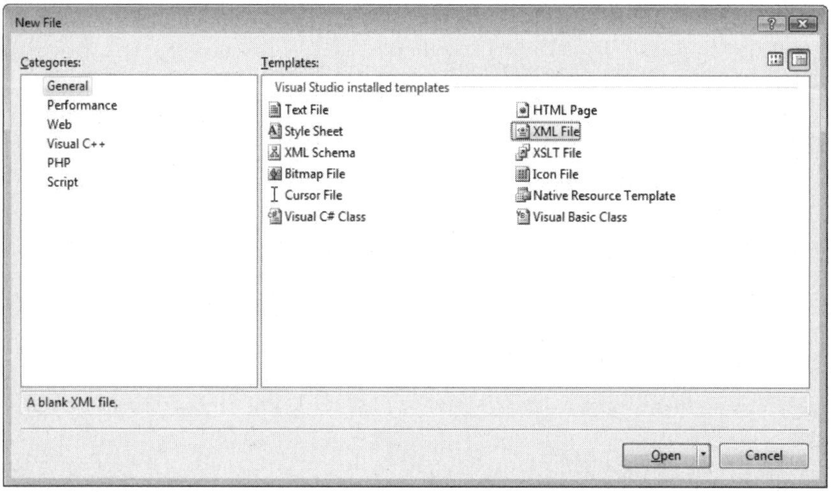

Figure 15-12

Click Open, and a blank XML file will be displayed in Visual Studio. Paste the following into the text editor window, replacing the existing text:

```
<?xml version="1.0" encoding="utf-8"?>
<WorkflowInfo Language="en-us">
 <Actions Sequential="then" Parallel="and">
   <Action Name="" ClassName="" Assembly="" AppliesTo="all" Category="">
     <RuleDesigner Sentence="">
     </RuleDesigner>
     <Parameters>
     </Parameters>
   </Action>
 </Actions>
</WorkflowInfo>
```

Now that you have a template to edit, you can start filling in values for your custom action. You will have to use the Strong Name Utility to get the PublicKeyToken portion of the value for the Assembly attribute. Follow these steps:

1. If it is not already open, open the Output window by selecting View ⇨ Output.

2. Build the custom action assembly by selecting Build ⇨ Build Solution.

3. Note the location of the compiled DLL. For example:

   ```
   CustomActionsLibrary -> C:\Users\username\Documents\Visual Studio
   2008\Projects\ CustomActionsLibrary\bin\CustomActionsLibrary.dll
   ```

4. Open the Visual Studio Command prompt by clicking Start ⇨ All Programs ⇨ Microsoft Visual Studio 2005 (or 2008) ⇨ Visual Studio Tools ⇨ Microsoft Visual Studio 2005 (or 2008) Command prompt.

5. Type **sn.exe –T** *assemblypath*, where *assemblypath* is the location of the DLL from step 3. If *assemblypath* contains spaces, you must enclose it in quotation marks.

6. Note the public key token indicated. In the following example output, the key token is a4d44e6df3f4f726:

   ```
   Microsoft (R) .NET Framework Strong Name Utility  Version 3.5.21022.8
   Copyright (c) Microsoft Corporation.  All rights reserved.

   Public key token is a4d44e6df3f4f726
   ```

7. Specify these values for the attributes in the `Action` element:

Attribute	Element
Name	Create Subsite
ClassName	CustomActionsLibrary.CreateSiteAction
Assembly	CustomActionsLibrary, Version=1.0.0.0, Culture=neutral, PublicKeyToken=XXXXX where XXXXX is the value obtained from step 6
Category	Custom Actions

8. Specify the following as the value for the `RuleDesigner` element's `Sentence` attribute:

```
Create subsite with these settings: %1, %2, %3, %4 and %5
```

9. Inside the `RuleDesigner` element, paste the following code five times:

```
<FieldBind Field="" Text="" Id="" DesignerType="TextArea"/>
```

10. Specify 1 through 5 for the `Id` attribute of the new `FieldBind` elements.

11. For each property of the custom action, set the `Field` attribute to the property's name, and supply a user-friendly name for the `Text` attribute of the new `FieldBind` element. Fill out one `FieldBind` element for each of these properties:

- ❏ SiteUrl
- ❏ SiteTitle
- ❏ SiteDescription
- ❏ SiteTemplate
- ❏ InheritPermissions

The `FieldBind` element for `SiteUrl` should look like this:

```
<FieldBind Field="SiteUrl" Text="url" Id="1" DesignerType="TextArea"/
```

12. Inside the `Parameter` element, paste the following code five times:

```
<Parameter Name="" Type="System.String, mscorlib" Direction="In" />
```

13. For each property of the custom action, set the `Name` attribute of the new `Parameter` element to the property's name. Fill out one `Parameter` element for each of these properties:

- ❏ SiteUrl
- ❏ SiteTitle

❑   `SiteDescription`

❑   `SiteTemplate`

❑   `InheritPermissions`

The `Parameter` element for `SiteUrl` should look like this:

```
<Parameter Name="SiteUrl" Type="System.String, mscorlib" Direction="In" />
```

14.   Change the `Type` attribute of the `Parameter` element for the `InheritPermissions` property from `"System.String, mscorlib"` to `"System.Boolean, mscorlib"`.

15.   Finally, to pass your activity the workflow's context, add this to the `Parameter` element:

```
<Parameter Name="__Context"
    Type="Microsoft.SharePoint.WorkflowActions.WorkflowContext,
    Microsoft.SharePoint.WorkflowActions" Direction="In"/>
```

The resulting code should look as follows:

```
<?xml version="1.0" encoding="utf-8"?>
<Action Name="Create Subsite" ClassName=⏎
"CustomActionsLibrary.CreateSiteAction" Assembly="CustomActionsLibrary, ⏎
Version=1.0.0.0, Culture=neutral, PublicKeyToken=a4d44e6df3f4f726" ⏎
AppliesTo="all" Category="Custom Actions">
  <RuleDesigner Sentence="Create subsite with these settings:  %1, %2, ⏎
%3, %4 and %5">
    <FieldBind Field="SiteUrl" Text="url" Id="1" DesignerType="TextArea"/>
    <FieldBind Field="SiteTitle" Text="title" Id="2" ⏎
DesignerType="TextArea"/>
    <FieldBind Field="SiteDescription" Text="description" Id="3" ⏎
DesignerType="TextArea"/>
    <FieldBind Field="SiteTemplate" Text="site template" Id="4" ⏎
DesignerType="TextArea"/>
    <FieldBind Field="InheritPermissions" Text="inherit permissions" ⏎
Id="5" DesignerType="TextArea"/>
  </RuleDesigner>
  <Parameters>
    <Parameter Name="SiteUrl" Type="System.String, mscorlib" ⏎
Direction="In" />
    <Parameter Name="SiteTitle" Type="System.String, mscorlib" ⏎
Direction="In" />
    <Parameter Name="SiteDescription" Type="System.String, mscorlib" ⏎
Direction="In" />
    <Parameter Name="SiteTemplate" Type="System.String, mscorlib" ⏎
Direction="In" />
    <Parameter Name="InheritPermissions" Type="System.Boolean, mscorlib" ⏎
Direction="In" />
    <Parameter Name="__Context"
        Type="Microsoft.SharePoint.WorkflowActions.WorkflowContext,
        Microsoft.SharePoint.WorkflowActions" Direction="In"/>
  </Parameters>
</Action>
```

Save the ACTIONS file by selecting File ⇨ Save, entering custom.ACTIONS as the filename, selecting All Files from the Save as Type dropdown list, and clicking Save. Double-check the file extension of the saved ACTIONS file to ensure that it is ACTIONS and not XML.

Now that the ACTIONS file has been created, you can deploy your custom action to SharePoint and test it. The next section details those steps.

Deploying and Configuring Your Custom Action

There are three steps to deploying your custom action:

1. Add the assembly to the Global Assembly Cache.

2. Deploy the custom.ACTIONS file.

3. Update the web.config file.

Adding the Assembly to the Global Assembly Cache

The Global Assembly Cache stores assemblies that are shared among server processes. Most SharePoint-related assemblies must be placed in the Global Assembly Cache before SharePoint can use them. This restriction also applies to custom actions. However, placing assemblies in the Global Assembly Cache can be very dangerous, since these assemblies are accessible to the entire SharePoint farm and run without any restrictions on what code is allowed to run inside SharePoint. You can reduce this risk by examining the code of all assemblies to be placed in the Global Assembly Cache, including those from third parties. It is better to err on the side of caution than to risk the health and stability of your SharePoint farm.

To deploy the assembly to the Global Assembly Cache, open Windows Explorer and navigate to the C:\Windows\Assembly folder. Then, drag your DLL file into the folder, and it will automatically be added to the Global Assembly Cache. If you previously added your assembly to the Global Assembly Cache, you must restart IIS before your assembly will be recognized by SharePoint.

To restart IIS, open the Run dialog by clicking Start and choosing Run. Type **iisreset** into the Run box, and click OK.

Deploying the ACTIONS file

To deploy the ACTIONS file, simply copy the custom.ACTIONS file to the C:\Program Files\ Common Files\Microsoft Shared\Web Server Extensions\12\TEMPLATE\1033\Workflow folder on the SharePoint server. SharePoint monitors this folder for files with the ACTIONS file extension and uses the information inside to determine which actions to display in SharePoint Designer and how to display them.

Updating the web.config File

Finally, you need to update the `web.config` file to allow SharePoint Designer to use your custom action. Be aware that code running in the Global Assembly Cache runs without code restrictions and that updating the `web.config` file will enable this code to run inside SharePoint. Be careful about which assemblies you add to the Global Assembly Cache and which of those assemblies are allowed to run inside SharePoint.

Follow these steps to add the appropriate tags to the `web.config` file:

1. Back up your `web.config` file. If you misconfigure the `web.config` file, your SharePoint site will not function until you correct the file. The default location of the `web.config` file is `C:\inetpub\wwwroot\wss\VirtualDirectories\`*portnumber*`\web.config`, where *portnumber* is the port number of your SharePoint web application.

2. Open the `web.config` file.

3. Locate the tag named `<System.Workflow.ComponentModel.WorkflowCompiler>`.

4. Inside the tag named `<authorizedTypes>`, add a tag named `<authorizedType>` with the following attributes:

Attribute	Value
Assembly	Use the same value as the `Assembly` attribute of the `Action` element in your ACTIONS file.
Namespace	CustomActionsLibrary
TypeName	*
Authorized	True

The resulting code should look like this:

```
<!-- snipped code -->

<System.Workflow.ComponentModel.WorkflowCompiler>
  <authorizedTypes>

<!-- snipped code -->

    <authorizedType Assembly="CustomActionsLibrary, Version=1.0.0.0, ⏎
Culture=neutral, PublicKeyToken=c7353bc82ef93acf" ⏎
Namespace="CustomActionsLibrary" TypeName="*" Authorized="True" />

<!-- snipped code -->

  </authorizedTypes>
</System.Workflow.ComponentModel.WorkflowCompiler>

<!-- snipped code -->
```

Note that the `PublicKeyToken` value for your assembly *will* be different from the one in this example.

5. Save the `web.config` file.

Testing Your Custom Action

To test your custom action, you must create these items:

❑ A list or document library.

❑ A workflow in SharePoint Designer that uses your action and is attached to the list or document library.

❑ A list item or document in the list or document library.

Creating a Custom List

Because it is easier to test using a custom list, create a custom list by opening your browser and navigating to your SharePoint site. Choose Create from the Site Actions menu. If you cannot see the Site Actions menu, log in to the site as a site owner. Once you click Create, the Create page is displayed (see Figure 15-13). Depending on your edition of SharePoint and optionally installed features, you may have more or fewer options displayed on the Create page.

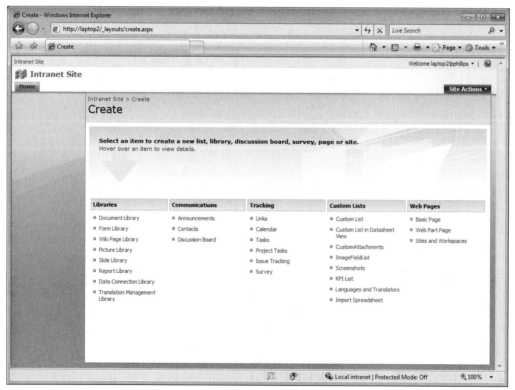

Figure 15-13

Choose Custom List under the Custom Lists column. On the New page, enter **WorkflowTestList** as the name of the list, keep the default values for the other controls, and then click Create. The All Items page is displayed.

To test your custom action, you will need to create a column for each property on the custom action. To create a new column, select Create Column from the Settings menu, and the Create Column page will be displayed (Figure 15-14). Create the five columns in the following table, using the values provided:

Column Name	Type
SiteUrl	Single line of text.
SiteTitle	Single line of text.
SiteDescription	Multiple lines of text. Select the Plain Text option.
SiteTemplate	Choice Enter these values for the Type of each choice on a separate line text box: Team Site Blank Site Document Workspace Wiki Site Blog
InheritPermissions	Yes/No (check box).

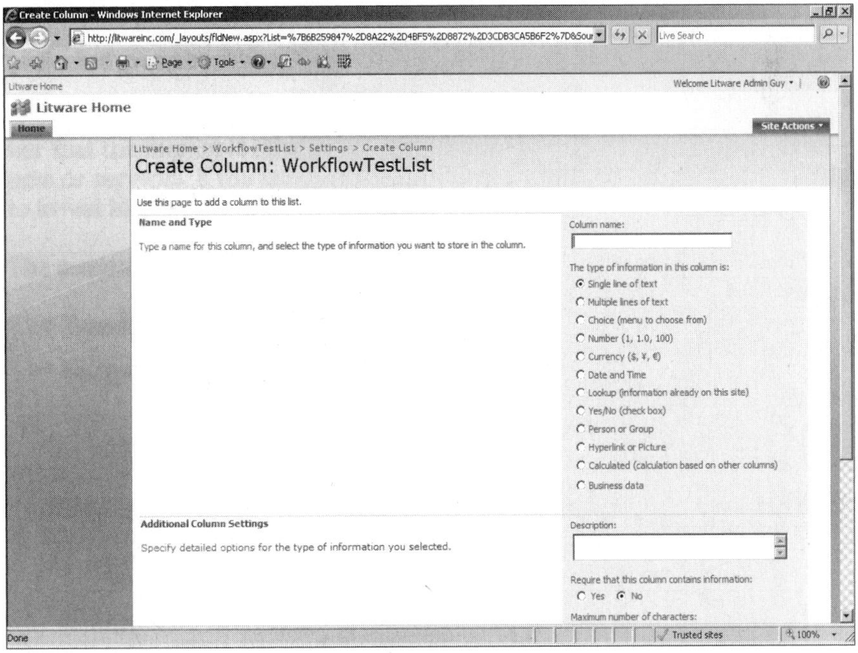

Figure 15-14

Now that you have created a test list, open SharePoint Designer to design a workflow that uses it.

Creating a Workflow in SharePoint Designer

In SharePoint Designer, open the site where you created the test list. Then, choose File ⇨ New ⇨ Workflow. On the initial Workflow Designer screen (Figure 15-15), select WorkflowTestList from the dropdown list and check the check boxes for the following:

❑ Allow this workflow to be manually started from an item.

❑ Automatically start this workflow when a new item is created.

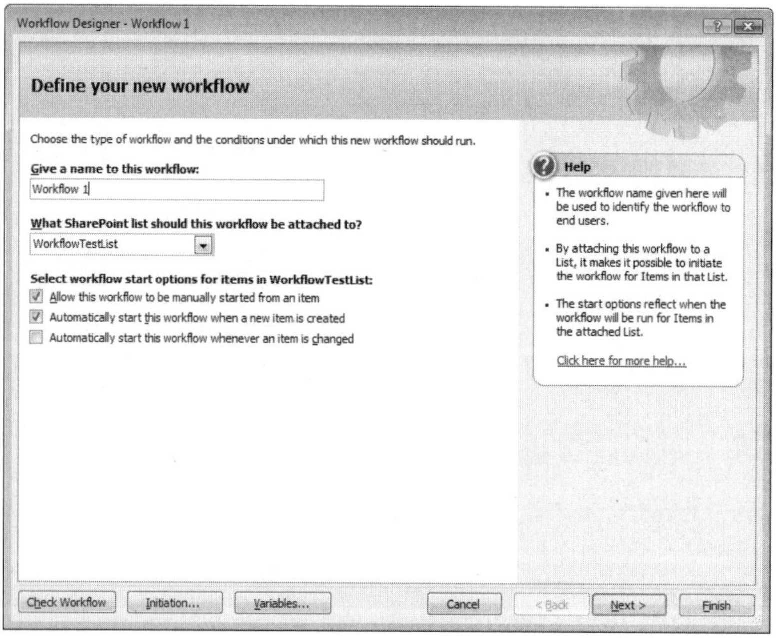

Figure 15-15

Finally, click Next.

On the next Workflow Designer screen (see Figure 15-16), enter **Step 1** for the Step Name. Then, click the Actions button, and select More Actions from the list that appears.

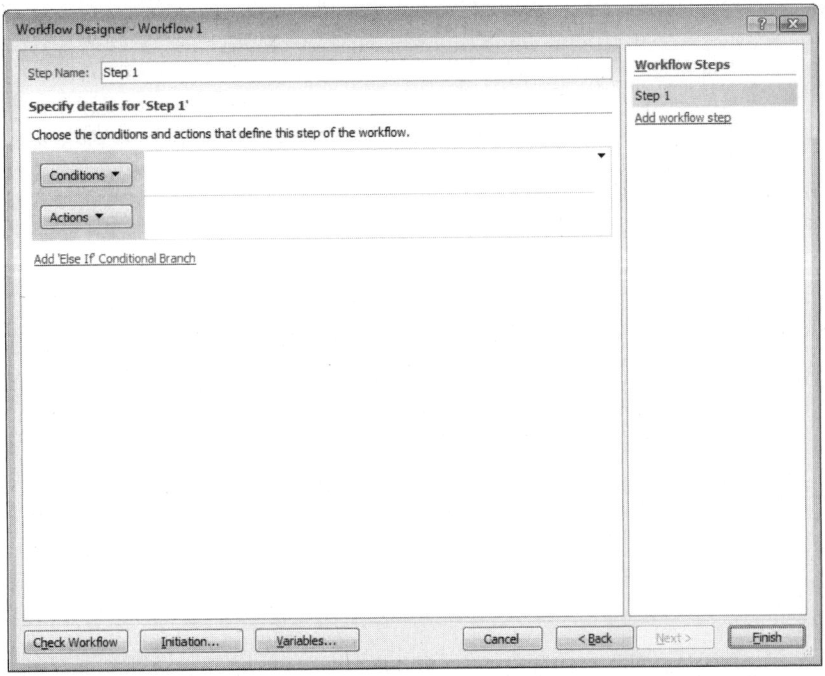

Figure 15-16

When the Workflow Actions dialog appears (Figure 15-17), choose Custom Actions from the Select a Category dropdown list, and your custom action will be displayed. With your custom action selected, click Add.

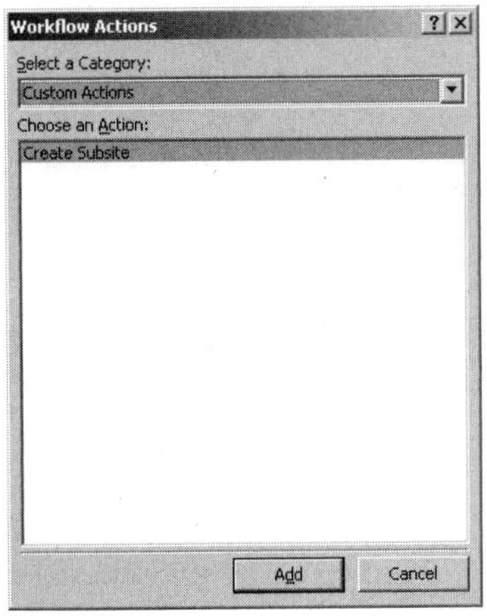

Figure 15-17

Now that your custom action has been added to the step, you can configure it by clicking each underlined word, clicking the *fx* button, and choosing the appropriate field from the list you created (Figure 15-18).

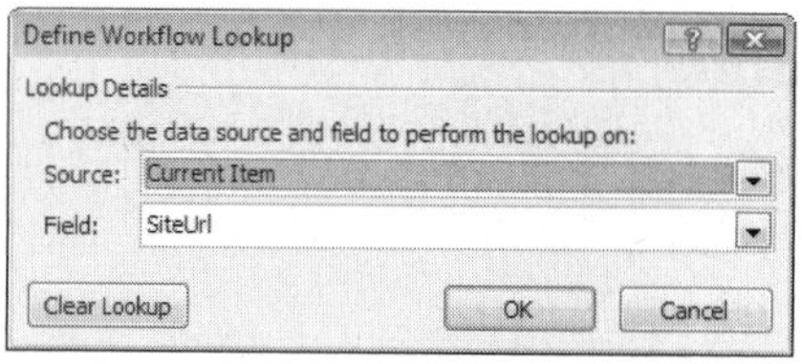

Figure 15-18

After your action is configured (Figure 15-19), click the Check Workflow button to check your workflow for errors. Finally, click Finish to save your workflow to SharePoint.

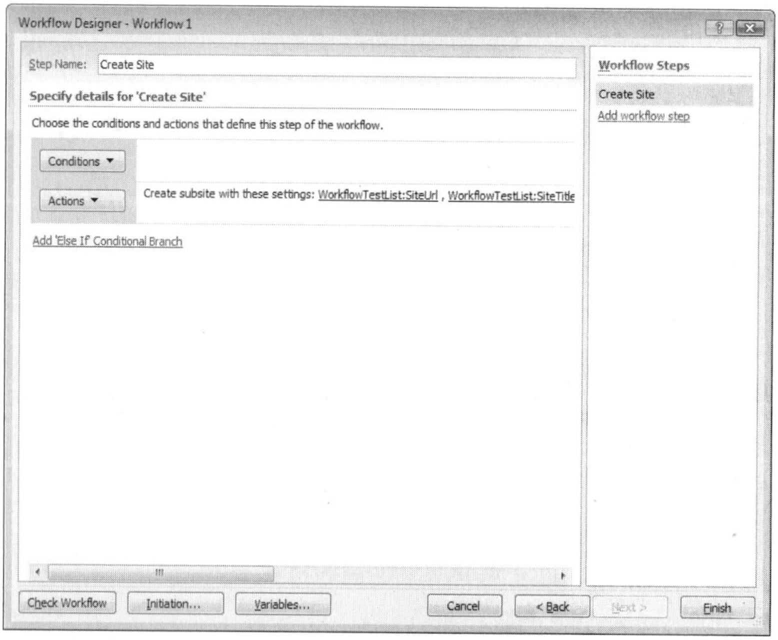

Figure 15-19

The workflow created in this section is a very basic one used solely to test the custom action. Normally, the custom action would be used as a part of a comprehensive workflow that could include sending a notification to the site collection administrators and requesting approval of the new site before it is created.

Adding an Item to the Custom List

You configured your workflow to start when an item is inserted in the WorkflowTestList list, so navigate to the list and click the New menu item. On the New Item screen (see Figure 15-20), fill out the fields and click the OK button to return to the list.

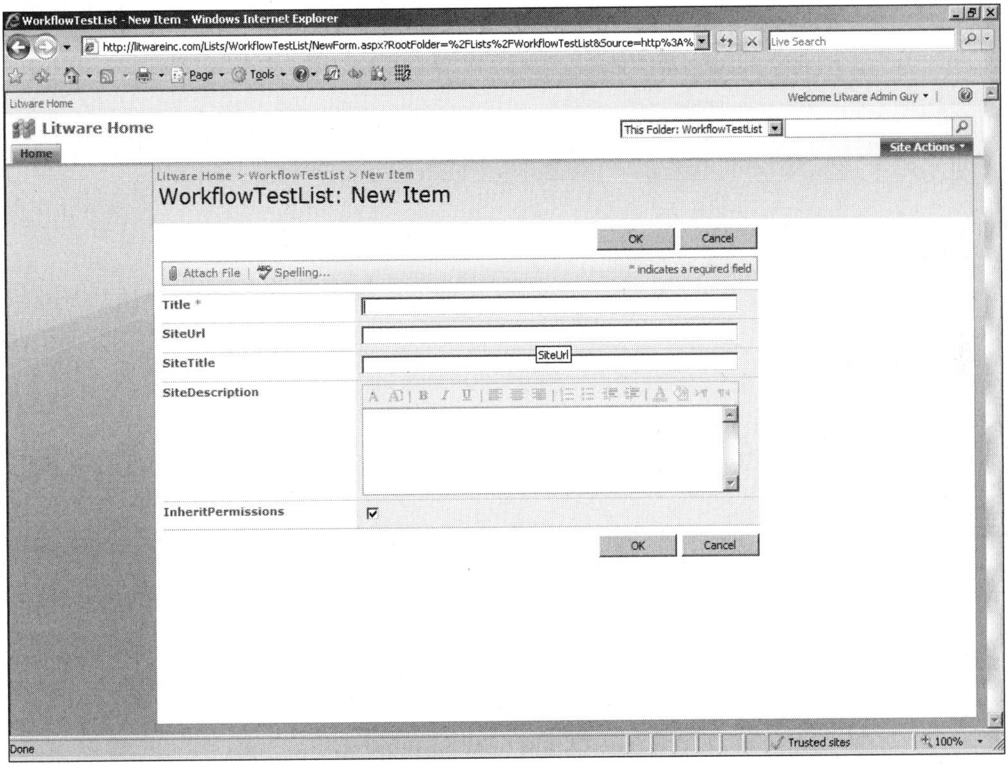

Figure 15-20

SharePoint automatically starts your workflow and adds a new column to the end of the list to display the workflow's status for your list item (see Figure 15-21).

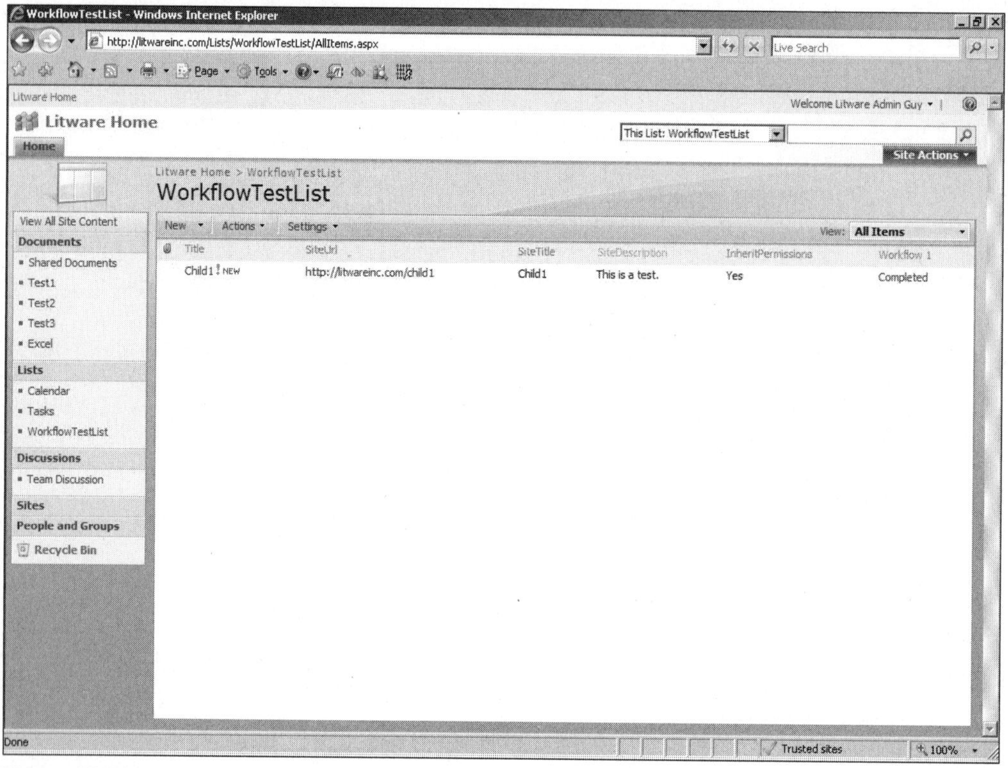

Figure 15-21

Initially, your workflow will show a status of In Progress. If the workflow completes successfully, the workflow's status changes to Completed; otherwise, it changes to Error Occurred. To verify that the site was created, click the Sites link from the Quick Launch bar at the left, and then click the name of the site on the All Site Content Page to navigate to the newly created site.

Troubleshooting Problems

During the process of creating, deploying, and using your action in SharePoint Designer, you can encounter various errors. This section explains how to resolve the most common errors.

❑ **Error: Your custom action does not appear in SharePoint Designer.**

❑ Ensure your custom ACTIONS file has been deployed to the C:\Program Files\Common Files\ Microsoft Shared\Web Server Extensions\12\TEMPLATE\1033\Workflow\ folder and that you have restarted IIS.

❑ **Error: You have updated your custom action, but the workflow does not appear to use the updated version of the action.**

❑ Ensure that you have added your assembly to the Global Assembly Cache and that you have restarted IIS.

❑   **Error: Your workflow passes validation after clicking the Check Workflow button, but not after clicking the Finish button.**

❑   Ensure that you have added your assembly to the AuthorizedTypes section of the `web.config` file and that your assembly's strong name is correct and matches the strong name you configured in the ACTIONS file.

Summary

With SharePoint Designer custom actions, you can greatly extend the power of custom SharePoint Designer workflows. Additionally, these custom actions are reusable and, once deployed, can be used across all sites in your SharePoint farm. Business process automation is very popular these days, and by creating domain-specific custom actions, you will arm your SharePoint Designer users with the tools they need to maximize SharePoint's workflow capabilities.

16

Creating Custom Web Parts

Chapter 2 introduced the built-in Web Parts in SharePoint and explained how they could be used to assemble a portal web site. Other chapters introduced the Data View, Data Form, and Content Editor Web Parts, which allow you to handle many sophisticated tasks on the web client side. This chapter takes you even further by showing you how to create and deploy your own Web Parts — configuring them to work inside SharePoint Designer. You'll:

❑   Look at the role of custom Web Parts.

❑   Create a custom Web Part.

❑   Deploy and configure your custom Web Part.

❑   Test your Web Part.

What You Need to Get Started

Before you can jump in and create new Web Parts, ensure that you have the correct tools:

❑   Microsoft Visual Studio 2008 (not Visual Studio Express).

❑   Windows SharePoint Services 3.0 SDK (`http://microsoft.com/downloads/details .aspx?FamilyID=05e0dd12-8394-402b-8936-a07fe8afaffd&DisplayLang=en`) or Microsoft Office SharePoint Server 2007 SDK (`http://microsoft.com/downloads/ details .aspx?FamilyID=6D94E307-67D9-41AC-B2D6-0074D6286FA9&displaylang=en`)

❑   Windows XP or Windows Vista. (I used Windows Vista.).

I chose General Development Settings when configuring Visual Studio 2008 for the first time. If you chose different settings, your screens may differ from the screenshots in this chapter.

If you want to reset your Visual Studio 2008 settings, select Tools ➪ Import and Export Settings, and use the wizard to reset your settings. In the wizard, you have the option of backing up your existing settings if you want to revert to them later on.

About Custom Web Parts

The built-in Web Parts in SharePoint are a good starting point for assembling portal-style functionality in SharePoint, and providing basic data access. But sometimes you may need a custom Web Part that adds functionality to your web site, or that allows users to truly interact with back-end line-of-business systems in a way far beyond what Data Views and Data Forms can provide. Custom Web Parts let you take the next step. They enable you to create reusable pieces of user interface and functionality to use among the sites in your SharePoint farm. Once you have deployed a Web Part to SharePoint and configured it to run, it appears in the Add Web Parts dialog (see Figure 16-1).

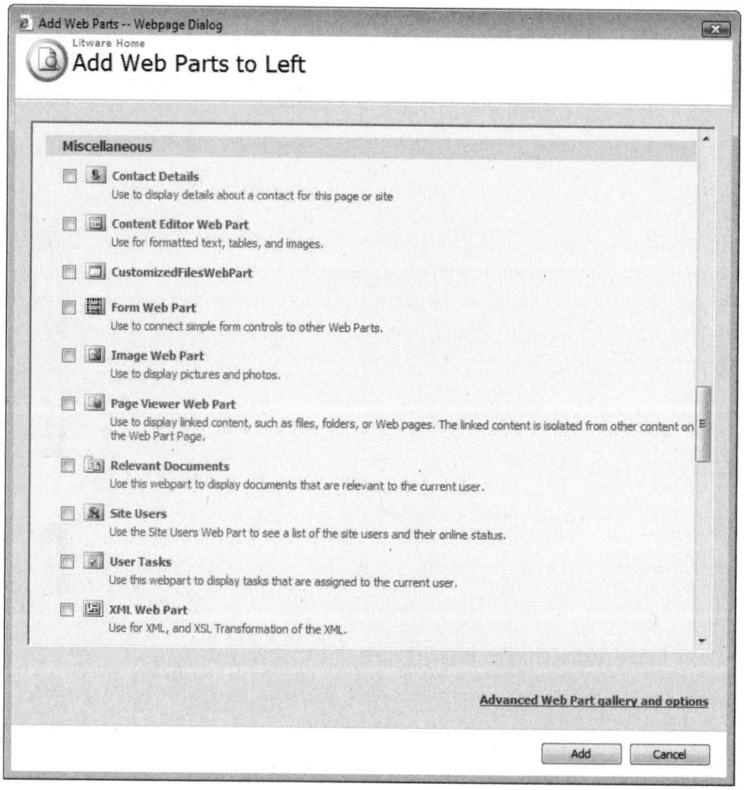

Figure 16-1

Through the exercises in this chapter, you will create, deploy, and test a custom Web Part that displays a list of the customized files in the SharePoint site and gives the user the option to uncustomize any of those files. This is called reverting to the site definition. Uncustomized files are processed faster than customized files because they are read from the file system rather than from the SharePoint content database. Files become customized whenever a user saves a file in SharePoint Designer that causes SharePoint to store the file in the SharePoint content database. SharePoint Designer is never allowed to modify files on the SharePoint server's file system. Because customized files affect the web application's overall performance, you can use this chapter's example Web Part to monitor these files. Refer to chapter 5 for the full description of the effects of customization.

Creating a Web Part

You begin the process of creating a custom Web Part by opening Visual Studio and selecting File ⇨ New ⇨ Project. The result is the New Project dialog. Figure 16-2 shows the dialog with Visual Basic as the selected language, and Figure 16-3 shows the C# choice.

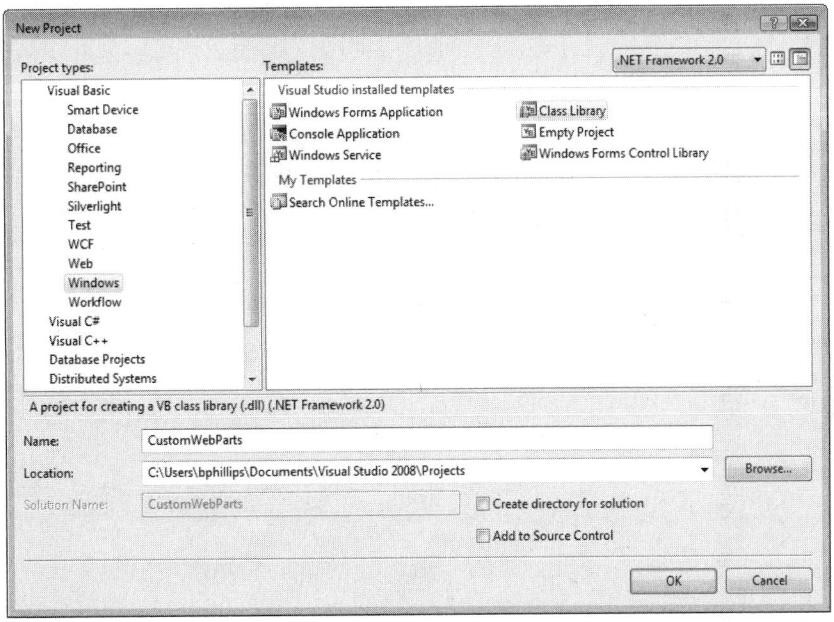

Figure 16-2

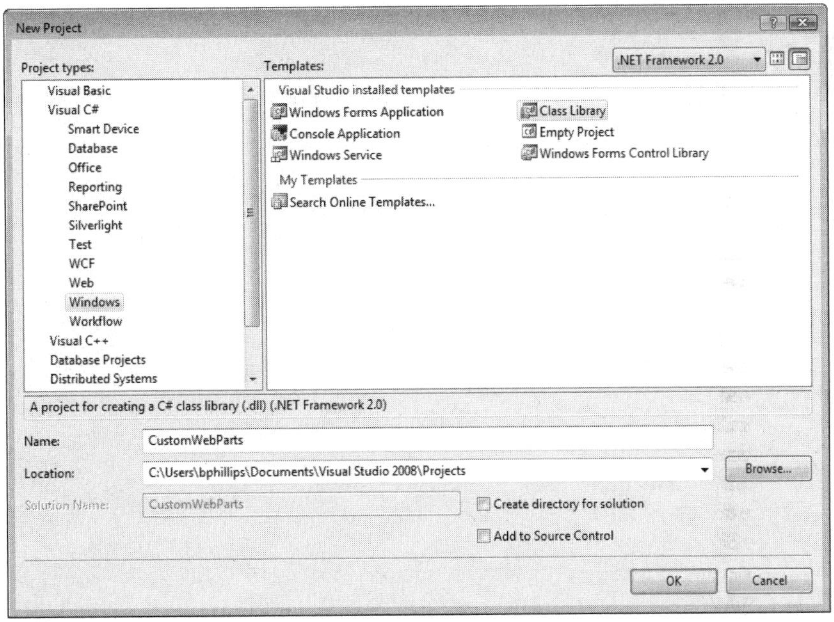

Figure 16-3

To choose the Project template for your custom Web Part, ensure .NET Framework 2.0 is selected in the dropdown list in the upper-right corner of the dialog, expand either the Visual Basic (for this example) or Visual C# node in the tree, and click the Windows folder. A list of Project templates is displayed on the right. Select the Class Library template and then enter a name — CustomWebParts, for this Project — and location for the Project. Click OK to create the Project to contain your custom Web Part (Figure 16-4 shows the VB Project on the left and C# Project on the right).

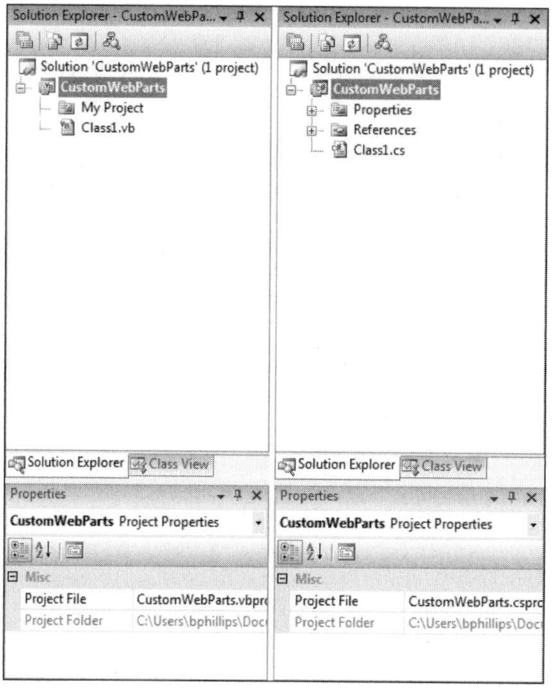

Figure 16-4

By default, Visual Studio automatically creates a file named `Class1.vb` or `Class1.cs` that you can re-use for your Web Part. Just right-click `Class1.vb` or `Class1.cs` in the Solution Explorer window and select Rename from the context menu. Rename the file to `CustomizedFilesWebPart.vb` or `CustomizedFilesWebPart.cs`. A confirmation dialog appears; click Yes to confirm the rename and allow Visual Studio to rename the class inside the file.

Assemblies that contain custom Web Parts must be strong-named to run inside SharePoint. To configure the Project to have a strong name, right-click the assembly name (CustomWebParts) in the Solution Explorer window, and select Properties to open the Project properties screen (Figure 16-5 shows the VB screen; Figure 16-6 shows the C# screen).

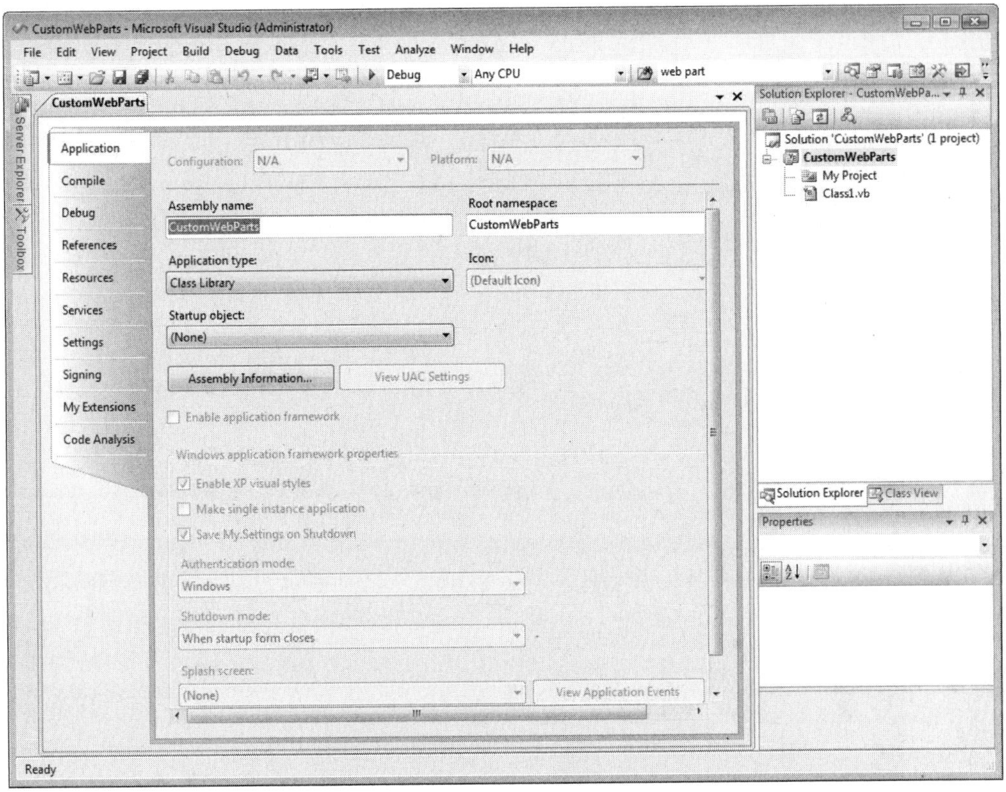

Figure 16-5

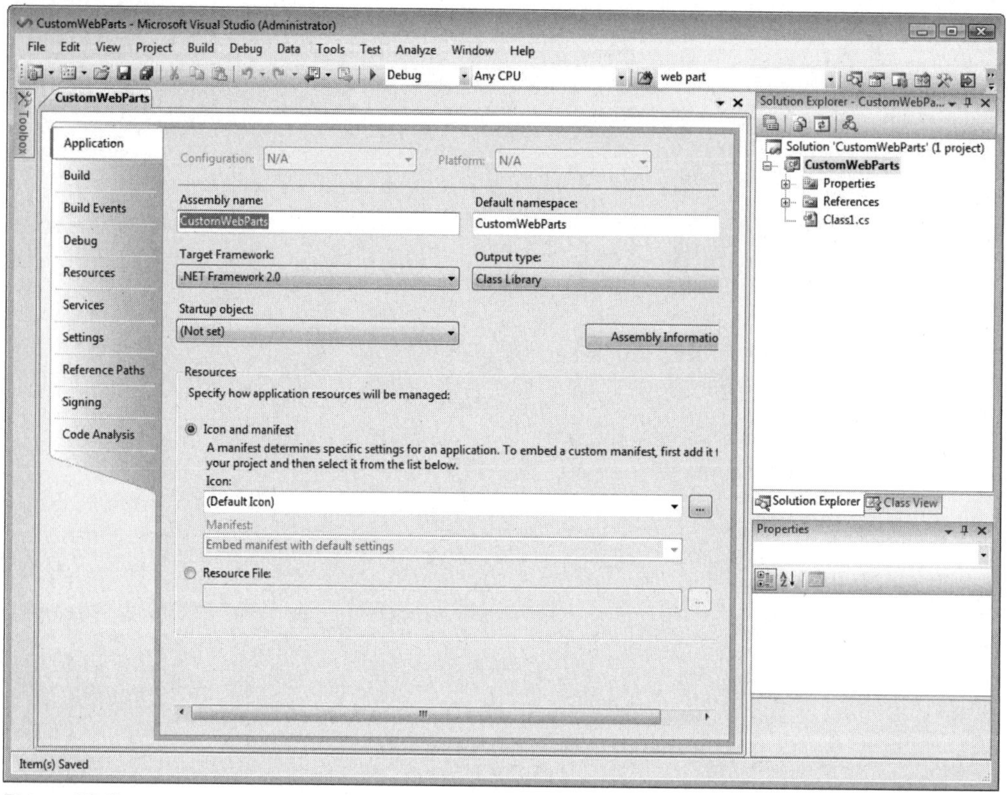

Figure 16-6

Go to the Signing tab and click the Sign The Assembly check box. Select New from the dropdown list, and the Create Strong Name Key dialog (see Figure 16-7) opens. Enter Key.snk in the Key file name text box, uncheck the Protect my key file with a password check box, and click OK. Close the Project properties screen.

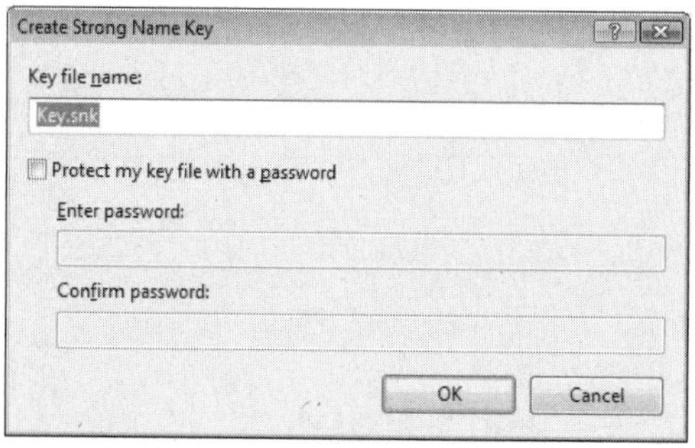

Figure 16-7

Before you add your Web Part, you must add references to the SharePoint assemblies (DLLs) that will allow your Web Part to access the SharePoint object model. Right-click the assembly name (CreateWebParts) in the Solution Explorer window, and select Add Reference. In the Add Reference dialog's .NET tab (see Figure 16-8), press and hold the Ctrl key while clicking on the following components:

- ❑ System.Web

- ❑ Windows® SharePoint® Services

- ❑ Windows® SharePoint® Services Security

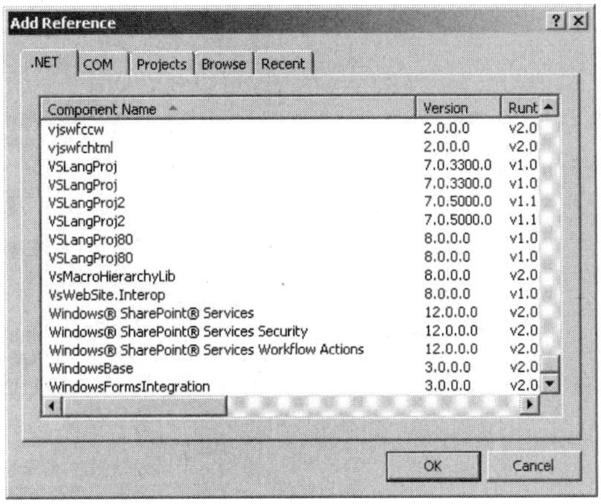

Figure 16-8

Then click OK.

Double-click the `CustomizedFilesWebPart.vb` or `CustomizedFilesWebPart.cs` file in Solution Explorer. Visual Studio opens the file in Code view. You will see the following code displayed:

VB.NET

```
Public class CustomizedFilesWebPart
End Class
```

C#

```
using System;
using System.Collections.Generic;
using System.Text;
namespace CustomWebParts {
    public class CustomizedFilesWebPart {
    }
}
```

Now, you can start modifying this code to provide a user interface for your Web Part.

To make it easier to use the classes in SharePoint, add these statements to the top of the file:

VB.NET

```
Imports Microsoft.SharePoint
Imports Microsoft.SharePoint.WebControls
Imports System
Imports System.Collections.Generic
Imports System.Web.UI.WebControls
```

C#

```
using Microsoft.SharePoint;
using Microsoft.SharePoint.WebControls;
using System.Collections.Generic;
using System.Web.UI.WebControls;
```

These statements allow you to use the shortened names of classes in SharePoint instead of their fully qualified names.

The final step is to modify the `CustomizedFilesWebPart` class to inherit from the `System.Web.UI.WebControls.WebParts.WebPart` class. Inheriting from a class allows you to re-use its basic functionality and add your own custom functionality. To inherit from the `System.Web.UI.WebControls.WebParts.WebPart` class, modify the `CustomizedFilesWebPart` class so that it looks like this:

VB.NET

```
Public Class CustomizedFilesWebPart
    Inherits System.Web.UI.WebControls.WebParts.WebPart
End Class
```

C#

```
public class CustomizedFilesWebPart : System.Web.UI.WebControls.WebParts.WebPart
{
}
```

Creating a User Interface for Your Custom Web Part

The user interface for a Web Part is provided by the web controls it contains. The controls are not automatically added to the Web Part because each Web Part can look different, based on its functionality. You must do two things to add web controls to your Web Part:

❑ Add a private field for each control.

❑ Override the `CreateChildControls` method.

Private fields are variables declared at the class level and are shared among the class's methods. By creating a private field for each control, you can manipulate the controls, based on the user's input, and interact with your Web Part. This example uses an SPGridView control, which is SharePoint's version of the ASP.NET GridView control. The SPGridView displays data to the user in a tabular format that is styled to match the SharePoint site in which it is displayed. To put the SPGridView control in your Web Part, add the following code inside your Web Part class:

VB.NET

```
Private WithEvents GridView1 As SPGridView
```

C#

```
private SPGridView GridView1;
```

Now that the SPGridView has been declared, add this code to override the CreateChildControls method:

VB.NET

```
Protected Overrides Sub CreateChildControls()


End Sub
```

C#

```
protected override void CreateChildControls() {


}
```

The `CreateChildControls` method is used to instantiate and configure the web controls in the Web Part. All controls require a value for the ID property. It is a good practice to specify a value for ID that matches the name of its variable. Use GridView1 as the value for ID.

Because the SPGridView control renders a table to the browser, you have the option to have it automatically generate columns or to specify your own. This example cannot use the automatically generated columns, so set the `AutoGeneratedColumns` property to `False`.

The SPGridView can also associate each row it renders with a data key to uniquely identify it. Each row in this Web Part's SPGridView represents a customized file, and you use the row's unique identifier to revert a file if the user chooses to do so. The following code sample sets the `DataKeyNames` property to `UniqueId`.

Finally, you might not have any customized files in your site. When the SPGridView does not have any rows to display, it displays the text stored in the `EmptyDataText` property. That property will be set to `No files have beencustomized`.

Add this code to the `CreateChildControls` method to instantiate the SPGridView control and configure it as previously described:

VB.NET

```
Protected Overrides Sub CreateChildControls()
    GridView1 = New SPGridView()
    GridView1.ID = "GridView1"
    GridView1.AutoGenerateColumns = False
    GridView1.DataKeyNames = New String() {"UniqueId"}
    GridView1.EmptyDataText = "No files have been customized."
End Sub
```

C#

```
protected override void CreateChildControls() {
    GridView1 = new SPGridView();
    GridView1.ID = "GridView1";
    GridView1.AutoGenerateColumns = false;
    GridView1.DataKeyNames = new string[] { "UniqueId" };
    GridView1.EmptyDataText = "No files have been customized.";
}
```

Because you have set the `AutoGenerateColumns` property to false, you have to write code to create columns and add them to the SPGridView. You need to create columns to display these values for each customized file:

❑ The name of the file.

❑ The parent folder of the file.

❑ Who last modified the file.

❑ When the file was last modified.

The `BoundField` class is used to add text columns to the `SPGridView` class. You will add one BoundField for each of the columns above. The BoundField has two important properties: `DataField` and `HeaderText`. The `DataField` property indicates what data to display, while the `HeaderText` property is used for the column's header at the top of the table generated by the `SPGridView` class. Enter the following code just before the end of the `CreateChildControls` method to create the four `BoundField` classes and add them to the SPGridView:

VB.NET

```
Dim nameField As New BoundField()
nameField.DataField = "Name"
nameField.HeaderText = "Name"
GridView1.Columns.Add(nameField)

Dim folderField As New BoundField()
folderField.DataField = "ParentFolder"
folderField.HeaderText = "Path"
GridView1.Columns.Add(folderField)

Dim modifiedByField As New BoundField()
```

```
modifiedByField.DataField = "ModifiedBy"
modifiedByField.HeaderText = "Modified By"
GridView1.Columns.Add(modifiedByField)

Dim modifiedDateField As New BoundField()
modifiedDateField.DataField = "TimeLastModified"
modifiedDateField.HeaderText = "Modified Date"
GridView1.Columns.Add(modifiedDateField)
```

C#

```
BoundField nameField = new BoundField();
nameField.DataField = "Name";
nameField.HeaderText = "Name";
GridView1.Columns.Add(nameField);

BoundField folderField = new BoundField();
folderField.DataField = "ParentFolder";
folderField.HeaderText = "Path";
GridView1.Columns.Add(folderField);

BoundField modifiedByField = new BoundField();
modifiedByField.DataField = "ModifiedBy";
modifiedByField.HeaderText = "Modified By";
GridView1.Columns.Add(modifiedByField);

BoundField modifiedDateField = new BoundField();
modifiedDateField.DataField = "TimeLastModified";
modifiedDateField.HeaderText = "Modified Date";
GridView1.Columns.Add(modifiedDateField);
```

You also need to create a column to contain the link that the user will click to revert the file to the site definition, so the final column is created using the CommandField class. It's the class that's used whenever you want to display a link or button to the user that, when clicked, will run code using that row's data. You could write code that selects the row, making it stand out to the user in the web page; delete the row; put the row in edit mode, to allow the user to edit the row's values; and save the row or cancel changes to the row. Here you create a CommandField that deletes the row because that action is analogous to uncustomizing a file, which makes it not appear in the table anymore. Add the following code to create the CommandField and configure it:

VB.NET

```
Dim revertField As New CommandField()
revertField.DeleteText = "Revert"
revertField.ShowDeleteButton = True
GridView1.Columns.Add(revertField)
```

C#

```
CommandField revertField = new CommandField();
revertField.DeleteText = "Revert";
revertField.ShowDeleteButton = true;
GridView1.Columns.Add(revertField);
```

The final step to complete the `CreateChildControls` method is to add an event handler to run code whenever the CommandField is clicked in the browser, and add the SPGridView to the Web Part's Controls collection. Event handlers link the action that a user takes in the browser with code on the server that is to run when the action is taken. Because the CommandField you added deletes rows, you need to add an event handler for the SPGridView's `RowDeleting` event. Add this code to the end of the `CreateChildControls` method to create the event handler that will call the soon-to-be-created `GridView1_RowDeleting` method, and add the SPGridView to the Web Part's Controls collection:

VB.NET

```
AddHandler GridView1.RowDeleting, AddressOf GridView1_RowDeleting
Me.Controls.Add(GridView1)
```

C#

```
GridView1.RowDeleting += new GridViewDeleteEventHandler(GridView1_RowDeleting);
this.Controls.Add(GridView1);
```

The resulting class should look like this:

VB.NET

```
Imports Microsoft.SharePoint
Imports Microsoft.SharePoint.WebControls
Imports System
Imports System.Collections.Generic
Imports System.Web.UI.WebControls

Public Class CustomizedFilesWebPart
    Inherits System.Web.UI.WebControls.WebParts.WebPart

    Private WithEvents GridView1 As SPGridView

    Protected Overrides Sub CreateChildControls()
        GridView1 = New SPGridView()
        GridView1.ID = "GridView1"
        GridView1.AutoGenerateColumns = False
        GridView1.DataKeyNames = New String() {"UniqueId"}
        GridView1.EmptyDataText = "No files have beencustomized."

        Dim nameField As New BoundField()
        nameField.DataField = "Name"
        nameField.HeaderText = "Name"
        GridView1.Columns.Add(nameField)

        Dim folderField As New BoundField()
        folderField.DataField = "ParentFolder"
        folderField.HeaderText = "Path"
        GridView1.Columns.Add(folderField)

        Dim modifiedByField As New BoundField()
        modifiedByField.DataField = "ModifiedBy"
        modifiedByField.HeaderText = "Modified By"
```

```
        GridView1.Columns.Add(modifiedByField)

        Dim modifiedDateField As New BoundField()
        modifiedDateField.DataField = "TimeLastModified"
        modifiedDateField.HeaderText = "Modified Date"
        GridView1.Columns.Add(modifiedDateField)

        Dim revertField As New CommandField()
        revertField.DeleteText = "Revert"
        revertField.ShowDeleteButton = True
        GridView1.Columns.Add(revertField)

        AddHandler GridView1.RowDeleting, AddressOf GridView1_RowDeleting
        Me.Controls.Add(GridView1)
    End Sub
End Class
```

C#

```csharp
using Microsoft.SharePoint;
using Microsoft.SharePoint.WebControls;
using System;
using System.Collections.Generic;
using System.Text;
using System.Web.UI.WebControls;

namespace CustomWebParts
{
    public class CustomizedFilesWebPart : System.Web.UI.WebControls.WebParts.WebPart
    {
        private SPGridView GridView1;

        protected override void CreateChildControls()
        {
            GridView1 = new SPGridView();
            GridView1.ID = "GridView1";
            GridView1.AutoGenerateColumns = false;
            GridView1.DataKeyNames = new string[] { "UniqueId" };
            GridView1.EmptyDataText = "No files have beencustomized.";

            BoundField nameField = new BoundField();
            nameField.DataField = "Name";
            nameField.HeaderText = "Name";
            GridView1.Columns.Add(nameField);

            BoundField folderField = new BoundField();
            folderField.DataField = "ParentFolder";
            folderField.HeaderText = "Path";
            GridView1.Columns.Add(folderField);

            BoundField modifiedByField = new BoundField();
            modifiedByField.DataField = "ModifiedBy";
            modifiedByField.HeaderText = "Modified By";
```

```
            GridView1.Columns.Add(modifiedByField);

            BoundField modifiedDateField = new BoundField();
            modifiedDateField.DataField = "TimeLastModified";
            modifiedDateField.HeaderText = "Modified Date";
            GridView1.Columns.Add(modifiedDateField);

            CommandField revertField = new CommandField();
            revertField.DeleteText = "Revert";
            revertField.ShowDeleteButton = true;
            GridView1.Columns.Add(revertField);

            GridView1.RowDeleting += new GridViewDeleteEventHandler
    (GridView1_RowDeleting);
            this.Controls.Add(GridView1);
        }
    }
}
```

The final step in creating a custom Web Part is to add the functionality itself. You need to add code to the `OnLoad` method of the Web Part and handle the events of the controls inside your Web Part. The `OnLoad` method is called whenever the page loads for the first time or posts back to the server to run code. The `OnLoad` method is where you will put the code to populate the SPGridView with the list of customized files. The code only needs to populate the SPGridView the first time the page is loaded. The `IsPostBack` property of the Page class can be used to determine if the page is loading for the first time or loading because the user caused the page to post back to the server. Add this code after the `CreateChildControls` method, to override the `OnLoad` method and call the `BindData` method when the page is loaded for the first time:

VB.NET

```
Protected Overrides Sub OnLoad(ByVal e As System.EventArgs)
    If Not Page.IsPostBack Then
        BindData()
    End If
End Sub
```

C#

```
protected override void OnLoad(System.EventArgs e) {
    if (!Page.IsPostBack) {
        BindData();
    }
}
```

Next, you create the `RecurseHierarchy` method. The virtual file system inside SharePoint is represented using files and folders in the same way as in Windows Explorer. Files and folders are nested and create a tree or hierarchy. SharePoint provides the `SPFolder` and `SPFile` classes so that you can access these folders and files, but you have to write the `RecurseHierarchy` method in such a way that the method will call itself repeatedly for each child folder. This technique is called *recursion*. Recursion is commonly used to navigate a hierarchical structure, and you will use it to navigate your SharePoint site's virtual file system. You also need to create another private-class–level variable to store the list of customized files found during recursion. Add this code just after the declaration of the SPGridView to declare the List variable to contain the list of customized files:

VB.NET

```
Private fileList As List(Of SPFile)
```

C#

```
private List<SPFile> fileList;
```

This List variable looks different from other variables because it contains the name of another variable type inside the declaration. That means the List variable can only contain SPFile objects.

When the List variable has been declared, you can create the RecurseHierarchy method. Unlike some of the other methods created in this chapter, RecurseHierarchy requires an SPFolder parameter to indicate where in the hierarchy to look for files. Add the following code just before the end of the class to declare the RecurseHierarchy method:

VB.NET

```
Private Sub RecurseHierarchy(ByVal parentFolder As SPFolder)
End Sub
```

C#

```
private void RecurseHierarchy(SPFolder parentFolder) {
}
```

Using the SPFolder parameter and a for-each statement, you can loop through the files in the SPFolder and examine the CustomizedPageStatus property to see if the file has beencustomized. Additionally, the SPFolder class has a SubFolders property that you can also loop to work your way down the virtual file system. Add this code inside the RecurseHierarchy method to gather the customized files in the SPFolder and recurse its subfolders:

VB.NET

```
For Each file As SPFile In parentFolder.Files
    ' We only want customized pages.
    If file.CustomizedPageStatus = SPCustomizedPageStatus.Customized Then
        fileList.Add(file)
    End If
Next

For Each folder As SPFolder In parentFolder.SubFolders
    ' Ignore files in the Web Part Gallery.
    If folder.Name <> "wp" Then
        RecurseHierarchy(folder)
    End If
Next
```

C#

```csharp
foreach (SPFile file in parentFolder.Files) {
    // We only want customized pages.
    if (file.CustomizedPageStatus == SPCustomizedPageStatus.Customized) {
        fileList.Add(file);
    }
}

foreach (SPFolder folder in parentFolder.SubFolders) {
    // Ignore files in the Web Part Gallery.
    if (folder.Name != "wp") {
        RecurseHierarchy(folder);
    }
}
```

Notice that this code excludes folders named `"wp"`. The Web Part gallery that contains the list of Web Parts that are allowed to be used in the site always contains customized files, and you will not want to allow the user to revert them.

The next method to create is called `BindData`. It is called by the `OnLoad` method and in turn calls the `RecurseHierarchy` method using the root folder of the SharePoint site. It also calls a method named `EnsureChildControls`, which calls the `CreateChildControls` method if it has not already done so. Call the `EnsureChildControls` method at the top of any method that accesses the controls in the Web Part, or you risk getting an error because the control might not have been created yet. However, never call the `EnsureChildControls` method from the `CreateChildControls` method, or you could crash the SharePoint server. Add the following code to define the `BindData` method and call the `EnsureChildControls` method:

VB.NET

```vbnet
Private Sub BindData()
    EnsureChildControls()
End Sub
```

C#

```csharp
private void BindData() {
    EnsureChildControls();
}
```

Before you can call the `RecurseHierarchy` method, you need to instantiate the `List` variable used to store the customized files and get a reference to the current SharePoint site to pass its root folder as a parameter. The current SharePoint site can be obtained using the `SPControl` class's `GetContextWeb` method. `GetContextWeb` returns an SPWeb object that represents the current SharePoint site. The `SPWeb` class has a `RootFolder` property that returns an SPFolder object representing the root folder of the site. Add the following code to the end of the `BindData` method to instantiate the `List` variable, get a reference to the current SharePoint site, and call the `RecurseHierarchy` method:

VB.NET

```vbnet
Dim site As SPWeb = SPControl.GetContextWeb(Me.Context)
fileList = New List(Of SPFile)()

RecurseHierarchy(site.RootFolder)
```

C#

```
SPWeb site = SPControl.GetContextWeb(this.Context);
fileList = new List<SPFile>();

RecurseHierarchy(site.RootFolder);
```

The final step in completing the BindData method is to bind the List variable to the SPGridView. The DataSource property of the SPGridView class is used to set the source of data from which it creates rows. The DataBind method of the SPGridView class is called to cause the SPGridView to create the rows from its DataSource property. Add this code to finish the BindData method:

VB.NET

```
GridView1.DataSource = fileList
GridView1.DataBind()
```

C#

```
GridView1.DataSource = fileList;
GridView1.DataBind();
```

Your BindData method should now look like this:

VB.NET

```
Private Sub BindData()
    EnsureChildControls()

    Dim site As SPWeb = SPControl.GetContextWeb(Me.Context)
    fileList = New List(Of SPFile)()

    RecurseHierarchy(site.RootFolder)

    GridView1.DataSource = fileList
    GridView1.DataBind()
End Sub
```

C#

```
private void BindData()
{
    EnsureChildControls();

    SPWeb site = SPControl.GetContextWeb(this.Context);
    fileList = new List<SPFile>();

    RecurseHierarchy(site.RootFolder);

    GridView1.DataSource = fileList;
    GridView1.DataBind();
}
```

The final method to create is `GridView1_RowDeleting`, which is called when the user clicks the CommandField of the SPGridView. This method has a `GridViewCommandEventArgs` parameter that indicates which row was clicked by the user. Once the row has been determined, you can get an `SPFile` class and revert the file. Begin creating `GridView1_RowDeleting` with the following code:

VB.NET

```
Protected Sub GridView1_RowDeleting(ByVal sender As Object, ByVal e As
System.Web.UI.WebControls. GridViewDeleteEventArgs)

End Sub
```

C#

```
protected void GridView1_RowDeleting(object sender, GridViewDeleteEventArgs e) {


}
```

Then use the `RowIndex` property of the `GridViewDeleteEventArgs` parameter to get the unique ID of the file. Add this code inside the `GridView1_RowDeleting` method:

VB.NET

```
Dim fileUniqueId As Guid = CType(GridView1.DataKeys(e.RowIndex).Value, Guid)
```

C#

```
Guid fileUniqueId = (Guid) GridView1.DataKeys[e.RowIndex].Value;
```

Now that you have the unique ID of the file, you need to get a reference to the SPWeb representing the current site and call its `GetFile` method to get the SPFile that you need to revert. Add this code just before the end of the `GridView1_RowDeleting` method:

VB.NET

```
Dim site As SPWeb = SPControl.GetContextWeb(Me.Context)
Dim file As SPFile = site.GetFile(fileUniqueId)
```

C#

```
SPWeb site = SPControl.GetContextWeb(this.Context);
SPFile file = site.GetFile(fileUniqueId);
```

To complete the `GridView1_RowDeleting` method, call the `RevertContentStream` method of the `SPFile` class, which will revert the file and restore it to its original, uncustomized state. Afterward, call the `BindData` method to refresh the rows in the SPGridView. Add the following code to the end of the `GridView1_RowDeleting` method:

VB.NET

```
file.RevertContentStream()

BindData()
```

C#

```
file.RevertContentStream();

BindData();
```

The finished `GridView1_RowDeleting` method should look as follows:

VB.NET

```
Protected Sub GridView1_RowDeleting(ByVal sender As Object, ByVal e As
System.Web .UI.WebControls.GridViewDeleteEventArgs)
Dim fileUniqueId As Guid = CType(GridView1.DataKeys(e.RowIndex).Value, Guid)

Dim site As SPWeb = SPControl.GetContextWeb(Me.Context)
Dim file As SPFile = site.GetFile(fileUniqueId)

file.RevertContentStream()

BindData()
End Sub
```

C#

```
protected void GridView1_RowDeleting(object sender, GridViewDeleteEventArgs e)
{
    Guid fileUniqueId = (Guid)GridView1.DataKeys[e.RowIndex].Value;

    SPWeb site = SPControl.GetContextWeb(this.Context);
    SPFile file = site.GetFile(fileUniqueId);

    file.RevertContentStream();

    BindData();
}
```

Compile your Web Part Project by selecting Build ⇨ Build Solution and fix any compilation errors.

Your custom Web Part is now complete, so you can deploy it to SharePoint and test it. The next section provides the details.

Deploying and Configuring Your Web Part

There are three steps to deploying your Web Part:

❑ Add the assembly to the Global Assembly Cache.

❑ Update the `web.config` file.

❑ Add your Web Part to the Web Part gallery.

Adding the Assembly to the Global Assembly Cache

The Global Assembly Cache stores assemblies that are shared among server processes. Most SharePoint-related assemblies must be placed in the Global Assembly Cache before SharePoint can use them. This restriction also applies to custom actions. However, placing assemblies in the Global Assembly Cache can be very dangerous because the assemblies are accessible to the entire SharePoint farm and run without any restrictions on the code allowed to run inside SharePoint. You can reduce this risk by examining the code of all assemblies to be placed in the Global Assembly Cache, including those from third parties. It is better to err on the side of caution than to risk the health and stability of your SharePoint farm.

To deploy the assembly, open Windows Explorer and navigate to the c:\windows\assembly folder. Drag your DLL file into the folder, and it is automatically added to the Global Assembly Cache. An easy way to find the location of your compiled DLL is to check the Output window in Visual Studio. If you cannot see the Output window, select View ⇨ Output in Visual Studio. Make sure the dropdown list in the Output window is set to Build. If you previously added your assembly to the Global Assembly Cache, you must restart IIS before your assembly is recognized by SharePoint. To restart IIS, choose Start ⇨ Run, type **iisreset** into the Run box, and click OK.

Update the web.config File

You need to update the web.config file to allow SharePoint to use your Web Part. Follow these steps to add the appropriate tags to web.config:

1. If it is not already open, open the Output window by selecting View ⇨ Output.

2. Build the custom Web Part assembly by selecting Build ⇨ Build Solution.

3. Note the location of the compiled DLL. For example:

```
CustomWebParts -> C:\Users\username\Documents\Visual Studio 2008\Projects\
CustomWebParts\bin\CustomWebParts.dll
```

4. Open the Visual Studio Command Prompt by clicking Start ⇨ All Programs ⇨ Microsoft Visual Studio 2005 (or 2008) ⇨ Visual Studio Tools ⇨ Microsoft Visual Studio 2005 (or 2008) Command prompt.

5. Type sn.exe -T *assemblypath*, where *assemblypath* is the location of the DLL from step 3. If *assemblypath* contains spaces, you must enclose it in quotation marks.

6. Note the value indicated. For example:

```
Microsoft (R) .NET Framework Strong Name Utility  Version 3.5.21022.8
Copyright (c) Microsoft Corporation.  All rights reserved.

Public key token is a4d44e6df3f4f726
```

7. Back up your `web.config` file. If you misconfigure the `web.config` file, your SharePoint site will not function anymore until you correct the file. The default location of `web.config` is `C:\inetpub\wwwroot\wss\VirtualDirectories\`*portnumber*`\web.config`, where *portnumber* is the port number of your SharePoint web application.

8. Open the `web.config` file.

9. Locate the tag named `<SafeControls>`. Inside it, add a tag named `<SafeControl>` with these attributes (without quotes):

Attribute	Value
Assembly	`"CustomWebParts, Version=1.0.0.0, Culture=neutral, PublicKeyToken=XXXXX"`
	where XXXXX is the value obtained from step 6
Namespace	`"CustomWebParts"`
TypeName	`"*"`
Safe	`"True"`
AllowRemoteDesigner	`"True"`

10. Save the `web.config` file.

Your `web.config` should look like this:

```
<!-- snipped code -->

<SafeControls>

<!-- snipped code -->

<SafeControl Assembly="CustomWebParts, Version=1.0.0.0, Culture=neutral,
PublicKeyToken=XXXXX"
             Namespace="CustomWebParts"
             TypeName="*"
             Safe="True"
             AllowRemoteDesigner="True" />
<!--  where XXXXX is the value obtained from step 6. -->

<!-- snipped code -->

</SafeControls>

<!-- snipped code -->
```

Where XXXXX is the value obtained in step 6.

Add Your Web Part to the Web Part Gallery

To add your Web Part to the Web Part gallery, navigate to your SharePoint site and choose Site Actions ⇨ Site Settings. After the Site Settings screen is displayed (see Figure 16-9), click the Web Parts link in the Galleries section.

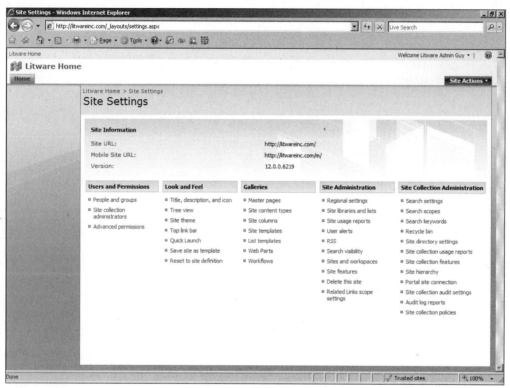

Figure 16-9

On the Web Part Gallery screen (see Figure 16-10), click New.

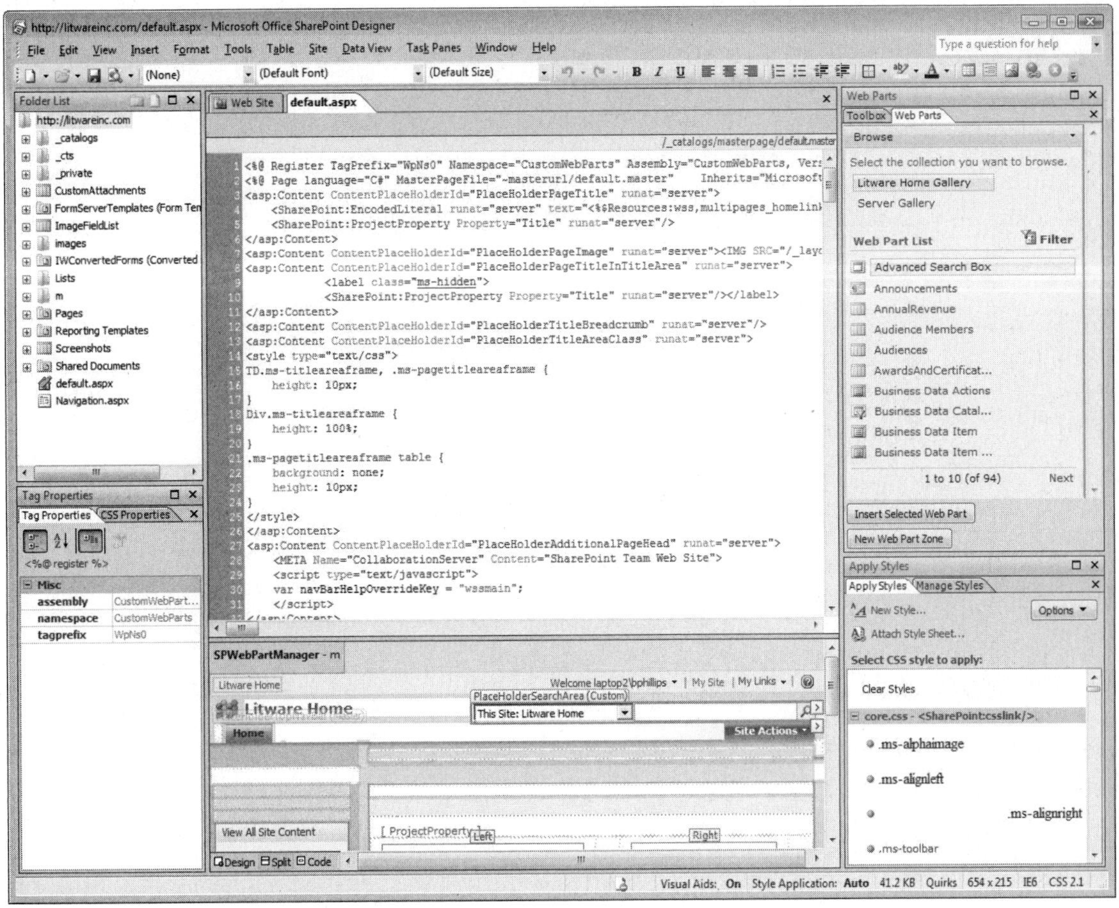

Figure 16-10

The New Web Parts screen (see Figure 16-11) opens. Locate the Web Part named `CustomWebParts` `.CustomizedFilesWebPart` and check the check box to the left. Finally, click the Populate Gallery button to return to the Web Part Gallery.

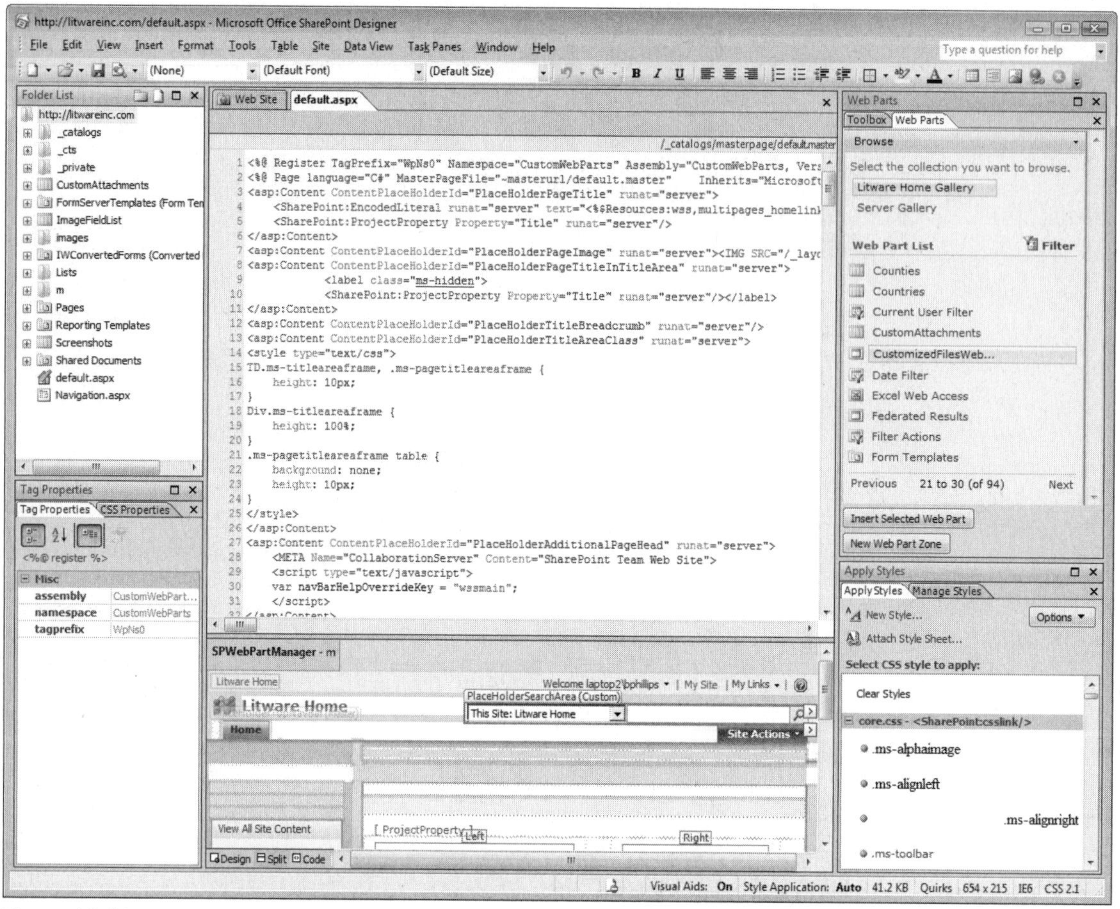

Figure 16-11

Testing Your Web Part

To test your custom Web Part, open SharePoint Designer and navigate to your SharePoint site by selecting File ➪ Open Site, entering the URL to your SharePoint site in the Site name text box of the Open Site dialog, and clicking OK. Open the `Default.aspx` page (see Figure 16-12) by double-clicking it. If the Web Parts task pane is not visible, open the task pane by choosing Task Panes ➪ Web Parts from the menu bar. Once the task pane is displayed (Figure 16-12), click Next until `CustomizedFilesWebPart` is displayed in the list.

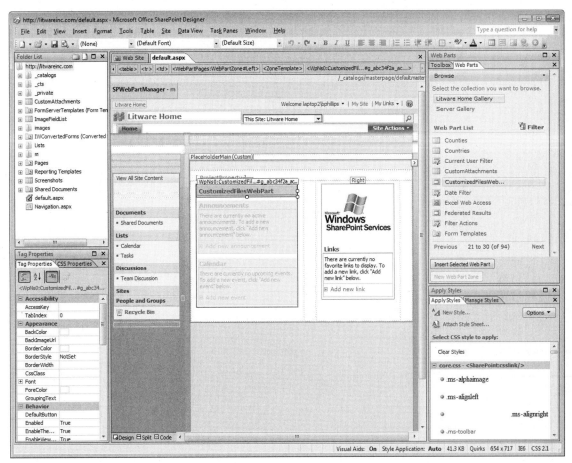

Figure 16-12

To add the Web Part to the page, drag the Web Part from the task pane and drop it into one of the Web Part Zones on the page. Web Part Zones are the locations on the page where Web Parts can be added and positioned. They have labels above them describing their relative position on the page. In Figure 16-13, the two Web Part Zones are named Left and Right. Your page should look like Figure 16-13 in SharePoint Designer.

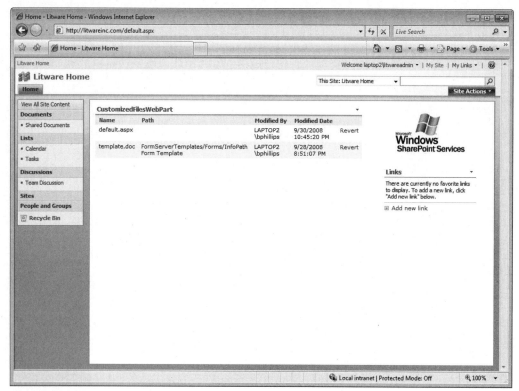

Figure 16-13

Once you save your page, you get a warning dialog. Click Yes to continue. Navigate to the page in the browser, and the Web Part should display the list of customized files in your site (see Figure 16-14).

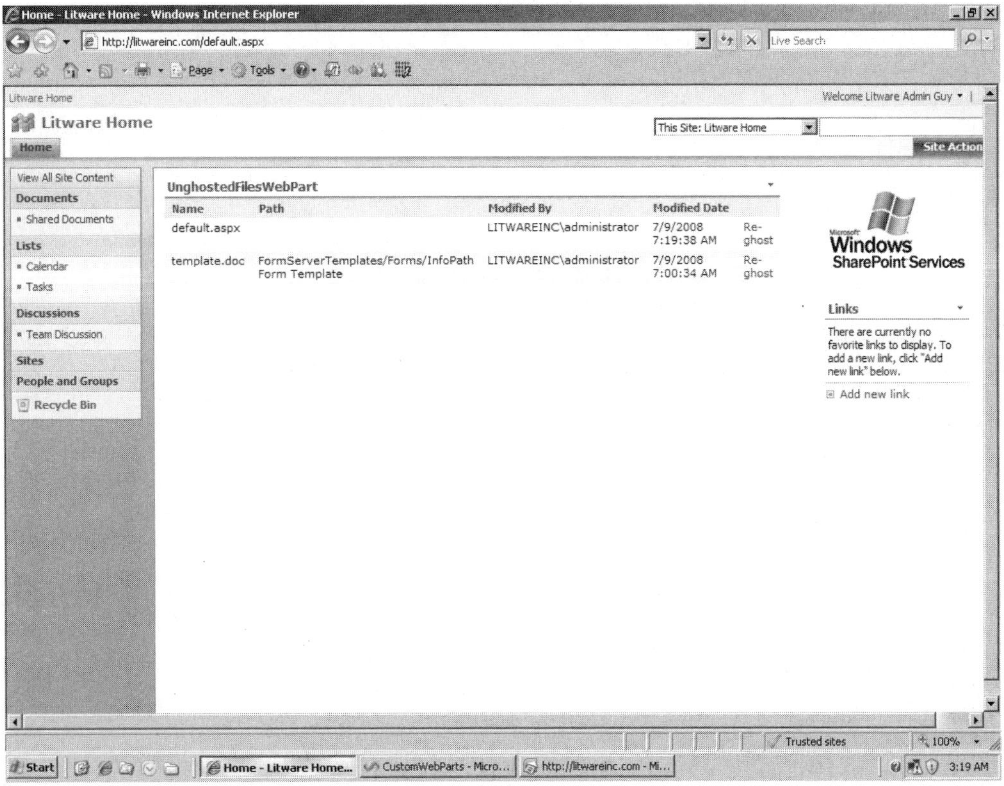

Figure 16-14

To test the functionality of the Web Part, customize a file in SharePoint Designer. In the browser, refresh the page and click the Revert link beside your customized file. The Web Part will undo your customization. If you refresh your files and folders in SharePoint Designer, you will note that the file is no longer customized.

Troubleshooting Problems

During the process of creating your Web Part, deploying it, and using it in SharePoint Designer, you can encounter various errors. This section will list some of those errors and how to resolve them.

❑ **Error: Your custom Web Part does not appear in SharePoint Designer.**

❑ Ensure that your assembly has been added to the Global Assembly Cache, the `web.config` file has been updated to mark your Web Part as Safe, and the Web Part Gallery has been populated.

❑ **Error: You have updated your custom Web Part, but the Web Part does not appear to have been updated.**

❑   Ensure that you have added your assembly to the Global Assembly Cache and that you have restarted IIS.

❑   **Error: You cannot add your Web Part to a Web Part Zone.**

❑   Ensure that `web.config` has been updated to mark your Web Part as Safe and that the Web Part Gallery has been populated.

Summary

People commonly create custom Web Parts to extend the functionality of SharePoint, as in this chapter's example, or to display information from other line of business systems and SharePoint itself. With custom Web Parts, you can greatly enhance the SharePoint user experience through the creation of customizable portals, dashboards, and workspaces, and take your SharePoint farm to the next level.

17

Creating SharePoint Designer Add-ins

You've already seen how to extend the power of SharePoint with custom-written actions and Web Parts, and how to use those enhancements in SharePoint Designer. Now this chapter shows you how to extend the power of SharePoint Designer itself, by creating add-ins using Visual Studio .NET.

This chapter:

❑ Explains how to install SharePoint Designer add-in templates.

❑ Leads you through creating a SharePoint add-in.

❑ Describes how to test your add-in.

❑ Shows you how to deploy your add-in.

What You Need to Get Started

Before you can jump in and create new add-ins, ensure that you have the correct tools:

❑ Microsoft Visual Studio 2008.

❑ Visual Studio Tools for Office templates for SharePoint Designer add-ins available from `www.codeplex.com/VSTO/Release/ProjectReleases.aspx?ReleaseId=17375`

Introducing Visual Studio Tools for Office Add-ins

Visual Studio Tools for Office (VSTO) provides the functionality to create add-ins for Office 2007 applications, including Excel, InfoPath, Outlook, PowerPoint, Project, Visio, and Word. SharePoint Designer isn't on that list because creating binary add-ins for SharePoint Designer with VSTO is not officially supported by Microsoft. The good news is that there's still enough of the plumbing inside Visual Studio Tools for Office for you to create SharePoint Designer add-ins regardless. To make the creation of these add-ins much easier, install the SharePoint Designer add-in Project templates.

Installing the SharePoint Designer Add-In Project Templates

If you haven't already done so, download the Project templates from the CodePlex web site. Extract the zip file to any directory. Double-click the extracted file, `VSTOSPD2007AddInTemplates.vsi`, to open the Visual Studio Content Installer dialog (see Figure 17-1). Choose to install the add-in Projects for Visual Basic.NET, C#, or both.

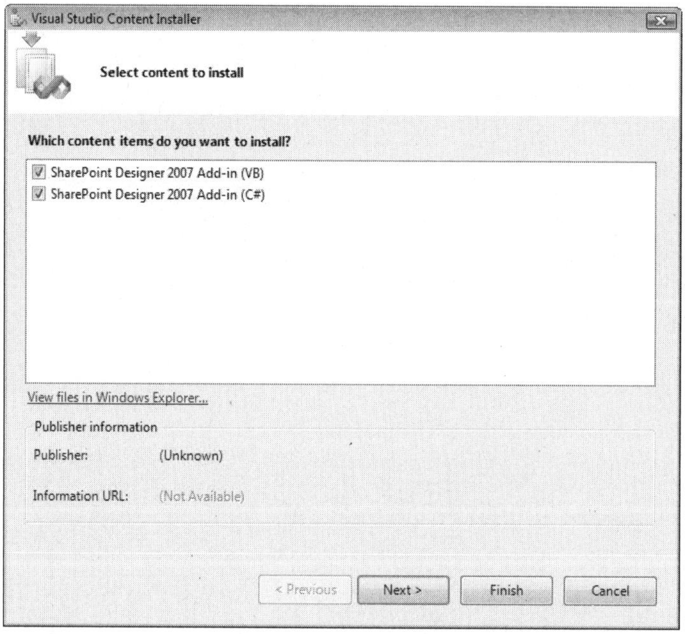

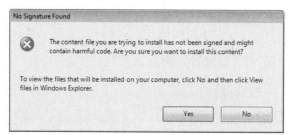

Figure 17-1

After selecting the add-in Projects you want to install, click Next. If you get the dialog shown in Figure 17-2, click Yes. Afterward, click Finish to start the process of importing the templates.

Figure 17-2

If you are reimporting the templates, you get the File exists dialog (see Figure 17-3). Select the option Overwrite the file with the same name, and click OK. The dialog serves as a warning because it will be overwriting the previously imported templates. Be aware that the dialog appears each time it needs to overwrite a file.

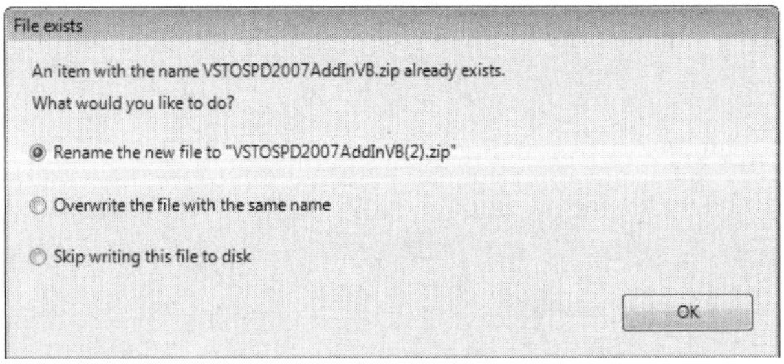

Figure 17-3

The installer shows the results of the installation (see Figure 17-4). Click Close to exit the Visual Studio Content Installer.

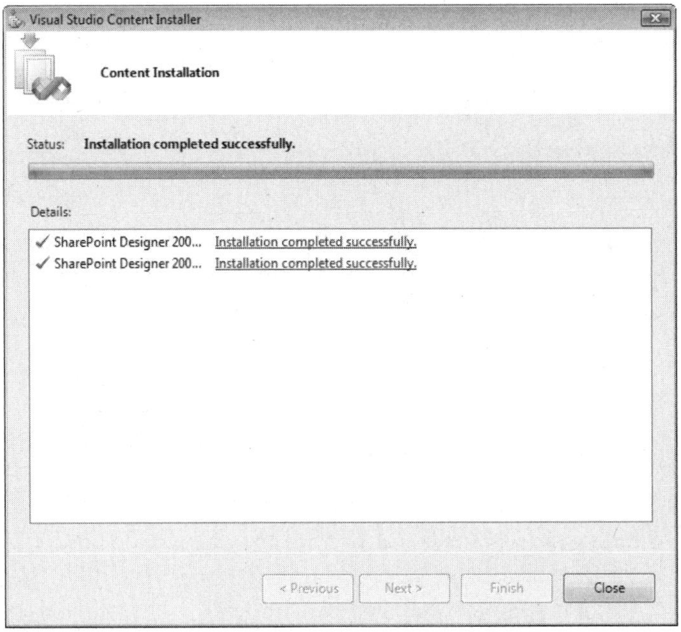

Figure 17-4

With the Project templates installed, you're ready to create your first SharePoint Designer add-in. The next section shows how to create a SharePoint Designer add-in that can export a SharePoint Designer workflow for use in Visual Studio.

Note that, while the source code for the add-in is provided in both C# and Visual Basic.NET, the add-in being created only generates workflow source files for C#.

437

Creating Your Add-In

Chapters 9 and 15 showed you how to build workflows using SharePoint Designer with built-in and custom-written actions. While those workflows are powerful, they are not easily portable. In fact, those workflows cannot be associated with any other lists or document libraries, as built-in workflows or Visual Studio–created workflows can. However, by exporting the workflow files and making a few modifications, these SharePoint Designer–created workflows can be transformed into Visual Studio workflows.

To create a SharePoint Designer add-in, open Visual Studio 2008 and select File ⇨ New ⇨ Project. The New Project dialog (Figure 17-5) appears. Select either Visual C# or Visual Basic from the Project types list, and select SharePoint Designer 2007 Add-in Project from the templates list. Enter **SPDWorkflowExporter** as the name for the Project, and click the OK button.

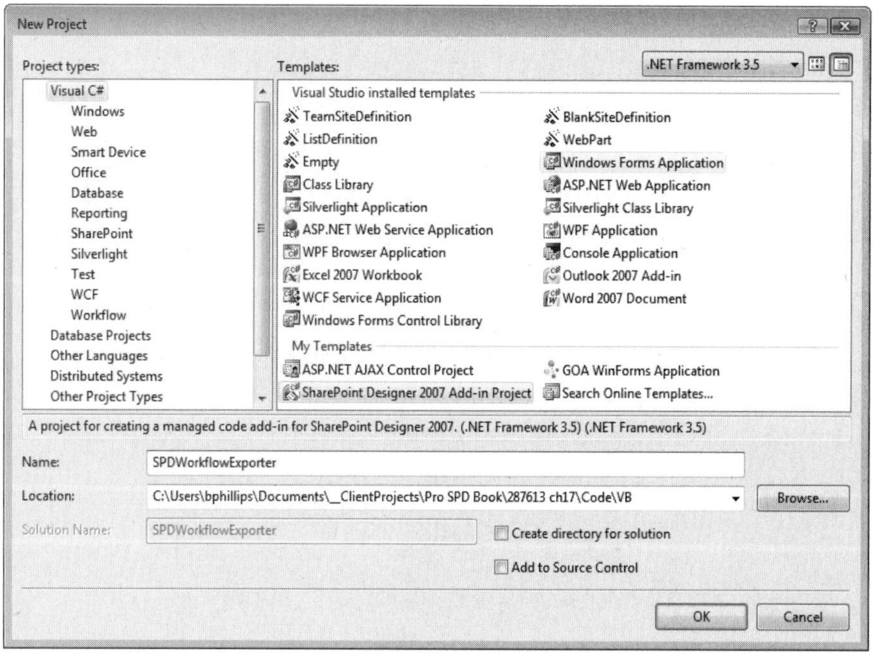

Figure 17-5

Because the Project templates are not marked as safe in the Registry, the Security Warning dialog shown in Figure 17-6 will appear. Select the option Load Project normally, and click the OK button. You can click More Details if you want instructions on disabling the warning for these Project templates.

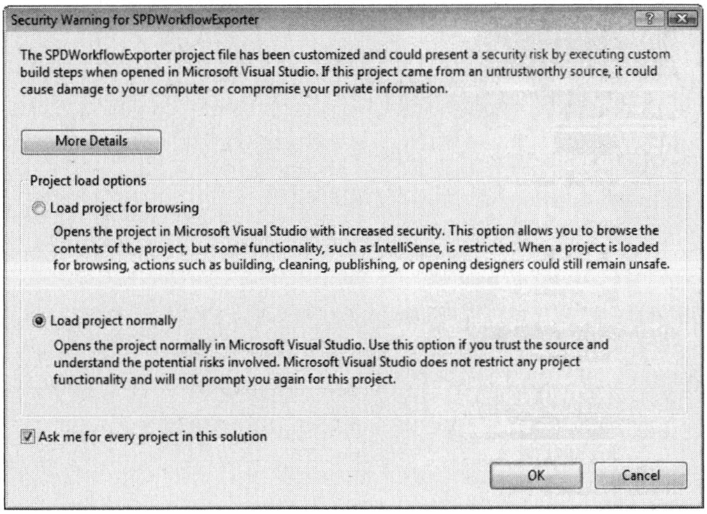

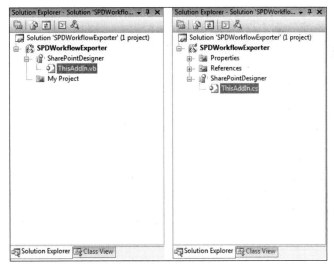

Figure 17-6

Visual Studio creates the Project, and presents it to you (Figure 17-7 shows the VB version on the left and the C# one on the right). If the file is not already open, open the `ThisAddIn.vb` or `ThisAddIn.cs` file to begin adding code to extend SharePoint Designer. The `ThisAddIn` file contains two methods: `ThisAddIn_Startup`, which is called when the add-in is loaded, and `ThisAddIn_Shutdown`, which is called when the add-in is unloaded.

Figure 17-7

Before you enter code in the `ThisAddIn` file, add these statements to the top of the file replacing any existing Imports or using statements:

VB.NET

```
Imports Microsoft.Office.Core
Imports Microsoft.Office.Interop.SharePointDesigner
Imports System.Diagnostics
Imports System.IO
Imports System.Reflection
Imports System.Windows.Forms
Imports System.Xml
```

C#

```
using Microsoft.Office.Core;
using Microsoft.Office.Interop.SharePointDesigner;
using System;
using System.Diagnostics;
using System.IO;
using System.Reflection;
using System.Windows.Forms;
using System.Xml;
```

Now, you can start modifying the code to add a new option to the context menu of SharePoint Designer that will run your code whenever the user selects it. Inside the `ThisAddIn_Startup` method, add the following code, which creates an option named "Export workflow" that will call the `exportButton_Click` method when selected:

VB.NET

```
For Each commandbar As CommandBar In Me.Application.CommandBars
    If commandbar.Id = 1324 OrElse commandbar.Id = 1319 Then
        Dim exportButton As CommandBarButton = _
CType(commandbar.Controls.Add(MsoControlType.msoControlButton, 1, _
Nothing, 1, True), CommandBarButton)
        exportButton.Caption = "Export workflow"
        AddHandler exportButton.Click, AddressOf exportButton_Click
    End If
Next
```

C#

```
foreach (CommandBar commandbar in this.Application.CommandBars) {
    if (commandbar.Id == 1324 || commandbar.Id == 1319) {
        CommandBarButton exportButton = (CommandBarButton) ←
commandbar.Controls.Add(MsoControlType.msoControlButton, 1, null, 1, true);
        exportButton.Caption = "Export workflow";
        exportButton.Click += new
_CommandBarButtonEvents_ClickEventHandler(exportButton_Click);
    }
}
```

Next, create the `exportButton_Click` method by adding the following code inside the `ThisAddIn` class:

VB.NET

```vbnet
Private Sub exportButton_Click(ByVal Ctrl As CommandBarButton, _
ByRef CancelDefault As Boolean)

End Sub
```

C#

```csharp
private void exportButton_Click(CommandBarButton Ctrl, ref bool CancelDefault) {

}
```

The exportButton_Click method will contain the functionality to export the workflow files from SharePoint Designer and modify them. To clean up memory and display a message to the user should an error occur, add the following code inside exportButton_Click. You must add a try-catch block to the method to display a message to the user when exceptions occur. SharePoint Designer suppresses unhandled exceptions, leaving your user in the dark when your functionality does not work.

VB.NET

```vbnet
Dim dialog As FolderBrowserDialog = Nothing
Dim process As Process = Nothing

Try

Catch ex As Exception
    MessageBox.Show("Error exporting workflow:" + ex.Message)
Finally
    If dialog IsNot Nothing Then
        dialog.Dispose()
    End If

    If process IsNot Nothing Then
        process.Dispose()
    End If
End Try
```

C#

```csharp
FolderBrowserDialog dialog = null;
Process process = null;

try {

} catch (Exception ex) {
    MessageBox.Show("Error exporting workflow:" + ex.Message);
} finally {
    if (dialog != null) {
        dialog.Dispose();
    }

    if (process != null) {
        process.Dispose();
    }
}
```

Because there is not a separate context menu for the workflows in the SharePoint site's Workflows folder, you must determine if the user has selected a folder in SharePoint Designer and if that folder contains a workflow. Otherwise, the user could click Export, and the code would try to export a workflow that did not exist. All workflow folders contain a file with the XOML extension. Add the following code inside the `try` section of the `try-catch-finally` block to implement these checks:

VB.NET

```
If Me.Application.ActiveWebWindow.SelectedFolders.Length <> 1 Then
    Return
End If

Dim workflowFolder As WebFolder = Me.Application.ActiveWebWindow.SelectedFolders(0)

' Check if folder selected contains a workflow.
Dim isWorkflowFolder As Boolean = False
For Each file As WebFile In workflowFolder.Files
    If file.Name.EndsWith("xoml") Then
        isWorkflowFolder = True
        Exit For
    End If
Next

If Not isWorkflowFolder Then
    Return
End If
```

C#

```
if (this.Application.ActiveWebWindow.SelectedFolders.Length != 1) {
    return;
}

WebFolder workflowFolder = (WebFolder) ↩
this.Application.ActiveWebWindow.SelectedFolders.GetValue(0);

// Check if folder selected contains a workflow.
Boolean isWorkflowFolder = false;
foreach (WebFile file in workflowFolder.Files) {
    if (file.Name.EndsWith("xoml")) {
        isWorkflowFolder = true;
        break;
    }
}

if (!isWorkflowFolder) {
    return;
}
```

If the running code has not exited at this point, the `workflowFolder` variable will contain a reference to the folder containing the workflow files. Now, you need to prompt the user for the destination folder for the exported files. Add the following code before the end of the `try` section of the `try-catch-finally` block to use the `FolderBrowserDialog` to get the user's desired export path:

VB.NET

```
dialog = New FolderBrowserDialog()
dialog.Description = "Select an output path for the workflow."

If dialog.ShowDialog() = DialogResult.OK Then
    Dim outputPath As String = dialog.SelectedPath

    If Not outputPath.EndsWith("\") Then
        outputPath &= "\"
    End If

End If
```

C#

```
dialog = new FolderBrowserDialog();
dialog.Description = "Select an output path for the workflow.";

if (dialog.ShowDialog() == DialogResult.OK) {
    string outputPath = dialog.SelectedPath;

    if (!outputPath.EndsWith("\\")) {
        outputPath += "\\";
    }
}
```

If the user selects a path and clicks OK in the `FolderBrowserDialog` form, you can export the workflow files. SharePoint Designer does not allow your code to directly access the content of XOML files, but it does provide the `WebPackage` class that allows you to package up any number of files and download them as a single unit. Add this code to the end of the `exportButton_Click` method to package the selected workflow's files and download them to the destination folder:

VB.NET

```
Dim workflowName As String = workflowFolder.Name
Dim outputPackagePath As String = outputPath & workflowName & ".fwp"
Dim extractPath As String = outputPath & workflowName

' Export the files via a web package.
Dim package As WebPackage = Me.Application.ActiveWeb.CreatePackage(workflowName)

For Each file As WebFile In workflowFolder.Files
    package.Add(file.Url, PackageDependencyFlags.PackageDependencyNone)
Next

package.Save(outputPackagePath, True)
```

C#

```
string workflowName = workflowFolder.Name;
string outputPackagePath = outputPath + workflowName + ".fwp";
string extractPath = outputPath + workflowName;

// Export the files via a web package.
```

```
WebPackage package = this.Application.ActiveWeb.CreatePackage(workflowName);

foreach (WebFile file in workflowFolder.Files) {
    package.Add(file.Url, PackageDependencyFlags.PackageDependencyNone);
}

package.Save(outputPackagePath, 1);
```

Once the package has been downloaded, it must be extracted to manipulate the files. This package is in CAB format, which is not supported in the .NET Framework. Instead, you can use the `Process` class to run the `expand.exe` utility to extract the package. Insert the following code just after the previous code, to extract the downloaded package:

VB.NET

```
' Create temp folder.
If Not Directory.Exists(extractPath) Then
    Directory.CreateDirectory(extractPath)
End If

' Extract the files.
Dim commandLine As String = """" & outputPackagePath & """ -F:* """ & ←
extractPath & """"

Dim startInfo As New ProcessStartInfo("c:\windows\system32\expand.exe", ←
commandLine)
startInfo.UseShellExecute = False

process = New Process()
process.StartInfo = startInfo
process.Start()
process.WaitForExit()
```

C#

```
// Create temp folder.
if (!Directory.Exists(extractPath)) {
    Directory.CreateDirectory(extractPath);
}

// Extract the files.
string commandLine = "\"" + outputPackagePath + "\" -F:* \"" + extractPath + "\"";

ProcessStartInfo startInfo = new ←
ProcessStartInfo(@"c:\windows\system32\expand.exe", commandLine);
startInfo.UseShellExecute = false;

process = new Process();
process.StartInfo = startInfo;
process.Start();
process.WaitForExit();
```

Finally, the extracted files are ready for processing. Web packages contain a file named `manifest.xml`, which lists the files in the package and their real names. The following code snippet uses `manifest.xml` to rename the extracted files to their original names. Add the code just after the previous snippet:

VB.NET

```
' Rename extracted files.
Dim manifest As New XmlDocument()
manifest.Load(extractPath & "\manifest.xml")

For Each fileNode As XmlElement In manifest.SelectNodes("//File")
    If File.Exists(outputPath & fileNode.Attributes("Name").InnerText) Then
        File.Delete(outputPath & fileNode.Attributes("Name").InnerText)
    End If

    File.Move(extractPath & "\" & fileNode.Attributes("Src").InnerText, _
outputPath & fileNode.Attributes("Name").InnerText)
Next

' Remove temp folder.
If Directory.Exists(extractPath) Then
    Directory.Delete(extractPath, True)
End If

' Remove package.
If File.Exists(outputPackagePath) Then
    File.Delete(outputPackagePath)
End If
```

C#

```
// Rename extracted files.
XmlDocument manifest = new XmlDocument();
manifest.Load(extractPath + @"\manifest.xml");

foreach (XmlElement fileNode in manifest.SelectNodes("//File")) {
    if (File.Exists(outputPath + fileNode.Attributes["Name"].InnerText)) {
        File.Delete(outputPath + fileNode.Attributes["Name"].InnerText);
    }

    File.Move(extractPath + "\\" + fileNode.Attributes["Src"].InnerText, ↩
outputPath + fileNode.Attributes["Name"].InnerText);
}

// Remove temp folder.
if (Directory.Exists(extractPath)) {
    Directory.Delete(extractPath, true);
}

// Remove package.
if (File.Exists(outputPackagePath)) {
    File.Delete(outputPackagePath);
}
```

The final step to process the workflow files is to modify their contents. The following code renames the workflow's rules file, if one exists; adds an event handler to the workflow; removes an unnecessary workflow activity; and exports a C# class file containing the workflow's event handlers. This code finishes the add-in:

VB.NET

```
If File.Exists(outputPath & workflowName & ".xoml.rules") Then
    ' Rename rules file.
    If File.Exists(outputPath & workflowName & ".rules") Then
        File.Delete(outputPath & workflowName & ".rules")
    End If

    File.Move(outputPath & workflowName & ".xoml.rules", outputPath & ↵
workflowName & ".rules")
End If

' Process the workflow file.
Dim xomlFile As New XmlDocument()
xomlFile.Load(outputPath & workflowName & ".xoml")

' Modify workflow activation code.
Dim activationActivity As XmlNode = xomlFile.SelectSingleNode("//*[local-↵
name()='OnWorkflowActivated']")
Dim invokedAttribute As XmlAttribute = xomlFile.CreateAttribute("Invoked")
invokedAttribute.InnerText = activationActivity.Attributes("x:Name").InnerText ↵
& "_Invoked"
activationActivity.Attributes.Append(invokedAttribute)
Dim applyActivation As XmlNode = xomlFile.SelectSingleNode("//*[local-↵
name()='ApplyActivation']")
applyActivation.ParentNode.RemoveChild(applyActivation)
xomlFile.Save(outputPath & workflowName & ".xoml")

' Export cs file.
Dim asm As Assembly = Assembly.GetExecutingAssembly()
Dim stream As Stream = ↵
asm.GetManifestResourceStream("SPDWorkflowExporter.Workflow.cs")
Dim b(stream.Length) As Byte
stream.Read(b, 0, b.Length)
stream.Close()

If File.Exists(outputPath & workflowName & ".xoml.cs") Then
    File.Delete(outputPath & workflowName & ".xoml.cs")
End If

Dim writer As FileStream = File.Create(outputPath & workflowName & ".xoml.cs")
writer.Write(b, 0, b.Length)
writer.Close()

MessageBox.Show("Workflow exported successfully.")
```

C#

```csharp
if (File.Exists(outputPath + workflowName + ".xoml.rules")) {
    // Rename rules file.
    if (File.Exists(outputPath + workflowName + ".rules")) {
        File.Delete(outputPath + workflowName + ".rules");
    }

    File.Move(outputPath + workflowName + ".xoml.rules", outputPath + 
workflowName + ".rules");
}

// Process the workflow file.
XmlDocument xomlFile = new XmlDocument();
xomlFile.Load(outputPath + workflowName + ".xoml");

// Modify workflow activation code.
XmlNode activationActivity = xomlFile.SelectSingleNode("//*[local-
name()='OnWorkflowActivated']");
XmlAttribute invokedAttribute = xomlFile.CreateAttribute("Invoked");
invokedAttribute.InnerText = activationActivity.Attributes["x:Name"].InnerText 
+ "_Invoked";
activationActivity.Attributes.Append(invokedAttribute);
XmlNode applyActivation = xomlFile.SelectSingleNode("//*[local-
name()='ApplyActivation']");
applyActivation.ParentNode.RemoveChild(applyActivation);
xomlFile.Save(outputPath + workflowName + ".xoml");

// Export cs file.
Assembly asm = Assembly.GetExecutingAssembly();
Stream stream = asm.GetManifestResourceStream("SPDWorkflowExporter.Workflow.cs");
Byte[] b = new Byte[stream.Length];
stream.Read(b, 0, b.Length);
stream.Close();

if (File.Exists(outputPath + workflowName + ".xoml.cs")) {
    File.Delete(outputPath + workflowName + ".xoml.cs");
}

FileStream writer = File.Create(outputPath + workflowName + ".xoml.cs");
writer.Write(b, 0, b.Length);
writer.Close();

MessageBox.Show("Workflow exported successfully.");
```

The final contents of the `ThisAddIn` class file should look like this:

VB.NET

```vbnet
Imports Microsoft.Office.Core
Imports Microsoft.Office.Interop.SharePointDesigner
Imports System.Diagnostics
Imports System.IO
Imports System.Reflection
Imports System.Windows.Forms
Imports System.Xml


Public Class ThisAddIn

    Private Sub ThisAddIn_Startup(ByVal sender As Object, ByVal e As ←
System.EventArgs) Handles Me.Startup
        For Each commandbar As CommandBar In Me.Application.CommandBars
            If commandbar.Id = 1324 OrElse commandbar.Id = 1319 Then
                Dim exportButton As CommandBarButton = _
                CType(commandbar.Controls.Add(MsoControlType.msoControlButton, 1, _
                Nothing, 1, True), CommandBarButton)
                exportButton.Caption = "Export workflow"
                AddHandler exportButton.Click, AddressOf exportButton_Click
            End If
        Next
    End Sub

    Private Sub ThisAddIn_Shutdown(ByVal sender As Object, ByVal e As ←
System.EventArgs) Handles Me.Shutdown

    End Sub

    Private Sub exportButton_Click(ByVal Ctrl As CommandBarButton, ByRef ←
CancelDefault As Boolean)
        Dim dialog As FolderBrowserDialog = Nothing
        Dim process As Process = Nothing

        Try
            If Me.Application.ActiveWebWindow.SelectedFolders.Length <> 1 Then
                Return
            End If

            Dim workflowFolder As WebFolder = ←
Me.Application.ActiveWebWindow.SelectedFolders(0)

                ' Check if folder selected contains a workflow.
                Dim isWorkflowFolder As Boolean = False
                For Each file As WebFile In workflowFolder.Files
                    If file.Name.EndsWith("xoml") Then
                        isWorkflowFolder = True
                        Exit For
                    End If
                Next

                If Not isWorkflowFolder Then
```

```
                     Return
                 End If

                 dialog = New FolderBrowserDialog()
                 dialog.Description = "Select an output path for the workflow."

                 If dialog.ShowDialog() = DialogResult.OK Then
                     Dim outputPath As String = dialog.SelectedPath

                     If Not outputPath.EndsWith("\") Then
                         outputPath &= "\"
                     End If

                     Dim workflowName As String = workflowFolder.Name
                     Dim outputPackagePath As String = outputPath & workflowName ⏎
& ".fwp"

                     Dim extractPath As String = outputPath & workflowName

                     ' Export the files via a web package.
                     Dim package As WebPackage = ⏎
Me.Application.ActiveWeb.CreatePackage(workflowName)

                     For Each file As WebFile In workflowFolder.Files
                         package.Add(file.Url, ⏎
PackageDependencyFlags.PackageDependencyNone)
                     Next

                     package.Save(outputPackagePath, True)

                     ' Create temp folder.
                     If Not Directory.Exists(extractPath) Then
                         Directory.CreateDirectory(extractPath)
                     End If

                     ' Extract the files.
                     Dim commandLine As String = """" & outputPackagePath ⏎
& """ -F:* """ & extractPath & """"

                     Dim startInfo As New ⏎
ProcessStartInfo("c:\windows\system32\expand.exe", commandLine)
                     startInfo.UseShellExecute = False

                     process = New Process()
                     process.StartInfo = startInfo
                     process.Start()
                     process.WaitForExit()

                     ' Rename extracted files.
                     Dim manifest As New XmlDocument()
                     manifest.Load(extractPath & "\manifest.xml")

                     For Each fileNode As XmlElement In manifest.SelectNodes("//File")
                         If File.Exists(outputPath & ⏎
fileNode.Attributes("Name").InnerText) Then
```

```vb
                          File.Delete(outputPath & ↵
fileNode.Attributes("Name").InnerText)
                      End If

                      File.Move(extractPath & "\" & ↵
fileNode.Attributes("Src").InnerText, outputPath & ↵
fileNode.Attributes("Name").InnerText)
                  Next

                  ' Remove temp folder.
                  If Directory.Exists(extractPath) Then
                      Directory.Delete(extractPath, True)
                  End If

                  ' Remove package.
                  If File.Exists(outputPackagePath) Then
                      File.Delete(outputPackagePath)
                  End If

                  If File.Exists(outputPath & workflowName & ".xoml.rules") Then
                      ' Rename rules file.
                      If File.Exists(outputPath & workflowName & ".rules") Then
                          File.Delete(outputPath & workflowName & ".rules")
                      End If

                      File.Move(outputPath & workflowName & ".xoml.rules", ↵
outputPath & workflowName & ".rules")
                  End If

                  ' Process the workflow file.
                  Dim xomlFile As New XmlDocument()
                  xomlFile.Load(outputPath & workflowName & ".xoml")

                  ' Modify workflow activation code.
                  Dim activationActivity As XmlNode = ↵
xomlFile.SelectSingleNode("//*[local-name()='OnWorkflowActivated']")
                  Dim invokedAttribute As XmlAttribute = ↵
xomlFile.CreateAttribute("Invoked")
                  invokedAttribute.InnerText = ↵
activationActivity.Attributes("x:Name").InnerText & "_Invoked"
                  activationActivity.Attributes.Append(invokedAttribute)
                  Dim applyActivation As XmlNode = ↵
xomlFile.SelectSingleNode("//*[local-name()='ApplyActivation']")
                  applyActivation.ParentNode.RemoveChild(applyActivation)
                  xomlFile.Save(outputPath & workflowName & ".xoml")

                  ' Export cs file.
                  Dim asm As Assembly = Assembly.GetExecutingAssembly()
                  Dim stream As Stream = ↵
asm.GetManifestResourceStream("SPDWorkflowExporter.Workflow.cs")
                  Dim b(stream.Length) As Byte
                  stream.Read(b, 0, b.Length)
                  stream.Close()
```

```
                If File.Exists(outputPath & workflowName & ".xoml.cs") Then
                    File.Delete(outputPath & workflowName & ".xoml.cs")
                End If

                Dim writer As FileStream = File.Create(outputPath & ↩
workflowName & ".xoml.cs")
                writer.Write(b, 0, b.Length)
                writer.Close()

                MessageBox.Show("Workflow exported successfully.")
            End If
        Catch ex As Exception
            MessageBox.Show("Error exporting workflow:" + ex.Message)
        Finally
            If dialog IsNot Nothing Then
                dialog.Dispose()
            End If

            If process IsNot Nothing Then
                process.Dispose()
            End If
        End Try
    End Sub
End Class
```

C#

```
using Microsoft.Office.Core;
using Microsoft.Office.Interop.SharePointDesigner;
using System;
using System.Diagnostics;
using System.IO;
using System.Reflection;
using System.Windows.Forms;
using System.Xml;

namespace SPDWorkflowExporter
{
    public partial class ThisAddIn
    {
        private void ThisAddIn_Startup(object sender, System.EventArgs e)
        {
            foreach (CommandBar commandbar in this.Application.CommandBars) {
                if (commandbar.Id == 1324 || commandbar.Id == 1319) {
                    CommandBarButton exportButton = (CommandBarButton) ↩
commandbar.Controls.Add(MsoControlType.msoControlButton, 1, null, 1, true);
                    exportButton.Caption = "Export workflow";
                    exportButton.Click += new ↩
_CommandBarButtonEvents_ClickEventHandler(exportButton_Click);
                }
            }
        }

        private void exportButton_Click(CommandBarButton Ctrl, ref bool ↩
CancelDefault) {
```

```
                    FolderBrowserDialog dialog = null;
                    Process process = null;

                    try {
                        if (this.Application.ActiveWebWindow.SelectedFolders.Length != 1) {
                            return;
                        }

                        WebFolder workflowFolder = (WebFolder) ↩
                this.Application.ActiveWebWindow.SelectedFolders.GetValue(0);

                        // Check if folder selected contains a workflow.
                        Boolean isWorkflowFolder = false;
                        foreach (WebFile file in workflowFolder.Files) {
                            if (file.Name.EndsWith("xoml")) {
                                isWorkflowFolder = true;
                                break;
                            }
                        }

                        if (!isWorkflowFolder) {
                            return;
                        }

                        dialog = new FolderBrowserDialog();
                        dialog.Description = "Select an output path for the workflow.";

                        if (dialog.ShowDialog() == DialogResult.OK) {
                            string outputPath = dialog.SelectedPath;

                            if (!outputPath.EndsWith("\\")) {
                                outputPath += "\\";
                            }

                            string workflowName = workflowFolder.Name;
                            string outputPackagePath = outputPath + workflowName + ".fwp";
                            string extractPath = outputPath + workflowName;

                            // Export the files via a web package.
                            WebPackage package = ↩
                this.Application.ActiveWeb.CreatePackage(workflowName);

                            foreach (WebFile file in workflowFolder.Files) {
                                package.Add(file.Url, ↩
                PackageDependencyFlags.PackageDependencyNone);
                            }

                            package.Save(outputPackagePath, 1);

                            // Create temp folder.
                            if (!Directory.Exists(extractPath)) {
                                Directory.CreateDirectory(extractPath);
```

```
                    }

                    // Extract the files.
                    string commandLine = "\"" + outputPackagePath ↵
+ "\" -F:* \"" + extractPath + "\"";

                    ProcessStartInfo startInfo = new ↵
ProcessStartInfo(@"c:\windows\system32\expand.exe", commandLine);
                    startInfo.UseShellExecute = false;

                    process = new Process();
                    process.StartInfo = startInfo;
                    process.Start();
                    process.WaitForExit();

                    // Rename extracted files.
                    XmlDocument manifest = new XmlDocument();
                    manifest.Load(extractPath + @"\manifest.xml");

                    foreach (XmlElement fileNode in ↵
manifest.SelectNodes("//File")) {
                            if (File.Exists(outputPath + ↵
fileNode.Attributes["Name"].InnerText)) {
                                    File.Delete(outputPath + ↵
fileNode.Attributes["Name"].InnerText);
                            }

                            File.Move(extractPath + "\\" + ↵
fileNode.Attributes["Src"].InnerText, outputPath + ↵
fileNode.Attributes["Name"].InnerText);
                    }

                    // Remove temp folder.
                    if (Directory.Exists(extractPath)) {
                        Directory.Delete(extractPath, true);
                    }

                    // Remove package.
                    if (File.Exists(outputPackagePath)) {
                        File.Delete(outputPackagePath);
                    }

                    if (File.Exists(outputPath + workflowName + ".xoml.rules")) {
                        // Rename rules file.
                        if (File.Exists(outputPath + workflowName + ".rules")) {
                            File.Delete(outputPath + workflowName + ".rules");
                        }

                            File.Move(outputPath + workflowName + ↵
".xoml.rules", outputPath + workflowName + ".rules");
                    }

                    // Process the workflow file.
                    XmlDocument xomlFile = new XmlDocument();
```

```
                        xomlFile.Load(outputPath + workflowName + ".xoml");

                        // Modify workflow activation code.
                        XmlNode activationActivity = ←
xomlFile.SelectSingleNode("//*[local-name()='OnWorkflowActivated']");
                        XmlAttribute invokedAttribute = ←
xomlFile.CreateAttribute("Invoked");
                        invokedAttribute.InnerText = ←
activationActivity.Attributes["x:Name"].InnerText + "_Invoked";
                        activationActivity.Attributes.Append(invokedAttribute);
                        XmlNode applyActivation = ←
xomlFile.SelectSingleNode("//*[local-name()='ApplyActivation']");
                        applyActivation.ParentNode.RemoveChild(applyActivation);
                        xomlFile.Save(outputPath + workflowName + ".xoml");

                        // Export cs file.
                        Assembly asm = Assembly.GetExecutingAssembly();
                        Stream stream = ←
asm.GetManifestResourceStream("SPDWorkflowExporter.Workflow.cs");
                        Byte[] b = new Byte[stream.Length];
                        stream.Read(b, 0, b.Length);
                        stream.Close();

                        if (File.Exists(outputPath + workflowName + ".xoml.cs")) {
                            File.Delete(outputPath + workflowName + ".xoml.cs");
                        }

                        FileStream writer = File.Create(outputPath + ←
workflowName + ".xoml.cs");
                        writer.Write(b, 0, b.Length);
                        writer.Close();

                        MessageBox.Show("Workflow exported successfully.");

                    }

            } catch (Exception ex) {
                MessageBox.Show("Error exporting workflow:" + ex.Message);
            } finally {
                if (dialog != null) {
                    dialog.Dispose();
                }

                if (process != null) {
                    process.Dispose();
                }
            }
        }

        private void ThisAddIn_Shutdown(object sender, System.EventArgs e)
        {
```

```
        }

        #region VSTO generated code

        /// <summary>
        /// Required method for Designer support - do not modify
        /// the contents of this method with the code editor.
        /// </summary>
        private void InternalStartup()
        {
            this.Startup += new System.EventHandler(ThisAddIn_Startup);
            this.Shutdown += new System.EventHandler(ThisAddIn_Shutdown);
        }

        #endregion
    }
}
```

The last snippet of code exports a class file for the workflow. The class file does not currently exist in the Project, so add it by right-clicking the Project in Solution Explorer and selecting Add New Item. Choose Text File from the Templates list and enter `Workflow.cs` as the filename. Click Add to add the file to your Project.

In the Properties tool pane, change the Build Action to Embedded Resource. Paste the following code into the `Workflow.cs` file and save it:

```
namespace Microsoft.SharePoint.Workflow {
    using System;
    using System.Drawing;
    using System.ComponentModel;
    using System.ComponentModel.Design;
    using System.Workflow.ComponentModel;
    using System.Workflow.ComponentModel.Design;
    using System.Workflow.ComponentModel.Compiler;
    using System.Workflow.ComponentModel.Serialization;
    using System.Workflow.Runtime;
    using System.Workflow.Activities.Rules;
    using System.Collections;
    using System.Collections.Generic;
    using System.Workflow.Activities;
    using Microsoft.SharePoint.WorkflowActions;

    public partial class ROOT :
Microsoft.SharePoint.WorkflowActions.RootWorkflowActivityWithData {
        private void ID1_Invoked(object sender, ExternalDataEventArgs e) {
            __context = new WorkflowContext();
            __context.Initialize(__initParams);
            __list = __initParams.List.ToString();
            __item = __initParams.ItemId;
            __workflowId = __initParams.WorkflowId;
        }
    }
}
```

Your SharePoint Designer add-in is now complete. The next section shows you how to test your add-in inside SharePoint Designer.

Testing Your Add-In

To test your add-in, press F5. Visual Studio builds your add-in, registers it to load when SharePoint Designer starts, and starts the SharePoint Designer program itself. Once SharePoint Designer opens, the site from your last session automatically opens, unless the user has disabled that option. You may need to open another site by selecting File ⇨ Open Site from the menu bar. If you open another site, SharePoint Designer launches a new instance of itself, which prevents your add-in from being debugged. To get around this problem, select Debug ⇨ Stop Debugging in Visual Studio; that will close the original instance of SharePoint Designer. Next, close the new instance of SharePoint Designer that will remember your site and reopen it the next time SharePoint Designer loads. Finally, press F5 key again to load SharePoint Designer and debug your add-in.

In SharePoint Designer, create a new workflow by selecting File ⇨ New ⇨ Workflow. In the Workflow Designer dialog (see Figure 17-8), enter **SPDWorkflow** as the name of the workflow, and select any SharePoint list from the dropdown list. Click Next to continue.

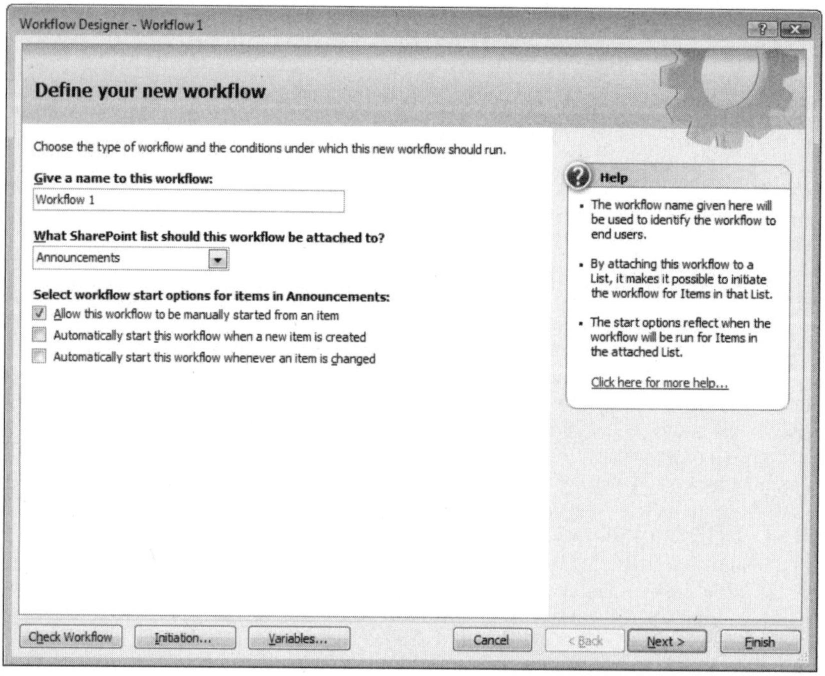

Figure 17-8

On the Step 1 screen (see Figure 17-9), click the Actions button and select the More Actions option.

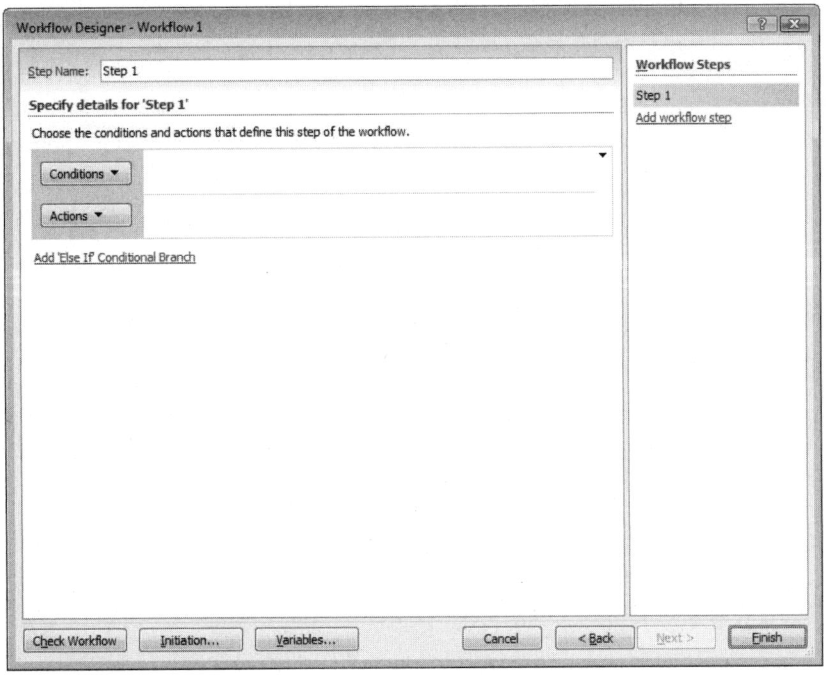

Figure 17-9

The Workflow Actions dialog (Figure 17-10) opens; select the Build Dynamic String option and click Add. Repeat these steps one more time to select the Log to History List option.

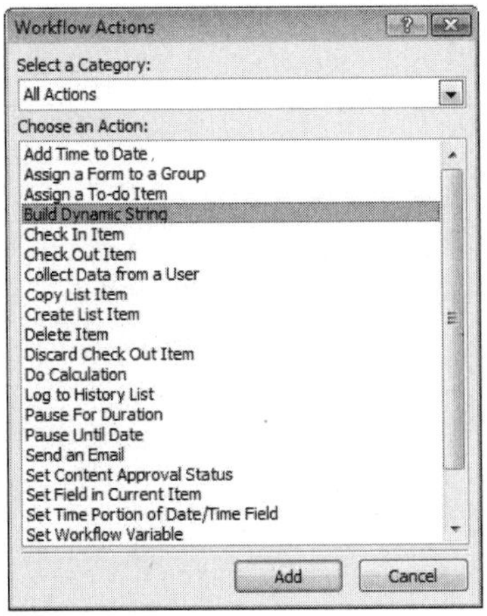

Figure 17-10

Configure the Build Dynamic String action by clicking the `dynamic string` hyperlink to display the String Builder dialog (see Figure 17-11). In the dialog, enter the text **You entered:** and click Add Lookup.

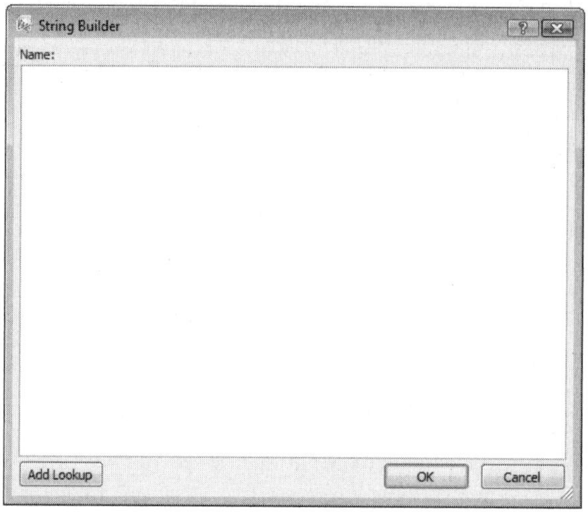

Figure 17-11

In the Define Workflow Lookup dialog (see Figure 17-12), select Current Item from the Source dropdown and Title from the Field dropdown. Click OK to close the lookup dialog, and then click OK to close the String Builder dialog.

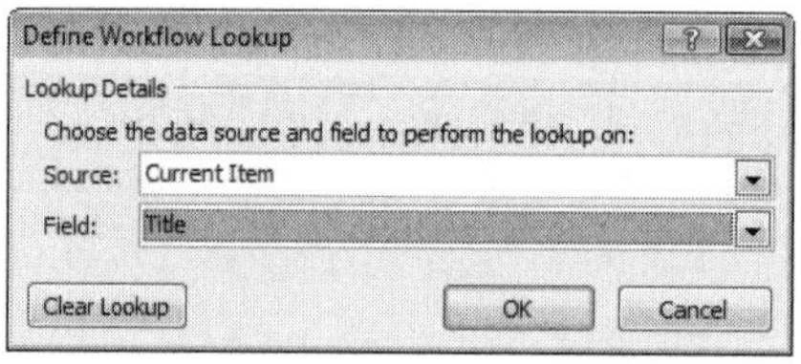

Figure 17-12

Configure the Log to History List action by clicking the `this message` hyperlink and then clicking the fx button. In the Define Workflow Lookup dialog, select Workflow Data from the Source dropdown and Variable: variable from the Field dropdown. Click OK to close the lookup dialog, and then click Finish to save the workflow to SharePoint.

Navigate to your list and test your SharePoint Designer workflow. Once you have confirmed that the workflow executes correctly, expand the Workflows folder in the Folder List tool window (see Figure 17-13), right-click the SPDWorkflow folder, and select Export Workflow from the context menu.

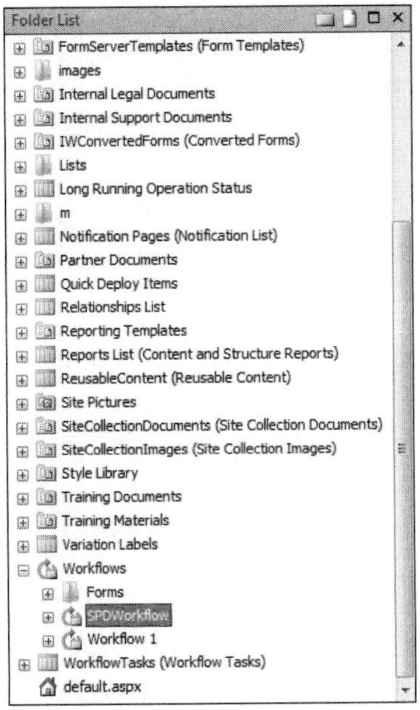

Figure 17-13

In the Browse For Folder dialog (Figure 17-14), select a folder for the exported files and click OK. Wait for your add-in to display the "Workflow exported successfully" message.

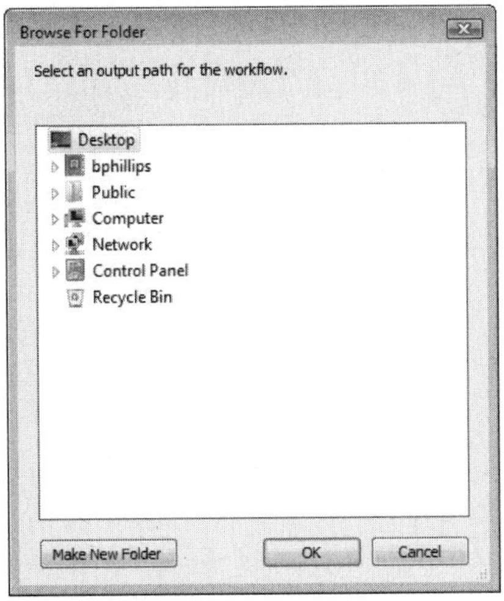

Figure 17-14

You have successfully exported a workflow from SharePoint Designer. Now, you can create a SharePoint workflow Project to make your exported workflow reusable. Open another instance of Visual Studio and select File ⇨ New ⇨ Project to display the New Project dialog. Select Visual C# ⇨ Office ⇨ 2007 from the Project Types list, and select the SharePoint 2007 Sequential Workflow Project from the Templates list. Enter **SPDWorkflow** in the Name text box and click OK.

When Visual Studio creates the Project, the New Office SharePoint Workflow dialog (see Figure 17-15) appears. Enter a valid URL for a site collection in your SharePoint farm in the second text box, and click Next.

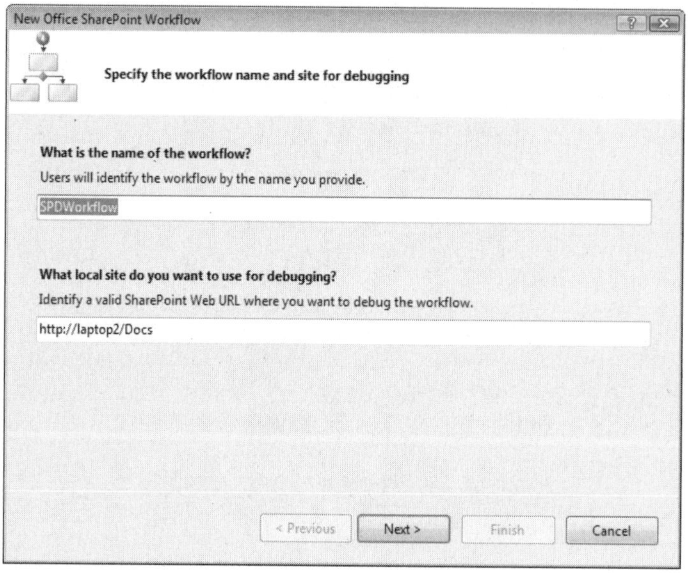

Figure 17-15

The dialog shown in Figure 17-16 allows you to automatically associate the workflow with a list or document library from the site collection you chose. If you plan on associating to the same list as the SharePoint Designer workflow, delete the SharePoint Designer workflow to prevent any conflicts later. Click Next to continue.

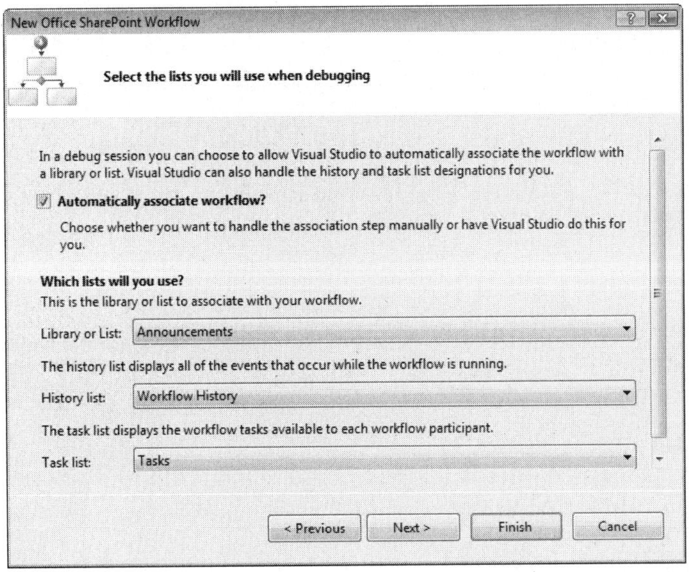

Figure 17-16

The final dialog, shown in Figure 17-17, enables you to choose the circumstances under which the workflow should execute. Make your selections and then click Finish to close the dialog. Remove the `Workflow1.cs` file by right-clicking it and selecting Delete.

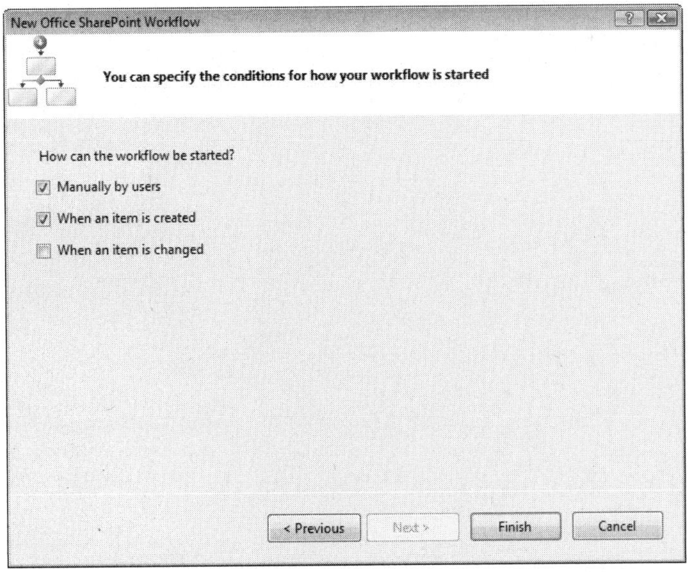

Figure 17-17

To add your workflow to the Project, right-click the Project in Solution Explorer and select Add Existing Item. In the existing item dialog, navigate to the folder with the workflow files, select the `SPDWorkflow` `.xoml` file, and click Add. Repeat the process for the `SPDWorkflow.rules` file, if one exists, and for the `SPDWorkflow.xoml.cs` file. You must adhere to the order of the files, or Visual Studio cannot correctly relate the files in the Project.

Open `workflow.xml` in the Project, and change the `CodeBesideClass` attribute of the Workflow element to the following:

```
CodeBesideClass="SPDWorkflow.ROOT"
```

Open `SPDWorkflow.xoml` to display the workflow in Visual Studio's graphical workflow designer. Locate any activities with `ListId` properties, and modify them to use the name of the list instead of the current GUID value.

Once you have made your changes, right-click the Project and select Deploy to install your workflow into your SharePoint site collection. Now, you can navigate to your list and confirm that the workflow still works. Go to the Workflow Settings screen of any list and note that you can now associate your workflow with it.

Summary

SharePoint Designer add-ins greatly enhance productivity by automating repetitive tasks in the SharePoint Designer user interface and providing new functionality, like the sample add-in created in this chapter. The sample add-in does not cover every situation in converting workflows, but it does automate the most common tasks you must perform to get your workflows to run in Visual Studio. These add-ins are just another gadget on your SharePoint Designer tool belt to take your SharePoint farm to the next level.

18

A Little Administration

The primary emphasis of this book has been on the tools SharePoint Designer provides to help you produce great SharePoint site designs and applications. Yet SharePoint Designer also provides many features that are useful for administering and maintaining web sites, but do not directly involve the creative process. This chapter describes some of those key features and shows you how to:

- ❏ Create usage reports with SharePoint Designer and SharePoint.
- ❏ Customize reports.
- ❏ Develop your own reports.
- ❏ Back up and restore SharePoint Designer sites.
- ❏ Save, move, and share list and library templates.

It also explains some ways to take the work you have done to customize a site and re-use it in other environments.

Reporting

A key part of administering a web site is monitoring usage, traffic, performance, and so on. SharePoint Designer offers a number of built-in reports to help site owners optimize their sites. In addition, SharePoint itself provides some web-based summaries. Finally, raw log information is available for you to analyze, using tools of your choice.

A Few Words about Web Reporting

Since the dawn of the Internet and the World Wide Web, site owners have been trying to improve their sites by monitoring site usage. Many usage analysis tools have been developed over the years. It is now fairly easy to get a good idea of what is popular and what is not.

What gives people trouble is trying to measure things like visits to their sites. While it is easy to determine how many times a server has sent a particular file to a particular web address, it is much harder to determine whether a user has come to a site for many short visits or a few longer ones. In addition, proxies and other forms of caching can reduce the number of times a server sends a file, compared to the number of times someone has seen it.

Different reporting tools use different strategies for dealing with this imprecision, which can result in slightly different actual numbers being reported for the same kinds of activities. Choosing slightly different start and end times for reporting periods can also result in discrepancies between tools, even of absolute numbers.

This does not make one tool right or another wrong. It is simply an artifact of the nature of web reporting. You should, therefore, be careful in trying to compare the results of one reporting system to another down to the hit-count level. Most web tools are self-consistent, however, and can allow you to reasonably gauge the relative usage of two similar items such as page hits. Just beware of assuming that numeric precision implies absolute accuracy.

Configuring SharePoint for Usage Reporting

As useful as reporting is, the logging required to collect the data for usage reports can be resource-intensive. SharePoint enables administrators to configure how usage information is collected and analyzed. Different aspects of SharePoint may be configured in different areas.

Although only usage logging is covered here, SharePoint offers considerable control over system diagnostic and user audit logging levels. Configuration and analysis of those logs is beyond the scope of this book.

To configure standard SharePoint usage logging and reports:

1. Launch the SharePoint Central Administration web site.

2. On the Logging and Reporting section's Operations tab, click Usage Analysis Processing.

3. On the Usage Analysis Processing page (see Figure 18-1), ensure that the Enable logging option is checked.

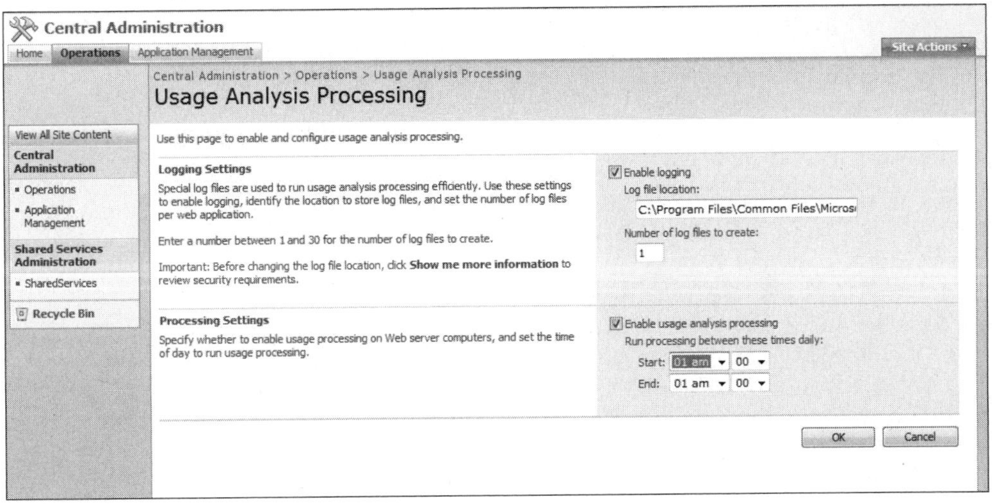

Figure 18-1

4. Specify where to store the log files. On busy sites, these files can become quite large, so you need to provide adequate space.

5. Determine how many log files to create per day per web application. A folder is created for each web application at the path provided, and each day's files are stored in a subfolder within it. Busier sites run more efficiently if you allow more (and therefore individually smaller) log files to be created.

6. Ensure that the Enable usage analysis processing option is checked.

7. Specify an appropriate time to process the log files.

8. Click OK.

On MOSS and Search Server, there is an additional level of usage analysis to configure:

1. On the Shared Services Home page, under Office SharePoint Usage Reporting, click Usage reporting. (On Search Server, the Search Administration page is shown by default when you enter the Shared Services provider. You will need to click the Home tab to get to the Home page.)

2. Ensure that both Enable advanced usage analysis processing, and Enable search query logging are checked.

3. Click OK.

Usage information is processed once per day, on the schedule you specified in the preceding step 7. The log files are collected from each web front-end server and processed, and the report information is then stored in the Content databases. It is this accumulated information that is used by SharePoint's built-in reports and by SharePoint Designer.

Daily usage information is retained in the database for 31 days. Thereafter, only monthly summary information is available from the built-in reporting tools and SharePoint Designer.

SharePoint Designer Reports

SharePoint Designer provides a broad array of reports that are useful to site designers and administrators. Some of these reports are drawn from analyzing the content of your site, while others are generated from server usage data. All SharePoint Designer reports are scoped to the currently open web, and do not include any information from parent or child sites.

There are two ways to access SharePoint Designer reports for the currently open web:

❑ Choose Site ➪ Reports, and navigate to the report you want to view, such as Site Summary.

❑ On the Web Site tab, select the Reports view from the View selector bar at the bottom of the window. This presents either the most recently viewed report or the Site Summary report, if no other report has yet been shown.

The selected report is displayed in the design surface area. At the top of the report window is a nonmovable toolbar that includes a report selector menu (the same list as is available from the Site Menu) and icons for selecting options appropriate to the currently displayed report.

Figure 18-2 shows a Site Summary report, which provides the totals, or top-line information, from each of the major SharePoint Designer reports.

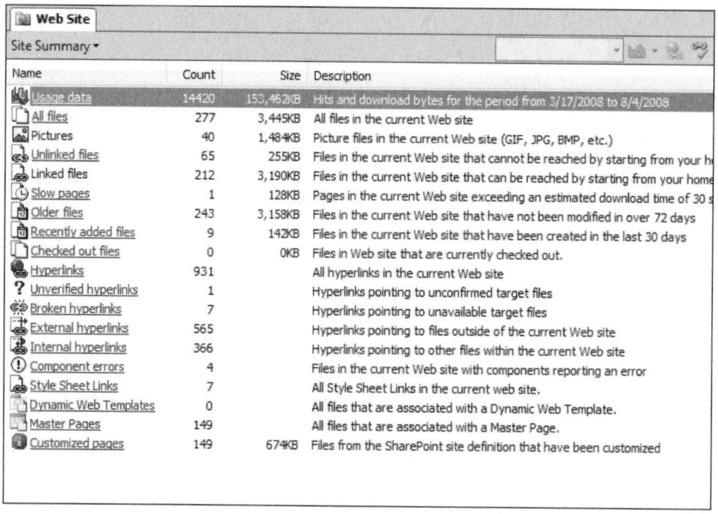

Figure 18-2

Most lines on the summary have further detail available. In those cases, the entry in the site summary provides a link that allows you to drill down to the detailed report. These are the same detail reports you can navigate to via the menus.

There are two main types of reports in SharePoint Designer:

❑ Content reports: Typically used to *enumerate*, or list, items on your site that fall into a particular category.

❑ Usage reports: Used to *quantify*, or count, the usage of items on the site over time.

Site Content Reports

SharePoint site content reports tell you about the files in your web. There are three main groups of content reports:

❑ Files

❑ Shared Content

❑ Problems

Files reports show you all of the files on your site in a single list (without your needing to drill through the folder structure). You can also see which files are new, recently updated, or oldest. Finally, you can see which files are checked out, and which are available for editing.

Shared Content reports let you know which pages are connected to particular Master Pages, style sheets, or Dynamic Web Templates. They also show which files are customized (unghosted) from their site definition.

Problems reports tell you which pages contain broken hyperlinks (links to nowhere, whose targets do not exist), how many pages link to a page, or how many other pages a particular page links out to. You can determine which files take longest to load, and which SharePoint Designer components are not correctly configured.

> **SharePoint Designer link reports do not report on Links lists or list and library fields that may contain hyperlinks. Only static links — those embedded in a page — are counted.**

When you display a hyperlinks report, you can choose to verify the hyperlinks on your site. To verify the links, SharePoint Designer attempts to open the target URL specified in the link. Successfully verified links are marked OK, and unsuccessful verifications are marked Broken. You can also invoke hyperlink verification with the icon at the far right of the toolbar. When viewing the Hyperlinks report, you can edit a hyperlink either from the link's context menu or by clicking the toolbar icon next to the verify hyperlink icon.

As you begin to fix broken links, you will see that not all links flagged as Broken are errors. Figure 18-3 shows a link in a workflow form, which cannot be verified because it is derived from an XSLT formula. These links are flagged only because SharePoint Designer cannot open the target URLs. While such links are usually functional at run time, you may choose to verify them manually by viewing the live page and testing the component (e.g., Data View or workflow) that contains the link.

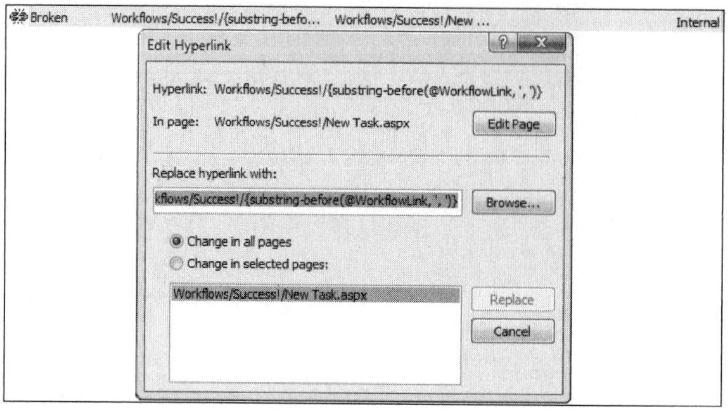

Figure 18-3

Content reports are live — that is, you can directly interact with the items listed. You can modify their properties, check them out (or in), reset customized files to their site definition, or even open them for editing. Figure 18-4 shows the "right-click" context menu of a typical file listed in a content report.

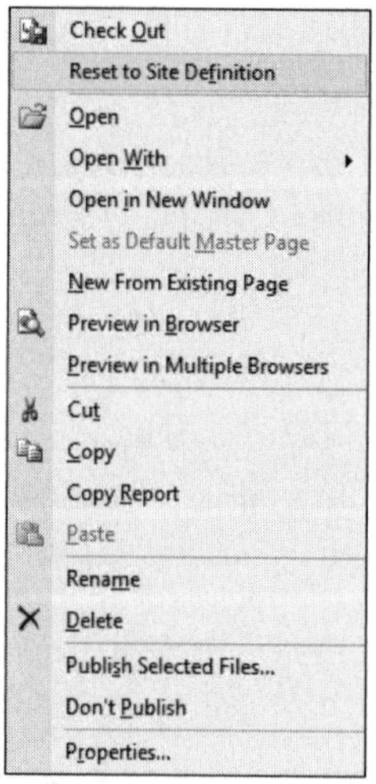

Figure 18-4

Site Usage Reports

Depending upon the kind of site you have, the site usage reports may be drawn either from the SharePoint logs or from IIS logging. These reports allow you to learn about the users of your site. You can find out which pages are popular, and which are not. You can observe trends in usage, as well as which browsers and operating system people are using.

The Usage Summary report (see Figure 18-5), like the Site Summary, gives a top-line overview of your site's usage, and you can drill down into the specific detail reports.

Name	Value	Description
Date of first data	Monday, March 17, 2008 3:00 AM	Usage data accumulated starting with this date
Date last updated	Monday, August 04, 2008 2:59 AM	Last time usage processing was run on the server
Total visits	11875	Number of pages viewed from external sources
Total page hits	14420	Number of hits on all pages.
Total bytes downloaded	153462 KB	Number of bytes downloaded
Current visits	230	Number of pages viewed from external sources for
Current page hits	256	Number of page hits received for this month (Aug-0
Current bytes downloaded	5328 KB	Number of bytes downloaded this month (Aug-08)
Top referrer	http://pro-spd/previewresults.aspx	Most frequent referrer this month (Aug-08)
Top referring domain	http://pro-spd	Most frequent referring domain this month (Aug-08
Top web browser	Internet Explorer 4.01	Most frequent browser used to view this Web site t
Top operating system	Windows NT 4	Most frequent operating system used by browsers
Top search terms		Most frequent search terms used to find this Web s
Top user	69-64-72-35\woodyw	Most frequent user to view this Web site this month

Figure 18-5

Unlike content reports, which look similar to each other, usage reports vary considerably in the data displayed. They do have a few things in common: They count the occurrences of something over time, they usually allow you to select subsets of the data through the dropdown Options selector in the report toolbar, and they enable you to create graphs of the usage data, as shown in Figure 18-6.

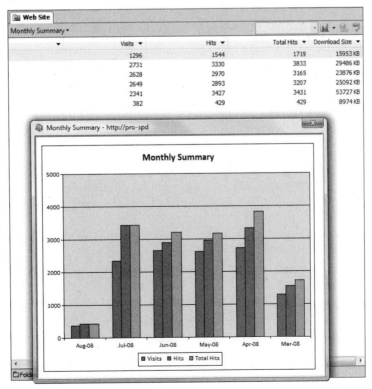

Figure 18-6

There are many graph types available, from pie and bar charts, for comparing quantities, to line and Ribbon graphs to let you plot trends over time. Both two- and three-dimensional versions of most chart types are available.

Customizing and Exporting Reports

You can customize most of the reports in SharePoint Designer, typically by sorting and by setting filters in the columns of data. Click a column header to sort using the information in that column. Clicking a second time reverses the order (changing lowest-to-highest into highest-to-lowest, for instance).

Column filtering works much like filtering a tabular view in SharePoint. The column title includes a dropdown arrow, which allows you to select a number of filter options: a specified value from the column, blank values, nonblank values, and a custom filter option. Custom filters can set conditions on up to two criteria per field, combined with AND or OR.

Reports and charts can also be exported. As the right-click context menu in Figure 18-7 indicates, charts can be saved directly to the file system (as GIF or BMP images), emailed, printed, or copied to the Clipboard. Text reports can be copied to the Clipboard as a table, which can then be pasted into other applications for further formatting or analysis.

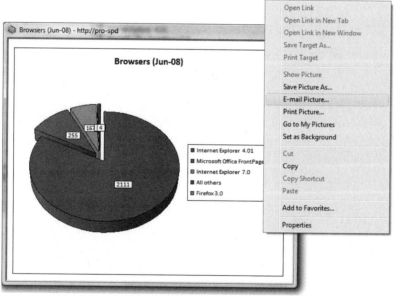

Figure 18-7

SharePoint Web-Based Reports

SharePoint provides site owners/administrators with usage reports through the web user interface. The exact reports available will depend upon the version of SharePoint installed, and the features activated on the site. There are reports available for the site collection and subweb levels, accessed through the Site Settings page of each site.

Basic Reports

Windows SharePoint Services and most sites on Microsoft Office SharePoint Server offer a set of basic text-based usage reports. At the site collection level, a top-line report provides an overview of total hits, assigned users, and server space used compared to available quota. The site collection Usage Summary (see Figure 18-8) is found at {site collection path}/_layouts/usage.aspx.

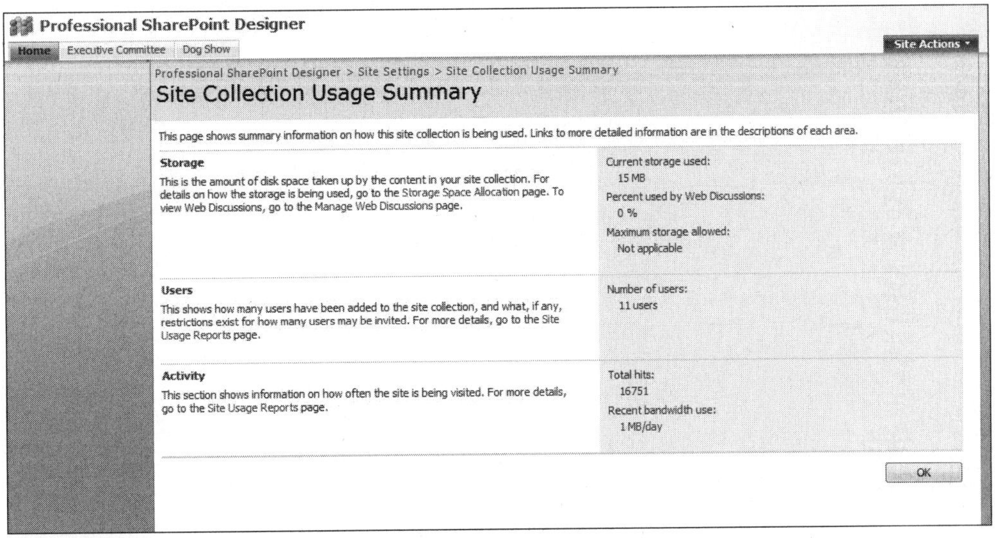

Figure 18-8

While many SharePoint and SharePoint Designer reports offer different useful views of similar information, the Site Collection Usage Summary (usage.aspx) is the only built-in report that provides information relating total storage to administrative quota, total registered users, or daily bandwidth utilization for an entire site collection.

At the subweb level, specific category usage reports — similar in scope to those available in SharePoint Designer — are supplied. Monthly summary and daily details views are provided for each report. Unlike the SharePoint Designer reports, however, these reports are text only, and do not have filtering options. The detailed Site Usage Report (see Figure 18-9) is at {web path}/_layouts/usagedetails.aspx.

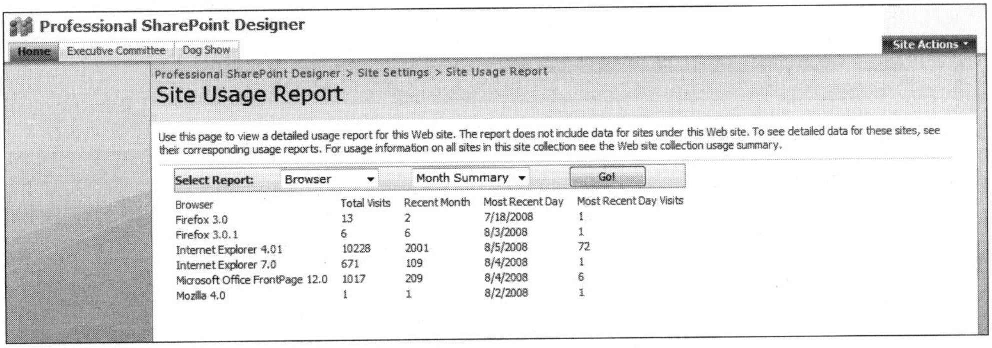

Figure 18-9

The `usagedetails.aspx` *report may be shown at the site collection root or at any subweb within the collection; however, like the SharePoint Designer reports, it only shows the usage detail for the specific web from which it was invoked.*

Advanced/Publishing Reports

On MOSS sites that have the Publishing features enabled, the report links in Site Settings provide a different set of reports. These Advanced/Publishing reports provide a graphical representation of the usage statistics for the web site.

Publishing reports are available for the site and site collection. Unlike the basic reports, the site and site collection reports are not as different in kind so much as in scope. Site collection–level reports contain information for the entire collection, rather than just the root web. In addition, the site collection reports offer access to the Search Reports for that collection.

Figure 18-10 shows a typical Site Summary report.

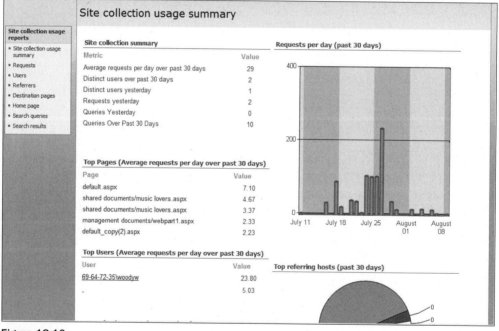

Figure 18-10

The site collection–level report is found at `{site collection path}/_layouts/spUsageSite.aspx`, and the web-level reports are at `{web path}/_layouts/spUsageWeb.aspx`.

On MOSS and Search Server, Publishing reports can be viewed in nonpublishing sites by directly entering the URLs above. Similarly, you can view the basic format reports for publishing sites by entering their respective URLs.

The Advanced/Publishing reports are not included with Windows SharePoint Services 3.0 (WSS 3.0).

Why Are These Reports Only Enabled on Publishing Sites?

As mentioned in the earlier sidebar, web usage reporting can be a tricky business, even under the best of conditions. In a database-based system like SharePoint, another complication is introduced. List-based content relies on a few "view" pages, for which parameters are provided to determine which item(s) should be displayed.

When generating reports in SharePoint, only the pages are counted. While you can easily see what List Views have been accessed from the logs, there is no easy way to determine which list items have been displayed from these pages.

In publishing sites, on the other hand, each Content Page is represented as a separate file in the Pages library. That gives the reporting tools an easy URL to grab onto, making for more meaningful reports.

That doesn't make these reports useless in other sites, however. It can still be helpful to see which general areas of your site people are visiting. Wikis, like publishing sites, are also based on a library file model, so they can benefit fully from these reports. And for sites in which document or image management is an important aspect, the file-level data available in these reports can be invaluable.

Search Reports

Learning what your users are looking for can help you plan your content. On MOSS and Search Server, there are two Search Report pages: Search Queries and Search Results. These reports are available in two scopes — site collection and farm. Each report has a number of panes which provide useful information. A typical Search Queries page is shown in Figure 18-11.

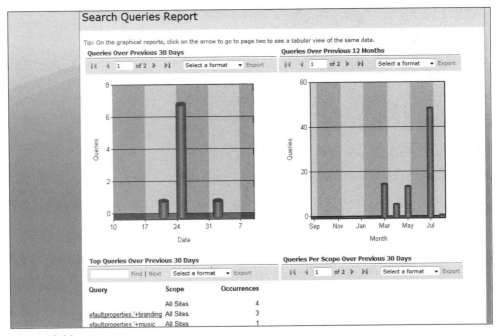

Figure 18-11

Building Your Own Reports

As flexible as the SharePoint Designer and SharePoint web-based reports are, there may be times when you want to build your own reports. As described earlier, this is easier said than done. While an analysis of different third-party reporting tools is beyond the scope of this book, you should at least be aware of the following, and their ramifications.

❑ **Scattered log files:** At the beginning of this chapter, you learned how to configure SharePoint for usage logging. As part of that configuration, you specified a path to store log files. While there is only one path specified, it is used locally by each web front-end server in your farm. This means you may need to collect log files from two or more systems, and consolidate them to get accurate reports.

❑ **Other information sources:** SharePoint sites run on Microsoft Internet Information Server (IIS). IIS has its own logging capability. You might find it useful to build a few reports from IIS logs. Once again, these are stored on each web front-end server, and will need to be gathered and consolidated. If you extend your web application into multiple zones, you will also want to accumulate logs from each zone on each server.

❑ **Different formats:** IIS logs are collected in a standard form, prescribed by the W3C (World Wide Web Consortium). Not so the SharePoint logs. Off-the-shelf reporting tools may not understand the SharePoint log file format, which stores much information in a numerically encoded form. To make these logs usable, you may need to preprocess them to put them in a format your reporting tool understands. Microsoft documents the SharePoint log file format and provides examples of preprocessing code on the MSDN web site.

At the time of this writing, the article was entitled "Usage Event Logging in Windows SharePoint Services 3.0," and located at `http://msdn.microsoft.com/en-us/library/bb814929.aspx`.

Backup Plans

"Save early, save often" has been a computing mantra ever since the first computer program stored information in memory. Even with the resilience of a server farm architecture, clustered database servers, and redundant disks, accidents happen. And when they do, there is no substitute for the comfort of having a complete, current backup.

Backing Up through SharePoint Designer

SharePoint Designer provides backup and restore options via Site ➪ Administration. These can be used both for standard file-based web sites and for SharePoint sites. Non-SharePoint sites can also be backed up by using the SharePoint Designer publishing feature to copy them to the file system or to a different server.

SharePoint Designer Backup

Backing up a site through SharePoint Designer is a simple process. It uses the SharePoint Server Content Migration API to package the site content into a file called a Content Migration Package (CMP), which is then downloaded onto the PC on which SharePoint Designer is running.

The Content Migration API is a large interface, used by many parts of SharePoint for various purposes. You may wish to consult the SharePoint SDK to learn more about its many facets.

When you select Site ⇨ Administration ⇨ Backup Web Site, the dialog shown in Figure 18-12 is displayed, and you can choose whether to include any subsites.

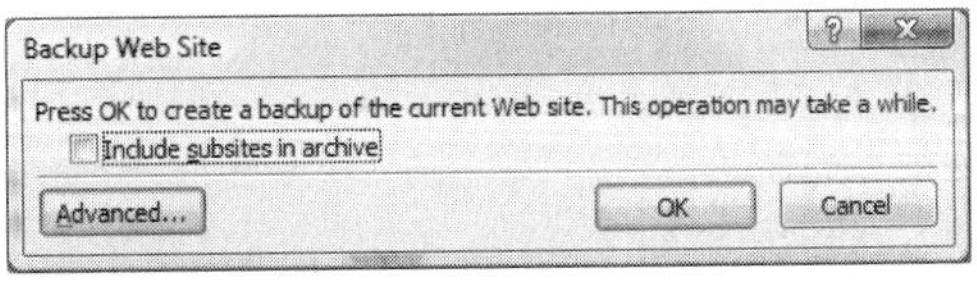

Figure 18-12

SharePoint server administrators can set storage quotas for site collections. Because the CMP is first assembled on the server, it is possible to exceed any quota that may exist. The Advanced button allows you to specify a different SharePoint site collection to hold the temporary CMP file until it is ready to download.

When you click OK in the Backup Web Site dialog, the File Save dialog appears, allowing you to specify where to save the CMP file after the assembly process completes. Enter a filename, and click Save. SharePoint assembles the CMP file, which SharePoint Designer then retrieves to the specified location. Finally, the temporary file is deleted from the site.

SharePoint Designer Restore

Although the act of restoring a site is simple, it takes a little planning. The portion of the Content Migration API used by SharePoint Designer does not support restoring over the top of existing content. Before starting a restore, therefore, you need to create an empty site to hold the restored content. In addition, ensure that all features and site definitions used by the originally backed-up site are installed and activated on the target server.

Your server administrator should be able to tell you of any custom features and/or site definitions that were installed in your original environment, and whether they are indeed installed on your intended restoration target.

Create a Blank Site

There are several ways to create an empty site. If you are restoring a single subweb, you can create a site through the web interface using the Blank Site template. You can also create an empty subweb through SharePoint Designer. To do this:

1. Create a folder at the root of the web that will be the parent of the restored site.

2. Right-click the folder and select Convert to Web. Click YES at the warning.

If you are creating a new site collection, you must either use Central Administration, or have Self Service Site Creation enabled on your web application. In either case, create a new site collection using the Blank Site template.

Restore the Archive File

Once you have a blank target site created, open that site in SharePoint Designer. Choose Site ➪ Restore, and select the CMP file you want to restore.

Sites should only be restored to like levels — that is, application root to application root, site collection to site collection, or subweb to subweb.

Post Restoration Clean-Up

After restoring your site, verify that everything is working correctly. Although all of your content will have been carried through the process, if you restore into a site with a different URL, certain elements may need manual updates to reflect the new address.

In addition, you may find that list GUIDs have changed. In some cases, functions that rely on them (such as Web Part connections) may need to be reestablished. Workflows that were in progress at backup time are probably disrupted and will need to be reinitiated.

SharePoint Designer Publishing

Non-SharePoint sites can be easily backed up or transferred to other environments through the publishing process. This function is largely carried over from the earliest days of FrontPage, and works well. Unlike site backup and restore, publishing is not all-or-nothing. You can select individual files or groups of files to publish. The source and destination sites can be of different types (such as an FTP site and the local file system).

Generally speaking, you should not use SharePoint Designer publishing for SharePoint sites, as only partial SharePoint information can be transferred in this way. On these sites, the process can transfer files, including those in document libraries, but does not include any information that is not represented as a file in SharePoint Designer. Document metadata, list item content, and workflows in progress cannot be transferred.

Any files that are transferred do not retain their SharePoint-ness — for instance, view definition files transferred via SharePoint Designer publishing are just pages to the target system, and have no association to any SharePoint lists or libraries. You can recover the code from any static Web Parts on these pages, but otherwise, there is no way to reestablish a SharePoint connection.

Other Backup Techniques

In addition to the SharePoint Designer–based techniques described in the previous section, SharePoint itself provides options for backing up and restoring your sites — through the command line via STSADM, and through the web interface. Your organization may also have acquired third-party backup tools. You should communicate with your system administrators to learn exactly what centralized backup options are in place for your SharePoint sites.

STSADM.EXE

The STSADM.EXE command-line utility provides modules for backing up and restoring site collections. The `Export` function uses the same Content Migration API as SharePoint Designer, but offers some more choices, including control over retention of version histories.

The STSAMD.EXE Backup function operates on the site collection level. This is a full-content fidelity backup, and works only for site collections. It can be used to move a site to a different farm, while retaining the element GUIDs.

STSADM.EXE Backup with the -backupmethod parameter allows you to back up entire web applications and various other SharePoint components. This uses a different API behind the scenes from site and web backups.

Backups through the Web Interface

For true disaster-recovery–level backups with built-in tools, the backup and restore options in Central Administration are your best bet. Almost all aspects of your SharePoint environment are backed up, and you can restore it onto fresh hardware. (You will still need to back up and restore any Solution Packages or other third-party software separately.) This uses the same API as STSADM backup with the -backupmethod parameter.

One element you can back up, but not restore, with the SharePoint tools is the configuration database. This means that to restore a SharePoint farm, you first need to create a new configuration by installing SharePoint itself and any feature packages needed by your environment.

Third-Party Tools

There are two types of third-party backup tools that may have been deployed in your organization:

❑ Dedicated SharePoint backup and restore programs. These are tools designed specifically to work with SharePoint sites. They generally offer the ability to restore granularly, down to the individual document or item level.

❑ SharePoint modules for general-purpose enterprise backup solutions. These modules allow an organization with very large scale implementations to integrate SharePoint with their disaster recovery plans, but usually do not allow for very granular component restoration.

Templates and Packages

Generally speaking, backup and restore are used for disaster recovery scenarios. There are other, more effective ways to move and re-use designs from one environment to another. Templates allow you to save your customizations — and even initial data — into a single file. Solution Packages provide an installation mechanism for virtually any kind of server-side SharePoint module.

List and Library Templates

The easiest way to get a design from one environment into another is to incorporate it into a SharePoint Template. Templates allow you to easily save most lists, libraries, and sites in SharePoint Template Package (.STP) files.

Saving a List Template

Although SharePoint has several built-in list and library types, very often you will customize a list. You may add fields, views, and default content that you want to re-use in other sites. To save a list as a template:

1. Navigate to a view of the list that contains the list toolbar.

2. Choose Settings ⇨ List Settings.

3. In the Permissions and Management section of the header, select Save List As Template.

4. Enter appropriate descriptive text in the form (see Figure 18-13).

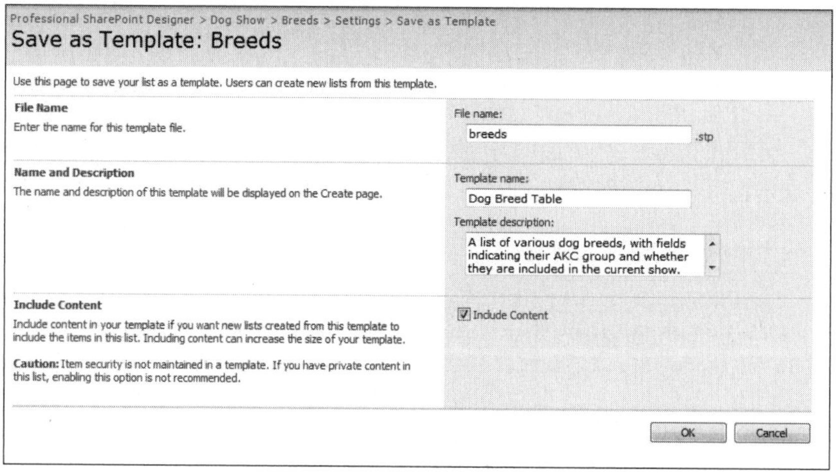

Professional SharePoint Designer > Dog Show > Breeds > Settings > Save as Template

Save as Template: Breeds

Use this page to save your list as a template. Users can create new lists from this template.

File Name
Enter the name for this template file.

File name:
breeds   .stp

Name and Description
The name and description of this template will be displayed on the Create page.

Template name:
Dog Breed Table

Template description:
A list of various dog breeds, with fields indicating their AKC group and whether they are included in the current show.

Include Content
Include content in your template if you want new lists created from this template to include the items in this list. Including content can increase the size of your template.

Caution: Item security is not maintained in a template. If you have private content in this list, enabling this option is not recommended.

☑ Include Content

[OK]   [Cancel]

Figure 18-13

5. If you want to save only the schema of the list (fields, views, and so on), leave the Include Content box unchecked. Check the box if you want to save the entire list, including the existing content (list items or documents).

6. Click OK.

After the template is saved, you can display the Template gallery or return to the list settings. The new template is now available on the Create page (see Figure 18-14) for use in any site within the site collection.

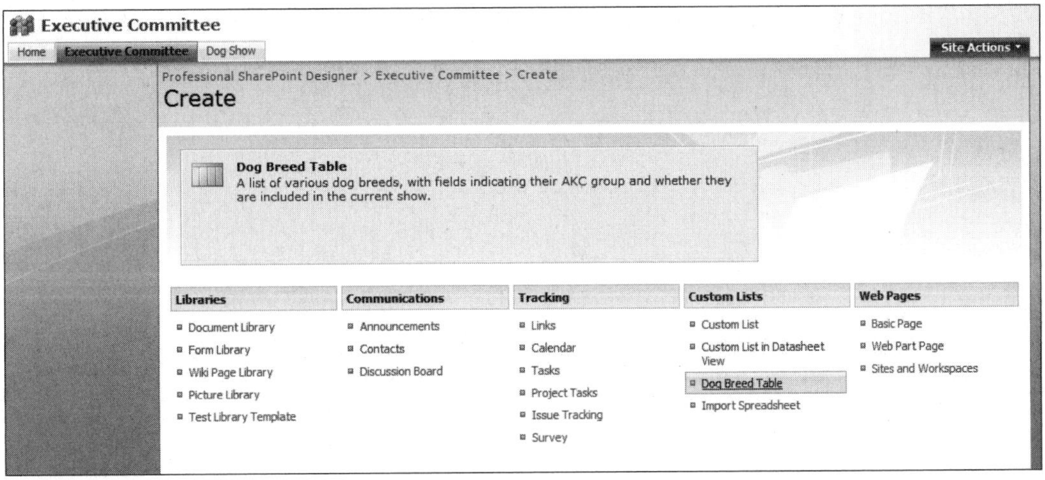

Figure 18-14

Saving a Site Template

Other than where the command resides, saving an entire site as a template is virtually identical to saving a list:

1. Choose Site Actions ⇨ Site Settings.

2. Under Look and Feel, click Save Site As Template.

3. In the form, fill in the appropriate descriptive text.

4. Check the box if you want to save content with your template.

5. Click OK.

The site is saved, and you can view the gallery or return to the site settings page. The site template is now available in the Custom tab of the New SharePoint site page's Template Selection section.

> **MOSS sites with the Office SharePoint Server Publishing feature active cannot be saved as templates.**

Moving a Template to Another Templates Gallery

List, library, and site templates saved as described earlier can be instantiated anywhere within the site collection in which they were created. To use them in other site collections or on other servers, you need to export the .STP files from the initial site, and import them into a new one.

Exporting a Template

To export a template, follow these steps:

1. Choose Site Actions ⇨ Site Settings.

2. If you are not in the root site of the collection, go there by clicking Go To Top Level Site Settings in the Site Collection Administration section.

3. Under Galleries, select either site templates or list templates.

4. Click on the name of the template you want to download.

5. Follow the prompts appropriate to your browser to save the file.

Importing a Template

Here's how to import a template:

1. Navigate to the site collection where you want to install the template. (This may be on a different server.)

2. Choose Site Actions ⇨ Site Settings.

3. Under Galleries, select either site templates or list templates, as appropriate.

4. In the toolbar of the gallery, click Upload.

5. Enter or browse to the address of the template file.

6. Click OK.

7. The Properties screen for the template is displayed, showing the values you entered when you created the template. You may edit them if needed. Once they are suitable for the current site, click OK.

You can now create instances of the list, library, or site within the new site collection.

Additional Template Info

Some key things to know about templates:

❑ Templates are only visible — and can only be instantiated — on sites created in the same language (such as English or Brazilian Portuguese) as the template.

❑ Custom lists and libraries are dependent upon underlying features, which are shown in the gallery as the Feature ID GUID.

❑ Templates can be instantiated only on sites that have the appropriate feature activated.

❑ Site templates that contain custom lists will generate errors if you attempt to instantiate them on servers for which the lists' parent features are not available.

❑   Template galleries are hosted in the root site of the site collection. Templates made from subsites are not included in these galleries, even if you select Include Content. However, any existing lists, libraries, or subsites in the template that were instantiated from these templates function normally.

❑   Permission assignments are not included in templates. Instantiated items will inherit the default security roles and permissions of the target site.

Sharing a Site Template at the Farm Level

The template galleries are great when you want to move a certain list or site template around without needing direct access to a server. However, sometimes you may want to use a particular site template at the root of a site collection. Because the site Template gallery doesn't exist until the site collection is created, it seems you are in a Catch-22 situation.

Fortunately, SharePoint offers the capability to install a site template at the server level, making it available for use as the root of a site collection. One of the operators in the STSADM utility can add a site template. To do this:

1.   Copy a site template saved with the method described above to a location accessible from the console of your SharePoint server.

2.   Open a Command prompt on the SharePoint server.

3.   Navigate to the bin directory in the 12 hive. The path is typically:

```
c:\program files\common files\microsoft shared\web server extensions\12\bin
```

4.   Execute the STSADM command with the `addtemplate` operator. `addtemplate` takes up to three parameters. The first two, `-filename` and `-title`, are required. The third, `-description`, is optional. Unlike adding the template to a site gallery, the embedded title and description are not carried over by the STSADM command. Below is an example of the command:

```
stsadm -o addtemplate -filename c:\templatefiles\dogshow.stp -title "Dog Show Site"
-description "A site for managing the entries in a dog show"
```

When the command completes, you will see the following:

```
Operation completed successfully.

IIS must be restarted before this change will take effect. To restart IIS, open a
command prompt window and type iisreset.
```

Site templates can be installed into the farm on which they were created, or on any other farm that contains all of the features used in the site. Once installed, the template appears in the Custom tab of any site creation screen for the language of the template. Figure 18-15 shows the template just installed being selected as the root of a new site collection.

Figure 18-15

Site Definitions

You have customized your site in SharePoint Designer. You have added lists and libraries, created workflows, and made some mash-up pages with Data View Web Parts. You have added your own flair with a custom Master Page and Theme. You have saved your site as a template, and deployed that template for all to use with STSADM. Life is good.

Or is it? The truth is, as in so many areas, "It depends."

The Great Debate

In chapter 5, you learned about the hybrid nature of SharePoint file service, that is, how some elements of a page are stored in the content database, and others are drawn from the file system. Most of the changes you make in SharePoint Designer result in pages that are customized, or unghosted, meaning that the entire pages are loaded from the database.

Throughout this book, you have been introduced to the powerful features of SharePoint, and how SharePoint Designer can be used to tame them. In this chapter, you saw that you can take your changes and save them in templates for re-use. But there are other ways to modify SharePoint to accomplish your goals.

The primary alternative to SharePoint Designer customization is the creation of *site definitions*. In WSS 3.0 and MOSS 2007, a site definition is a list of SharePoint Features, stapled together to define the components that will be created when you instantiate a site from that definition. All of the default site types available in SharePoint are based on site definitions.

The biggest question on some people's minds is whether SharePoint Designer should be used for customization at all. Should all customizations be done in the form of site definitions and/or stapled features? This question usually springs from one (or both) of two roots: performance and governance.

Performance

Customized pages load more slowly than noncustomized pages. That's commonly accepted as a fact. How much slower they are, however, is far less concrete. Perceived performance often depends on factors other than the page itself. Images on the page, retrieval of list and library items, and non-SharePoint data are far more likely to be bottlenecks.

In practice, then, there is little or no noticeable difference in loading speed between customized and noncustomized pages. The only time that may become an issue is on extremely busy sites — with many thousands of simultaneous users. Even in these instances, however, MOSS caching is typically employed, meaning that most items are not being served from the database at all.

Governance

Far more relevant than theoretical performance problems are governance issues, which can involve anything from permission and approval to application life-cycle management. This is far more likely to be an issue in a large organization than in a small or medium-sized business. Concerns may include:

❑ Giving the power of a tool like SharePoint Designer to a typical business user.

❑ Maintaining enterprise standards for look and feel (such as updating to existing sites to reflect new standards).

❑ Compatibility of customizations with new versions of SharePoint.

❑ Restricting user access to some but not all SharePoint and SharePoint Designer features.

These are all valid concerns, and should be carefully considered when planning to deploy SharePoint in an enterprise environment. SharePoint Designer is a powerful tool. It can be used in ways that minimize these concerns, and in ways that maximize them while solving other more pressing problems. While it is not the place of this book to make these decisions for you, there are some areas where you can feel secure in the use of SharePoint Designer, regardless of the size of your business and corporate development policies and procedures:

❑ SharePoint Designer is the best tool available for designing Themes or other CSS files, even if they are later to be deployed as part of a site definition or Feature.

❑ SharePoint Designer is an excellent general-purpose web editor, compatible with a number of industry standards.

❑ SharePoint Designer is an excellent prototyping tool. Even if you do not plan to use SharePoint Designer to modify production sites, it is fully aware of all SharePoint Features, and can be used by business analysts to mock up designs, workflows, and applications to be implemented later with Visual Studio.

> ### A Note about Upgrading
>
> One of the largest concerns in any SharePoint development effort is compatibility with future versions. In the previous version of SharePoint, the conventional wisdom was that your best bet for easing the path to upgrades would be to use custom site definitions rather than customized sites. When Microsoft finally moved from Version 2.0 to Version 3.0 of the SharePoint platform, however, the opposite turned out to be true.
>
> The massive changes in the underlying platform required that custom site definitions be rebuilt from scratch. Special feature-mapping tables had to be constructed before any kind of migration could be performed. Most FrontPage (SharePoint Designer's predecessor) customized sites, however, were easily upgraded in place, with minimal impact on the user's experience.
>
> Now, that's no guarantee that the same will be true with the next release, whenever it may come. Certainly, both Microsoft and independent developers learned valuable lessons from the 2.0 to 3.0 transition. Hopefully, both site customizers and server-side developers will be equally accommodated.

Converting a Customized SharePoint Site to a Site Definition

Microsoft has provided a tool to enable you to convert a customized SharePoint list or site into source code for a site definition and its constituent features. It's called the SharePoint Solution Generator, and it is included with the Visual Studio Extensions for Windows SharePoint Services (VSeWSS).

The VSeWSS is something of a super SDK (software development kit), in that it provides tools and guidance to make designing components for SharePoint much easier. There are separate versions of the VSeWSS for Visual Studio 2005 and Visual Studio 2008, but they have roughly similar features. You need at least the Standard edition of either version of Visual Studio to use the VSeWSS.

You can install the VSeWSS on any server that has both SharePoint and the appropriate version of Visual Studio installed. The SharePoint Solution Generator must be run on the SharePoint server containing the site or lists you want to convert. To run the SharePoint Solution Generator:

1. Select SharePoint Solution Generator from the Start menu to launch the wizard.

2. Select whether you want to create a Site Definition or a List Definition feature, and click Next. A list of the sites on the server appears.

3. Select the site containing the elements you want to use (see Figure 18-16). You may choose any site or subweb. Then, click Next.

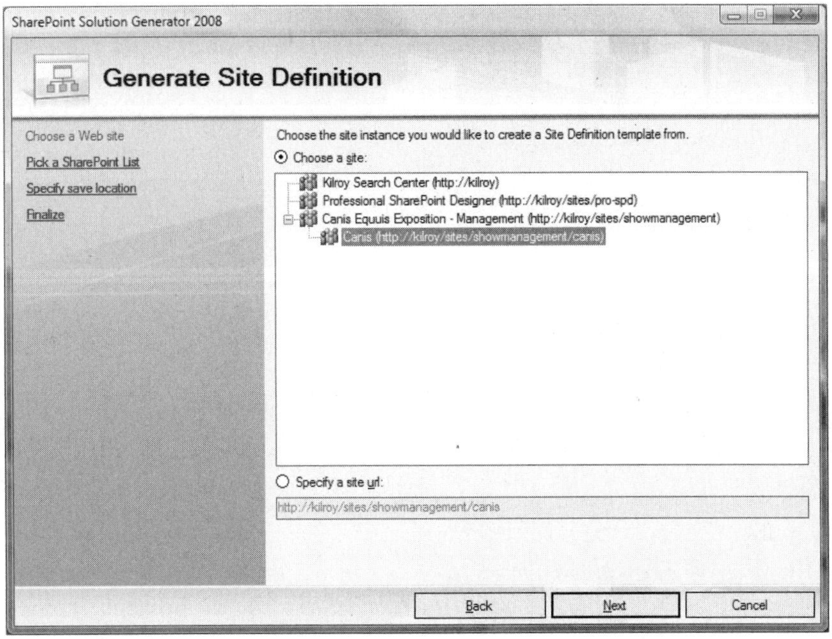

Figure 18-16

4.   Select the lists or libraries you want to include in the Project (Figure 18-17), and click Next.

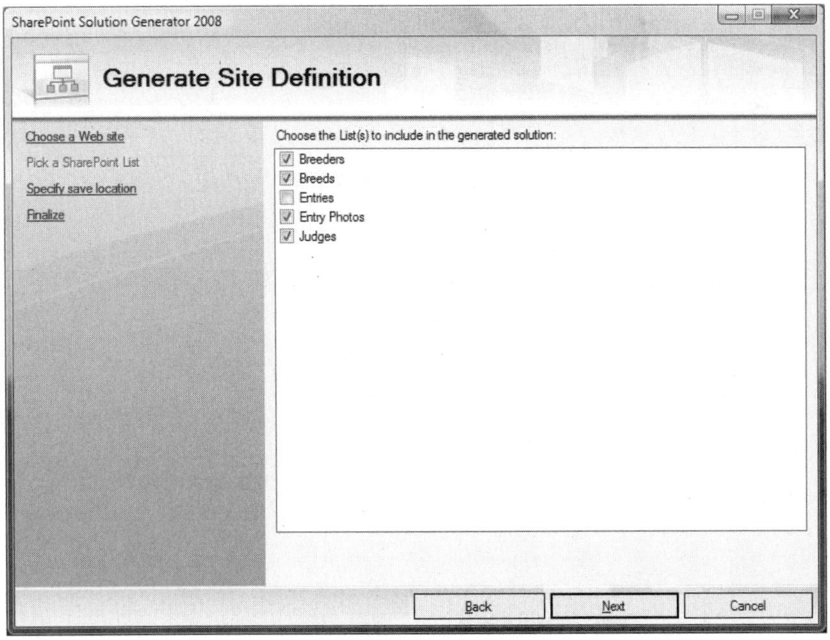

Figure 18-17

5. Enter a name and storage path for your Project, as shown in Figure 18-18, and click Next.

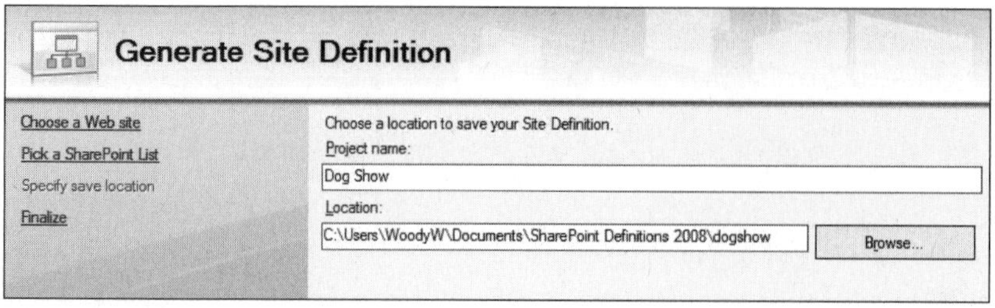

Figure 18-18

6. The steps the wizard will take are displayed, as shown in Figure 18-19. Click Finish to begin the process.

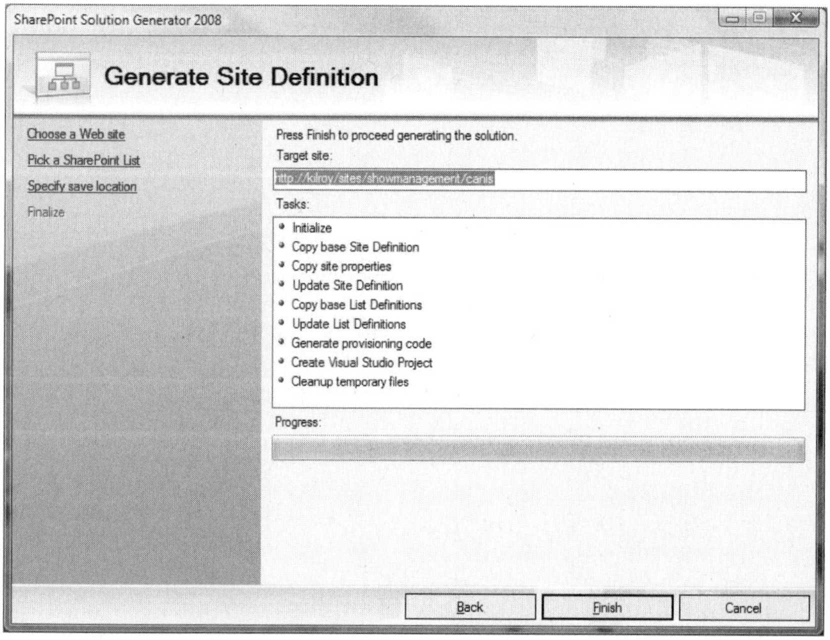

Figure 18-19

7. When the generation process is finished, you can either click Exit to close the wizard, or click a provided link to open the solution folder you specified in step 5.

8. A log of the process and a Visual Studio Project file are created in the root of the folder. Other supporting files are arrayed in appropriate subfolders. Double-click the Project to open the solution in Visual Studio.

9. Right-click the solution in the Solution Explorer, and select Deploy. Visual Studio will compile the solution and deploy its components to your SharePoint server.

The new site is now available as one of the templates in the New SharePoint Site page. By default, it is placed under the Development tab, as shown in Figure 18-20.

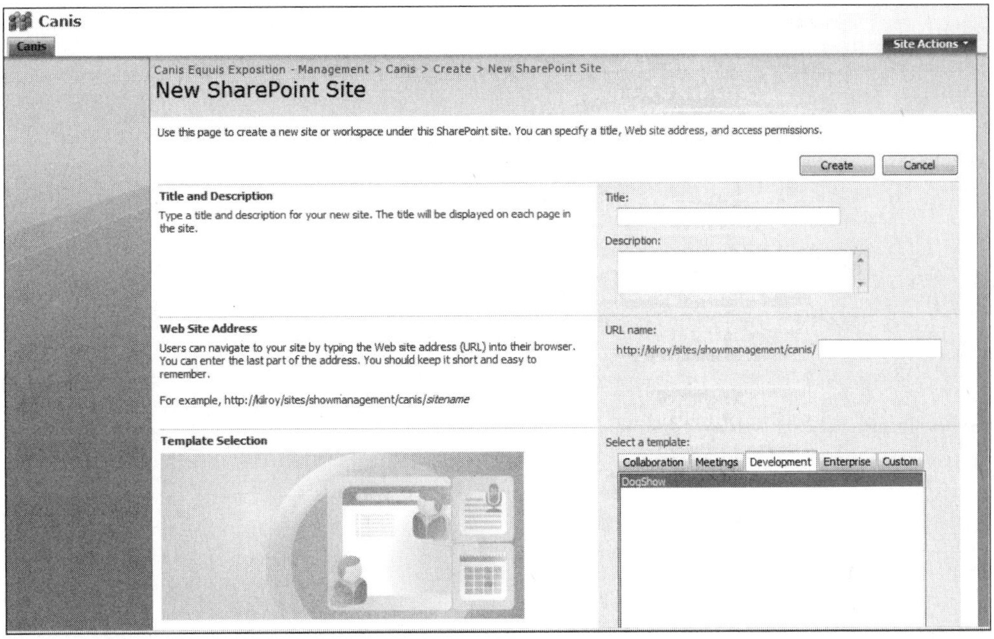

Figure 18-20

Once you have the Project in Visual Studio, you can also make any changes needed to the site definition or its constituent Features, just as though you had written them from scratch. Such modification of these items is beyond the scope of this book.

Summary

This chapter has shown you some of the administrative tools available in SharePoint Designer, as well as ways in which you can take the work you have done and share it throughout your organization. It also examined:

❑ Exporting SharePoint Designer reports for use in other tools.

❑ Several ways to export content from a SharePoint site, for both archival and deployment purposes.

❑ Using other tools to customize your SharePoint Designer sites.

❑ Using Microsoft's VSeWSS tool to convert SharePoint content from the form SharePoint Designer customizes into a form you can further edit in Visual Studio.

A Brief History of SharePoint and SharePoint Designer

This book has thoroughly introduced you to Microsoft Office SharePoint Designer 2007. Many readers will be satisfied understanding the present state of the product. Others, however, may find a history of this latest in a long line of web design tools from Microsoft useful. In particular, it may help in understanding those "What were they thinking?" moments. This appendix discusses the evolution of SharePoint Designer and Microsoft SharePoint Products and Technologies, and how they influenced each other.

From FrontPage to SharePoint Designer

The year was 1995. Although the Internet had been around for many years, only recently had its HyperText Transfer Protocol (HTTP) and the associated HyperText Markup Language (HTML) caught the public eye in the form of the World Wide Web. While the general public was falling in love with the Web through web browsers such as Mosaic, Netscape, and Internet Explorer, many companies were struggling to come up with ways to produce the content this new market was demanding.

One such company was Vermeer Technologies. Vermeer came up with a unique, modular approach to web design that it called FrontPage. It included prebuilt functionality for the server — the FrontPage Server Extensions (FPSE) — and modules for the design client (which it called WebBots. Unlike most web design tools, FrontPage included not only a WYSIWIG (what-you-see-is-what-you-get) editor (the FrontPage Editor), but full site management features for the client as well (the FrontPage Explorer). FrontPage 1.0 had only been on the market for a few months when the announcement came that Vermeer had been purchased by Microsoft, and that the FrontPage system was going to form the basis of Microsoft's web design strategy.

As advanced as it was, FrontPage was not immune to problems. In particular, the FrontPage editing client had a tendency to rewrite a page's code to meet its own specifications, which often resulted in nonfunctional scripts — a trait that most developers did not find endearing. While each subsequent release of FrontPage was better behaved than its predecessor, the damage to its reputation was done. Ultimately, the name FrontPage had to be retired. The following table shows the timeline of major milestones from the first release of FrontPage to SharePoint Designer 2007:

Date	Event	Description
Oct-95	Vermeer introduces FrontPage 1.0.	First version.
Jan-96	Microsoft announces purchase of Vermeer.	
Jan-96	Microsoft introduces FrontPage 1.1.	Microsoft branding.
Dec-96	Microsoft introduces FrontPage 97.	Improved features, first MS Office integration.
Jun-98	Microsoft introduces FrontPage 98.	New features — Navigation, Shared Borders, Themes.
Jan-99	Microsoft introduces FrontPage 2000.	Unified Explorer and Editor into a single interface.
May-01	Microsoft introduces FrontPage 2002 (XP).	Support for SharePoint Team Services.
Nov-03	Microsoft introduces FrontPage 2003.	Support for Windows SharePoint Services 2.0 and SharePoint Portal Server 2003, improved support for web standards.
Nov-06	Microsoft replaces FrontPage with two products — Expression Web 1.0 and SharePoint Designer 2007.	Expression Web: supports web standards, but has no support for SharePoint-based sites.
		SharePoint Designer: supports all previous FrontPage features, and provides support for Windows SharePoint Services 3.0 and Microsoft Office SharePoint Server 2007.

The SharePoint Family Tree

Meanwhile, back on the server, the FrontPage Server Extensions (FPSE) were being enhanced until, in the Microsoft Office 2000 releases, a new layer was created over the FPSE called the Office Server Extensions (OSE). The OSE added services for managing discussions and sending email alerts. In addition, file management protocols — including the then-new WebDAV — were added, allowing the Office client applications such as Microsoft Word and Microsoft Excel to both read from and write to web sites directly for the first time.

Office 97 applications supported reading and writing via the FTP protocol.

The Years BSP (before SharePoint)

There were many other web server initiatives taking place at Microsoft during this time frame. Two of them — Microsoft Site Server 3.0 and the Digital Dashboard Resource Kit (DDRK) — warrant special notice as ancestors of SharePoint, as shown in the family tree in Figure A-1.

The SharePoint Family Tree

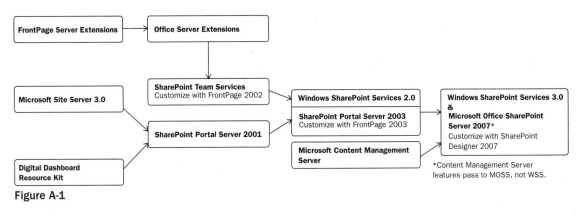

Figure A-1

Microsoft Site Server 3.0 was a massive product with many parts that were not directly related to one another beyond being installed and accessed through a common user interface. Several of these components, however, form conceptual (if not direct code) predecessors to components of Microsoft Office SharePoint Server 2007. First, Site Server included content management and deployment functionality, allowing the staging and incremental updating of web sites. Second, Site Server contained a Knowledge Management framework, which let administrators define property sets that could be applied to items of content. Finally, Site Server introduced Microsoft's first Enterprise-class search engine (Site Server Search).

The Digital Dashboard Resource Kit (DDRK) was a set of tools to present pieces of content on a special web page called a dashboard. The pieces were called Web Parts and could be sourced a number of ways, from static content to JavaScript to ASP code. The dashboards and Web Parts were stored server-side — either in the file system, a SQL Server database, or an Exchange message store — accessed via standard HTTP, and managed through the WebDAV protocol.

Fraternal Twins — It's All in the Name

The first products to actually bear the name *SharePoint* were released at about the same time as Microsoft Office XP (whose individual components were known as the 2002 Office Products). There were two distinct products named SharePoint: SharePoint Portal Server 2001 (SPS), and SharePoint Team Services (STS). While there was some functional overlap, they were architecturally very different.

SharePoint Team Services (1.0)

SharePoint Team Services was an enhancement to the Office Server Extensions, and was shipped with Microsoft Office XP Professional. Unlike the OSE and the FrontPage Extensions, however, SharePoint Team Services functioned as a full web-based application in its own right. STS included predesigned web pages, and introduced several key concepts — particularly lists, document libraries, and views. Although still conceptually present in current versions of SharePoint, these objects are very dissimilar in implementation from the way they were in STS. For example, STS used the web server's file system to store all pages and the physical documents for libraries, but kept configuration info, lists, and document metadata in a database. The present architecture is discussed in detail in Part I of the book, and described briefly later in the appendix.

One of the key ways of manipulating these objects in code is called the *Collaborative Application Markup Language* (*CAML*). CAML was introduced in STS, has evolved considerably (like the objects it is designed to manipulate), and is still a key part of programming for SharePoint. For example, the query used by the modern Data View (a concept that did not exist in STS) of a SharePoint list or library is generated in CAML, not SQL.

Figure A-2 shows a typical SharePoint Team Services site. FrontPage 2002 was "aware" of all SharePoint Team Services features, and could be used to customize and configure STS pages, lists, and libraries.

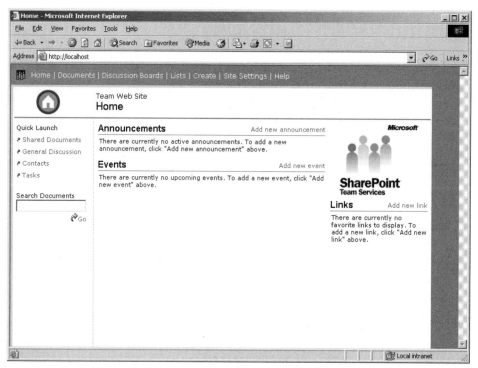

Figure A-2

SharePoint Portal Server 2001

SharePoint Portal Server 2001 made use of the Digital Dashboard technology from the DDRK, and backed it up with many powerful server-side capabilities. Unlike the multiple back-end options provided for the DDRK, SPS exclusively used an updated version of the Exchange message store, which was renamed the *Web Storage System*. The Web Storage System held dashboard pages and Web Parts, as it did with the DDRK, but in SPS it also stored documents and other content.

SPS also included document library functionality, although it was very different from that provided in STS. SPS document libraries offered workflow and granular control over permissions. SPS also included an updated version of the enterprise search engine from Site Server, allowing SPS to crawl and index information from a wide variety of corporate data sources. Figure A-3 shows a typical SharePoint Portal dashboard.

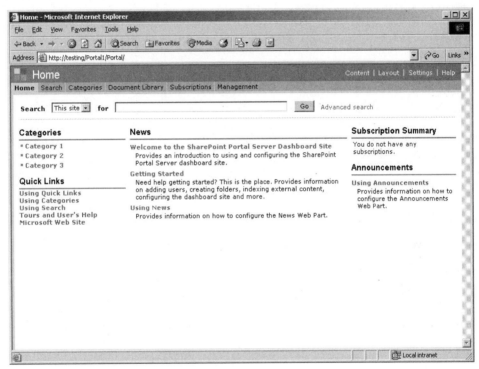

Figure A-3

Let's Get Together — Casting the (dot) Net

By the year 2003, SharePoint Team Services and SharePoint Portal Server had each secured a following, but there was a great deal of confusion because of the combination of similar names and superficially similar functionality with vast differences in architecture, programming models, and user interface between the two products. There had also been many changes to web programming. Microsoft had introduced the .NET framework and with it ASP.NET. Web services and the SOAP protocol were starting to make inroads, and XML was becoming the lingua franca of data interchange.

Windows SharePoint Services — A Platform Is Born

For the next wave of SharePoint products, Microsoft attempted to resolve some of the confusion by moving both SharePoint Team Services and SharePoint Portal Server onto the .NET platform. This required a significant amount of rework to both the STS and SPS platforms, as well as going beyond the standard ASP.NET 1.1 ways of doing things. When the dust had settled, a new SharePoint foundation had been created.

This new child contained elements of both parents, as well as several characteristics of its own. In the process, SharePoint Team Services had earned a new name, *Windows SharePoint Services (WSS)*, and a new place in the family tree. WSS would now be considered part of Windows Server, rather than Microsoft Office. As acknowledgment of its STS predecessor, WSS was deemed a 2.0 (version 2) product.

From SharePoint Portal Server 2001, Windows SharePoint Services inherited the concept (but not the implementation) of Web Parts as easily configurable modules to display content of various types on pages (now called *Web Part Pages* rather than dashboards). From SharePoint Team Services, WSS gained easily customizable lists, libraries, and views. Most of these elements, as well as library documents and other site-specific files, were now served from a re-architected content database.

Web Part Pages were a special case. Templates for Web Part Pages, and site definitions for the core web site types, were housed on the file system. When one of these elements was instantiated, a placeholder, or ghosted item, was placed in the content database. The ghosted item contained a pointer to the original file, and the instance information needed to make the item unique. These pages could be customized, however, by an editing tool such as FrontPage 2003, and in the process, a full instance of the customized file was stored in the database. That was called *unghosting* the file, and it could result in performance degradation, as well as complications when broader-scale changes needed to be made to all pages in a site.

Finally, the new platform introduced the capability to spread its functions across multiple servers and to serve the same content from multiple web front ends. This farm system was critical to improving SharePoint's scalability and resilience.

Opening a New Portal

SharePoint Portal Server 2003 was built upon the WSS foundation, and therefore contained all of the WSS functionality. However, many features that were carried forward from SPS 2001 but not included in WSS were implemented through custom code in SPS 2003. In particular, portal sites and areas used a different page model and site hierarchy than standard WSS sites. Also, because the WSS document storage framework did not implement certain features that were present in SPS 2001 document libraries (such as item-level permissions and workflows), an option was provided to use a special backward-compatible document library, which continued using the Web Storage System instead of the new content database structure. Figure A-4 shows a typical page from a WSS or SPS 2003 site.

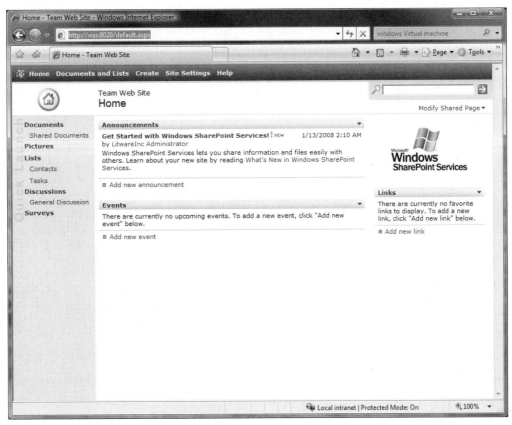

Figure A-4

SharePoint and SharePoint Designer Today

For the 2007 Microsoft Office System, Windows SharePoint Services was again significantly enhanced over its predecessor. WSS 3.0 is built on the ASP.NET 2.0 framework, which itself was enhanced with several concepts taken from SharePoint — specifically, ASP.NET 2.0 includes support for a Web Part framework. WSS 3.0 also makes use of the Windows Workflow Foundation and ASP.NET 2.0 authentication models. In addition, many weaknesses of WSS 2.0 are addressed in WSS 3.0, including the following:

❑   Item-level security is now allowed in lists and libraries.

❑   Security trimming is implemented to hide items and functions a user does not have permission to use.

❑   An extensibility framework has been created to make it easier to create and deploy new functionality on the Windows SharePoint Services platform.

❑   New site types, including basic blogs and wikis, have been added.

Appendix A: A Brief History of SharePoint and SharePoint Designer

SharePoint Portal Server 2003 was replaced with Microsoft Office SharePoint Server 2007 (MOSS). As the name implies, MOSS is far more than a portal product. Enterprise Content and Records Management, enhanced social networking through My Sites, and the latest version of Microsoft's Enterprise Search technology are just the starting point.

A new level of MOSS functionality is available through the Enterprise Features. While these Features are installed on all MOSS servers, they need to be enabled with a special code, and can only be accessed by users who have an Enterprise Client Access License (CAL). Enterprise CALs are an extra-cost option. They permit access to server-side Excel Services, an InfoPath Forms engine, business reporting functions such as KPIs, and easy integration with third-party systems through the Business Data Catalog (BDC). Figure A-5 shows a default MOSS home page.

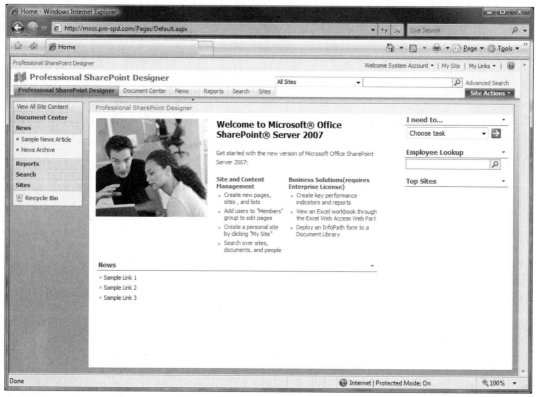

Figure A-5

Notice the distinct family resemblance in all of the screenshots shown in this appendix. The number one request of people implementing SharePoint has historically been, "Can you make it look less like SharePoint?" As you have learned throughout this book, with your mastery of Microsoft Office SharePoint Designer 2007 the answer is a resounding "Yes!"

Index

M